Global Trends of Modernization in Budgeting and Finance

Denis Ushakov
Suan Sunandha Rajabhat University, Thailand

A volume in the Advances in Finance, Accounting, and Economics (AFAE) Book Series

IGI Global
DISSEMINATOR OF KNOWLEDGE

Published in the United States of America by
IGI Global
Business Science Reference (an imprint of IGI Global)
701 E. Chocolate Avenue
Hershey PA, USA 17033
Tel: 717-533-8845
Fax: 717-533-8661
E-mail: cust@igi-global.com
Web site: http://www.igi-global.com

Library of Congress Cataloging-in-Publication Data

Names: Ushakov, D. S. (Denis Sergeevich), editor.
Title: Global trends of modernization in budgeting and finance / Denis Ushakov, editor.
Description: Hershey, PA : Business Science Reference, [2019]
Identifiers: LCCN 2018034974| ISBN 9781522577607 (hardcover) | ISBN 9781522577614 (ebook)
Subjects: LCSH: Corporations--Finance. | Managerial accounting. | Budget. | International finance.
Classification: LCC HG4026 .G6226 2019 | DDC 658.15--dc23 LC record available at https://lccn.loc.gov/2018034974

This book is published in the IGI Global book series Advances in Finance, Accounting, and Economics (AFAE) (ISSN: 2327-5677; eISSN: 2327-5685)

British Cataloguing in Publication Data
A Cataloguing in Publication record for this book is available from the British Library.

All work contributed to this book is new, previously-unpublished material. The views expressed in this book are those of the authors, but not necessarily of the publisher.

For electronic access to this publication, please contact: eresources@igi-global.com.

Advances in Finance, Accounting, and Economics (AFAE) Book Series

Ahmed Driouchi
Al Akhawayn University, Morocco

ISSN:2327-5677
EISSN:2327-5685

Mission

In our changing economic and business environment, it is important to consider the financial changes occurring internationally as well as within individual organizations and business environments. Understanding these changes as well as the factors that influence them is crucial in preparing for our financial future and ensuring economic sustainability and growth.

The **Advances in Finance, Accounting, and Economics (AFAE)** book series aims to publish comprehensive and informative titles in all areas of economics and economic theory, finance, and accounting to assist in advancing the available knowledge and providing for further research development in these dynamic fields.

Coverage

- Behavioral Economics
- Applied Finance
- Finance and Accounting in SMEs
- Fiscal Policy
- International Economics
- Managerial Accounting
- Macroeconomics
- Accounting information systems
- Economic Policy
- Economics of Intellectual Property Rights

IGI Global is currently accepting manuscripts for publication within this series. To submit a proposal for a volume in this series, please contact our Acquisition Editors at Acquisitions@igi-global.com or visit: http://www.igi-global.com/publish/.

The Advances in Finance, Accounting, and Economics (AFAE) Book Series (ISSN 2327-5677) is published by IGI Global, 701 E. Chocolate Avenue, Hershey, PA 17033-1240, USA, www.igi-global.com. This series is composed of titles available for purchase individually; each title is edited to be contextually exclusive from any other title within the series. For pricing and ordering information please visit http://www.igi-global.com/book-series/advances-finance-accounting-economics/73685. Postmaster: Send all address changes to above address.

Titles in this Series

For a list of additional titles in this series, please visit: www.igi-global.com/book-series

Techno-Social Systems for Modern Economical and Governmental Infrastructures
Alexander Troussov (The Russian Presidential Academy of National Economy and Public Administration, Russia) and Sergey Maruev (The Russian Presidential Academy of National Economy and Public Administration, Russia)
Business Science Reference • copyright 2019 • 351pp • H/C (ISBN: 9781522555865) • US $205.00 (our price)

Perspectives, Trends, and Applications in Corporate Finance and Accounting
Constantin Zopounidis (Technical University of Crete, Greece) Apostolos G. Christopoulos (National and Kapodistrian University of Athens, Greece) and Petros Kalantonis (Technological Education Institute (TEI) of Piraeus, Greece)
Business Science Reference • copyright 2018 • 354pp • H/C (ISBN: 9781522561149) • US $215.00 (our price)

Microfinance and Its Impact on Entrepreneurial Development, Sustainability, and Inclusive Growth
Ramesh Chandra Das (Katwa College, India)
Business Science Reference • copyright 2018 • 385pp • H/C (ISBN: 9781522552130) • US $245.00 (our price)

Maintaining Sustainable Accounting Systems in Small Business
Luísa Cagica Carvalho (Open University, Portugal & University of Évora, Portugal) and Elisa Truant (University of Turin, Italy)
Business Science Reference • copyright 2018 • 387pp • H/C (ISBN: 9781522552673) • US $215.00 (our price)

Agricultural Finance and Opportunities for Investment and Expansion
Augustine Odinakachukwu Ejiogu (Imo State University, Nigeria)
Business Science Reference • copyright 2018 • 236pp • H/C (ISBN: 9781522530596) • US $195.00 (our price)

Regaining Global Stability After the Financial Crisis
Bruno Sergi (Harvard University, USA) Filip Fidanoski (University of New South Wales, Australia) Magdalena Ziolo (University of Szczecin, Poland) and Vladimir Naumovski (University American College Skopje, Macedonia)
Business Science Reference • copyright 2018 • 383pp • H/C (ISBN: 9781522540267) • US $215.00 (our price)

Employment Protection Legislation in Emerging Economies
Samir Amine (Universite du Quebec en Outaouais, Canada)
Business Science Reference • copyright 2018 • 301pp • H/C (ISBN: 9781522541349) • US $195.00 (our price)

Fractal Approaches for Modeling Financial Assets and Predicting Crises
Inna Nekrasova (Southern Federal University, Russia) Oxana Karnaukhova (Southern Federal University, Russia) and Bryan Christiansen (PryMarke, LLC, USA)
Business Science Reference • copyright 2018 • 306pp • H/C (ISBN: 9781522537670) • US $215.00 (our price)

IGI Global
DISSEMINATOR OF KNOWLEDGE

701 East Chocolate Avenue, Hershey, PA 17033, USA
Tel: 717-533-8845 x100 • Fax: 717-533-8661
E-Mail: cust@igi-global.com • www.igi-global.com

Table of Contents

Detailed Table of Contents

The global financial crisis has greatly limited access to both public and private sources of finance in the recent decades. Markets and national governments emitted low interested and multi-structured financial means with low liquidity. In the post-crisis period national governments tend to regulate their financial sectors more strictly, paying more attention to risky and low interest financial sources, necessary for investments, on which private equity is dependent. Private equity funds grew significantly in the last two decades, both in the USA and in Europe. Such new ways of debt financing and cheap money support massive growth in the industrial sectors of individual countries. This research is studying the positive impact of private equity on management of the whole industries and economies in Europe. Our analysis stems from the general assumption that private equity has positive influence on industrial performance and our empirical data evidences that private equity reacts to economic decrease more intensively than under the business model without financial leverage. The goal of this chapter is to show how private equity contributes to the growth of industrial sectors, performance of industrial companies, with a special emphasis on the mining sector.

Under the conditions of megarisks, the general level of the world economy's instability rises, the number of unprofitable organizations with overdue debts increases, thus, creating additional threats to the financial security of states. In this regard, presented here, research results have scientific and applied importance for risk management and financial security of economic entities on the basis of the control and analytical concepts which cover: monitoring, diagnostics, prevention of crisis situations, including bankruptcy, corporate fraud and various other financial irregularities in the economy. Accounting for the specifics of economic entities in the course of analysis, diagnostics, and control over their activities is aimed at the creation of effective corporate fraud prevention and bankruptcy management systems. The conceptual principles of information and analytical support, improved methods for analyzing, and evaluating and monitoring financial security contributes to the development of a common methodology for economic analysis and control activities, ensuring their effectiveness and transparency. The comprehensive toolkit for diagnosing financial security allows identifying the areas of increased bankruptcy risks, fraudulent actions or ineffective business management; and unifies the control process, thereby reducing labor intensity and improving the quality of control measures.

Instruments of financing at the housing market allow increasing the efficiency of branch operation, accumulating more money resources, and redistributing them among the segments of this market. The chapter is based on the analysis of the housing markets' functioning in different countries, taking into account the possibilities of their financing. Recommendations have been formulated on the use of the foreign countries' experience in Russian practice in order to improve the efficiency of financing for the housing market in Russia. It is determined that the main instrument of financing at the majority of national housing markets is mortgage lending. The author has analyzed single-level and two-level models of mortgage lending to determine the advantages and disadvantages each of them has. In the German model, such a mechanism is implemented as a system of "building saving," which involves gradual accumulation of the initial contribution.

In this chapter, the authors, operating the criteria of rigid and comfortable national taxation regimes, attempt to evaluate the stimulating impact of country's taxation systems on the dynamics of their macroeconomic growth and country's participation in the world trade. Therefore, the chapter presents the authors' conclusions concerning the efficiency of fiscal instruments for economic growth stimulation and external trade attractiveness increase as applied to the majority of contemporary states. Based on correlation of indices of tax reformations and trends of the modern countries macroeconomic development, the co-authors present their conclusions on the priority importance of the so-called "taxation comfort" in the context of country's positioning in the global rankings. Research proved a taxation effect in countries' macro-economic growth and external attractiveness stimulating, as well as this effect dependence on the level of countries material wellbeing and infrastructural conditions.

This chapter systematizes the main components of the socio-market model of the economy. Its basis is formed by market economy and public-private partnership as the mechanism stimulating the attraction of private investments. Using the opportunities of the market economy and PPP mechanism creates a real opportunity for the formation of a new model of socio-market economy. This model does not imply the weakening the role of the state and infringement of democracy as such, but rather strengthening of institutions and PPP mechanisms with the aim to attract private investments and improve social relations at the same time. This chapter is thus aimed at revealing the main elements of this socioeconomic model along with the theoretical, methodological, and practical aspects of its main components: the market economy and the PPP mechanisms.

Tax system and tax policy today are becoming the most important instruments of national economic policy. Globalization process is objective in nature and is also inherent in market economy, whereas the neoliberal model of globalization is constantly getting more popular in both developed and developing countries. While developing countries in this regard are concentrating mostly on a multitude of potential reforms and resolving their numerous economic and social problems which are getting only more complicated, the interest of developed countries concerns mostly newest innovative technological trends and their application in a specific economic context. That is, in order to provide better conditions for full convergence of socioeconomic systems with higher rates of economic growth reforms, tax systems and tax policies are needed to reduce the barriers to free and global movement of goods, services, capital, and manpower.

Preface

Finance serve as the means for universalization of economic relations, of economic subjects' interests, regardless of their forms of ownership and property or the priorities stated for their activities. Finance also determine the efficiency of markets' functioning from the standpoint of the resource provision necessary for further development, for economic expansion (including transnational one). Also, finance regulate and shape the system of world economic instability prevention, thus guaranteeing stability even in the periods of crisis when the strategic interests of national states still have to be followed.

Capitalist economy is essentially of credit nature; thus, it constantly requires advance investments. The latter are formed predominantly by borrowed funds concentrated as the assets of various financial organizations which can be state-owned or private (owned by businesses). Therefore, it is rather obvious that financial relations established in the course of new business creation go first, prior to the emergence of production, tangible relations. Thus, the efficiency of financial relations (including the adequacy of interest rates on loans as expected by a future entrepreneur) always predetermines the efficiency of the future production process along with its expediency as such.

Financial environment (for example, inflation rates, taxation rates, foreign currencies' exchange rates) is always an integral element of competitiveness. And the latter means competitiveness of separate enterprises, of a certain sector and of national economy as a whole. Regulation of finance thus becomes an additional and quite a powerful instrument for stimulation of business development. Moreover, finance serves as the basis for this business' integration into the world economic relations in the context of a particular country's positioning within the world economy. Under the conditions of competitive fight going global, financial markets are becoming more and more interesting for the businesspersons worldwide, for public authorities' representatives and also for the academia, no matter what is the ideological standing of a particular researcher - liberalism, etatism, or dirigism.

Throughout the whole 20th century, economic progress as such, evolution of the world economic thought and state reforms worldwide were directed at the creation of the capacious and resourceful financial infrastructure along with the set of various mechanisms (mostly regulatory ones) so that to "connect" states and separate business units to this infrastructure. Another important direction in the financial infrastructure creation was universalization of the game rules at the financial markets worldwide and standardization of regulatory competences assigned to national governments at financial markets. Formation of a supranational infrastructure for financial regulation is supposed to establish and maintain the stability of financial markets globally.

The leading ideas behind long-term modernization of financial relations on the global scale are as follows:

- Formation of a supranational (autonomous from state regulation), capable and mobile infrastructure for the financing of businesses and even of states themselves. This supranational infrastructure is supposed to have truly colossal economic power.
- Narrowed competences of national states when it comes to regulation of national financial markets. This has become possible due to introduction of common rules for financial administration and control with the aim to eliminate unfair competition of the global level.
- Limited capacities of national governments in carrying out their autonomous investment policies. This has become possible due to active liberalization of markets worldwide, growing mobility of national capital, more influential role of gold reserves of the national governments etc.

Meanwhile, the very end of the 20th century saw the most negative consequences from financial modernization. These consequences made some of the national governments and academic world question the efficiency of the global financial infrastructure and its capacity to resist the global financial crises. Moreover, popular became the idea that the very existence of the world financial infrastructure is the key precondition and the major cause of financial crises. Also questionable became universalization of national financial policies as the instrument for "levelling" national economic systems and construction of one common and global production-distribution system. All these doubts have caused a huge inflow of theoretical studies on the issues related to financial autonomy of states, their limited participation in supranational financial relations, stabilization policies for the world financial system, the degrees of its freedom and control over it. An important aspect in all these studies concerned the gap between financial markets on the one side and actual production and trade in real commodities on the other.

Therefore, at the very beginning of the 21st century the issues of correlation between the finances of corporate, national and global levels, financial potential for further economic growth and competitiveness not only remained to be relevant and topical but also got new manifestations due to the priority of solving all these issues. For example, anti-crisis and anti-sanctions financial policies became a popular issue as well as the development of national instruments for limited integration into the world financial space, efficiency of national financial resources' management, correlation between national economic security and commercial interests of the largest national businesses etc.

The core aims of this monograph include: theoretical analysis and assessment of the financial reforms' consequences in various countries of the world; determination of the most constructive directions in modernization of national and corporate systems of finance and budgeting (under "constructive" we mean here those that are aimed not at full destruction of the currently existing world financial system but at its restructuring and further adjustment to national financial administrations while the latter are trying to follow their aims of maintaining economic sovereignty and security).

Following these aims the monograph is supposed to solve such tasks as:

- To analyze the major impacts of financial crises on the structure and the dynamics of entrepreneurial activities along with the efficiency factors of the anti-crisis policies implemented today by enterprises and national financial administrations;
- To evaluate the corporate instruments used in financial stabilization and in maintaining economic security and business solvency under the constantly changing conditions at the national and world financial markets; to consider what are the key instruments applied for assessment of financial risks by contemporary enterprises and also for forecasting the situation at financial markets (such forecasting can be carried out by consumers of financial services or by the agents forming the proposition at national financial markets);

- To describe the common practices of sectors' stabilization by means of their more efficient integration with national and/or international financial markets;
- To assess the efficiency of the most popular instruments used in the course of state financial policy implementation at the national and/or regional levels; to consider the related issues of public-private partnership development in the aspect of financial provision for business development;
- To describe the role of the national tax system in stimulation of the general economic system development along with the accumulated experiences of tax regimes' modernization in various countries worldwide, including those that are actively integrating today into supranational economic organizations.

The research object in the monograph is financial relationship emerging between businesses, national states and/or international organizations in the course of following own economic interests by all sides involved.

The research subject in this monograph is the adaptation mechanism as applied to the economic interests of various businesses, states and international organizations in the course of financial markets' modernization and capitalist financial relations' development.

This collective monograph consists of two larger parts which, in their turn consist of chapters, so that to analyze together the problem of financial relations' modernization from the standing point of smaller businesses and corporate sector as the key consumer and supplier of financial services (the first section of this book) and then, from the standing point of the state authority as the financial administrator and regulator responsible for implementation of its independent national policy aimed at economic security maintenance, taking into account the megatrends of the today's financial markets (the second section of this book).

The first section titled "Financial Provision of Entrepreneurial Efficiency: Today's Priorities in Modernization of Corporate Budgeting" consists of eight chapters which together analyze a wide circle of issues directly related to the problems of business financing, corporate financial management and accounting in today's globalized world.

Results of international research conducted by Krongthong Khairiree and Denis Ushakov are presented in chapter "Budgeting Administration and Economic Growth Dynamics in Conditions of National Markets' Integration." Co-authors analyzed the macroeconomic indicators of the modern economies, determined the level of impact from their involvement in the world trade on the stability of their economic development. Authors offered original method to determine the index of economic growth stability, evaluated correlation between economic growth stability and external trade activeness of the today's economies. This chapter offered some strategies for fair and effective social compensation, as well as methodology for calculating the indicators of social compensation feasibility, recommendations on modernization the social compensation policy in the dynamics of integrating markets were also offered.

The next chapter, written by Russian experts Nadezhda Krasovskaya, Elena Danilova and Larisa Zamuraeva, evaluates the consumption of financial services on the example of the Russian Federation. This group of authors offers their own vision of what is "financial behavior of population" from the standpoint of risks (related to the decision made by investors and also those made by citizens). The authors also assess the factors shaping the specificity of population's financial behavior in Russia. Further, the authors make an attempt to assess the dynamics of changes in consumer behavior of the Russians at their financial markets (on the case study of one large city - Tyumen). The authors demonstrate how patterns of financial behavior correlate with demographic and socioeconomic changes in the city in question (for example, with the level of education, changes in the level of income, place of residence, nature of work). On the basis of the established correlation the authors also outline the key directions in modernization of corporate financial strategies of the local enterprises and also key necessary changes to be made in the marketing strategies of financial institutions operations at the regional markets inside the Russian Federation.

Theoretical research on the influence of political and economic risks on the dynamics of FDI has been carried by Turkish Assistant Professor Fatih Ayhan in his dedicated chapter. The researcher has provided a rather detailed definition of political and economic risks and has also offered an original model to be applied to determine the correlation between the factors defining the scale of risks and the degree of their perception by foreign investors. The author has also carried out the analysis of the established correlation between the indicators of economic and political risks by countries, taking into account the dynamics of foreign investments' inflows into these countries. On the basis of the carried out analysis the author has also determined the key patterns which later have served as the basis for author's original recommendations.

Igor Keri, Elena Gromova and Nadezhda Sinelschikova represent the younger generation of scientists from Plekhanov Russian University of Economics. In their chapter titled "Features of Financial Policy Development by Russian Companies in Today's Conditions" the authors study the problems of corporate financial system modernization and determine the alternative approaches to assessment of credit and investment resources in the context of corporate trade strategy and pricing strategy. The authors' assessment of investment resources available for Russian enterprises along with the sources of crediting and the structure of business spending in Russia takes into account low investment attractiveness of the Russian Federation as such and the ongoing sanctions imposed on Russia by a range of Western countries. After this detailed assessment the authors offer their original recommendations on more efficient use of the available financial resources by Russian companies. In particular, they recommend directing such resources into innovative development of companies. Other authors' recommendations concern the flexibility of pricing policies at both external and internal markets etc.

Specific aspects of national instruments applied for financial support of local businesses under the conditions of active integration of national states into supranational organizations have been considered by the group of Slovak authors - Katarína Čulková, Adriana Csikósová and Mária Janošková. These authors have formulated the key task of their research as follows: to assess the contribution of private equity financing on the example of European industrial companies through determination of individual types of investments and specific description of the private equity market with its influence on the performance of industrial sectors and national economies. The central point of this chapter is that the mentioned above authors have analyzed the private equity investments in several members of the European Union so that to assess more specifically the determining role of private equity financing for investment attractiveness. The authors have also determined certain regularities in stimulation of sectoral entrepreneurship under the influence of private equity financing on the example of the mining sector in the EU.

Financial security of businesses and methodologies to be applied to assess financial risks in the context of corporate financial management have always been "hot topics," however, they became especially relevant and topical recently, due to the escalating political instability and volatility at the world markets of raw materials. The next chapter, prepared by Russian researchers Natalia Kazakova and Anna Sivkova, considers the key problems in the course of efficiency system formation for financial risks' accounting. This system is supposed to cover not only the assessment of financial assets and financial results but also the distribution of security indicators between the strategic centers of control as well as the indicators of current business activity, market environment and a range of specific features of the internal corporate environment.

One more representative of the Plekhanov Russian University of Economics, Mariia Ermilova, in her chapter titled "Financing at the Housing Market: The Analysis of Best Practices in the Selected Countries" explains the vital role and value of the state financing programs at the housing market, stemming from the importance of the latter as the driver of economic development for the whole country. At the same time, specificity of the housing market and housing as a commodity assumes more serious regulation of the related environment with application of specific financial instrument. The housing sector as such assumes its close connection (if not partial integration) with the national financial system, actually. In this chapter its author analyzes the international experience in the field of state financing at the housing markets, and after this analysis the author offers her own building-savings model, the application of which in Russia specifically may boost the investment process in the construction sector, thus directly contributing to accessibility of crediting programs for housing purchases by Russian population.

One more research tandem from Russia, Oleg Patlasov and Olga Mzhelskaya, has chosen the instruments of financial risks' and bankruptcy risks' forecasting as their research object. They started with the analysis of the available today methodologies of financial risks' assessment and planning used by corporations and then offered their own model based on the assessment of bankruptcy symptoms. The key benefit of their study is that it is directly connected to real practice of today's banking sector in Russia since the authors managed to use the real data on two largest banks that are specializing in agricultural crediting these days. The offered model is already adapted to the current situation in the banking sector of Russia (including the sanctions imposed by the West) and it also takes into account the dynamic nature and high instability of the sectoral markets in the Russian Federation.

The second part of this collective monograph is titled "The State at the Financial Market: Making the National Financial Policy Efficient." It consists of seven chapters, all of which consider the problems of national financial policies in the contemporary states. Also, financial reforms that have been taking place in the selected countries during the two recent decades are studied.

The second section of the book starts with the chapter by Russian researchers Anastasia Ostovskaya and Irina Pavlenko. Their study under the title "Financial Instruments of Regional Economic Policy Implementation" considers the theoretical and methodological principles of regional economic policies' implementation. According to the authors, the most instrument tool for these regional policies consists of the state financing programs. The key benefit of this chapter is that its authors managed to evaluate not only the current economic condition of Russia's regions in general but also the efficiency of state financial support programs in these regions. They applied their own methodology for this analysis and it enabled them offer a complex of measures boosting the growth of quality in financial management regionwide. The offered methodology is also able to help smoothing the interregional differences in the volumes of state financial support.

The next chapter has been prepared by Slovak scientists representing the University of Economics in Bratislava, Marcela Rabatinová, Juraj Válek, and Jana Kušnírová. These authors consider the issues of the national taxation systems' modernization under the condition of common financial space in Europe. They describe in detail various advantages (including semilegal and illegal ones) of tax avoidance in the context of studying what are the most comfortable, in terms of taxation, jurisdictions within the EU. The authors have selected three important taxes for their analysis - corporate income tax, excise tax on alcoholic beverages and value added tax. All three are often considered to be the most risky ones in terms of tax evasion. In this context, the mentioned authors assess the major problems the fiscal system of Slovakia is facing today. The authors also offer their own recommendations on the normalization of tax rates taking into account the "tax sensitivity" of Slovak consumers and local businesses. Budget needs and the potential ways to avoid taxation using the newly emerged advantages of the integrated financial markets and businesses' transnationalization within the EU are also considered in this chapter.

Denis Ushakov and Tran Ai Huu, in the following chapter, are considering the potential of taxation regimes of various contemporary states in terms of overcoming the major problem of today's market economy - unequal distribution of income between market agents. This problem is considered in the context of a larger problem - formation of the resources for further national economic growth. This chapter is titled "Taxation Regime and Macroeconomic Systems' Dynamics" and it is based on thorough research of the statistical indicators on macroeconomic dynamics of the selected states worldwide. The author makes the conclusion concerning the correlation between the stimulating impact of tax instruments on economic growth (tax rate and taxation comfort) and the achieved indicators of material welfare in the selected countries along with the role of state in their economic systems. The authors formulate rather original conclusions concerning the growth of stimulating influence demonstrated by taxation comfort (as compared to the tax rate) in relation to economic growth in the context of growing welfare. Another interesting conclusions concerns the importance of the tax rate level for export stimulation in the countries with high income per capita and also for import stimulation in the countries with low income per capita. Inter alia, the author proves that the influence of taxation comfort is larger for per capita indicators as opposed to gross indicators of GDP. In the author's view, all these conclusions may help reformulate the guidelance and reconsider the tools used for modernization of national taxation regimes today.

Russian scientists Alexey Zeldner, Vladimir Osipov and Tatiana Skryl in their chapter which goes next have grounded the absolute inefficiency of specialization in raw materials today. This inefficiency is proved to be valid at the level of national governance and also at the level of corporate management of large national companies. In this context, the authors study the issues related to stimulation of investment flows (both internal and of foreign origin) into the most innovative, socially oriented and high-tech sectors of Russian economy. Special attention in the context of this larger problem is paid to the development of public-private partnerships in Russia. These authors are of the opinion that taking into account the specificity of investment flows and the forms of PPP used in Russia today may help shaping a brand new model of social-market economy. The latter has a huge strategic potential for growing national economy's competitiveness and efficiency.

Indepth analysis of tax reforms as applied to the bank sectors of the Balkan countries has been carried out by Serbian Professor Sofija Adžić. In this analysis economic and market consequences of the mentioned reforms have been considered, inter alia. As the author of this chapter notes, the problems of Serbian economy are very much similar to the problems other Balkan countries are facing these days too. Namely, despite the permanent fall of GDP, authorities in all these countries are more and more inclined to increase the taxation load. At the same time, the national budget inflows (even when considered in the short term only) tend to fall. This becomes yet another proof that national taxation systems in Serbia and in other Balkan countries need to be urgently modernized. Also, this proves that the policy of tax expansion, in this particular case, is highly ineffective. The key result from the analysis carried out by the author is the brand new paradigm for taxation modernization in Serbia. The presented paradigm rests on efficient management of national debt as well as on the alternative methodologies of determining fiscal capacity, diversification of taxation regimes in favor of high-tech sector since the latter are most able to attract significant flows of foreign direct investments to the Balkan countries.

The next chapter with the title "The Impact of Budget and Fiscal Policy on Entrepreneurial Activity and Country's Competitiveness: The Case of Ukraine" was contributed by the authors Yuriy Holynskyy and Irina Onyusheva. They assess the efficiency of tax reforms in Ukraine as applied to stabilization of Ukrainian economy and its long-term growth. The country in question has been in rather extreme conditions for the last several years, due to a range of political and economic problems it is facing. For this and other reasons, Ukraine need to revise its national economic system as soon as possible so that to be able to integrate most efficiently into the common economic space of the EU. The authors provide their own assessment of Ukraine's competitiveness indicators in the context of the world economy, and this assessment has helped the authors to evaluate objectively the today's problems Ukraine is facing along with the potential challenges and threats to its development. On this basis, the authors offer a wide range of measures, all of them being of fiscal and/or budget nature and oriented on the development of economic motivation for both foreign and internal investors. Formation of new, truly innovative sectors of the economy which would positively exploit the intellectual potential of the national has been also considered in the context of socioeconomic stabilization of Ukraine and elimination of this country's heavy dependence on various raw materials.

Ecologization of consumption and transformation of consumer preferences in favor of "green" products and technologies have already become the next big thing in the absolute majority of both developed and developing nations worldwide. These "going green" trends are rather promising in terms of competitiveness growth for separate businesses as well as for national sectors overall. In this particular context, Professor Prateep Wajeetongratana from Bangkok, Thailand, has been considering the issues around the environmental accounting introduction on the example of Thai business sector. The final chapter of the monograph presents the results of the survey carried out among Thai business representatives, and also within expert community and even inside the regulator (the Ministry of Finance). The survey covered the issues concerning the potential introduction of innovations in national accounting with the aim to make the latter "more green." After the analysis of this survey results the author offers a range of innovations for the existing system of accounting. These innovations would make it possible to monetize the efforts of businesses aimed at own ecologization and also to commercialize the measures aimed to environmental protection and ecologization of national consumption.

As a conclusion, the chief editor of this monograph would like to note that all presented here research studies have passed rather strict review procedures, including double-blind reviews and numerous corrections and adjustments. Thus, we can assure all our readers that here we present the most outstanding results of the scientists representing very different parts of our world. These are the results of international research, all of which took many years to summarize. And we can rest assured that the conclusions of these authors really mirror the actual situation in the countries these authors are representing. Moreover, all these conclusions can help solving the most topical problems today's financial markets are facing.

I would also like to take this opportunity to say thank you to IGI Global for the opportunity to present all these materials collected worldwide to a wider audience. This is a truly unique chance for fruitful, interpersonal and international cooperation which only became possible once we came up with the idea of this monograph. We have high hopes this cooperation would be continued in the near future already.

Many thanks to everyone who had contributed to shaping and publishing of this book!

Denis Ushakov
Suan Sunandha Rajabhat University, Thailand

Section 1

Financial Provision of Entrepreneurial Efficiency: Today's Priorities in Modernization of Corporate Budgeting

Chapter 1
Budgeting Administration and Economic Growth Dynamics in Conditions of National Markets' Integration

Krongthong Khairiree
Suan Sunandha Rajabhat University, Thailand

Denis Ushakov
Suan Sunandha Rajabhat University, Thailand

ABSTRACT

In this chapter we analyze the macroeconomic indicators of the contemporary economies so that to determine the level of impact from their involvement in the world trade on the stability of their economic development. A new, author's method is offered here to determine the index of economic growth stability for the economies of the 21st century. A correlation is revealed being between economic growth stability and external trade activeness of the today's economies. In the chapter based on the authors' approach to the definition of strategies for fair and effective social compensation, as well as a proposed methodology for calculating the indicators of social compensation strategies feasibility, the conclusions regarding macroeconomic conditions of selecting a state participation program in the process of economic achievements converting into social conditions were done, recommendations on modernization the social compensation policy in the dynamics of integrating markets were also offered.

INTRODUCTION

Under today's conditions of the world economy globalization and transnationalization of production & distribution system more topical and urgent are becoming the issues related to stabilization of economic development trends and overall progressive development of macroeconomic systems (Rodionov & Rudskaya, 2017, 2017a). This stabilization, on the one hand, is supposed to maintain the dynamics of national economy's integration into the world economic space and all related processes, and on the other

DOI: 10.4018/978-1-5225-7760-7.ch001

hand, it is also supposed to guarantee the priority of national economic interests and national economic security in particular. Stable economic growth of a country means this country has internal economic efficiency, and its internal system of resource use and welfare distribution (between the state and the business, between citizens and various social strata, etc.) is in full compliance with the demands of all active participants of the national socioeconomic system. Moreover, stable economic growth is yet another confirmation of country's external (or even global) competitiveness and is a decisive factor when it comes to country's attractiveness for international finances (Rodionov & Rudskaya, 2017a), migrating highly qualified labor, potential trade partners (Kudryavtseva, Ivanova, Kozlova, & Skhvediani, 2017) etc. Only internal economic stability can rescue national economy from the fluctuations at the world markets and from all uncertainties of the global economy today.

At the same time, efficient implementation of national economic growth stabilization strategy today may face a range of obstacles, most serious of which are related to the limited capacities of national governments under globalization conditions (Ushakov, Elokhova, & Kozonogova, 2017) and these limited capacities of public authorities are related not only to external trade, but often also to internal markets, national business development, taxation, labor conditions, etc. (Ushakov, 2017a).

Unification of doing business conditions and common rules of market regulation, similar patterns of privatization processes and liberalization of trade and other forms of external economic activities, freer than ever international exchange of technologies and capital – all these key features of today's world tend to negate all "natural" competitive advantages of the countries including their special regimes of economic regulation, specific policies and preferences etc. Extremely rapid development of multinational businesses promote nearly absolute automation of corporate production & distribution systems, thus, the latter become nearly fully protected from any state control and/or intrusion, since nearly any corporate asset today can be transferred, in a matter of seconds, to another jurisdiction, which seems to be more attractive and/or favorable in terms of taxation, customs, internal market etc.

Therefore, studying the factors which have their influence on the stabilization of national economic growth remain topical today, especially taking into account the rate and the extent of countries' economic interdependence (one of the manifestations of which is state's participation in export-import operations) (Kharchenko, 2017).

The success of modern state economic progress is connected not only with its achievement of a certain level of material prosperity, forming of comfortable conditions for doing business necessarily reflected in the country's attractiveness to foreign capital, but with efficiency of country's economic success converting in the quality of own citizens life (the level of personal incomes, the state of social infrastructure, the completeness and targeting of social programs, the development of human potential and so on).

In this paper we used the term "social compensation", which in the authors' interpretation is understood as the conversion of macroeconomic achievements and economic results of the national (and attracted foreign) business to high standards of the quality of population life implemented with the participation of the state. At the same time, the state can act as a benefits redistributor from business to the population (fair strategy of social compensation) or as a stimulator of this conversion through creating of comfortable conditions (effective strategy of social compensation).

The research problem lies in the fact that the state needs to determine the conditions under which the choice of the first or second social compensation strategy will be more appropriate, as well as to assess the prospects for the social compensation strategies implementing in the dynamics of world and national markets.

Thus, our research aim is to analyze the macroeconomic statistics and the rate of economic progress in various countries of the world so that to determine the correlation between the stability of national economic growth on the one hand and the depth of country's integration into the world markets on the other; to develop a set of conceptual recommendations based on the macroeconomic indicators analysis and aimed at modernizing the national strategy of social compensation, adequate to the globalization dynamics of the 21st century.

In accordance with the research aim we set forward the following research tasks:

- Using the author's original methodology, we will determine the stability index for economic development of various contemporary countries worldwide. The study period covers the most recent 15 years for which the full data is available. Then, the countries will be classified according to their values of this index, and these values will be compared and correlated with other important macroeconomic features of the same countries (for example, GDP per capita, natural resource potential, consumer market capacity)
- A correlation will be determined between the indicators of economic growth stability and external trade activity of the selected contemporary countries, the latter will be again classified, now depending on the dynamics of their trade balance
- To outline the most contemporary factors of national economic growth stabilization, all being correlated with the dynamics of external trade of the selected countries. To offer author's recommendations concerning the possible strategic guidelines as per stabilization of national economic development rates
- Propose authorial indices reflecting the role of the state in social compensation policy implementing (fair policy and effective policy) that are possible for calculation using available secondary information, macroeconomic indicators of the countries of the world
- Analyze these indices changes with dynamics of Ginny coefficient in the countries of the world, assess the effectiveness of the national social compensation program in countries grouped by the level of per capita income
- Give recommendations on directions and principles of national policy of social compensation modernization which is relevant for the dynamics of the global market situation

Research Hypotheses

1. Availability of strategic supply of natural resources and also agricultural lands are not the most decisive factors of economic growth stabilization for today's countries;
2. Countries with high indicators of material welfare will demonstrate not high, but still very stable rates of economic development;
3. Dynamic (or intensive, that is, at least 4% per annum) rate of economic growth during the whole period in question (15 years) simple cannot be stable all the time;
4. There is a direct correlation between stability of national export growth and stability of country's economic growth overall;
5. The most vital factors of economic growth stabilization are not the impressive indicators of national export or import but the dynamics of their change in time;

6. The strategy of effective social compensation, despite its obvious advantages, does not contribute to the formation of a sustainable model of interaction between business, the state and society, even in economically successful and wealthy states.
7. In modern conditions, budgetary fiscal policy seems more oriented towards maintaining the social stability and lower level of material differentiation of the population than the policy of effective social compensation.
8. There is a direct correlation between the fairness / efficiency of the state budget policy and the level of property differentiation in the countries of the world.
9. High effectiveness of the fair policy of social compensation application is typical only for countries with a high level of per capita income, and consequently, with a capacious domestic consumer market.

LITERATURE REVIEW

Due to their absolute top priority, the general problems of economic growth along with the factors of its provision under the conditions of market instability have been already quite thoroughly developed by the representatives of nearly all schools of economic thought.

Due to current multimodality of the world economy, functioning of various economic systems differ by their fundamental features (the very construction of the national socioeconomic system, the type and practices of reproduction, the role of the state, the functions of business etc.). Obviously, these national socioeconomic systems also have differences in terms of their geographical and climatic features, natural resource potential etc. For this and other reasons, cross-country studies are always of significant scientific interest, since only such studies can provide the necessary conclusions and recommendations concerning the specificity of national economic growth strategies' development and implementation.

For example, Robert J. Barro (1996) analyzed the data on 100 contemporary (at that time) economies during the period of their economic establishment and development (1960 till 1990) and came to the conclusion that growth is negatively related to the initial level of real per capita GDP and also that political freedom has only a rather weak effect on growth, and also that once a moderate level of democratic development is reached – its further expansion would only reduce the growth.

Kevin B. Grier and Gordon Tullock (1989) used the pooled cross-section/time-series data on 113 countries to investigate the empirical regularities in the post-war economic growth and found that the growth of government consumption is significantly negatively correlated with the economic growth in the OECD and that political repression is negatively correlated with growth in Africa as well as in Central and South America.

A separate direction in the research is represented by the studies on the internal peculiarities of national economic systems and their global competitive advantages which are, to a large extent, the key factors in maintaining stable and long-term economic growth. For example, Emil E. Malizia, Shanzi Ke (1993) clarified the influence of economic diversity on unemployment and instability in regional economies of the United States, the United Kingdom, and Canada and indicated that metropolitan areas which are usually more diverse experience lower unemployment rates and less instability than the areas which are smaller and less diverse.

Shungo Sakaki (2004), in the same research context, came to the conclusion that income distribution is independent from long-term economic growth, and that management of the income distribution ratio enables the promotion of the growth driven by the replacement of the existing technology with new knowledge stock. In the countries where income is not that highly concentrated and larger share of it operates within market economy, the consumer demand-driven economic policy is effective. On the other hand, in a society where income is highly concentrated, the investment demand promotes growth by increasing concentration at the growth phase, while in the sluggish phase, a temporary equalization of distribution enables the creation of a new growth course by inducing a technological change brought about by consumer demand.

Arusha Cooray (2009) investigates the role of national governments in economic growth by extending the neoclassical production function to incorporate two dimensions of government as a phenomenon – the size and the quality dimensions, indicating that both these parameters of governments are important for country's economic growth.

William Easterly (1993) found a strong association between development level and fiscal structure: poor countries rely heavily on international trade taxes, while income taxes are important mostly for developed economies; fiscal policy is influenced by the scale of the economy, measured by its population; investment in transport and communications is consistently correlated with overall economic growth, while the effects from taxation are difficult to isolate empirically.

Jiandong Ju, Yi Wu and Li Zeng (2010) studied the external preconditions for economic growth stabilization in contemporary countries (in particular, active involvement in external economic operations). And they revealed that liberalization of markets and of external economic activities worldwide has its negative impact on stable growth of national economic systems.

Dependence of today's economies' growth on export diversification was also evaluated by Badri Narayan Rath, Vaseem Akram (2017) on the sample of South Asian countries. They came to the conclusion that export diversification causes economic growth in the long run, whereas no causality found in the short run, thus, they suggested that export diversification is crucial for avoiding the volatility in export growth and for enchantment of productivity growth, at least for the economies of the South Asian region.

Gershon Feder (1983) indicated that marginal factor productivities are significantly higher in the export sector and that growth can be generated not only by increases in the aggregate levels of labor and capital, but also vie reallocation of the existing resources from less efficient non-export sectors to higher productivity export sector. Bela Balassa (1978) also investigated the relationship between exports and economic growth on the group of 11 developing countries that have already established their industrial base.

Ann Harrison (1996) tested the association between openness and growth, namely, the correlation across different types of openness and growth and different measures of openness. Hamid Davoodi (1998) investigated the relationship between fiscal decentralization and economic growth and found a negative relationship between fiscal decentralization and growth in developing countries, but nothing of the like for developed countries.

Shantayanan Devarajan, Vinaya Swaroop, Heng-fu-Zou (1996) focused on the link between public expenditure volumes and growth, thus, they managed to describe the conditions under which a change in the composition of expenditure leads to higher steady-state growth rate of the economy. Using data from 43 developing countries over 20 years these co-authors show that an increase in the share of current expenditures has positive and statistically significant growth effects. By contrast, the relationship between the capital component of public expenditure and per capita growth is nearly always negative.

Hadi Salehi Esfahani (1991) showed that the correlation between export/import and economic growth has been mainly due to the contribution of exports to the reduction of import shortages which tend to restrict output growth. In this sense, export promotion is particularly important for those countries which cannot obtain sufficient foreign aid or capital.

The problem of the state's social spending impact on economic growth stimulating was explored in the context of cross-country analysis, and also at the theoretical level of budget expenditures redistribution and sectoral development stimulating modeling.

In the category of cross-country studies, for example, Axel Dreher, Jan-Egbert Sturm and Heinrich W. Ursprung (2008) considered the impact of globalization on the composition of government expenditures on the example of 60 countries and determined that globalization did not influence the composition of government expenditures in a notable way, even taking in account that governments may attempt to curtail the welfare state, which is often seen as a drag on international competitiveness, by reducing especially their expenditures on transfers and subsidies.

A similar study, but in the case of OECD countries (Dreher, 2006), also show that globalization (measured by an index encompassing 23 variables) did not in general decrease leeway for independent national economic policy, increasing social integration also influences policies, while political integration does not matter for economic policy in most specifications.

In direction of modeling the process of budget funds redistributing for economic growth and quality of life stimulation Robert J. Barro (1990) extended endogenous-growth models to include tax-financed government services that affect production or utility и продемонстрировал, что Growth and saving rates fall with an increase in utility-type expenditures; the two rates rise initially with productive government expenditures but subsequently decline.

More "socialized" research (Scully, 2001), based, in part, on the author's original aggregated index of the "quality of life" led to the unexpected conclusion that government consumption expenditure is considerably higher than is necessary to maximize the physical quality of life, and that a reduction in government consumption expenditure would not lower quality of life.

Hannu Tanninen (2010) investigated the relationship between income inequality and growth by utilizing the recently published Deininger-Squire data set and found a negative relationship between inequality and growth on the basis of reduced-form growth equations (high level of income inequality leads to a higher demand for redistribution, which in turn affects growth through resource allocation out of investment or through incentive-distorting taxes needed to fund the redistribution).

Trish Kelly (1997) traced the dynamics of the social programs affecting economic growth, he also identified factors that determine the quality of the process of budget funds redistribution in modern macroeconomic conditions.

Studies by Peter H. Lindert (1996) and James R. Hines (2006) have affected not only the budget distribution issues, but also the formation of budgetary funds for the social programs implementation. So, the first one, assessed limits of social taxation, and the second analyzed the effectiveness of social compensation tools using at the expense of budget expenditures and stimulating of business social programs.

Robert A Amano, Tony S Wirjanto (1998) considered a two-good permanent-income model and estimated preference parameters to shed some light on whether private and public consumptions are best described as complements, substitutes, or unrelated occurrences.

Studies of correlation of public spending and quality of life, as well as state of business environment, were conducted in many countries and international associations. However, the results obtained differed and sometimes significantly.

For example, in Malaysia, the growth of the state's social expenditures (in the direction of new jobs creating) stimulated the quality of life and the fairness of the distribution of material goods only until the mid-1990s, after which the stratification of Malay society significantly increased (Shari, 2000). In China, according to a study conducted by Shujie Yao (2007), high social injustice remains in the sphere of National budget distributions (in comparison with the labor incomes). In the Middle East, the role of public budget spending in stimulating economic growth (primarily through local consumption) remains high importance (Al-Yousif, & Yousif Khalifa, 2000).

Continuing in this chapter, we plan to assess and explain the export-import dynamics (in its absolute and relative terms) as a factor of economic growth stabilization for the selected group of countries, data as of early years of the current, 21st century. Using the data on this century makes this research different from all of the abovementioned, since economic growth, at least so far, has been predominantly studied on the data from the previous century. This analysis gives us an opportunity to analyze and evaluate the factors behind economic growth stabilization which are relevant specifically for the context of the emerging century, not the previous one.

The present study using the achievements of cross-state assessments of the economic role of budgetary social expenditures in the countries of the world, as well as theoretical conclusions on the correlation between the dynamics of public expenditure and economic growth, attempts to evaluate an effectiveness of social compensation in countries of the world.

CONDITIONS OF ECONOMIC GROWTH: CROSS-COUNTRY ANALYZE

In our research and analysis we have been mostly operating the statistical information of the World Bank (from their official site - worldbank.org). From this large massive of data, we have extracted the needed information on the 150 countries of the world, the study period being from 2000 till 2015. Table 1 shows, on the example of Albania, which specifically data we had in use.

Table 1. Statistical indicators used in our research

Albania							
Years	**GDP Growth (Annual Growth Rate, in %)**	**Exports of Goods and Services (% Share of GDP)**	**Imports of Goods and Services (% Share of GDP)**	**Years**	**GDP Growth (Annual Growth Rate, in %)**	**Exports of Goods and Services (% Share of GDP)**	**Imports of Goods and Services (% Share of GDP)**
2000	6,66	17,86	38,05	2008	7,53	29,59	56,43
2001	7,94	18,43	38,99	2009	3,35	29,6	53,75
2002	4,23	19,59	44,33	2010	3,71	32,44	53,02
2003	5,77	20,35	45,08	2011	2,55	34,01	56,74
2004	5,7	21,98	44,37	2012	1,42	33,35	51,98
2005	5,72	22,82	47,47	2013	1,11	35,44	53,48
2006	5,43	24,93	48,52	2014	1,8	28,23	47,22
2007	5,9	28,08	54,78	2015	2,59	27,25	44,52

(On the example of Albania, authors' extraction and calculation from the World Bank data)

In order to determine the indicators of economic growth stability we have used the statistical method of mean-square deviation calculation in the indicators of economic growth dynamics as well as the indicators of national export and import growth for all the analyzed countries during these 15 years in question. The obtained results are presented in Table 2.

As it is shown in Table 2, during the period of 2000-2015 the most stable economic growth has been demonstrated by the developing countries of Asia and Africa, and also by some developed – but noteworthy, distanced from the global economic processes and world turmoil overall Australia and Norway. Both these countries, apart from having powerful technological and industrial platforms for such an impressive economic growth, also have sufficient strategic reserves of natural raw materials. Among other developed countries rather stable economic growth has been observed in France, USA, Canada, Austria and Denmark.

At the same time, economic growth stability of Japan turns out to be on the same level with Tunisia (a country still feeling the consequences of the severe political crisis), while the dynamic economic growth of India was rather unstable, thus, the indicator of this country turns out to be on the same level with Italian economy (the latter demonstrated mostly negative dynamics in the several recent years). The absolute leader in terms of economic growth stability during the first 15 years of the 21 century became Norway, while its closest geographical neighbor, Sweden, has found itself on the same level with Mexico and Brazil (the indicators of Finland are even lower). Most of fluctuations in economic growth among the well-to-do countries have been demonstrated by Ireland and Iceland. Countries, exporting raw materials (first of all – hydrocarbons) and thus having low diversification of their trade and economy overall, such as Azerbaijan, Nigeria, Russia and the United Arab Emirates – all find themselves in the last third of the list (100-150 ranks). Therefore, we can state that our hypothesis #1 is confirmed.

As Table 3 clearly shows, among the countries with the maximum average rate of economic growth during the 2000-2015 period, there is no leader as such in terms of economic dynamics' stability. Moreover, correlation between macroeconomic indicators is 0,06, which basically means no correlation as such between them. Analysis of the obtained data confirms that high indicators of economic growth during the period in question (high here means at least 4% per annum) in the majority of countries is demonstrating it was accompanied by great deal of economic instability (however, with the exception of 9 countries, namely, Bangladesh, Bolivia, China, India, Indonesia, Malaysia, Tanzania, Thailand, Vietnam). This confirms our hypothesis #2.

At the second stage of our research we calculate the correlation between the indicators of economic growth stability and the volumes of exports and imports, as well as with the indicators of exports/imports growth stability (in dynamics). At this, we have obtained the following correlations (see Table 4).

As Table 4 clearly shows, there is literary zero correlation between the indicators of economic growth stability and the volumes of national import, export and payment balance (measured as % of national GDP). However, if we take the indicators of external economic activity of countries in their dynamics (stability of national export/import growth and stability of payment balance) – those demonstrate certain connection with stability of countries' overall economic growth. Therefore, for economic stability maintenance the most important factor is stability of export/import growth but not the actually achieved indicators of export/import. Thus, we can state that our hypothesis #3 is partially confirmed. There is an obvious dependence of economic growth stability from the relative indicators of export and import, but not from their absolute values. This means hypothesis #4 is fully confirmed.

At the final stage of our research countries of the world have been classified into four groups according to the values of their payment balance (positive or negative) and also taking into account the dynamics

Table 2. Indicators of economic growth stability and of external economic activeness of the countries, 2000 to 2015

Stability of Economic Growth			Stability of National Export Development			Stability of National Import Development		
#	Country	Indicator	#	Country	Indicator	#	Country	Indicator
Leading Countries								
1	Vietnam	2,83	1	Malaysia	14,92	1	Ethiopia	9,4
2	Indonesia	2,93	2	Senegal	15,14	2	Russia	13,23
3	Australia	2,98	3	Thailand	16,22	3	Norway	14,4
4	Bangladesh	3,35	4	C. Rica	16,34	4	Canada	14,41
5	Lao	3,78	5	Sweden	16,92	5	Lesotho	15,89
6	Cameroon	4,48	6	Poland	17,29	6	Australia	16,44
7	Tanzania	4,67	7	France	18,11	7	Malaysia	16,53
8	Guatemala	4,99	8	Mexico	18,59	8	Swaziland	17,53
9	Norway	5,21	9	Cyprus	19,11	9	Mexico	18,26
10	Bolivia	5,47	10	Croatia	19,21	10	UK	18,46
A Separate Group of Large Countries								
17	USA	6,38	11	UK	19,81	22	Germany	23,75
26	South Africa	6,9	15	Germany	21,58	42	Italy	27,95
32	UK	7,49	20	Russia	23,33	50	Turkey	29,82
35	China	7,61	40	USA	28,12	62	Brazil	33,58
47	India	8,44	70	S. Africa	36,03	73	Thailand	37,38
48	Italy	8,45	78	India	39,23	86	S. Africa	39,71
53	Germany	9,02	86	China	41,87	96	China	42,05
63	Thailand	9,78	93	Turkey	43,24	101	India	44,29
Outsiders								
146	CAR	39,55	146	Congo	135,97	146	Nigeria	135,04
147	Zimbabwe	39,83	147	S. Leone	141,03	147	Congo	148,86
148	S. Leone	40,13	148	Chad	142,9	148	Chad	150,4
149	Liberia	43,76	149	Liberia	144,81	149	Serbia	159,46
150	S. Sudan	51,36	150	Argentina	148,1	150	Liberia	511,59

(Calculated by the author on the basis of the World Bank statistics)

of their economic growth (here, dynamic growth means at least 4% a year, on average, throughout the whole period in question – 2000 to 2015; in the opposite case the growth is considered to be slow). For these groups we got the following correlations (see Tables 5 and 6).

Our results from evaluation of correlation between economic growth stability and dynamics of key macroeconomic indicators for the groups of countries, as described above, shows that this correlation is much more significant for the countries with positive trade balance (these are 49 countries from the analyzed) and also for the countries with rather slow but still average economic growth (around 4%) throughout the whole period of 2000-2015.

Table 3. Stability of economic growth vs average rate of economic growth by countries of the world, 2000-2015

#	Country	Average Rate of Economic Growth, 2000-2015	#	Country	Stability of Economic Growth
Leading Countries					
1	Azerbaijan	10,94	1	Vietnam	2,83
2	China	9,59	2	Indonesia	2,93
3	Ethiopia	9,03	3	Australia	2,98
4	Turkmenistan	8,51	4	Bangladesh	3,35
5	Chad	8,31	5	Laos	3,78
6	Rwanda	8,03	6	Cameroon	4,48
7	Tajikistan	7,83	7	Tanzania	4,67
8	Cambodia	7,82	8	Guatemala	4,99
9	Bhutan	7,61	9	Norway	5,21
10	Nigeria	7,54	10	Bolivia	5,47
Outsiders					
141	Brunei Darussalam	1,02	141	Kosovo	31,72
142	South Sudan	0,95	142	Chad	33,68
143	Yemen	0,94	143	Yemen	34,69
144	Japan	0,89	144	Azerbaijan	37,84
145	Jamaica	0,69	145	CAR	39,55
146	Portugal	0,42	146	Zimbabwe	39,83
147	Italy	0,24	147	Sierra Leone	40,13
148	Greece	0,16	148	Liberia	43,76
149	CAR	-0,01	149	South Sudan	51,36
150	Zimbabwe	-0,01	150	Iraq	64,73

(Compiled by the author on the basis of the World Bank statistics)

Table 4. Correlation between the indicators of economic growth, national export, national import and payment balance (in % of national GDP, 2000-2015)

Indicators in Correlation	Correlation Values		
	National Export Volume	**National Import Volume**	**Payment Balance of the Country**
Stability of national economic growth	0,12	0,19	-0,09
	Stability of national export growth	Stability of national import growth	Stability of payment balance growth
Stability of national economic growth	0,53	0,58	0,54

(Calculated by the authors)

Table 5. Correlation between economic growth, national export, national import and payment balance (in % of national GDP during 2000-2015) in the countries with negative and positive payment balance

Indicators in Correlation	Stability of National Export Growth		Stability of National Import Growth		Stability of Payment Balance Growth	
	Countries With Positive Balance of Payments1	Countries With Negative Balance of Payments	Countries With Positive Balance of Payments	Countries With Negative Balance of Payments	Countries With Positive Balance of Payments	Countries With Negative Balance of Payments
Stability of economic growth	0,57	0,34	0,58	0,42	0,72	0,41

(Calculated by the author)

Table 6. Correlation between the indicators of economic growth, national export/import and payment balance (in % to national GDP, 2000-2015; calculated separately for the countries with dynamics and with slow economic growth)

Indicators in Correlation	Stability of National Export Growth		Stability of National Import Growth		Stability of Payment Balance Growth	
	Countries With Dynamic Economic Growth	Countries With Slow Economic Growth	Countries With Dynamic Economic Growth	Countries With Slow Economic Growth	Countries With Dynamic Economic Growth	Countries With Slow Economic Growth
Stability of economic growth	0,5	0,72	0,52	0,68	0,54	0,71

RESEARCH METHODOLOGY

For the study we used the World Bank's statistical information and following macroeconomic indicators of the world's development in 2016: state budget revenues; average tax rate in the countries; countries' GDP; average rate of loans for business in the countries; inflation rate in the national economies.

The study evaluated statistical information of 95 world's largest countries with a relatively stable socio-economic situation in 2016.

The study was based on a comparison of synthetic indicators reflecting the fairness of social compensation of tax payments received from business; the fairness of social compensation of business contribution to the national GDP formation.

The logic of these indicators selecting based on the Government role as a redistributor of budget funds collected from business in tax form in favor of social programs, and the Government efficiency in spending of the national GDP part (also generated by business) on the needs of social development.

As a reference point we used a hypothesis that in the effective state the first indicator (social compensation of taxes paid by business) should be lower than the second (social compensation of business contribution to GDP), since social compensation can be maintained at a high level not only due to high taxes, but also public-private partnership, social investment, outsourcing (for example, development of insurance medicine, private education, etc.), encouraging a small business and so on. In this case, the high budget expenditures on the social sphere will be compensated not only by .tax payments of the business, as by, for example, the state (municipal) quota (a fixed state / municipal quota of places in private schools), tax preferences (for example, for new technologies development, increase of administration and market regulation effectiveness, implementation of business social responsibility programs) and so on. An effective state focuses on business stimulating to co-execute the function of social compensation.

On the other hand, the fair state accentuates own role of budgets redistributor. High level of social compensation in such states is justified by high tax payments from business. A fair state is more independent in the process of making decisions about social compensation, but it may be less attractive to business (this strategy is effective only in the case of insignificant demand in domestic markets), and also to assume the emergence of corruption schemes in budget distribution.

The calculation of the coefficients of the state policy of social compensation efficiency and fairness was carried out on the basis of comparing the shares of a particular country in the global amount of paid taxes, social payments and GDP in 2016 (World Bank statistics).

Table 1 shows the indicators of social compensation of taxes paid by business and indicators of social compensation of business contribution to national GDP formation in the countries of the world in 2016.

According to Table 6 it can be seen that the indices of social compensation of taxes paid by business are the lowest in countries with low government expenditures on the social sphere and relatively medium or low tax rates for business. The outsiders of the rating are countries in which state high social expenditures are formed not due to the business tax payments (but for example, by exploiting the country's resource potential, activities of state corporations, or loans from international organizations).

Indicators of social compensation of business contribution to national GDP formation are low in countries where the share of government social spending remains at a minimum (Guinea, Ukraine, Zimbabwe, Bangladesh, Philippines), or where the largest contribution to GDP was realized not by private business but by state companies (Russia, Iran, India). In the end of the rating there are mostly highly developed countries, in which both public spending on social programs and the contribution of private businesses to GDP are high.

As can be seen from Table 7 countries that implement a fair policy (social compensation of the business contribution to GDP higher than a similar compensation of paid taxes) are world economically developed countries, whereas countries with effective budget policy are mainly represented by states with a high share of the profitable public sector (Iran, Algeria, Saudi Arabia), or the either countries consciously implementing liberal reforms (Paraguay, Ukraine, Tunisia), or simply feeling a severe shortage of their own budget sources (Bangladesh, Burundi, Niger).

At the second stage of the research the social compensation (of tax paid by business and business contribution in national GDP formation) indicators of the countries of the world in 2016 were compared (Table 8).

We can note the first interesting conclusion: that among the countries with effective budget policy there is practically no successful economically developed and stable one (with the exception of countries where state companies exploit natural potential).

Moreover, conscious liberalization of the state budget policy, development of extra-tax and extra-budget schemes of social compensation, most likely simply deprives the state of regulatory competencies and its effectiveness as an actor of own economic system and economic sovereignty. The problem of budgetary policy liberalization is repeatedly reinforced in countries with non-clear near-budgetary relations and corruption, which reduce the effectiveness of social compensation programs, their targeting and expediency (Ukraine, the Philippines, the countries of Africa).

Table 7. Indicators of social compensation of taxes paid by business and indicators of social compensation of business contribution to the National GDP formation in the world in 2016

Indicators of Social Compensation of Taxes Paid by Business			Indicators of Social Compensation of Business Contribution to the National GDP Formation		
N°	Country	Indicator	N°	Country	Indicator
1	Poland	49,31	1	Guinea	16,14
2	Argentina	63,12	2	India	20,96
3	India	63,83	3	Zimbabwe	24,22
4	Korea, South	68,38	4	Ukraine	24,85
5	Botswana	72,8	5	Burundi	26,08
6	United States	72,82	6	Iran	30,81
7	Israel	73,29	7	Bangladesh	31,33
8	Moldova	83,07	8	Mauritius	32,06
9	China	83,22	9	Philippines	32,11
10	Turkey	83,8	10	Russia	32,75

(Made by co-authors)

Table 8. Indicators of social compensation of the countries of the world in 2016

Leaders				Outsiders			
N°	Country	Comparison of Indicators of Social Compensation	Ginny Coefficient	N°	Country	Comparison of Indicators of Social Compensation	Ginny Coefficient
1	Switzerland	0,46	0,62	76	India	3,04	0,72
2	Israel	0,47	0,67	77	Coted'Ivoire	3,06	0,71
3	Belgium	0,51	0,66	78	Uganda	3,17	0,72
4	France	0,52	0,64	79	Philippines	3,27	0,71
5	Austria	0,53	0,64	80	Indonesia	3,362	0,76
6	NewZealand	0,55	0,65	81	Mali	3,394	0,75
7	Finland	0,56	0,59	82	SaudiArabia	3,458	0,73
8	Iceland	0,6	0,66	83	ElSalvador	3,6	0,74
9	Germany	0,62	0,66	84	Zimbabwe	3,63	0,84
10	Ireland	0,62	0,58	85	Mauritius	3,64	0,66
11	China	0,67	0,55	86	Paraguay	3,76	0,76
12	UK	0,71	0,69	87	Mozambique	3,9	0,68
13	Italy	0,73	0,6	88	Kyrgyzstan	3,93	0,68
14	Australia	0,74	0,62	89	Burundi	3,97	0,69
15	Spain	0,75	0,57	90	Ukraine	4,43	0,66
16	Canada	0,79	0,68	91	Niger	4,66	0,72
17	Korea,South	0,82	0,57	92	Tunisia	4,86	0,69
18	Estonia	0,85	0,67	93	Bangladesh	6,14	0,66
19	Slovenia	0,88	0,62	94	Algeria	6,5	0,67
20	UnitedStates	0,93	0,8	95	Iran	8,17	0,7

(Made by co-authors)

Thus, the desire for effective budgetary policy, which consists in the implementation of social compensation programs through extra-tax budget revenues, the development of quota mechanisms, business social responsibility programs, etc., anywhere in the world (except countries with state-owned companies with exclusive rights to exploit natural potential) did not lead to the formation of a stable, developed and sufficient socio-economic system. Hypothesis regarding the preservation of the social irresponsibility of business, even using preferences and benefits, is confirmed.

At the final stage of the study, the fairness / efficiency indicators of the countries budget policy were compared with the indicator of the equality of wealth distribution in the social and economic system (Ginny coefficient). It was estimated that, on average, the Ginny coefficient in countries implementing an fair budget policy (24 countries of the analyzed) was 0.65, while the 71 countries implementing a more or less effective budget strategy had an average Ginny coefficient of 0.71. Given that for 95 analyzed countries, the Ginny coefficient varies from a minimum of 0.54 in Japan to a maximum of 0.84 in Namibia, a difference of 0.6 is very significant (20% of the assessment range).

It can be concluded that in countries with a budget policy aimed at maximizing accumulation and further spending of budgetary funds on behalf of the state, wealth among property groups is distributed more evenly (by about 20%), thus, fair budgetary policy seems more oriented to maintain social stability and low level of material differentiation.

After analyzing the countries grouped for dozens by increasing of social compensation indicators (Table 3), one can see that the corresponding average Ginny coefficient changes wavy, starting from a minimum in countries with fair social compensation, reaching a maximum in the countries of the sixth dozen (that are already focusing on an effective model of social compensation) and again falling to the last dozen. Consequently, there is no direct correlation between the fairness / efficiency of the state budget policy and the level of property differentiation in the countries of the world.

That allows making a conclusion that in their maximums, state programs of fair and effective compensation are highly effective and leading to property differentiation reduction in the society. However, as can be seen from the results of the last column of Table 9, the impact of fair social compensation will

Table 9. Indicators of social compensation, Ginny coefficient and GDP per capita in the world (by dozens of the countries, 2016)

	Countries	Correlation of Social Compensation Indicators	Ginny Coefficient	GDP per Capita
1	Switzerland, Belgium, France	0,46 - 0,62	0,63	82911
2	China, UK, Australia, United States	0,67-0,93	0,64	78494
3	Argentina, Brazil, Turkey, Japan	0,94 -1,04	0,67	41314
4	Portugal, Poland, Hungary, Zambia	1,04 -1,22	0,68	26942
5	Singapore, Jordan, Kenya, Azerbaijan	1,25-1,62	0,7	22184
6	Namibia, South Africa, Malaysia	1,62-2,09	0,73	9984
7	Colombia, Egypt, Russia, Thailand	2,11-2,77	0,71	10940
8	Georgia, India, Philippines, Indonesia	2,83-3,36	0,72	6977
9	Saudi Arabia, Paraguay, Ukraine	3,39-4,43	0,72	13900
10	Tunisia, Bangladesh, Algeria, Iran	4,66-8,17	0,69	10057

be high in high-income countries (maximum per capita income in the top ten countries is about 83000 USD), and effective budget policy - in poor countries (per capita income is about 10000 USD).

To confirm this conclusion, we can detail the first dozen and the last five of the analyzed states (Table 9).

As can be seen from Table 9, in general, more affluent states of the ten use fair social compensation policy which shows the highest effectiveness in reducing property differentiation (for example, in Ireland, France and Switzerland). For example, in Iceland, social compensation is more fair than in Ireland, but less effective (Iceland is poorer than Ireland), a similar situation in the pair Israel-Switzerland or Austria-France.

Among the countries of the latter group (five), an effective policy of social compensation does not have high achievements in Niger (the poorest country of the group) and Iran (which, although is the richest state in the group, cannot be considered as a demonstration example because of the huge public sector that actively exploits the country's natural potential and form the revenue side of the country's budget not only by tax payments, but also, for example, by profits). A detailed analysis of the countries of group 9 (ten states) also demonstrates a certain "wave" of the ratio of social compensation indicators with GDP per capita growth (Table 10). The wave reaches its maximum (the maximum efficiency of the social compensation policy) in Ukraine, which occupies an average position in the ranking of the countries of the group on per capita income.

A detailed analysis of groups of countries suggests that the high effectiveness of fair policy of social compensation applying is a characteristic of countries with high per capita income, whereas in poor countries of the world, fair social compensation loses its effectiveness and expediency, giving way to effective social compensation. In rich countries with a strong domestic demand, the business is able to concentrate significant amounts and pay high taxes for the realization of own access to large consumer markets. The high level of taxes will not turn into a factor of investment attractiveness and country high competitiveness reducing if these payments are compensated by high domestic demand and state efficiency as a redistributor of budgetary funds (rational policy of social compensation).

Table 10. Indicators of social compensation, Ginny coefficient and GDP per capita in the world (the first dozen, 2016).

	Countries	Correlation of Social Compensation Indicators	Ginny Coefficient	GDP per Capita
1	Finland	0,56	0,59	53154
2	New Zealand	0,55	0,65	55823
3	Israel	0,47	0,67	64633
4	Austria	0,53	0,64	73047
5	Iceland	0,6	0,66	81945
6	Belgium	0,51	0,66	86205
7	Germany	0,62	0,66	90768
8	Ireland	0,62	0,58	91432
9	France	0,52	0,64	94557
10	Switzerland	0,46	0,62	137549

In the world poorest countries with limited domestic demand, the state's task is not only to ensure the social peace and stability, but also to maintain a high investment attractiveness and competitiveness of the national business environment. In addition, in poor countries that are prone to corruption, business is often able to carry out social compensation more rationally and efficiently than the authorities. In this connection, the rationality of effective social compensation increases dramatically.

CONCLUSION AND RECOMMENDATIONS

Our analysis of correlations between economic growth indicators and dynamics of external trade operations for various countries of the world (2000-2015) proves that growth of both export and import may have quite a stabilizing influence on the economic development of the countries, however, only provided the trade balance is positive. A separate analysis of this correlation by the decile groups of countries (divided according to the volume of their trade balance) demonstrates that the highest correlation is observed for the top deciles (the countries with the maximum positive trade balance - Ireland, Turkmenistan, Brunei Darussalam, Gabon, Switzerland, Thailand, Netherlands, Maldives, Slovenia, Hungary) and also in the countries where trade balance is close to zero (Cyprus, Bulgaria, Greece, Nigeria, Belarus, Chile, Finland, Japan, Uruguay, Swaziland). At the same time, for the countries with the negative balance of payments external trade operations have very little or none at all influence on economic growth and its stability.

Therefore, we can make a theoretical conclusion that even in the 21st century maintaining positive trade balance is still the key decisive factor for economic growth and development of countries, regardless the availability of many other options for growth and development – such as instruments of the international financial market, well-developed service sector, transfer of innovations etc. However, there is a big difference from the classical times of traditional mercantilism: nowadays growth of import can lead to economic stability only provided export growth is still higher (even if insignificantly, when the trade balance is still quite close to zero). Negative trade balance, in the majority of cases worldwide, is still among the most destabilizing factors for economic growth.

Rapid economic growth tends to have mostly negative influence on the stability of economic systems. This is quite logical if we take into account the imminent restructuring of the whole economic system in favor of most dynamically developing sectors, temporary financial misbalance (and a significant one), investment "overheating", limiting state capacities in timely and efficient regulation of the economic system which is developing too quickly (and states, traditionally, tend to be always late in their reaction). Under the conditions of rather dynamic economic growth indicators of external trade may change suddenly and dramatically: for example, export of readymade product from the developing sectors may suddenly grow, thus causing also quite sudden growth in imports of the related raw materials and technologies. All these quick changes will cause abrupt fluctuations in trade balance and balance of payments, they may also lead to significant changes in international labor migration, cross-country investment flows etc. Obviously, all these changes – being abrupt and often not quite predictable – will have their negative influence on the stability of economic growth of countries. Finally, too rapid economic growth may lead to overdependence of a country from foreign consumption due to fluctuations of the world prices. In a longer term, this can limit the economic development horizon as such (the most typical scenario will include full degradation of the non-growing sectors because all their resources have been moved to more profitable sectors which sooner or later will have its negative impact on internal consumption). All these trends and manifestations tend to increase destabilization effects manifold, even if annual reduction of GDP rate is not that significant (in such a situation skeptical sentiments or even panic emerge too easily, thus causing capital outflow from a country, lower prices of raw materials, higher prices at consumption markets etc.).

Thus, taking into account the outlined specificity of economic development of the countries during the early years of the 21st century, we can also formulate a range of vital requirements to the process of strategy development and implementation so that to make national economic growth more stable and long-term, even under all the risks and uncertainties related to unavoidable integration of the world markets.

Today, dynamic economic growth (again, dynamic here means more than 4% per annum) would be nearly impossible without intensive external trade and cross-country borrowing of production factors. Many countries worldwide do not have enough internal capacities for economic development this quick. This means neither they have the economic strength to guarantee own long-term and stable economic growth on the basis of external trade only (as statistical analysis clearly shows this trade potential survives usefulness during some 8-10 years only). Among all 150 countries we have analyzed here only two (Croatia and Guinea Bissau) had outstripping economic growth (meaning every new year the indicator was always higher than in the previous year) during at least 12 years (out of 15 overall). In 19 more countries (including India, UAE and Pakistan) such outstripping growth was observed for 11 years. And in Germany, Russia and Denmark it was recorded only for 6 consecutive years. The worst indicator in this regard got Southern Sudan – 4 years since the year this country got independence. In the absolute majority of the studied countries (72 out of 150) this outstripping growth lasted for 8-9 years, and this rather short term significantly limits governmental efforts when it comes to change of priorities and strategic guidelines in national economic development.

Relatively small volumes of national export or import do not necessarily mean lack of economic growth. For example, to the group of 20 countries with the smallest volumes of national exports belong Pakistan, Haiti and Columbia, and all three economies have also demonstrated rather average dynamics of GDP growth – slightly less than 3%. Majority of the analyzed countries, including the United States, had the economic growth on the level of 3,8-4,5% throughout the studied period.

If we analyze the import indicators separately – the situation is more explicit. To the group with minimum import volumes belong very different countries, including Brazil (the average rate of economic growth – 4,2%), Japan (7%), USA (3,8%), China (5,1%), India (3,7%), Indonesia (1,6%). Therefore, we can state that slow-but-steady economic development by means of internal reserves is possible even in the 21st century, and the only major problem for the governments striving to develop their countries under sanctions, for example, or under high external competition with neighbors would be finding sufficient internal reserves for this growth. And the key sources for these resources are internal consumption and internal competitive environment. Better internal consumption means internal demand must be efficiently satisfied (and this, in turn, means that internal demand will develop qualitatively further), while more competitive internal environment means that the most competitive enterprises and sectors must be developed in a country.

In the case when a state is actively integrating into the world markets, its strategies of economic growth stabilization must guarantee, in the first place, not necessarily high indicators of export, import and trade balance – but stability of positive dynamics in these indicators, even under global instability and constant fluctuations at the strategic markets of raw materials, food products and electronic services. This is why stabilization of economic growth in a country must be seen as, first of all, reducing its dependence from externalities, for example, through diversification of external economic activities. This diversification should include the following items: monitoring the contributions of all important trade partners making sure none of them is getting too risky large share in export or import; stimulation of competition between foreign agents and at foreign markets; widening the area of export activities etc. At the same time, development of internal markets must rest on maintaining the sectoral balance in national economy (for example, through introduction of mandatory quotas for all large exporters of what they must sell internally; flexible taxation and budget policies, both aimed at regulation of intersectoral flows of investments, labor force, resources etc.; promotion of regional cooperation which would allow, on the one hand, to accumulate the advantages of external trade (foreign distribution, availability of resources and production factors), and on the other – to localize many economic processes so that they can be better regulated, controlled and forecasted by regional authorities.

The conducted research and hypotheses testing allow to set a number of recommendations for modernization of the national policy of social compensation.

- Based on conclusion that nowhere in the world (neither rich nor poor) the effective strategy of social compensation has led to the formation of stable society with a minimum property differentiation, that confirms the persistence of business social irresponsibility in the 21st century, it can be determined that the state does not should be eliminated from social compensation programs, allowing the business to independently implement social responsibility strategies in exchange for tax benefits and preferences. With all the existing inefficiencies of the authorities and governments, the state should coordinate the interactions between business and society, not allowing its own merging with either the first (oligarchy) or the second (radical socialism);
- The government's balance between society and business should be ensured by combining a fair and effective social compensation policy, which effectiveness changes with the welfare of society (the growth of the country material well-being should be accompanied by a transition to more fair social compensation, primarily due to tax increase, and vice versa, the government must make effective social compensation in case of living or business conditions deterioration in the country);
- As it was determined in the study, often the obtained results cannot be considered as demonstrative due to the powerful public sector in the economy of analyzed countries, which exploits the natural resource potential and generates the revenue part of national budget not only by paid taxes, but also, for example, by own income.

In connection with this, in the future, the co-authors research activities can expand the number of indicators of the world's countries (for example, state's share in the economy, share of natural resource exploiting in the national GDP) which will help to determine conclusions more relevant to the modernization of national programs of social compensation in the conditions of globalization dynamics.

REFERENCES

Al-Yousif, Y. K. (2000). Do government expenditures inhibit or promote economic growth: Some empirical evidence from Saudi Arabia. *The Indian Economic Journal*, *48*(2), 92.

Amano, R. A., & Wirjanto, T. S. (1998). Government expenditures and the permanent-income model. *Review of Economic Dynamics*, *1*(3), 719–730.

Balassa, B. (1978). Exports and economic growth: Further evidence. *Journal of Development Economics*, *5*(2), 181–189. doi:10.1016/0304-3878(78)90006-8

Barro, R. (1998). *Determinants of Economic Growth: A Cross-Country Empirical Study.* The MIT Press.

Barro, R. J. (1990). Government spending in a simple model of endogeneous growth. *Journal of Political Economy*, *98*(5, Part 2), S103–S125.

Cooray, A. (2009). Government Expenditure, Governance and Economic Growth. *Comparative Economic Studies*, *51*(3), 401–418. doi:10.1057/ces.2009.7

Davoodi, H., & Zou, H. (1998). Fiscal decentralization and economic growth: a cross-country study. *Journal of Urban Economics*, *43*(2), 244–257. doi:10.1006/juec.1997.2042

Devarajan, S., Swaroop, V., & Zou, H. F. (1996). The composition of public expenditure and economic growth. *Journal of Monetary Economics*, *37*(2), 313–344.

Dreher, A. (2006). The influence of globalization on taxes and social policy: An empirical analysis for OECD countries. *European Journal of Political Economy*, *22*(1), 179–201.

Dreher, A., Sturm, J. E., & Ursprung, H. W. (2008). The impact of globalization on the composition of government expenditures: Evidence from panel data. *Public Choice*, *134*(3-4), 263–292.

Esfahani, H. (1991). Exports, imports, and economic growth in semi-industrialized countries. *Journal of Development Economics*, *35*(1), 93–116. doi:10.1016/0304-3878(91)90068-7

Feder, G. (1983). On exports and economic growth. *Journal of Development Economics*, *12*(1-2), 59–73.

Grier, K., & Tullock, G. (1989). An empirical analysis of cross-national economic growth, 1951–1980. *Journal of Monetary Economics*, *24*(2), 259–276. doi:10.1016/0304-3932(89)90006-8

Harrison, A. (1996). Openness and growth: A time-series, cross-country analysis for developing countries. *Journal of Development Economics*, *48*(2), 419–447. doi:10.1016/0304-3878(95)00042-9

Hines, J. R. Jr. (2006). Will social welfare expenditures survive tax competition? *Oxford Review of Economic Policy*, *22*(3), 330–348.

Ju, J., Wu, Y., & Zeng, L. (2010). The impact of trade liberalization on the trade balance in developing countries. *IMF Staff Papers*, *57*(2), 427–449. doi:10.1057/imfsp.2009.19

Kakwani, N., & Krongkaew, M. (2000). Economic growth, poverty and income inequality in the Asia-Pacific region. *Journal of the Asia Pacific Economy*, *5*(1-2), 9–13.

Kavoussi, R. (1984). Export expansion and economic growth: Further empirical evidence. *Journal of Development Economics*, *14*(1), 241–250. doi:10.1016/0304-3878(84)90052-X

Kelly, T. (1997). Public expenditures and growth. *The Journal of Development Studies*, *34*(1), 60–84.

Kudryavtseva, T. J., Ivanova, E. A., Kozlova, E. A., & Skhvediani, A. E. (2017). Pricing and assessment of competitiveness of innovative medical devices in the context of commercialization strategy. *Academy of Strategic Management Journal*, *16*(1), 110–122.

Lindert, P. (1996). What Limits Social Spending? *Explorations in Economic History*, *33*(1), 1–34. doi:10.1006/exeh.1996.0001

Malizia, E. E., & Ke, S. (1993). The influence of economic diversity on unemployment and stability. *Journal of Regional Science*, *33*(2), 221–235.

Narayan Rath, B., & Akram, V. (2017). Export diversification and total factor productivity growth in case of South Asian region. *Journal of Social and Economic Development*, *19*(1), 196–210.

Rodionov, D. G., & Rudskaya, I. A. (2017). Regional Innovative Environment in National Economic Development (The Case of Russia). *International Journal of Economic Development*, *32*(4), 20–28.

Rodionov, D. G., & Rudskaya, I. A. (2017a). Econometric modeling as a tool for evaluating the performance of regional innovation systems (with regions of the Russian Federation as the example). Academy of Strategic Management Journal, 16(2), 12-21.

Sakaki, S. (2004). Income distribution management to sustain long-term economic growth: Does the equalization of income distribution contribute to long-term economic growth? *The Annals of Regional Science*, *38*(2), 199–218.

Scully, G. (2001). Government Expenditure and Quality of Life. *Public Choice*, *108*(1), 123–145. doi:10.1023/A:1017518926640

Shabunina, T. V., Shchelkina, S. P., & Rodionov, D. G. (2017). An innovative approach to the transformation of eco-economic space of a region based on the green economy principles. Academy of Strategic Management Journal, 16(1), 176-185.

Shari, I. (2000). Economic growth and income inequality in Malaysia, 1971–95. *Journal of the Asia Pacific Economy*, *5*(1-2), 112–124.

Tanninen, H. (2010). Income inequality, government expenditures and growth. *Applied Economics*, *31*(9), 1109–1117.

Ushakov, D. (2016). Dynamics of international economical relationships in the global context of Innovative Modernization. *International Journal of Environmental and Science Education*, *18*, 10160–10165.

Ushakov, D. (2017a). Information Technologies Within Market Economy: How Communication Tools Became A Field Of Activity. *The EUrASEANs*, *1*, 7–18.

Ushakov, D., Elokhova, I., & Kozonogova, E. (2017). Post industrialization prospects in the dynamics of socioeconomic transformations: Cluster approach. *International Journal of Ecological Economics and Statistics*, *38*(2), 46–57.

Yao, S. (2007). Economic growth, income inequality and poverty in china under economic reforms. *The Journal of Development Studies*, *35*(6), 104–130.

ENDNOTES

1 Trade balance of countries – as of 2015

2 We took into account the average indicators of GDP growth by countries, 2000 to 2015

Chapter 2
Financial Behavior of Russian Population under Crisis Phenomena

Krasovskaya Nadezhda
Tyumen State University, Russia

Danilova Elena
Tyumen State University, Russia

Zamuraeva Larisa
Tyumen State University, Russia

ABSTRACT

Basing on the analysis of contemporary literature sources, the category "financial behavior of population" is defined. Analysis of the factors influencing financial behavior of households under the conditions of ongoing crisis is carried out. Our quantitative study was carried out to identify the motives behind the financial strategy and the reasons limiting the financial behavior of population. Trends in the use of monetary incomes by population have been revealed, dynamics of the structure and the volume of savings has been shown. Transformations of financial strategies of households during the crisis are also demonstrated. A typology of households was developed according to the criterion of money management depending on sociodemographic characteristics, taking into account the age of the respondents, their financial standing and also their lifestyle. The purpose of this study is to determine the contents, the structure, characteristics, dynamics and other factors of financial behavior of a mass actor on the example of the Tyumen region.

INTRODUCTION

At present, Russia is facing an important task of shifting from the resource-oriented economy to an innovative one. Population of the Russian Federation became familiar with the notion of mass investment only at the end of the 20th and beginning of the 21st centuries. Therefore, development of this type of

DOI: 10.4018/978-1-5225-7760-7.ch002

investment in Russia seriously lags behind similar processes in many other countries. There are various explanations for this situation, including low level of citizens' trust in Russian financial institutions, in the first place.

The mass actor of financial behavior in Russia has not been formed yet. The process of its formation and actualization is quite complex and contradictory, and it also requires proper understanding of the motivation of potential investors. In this regard, theoretical and empirical studies of financial behavior, exacerbated by the global financial and economic crisis, are becoming particularly relevant.

The purpose of this study is to determine the contents, structure, characteristics, dynamics and factors behind financial behavior of a mass actor on the example of the Tyumen region.

The main objectives of the study have been as follows:

- To determine the content of financial behavior of economic entities and the category of crisis phenomena on the basis of the analysis of the existing sociological and economic approaches
- To determine the structure of financial behavior of economic entities in the context of the theory of economic behavior
- To reveal the nature and the impact of risks and uncertainty on financial behavior in the dynamics of crisis phenomena
- To conduct a statistical analysis of specific features of the investment environment in today's Russia
- To identify the structure, factors and features of the formation of a mass actor of financial behavior

The core object of the study is financial behavior.

The subject of the study is investment behavior of economic entities in the context of socioeconomic changes.

General Context of the Study

The current socioeconomic situation actualizes the problem of financial behavior of Russian population, especially when it comes to long-term investments. An important tool to attract this money to national economy is to stimulate mass financial behavior. Today's population in the Russian Federation not only spends, but also accumulates funds, including those concentrated in banks. Banks, in turn, instead of lending all these funds to the real economy sector, prefer investing in the short term, that is, be engaged in consumer lending. Thus, the risk of money loss and non-receipt of possible incomes is exacerbated by the risk of incorrect investments, and the latter, in its turn, leads to various social risks.

BACKGROUND

There is a rather large number of definitions, understandings and interpretations of the essence of financial behavior. Different authors have defined them in their own way, reflecting the development of this category during a certain period of time. Financial activity in its various aspects has been and is the subject of research for many scientists.

Theoretical foundations were laid in the scientific studies of the classics, beginning with K. Marx, Ricardo and A. Smith. Today, this legacy forms the basis of general ideas about the regularities of the functioning of financial relations systems. These are the results of the works of M. Alla, E. Domar, J. Keynes, N. Kondratiev, V. Leontiev, A. Marshall, G. Mensch, L. Pasinetti, J. Robinson, A. Sen, R. Solow, M. Friedman, E. Hansen, R. Harrod, J. Hicks, I. Schumpeter, and many others.

Defining the author's interpretation of the basic approaches to understanding finance, one must accept the judgments of such scientists as B. Boyd, E. Dolan, G. Manshuani, V. Oiken, P. Samuelson etc. It should be noted that the issues of savings' transformation into investments have not found sufficient reflection in the studies carried out in our country, while scientific understanding of investments according to the contemporary approaches of Russian economists were proposed in the works of O. Bestuzheva, I. Blank, V. Kossova, A. Krutik, I. Lipsitsa, V. Milovidova, E. Nicholas.

Financial behavior has become a subject of thorough studies in both economics and sociology. Scientific works by the classics of economic sociology, M. Weber, G. Simmel, J. Coleman, T. Parsons, H. White, had a strong influence on the formation of theories of financial behavior. There are also studies in the field of financial behavior belonging to domestic scientists: V. Verkhovin, D. Demin, O. Kuzina, V. Radaev, D. Strebkov and others.

Investigations on the problems of risk and uncertainty, which are integral part of any financial process, and in many respects are characterizing the current stage of the transition economies, can be found in the classic works of R. Catillon and F. Knight, as well as in the works of foreign and domestic scientists A. Algin, I. Balabanov, D. Barlet, V. Glazunov, D. Gladstone, V. Dorodnikov, V. Z. Zubkov, N. Ilyenkov, L. Rusaleva, E. Smirnova, A. Streltsov, D. Timmons, A. Folomiev, T. Shestovskikh, and others who examined, inter alia, the current issues related to risks within economic behavior.

In this context, the problem of studying financial behavior from the point of view of the economic-sociological approach is still not yet fully developed. These circumstances have predetermined the choice of this topic, the definition of the object and the subject for this research, its goals and objectives.

The newest (post-Soviet) Russian economic history has already had four periods of instability: 1987-1992, 1998-2000, 2008-2009, 2014 - ongoing.

It is important to note here that the feature that unites all these periods is the greatest degree of instability in the financial sector which is traditionally more sensitive to various sudden changes and fluctuations. The situation is exacerbated by a large proportion of foreign loans taken by companies and banks, as well as by general crisis in the banking sector. The situation with enterprises is also quite complicated due to decline in production and reduction of domestic demand for products and services in virtually all sectors of the economy. Even the largest companies have closed down many investment programs so that to reduce the expenditure part of their budget, and this, in turn, entails a massive layoff and job cuts.

From the theoretical point of view, crisis phenomena are characterized by risk and uncertainty, both being the key features of financial behavior at the same time. Let's consider the history of the comprehensive history of the development of theories and methods related to risk assessment in financial behavior.

The term "risk" as such was introduced into scientific use at the beginning of the eighteenth century in connection with active development of economic theories of entrepreneurship. Richard Cantillon, who is often referred to as the "mystery man", studied the most mysterious processes of extracting entrepreneurial income. According to R. Cantillon, an entrepreneur is a person who puts himself at risk of inconsistent income: a peasant, an artisan, a merchant and even a robber and a beggar, but not a worker or an official with constant salary, and not a landowner living on rent (Avtonomov,1993). It is the discrepancy between market demand and supply that allows an entrepreneur take risks through buying cheap and selling expensive. After him, uncertainty and risk of entrepreneurial behavior was studied, at least to some extent, by virtually all economists and sociologists.

Categories "risk" and "uncertainty" have long attracted the attention of scientists of various specialties. One of the first researchers of the phenomena of uncertainty and risk was the American economist F. Knight. It was after the publication of his book under the title "Risk, Uncertainty and Profit" back in 1921, that the topic became especially actual in the scientific community. In his work, F. Knight noted that in order to construct a reasonable behavior, the economic subject (actor) must establish causal (cause-effect) relationships between solutions and their consequences. However, due to greater uncertainty of the economic environment, the actor can resort only to determining the probabilities from the implementation of events. F. Knight distinguished three types of such probabilities: a priori, statistical probabilities and also estimates (Knight, 1994).

Determination of a priori probabilities is carried out using mathematical calculations and is applicable in the cases of completely homogeneous and independent events. Statistical probability is based on artificial grouping of events, which we conditionally consider identical. In this case, probabilistic information can be obtained only as a result of statistical processing of data on the already accomplished facts. F. Knight believed that determining a priori probabilities in economic behavior is practically not implementable, while determination of statistical probabilities in some cases is possible.

It is necessary to understand here that the more we approach the investment sphere, the more meaningful is the significance of unique events, the mathematical calculation of the probability of which is impossible.

To preserve the distinction between mathematically measurable and immeasurable uncertainty, F. Knight suggested that the uncertainty of the first type should be called risk, while for the second one the term "uncertainty" itself should be left out (Knight, 1994). Such a breeding of the concepts of risk and uncertainty is still relevant in science and with small changes in interpretation is still supported by many scientists today. We will also adhere to this scientific understanding of the notions of risk and uncertainty.

In the process of economic entities' activities, the following types of financial risks are distinguished:

- The risk of using only own funds or assets
- The risk of non-return of borrowed funds secured by collateral
- The risk of devaluation

There is an opinion that business entities (investors in our case) cannot know exactly what margin they will receive from investments, therefore, the only option for them is to use only their own or borrowed savings based on personal experience and knowledge of economic laws, the reliability of which cannot be guaranteed for 100% in the context of constantly changing socioeconomic environment.

In a volatile situation, investments in assets by public entities should be clearly planned, if necessary, this plan should be quickly adjusted in the online regime. At the same time, the bigger is the organization or business entity, the more time it will take to make a decision and respond to the emerging situation. In this case, there are pluses and minuses, namely, if an unfavorable situation occurs, the inert economic entity will have time to correct everything. Factors of uncertainty may include increases or decreases in the cost of fixed assets, associated with moral and physical deterioration, force majeure circumstances or sharp price fluctuations.

At the end of the 20th century, a whole layer of works devoted to economic analysis of risk appeared in Russian science. Those mainly concerned approaches and methods to be applied when quantifying economic risk measures, while social aspects of risk began to be reflected in studies only since recently. Great contribution to the development of the domestic theory of risk has been made by A. Algin (Algin,

1991). In contrast to the probabilistic risk concept of F. Knight, the concept of A. Algin is cumulative: the risk arises in the event of uncertainty accumulation and is identified with the possible damage caused by a wide variety of factors, including inflation, accidents, bankruptcy. Risk is one of the key elements of investment behavior. Each decision taken by an actor is inevitably associated with risk. Domestic authors suggest different approaches to the definition of the category of "risk".

For example, I. Balabanov (Balabanov, 1996) under the risk understands possible danger of loss, proceeding from certain types of society's activities and the specifics of certain natural phenomena, determining risk, primarily as a historical and economic category. According to A. Streltsov (Streltsov, 2000), under the risk should be understood the possibility/probability of the following events: first, the actor's loss of some of the available resources; secondly, losses while attracting resources in the course of achieving goals; thirdly, shortage of income or identification of additional costs in the course of economic activity.

E. Smirnova (Smirnova, 2001) states that risk is a very dynamic phenomenon that is in constant movement and development. Such a movement is a mechanism of risk, which is expressed in the level of risk taken at each moment of time. There are risks with a visible time horizon, the time of completion of which we know and the risk without a visible time horizon, when the risk mechanism is endless. In the conditions of such mechanisms lies the contentious contradiction caused by the general laws of existence of risk. First, we are talking about the inconsistency of the forms of manifestation of risk. The risk can be either positive, yielding, or negative, damaging. The path of risk development can go beyond permissible limits. Secondly, there is a contradiction of the elements of necessity and randomness contained in the risk. Randomness is not determined by anything, it arises unexpectedly, and necessity is something that should naturally take place. Thirdly, there is a temporary inconsistency, determined by the fact that the time of occurrence and the moment of risk manifestation often do not coincide in time.

Thus, risk is a universal phenomenon, and any economic entity that makes a decision about investing must evaluate possible risks. In this regard, the search for new approaches to accounting and measuring investment risk is becoming particularly relevant. Studying the risk in the structure of investment behavior, we turn to the concept of V. Verkhovin (Verkhovin, 1994). According to him, the ratio of costs and benefits is not always achieved, therefore, under the conditions of socioeconomic changes, activities of subjects cannot be constantly based on the postulates of rational choice. The existing uncertainty generates a discrepancy between reality and real expectations of business entities.

For each type of business entities, T. Shestovskikh (Shestovskikh,1998) identified possible components of socioeconomic risk. Among a large number of market actors, she singled out the following: producer, buyer, seller, merchant, investor, owner, saver and consumer.

In the process of producing a certain product, the manufacturer may face the following risks:

- The risk of irrational choice of location for the organization of production. The place of production organization should be chosen optimally, taking into account the location of resources to be consumed in the course of production process, as well as locations of both suppliers and customers (the latter - in the case of direct sales)
- The risk of an error while determining the demand for a manufactured product. Such an error can lead to an increase in residual commercial products in the warehouse
- The risk of inefficient and inconsistent recruiting of human resources and/or involving material and technical resources. The competence of production personnel, production technology, productive capacity of equipment must meet the most advanced requirements possible

The buyer may experience the following risks:

- The risk of acquiring a substandard product that does not meet the expectations of this buyer
- The risk of profits' loss due to acquiring goods at a price higher than the market average
- The risk of exceeding the costs of finding the most optimal combination cost-quality of the good over the benefit of acquiring the first good that meets the buyer's requests based on a quick purchase, thus excluding the search costs as such

In the process of implementing the purchase of goods, the seller can feel the impact of the following risks:

- The risk of incorrect calculations when determining the price, which can lead to losses from sales
- The risk of losses in the event of a need for long-term storage of a product that can lose its consumer properties
- In the course of carrying out its functions, a merchant may face the following risks:
    - The risk of exceeding the costs of storage and transportation of goods over the expected net income
    - The risk of acquiring a good for resale at a price higher than the market average, which will cause difficulties in setting the desired level of margin
    - The risk of forced sale of goods at a price lower than estimated, which will not allow achieving the expected level of profit
    - The risk of losses due to longer term of storage of a product
    - The risk of losses is higher than the normative when transporting the product from the point of purchase to the point of sale

When investing in certain objects an investor may face the following risks:

- The risk of a partial or total loss of funds, when investing in non-viable projects
- The risk of income loss due to non-optimal distribution of funds between several projects
- The risk of impairment of securities in the case of financial investments
- The risk of losses when investing in economically unsustainable financial institutions

The owner's risk includes the following components:

- The risk of loss or damage of property due to the influence of political, military factor or natural disasters
- The risk of acquiring property that is characterized by fluctuations in market value

The following probable risks await for the savings bank

- The risk of irrational choice of the form of saving values
- The risk of an erroneous choice of a financial institution when investing in valuables, including the possibility of becoming a victim of a financial pyramid or a one-day company
- The risk of losses due to bank's freezing all accounts in the event of a financial crisis

- The risk of loss in case of untimely investment or withdrawal of funds from a bank account

In the process of consumption, the actor may face the following risks:

- The risk of consuming poor-quality goods
- The risk of consuming the good, which can have a significant negative impact on the consumer
- The risk of consuming goods that are not able to satisfy the actual needs of the consumer
- The risk that can arise when consuming dangerous goods
- The risk of consuming a high-quality product that is not able to satisfy consumer demands when used under certain conditions

In the general case, risk is defined as the probability of losses in the form of financial loss or damage occurring under the influence of a number of objective and subjective factors.

In contemporary economic theory, it is believed that a necessary and sufficient condition for determining the quantitative characteristics of probable risk is the presence of two reasonable values: mathematical expectation and standard deviation. In the absence of these values, most economists, following the tradition once introduced by F. Knight, speak of uncertainty.

Of course, for economics that studies relatively isolated and supposedly rational economic entities, this approach, which allows to build formalized mathematical models of behavior, is pragmatically useful, but it is not that fully acceptable when studying economic risks in economic sociology, which studies not only rational economic behavior, but all the real diversity of socioeconomic actions.

Undoubtedly, investment behavior in comparison with other types of social behavior is the most rational one. Economic entities, building a vector of their behavior, calculate profits and losses, costs and compensations, compare prices for various resources etc. However, these calculations, as it has been already sufficiently, numerously and convincingly proved by scientists, in the vast majority of cases have nothing to do with mathematical calculations: people weigh the subjective utility of goods and calculate the subjective probabilities of the available alternatives. They do this even in those rare cases when they have full information, know the mathematical methods of calculating probabilities and have enough time for such calculations. Subjective probabilities that are different for different economic entities in the same situations are determined based on qualifications and experience, and also depend on the degree of one's self-confidence, the level of claims and various other psychological and social features.

In the absence of a tangible difference between alternatives or lack of information about them, an economic decision, especially in investment activities, is made on the basis of a flair, moral or aesthetic predilections. However, from the standpoint of an economic subject acting randomly, there is also a risk of inaction and also a risk of a missed chance.

Hence, the conclusion is that if we only rely on the possibility of a mathematical definition of probabilities to determine the risk, or in addition to this, we will refer to risky situations with the possibility of qualitative assessment (for example, through an expert survey), it turns out that risky actions can take (and this is by no means always the case) only large enough economic organizations, and practically all individual economic behavior will be characterized only by uncertainty.

As it was said before, there are own and borrowed sources for financing of investment activity. Among borrowed sources, the most common are credit facilities of banks and other intermediary financial structures. Thus, it is necessary to note the serious influence of credit risks on the investment behavior of actors. Credit risk is the financial risk associated with improper regulation of obligations to repay the loan and interest.

For example, Barinov identified three types of credit risk (Barinov, 2001):

- **Credit Risk Without Recourse to the Borrower:** The actor, who is the lender evaluates only the amount of cash flow from the project, directed to repay the loan, taking care of all the political and commercial risks associated with the project;
- **Credit Risk With Full Recourse to the Borrower:** The actor, who is the lender assumes minimal risks without limiting their participation to only giving means, but also by analyzing the amount of income that the company-borrower will receive from a project;
- **Credit Risk With Limited Recourse to the Borrower:** The actors with investment behavior assess fully all the risks associated with the investment project. The parties that are participants in the project, take responsibility for the scope of works (services), the execution of which is directly dependent on them.

On the territory of Russia, the most common one is the second type of credit risk. Thus, we can state that credit and project risks are nearly always interrelated.

Project risks mean a defined set of risks, characterized by the ability to occur due to a range of objective and subjective reasons, which pose threats to economic viability of a project, resulting in a negative impact on cash flows. Literature describes the following group of project risks: risks associated with the introduction of a project; operational risks, defined by failures in the production process; management risks associated with the lack of qualified specialists of the enterprise and, as a consequence, low level of organization and project management; sales risks related to changes in market conditions, changes in prices of manufactured products;

There are also other classifications of investment risks, of course. For example, according to V. Krivov (Krivov, 2000), investment risk can be unpredictable or predictable, but uncertain.

Unpredictable in terms of investment risks of the project include:

- Macroeconomic risks (political instability, changes in the external economic situation, unexpected measures of state regulation, new standards, changes in environmental protection and the use of natural resources, etc.)
- Environmental risks (accidents and natural disasters)
- Socially dangerous threats and risks
- Risks associated with the occurrence of force majeure. This manifest themselves in the form of unforeseen disruptions, for example, bankruptcy of contractors, various accidents and equipment failure, manufacturing defects, etc.

External predictable, but uncertain risks include:

- Market risk associated with acquiring raw materials from new sources or sudden increase in its value, abrupt changes in consumer demand, increased competition, the loss of market position
- Operational risks, defined as the inability to maintain the operating state of the elements of the project, security breach, deviation from the initial objectives of the project

Thus, in terms of socioeconomic changes, any activity is characterized by certain risks. According to V. Zubkov (Zubkov, 2001), risks can be divided into several categories. Their great diversity can be explained by the presence of factors that characterize specific traits of uncertainty and particular types of activity. Apart from that, there are also risk-creating factors.

All risk-creating factors can be divided into two groups based on the nature of risk. The first group consists of the internal factors that arise in the course of activity of a managing company (companies). The reason for their occurrence is the specific activity of a company in the areas of management, production and circulation, which allows implementing a scientific approach to management activities and related services of the company so that to develop an effective development strategy, systematically and according to the the level of staff competence. The second group consists of the external factors that exist outside the company and identify trends in the changing socioeconomic environment. Among them are scientific and technical, political, socioeconomic and environmental factors.

Socioeconomic life of economic subjects is always full of risks. In the course of making investment decisions it would be nearly impossible to find an alternative that may result in certain, known in advance consequences.

Therefore, basing on the analysis of the existing approaches to determining the risk category as such, investment risk can be interpreted in detail. In our own formulation, investment risk is a probable variability of anticipated benefits from certain forms of investment. In a general sense, the structure of investment risk includes the risk of loss of profits, the risk of reduced yields and the risk of direct financial losses. In particular, the investment risks components may differ depending on which types of investment behavior are already revealed in action.

RESEARCH METHODOLOGY

The first stage of our study was dedicated to studying and interpretation of various economic and sociological approaches to financial behavior.

At the second stage, statistical analysis of the use of monetary incomes of Russian population, the volume and the structure of accumulations, as well as other parameters characterizing the subject of the study was carried out.

At the third stage, a survey was conducted in the city of Tyumen and in the Tyumen Region so that to determine the views of various groups of respondents on the specifics of financial behavior in the context of ongoing socioeconomic changes. The face-to-face interview method was applied.

Types of Financial Behavior

Reinterpreting the risks' classification by T. Shestovskikh, we determine risks by their allocation and also by investment behavior, as well as by possible areas of investment companies' functioning. We propose the concept of investment resources, which includes cash and intangible assets, the latter driving both material and financial assets: knowledge, skills and experience of professional participants of investment process together predetermine their behavior, and without them investment funds do not have any market value as such; methods and technologies bringing these resources into effect; confidential information, statuses and roles, which are indispensable for effective promotion of investment resources at various markets.

The nature and the objectives of investment behavior of "pure" (real) investors (companies) and the mass of external investors (population) are different. Same different are the approaches to the contents and the effects of investment activity, so the authors of this chapter share the typology of the investment behavior of population and the directions in investment behavior of companies.

It would be important to note here that any feature of this typology cannot be interpreted as a principle for all behaviors. For example, the same person can act as a consumer, a saver and also as an active investor. Companies, in their turn, are always managed by people, hired managers or owners, both of which are subject to risks, direct and/or indirect, operate under the conditions of uncertainty and competition, often making choices under the conditions of incomplete or distorted information.

Direct-investment type of risk is characterized as the risk of partial or complete loss of funds due to investment in a non-viable project; lost revenue as a result of sub-optimal allocation of resources between multiple projects; impairment of securities in the case of financial investments; losses by investing values in economically unstable financial institutions.

Investment-saving type of risk is closely related to the irrational choice of savings; wrong choice of a financial institution to entrust savings to and/or the probability of becoming a victim of a financial pyramid, or one-day companies; losses in case the bank chooses to freeze the accounts due to financial crisis; losses in the event of untimely investment or withdrawal of funds held in a bank account.

Investment-consumer type of risk is characterized by the following features: low-quality goods being in use; consumer goods with a significant negative impact on consumers; consumer goods are not able to meet the current demands of customers; consumption of high-quality products that still are unable to meet the demands of consumers under the existing conditions.

Investment behavior of a person as an economic entity is a multidimensional and complex process characterized by a certain socioeconomic orientation. On the one hand, carrying out investments, people tend to be rational and concentrate on the potential benefits from the investment process. However, this behavior is social in nature, as investing, people enter into a certain relationship. In addition, investment behavior is influenced by various non-economic factors, among which are values, expectations, social norms etc.

A person is an entity that is actively involved (consciously or unconsciously) in economic exchange. Thus, it would be logical to assume that investment behavior of population and of separate individuals is the reflection of crisis in its dynamics.

Statistical Analysis of Financial Behavior of the Russian Population

The constantly increasing complexity of the economic situation, the instability of geopolitical situation, the fall of national currency, only rising unemployment, declining real incomes together had their significant adjusting impacts on the financial behavior of population in Russia. Let us consider the dynamics of average per capita income, for example (Table 1).

As it can be seen in the table, in the years 2009-2011, 2014, 2016 there was a decrease in the growth rates of per capita monetary incomes in the Russian Federation. The dynamics of real disposable money incomes of the Russian Federation's population, taking into account inflation, is shown in Figure 2.

Dynamics of real money incomes of the population in general has a negative trend, the largest decline in growth relative to the previous period observed in 2011 and 2016.

To study the trends in the financial behavior of the population of the Russian Federation, let us consider the dynamics of the structure of the money incomes' use (Table 2).

Table 1. Dynamics of average per capita income of population in the Russian Federation, 2000-2016

Year	Rubles/Month	In % to the Previous Period
2000	2 281.1	137.5
2001	3 062.0	134.2
2002	3 947.2	128.9
2003	5 167.4	130.9
2004	6 399.0	123.8
2005	8 088.3	126.3
2006	10 154.8	125.5
2007	12 540.2	123.5
2008	14 863.6	118.5
2009	16 895.0	113.7
2010	18 958.4	112.6
2011	20 780.0	109.6
2012	23 221.1	111.0
2013	25 928.2	111.7
2014	27 766.6	107.1
2015	30 466.6	110.6
2016	30 744.4	100.9

(Source: compiled by the authors on the basis of the Rosstat data. http://www.gks.ru)

Analysis of the table above shows that financial behavior of the Russian population over the past 16 years has changed significantly. The maximum share of savings falls on the years 2003-2004, 2009-2010 and 2015. In the crisis years, the share of savings was minimal: 5.4% in 2008 and then 6.9% in 2014. During these years, there was an obvious correlation with the increased purchases of currency. Thus, the share of funds spent on the purchase of currency increases 1.3 times (in 2014) and 1.5 times (in 2008). Transferring part of savings into currency in cash can be explained by the motivation to save money from depreciation of Russian ruble. The share of population's expenses on purchasing goods and paying for services also increases. In the post-crisis years, the share of savings increases due to the desire of population to save part of the money for a rainy day.

To assess the financial behavior of population in Russia let us consider the consumer confidence index, also the Rosstat data, determined on the basis of opinion polls and calculated through partial indices. In the 1st quarter of 2015, relative to the previous period, this index is reduced by 14 pp, slightly behind its lowest level back in 2009.

According to the 2017 official statistics, the volume of cash savings of the population increased by 7.8% (Table 3). In this case, of interests is the transformation of cash into securities.

Next, let us consider the structure of turnover on loans attracted by credit organizations (deposits) of the Russian Federation during 2014-2017 (Table 4).

As it can be seen above, the share of turnover in the deposits of individuals of the Russian Federation attracted by credit organizations with the term of more than one year is declining. This testifies to the lack of confidence among population in the financial stability of the economy.

Table 2. Dynamics of the structure of the money incomes use by the population of the Russian Federation, 2000 to 2016

Year	Total Income Used, %	Divided, in %				
		Purchasing Goods and Paying for Services	Compulsory Payments and Contributions	Savings	Currency Purchases	Increment (+), Decrease (-)
2000	100	75.5	7.8	7.5	6.4	2.8
2001	100	74.6	8.9	8.9	5.6	2.0
2002	100	73.2	8.6	10.7	5.6	1.7
2003	100	69.1	8.3	12.7	7.2	2.7
2004	100	69.9	9.1	11.0	8.2	1.8
2005	100	69.5	10.1	10.4	8.5	1.5
2006	100	69.0	10.5	10.3	6.8	3.4
2007	100	69.6	11.8	9.6	5.2	3.8
2008	100	74.1	12.3	5.4	7.9	0.3
2009	100	69.8	10.5	13.9	5.4	0.4
2010	100	69.6	9.7	14.8	3.6	2.3
2011	100	73.5	10.3	10.4	4.2	1.6
2012	100	74.2	11.1	9.9	4.8	0.0
2013	100	73.6	11.7	9.8	4.2	0.7
2014	100	75.3	11.8	6.9	5.8	0.2
2015	100	71.0	10.9	14.3	4.2	-0.4
2016	100	73.1	11.2	11.1	4.0	0.6

(Source: the Rosstat data, http://www.gks.ru)

Table 3. Volume and structure of cash savings of the population in the Russian Federation in 2017, at the beginning of the month

Month	Total Savings, Billion Rubles	Including					
		Deposits		Cash		Securities	
		Billion Rubles	In % to the Total Amount of Savings	Billion Rubles	In % to the Total Amount of Savings	Billion Rubles	In % to the Total Amount of Savings
January	27350.9	18472.0	67.5	4617.7	16.9	4261.2	15.6
February	27082.9	18316.2	67.6	4454.6	16.5	4312.1	15.9
March	27450.3	18547.4	67.6	4539.4	16.5	4363.5	15.9
April	27608.7	18610.7	67.4	4567.3	16.5	4430.7	16.1
May	28023.0	18809.1	67.1	4743.5	16.9	4470.4	16.0
June	28178.1	18906.0	67.1	4775.6	16.9	4496.5	16.0
July	28705.5	19271.3	67.1	4881.8	17.0	4552.4	15.9
August	28890.4	19317.6	66.9	4975.7	17.2	4597.1	15.9
September	28976.0	19339.4	66.7	5001.4	17.3	4635.2	16.0
October	29136.9	19413.9	66.6	5035.1	17.3	4687.9	16.1
November	29243.4	19472.2	66.6	5032.5	17.2	4738.7	16.2
December	29489.1	19688.8	66.8	5038.5	17.1	4761.8	16.1

(Source: the Rosstat website. http://www.gks.ru)

Table 4. Structure of turnover in credit organizations' deposits of individuals in Russia, in %*

Years	Term of Attraction	
	Up to 1 Year, Including Deposits "On Demand"	Over 1 Year
2014	63.16	36.84
2015	78.99	21.01
2016	78.29	21.71
2017**	80.89	19.11

(Source: compiled by the authors on the basis of the data from the site of the Central Bank of Russia http://www.cbr.ru/statistics)

* Based on the average percentage of turnover

** Calculated on the basis of data for January-November 2017.

Table 5. Loans to individuals in Russia, 2010 to 2017, billion rubles

Index	At the Beginning of the Year								As of December 1, 2017
	2010	2011	2012	2013	2014	2015	2016	2017	
Volume, total	2 610.9	3 649.1	5 438.7	7 226.4	8 778.2	8 629.7	5 861.4	7 210.3	8 158.7
in rubles	2 482.9	3 506.7	5 289.2	7 075.4	8 612.6	8 461.4	5 765.8	7 100.6	8 067.1
in foreign currency	128.0	142.4	149.5	151.1	165.6	168.3	95.6	109.7	91.6
Debt, total	3 562.4	4 064.0	5 534.7	7 711.6	9 925.9	11 294.8	10 634.0	10 773.7	11 964.6
in rubles	3 167.2	3 715.3	5 218.0	7 474.2	9 698.9	11 005	10 366.8	10 619.2	11 855.2
in foreign currency	395.2	348.8	316.7	237.4	226.9	289.5	267.2	154.5	109.4
Including arrears, total	241.0	279.3	290.3	312.5	439.2	665.6	861.4	856.1	868.5
in rubles	207.5	235.7	244.4	276.9	406.5	620.3	802.7	810.1	833.3
in foreign currency	33.5	43.6	45.9	35.5	32.7	45.4	58.8	46.0	35.2

(Source: compiled by the authors on the basis of the CBR data, http://www.cbr.ru/statistics)

An important indicator of the economy and to the financial behavior of the population is a credit behavior. Currently, there is an active development of the market of credit services. In addition to opportunities to expand consumption, the use of loans and leads to the emergence of rising debt on loans due to the economic and social causes. Dynamics in the volume of credits and debts belonging to individuals in the Russian Federation is presented in Table 5.

According to Table 5, during the period of 2010-2016 the volume of loans issued to individuals increased by 2.7 times, and as of 11 months of 2017 it amounted to 8 158.7 billion rubles. At the same time, the share of loans issued in rubles is much higher. So, as of 11 months of 2017 this share was 98.5% of all loans.

During the period under consideration the proportion of debt went up threefold. Foreign currency denominated debt in absolute and relative terms has reduced. The average share of overdue debt is 6.28%, in 2016 the maximum specific weight of overdue credit debt is observed (8.09%).

Next, we examine the structure of the turnover on loans granted by credit institutions to individuals in Russia (Table 6).

Table 6. Structure of turnover on loans provided by credit institutions to individuals in Russia, 2014 to 2017, in %*

Years	With the Due Date	
	Up to 1 Year, Including Loans "On Demand"	Over 1 Year
2014	9,48	90,52
2015	11,47	88,53
2016	8,10	91,90
2017**	5,96	94,04

Source: compiled by the authors on the basis of the CBR data [http://www.cbr.ru/statistics]
* Based on the average percentage of turnover
** The data for January-November 2017

The Credit Optimism Index calculated by the All-Russian Center for the Study of Public Opinion shows how favorably the population of the Russian Federation assesses the current time for lending, and in Q1 of 2016 this index showed the worst value since 2009 - 18 p.p. For comparison: in the first and second quarters of 2014 the index was 40 p.p., and that was the maximum value for the period 2009-2017. In the crisis year of 2009 this index was 24 p. p. By September 2017 the credit confidence index was 29 p.p.

Empirical Study of the Financial Behavior of a Mass Actor on the Example of the Tyumen Region

Analysis of the financial behavior of population in accordance with the allocated earlier types has been carried out on the example of the Tyumen region. As the empirical base served the sociological data obtained from the population surveys. Thus, the object of our study is the Tyumen region's population of 18 years old and older. The subject of investigation is the financial behavior of this population under the conditions of socioeconomic changes.

Further, in accordance with the concept of work, under the financial behavior of population we will understand the behavior of the mass actor in relation to the investment of available free cash.

The analysis of population's financial behavior is fundamentally different from the analysis of companies' financial behavior. In the case of companies' financial behavior is, above all, economic behavior, focused on the investments in assets that generate net income, i.e., the focus is on results. When analyzing the financial behavior of the population, the main emphasis is not on personal net income, but on the intrinsic motivation behind economic behavior, which is characterized not only by the focus on increasing the value of all types of capital, but also by all related social impacts.

As an example, let's take the case of buying an apartment. The apartment does not bring the owner net income (except for the case when it is later rented out), on the opposite - there are additional costs for its maintenance. But this operation can be still considered as investment for the owner, because when buying, he/she was guided by rational reasoning (the price for apartments is growing and such a purchase is usually more profitable than plain cash investments). It is also assumed that there will be final benefits from this acquisition (the apartment can be used as the place of own residence, thus the person is saving money by not renting an apartment, or on the opposite - this new apartment can be rented out, thus bringing extra income). From the point of view of social effect, investing money into purchasing an apartment is also providing the feeling of confidence in the future, gives additional security since now this person already knows that new property is their future capital.

This approach is entirely consistent with the concept of D. Keynes, who, under the investment behavior of subject understands the purchase of any old or new property, the purchase of securities at a stock market, accumulation of stocks of finished goods and work in progress.

To directly measure the investment behavior of population, the following questions were used in the toolbox:

If you had available funds, where would you invest them? If you had to take a loan in the last 5 years, for what purpose would it be? Further, the variants of answers were grouped, proceeding from the concept of internal motivation behind investment behavior of population (Tables 7 and 8).

Consideration of linear distributions leads to the unequivocal conclusion that purchasing an apartment is the most desirable investment choice. Interestingly, when prices for apartments decreased - so did the intention to buy one (Table 7). This may be indicative of the share of people who wanted to buy an apartment not for the purposes of own living (consumption) but for extra profits (via lease or further resale). Analysis of regional differences leads us to the assumption that increase in the welfare level (KMAA is the most secure of all subregions in the Tyumen Region, while South Tyumen Region is the poorest one) people tend to give me credit to the idea of buying an apartment or a car (Table 8), but there is no serious change in the types of investment behavior - it is still predominantly consumer-oriented.

Further analysis is dedicated to checking this and other hypotheses aimed at identifying the structure of investment behavior of population in the region in question.

Basing on the analysis of empirical data and theoretical aspects of investment behavior, we have formed the following typology of investment behavior:

- **Direct-Investment Type:** Is characterized by the desire of an actor to invest money in securities or mutual funds to multiply their capital at their own risk;
- **Investment and Savings Type:** Is manifested through actor's pursuit to keep their savings with the possibility of their future saving in a bank with a certain interest rate and/or accumulating this money for future retirement;

Table 7. If you have spare cash, where would you put them? (in general in the Tyumen region, % of the respondents)

Variants of Answers / Years	2010	2016
I would buy a car	13	17
I would buy an apartment	59	46
I would buy shares (bonds)	11	7
I would put money on a bank account	15	15
I would save up for retirement	9	10
I would invest money in the Unit Investment Funds	2	2
Other	-	5
No answer	7	5
Answers in total *	108	107

* It was possible to indicate more than one answer

*Table 8. If you had to take a loan in the last 5 years, for what purpose was it? (as of 2016, % from the total number of the respondents)**

	South Tyumen Region	Khanty-Mansi Autonomous Area	Yamal-Nenets Autonomous Area
for business development	5	6	6
for an apartment (mortgage)	7	16	12
for a car	16	16	20
for household appliances	27	24	22
for other purposes	6	6	3
No, I did not take one	42	32	38
No response	3	6	4

* It was possible to indicate more than one answer

- **Investment and Consumer Type:** Manifests itself in cases when the investment of funds is aimed at satisfying consumer demand (most frequently - acquisition of movable and/or immovable property).

It is obvious that in the Tyumen region the prevailing type is the investment and consumer behavior of the mass actor. This can be explained by the fact that the absolute majority of local citizens still have great deal of mistrust in financial institutions. The smallest share has the behavior of the direct-investment type.

This is quite natural since for investments in shares and other securities one must have a certain level of economic literacy. Besides, such investments are still treated as the most risky ones.

We find it also interesting that in 2016 people began to save more, spending a little bit less and less invest in the future. *Why is it so?* Below we examine this situation and trend in more detail.

Analysis of the overall financial dynamics shows that in today's socioeconomic situation, investment behavior of population is really insignificant, moreover, it is only declining.

This reduction in the overall level of investment behavior is not associated with the rejection of investment as an idea (the share of those who refuse to invest as such remains approximately the same - at the level of 5-6%), however, greater caution is observed in some of the areas.

We can also note that the growth rate of the consumer type of investment in the Tyumen region demonstrates a slight decline as compared to Russia's average.

In today's socioeconomic situation and its general economic and financial instability in the first place, development of the investment component in the behavior of the mass actor in the Tyumen region has a negative trend. The total investment level decrease has been caused by the reduction of direct investments and less active investment consumer behavior overall. Occasional growth observed for some of the types of investment behavior does not compensate for that. This occasional growth is associated with the formation of institutional conditions that strengthen the public confidence in banks (deposit insurance, more solid state control over the banking sector etc.). These and other changes have been quickly and properly assessed by the population, and this suggests that the investment preferences of the mass actor in Russia are very flexible and also in direct and obvious dependence from the measures of state regulation in this sector.

It should be also noted that the initially low level of savings component, however, has increased even during the crisis, therefore, the potential for investment has reduced (both at the level of individuals and at the level of legal entities). This leads us to the conclusion about the effectiveness of the mechanisms used for social interaction between the microactors at the related market. Another conclusion is that there is great potential for what is called today the "investment model of growth". Clearly, this potential has not yet found its actual implementation, and as of today there are several constraints for such growth.

In 2010 the vast majority of people in the region invested in apartments (from 60% in the South of the region and in Khanty-Mansiysk Autonomous region to 54% in the Yamal-Nenets Autonomous region). In 2016, despite the decline in property prices due to the crisis, the interest in real estate also decreased significantly (to the levels of 48% in the South of the region, 43% in the Khanty-Mansiysk Autonomous region and 49% in Yamal-Nenets Autonomous region). This happened due to the fact that the majority of population was also suffering from the same crisis and thus was unable to buy property entirely at own expense, while the cost of borrowing money from banks has increased significantly during this period.

The rate of the savings type of investment behavior increased from 21% to 25%. This change took place due to a number of influencing factors. First, there was a gradual increase in confidence in the banking institutions (not the last role here was played by the state deposit insurance system). Secondly, the impact of the economic crisis resulted in increased prices and interest rates on loans (which led to some reduction in consumer activity), however, increased the public interest on deposits. Socioeconomic situation has developed in such a way that for general population bank deposits quickly became the most efficient and the least risky means of preserving and increasing the accumulated assets.

Further, we have determined the factors influencing the investment behavior of population in the Tyumen region on the basis of the cross-sectional data analysis.

The following investment behavior factors were considered: financial status, occupation, education, gender, age, marital status, values, the level of economic awareness, credit history, region, type of settlement and dynamic effects.

Financial Situation

With the increasing level of income significantly increases the proportion of direct-investment type of behavior (from 8% among the poor up to 20% among the rich). Given the nonadditivity forms (the sum is not equal 100% because the respondents were able to indicate more than one answer), the reduction in the share of a consumer group (for example, transition from wealthy to very rich) can only be explained by the fact that the question was formulated in a projective form (*How would you... if you have the money...*), while many of such respondents had actually done that.

Therefore, eliminating from consideration the most secured financially, top layer of the society we would get a much more realistic picture concerning the savings and investment components of the investment behavior. Moreover, this trend is typical for both 2010 and 2016, i.e., we observe a time-stable effect.

The subdivision of the sample into subsamples (STR, KMAA, YNAA, rural/urban, men/women, by age groups etc.) showed that this effect is fairly stable not only in time but also in social structure.

Let's note one more important feature: insufficient level of direct investment behavior is characteristic for all property layers, and the initial hypothesis that people do not invest in the long because they have nothing to invest is not confirmed.

Profession

Direct investment type of behavior is typical for entrepreneurs (26% of all surveyed entrepreneurs belonged to this type in 2010 and then 21% in 2016), saving type of investment behavior is more typical for agrarian managers, rural intelligentsia (2010) and other rural residents, including pensioners (2016). The consumer type of investment behavior is typical for those who do not work, do not study (2010) and also for students (2016).

Gender

Men are slightly more inclined to direct-investment type of behavior, whereas women are more likely to use money for consumption purposes. Thus, investment behavior of the population is indeed gender-dependent to some extent.

Age

Young people of about 25 years old tend to consume the maximum, they are little inclined to think about the future and their savings preferences are rather modest. With the age consumption desire is going down, while the desire to preserve money persists. This trend is quite traditional for many countries and has no scientific novelty. For our analysis, also important is the fact that dynamics of direct-investment type is going down with age much less than it was be expected. The lowest level (4%) of direct investment preferences is observed for those over 60 years, and the highest level is observed among the citizens of 35-39 y.o. (16% in 2010 and 13% in 2016). That is, first, investment behavior increases, then it decreases, as expected, but this change is rather gradual and prolonged in time. We should also pay special attention to the apparent lack of support for direct investments among the youth. The key reason why young people do not invest more actively is lack of financial literacy. And even among the most active sections of the middle-age group the support for this type of investment and the financial literacy are not yet at the sufficient level.

Education

The influence of education on investment behavior depends on the type of behavior. It is noticeable that the investment-consumer and direct-investment types of behavior expand with higher level of education, while the investment-savings type is narrowing. That is, more educated citizens are less likely to simply keep money in banks, they will prefer either to receive direct benefits by sending money to consumption, or will seek extra benefits in the future. Considering our indicators in their dynamics, we can see how consumer and direct-investment behavior declined during the crisis years. Activation of the savings component is provided by more educated sections of population, whereas less educated people, on the contrary, back in 2016, had less savings. That is, the actions of authorities directed at the insurance of deposits were perceived only by the educated strata of population.

Credit History

Direct-investment type of behavior is activated through the experience with lending for business development. At the same time, consumer type of investment behavior narrows down the lending experience. We have already noted that upper layers of the society consume more, but in the projective situation, this kind of behavior for them is less relevant. Therefore, while maintaining the explicit domination of consumption (50%), the structure of investment behavior becomes more balanced.

Type of Settlement

Direct-investment type of behavior is largely supported by the residents of medium-sized cities (100-500 thousands of residents). The level of savings behavior varies slightly, but the overall support of investment and consumer types of behavior is sharply higher among the residents of large cities (in our sample this would be only one city, the center of the region in question - Tyumen). The type and the size of settlement is one of the important factors for investment behavior due to the presence (or not) of the developed market infrastructure, availability of the advanced means of communication (access to the Internet, in the first place) and generally higher level of public awareness in cities as compared to town and rural settlements.

However, in big cities people are less (as compared to medium-sized cities (in our case - Surgut, Nizhnevartovsk, Novyi Urengoy)) ready to save money in banks or invest in stocks, or delegate them to investment funds. They usually seek to preserve their earnings through extra purchasing of real estate and various durable goods.

So, the real component of consumer investment behavior of people under the influence of crisis is certainly decreased, but much less than one would expect. A desired (projective) component of it remains almost unchanged, i.e., the nature of the consumer type of investment behavior has had only minor changes under the influence of the crisis.

It determined that in today's crisis socioeconomic situation, the overall financial and economic instability, the development of the investment component in the behavior of mass actor in the Tyumen region has a negative trend. This general decline in investment activity is due to a decrease in the level of investment by groups and direct-investment and investment-consumer types of behavior. And even some growth observed for the investment-saving type of behavior does not compensate for this.

The emergence of new institutional conditions that strengthen confidence in banks (deposit insurance, strengthened state control over the banking sector etc.) have been properly assessed by the population with the conclusion that the total collapse of the financial system could be prevented (thus, deposits would not be confiscated en masse). This allows us to assume that the investment preferences of the mass actor in Russia are elastic in relation to measures of state support in this sphere. It should be also noted that the initially low level of savings component increased, even during the crisis of 2014-2017 which has significantly reduced the opportunities for investment (at the level of individuals and at the level of legal entities).

This leads us to the conclusion about the sufficient effectiveness of social mechanisms in market interaction of microactors. Tyumen region indeed has a certain potential for the application of the so-called "investment model of growth", at least at the population level of investment activity. At the same time, as it was shown above, this potential has not yet found its actual implementation, as there are serious limitations to this growth. First and foremost, the restrictions concern the following: the overall level of education, financial literacy and awareness, the level of material well-being (which is not high enough to talk about any sort of saving and/or additional savings), economic features of local mentality (the limiting factors are ranked here in the descending order).

The main positive fact revealed in this work is an increase in the level of citizens' confidence in banks as a way to save money. However, this growth of confidence is observed mostly among less educated citizens and/or those who are less well-off financially, whereas the most educated (and/or financially secured) citizens, on the contrary, have shifted more to the idea of direct investment opportunities.

Thus, the identified here factors, significant at the empirical level, are affecting the investment behavior of the mass actor in the Tyumen region, namely: the sociodemographic factors, and also cultural and market ones. It was found that the most prevalent among them all are cultural factors, embodied in education, value orientations, economic awareness etc. More specifically, cultural factors have been found to have direct impact on the personal credit history of citizens. Among the sociodemographic factors dominates the financial situation, and among market factors the most serious is the global financial crisis, with its very much negative impact on the investment behavior. Also, we have observed the declining influence on the side of motivation and economic awareness, meanwhile, the growing importance has been observed for such factors as age, education level, occupation, financial status. More specifically, all of these factors tend to have immediate influence on the type of investment behavior. On the other hand, these factors have very different effects on different types of investment behavior.

SOLUTIONS AND RECOMMENDATIONS

The authors proposed the following typology of financial behavior of the mass actor: direct-investment type, which is characterized by the desire to invest own money, at own risk, in shares and other securities in order to increase own capital; investment-saving type, which manifests itself as the desire to maintain savings with the possibility of their future use by means of investing money into a bank deposit at an advantageous interest or by means of accumulation for retirement; investment-consumer type which manifests itself as the cases when investments are directed at satisfying direct consumer requests (investing in movable or immovable property).

It is established that in the Tyumen region the investment-consumer type of financial behavior of the mass actor is predominant. This choice of the local citizens can be explained by the low level of public confidence in financial institutions that has developed over the previous several decades. It is also revealed that, according to the authors' typology, the direct investment type constitutes the smallest share in the structure of mass financial behavior. This social fact is quite understandable and natural, since for the implementation of investments in stocks and other securities it would be necessary (besides the obvious availability of funds) to have a certain level of economic literacy, that is, to become active investors (professional participants of the investment market). In addition, this type of investment is the most risky one.

It is determined that in the current crisis socioeconomic situation, general financial and economic instability, development of the investment behavior of the mass actor in the Tyumen region has negative dynamics. This general decline in investment activity has taken place due to a decrease in the level of investment for the direct-investment and investment-consumer types of behavior. And even some growth observed for the investment-saving type of behavior did not manage to compensate for this. The emergence of new institutional conditions has strengthened the public confidence in banks (thanks to deposit insurance, increased state control over the banking sector). This was duly appreciated by population, moreover, there are reasons to believe that these measures have prevented the general collapse of the financial system (since general public got more confident in banks, deposits were not massively withdrawn from banks when the crisis period came). This trend allows us to assume that the investment preferences of the mass actor in Russia are flexibly dependent upon the measures of state support in this sphere.

The factors of significant influence on the investment behavior of the mass actor in the Tyumen region can be divided into the following groups: sociodemographic factors, cultural and market factors. As it turned out, cultural factors dominate among them, these factors are embodied in value orientations, associated with economic awareness and credit history of individuals.

Among the sociodemographic factors, the current financial position is the most meaningful one; and among the market factors the most significant one concerns various manifestations of the global financial crisis which, for several years, has been negatively affecting the financial behavior of population. Motivation and economic awareness were found to have the gradually decreasing influence on the financial behavior of population, while the growing importance has been getting the sociodemographic characteristics of respondents such as gender, age, education level, occupation and financial position.

REFERENCES

Algin, A. P. (1991). *The borders of economic risk.* Moscow: Knowledge.

Avtonomov, V. C. (1993). Man at mirror of economic theory (Essay on the history of Western economic thought). *Science.*

Balabanov, I. T. (1996). *Risk management.* Moscow: Finance and Prospects.

Barinov, A. E. (2001). Design and credit risks: The problem of their insurance. *Risk Management, 4,* 19–22.

Danilova, E. P. (2010). *Investment behavior of business entities in terms of socio-economic changes (in Tyumen region).* Tyumen: TSU Publishing House.

Knight, F. (1994). Concept of risk and uncertainty. *THESIS, 5,* 12-28.

Krivov, V. (2000). The problem of risk management decisions. *Risk Management, 4,* 15–17.

Shestovskikh, T. S. (1998). Risk in the structure of economic behavior. *Sociological Research, 5,* 116–119.

Smirnova, E. (2001). Manufacturing risk: The nature and management. *Risk Management, 1,* 3–5.

Streltsov, A. V. (2000). Risk assessment when updating production facilities. *Risk Management, 2,* 13–15.

Verkhovin, V. I. (1994). Economic behavior as a subject of sociological analysis. *Sociolinguistic Studies, 10,* 120–125.

Verkhovin, V. I. (2009). Investment behavior. *Economia e Sociologia (Evora, Portugal), 2,* 148–160.

Zubkov, V. I. (2001). Risk in the structure of economic behavior. *West. Ros. Univ. of Peoples'. Friendship, 2,* 76–93.

KEY TERMS AND DEFINITIONS:

Direct-Investment Type of Behavior of Population and Organizations: Is characterized by the risk of partial or complete loss of funds due to investment of certain values in a non-viable project; lost revenue in this case is the result of sub-optimal allocation of resources between multiple projects; impairment of securities in the case can be also observed as well as losses due to investment into economically unstable financial institutions.

Investment-Consumer Type of Risk: Is characterized by the following features: low-quality goods and/or services in use; consumer goods which could have a significant negative impact on consumers; consumer goods that are not meeting the current demands of customers; consumption of a high-quality product that is still unable to meet the demands of consumers under certain current existing conditions.

Investment Risk: A probable variability of anticipated benefits from certain forms of investment.

Investment-Saving Type of Risk: Is accompanied by irrational forms of savings; wrong choice of a financial institution which includes the possibility of becoming a victim of a financial pyramid or a one-day company; loss of assets due to freezing of a bank account in the event of crisis; losses due to untimely investment or withdrawal of funds from a bank account.

Chapter 3
The Effects of Political and Economic Risk on FDI:
A Theoretical Survey

Fatih Ayhan
Bandırma On Yedi Eylül University, Turkey

ABSTRACT

Foreign direct investments (FDI) are becoming the key element in achieving development in developing countries. On the global scale, FDIs reached the level of $1,75 trillion back in 2016. FDI also brings lots of economic benefits to host countries. However, beyond these economic indicators, political structure and social characteristics of a host country also have special importance for investors' decisions. Political risk indicators cover mainly democratization level, political/government instability, war, immigration problems, problems with neighboring countries, internal and external conflicts, corruption level, military and religious influence on politics, law and order, ethnics tensions, property rights protection, national security and geographic situation - all of these factors also deeply affect decisions on FDI. Also, some basic social characteristics for host countries can play the catalyzer role for FDI, such as literacy rate, education opportunities, etc. The aim of this study is to examine theoretically the relationship between political and economic risks on the one hand with FDI on the other. It is aimed to show the theoretical background for the political and economic risk factors. Statistical figures on the FDI trends worldwide will be also presented.

INTRODUCTION

Risk is a concept of daily life that affects economic and social decisions of individuals. Individuals direct their activities assessing the risk factors in the course of decision-making. Likewise, investors make their decisions on to invest or not by paying attention to the risk factors of their activities. Political risk, a type of risk that an investor is exposed to, is also one of the important factors affecting investment decisions. It is among the factors that investors primarily consider when deciding on foreign investments. Political risks that are not under their control and make it difficult to recover sunk costs are decisive for foreign direct investors.

DOI: 10.4018/978-1-5225-7760-7.ch003

Since the 1990s there have been significant increases in foreign direct investment volumes all over the world. Today, too quick changes in political risk elements require foreign investors to be more careful. This is especially concerns the influence of globalization, since both trade and investment can easily go beyond the borders. Both investors and host countries of FDI mutually benefit from this situation. Key advantages from cross-border investments can briefly be summarized as lower production costs, large market volume and high profit expectations.

Countries that are unable to save enough and have saving deficit, aim to increase their production volumes by hosting foreign direct investments, thus providing high earnings, employment potential and technology transfers. To this end, foreign direct investment is being encouraged for host countries. Foreign direct investment is a bigger priority for developing countries. In these countries, the inadequacy of capital accumulation and low level of savings can lead to inadequate investments. This situation causes the production level of the countries and the national income decrease accordingly. Inadequate production causes the level of employment fall below potential and income per capita stabilize at rather low levels. Thus, developing countries are constantly seeking to break this vicious circle of poverty, and one of the potential ways to do that is through foreign direct investments' inflow. In other words, developing economies often hope to find solutions to their chronic economic problems via FDI inflows.

The influence of globalization and neoliberal policies has increased the interdependence of all countries. This necessitates greater cooperation with foreign traders and investors, but also requires the presence of foreign trade in these countries. For this reason, they should not be independent of financial, political and socioeconomic developments in the world beyond their national boundaries. Any socioeconomic development experienced by trade partners in the course of their cross-border cooperation affects these countries rather spontaneously. Similarly, political risks posed by trading partners can affect trade and investment volumes on both sides of cooperation.

The tendency of developing countries' shares' increase in the global FDI volumes which is mostly due to political and economic vulnerability of the early 2000s is also reflected the investors' most worried factors. The World Investment and Political Risk (WIPR) Report of the Multilateral Investment Guarantee Agency (MIGA) as of 2013 shows that political risks are second only to macroeconomic stability with little difference (World Bank, 2014).

According to the UNCTAD database, by the end of 2016 the total FDI inflows in the world reached the level of approximately 1,8 trln USD, with 1 trln falling on developed countries and the rest of 600 bln - on developing countries. FDIs which demonstrated several falls before and after the global crisis, increased in 2015 and then in 2016. During the Arab Spring of 2010 which spread all over the Middle East and North Africa (MENA) countries and was triggered by socioeconomic reasons as well as political corruption, the effects of political risks on FDI volumes were felt quite strongly. Events related to political and global concerns such as the 9/11 attacks in the USA, the London subway attack, the Spanish attack, tensions in the Middle East, the Arab Spring, the Syrian crisis and the immigrant problems show how political risks can affect FDI volume and how difficult it can be to foresee those risks due to the impossibility to predict such events. In addition, security threats and terrorist attacks in developed countries confirm the assumption that political risks are not be limited only to developing countries with their governmental instability. This situation makes FDI investors' decision-making an even more difficult task.

This study attempts to theoretically examine the effects from political risks on foreign direct investment decisions. First, the concept of risk will be defined, then the concept and types of political risk will be explained. Statistical data on both variables will be presented, specifying the foreign direct investments and the key determinants behind them. After clarifying the theoretical effect of political risks on FDI decisions, the study will be completed by giving a brief summary in the conclusion part.

BACKGROUND

Macroeconomic variables, political risks and institutional quality variables are often emphasized in literature as being the main determinants of foreign direct investments. Very different results though are obtained in different studies concerning the relation between political risks and FDIs. This is because different forms and manifestations of political risk are discussed, differences in the development level of certain countries also have their influence, different time periods are as well as different countries, country groups and regions. For example, some studies have found that political stability, corporate quality and corruption variables have their significant impacts on FDI inflows: Tallman (1988), Demirguc-Kunt and Maksimovic (1998), Wurgler (2000), Wei (2000), Asiedu (2006), Busse and Hefeker (2007), Daude and Stein (2007), Krifa-Schneider and Matei (2010), Baek and Qian (2011), Hayakawa et al. (2011), Aguiar et al. (2012), Sedik and Seoudy (2012), Al-Khouri and Khalik (2013), Erkekoğlu and Kilicarslan (2016) and Kirikkaleli (2016). Some other studies have found that political stability has zero impact on direct investment decisions: Wheeler and Mody (1992), Noorbakhsh et al. (2001), Steiner (2010).

Some studies have shown that political instability such as internal armed conflicts, political strikes, riots, terrorism acts, and external conflicts have negative impact on direct investment decisions: Nigh (1986), Schneider and Frey (1985), Erramilli and Rao (1993), Singh and Jun (1995), Gastanaga et al. (1998), Wei (2000), Rool and Talbott (2001), Stoever (2002), Kolstad and Tondel (2002), Trevino and Mixon (2004), Grosse and Trevino (2005), Demirhan and Masca (2008), Benacek et al. (2014), Khan et.al. (2013), Erkekoğlu and Kilicarslan (2016). Findings of these studies would be briefly and selectively presented below.

Stoever (2002) developed a model on the data of South Korea, covering the period from 1962 to 2000. This author found that less political risk stimulates increases in foreign direct investments.

Roll and Talbott (2001) analyzed the GNI per capita across 162 different countries, the data covering 1995 to 1999 years. They found that variation in GNI per capita depended on the freedom of press, political rights, property rights, government expenditures and civil liberties. According to results these variables influenced the GNI per capita positively. But trade barriers, poor monetary policy, excessive regulation and black market activity had negative effect on GNI. They also found that democracy affects GNI positively.

Tallman (1988) examined the effects of economic and political conditions on FDI in developed countries, 1974 to 1980. According to their results, FDI decisions significantly depend upon political and economic conditions.

Wheeler and Moody (1992) found that corruption rate in a host country doesn't have any significant effect on foreign direct investments, however, we need to note that their study was carried out on the micro level and concerned USA only.

Erramilli and Rao (1993) examined the relationship between political risk and FDI on the data of 114 firms carrying out a survey for analyzing their decisions to enter foreign markets. They concluded that the sovereign risk tends to hinder the flow of foreign direct investment and for the same reason multinational companies hesitate to make new investment decisions in relation to countries that demonstrate higher political risks.

Singh and Jun (1995) performed an empirical analysis on the data between 1970 and 1993 and on 31 countries. They studied the macroeconomic and sociopolitical variables affecting the geographical distribution of foreign direct investments. Political risk and business conditions were found to be quite influential determinants of FDI.

Grosse and Trevino (1996) analyzed the relationship between political risks and FDI in the case of the USA for the period from 1980 to 1991. They found a statically significant effect of political risk on FDI in the USA.

Wei (2000) concluded that there is a significant relationship between corruption rate and FDI. According to their results, corruption decreases FDI volumes and also influences import capital in terms of both volume and structure.

Noorbakhsh et al. (2001) found that democracy and political risk had no significant effect on FDI for 36 different developing countries from Africa, Asia and Latin America. They analyzed the data covering the years from 1980 to 1994.

Kolstad and Tondel (2002) found that corruption had no significant effect on FDI. But political rights, civil freedom, democratic accountability, religious and ethnic tensions and other forms of internal conflict had important effects on FDI for 61 different developing countries, 1989 to 2000.

Trevino and Mixon (2004) concluded that institutional reform can be a significant variable for FDI in the case of Latin America (Argentina, Brazil, Chile, Colombia, Mexico, Peru and Venezuela). Their dataset covered the years between 1988 and 1999.

Grosse and Trevino (2005) conducted a study on the relationship between institutional variables and FDI for Central and Eastern European countries. They found that corruption, political risk and foreign direct investment flows were negatively related.

Daude and Stein (2007) analyzed the nexus between institutional quality on foreign direct investment for 34 source countries and 152 host countries. They used the data for 1982 and 2002 years and found that institutional quality affects FDI flows positively.

Busse and Hefeker (2007) investigated the relationship between political risk and FDI flows in 83 developing countries. Their analysis captured the data in the period from 1984 to 2003. According to their findings, government stability, internal and external conflicts, corruption and ethnic tensions, law and order, democratic accountability of the government and the quality of bureaucracy variables are all statistically significant for FDI.

Krifa-Schneider and Matei (2010) performed the analysis of the relationship between political risk, business environment and FDI for 33 different developing and transition countries. They found that lower political risk level induced higher rates of FDI and also that business climate is a significant determinant for FDI inflows.

Hayakama et al. (2011) conducted the analysis for 93 countries (1985 to 2007) in order to determine the effects of political and financial risks on FDI inflows. They found that political risk affects FDI inflows and also that socioeconomic conditions, investment conditions and the presence of external conflict are quite affecting variables for FDI.

Baek and Qian (2011) carried out a panel analysis for 22 industrialized and 94 developing countries between the years 1984 and 2008. They aimed to find whether political risk affects FDI or not. According to their findings, political risk is statistically significant for FDI. And after the 9/11 attacks political risk got even higher importance for determining the FDI volumes in developed countries. They used 12 different political risk variables in their analysis.

Aguiar et al. (2012) investigated the effects of political risk on FDI inflows into 180 different countries. Their findings showed that higher political risk decreased FDI inflow into a host country.

Sedik and Seoudy (2012) analyzed the relationship between country risk and FDI for 20 MENA countries. Their data included the years 1999 and 2010. Their findings showed that lower political risk affects FDI positively, but economic and financial risks have insignificant and positive effects on FDI.

Sissani and Belkacem (2014) investigated the relationship between FDI and political and financial risk during 1992-2012. According to their results for Algeria, FDI was negatively affected by political risk factors.

Benacek et al. (2014) investigated the relationship between political and economic risk on FDI for 35 host countries in Europe, their data covered the years between 1995 and 2008. And their findings indicated that these risks don't always affect FDI negatively.

Al-Khouri and Khalik (2013) analyzed political, financial and economic risk effects on FDI in 16 MENA countries. Their data covered the time period between 1984 and 2011. And these authors found a significant relationship between FDI, market size, political risk and foreign direct investment. They also highlighted that corruption level, external conflict (tension) and FDI were closely correlated in the context of 12 political risk variables.

Erkekoğlu and Kilicarslan (2016) analyzed the impact of political risk on FDI for 91 different countries using the panel data that covered the period of 2002-2012. According to their results, higher political stability, absence of violence and management effectiveness reduce FDI. However, higher value of exportation of goods and services, population, GDP growth and regulatory quality increases FDI volumes, and this result is applicable to all 91 countries.

Kirikkaleli (2016) explored the relationship between financial, economic and political risk variables for seven Balkan countries. According to his results, financial and economic stability had positive relationship, but financial stability influenced the political stability negatively in the long run. Also, financial and economic stability had significant effect on political stability.

THEORETICAL RELATIONSHIP BETWEEN POLITICAL AND ECONOMIC RISK AND FDI

Issues, Controversies, Problems

All countries, especially developing ones, need foreign direct investment / investors' interest for achieving their economic growth goals. But the most important elements that attract foreign investment into a country are positive development of macroeconomic indicators and the reduction of political risks. For this reason, countries that aim to be hosts for foreign direct investment are supposed to maintain stability in both macroeconomic situation and political life. After the conceptual analysis of political risks and foreign direct investments in the following sections, the prevailing and recent trends of FDI development will be presented statistically.

1. Definition and Types of the Risk Concept

Before analyzing the relationship between political risk and FDI, it would be appropriate to determine risk as such along with its components. Risk is a daily-life concept with direct and immediate relation to human nature. People are exposed and expose others to risk in all of their daily decision-making processes.

Risk is a concept that covers an action's potential harm. Risk can be seen as a potential action or a condition which would bring about damage to a business, provided that this risk comes true. The gauge of risk can be attributed to its probability of happening and the scale of its influence. Their total size shows the overall risk damage (McKellar, 2010:3). Clark and Marois (1996) came up with a definition of risk as the probability of an event happening and negative results (costs) for the related groups.

It is quite obvious that risk potentially carries harm and hazard. The main goal of businesses is to reach a certain level of profit. The loss of an enterprise from an activity thus also means there is insufficient profit on the one hand. But if one focuses only on businesses with less of potential damages, it would be difficult to see the critical factors behind the achievement of international success on the other hand. For example, an actual political risk may damage reputation of a company and thus reduce the belief of its key stakeholders in a project implemented by this company (McKellar, 2010:4).

Cross-border trade and investment have their own, additional risks. Companies that are operating internationally and thus are actively engaged in foreign trade are usually exposed to totally different types of risks. Country risk depends on the variables which affect international capital flows, e.g., GDP rate, the volume of international reserves, political and economic stability and the probability of default. Country risk covers all risks arising from political and social conditions inside a certain country. Types of country risks include economic, commercial and political risks.

- Economic risk covers country's macroeconomic development indicators like interest rates and exchange rates.
- Commercial risk is a kind of investment-related risk in itself and it depends on the fulfillment of obligations between international companies and their local partners.
- Political risk affects international investments via political decisions or events in a country. So international investor makes less profits than it has been expected or suffers a loss due to host country's political actions.

Depending on macroeconomic variables, government policies and regulations, geographical factors and monetary policy changes, international investors could be exposed to country risk. For this reason, country risk makes business environment more dangerous, and it may also reduce the potential profits from international investments. The three most important components of the country risk are economic, financial and political risk. In relation to international investment decisions, the most important of these three is political risk and it tends to have a multifaceted impact on FDI (Krifa-Schneider & Matei, 2010, p. 55).

Therefore, there are also economic and commercial consequences of the political decisions which aim to organize the society. Decisions and attitudes of politicians are not limited only to their regions of location. Political decisions and attitudes can also determine the volume and the direction of international investments and trade. The capacity of politicians and governments to hold the official power of influence in their hands is beyond the limits. In this sense, political attitude, discourse and behavior carry an important responsibility. In particular, political risks of developing and transition economies that need foreign investors have the decisive influence on the investment decisions made outside a country.

2. Definition of Political Risk

It would be appropriate to start with the definition of political risk prior to FDI analysis. Political risk refers to the damage or influence of businesses as a result of attitudes and behaviors demonstrated by politicians along with the costs of the related political (McKellar, 2010:3). Political risk is of non-commercial nature, but it is still strongly correlated with market conditions (Kansal, 2015). Political risk usually covers various internal and external conflicts, terrorist acts, riots, wars, questionable government regulations, too heavy tax burden, corruption, protectionism measures, trade unions restrictions, tariffs, price controls, currency convertibility, restrictions imposed on repatriation of profits, expropriation of assets, potential risk of nationalization, etc.

The most common form of political risk is imposing special requirements or taxes on foreign trader and investors with the aim to make foreign companies' profit transfers difficult, thus providing an additional incentive to local firms. Besides, inconvertibility of a host country's currencies can be evaluated within the scope of political risk for FDI. However, the most important political risk factors - the ongoing war or a war threat - can have much more devastating effects on foreign investment. In addition, excessive bureaucracy and high corruption rates as a political risk factor also lower the profitability of companies by imposing additional costs while making the work environment more hazardous (Dzidrov & Dzidrov, 2010, p. 553).

3. The Importance of Political Risk for Developing Countries

Globalization allows companies realize their growth potential by catching opportunities in developing countries. Multinational companies need to consider international opportunities in order to be able to realize competitive advantages and growth goals. But in addition to the growth opportunities in developing countries, it is necessary to be cautious about whether political risks are widespread in a chosen for investing region. Companies that have clear understanding how to manage all related political risks can increase their profits. This is why managing political risk is an important element in achieving success at emerging markets and growing at international platforms. Political risk as such, putting it simply, is preventing or making it difficult to enter emerging markets in general (McKellar, 2010,p. 7).

The increase in political risk and instability tends to damage macroeconomic indicators as well as financial infrastructure. For this reason, political risk must be taken into account in both financial development and foreign capital inflows. Political stability reduces the risk of expropriation and increases the credibility of governments in the eyes of potential investors. Such developments would encourage the growth of foreign investment while ensuring that investors are more confident and feel secure enough about a host country. High level of political instability will always constitute an obstacle for foreign direct investments' inflow (Dutta & Roy, 2008).

The groups potentially affected by political risks are quite different. Not only investors, but also project sponsors, creditors and governments can be affected by these risks. Therefore, there are multidimensional effects of political risks. Developing countries usually have high political risk factors, however, developed countries too have demonstrated recently quite a range of own political risks. For example, the 9/11 attacks in the USA, 11/3/2004 Madrid train bombing, 7/7/2005 London Bombing, the political issues related to the presence of Syrian refugees in various European countries, the Arab Spring. These and other facts clearly demonstrate that political tensions today are not only limited to developing countries. And this increase in political risks due to the increase in political tensions in developed countries also influences investors' decisions worldwide.

4. Types of Political Risk

It is obvious that political risk, similar to other types of risk, has its negative influence on every economy. Political risk can arise from local elections, internal and external riots, rebellions, economic stagnation or war threats. Increased political risk can deter foreign investors due to potential confiscation of their assets, sudden increase in taxes and/or tariffs, more incentives provided to local investors, high costs of local raw materials and/or intermediaries' services, or difficulties with money convertibility etc. The net macroeconomic effects from the decline in foreign investors' activities due to increased political risk may lead to delays or halt of production, loss of property, increase of import costs, reduction of incomes, managerial obstacles, higher operating costs or transfer of profits into another country. On the macrolevel, mismanagement of the economy leads to increased costs due to increases in inflation and interest rates, thus making long-term investment decisions more difficult (Bhalla, 1983; McGowan & Moeller, 2009; Kruja & Dragusha, 2014).

Different types of tensions between countries have different consequences for international investment and trade decisions. Strategic and economic tensions between national governments arise for a variety of reasons. This can be a long-lasting unresolved border conflict that is gradually becoming an armed one (as in the Arab-Israeli case). Fundamental differences in national ideologies can also cause countries to see other countries as being inadequate (for example, the liberal capitalist Western Bloc vs. the authoritarian communist Eastern Bloc during the Cold War, or the conflict between Iran and the West today). When there is distrust on the cultural and historical levels, it may also cause tensions between countries. Tensions between countries can disrupt supply chains or cause other external economic damages. Governments' campaigns for providing preferences and consuming more of domestic goods as well as tariffs on foreign trade can create serious barriers to market entry (as it happened during the US-Japanese trade wars) (McKellar, 2010, pp. 12-14).

Hamada et al. (2004) divided political risk into three broad categories (see Figure 1):

- Expropriation risk is the risk of damage an investor may incur due to the loss of ownership or control over the investment after certain actions taken by a host government. Moreover, in the case of debt, project enterprise can't meet the lender's demands. Today, expropriation or "lack of wealth" can emerge in different ways: it can be either an expropriation of an investment, or a complete, physical takeover.
- Transfer risk is the difficulty with converting local currency (capital, interest, profit, royalties and other charges) into foreign ones. Sometimes local governments can make it difficult for foreign investors to transfer capital. This situation harms the interests of foreign investors and thus discourages them from investing into this particular country.
- Political violence risk is a loss and harm that will result from the destruction of physical assets as a result of political directives or as caused by government-related events such as revolution, terrorism, sabotage, military uprising, revolt, insurrection, coup, war or civil disorder (Kruja & Dragusha, 2014).

Figure 1. Types of Political Risk
(Hamada, Haugerudbraaten, Hickman, & Khaykin, 2004)

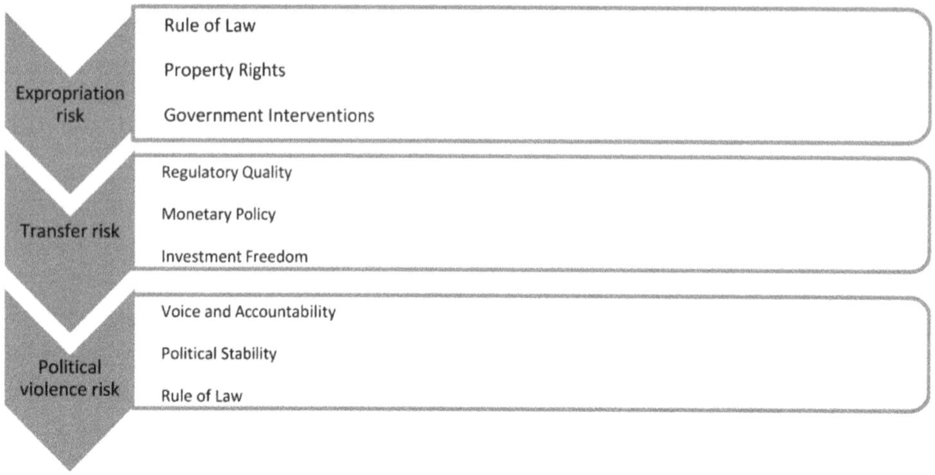

5. Definition and Types of FDI

Foreign direct investments aim to achieve continuous gains in a foreign country with a 10% (for example) share in management through an entrepreneur settled in this foreign country (Jensen, 2012, p. 56). It may be the establishment of a factory or another production facility in a foreign country, or it may be done through purchasing stocks in order to take over management control (Currie, 2011, p. 3).

FDIs are often preferred and welcomed by developing countries, and various government policies are being implemented to attract foreign investors due to long-terms nature of most FDIs. Main contributions of FDI for a host country include: new employment opportunities, internalization of new production technologies, increases in foreign trade volumes and in production capacity.

Investments to be made beyond national borders due to profit-seeking behavior of entrepreneurs cannot be realized without certain risk. The risks of foreign direct investments are always greater than those related to domestic investments. As developed countries are already very much integrated with each other, they tend to reorient onto developing countries which are offering potentially higher profit opportunities and thus - increased profit expectations. However, this also means that they pose greater risks for foreign investors (from developed countries).

Currie (2011) summarized the key risks faced by international investors as follows:

- Country risk is the risk that the political or economic situation in a country will affect the value of an investment in that country. Country risk is affected by the degree of country's development, the attention that a country's politicians pay to international investors, and the degree of confidence the global investors have in this country and its administrators.
- Exchange rate risk is the risk that a country's currency will appreciate or depreciate at the global currency market so that it affects the return one receives on their investment.
- Credit risk is the risk that whoever you lend money to will not repay it. Credit risk is the most widespread risk associated with lending, because there always is a chance that a person, a company, or government to whom you lend money will not pay you back. A synonym for credit risk is

default risk. Owners of mortgage-backed securities around the world encountered credit risk when home owners in the USA, Spain, and several other countries who were unable to make mortgage payments in 2008 and later due to the global financial crisis.

- Business risk is related to the performance of an industry in which the firm operates. Economic conditions may change so that the industry performs better than previously, or they may change so that this industry deteriorates. A good example of business risk is what happened to the world automobile industry back in 2008 and 2009, when even the industry leaders experienced sales declines and several globally known firms faced bankruptcies.
- Financial risk reflects how a firm is financed. Firms that are financed through borrowing rather than owner's investments have a higher degree of financial risk. Financial risk relates to a firm's leverage, which is debt relative to equity. Leverage is great during good times because it aggrandizes returns to owners, but it is deadly during bad times because it also aggrandizes losses. The financial crisis of 2008 showed that many firms had incurred too much financial risk because they borrowed a lot when times were good. When the downturn came, these firms were unable to repay the interest and principal on those borrowings.
- Liquidity risk measures how easy or difficult it is to sell an asset in exchange for cash. A characteristic of financial markets in many developed countries is that they are liquid: it is relatively easy to sell a stock or a bond when you want to cash out. Of course, during panics you cannot expect a high price, but at least you can liquidate the previous investment. Many homeowners in the USA back in 2008 were unable to sell their houses because prices were declining, people were not willing to buy houses, and willing buyers found it difficult to obtain credit financing for such purposes. The housing market was not liquid overall.

6. The Importance of FDI for Developing Countries

FDI is often regarded to be the driving force and the engine of growth for developing countries in their strive to achieve economic growth goals. It is frequently stated that FDIs contribute to economic development of a host country through the provided financial capital, technology transfer, managerial skills' exchange, new employment opportunities and various spillover effects (Alfaro, Chanda, Kalemli-Ozcan, & Sayek, 2004). With the FDI inflow, companies are expected to be more competitive in terms of their liquidity and also while facing various production constraints (Krifa-Schneider & Matei, 2010:55). In addition to this, via FDI host countries can be integrated more easily into the world economy which basically means they are able to become truly global actors.

In addition, FDIs boost both economic and production efficiencies, thus contributing to country's foreign exchange reserves through increasing the production level and satisfying the need in capital. FDI indirectly also increases the trade openness rate. Finally, FDIs assist developing countries in coping with economic problems by means of lowering the saving-investment deficit and expanding the knowledge spillover effect.

7. Theoretical Relationship Between Political and Economic Risks and FDI

Most of political risks arise from government interventions into business operations, local or international.

The whole variety of political risks can be largely divided into macropolitical and micropolitical risks. Macropolitical risks concerns expropriation most often, they can be also generally presented as the risks affecting all foreign firms operating in the same country. These include: tax law amendments, price control, strict environmental regulations, restrictions on capital transfers, and restrictions on foreign ownership. Micropolitical risks usually affect certain sectors only and they may vary by industry, project or firm (Bayraktutan & Tari, 2016, p. 93).

Nowadays, policies on foreign investments are becoming increasingly complex and uncertain. Besides, it is becoming increasingly difficult for governments to develop these policies, not contradicting globalization trends at the same time. The factor of hypothetical government intervention hinders the predictability of international investments. In order to reduce uncertainty and establish a regular investment relationship in today's business world, there is a need for reliable and comprehensive investment regimes, open to cooperation and supporting the sustainable development (UNCTAD Investment Report, 2017).

Multinational corporations need to find a balance between developing countries with their usually low political risks and low costs on the one side and developed countries with their high political stability but also higher costs of hosting, on the other. In many cases multinational businesses already had a chance to prove that developing countries have a more stable political structure due to decreased political risks (Baek & Qian, 2011, p. 14).

The countries with higher democratic accountability tend to absorb more FDI flows. Democratic accountability reduces economic turmoil and provides a more robust business environment for foreign investors (Büsse & Hefeker, 2007).

Political risk goes way beyond the commercial risks, also, they may be limited to the host country only or may belong to the international environment. Unlike with some other determinants, political risks, in most cases, can't be precisely predicted, thus they can quickly lead to a deterioration of the investment climate, weakening of the investors' rights, problems with their ownership of assets etc. - all due to sudden changes in the political environment of host countries (Bayraktutan & Tari, 2016, p. 92).

Effects from political risks on investment decisions can be narrowed down, actually. One of the political risk indicators is, for example, corruption, it always has a major impact on FDI decisions. Same applies to bureaucracy, transparency of government policies and actions, the risk of expropriation and nationalization of the assets, public intervention in the course of doing business etc.

According to the survey conducted by the World Bank on the most important constraints imposed on foreign investment decisions (see the results of this research in Table 1 below), the major of them are as follows: the lack of talented employees, financial difficulties, macroeconomic instability, while political risks and corruption also got quite many votes, inter alia.

According to the results of the same World Bank survey, the most important political risks for the investors entering the markets of developing countries have been identified. According to the results in Table 2, the most important political risks concern: regulatory changes, breach of contract, transfer and convertibility restrictions, civil disturbance, non-honoring of financial obligations, expropriation, terrorism and war.

According to the MIGA's survey, the most influential factors often violating of the investors' contracts are listed as follows: crisis (29%), political regime change in the destination country (14%), corruption/red tape (11%), sovereign state default (10%), political instability/war (9%), non-discriminatory regulatory or policy changes (e.g., increase of tax rates, subsidy cuts, deprival of licenses) (6%), frequent and/or sudden changes in input prices (5%) (World Bank, 2014).

Table 1. Major Constraints to FDI (%)

	2010	2011	2012	2013
Number of respondents	94	316	438	459
Limited size of the local market	9	7	7	5
Lack of investment opportunities	7	-	-	-
Poorly developed infrastructure	9	11	8	7
Lack of qualified staff	10	17	18	18
Lack of assets to carry out the investment	5	11	13	13
Political risks	21	18	22	19
Macroeconomic instability	16	15	20	21
Lack of information on the country's business environment	2	-	-	-
Weak government institutions/red tape/corruption	19	13	8	10
Increased government regulation in the aftermath of the global financial crisis	-	5	3	4

Table 2. Types of Political Risks that Concern Investors in Developing Countries the Most (%)

	For the Next 3 Years	For the Next 12 Months
Adverse regulatory changes	58	56
Breach of contract	45	45
Transfer and convertibility restrictions	43	37
Civil disturbance	33	30
Non-honoring financial obligations	31	27
Expropriation	24	19
Terrorism	13	11
War	7	6

(WIPR-2013:7)

7. Key Factors Influencing Future FDI Flows

FDI movements are determined by push and pull factors. The push factors are mostly related to the supply side of the economy, they are often predetermined by international and global conditions. Pull factors are related to local conditions of a host country, affected by changes in demand, for example. Push factors encourage multinational corporations increase their market share through competitive advantages. Using these push factors corporations are able to benefit from low production factor costs in host countries. On the other hand, pull factors are the institutional measures taken by liberalization of developing countries, infrastructure development, increase in human capital investments and investment incentives. In addition to these factors, macroeconomic stability, availability of finance, presence of well-educated labor, market size, corruption rate and some other political risks are the crucial factors determining the host countries' FDI opportunities (Bayraktutan & Tari, 2016).

Jensen et al. (2012) summarized the main determinants of FDI in five different categories. These are: macroeconomic conditions and characteristics of a host country, economic reforms, good governance including democratization and political risks, protection of intellectual property rights and security and geographical evaluations.

In addition to that, Elleuch et al. (2015) stated that the level of socioeconomic infrastructure development, market size, the level of capital development, distance between countries, labor costs and differences in them, the level of international trade openness, political changes, financial incentives, political stability, interest rate, monetary policy, the level of financial liberalization and economic growth potential are the influential elements for the FDI being directed into a host country.

For example, increasing GDP per capita, constant growth potential and higher GDP overall are preferred by FDI-oriented investors, in addition, such factors as higher literacy rate and higher qualificational level of human capital are also quite influential factors when it comes to FDI decision-making (Jensen, Biglaiser, Malesky, Pinto, Pinto, & Staats, 2012).

The main variables determining the directions and the regions of foreign direct investment flows can be summarized as follows:

- **Wage Rates:** Lower wage levels help multinational companies reduce their production costs through the right FDI decisions
- **Labor Skills:** The decision to invest abroad by the companies operating in the sectors that need qualified labor is significantly affected by both lower wages and higher labor productivity at the same time
- **Tax Rates:** One of the most important factors in investment decisions of multinational companies is undoubtedly the choice of countries that have lower tax rates, on profits especially
- **Transport and Infrastructure:** Transportation, shipping and infrastructure facilities are effective in shaping FDI decisions as all of them can facilitate production and marketing opportunities
- **Size of an Economy/Its Potential for Growth:** The size of a market and its potential for growth are significant influences for the multinational companies that are expanding their sales volumes in an attempt to reach wider customer circles
- **Political Stability / Property Rights:** To the most important variables for FDI investors belong uncertainty, country risk, probability of crisis, reliability of institutions, corruption, law & order, reliability of the legal system
- **Exchange Rate:** Lower exchange rate is an important variable in FDI decisions as the cost of production for multinational companies operating in host countries can be reduced through it. In addition to this, the exchange rate volatility can be regarded as a deterrent for FDI

According to the UNCTAD (2017) survey results, the economic situation in developing Asia is the most influential factor, then goes the macroeconomic situation in the USA, technological change and the digital economy, rising commodity prices, progress of regional agreements - all being positive factors of influence in relation to FDI. At the same time, the following are the key negative factors of influence for FDI: the exchange rate volatility, higher interest rates, increasing debt rates in emerging economies, cyber threats and other problems related to data security, geopolitical uncertainties, terrorism threats, social instability and abrupt withdrawals from regional agreements.

8. Trends in FDI Global Statistics

According to the UNCTAD (2017) database, as it can be seen in Table 3, after a strong increase in FDI volumes on the global scale in 2015, a relative decrease was observed in 2016, when FDIs declined by 2%, to $1.75 trillion. In advanced economies alone though FDI increased by 5%. FDI, which was about $ 646 billion in developing countries, decreased by 14% then. The share of transition economies is $ 68 billion, it demonstrated the increase of 81% in 2016 as compared to the previous year. In LDC (least developed countries) which are structurally fragile and have weak economies, FDI decreased by 13% to the level of $38 billion. Although a moderate improvement in FDI flows is observed for the period of 2017-2018, it still does not reach the peak of 2007. It is estimated to be $ 1.8 trillion with an increase of 5% as of 2017.

When we look at regional differences (Table 3), FDI flows to developing Asia decreased by 15%, to the level of $443 billion in 2016. FDI flows to Africa reached $59 billion, which is 3% lower as compared to 2015. Latin America and the Caribbean had the decreased trend in FDI flows, the fall was around 14%, to the level of $142 billion, mostly due to economic recession, weak commodity prices and various pressures on exports. Least developed countries' FDI share also fell, by 13%, to the level of $38 billion.

Table 3. FDI Inflows by Group of Economies and Regions, 2014-2016, and the Projections for 2017 (in bln USD and %)

Group of Economies/Regions	2014	2015	2016	Projections for 2017
World	1324	1774	1746	1670 to 1870
Developed Economies	563	984	1032	940 to 1050
Europe	272	566	533	560
North America	231	390	425	360
Developing Economies	704	752	646	660 to 740
Africa	71	61	59	65
Asia	460	524	443	515
Latin America and the Caribbean	170	165	142	130
Transition Economies	57	38	68	75 to 85
Annual Growth Rate (%)				
World	-8	34	-2	(-4 to 7)
Developed Economies	-18	75	5	(-9 to 2)
Europe	-20	108	-6	-5
North America	-15	69	9	-15
Developing Economies	4	7	-14	(2 to 15)
Africa	-4	-14	-3	10
Asia	9	14	-15	15
Latin America and The Caribbean	-3	-3	-14	-10
Transition Economies	-33	-34	81	(10 to 25)

(UNCTAD Database)

Due to the increasing political uncertainties of global political developments in recent period, the FDI will decrease. Global developments such as Britain's exit from the EU (Brexit), electoral processes in European countries, separation of the United States from the Trans-Pacific Partnership and the start of negotiations with NAFTA, and the crisis in Syria seem to negatively affect FDI decisions.

According to UNCTAD (2017) report, China and developed countries will be the most important investor countries. Following China, the largest investor, the US, Germany and UK are the most important FDI investors. Developed economies such as Japan, Italy and Spain will also take up at the list. United Arab Emirates among emerging economies, the Republic of Korea and Turkey ranking places increased, but South Africa decreased. The USA, China, India and emerging economies will be the most favorite FDI directions. Indonesia, Thailand, Philippines, Vietnam and Singapore will be the most developing FDI countries in East Asia.

As can be seen from Figure 2, FDI, which has increased regularly in the world between 1990-2000, declined between 2000-2003, and then FDI, which increased significantly until 2007 before the global crisis, reached at the peak in 2007. FDI, which started to decline after the global crisis and started to increase again, showed a significant increase in 2015 and 2016. The FDI shares of developed economies with the most significant share showed significant changes during the period under review. The peak in 2007 decreased after the global crisis and followed a steady state in the following years. It's received the most important share in 2015 and 2016. The share of developing countries has also increased steadily since 2003, with the same share of developed countries in 2013. In 2014, it attracted more FDI than developed countries. The share of transition economies was relatively low compared to developed and developing countries.

In terms of country groups, FDI flows for the last ten years are shown in Figure 3. In this graph one can see that the FDI flows are directed mostly to the industrialized countries and their peaks falls on the year 2007. The highest next share belongs to the OECD members, followed by G-20, G-8 and the group of emerging countries, respectively. The share of the EU-28 is fluctuating in years, while the NAFTA countries have a more modest share.

Figure 2. FDI Inflows by Group of Economies 1990-2016, (Millions of Dollars)
(UNCTAD database)

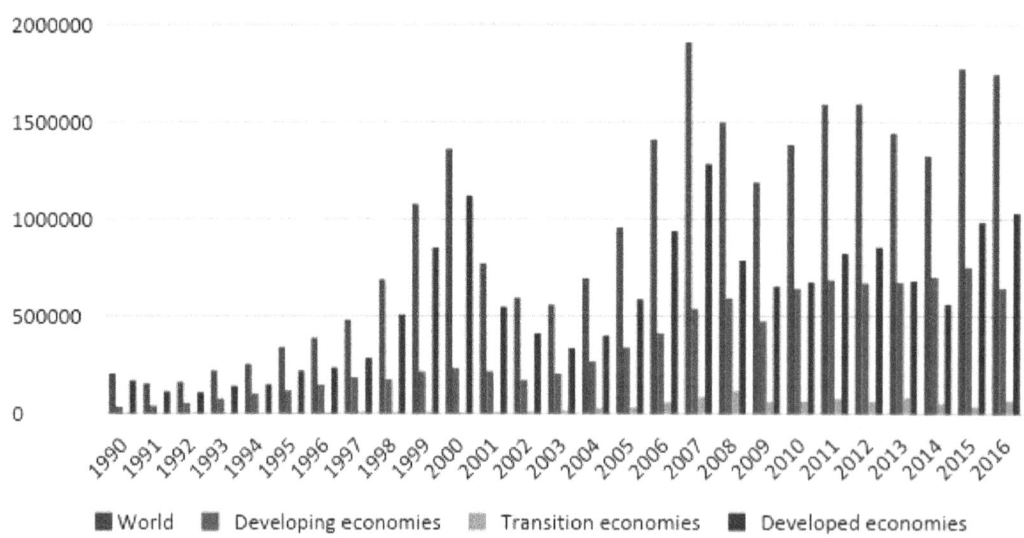

Figure 3. FDI Inflows by Groups, 2006-2016 (mln $)
(UNCTAD database)

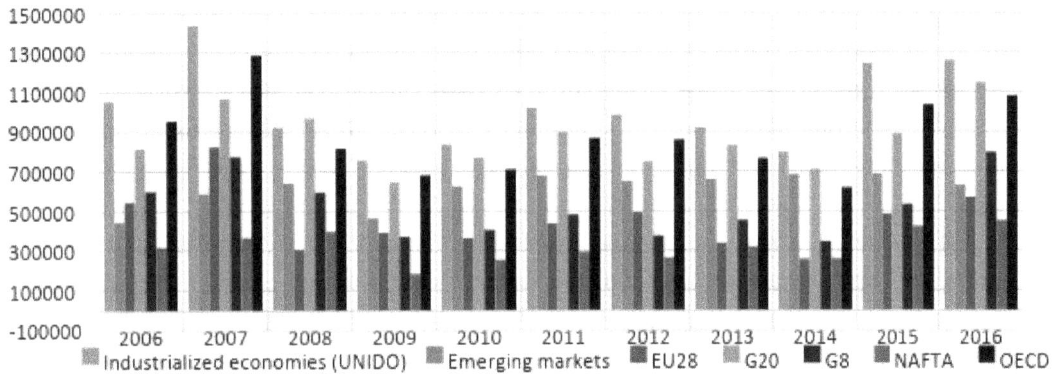

Moderate global growth is expected in the future, expectations of the increase in global trade and in profitability level are perceived as signs of FDI flow. It is also expected that FDI will reach the level of $ 1.85 trillion by the end of 2018. At the same time, political uncertainty and potentially increasing geopolitical risks prevent FDI increases, while changes in tax policies reduce foreign trade globally.

SOLUTIONS AND RECOMMENDATIONS

The ongoing debate so far has shown how direct foreign investments are influenced by the rise in political interest in addition to the instability of macroeconomic variables. It is emphasized that developing countries especially need direct foreign investments for their further economic growth and creation of new employment areas. In order for all economies to attract more foreign direct investment, especially developing ones, it is necessary to reduce both macroeconomic and political risks. For this reason, governments of developing countries have to take more precautions about their political risks in order to obtain more FDI.

FUTURE RESEARCH DIRECTIONS

For all further empirical studies on the same problem it is noteworthy important that similar data should be analyzed, of the uniform type and obtained from the same/similar sources. However, it is very different with political risks: those should be analyzed using the data from official institutions and that from alternative databases. This will enable the diversification of empirical studies and would provide more effective results on this subject. Differences in the development levels of countries cause macroeconomic variables to be also different, same applies to the political risk elements. For this reason, it will be beneficial to clarify the numerical data related to the political risk elements of developing countries and to present the use of these factors in practical terms.

CONCLUSION

Trade and investment decisions are strongly influenced by risk factors. International investment decisions, however, require taking into account quite different risks as opposed to domestic investments. Unlike portfolio investments and short-term capital movements, foreign direct investments have some difficulties due to additional reasons such as sunk costs, irreversibility of investment and difficulty in transferring profit and capital to a country. Similarly, political risks have a strongly negative impact on FDI decisions.

Over the last decade, FDIs have increased considerably on the global scale and has shown significant changes in the recent years. In developing countries, factor prices can become attractive centers for foreign investment due to their relatively lower costs, ease of competitiveness and wider market size. However, developing countries have a lower share of FDIs due to the high level of political risk variables.

In order to increase the share of FDI inflows with significant positive externalities and spillover effects for developing countries, it is necessary to reduce political risk factors as well as to improve macroeconomic variables. As a matter of fact, in recent years, countries with a large share of FDI inflows on the global scale, more or less macroeconomically sound and with less political risks, have managed to attract more FDI.

REFERENCES

Aguiar, S., Aguiar-Conraria, L., Gulamhussen, M. A., & Magalhaes, P. C. (2012). Foreign Direct İnvestment And Home-Country Political Risk: The Case of Brazil. *Latin American Research Review*, *47*(2), 144–165. doi:10.1353/lar.2012.0013

Al-Khouri, R., & Abdul Khalik, U. (2013). Does Political Risk Affect the Flow of Foreign Direct Investment into the Middle East North African Region. *Journal of Global Business and Technology*, *9*(2), 47–63.

Alfaro, L., Chanda, A., Kalemli-Ozcan, S., & Sayek, S. (2004). FDI and Economic Growth: The Role Of Local Financial Markets. *Journal of International Economics*, *64*(1), 89–112. doi:10.1016/S0022-1996(03)00081-3

Asiedu, E. (2006). Foreign Direct Investment in Africa: The Role of Natural Resources, Market Size, Government Policy, Institutions and Political Instability. *World Economy*, *29*(1), 63–77. doi:10.1111/j.1467-9701.2006.00758.x

Baek, K., & Qian, X. (2011). An Analysis on Political Risks and the Flow of Foreign Direct Invesment in Developing and Industrialized Economies. *Economics. Management and Financial Markets*, *6*(4), 60–91.

Bayraktutan, Y., & Tarı, Ö. M. (2016). Politik Riskler, İki Taraflı Yatırım Anlaşmaları ve Uyuşmazlıklar Bağlamında Doğrudan Yabancı Yatırımlar [Foreign Direct Investments at the Context of Political Risks, Bilateral Investment Agreements and Disputes]. *Uluslararası Ekonomik Araştırmalar Dergisi [International Journal of Economic Studies]*, *2*(4), 87–104.

Benáček, V., Lenihan, H., Andreosso-O'Callaghan, B., Michalíkov, E., & Kan, D. (2014). Political Risk, Institutions and Foreign Direct Investment: How Do They Relate in Various European Countries? *World Economy*, *37*(5), 625–653. doi:10.1111/twec.12112

Bhalla, B. 1983. How Corporations Should Weigh Up Country Risk. *Euromoney*, June, 66–72.

Busse, M., & Hefeker, C. (2007). Political Risk, Institutions And Foreign Direct Investment. *European Journal of Political Economy*, *23*(2), 397–415. doi:10.1016/j.ejpoleco.2006.02.003

Clark, E., & Marois, B. (1996). Managing Risk. In *International Business: Techniques And Applications*. USA: Thomson Business Press.

Currie, D. M. (2011). *Country Analysis: Understanding Economic and Political Performance*. NY, USA: Routledge Taylor and Francis.

Daude, C., & Stein, E. (2007). The quality of institutions and foreign direct investment. *Economics and Politics*, *19*(3), 317–345. doi:10.1111/j.1468-0343.2007.00318.x

Demirhan, E., & Masca, M. (2008). Determinants of foreign direct investment flows to developing countries: a cross-sectional analysis. *Prague Economic Papers*, *4*(4), 356–369. doi:10.18267/j.pep.337

Dutta, N., & Roy, S. (2008). Foreign direct investment, financial development and political risks. *Munich Personal RePEc Archive*. Retrieved from http://mpra.ub.uni-muenchen.de/10186/

Dzidrov, M., & Dzidrov, M. (2010). Political and economic risk analysis case study of Macedonia. In *The Conference on Web-Based Business Management*. Retrieved from http://file.scirp.org/pdf/18-1.8.14.pdf

Elleuch, N., Ilhem, M., Jaouadi, Z., & And Jaouadi, S. (2015). Examination of the impact of political and country risk on foreign direct investment inflows in Tunisia. *European Academic Research*, *2*(11), 14434–14445.

Erkekoglu, H., & Kilicarslan, Z. (2016). Do political risks affect the foreign direct investment inflows to host countries? *Journal of Business, Economics and Finance*, *5*(2), 218–232.

Erramilli, M., & Krishna, C. P. (1993). Service firms' international entry-mode choice: a modified transaction-cost analysis approach. *Journal of Marketing*, *57*(3), 19–38. doi:10.2307/1251852

Gastanaga, V. M., Nugent, J. B., & Pashamova, B. (1998). Host country reforms and FDI inflows: how much difference do they make? *World Development*, *26*(7), 1299–1314. doi:10.1016/S0305-750X(98)00049-7

Grosse, R., & Trevino, L. J. (1996). Foreign direct investment in the United States: an analysis by country of origin. *Journal of International Business Studies*, *27*(1), 139–155. doi:10.1057/palgrave.jibs.8490129

Grosse, R., & Trevino, L. J. (2005). New Institutional Economics and FDI Location in Central and Eastern Europe. *Management International Review*, *45*(2), 123–145.

Hamada, J., Haugerudbraaten, H., Hickman, A., & Khaykin, I. (2004). Pricing Political Risk within an Economic Capital Framework. In S. Wilkin (Ed.), *Country and Political Risk: Practical Insights for Global Finance*. Risk Books, England.

Hayakawa, K., Kimura, F., & Lee, H. (2011). How does country risk matter for FDI. Institute of Development Economies.

Jensen, N., Biglaiser, G., Malesky, E., Pinto, P., Pinto, S., & Staats, J. (2012). *Politics and Foreign Direct Investment*. USA: University of Michigan Press. doi:10.3998/mpub.3425019

Kansal, V. (2015). Political Risk: Conceptualization, Definition, Categorization and Methodologies. *The Journal of Politik Risk*, *3*(4).

Kirikkaleli, D. (2016). Interlinkage Between Economic, Financial, and Political Risks in the Balkan Countries: Evidence from a Panel Cointegration. *Eastern European Economics*, *54*(3), 208–227. doi:10.1080/00128775.2016.1168704

Kolstad, I., & Tondel, L. (2002). *Social Development and Foreign Direct Investment in Services. CMI Report 2002:11*. Bergen: Chr Michelsen Institute.

Krifa-Schneider, H., Matei, I., & Matei, I. (2010). Business Climate, Political Risk and FDI in Developing Countries: Evidence from Panel Data. *International Journal of Economics and Finance*, *2*(5), 54–65. doi:10.5539/ijef.v2n5p54

Kruja, A., & Dragusha, B. (2014). The Impact of Political Risk on Foreign Direct Investment. *Iliria International Review*, (2), 73–92. doi:10.21113/iir.v4i2.33

McGowan Jr, C. B., & And Moeller, S. E. (2009). A model for making foreign direct investment decisions using real variables for political and economic risk analysis. *Managing Global Transitions International Research Journal*, *7*(1), 27–44.

McKellar, R. (2010). *A Short Guide to Political Risk*. England: Gower Publishing Limited.

Mustaque, K. M., & Akbar, M. I. (2013). The Impact of Political Risk on Foreign Direct Investment. *MPRA*. Retrieved from http://mpra.ub.uni-muenchen.de/47283/

Nigh, D. (1986). Political Events and the Foreign Direct Investment Decision: An Empirical Examination. *Managerial and Decision Economics*, *7*(2), 99–106. doi:10.1002/mde.4090070205

Noorbakhsh, F., Paloni, A., & Youssef, A. (2001). Human Capital and FDI Inflows to Developing Countries: New Empirical Evidence. *World Development*, *29*(9), 1593–1610. doi:10.1016/S0305-750X(01)00054-7

Roll, R., & Talbott, J. (2001). Why Many Developing Countries Just Aren't. The Anderson School at UCLA. Retrieved from https://ssrn.com/abstract=292140

Schneider, F., & Frey, B. S. (1985). Economic and Political Determinants of Foreign Direct Investment. *World Development*, *13*(2), 161–175. doi:10.1016/0305-750X(85)90002-6

Sedik, W. M., & Seoudy, H. (2012). The Impact of Country Risk and New Institutional Economics on Foreign Direct Investment A Panel Data Analysis for Middle East and North Africa Region (1999-2010). In *The 16th Meeting of the International Society for New Institutional Economics*, University of Southern California.

Singh, H., & Jun, K. W. (1995). Some New Evidence on Determinants of Foreign Direct Investment in Developing Countries. *World Bank*. Retrieved from http://ssrn.com/abstract=623885

Sıssanı, M., & Belkacem, Z. (2014). The Effect of Political Risk on Foreign Direct Investment: The Case of Algeria, *Hyperion. Economic Journal (London)*, *3*(2), 29–35.

Stoever, W. (2002). Attempting to resolve the attraction-aversion dilemma: A study of FDI Policy in the Republic of Korea. *Transnational Corporations*, *11*(1), 49–76.

Talbott, J., & Roll, R. W. (2001). Why many developing countries just aren't. *The Anderson School at UCLA*.

Tallman, S. B. (1988). Home Country Political Risk and Foreign Direct Investment in The United States. *Journal of International Business Studies*, *19*(2), 219–233. doi:10.1057/palgrave.jibs.8490856

Trevino, L. J., & And Mixon, F. G. (2004). Strategic factors affecting foreign direct investment decisions by multinational enterprises in Latin America. *Journal of World Business*, *39*(3), 233–243. doi:10.1016/j.jwb.2004.04.003

UNCTAD. (2017). *World Investment Report 2017: Investment and The Digital Economy*. Geneva: UN Publication.

Wei, S. J. (2000). How taxing is corruption on international investors? *The Review of Economics and Statistics*, *82*(1), 1–12. doi:10.1162/003465300558533

Wheeler, D., & Moody, A. (1992). International investment location decisions: The Case of US Firms. *Journal of International Economics*, *33*(1-2), 57–76. doi:10.1016/0022-1996(92)90050-T

World Bank. (2014). *World Investment and Political Risk (WIPR)-2013: World Investment Trends and Corporate Perspectives, The Political Risk Insurance Industry, Breach of Contract*. Washington, D.C.: MIGA, World Bank Group.

KEY TERMS AND DEFINITIONS

Country Risk: Is the risk that political and/or economic situation in a country will affect the volume of investments into that country.

Credit Risk: Is the risk that whoever you lend money to - will not repay it.

Foreign Direct Investment: Investments aiming to achieve continuous gains in a foreign country with a certain share in management in this country.

Political Risk: Refers to the damage or negative influence on businesses as a result of the attitudes and behaviors of politicians and the costs of political events etc.

Risk: Probability of an event happening and its negative results (costs) for the related actors.

Chapter 4
Features of Financial Policy Development by Russian Companies in Today's Conditions

Igor Keri
Plekhanov Russian University of Economics, Russia

Elena Gromova
Plekhanov Russian University of Economics, Russia

Nadezhda Sinelschikova
Plekhanov Russian University of Economics, Russia

ABSTRACT

The chapter includes the proposals regarding the development of rational financial policies by Russian companies in today's conditions. The authors have identified the following areas of difficulties: sales; deficit of financial resources for investment in development and distribution; instability and unpredictability of external conditions. Changes in price policies, optimization of components and volume of trade account receivables are some of the suggested ways of how to improve company's sales. The solution to the lack of financial resources for company's investment development can be found through selecting more effective forms of financing. The authors also point out the limitations in investment activities' financing under the conditions of current import substitution while suggesting author's own and original composition of indicators for innovation activity. The study leads the readers to the conclusion that the state today faces the challenge of creating favorable conditions for strengthening the financial stability of companies.

DOI: 10.4018/978-1-5225-7760-7.ch004

INTRODUCTION

Implementation of a company's financial policy in practice is closely related to financial theory. At present, there is no systematic approach to the concept and formation of company's financial policy in financial theory. As a consequence, in real business practice most companies do not apply any holistic approach to the formation and implementation of financial policies, replacing it with disparate, and sometimes contradictory, managerial decisions in the field of financial management.

Categories "financial policy" and "financial management" should be highlighted here in the first place.

Financial policy is an independent concept, requiring a separate study and analysis in terms of both theory and practice.

Development and implementation of a financial policy by a company allows solving successfully its strategic and tactical tasks in comparison with the companies without a financial policy.

On a higher level, financial policy implemented by the state sets the vector for the formation of financial policies by all companies in the state (or in its specific region).

Directions of activities in the course of this research are put forward as follows:

- To overview of the already available research & development achievements in the field of company's financial policy
- To assess the impacts of internal and external challenges on the development of Russian companies in general
- To identify the key areas in the development of financial policies in terms of financial constraints

The purpose of the study is to define a systematic approach to the contents of a company's financial policy for practical use in creating an effective financial management system.

The objectives of this study, taking into account the directions above, are as follows:

- To determine the contents of a company's financial policy
- To develop recommendations on pricing policy, obligations of management, policy of attracting investment resources
- To justify potential state measures which should be aimed at creating favourable financial conditions for the development of Russian companies

BACKGROUND

Both globally and within Russian scientific community specifically, there has been a discussion as to the essence of a company's financial policy for quite a long time already. The following approaches to interpreting the scientific concept of "company's financial policy" have been identified by now: hierarchical, ideological, elemental, normative, managerial.

The hierarchical approach covers management of an economic entity from the perspective of different levels and is relatively rare in economic literature.

German scientist H. Hinterhuber (1996) considers "financial policy of an enterprise to be an element of strategic planning, which aims to increase the value of the enterprise through the implementation of operational and strategic plans".

The ideological approach assumes that company's financial policy should be formed in accordance with its corporate ideology. This approach implies the establishment of company's development goals and tasks arising from them as well as the choice of methods to be used for their solution.

H. Ulrich (1990) adheres to the financial and economic model of company's policy, "the formation stages of which are the formulation of financial and economic goals, the identification of the enterprise's potential and the development of strategies for further development".

V. V. Bocharov (2014) defines financial policy as the course, purpose, strategy, ideology of the company.

Elemental approach studies the composition of elements that reflect the direction of financial policy of an organization.

M.V. Romanovsky (2014) refers to the elements of company's financial policy as: accounting policy, credit policy, cash management policy, cost management policy, dividend policy.

A.S. Makarov (2008) examines financial policy "in terms of the types of activities of the organization: investment, supply, production, marketing, innovation, financial etc.".

The normative approach implies the development of norms and principles for the functioning of economic entities in order to achieve the set goals.

Z. Bodie, R. Merton (2007) emphasize that under certain conditions "financial policy is to conduct ... a dividend policy that establishes, for example, a regularity in payments to shareholders in the form of dividends of one-third (or a different share) of profit". It is obvious that these authors perceive the terms "dividend" and "financial policy" in general as a set of principles and norms used in financial management.

Bertonesh M., Nait R. (2004) do not provide their own definition for financial policy. However, they specifically mention the target values (norm) for debt-to-equity and dividend ratios (in %).

H.H. Hinterhuber (1996) defines policy as part of the strategic planning system and includes, as a direction of financial policy, "the choice of financial and economic criteria for evaluating development strategies and programs, as well as the contribution of individual units to increasing the market value of the enterprise".

Management approach is related to interpretation of company's financial policy as a set of activities (actions) for the purposeful formation and use of finance.

V.G. Kogdenko (2013) understands corporate financial policy as "a set of targeted actions for the effective formation and use of financial resources, focused on achieving the strategic and tactical goals of the corporation".

N.N. Simonenko and V. N. Simonenko (2017) consider financial policy to be a set of measures for purposeful raising, distribution and use of finance to achieve the objectives of an enterprise.

C. Drury (2005) in his work on management accounting addresses the importance of having the balance between correct structure of trade receivables account and its impact on company's activities as an integral part of financial policy.

In general, we can conclude that in economic specialized literature there is no uniform approach to the concept and the composition of company's financial policy. This prevents us from forming a complete understanding of this phenomenon as a whole. Moreover, many authors believe that financial policy and financial management are one and the same thing. As a consequence, no separate study is required for financial policy in theory and its formation and analysis in practice.

The authors of this study believe, however, that financial policy is subject to separate study and analysis, both in theory and in practice, in order to build an effective financial management system.

MAIN FOCUS OF THE CHAPTER

Issues, Controversies, Problems

The authors of the study consider it a practical necessity for any today's company to develop a financial policy which would cover all areas of financial management systematically in its operational, investment and financial activities.

Companies without a financial policy, that is, without systematized financial management, are unable to adequately take into account threats posed by changes in the external and internal environments, therefore, they are losing dynamism in their own development.

On the contrary, in companies that have a developed financial policy, a lot of attention is paid to monitoring factors and indicators of both external and internal environments. This allows taking into account the impact of specific factors and indicators while selecting the most optimal managerial decisions for certain areas of company's financial activities.

Attention to the investigated elements of financial policy enable companies respond quickly to serious economic challenges. The most significant challenge is currently the introduction of financial sanctions against Russia from the EU, the US and some other countries. The key consequence from such sanctions has been the deterioration of business climate, drastic changes in market conditions, increasing costs of doing business overall, reduced possibilities for attracting external and internal financial resources. Russian companies have been facing serious financial problems in such areas as sales, deficit and availability of financial resources for investment in own development and progress. The solution to all these problems directly concerns the improvements of companies' financial policies.

Selecting and monitoring the composition of financial indicators allows companies reasonably identify those areas of financial policy that require special attention at the moment. The following indicators have been selected for monitoring: the change in price indices, the dynamics and the ratio of trade receivables and payables accounts, the dynamics of external sources of investment in fixed assets, the volumes of loans, the change in average lending rates, the volume of foreign investments' inflow into Russian economy. The information base for this research has become the Federal State Statistics Service (Rosstat, in short) and the Bank of Russia.

We believe that companies, considering the current conditions, should pay special attention to their pricing policy. Price serves as the tool for resolving marketing and competitiveness issues.

Information about the level of prices for the production and distribution of electricity, gas and water is a significant factor shaping the pricing policy. Table 1 provides detailed information on price indices for the production and distribution of electricity, gas and water in the Russian Federation, intended for sale at the domestic market.

The data in Table 1 shows that during 2006-2016 there was a decrease in the growth of the price index in the production and distribution of electricity, gas and water, intended for sale domestically.

Solution of the current sales issues is largely dependent on how effective the ongoing activities related to management of accounts receivable and creditor debt, explicitly associated with it. The state of trade receivables accounts has a direct impact on company's profitability. Comparative analysis of the dynamics of a company's accounts receivable and payable allows us to identify the problems of selling products and making payments (Table 2).

Table 1. Price indices for production and distribution of electricity, gas and water in the Russian Federation, intended for sale at the domestic market

Year	Price Index, in %
2006	110,3
2007	113,3
2008	118,0
2009	118,3
2010	113,8
2011	105,1
2012	107,0
2013	108,1
2014	104,5
2015	109,3
2016	105,1

(Source: Russian statistical yearbook, 2017)

Trade receivables account management is aimed at decreasing its growth rate while increasing the volume of working capital. The dynamics of trade receivables accounts of Russian companies is demonstrated in Table 2.

Looking at the data provided in Table 2, one can notice the trend of constant growth in the volumes of trade receivables accounts of Russian companies, including overdue debts. The growth in the volume of trade receivables results in the growing need to borrow more and more of capital, thus increasing costs and reducing profitability of a company. Eventually, this may lead to company's bankruptcy.

Trade payables are one of the sources for financing of current activities carried out by Russian companies. The share of trade payables accounts varies between 40-50% of the total liabilities of Russian companies. As to the structure of trade payables accounts, about 50% is accounted for by debts to suppliers and contractors. This situation has been prevailing for quite a long period of time by now and thus has already become a trend.

Comparative analysis of the above indicators for Russian companies in general indicates that in the recent years the volumes of trade payables exceed trade receivables and this trend is growing all the time. This is yet another evidence that Russian companies are rather financially unstable.

In order to obtain more complete information about the state of trade payables accounts, it is necessary to analyze the companies' turnover too. Comparison of the terms of turnover of trade payables and receivables accounts of Russian companies by main types of economic activity is presented in Table 3.

With a slower turnover of trade payables in comparison with trade receivables, the former fully covers receivables and, moreover, serves as the source of financing for other elements of current assets. As a consequence, companies' liquidity and solvency are increasing.

But the risk of financial instability still increases. The Indicators of turnover by industry point at the existence of problematic issues in the regulation of accounts receivable, inter alia.

Solving strategic-level directly related to companies' transition to new technological structures means, in the first place, providing companies with a sufficient volume of investment resources. Analysis of

Table 2. The ratio of trade payables and receivables accounts, bln Rubles

Year	Trade Payables	The Share That Is Overdue	Trade Receivables	The Share That Is Overdue	By How Much Trade Payables Exceed Trade Receivables	By How Much Overdue Trade Payables Exceed Overdue Trade Receivables
2006	7697	821	7871	1040	–174	–219
2007	10653	833	11061	887	–408	–54
2008	13353	994	13783	1051	–430	–57
2009	14882	958	15442	1011	–560	–53
2010	17683	1006	18004	1048	–321	–42
2011	20954	1208	21797	1167	–843	41
2012	23632	1188	22867	1225	765	–37
2013	27532	1470	26264	1483	1268	–13
2014	33174	1881	31014	2016	2160	–135
2015	38925	2429	35736	2276	3189	153

(Source: Region of Russia. Socio-economic indicators. Statistical compendium, 2017)

indicators on the state of external investment resources, taking into account constant and long-term lack of own funds, allows determining the likelihood of solving these tasks.

Data on the structure of investment resources of Russian companies is presented in Figure 1.

Currently, there is a decrease in the share of external sources in financing of investment activities in the total volume of financial resources of companies. This is despite the trend being a continuous decline in profits for many companies and further ageing of fixed assets.

It should be also noted that in developed countries, investment funds are mostly originating from company's own funds (profit and depreciation), which, if necessary, are supported by external sources - bank loans, bonded loans, other means (including the issuance of shares). So, on average in the US industry, depreciation is about 60-70% of capital investment, being the main source of investment resources.

Figure 1 shows that the share of bank loans in the total volume of main capital investments is traditionally low - from 8 to 10%. Following a sharp increase in interest rates, lending volumes reached their peak at the end of 2014, after which they fell sharply in 2015 and still remain below the level of 2014 (Figure 2).

High interest rates on loans are the major issue which is preventing fixed capital in Russia from being updated. In response to the sharp fall in the ruble exchange rate in December 2014, the Bank of Russia raised the base rate to 17% in order to stabilize the financial situation in the country. After that banks also significantly raised their rates on loans (see Figure 3). In January 2015, for non-financial organizations, the average weighted rates on ruble loans for the period up to a year reached 19.9%, for over a year – 15.1%. Stabilization of the financial sector led to gradual reduction in these rates: in September 2016, the Bank of Russia lowered the key rate to 10%. At the same time, the rates of ruble loans for non-financial companies (12.7% and 13.7% in June 2016 for loans with the maturity of less than and more than a year, respectively) still remain above the level of November 2014 (12,0% and 12,6% accordingly).

Table 3. Average maturity (turnover) of payables and receivables of companies by types of economic activity

Year	Trade Payables, Total Days	Including: Mining	Manufacturing	Agriculture, Hunting and Forestry	Construction	Transport and Communications	Wholesale and Retail Trade	financial services	Housing and Communal Services	Trade Receivables, Total Days	Including: Mining	Manufacturing	Agriculture, Hunting and Forestry	Construction	Transport and Communications	Wholesale and Retail Trade	Financial Services	Housing and Communal Services
2006	60	75	50	88	102	55	51	37	132	54	52	51	60	80	45	55	35	89
2007	59	47	52	80	112	54	59	31	112	59	53	56	68	91	46	62	29	84
2008	65	51	56	79	138	56	58	49	95	63	58	58	73	104	48	61	45	77
2009	76	62	74	87	177	51	61	55	104	72	69	74	80	131	41	63	59	91
2010	66	53	71	83	170	59	64	13	102	63	62	69	81	124	49	63	16	92
2011	68	52	68	80	173	65	59	13	106	67	58	69	86	120	57	73	17	97
2012	75	61	68	198	184	65	60	19	113	70	66	65	104	128	55	67	28	108
2013	75	71	76	87	152	70	65	12	133	68	80	73	94	100	56	68	16	150
2014	81	68	79	80	235	71	71	23	148	74	80	79	88	165	51	66	27	170
2015	80	65	89	78	241	72	69	21	161	75	82	92	84	176	49	66	23	204

(Source: Region of Russia. Socio-economic indicators. Statistical compendium, 2017)

Figure 1. Dynamics of the main sources of external investments into main capital of Russian companies, in %
Source: Made up by authors based on Federal State Statistics Service data

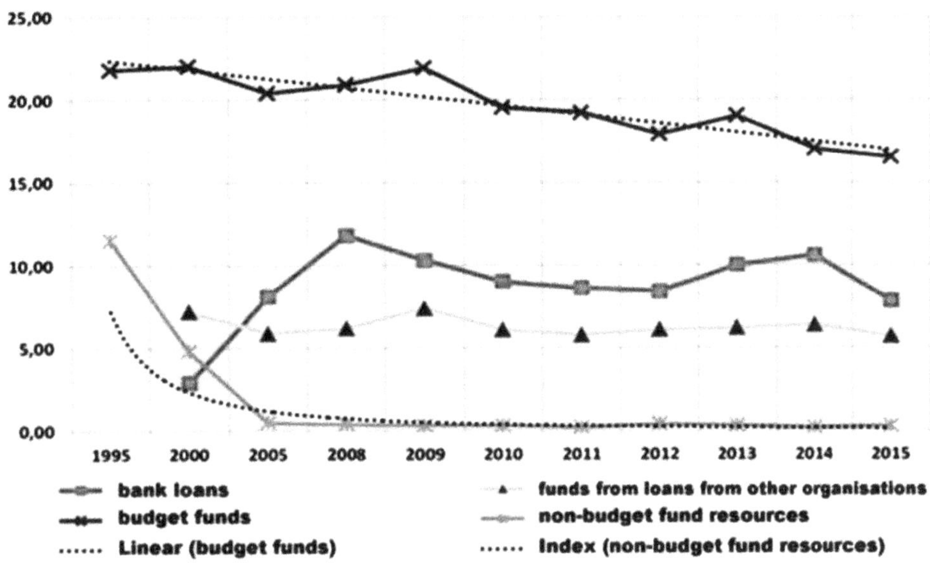

Figure 2. Change in volumes of loans provided to legal entities and individual entrepreneurs, 2012-2016, in current prices
(Made up by authors based on Bank of Russia data)

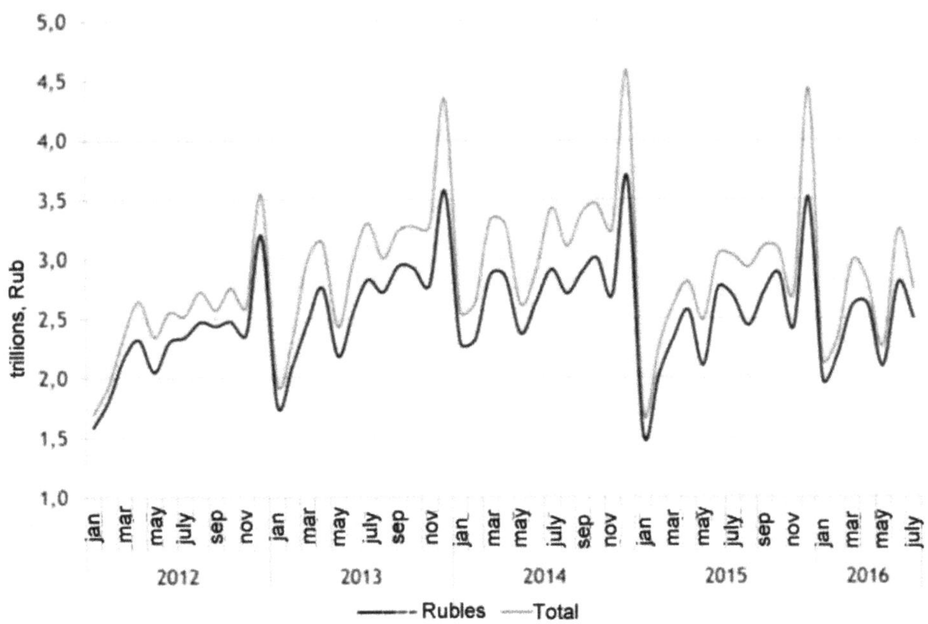

Figure 3. Weighted average interest rates on loans in rubles, 2014-2016 (in %)
(Made up by authors based on Bank of Russia data)

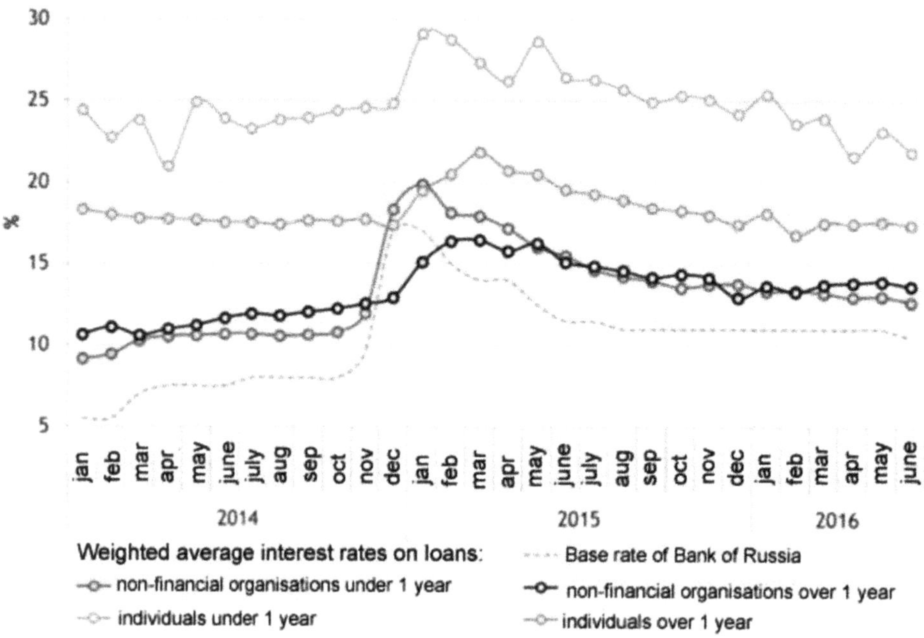

High interest rates on loans restrain investments of primarily small and medium-sized businesses that usually do not have access to other external sources of financing.

Understanding the possibility of attracting credit investment resources into Russian companies is a result of comparing average bank lending rates and profitability ratios of Russian companies (Table 4).

Table 4 shows that the profitability of assets is decreasing. In the analyzed period, the profitability of assets decreased from 6.5% to 3.7%. This indicates low return on invested capital. Decrease in the profitability of assets of Russian companies is also due to a decrease in profitability of sales.

Analysis shows that credit investment resources are unavailable for many Russian companies, since the average rates for these resources are much higher than the return on assets of companies.

The reduction in incoming direct investments in Russia by types of economic activity is shown in Figure 4.

Table 4. Changes in profitability of Russian companies, in %

Year	Assets' Profitability	Profitability of Sold Goods, Work and Services
2011	6,5	9,6
2012	6,1	8,6
2013	4,5	7,0
2014	2,5	7,3
2015	3,7	8,1

(Made up by authors based on Russian statistical yearbook data)

Figure 4. Direct investments in Russia in 2011-2015 by types of economic activity, mln USD
(Made up by authors based on Federal State Statistics Service data)

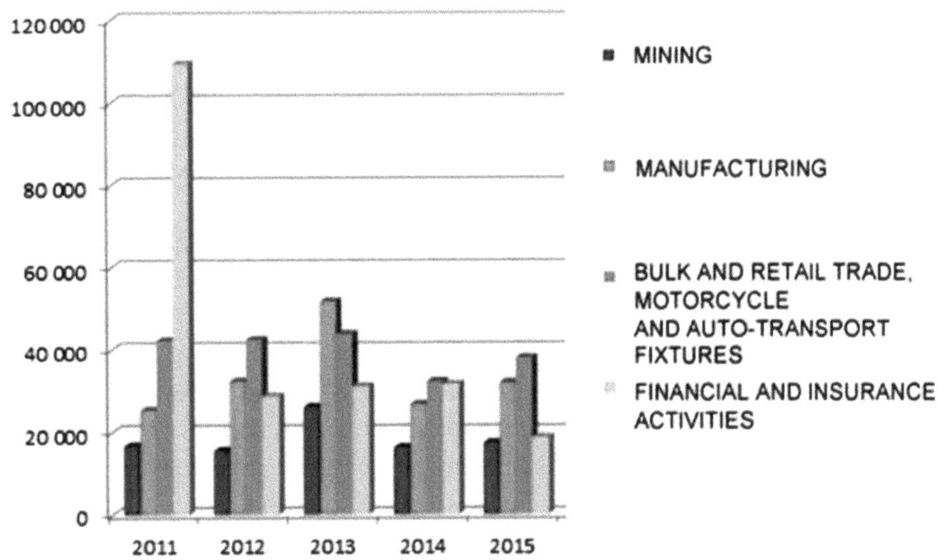

Due to the introduction of sanctions against Russia by the EU, the United States and a number of other states, permanent investment inflows into Russian economy from these countries declined drastically. This caused major issues in areas, where foreign investments were supposed to be distributed. Foreign companies have stopped investing their capital in engineering, high-tech production and in automobile manufacturing. Under these conditions, many Russian companies were forced to roll back investment resources, which is especially observable in healthcare as well as the pharmaceutical industry.

Development and implementation of a financial policy by a company, within the framework of which a systematic approach is taken in analyzing the factors and indicators of the external and internal environments, will allow for a full and qualitative assessment of financial activities and identify areas that need to be improved. According to the results of the study, such areas are recognized as pricing policy, management of receivables and payables, investment and innovation policies.

The influence of direct or indirect factors investigated and indicators of external influence on financial policy (for example, indices of prices for the production and distribution of electricity, gas and water in the Russian Federation, intended for sale at domestic markets, weighted average rates for ruble loans) is carried out through certain state measures. The main directions of the state's actions directly related to companies' financial policy are: development of state tax policy, regulation of prices for natural monopolies, regulation of money supply and inflation, targeted state support for promising industrial projects, development of currency regulation and control system.

SOLUTIONS AND RECOMMENDATIONS

The authors believe that "financial management" and "financial policy of a company" are two distinct categories. Financial management is an action, and financial policy is a mode of action. The image of action (management) is represented in the norms and principles applied in the process of making managerial decisions.

So, under price policy we understand the general principles to which the company is going to adhere in what concerns pricing. Management of accounts receivable assumes that a credit policy in relation to debtors is put in place. Investment policy is a documented set of norms, principles, in accordance with which management of activities based on company's investment cycle is carried out. Price policy, management of debt receivable and investment policy are all elements of a financial policy and, therefore, can be included in the definition of financial policy.

Interpretation of the category "financial policy of a company" along with the directions in the development of its key elements are proposed. Financial policy of a company consists of setting goals and objectives in financial management, developing an algorithm of actions, choosing forms and methods to be used in the course of its implementation. Solution to the current external and internal problems of the business environment is located in the field of improving such key areas of company's financial policy as pricing policy, receivables' and payables' management policy, investment and innovation policies.

Marketing-related issues require companies to change their pricing policies. Under the conditions of limited market demand caused by falling incomes of population and limited potential for economic growth in the country, the most important goal of company's pricing policy is to maintain the sales' volume and market share. Achieving this goal is possible through quicker development and adjustment of the price policy, taking into account changes in the system of state regulation of economic activity in the country and adverse external influences.

Along with the issues surrounding price policies, in order to improve sales it is necessary to pay attention to optimization of the structure and the volume of trade receivables. When managing trade receivables accounts companies need to take into account the following factors: the total sales volume and the share of it that will go towards subsequent payments; terms of settlements with customers and suppliers; rigidity of the collection system of trade receivables accounts; payment discipline of buyers and the general economic state of those industries, to which they are affiliated; quality of the analysis of receivables and consistency in the use of its results.

In order to minimize the risks associated with overdue trade receivables accounts, companies need to take various preventive measures. Among the preventive measures (Memba & Njery, 2016) in monitoring the level of receivables, effectiveness of the system of settlements with counterparties should be mentioned, as well as monitoring the solvency of buyers and customers, insurance of bad debts along with the possibilities for their refinancing. At the same time, the most popular and widely used method is refinancing trade receivables accounts, the main forms of which are factoring (Cengher, 2011), forfeiting and bills of exchange.

An important issue in financial management is the ratio of trade receivables and payables. In Russia, it is often the case that decline in receivables doesn't bring profit without changing creditor's debt. This is due to a decrease in coverage ratio, as a result of which the company acquires signs of insolvency and becomes vulnerable in relation to state bodies and creditors. In this case, it is crucial to not only reduce receivables, but also balance them with trade payables accounts.

Trade payables accounts have been used by Russian companies as a source of financing activities for a long time, since it is the most affordable and also a relatively cheap financial source.

At the same time, the use of trade payables accounts, which is inherently short-term, for financing long-term goals of companies often entails significant risks, including financial instability.

Obviously, future development of companies is associated with the expansion, updating and modernization of their activities and should be financed by long-term sources of financing. In today's Russia, for the companies operating in various industries, the issue of access to long-term investment resources is often troublesome. The inflow of foreign capital as an additional investment resource is currently very limited.

Low investment attractiveness status of Russia has been confirmed by the studies of the International Financial Research Centre, Faculty of Business, University of Navarra (IESE's International Centre for Finance Research) and also by Ernst & Young (Groh, Liechtenstein & Li, 2016). The index of countries' attractiveness for venture and direct investment funds shows that Russia comes 41st (out of 125), thus between Lithuania (40) and the Philippines (42). This means that investment in Russia is subject to significant country risks. At the same time, all other BRICS countries, excluding Brazil (which is 54th), are ranked above Russia. In particular, China is ranked 24th, India goes 29th, South Africa - 32nd. According to the key indicators of the Doing Business ranking (The World Bank, 2017), Russia's position, in comparison with advanced economies, is also rather weak. In terms of "protection of investors" our country is on the 53rd place, in terms of "receiving a loan" - on the 44th place. Russia's rating indicators for today are a deterrent to the influx of foreign investment into Russian economy.

Assessments of the mentioned above ratings show that in the short-term Russia will have low investment attractiveness for both foreign and domestic investors due to poor quality of the institutional environment and growing risks, both macroeconomic and geopolitical. As a result, the problem with shortage of financial resources for development in the near future will remain to be relevant for Russian companies.

This is also supported by the statistics concerning the volume of direct foreign investments in Russia. According to the UN Conference on Trade and Development, in 2015, it declined by 92%. Of the total investment in fixed assets in Russia in 2015, according to the Federal State Statistics Service, foreign banks' loans accounted for only 2%, while other foreign investments accounted for about 1%.

Mechanisms put in place with the purposes of attracting domestic investments do not actually work. Contribution of domestic banks to financing of fixed capital of companies amount to merely 6%. Issuance of corporate bonds provide 1.6% more, issuance of shares - only 0.5%. More than half of the total volume of investments in Russian companies' fixed assets was financed by own funds.

Decrease of investment activity below the threshold in any country would be treated as a serious threat to national security (Voronkova, 2011).

The authors believe that Russia has sufficient resources to increase domestic investment and thus overcome the current crisis. First of all, these are the funds accumulated by companies. In 2015, the balanced profit of Russian companies, according to the Federal State Statistics Service, rose by 53% and reached the level of 8.4 trln rubles. At the same time, all sectors of the economy grew too. Deposits of Russian legal entities, according to the Bank of Russia, reached the level of more than 12 trln rubles, the deposits of citizens - about 23 trln rubles.

Another significant reserve of domestic investment resources in Russia consists of pension accumulations of the country's population. There are about 2 trln rubles worth of savings under the management of non-state pension funds, and then also 1.8 trln rubles more under the management of state management company (VEB). At the end of 2015, 60% of the savings in non-state pension funds were invested in shares and bonds issued by Russian companies. But another 1.5 trln rubles were not included in the funded system due to the fact that this part of payments was frozen.

The possibility of active use of domestic investment resources will require the state to take appropriate legislative actions. It is necessary, inter alia, to simplify the procedures related to issuing and acquiring corporate bonds. There would be more interest of general population in this type of investing in case such bonds would become tax deductible. Taxation conditions and protection of the stock market through bank deposits should become more favorable.

In order to boost the investment activities of companies, it is necessary to develop special instruments of state support, while the latter should become more active overall.

Company's investment policy is largely predetermined by its dividend policy. In recent years, companies used to pay large dividends, as a consequence, the investment ability of such companies has been only falling. Perhaps shareholders, in many cases, should have reinvested the dividends they received. However, at present there is a shortage of investment demand and infrastructure so needed for the investment process is still underdeveloped in Russia. Potential investors often face the need for additional investments in infrastructure facilities, and this increase the overall project costs.

Russian companies should take into account the positive experience of the representatives of Western management schools in the field of non-standard methods used for reducing the investment budgets. The most popular methods of reducing investment costs these days include: outsourcing (delegating all supporting processes to the outside structures); outstaffing (transfer of support staff outside the core company); leasing; franchising; factoring (a type of banking service to expedite settlements with the buyer); crowdfunding (a form of cooperation between donors regarding an investment idea, supporting the initiator through relatively small contributions); bootstrapping (the methodology for implementing a project in the paradigm of deliberate abandonment of insignificant investment costs).

Investment activities of Russian companies are closely connected with the development of innovative activity. At the same time, the system of parameters for assessing the innovative potential of a company should include the integrated indicators of financial development of companies (Aliev, 2016).

Sufficient funding ensures the success of innovative development. It is necessary to develop market mechanisms for financing innovations - venture investments, project financing, equipment leasing etc. Innovative vouchers are widely used abroad and are attracting the attention of many Russian companies. An innovative voucher is a certificate that gives its holder the opportunity to get scientific or consulting support in the implementation of a project. Using an innovative voucher involves interaction between small and medium-sized businesses on the one side and research centres and universities on the other so that to gain access to research resources.

Special attention should be paid to creating innovative models of management behavior which should become the dominant one in their development. Creating such a model is possible if there are strategic standards in place that characterize the buildup of company's innovative potential and quantify necessary rates of growth. The authors propose to use the following indicators to stimulate the innovative activity of company's management: the standard of expenses for the maintenance of the Board of Directors or the rate of profits' distribution, depending on innovation activity. The authors in this particular case would like to mention the following indicators of innovative activity: the share of technological innovations in the volume of shipped products; the share of costs for all types of innovation in the volume of shipped products.

The share of technological innovations in the volume of shipped products is defined as the share of revenue from the sale of innovative goods, works, and services produced using technological innovations in total revenues in percent. The share of total costs for all types of innovation (technological, marketing and organizational innovations) in the volume of shipped products in percent is defined as the ratio of total costs for technological, marketing and organizational innovations to the amount of revenue from shipment from the sale of own production, as well as works and services, executed in-house.

The authors believe that a company's stable financial condition depends, to a large extent, on state measures aimed at creating of conditions for more stable financial positioning of companies in the real sector of the economy. Main directions of state actions in the field of ensuring financial stability of companies include: development of state tax policy, regulation of prices in the areas of natural monopolies, regulation of money supply and inflation, targeted state support of promising industrial projects, currency regulation and control.

As part of the development of a company's financial policy and overcoming external and internal problems, practical proposals have been made to adjust the key elements of financial policy as follows.

Company's pricing policy should be constantly assessed on the basis of actual results achieved and forecasts of economic parameters at the macroeconomic, sectoral and regional levels and, if necessary, adjusted. Under the conditions of constant changes in the economic situation, this is possible on the basis of multivariate business planning. However, in the case of medium-sized and small companies, so far, this approach has not been implemented due to the lack of appropriate specialists in planning and information from regional and sectoral management bodies on the forecast parameters for the development of industrial and regional markets of differentiated products.

High costs associated with pricing, which go towards ensuring the production activities of the company, including costs for products (services) of natural monopolies are an important issue for Russian companies to consider. The problem of high costs for production activities primarily concerns the companies importing some or all of their raw materials. It is the costs associated with the import of raw materials and other materials due to ruble depreciation that is the reason for growing prices for the end products of these companies. When companies create their own raw materials bases in Russia this situation can be avoided, which is especially important for the companies producing consumer goods. Companies are forced to do this to reduce the cost of production in future, while at the current moment they have significant costs and are also forced to pay high interest on credit resources. The lowered base rate from the Bank of Russia allows banks get lower rates on credit resources which will, in turn, allow Russian companies reduce costs and increase the price competitiveness of their goods.

It should be also noted that the latest state measures aimed at solving the problems with companies' pricing turned out to be rather positive. The government's decisions to limit the growth of prices and tariffs for natural monopoly products (services) within the inflation rate (4% in 2018-2020) will allow companies determine costs and prices more accurately, and as a result, to predict more reasonably the financial results from their activities. This will, in turn, allow companies plan their development primarily at their own expense.

Another positive trend of the present time concerns the reduction of companies' costs through diversification of production capacities and types of products produced at these capacities across the regions of Russia in order to bring production capacities closer to the raw materials base. However, weak infrastructure in many regions often leads to unnecessary investment costs and makes such investment projects unattractive. Strengthening the role of regional development plans and their provision for inter-regional projects through better financing would reduce the investment costs for projects and thus would also lower the prices for manufactured products.

Branding is an important aspect of price-making, which largely drives the increase in demand for products. Companies tend to create and maintain at least one strong brand in every segment of their products. Price ranges of brands are calculated for groups of population with different levels of welfare. However, for medium and small companies, brand advertising is a very expensive task; therefore, the share of well-known domestic brands is never large. Promotion of domestic brands at home and abroad should become an element of state policy.

Exceeding the growth rate of trade receivables accounts over the rate of increase in revenue from sales indicates a decrease in the level of management of trade receivables accounts. Management of trade receivables accounts should be aimed towards a relative decrease in the rate of its growth and a corresponding increase in working capital. At the same time, the main task in managing trade receivables accounts is to optimize the amount of receivables for settlements with customers, accounting for 80-90% of the total volume of trade receivables accounts of Russian companies.

In an attempt to reduce the turnover of trade receivables accounts, various payment options for products should be made available. The most common form of payment is a partial advance payment, which combines prepayment and sale on credit. A more effective form of payment with regular customers with whom long-term commercial relations have been already established would be a phased calculation for the works performed and services rendered. A bank guarantee should be used when concluding foreign economic contracts in order to minimize economic risks. In this case, the bank reimburses the required amount in the event of default of a debtor to pay under their obligations.

When choosing a system of settlements with customers, it is necessary to take into account that the provision of more favorable terms of settlements is accompanied by an increase in the balance of receivables. In order to maximize the flow of funds, it would be wise to develop a system of contract models with flexible payment terms and flexible pricing.

Discounts for advance payment of products or for early payments when providing a loan are an effective instrument of credit relations between companies and customers. However, providing discounts is appropriate only in the following situations:

discounts lead to increased sales and an increase in the total profit from the sale of this product, subject to a high proportion of fixed costs and high elasticity of the product; the system of discounts provides the inflow of money resources under the conditions of their deficiency; the system of discounts for speeding up payments is more effective than the system of penalties for late payments.

A system of discounts and penalties, in the opinion of the authors, will allow companies maximize the inflow of cash and reduce the risk of overdue trade receivables accounts. A system of calculating discounts and penalties for violation of payment terms established by the schedule of debt repayment should be provided under every single contract. Discounts should be given depending on the period of payment for goods: for example, when there is a full prepayment - a 3% discount on the price of goods can be provided, when there is a partial prepayment (more than 50% of the shipment cost) - a 2% discount, if paid on the fact of shipment - a 1% discount.

At present, when entering into contractual relations, it is very useful for companies to apply the anti-money laundering scheme - combating money laundering, preventing the legalization of criminal money transactions. This procedure involves checking potential buyers and other counterparties by Russian and/or international credit agencies, including Coface, D&B, Euler Hermes, IGK etc. This will allow companies avoid the risk of working with counterparties representing the informal sector of economy.

An important part of receivables management should be the motivation of company's employees involved in this process. To increase the effectiveness of the motivation system, aimed at reducing the volume of overdue trade receivables accounts, employees should be interested in achieving the planned level of receivables. A system of bonuses must be counterbalanced by a system of penalties. Applying penalties to overdue trade receivables accounts is necessary, especially in the cases of violation of rules and procedures in management of trade receivables accounts. A system aimed at motivating staff should be described in detail in company's regulatory documents.

Regulation of the state of trade receivables accounts is connected with the control of trade payables accounts. Reducing the volume or changing the form of obligations to suppliers and contractors can be achieved by introducing the following instruments into everyday practice of companies: conducting mutual settlements; carrying out debt novation; designing the compensation; transferring the debt to a creditor or to a third party that has receivables due; redeeming trade payables accounts (with a discount) by a solvent, a friendly legal entity; exchange of debt for additionally issued shares of the debtor company; the use of credit instruments; change in terms of the return of debts to suppliers and contractors (debt restructuring); conversion of debt into long-term company bonds, acquiring discounted claims to the creditor company with subsequent netting.

The authors believe that forming company's effective financial policy would be impossible without the creation of favorable conditions for business development of business on the side of the state. Recently, a number of important decisions have been made by the state: a policy of import substitution has been announced, subsidies have been granted to producers, separate R&D projects have been supported, and concessional loans have been granted by the Industrial Development Fund. But these measures will have a rather limited effect without implementing a favorable state industrial policy in general, which must directly involve, inter alia, the Bank of Russia. Therefore, in order to modernize companies, update their current assets, the cost of credit resources should not to exceed the profitability level of company's assets. And this rate should not be more than 5% per year in the short term and at the rate of "inflation plus 1%" in subsequent years.

For broader and more active development of innovative activities in the country, it is necessary to support innovative enterprises and private investors that fund them. This would be possible through provision of income tax relief and exemption of innovation-related items from the value added tax on goods and services related to research activities. Also, the state can ensure the provision of low-interest loans to venture businesses, reducing their rent for premises, for example. In addition, an effective way to support innovative companies can be through government orders for research and development.

Regulation of prices for products of natural monopolies is the next important direction in the influence of the state industrial policy on financial stability of companies.

An important direction of the state industrial policy, which affects the financial stability of enterprises, is regulation of money supply and inflation. Implementation of this direction is connected with creation of favorable economic environment that facilitates investments and redistribution of financial flows into the real sector. The Bank of Russia should pursue a favorable monetary policy aimed at creating objective prerequisites for savings to be made by companies and population as well as subsequent transformation of these savings into productive investments. This can be achieved through targeting inflation, stronger stability of the national currency, gradual lowering of interest rates, introduction of state guarantees for foreign currency deposits in credit institutions, and also creation of a currency deposit insurance system.

Innovations related to tax reform do not lead to reduction of the tax burden for many efficiently operating companies. The increase in revenues' inflows into the budget should not be at the expense of increasing tax rates, but due to the growth of the taxable base, i.e., due to the growth of production volumes. It is necessary to introduce a 50% investment benefit on income tax to stimulate investment in Russian production. We cannot agree with the proposals to reduce the rate of insurance premiums simultaneously with the increase in the value added tax. Such pseudo-improvement of the taxation system will only lead to heavier tax burden on companies and this, in turn, will have only negative impacts on the competitiveness of Russian products.

Increasing the financial stability of industrial companies is largely possible due to selective, targeted state support. The following forms of it might be most effective in the case of the Russian Federation: state support on the basis of co financing or in other forms, with the responsibility for the completion of the project imposed on companies; financial support provision only to applicants who won in public, transparently organized competitions.

It is also advisable to implement public-private partnership programs more actively and widely. A certain influence on the financial stability of industrial enterprises can be exerted by the measures of the state in the field of currency regulation and control. It is necessary to decide on the issue of rejecting the liberal monetary policy. The liberal regime of foreign economic activity is expedient only under the conditions of economic and political stability.

We believe that effective financial policy is the key prerequisite for successful operations of a company, competent investment, rational pricing, overcoming the cash deficit due to competent management of company's obligations. The main goal of any company's financial policy development is optimization of financial management in order to achieve strategic and tactical goals of company's activities.

FUTURE RESEARCH DIRECTIONS

A successful trajectory of development for Russian companies in the conditions of increasing competition is possible when developing and implementing a flexible financial policy that reacts promptly to changes in the external and internal environments of business. Producing such a financial policy enables the company solve most complex issues concerning current and strategic development.

Prospects for further study should be determined by the current and potential future trends that influence the formation of company's financial policy. It is necessary to specify the ideas on the formation of a price policy under the conditions of import substitution, innovations in management of obligations, implementation of the investment policies aimed at innovative development, taking into account financial constraints.

The authors of this chapter see further development of this research within the framework of improving the financial policies of companies in the following areas: dividend policy, inventory and cash management, tax policy.

Of serious practical interest would be also collection information, generalization, popularization of the best practices of Russian and foreign companies in the field of financial policy development.

The authors also set the task for developing recommendations concerning potential state measures aimed at creation of favourable conditions for conducting and developing businesses of all sizes and from all sectors.

CONCLUSION

Stability and growth of country's economic development can be achieved through successful development of companies in the real sector, first of all. This can be realized through a flexible financial policy of companies which would allow more efficient and prompt managerial decisions in the field of finance.

The authors of this study consider it a practical necessity for all Russian companies to have a financial policy systematically covering all the areas of financial management. Proposals of the authors on such key areas of financial policy as pricing policy, commitment management, investment and innovation policies may enable Russian companies adequately respond to current external and internal challenges.

In the opinion of the authors, all state measures in the field of improving banking and tax policies, state regulation of prices for products of natural monopolies should be focused, first of all, on creating favourable conditions for business development.

Effective financial policy is the key prerequisite for successful operations within a company, competent investment decision-making, rational pricing and also for overcoming the cash deficit.

REFERENCES

Aliev, A.A. (2016). Methodological approach to assessing financial potential of innovation development using the example of the Socar oil and gas company. *Economic Analysis: Theory and Practice (* 7), 153-161.

Bertonesh, M., & Nait, R. (2004). *Cash flow management*. St. Petersburg: Piter Publ.

Bocharov, V. V. (2008). *Corporate finance*. St. Petersburg: Piter Publ.

Bodie, Z., & Merton, R. (2007). *Finance*. Moscow: Williams Publ.

Doing Business. (2017). Doing business 2017. Retrieved from http://www.doingbusiness.org/reports/global-reports/doing-business-2017

Drury, K. (2005). *Management and production accounting. Introductory course* (Tutorial). Unity.

Gengher, E. (2011). *Best Practice in Accounts Receivable Reconciliation*. Analytical report of Citi Group. Retrieved from http://www.citigroup.com/transactionservices/home/about_us/articles/docs/accounts_receivable.pdf

Global Venture Capital and Private Equity Country Attractiveness Index. (2016). Retrieved from https://www.iese.edu/research/pdfs/ESTUDIO-143-E.pdf

Hinterhuber, H. (1996). *Strategische Unternehmensführung*. Berlin, Germany: Walter de Gruyter.

Kogdenko, V.G. (2013). Corporate financial policy: features of development and implementation. *Financial analytics: problems and solutions,* (25), 2-13.

Makarov, A.S. (2008). The financial policy of the organization, its types, instruments of formation and implementation. *Finance and credit,* (10), 54-60.

Memba, S. F., & Njeru, A. (2016). Effect of accounts receivable on financial performance of firms funded by government venture capital in Kenya. *Journal of Economics and Finance*, *7*(1), 62–69.

Romanovsky, M. V. (2014). *Corporate finance*. St. Petersburg: Piter.

Simonenko, N. N., & Simonenko, V. N. (2017). *Short-term and long-term financial policy of the firm: Textbook. M.: Master*. SIC INFRA-M.

Ulrich, H. (1990). *Unternehmungspolitik*. Bern, Stuttgart: Haupt.

Voronkova E.K. (2011). The balance of the economy and the investment policy of the Russian Federation. *Business in law,* (6), 300-306.

KEY TERMS AND DEFINITIONS

Financial Policy of a Company: Setting goals and objectives in financial management, developing an algorithm for action, choosing forms and methods for its implementation.

Innovation: A new achievement in the field of technologies or management, intended for use in the operating, investment or financial activities of a company.

Investment Policy of a Company: Selection and implementation of effective forms of investment that ensure the achievement of company's goals.

Investment Resources of a Company: All types of monetary and other assets of a company used for investment activities. The main sources of investment resources include: profit, depreciation, IPO, long-term loans of banks, issuance of long-term bonds, leasing.

Price Policy of a Company: Set of measures for choosing a system of prices for manufactured and/or sold products (services) along with their pricing strategies and pricing methods.

Trade Payables Accounts: Short-term liabilities of a company in relation to other legal entities and individuals. The main types of trade payables accounts are: suppliers and contractors; company's personnel; to state off-budget funds; debts on taxes, duties and other mandatory fees.

Trade Receivables Accounts: Debt in favour of the company represented by obligations of legal entities and individuals in relation to this company. The main kinds of trade receivables accounts are: for goods, works and services; on bills received; on payments to the budget.

Chapter 5
Financing of International Business Through Private Equity:
European Industry Case Study

Katarína Čulková
Technical University of Košice, Slovakia

Adriana Csikósová
Technical University of Košice, Slovakia

Mária Janošková
Technical University of Košice, Slovakia

ABSTRACT

The global financial crisis has greatly limited access to both public and private sources of finance in the recent decades. Markets and national governments emitted low interested and multi-structured financial means with low liquidity. In the post-crisis period national governments tend to regulate their financial sectors more strictly, paying more attention to risky and low interest financial sources, necessary for investments, on which private equity is dependent. Private equity funds grew significantly in the last two decades, both in the USA and in Europe. Such new ways of debt financing and cheap money support massive growth in the industrial sectors of individual countries. This research is studying the positive impact of private equity on management of the whole industries and economies in Europe. Our analysis stems from the general assumption that private equity has positive influence on industrial performance and our empirical data evidences that private equity reacts to economic decrease more intensively than under the business model without financial leverage. The goal of this chapter is to show how private equity contributes to the growth of industrial sectors, performance of industrial companies, with a special emphasis on the mining sector.

DOI: 10.4018/978-1-5225-7760-7.ch005

INTRODUCTION

Global growth of private equity has become an important development factor in the last two decades. This growth was achieved mainly in the USA, though other impressive results in terms of growth have been also recorded in Europe. Private equity and risk capital have become popular types of investments in the USA, and that means this sector of financial activity will only gain more popularity in the future. At the same time, there are certain geographic, institutional, social and political features of private equity, which is orientated mainly on the expected revenue and risks of the companies and industries with under evaluated price and performance. Thus, there is a growing demand to identify the main basis for improving the attractiveness of enterprises and sectors from the standpoint of private equity and risk capital for investors, which includes, inter alia, the development of capital market, protection of investors and financial infrastructure. Strong and developed capital market is able to provide a broad scale of financial sources (Zámborský, 2016). When a foreign private equity fund is attracted to a certain country, it will be profitable for local economy and it will have also its positive impact on future investments' volume into the same country.

The goal of this chapter is to estimate the contribution of private equity financing on the example of European industrial companies. This is achieved through determination of individual types of investments and specific description of the private equity market with its influence on the performance of industrial sectors and national economies. The influence of private equity is analyzed as applied to individual countries' attractiveness from the investors' standpoint. The results are confirmed by the analysis of private equity influence in the mining industry. Private equity evaluation and its impact on the industries is oriented on the development capital as a whole with the emphasis on certain differences present among individual sectors with high, low or zero participation of private equity. The research results serve to set the measure, at which private equity investors become more vulnerable during the times of general economic crisis.

BACKGROUND

Foreign Direct Investments in the European Union

Foreign investments present one of the ways how long-term international capital flows, and they can be divided into:

- **Portfolio Investments:** When an exporter does not manage a company abroad, and only revenues from capital are flowing from abroad (interests, dividends, profit sharing etc.);
- **Direct Investments:** When investor is located abroad with the goal to obtain control over a company, into which they intend to invest on a long-term basis. Investor is therefore participating not only in company's profit, but also in its property to the extent they could manage and/or control this company (Dorożyński & Kuna-Marszałek, 2016).

Foreign direct investment can be defined in many various ways. According to the U.N.O. definition these are investments, based on the long-term relation and permanent interest of the subject with a seat in one country (direct investor) to control a subject with the seat in another country. The usual key goal of direct investors is imposing their considerable level of influence on the organization management, which has a seat in the country of investor. Foreign direct investment also includes some sort of initial transaction between two subjects as well as all consequent transactions between the associated companies. FDI for the company's needs of payment means that FDI is basically providing a loan to a company abroad or purchasing the property of this company. From this definition, FDI represents not only the move of financial means, but also the move of management, skills, business know-how, technologies, licenses, marketing strategies etc. FDI is also connected with a certain level of control over it. However, the scale of this control is mostly defined by the owner of the invested capital. In some cases, even 100% ownership does not provide absolute control, for example, when a company is subject to certain restrictions on the side of a host country government. However, most of the authors agree that the rate of control from 10% to 25% may serve as the basis to classify any investment as direct investments.

Foreign investors evaluate the attractiveness of a country using two key indices:

1. Advantages of country as a business destination, speaking generally. Here belong, for example, such parameters as the volume of the market, GDP growth rate, rank of this country according to the international rankings, the state of business environment etc. Same parameters are actually also used by domestic business subjects, but mostly with a slightly different aim – to determine what can be their potential competitive advantages as compared to international competitors.
2. Specific policy of state concerned, eventually other local institutions, oriented towards FDI support. Such form of FDI support, however, leads to significant discrimination of domestic businessmen, but, on the other hand, it contributes to the overall development of business environment. Generally positive relationship is confirmed to be between GDP growth and the world movement of FDIs. What concerns European countries and their total FDI flows, it is obvious that investments are moving mostly to the Eastern part of the continent. From the standpoint of investors, most interesting areas in Central Europe are Czech Republic, Hungary and also South-Eastern part of Poland. Slovakia is interesting in the context of the triangle Bratislava-Vienna-Budapest.

Most important sector in Slovakia, from the investors' standpoint, is its automotive industry. 10% of all investments inflowing to Slovakia fall on this sector, however, this volume should be also divided into production of cars and production of automotive components. These are mostly investors, who are trying to find new measures for costs cut and thus come to Central and Eastern Europe. The sector of services is considered to be the sector with highest potential, with the most promising areas being computer and information technologies, construction, real estate and transportation (Birnleitner, 2014; Jackson & Markowski, 1996). Table 1 illustrates FDI development in the EU from the standpoint of their direction.

According to much estimation, the European Union today is the main economy in the world. Rapid economic growth in the new member states only strengthens this ranking. The EU is also much more actively involved in doing business, as compared to many other large economies (Csikósová, Mihalčová, & Antošová, 2015). The data on the EU-25 shows that the EU has the highest rate in the whole world in terms of foreign trade. The EU also gets the highest scores for its FDI into the economies and industries of foreign countries – almost twice more than from other territories. The EU is also a massive investor in the growing economies of Asia and Latin America. It has strong positive balance in terms of exporting FDI, and this proves strong desire of the EU organizations to engage in foreign partnerships.

Formation of the common market and introduction of the common currency also contributed to strengthening European businesses worldwide. Such experience makes the EU market very open for

Table 1. FDI development in Europe (in thousand EUR)

Year	Inwards FDI	Outwards FDI
2008	1 031 156 637	61 891 601
2009	33 495 438	2 169 705
2010	34 998 379	2 563 195
2011	36 690 150	3 070 644
2012	38 428 088	3 542 982
2013	38 926 047	3 435 124
2014	37 492 006	2 228 199
2015	38 394 685	2 193 553
2016	37 924 919	2 391 007

businesses and also very attractive due to its volumes as the net exporter of goods. In the absolute majority of the global financial centres the EU is being represented by a number of the world largest banks. From the business viewpoint, European organizations may experience some difficulties with becoming truly global institutions due to the split of national economies. But in the framework of the EU single market these companies are only extending their activity in terms of both sales volumes and brand power.

PRIVATE EQUITY CHARACTERISTICS

Private equity can be defined as a type of foreign investment, which is representing four main forms of investments. Leveraged buyout (LBO), or leverage through debt, is the first form of investment and it basically means leverage, when a small number of investors leverage the whole company or its part, and in such a way significant level of debt is incorporated by the transactions. LBO investments are orientated on a broad spectrum of companies, no matter whether this company is young or already well established at the market. In this regard, all companies have one common factor – they all have the ability to produce high positive cash flow. According to this factor, private equity companies use LBO investments and thus are able to manage and pay debt more quickly, thus decreasing indebtedness more effectively.

The second type of private equity is "growth capital", or development capital that is mostly defined as a minority investment into the target company. In this case investor would obtain some control over the company, but increasing of capital possibilities enables this company realizes its future investment plans more independently, for example, it may turn to acquisition, entering new markets etc. Further investment access to private equity investments is the so-called investment through "mezzanine capital", which is the investment to priority shares, or subjected debt. Company could obtain voting rights in the board of supervisors. Consequent type of investment is represented by "venture capital", which is basically investing at the earliest stages of company's development, and such type of investments obviously has the highest level of risks for investors, but – in some cases – it may also bring much higher revenues (Stowell, 2010).

In expert literature private equity is usually represented as various investment types, for example, Bloomberg business platform has it as going private (transforming to a private company), or management buyout – MBO (buyout of a company by its management), or other private equity types. LBO investments are commonly considered as net private equity investments, while mezzanine capital, venture capital and growth capital investments are considered more and more as individual investment types. Big and international private equity companies are orientated on all types of private equity investments, and thus the group of participants engaged in the private equity transactions, becomes rather big (Chemla, 2005).

Generally speaking, today's investment world distinguishes three types of investors – strategic investor, financial investor and speculative investor. Private equity investors are considered as financial investors, since they do not bring synergy in the course of investment transactions, which is the opposite of strategic investor access. Strategic investor usually represents some company with a strong position in the target industry, but the chance and the measure of success while applying for this target company might be lower than the offers from a private equity company. Therefore, private equity companies can have more aggressive investing, even under lower level of invested capital, higher rate of debt to own sources and less powerful position in a given industry. The main reasons for stronger success of private equity companies in particular industries and countries are the local antimonopoly rules that often become a considerable obstacle for the recently established subjects, new to this market. This reason only enables private equity investors to choose more aggressive behavior in relation to future cash flow, to providing more acceptable debt conditions and more flexible investment strategies (Gompers & Lerner, 1998).

Subjects, Participating at Private Equity Investments

To the major participants of the private equity market belong the following: private equity companies, investment banks, investors, top managers and other professional advisors. Key steps, leading to the initialization of private equity investment by a private equity company are the following ones: selection of a target market/company, negotiations on the merger/sale price, defining the debt financing way, realization of sale transaction and selection of the operation management mode for the company from the already existing or newer management options. The next steps are: supervision over the performance or this company, regulation of important operational and financial decisions, especially during the final stage of the investment cycle, when there takes place the final selection or exit – sale of the target company (Jeng & Wells, 2000).

The main advisors in the course of such private equity transactions are investment banks, functional responsibilities of which may be defined as follows: presentation of potential buyers to the target company, assistance during the negotiations; the following services included: negotiating the price, conditions of purchasing, debt financial services (for example, credit, recapitalization, merger/ acquisition etc). The main investment banks, participating in the world most known private equity transactions, according to the Bloomberg portal (www.bloomberg.com/europe) and according the actual financial volumes of such transactions, are Credit Suisse and Goldman and Sachs (Cetorelli & Gamera, 2001).

Other participants in the sector of private equity are investors that are, in most cases, grouped into consortiums so that to represent particular private equity companies. In this case private equity companies must provide only small part of investment capital, but they still are able to maintain significant control over the target company and its profits. Situation is rather different in the case of private equity funds, when their profit falls on 20% to private equity companies and is mostly realized during the exit stage (sale of the company), while 2% falls on the management of private equity company. Investors are commonly profiled as institutions, but there may be also investors with great net wealth or simply rich individual subjects that are able to obtain ownership (even under limited competences) via an investment fund, organized and managed by a private equity company. "Limited partnership" in the framework of private equity fund provides finances to fund in certain group payments, not as one big investment payment. Private equity funds are being invested in the framework of broad scale of industries/companies in the range from short investment cycles (up to 5 years) to longer cycles (covering 10-15 years). Living cycle of a standard private equity fund is commonly about 15 years, with the average volume reaching several hundred million EUR. As it was mentioned previously, resulting transaction from investment is called "exit", and it is presented mostly as a classical sale of a company or company's entry to the exchange market (EIF & EVCA, 2010).

The last dominant participant of the private equity transactions is company's management that invests via a private equity fund into a target economy. Management that is treated as an entity in this case, is responsible for operational activities and decisions in the course of private equity investment. Its performance is evaluated through annual managerial fees which go together with wages and options, their key goal being to eliminate the agency problem (the inconsistency between the interests of management and shareholders) and also to provide successful results from the private equity investment, mostly through managerial stimulus (Kaplan, 1989). Professional services of lawyers, accountants and other professionals are also very important due to the necessity to have specialized advice during the work of investors and managers, throughout the whole course of investment – from entrance to exit. Advisors, employed by a private equity company are usually mostly concentrated on the managerial problems of investment, thus, their work is highly specialized and demands very specific skills (Chemla, 2005).

Impact of Private Equity on Various Industries and Economies in General

Presence of private equity companies has its positive impact on management practices, on the level of both separate industries and economies overall. Higher level of competition forces companies to demonstrate better performance and introduce more effective managerial practices into their daily business routine. As presented by (Farrell, 2007) and (Stowell, 2010), private equity is able to influence both separate companies and whole markets (see Figure 1 for more details).

PRIVATE EQUITY IN THE FRAMEWORK OF SEPARATE INDUSTRIES

Private equity presents the type of investment that exists in Western European countries for several decades already, while presence of this investment concept in Eastern European countries is much shorter. Many expert studies are dealing with private equity's influence in the context of particular industries, as well as its effects on these industrial sectors. Our chapter is dealing with private equity impact on various areas of industries and consequently also with the private equity interaction with different stage of economic cycles (Bernstein, Lerner, Sørensen, & Strömberg, 2010).

Figure 1. Direct and indirect impacts of private equity
(Farrell, 2007; Stowell, 2010)

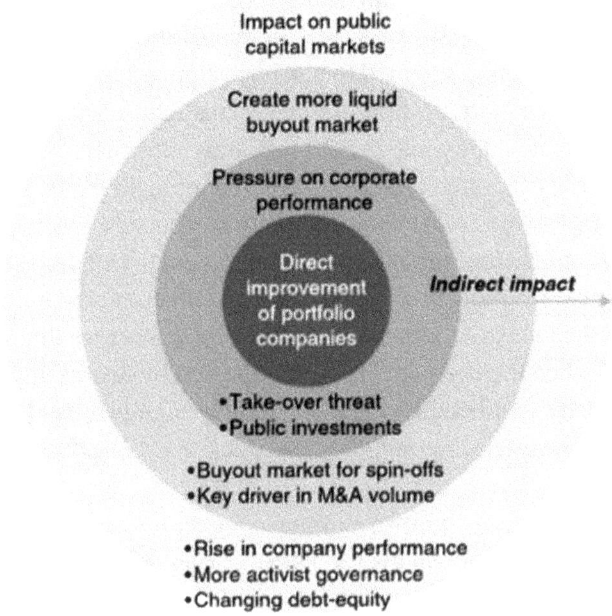

During this research on the private equity influence on various industries our final hypothesis had been orientated on finding whether private equity has any influence to the performance of the selected industries. Our assumption is based on the research carried out many years ago by Jensen (1989), according to which private equity improves operation performance of companies positively. Overall, companies supported by private equity usually record better results, mostly due to a chain of managerial improvements that also have their positive impact to the industry overall, or due to increasing of competition at a particular market. John et al. (1992) provided sufficient empirical evidence to state that the fear or sale or taking over the company by another company normally increase the motivation of a given company and thus, performance of this company increases. In a similar manner, private equity influences the consolidation of a business model of a company. As it was already mentioned above, private equity companies´ number may increase depending on the performance of a particular industry, and this has been supported by various empirical researches.

One of the most interesting studies in this regard is the study carried out by (Kaplan, 1989), in which the author tested 76 managerial takeovers of the companies for 6 years. The results of that study confirm that private equity companies help increase profit in target companies, improve cash flow and also other financial indexes (Janošková, Csikósová, & Čulková, 2018).

Similar results were also achieved by other researches, for example, in the study by Guo et al. (2009), where the research was orientated on transformation of companies from public to private ones; or as in the study by (Muscarella & Vetsuypens, 1990), who were studying in detail the debt purchases of companies. The results of the mentioned studies provide quite comparable results in the framework of various private equity segments, and these results only strengthen the popular opinion concerning the positive effect of private equity investments.

The already mentioned above studies confirm that private equity has a positive impact on the industries, to which private equity is orientated. There are also other studies, concentrating on a slightly different angle. For example, a study by Bloom et al. (2009) was searching to determine the managerial contribution to the total private equity position as well as to the following private equity benefits from the managerial view mostly. The results confirmed that private equity management is more successful than management in other companies in the framework of various industries. As it was already mentioned, companies, supported by private equity, record, immediately after being taken over by private equity investor, improvement in their economic indicators and operational results, but this does not mean that any private equity investment to the company is automatically successful.

Success depends on economic conditions and managerial quality of a given private equity property. Moreover, we can state that some industries record better results as compared to others, and this factor has also positive effect on the industries as a whole. There also cases revealing the opposite effects from private equity investment, when the company's sale is followed by dismissing of the larger share of the workforce, while the company is still achieving considerably high profits. This phenomenon has been described, for example, in (Bernstein, Lerner, Sørensen, & Strömberg, 2010) and also in (Rasmussen, 2008).

According to this previous information we can make a conclusion that private equity is vulnerable during the periods of changes in economic cycles. Due to easier access to low-cost financial sources at the market, the volume of private equity transactions is growing significantly. On the other side, when there is lack of cheap financial means private equity investments record deep decrease. This can be easily observable in the results of the last several years, when the financial crisis, rising in 2007, extended to the whole European continent. The main sectors with high level of debt financing in this period recorded big problems, production decrease and recession. The results of the research by (Axelson, Strömberg, Jenkinson, & Weisbach, 2009) show that debt financing is more influenced by debt conditions, which have bigger power of influence than the structure of industries and companies.

Traditional model of private equity is based on the use of the significant volumes of financial debt through financial leverage and this may lead to lack of trust during the recession period. The results of the already mentioned research present empirical evidences, according to which private equity reacts to economic decreases more intensively than the business model without financial leverage. The risk of using certain level of financial leverage and consequent growth of problems during economic recession can bring serious damage of private equity attractiveness. Situation when private equity companies force its competitors at the market to limitation of their potential can cause growth of bankruptcies in time of rapid economic change. Present economic decreases in the frame of national economies provide broad spectrum of evidences, according which we can search and validate various alternative economic scenarios. Companies, supported by private equity, have closely oriented managerial models of acting and these companies are mostly taken over and owned by properly capitalized companies. It means during economic decreases the companies supported by private equity are able to achieve better results as compared to their competitors at the market, mainly due to the stable core of the company and broad channel of financing. Companies that are supported by private equity investor achieve better market position, since management of such companies is much more flexible and is normally of higher quality. It is a well-known fact that companies, operating in the private equity sector, are much more oriented on obtaining skilled experts as their managers and at the same time they are able to stimulate their performance with interesting benefits. The research by (Jensen, 1989) mentioned, inter alia, that high level of indebtedness by private equity companies during transactions forced these companies turn to risk management and develop several various scenarios of further actions. This includes also better and more prompt reactions to changes in the framework of industries. Basically, all such skills are the results of managerial expertise. Studies by (Kaplan & Stein, 1993) and also by (Bernstein, Lerner, Sørensen, & Strömberg, 2010) provided the examples how big repurchases of companies, made through financial leverages and debt financing, reacted to financial problems and that included even repurchases that used high level of debt financing.

EVALUATION OF PRIVATE EQUITY COMPANIES BY INVESTORS

Evaluation of private equity companies, carried out by investors, is usually based on determination of the so-called righteous or internal value (often called "fair value") of a company and its assets, which are not public, which means outside the stock exchange market. Since the companies that are traded at the exchanges must publish their financial information, their evaluation is direct and basically does not cause much problems. But companies, which are private and are operating at a local market, for example, present some problems from the standpoint of their evaluation. During such evaluation of a company, it is not exactly possible to state the value of a single share, since such companies are not publicly traded at the exchange. Thus, the value of such companies is determined in the course of its immediate evaluation which often means at the time of its sale, or transformation of ownership rights. Due to the mentioned specificity, it is exceedingly important to use proper techniques in the course of company's evaluation, and this technique must reflect the typology of a company. The key factor for the selection of a proper evaluation technique is to determine which of the available techniques is able to evaluate this particular company most correctly and most accurately, including all relevant factors and events that are important for determination of the company's value.

During the determination of the company's value various factors must be taken into account. Processes and levels to be considered for the purposes of such evaluation include the following:

- Relative applicability of evaluation techniques according to the typology of the industry and actual market conditions
- Quality and reliability of data used in the course of evaluation
- Comparability of the company's transaction data
- Overall level of company's development
- The ability to generate sustainable profit and positive cash flow (Čulková, Csikósová, & Janošková, 2015)
- Other additional evaluation factors, unique for this particular company
- Results of testing (calibration) with the aim to replicate the resulting price of the investment during the company's further sale.

When it comes to private equity companies and investors, six key evaluation techniques are usually used with different access modes. Table 2 describes these techniques.

Table 2. Evaluation techniques for private equity to be used by investors

Evaluation Technique	Access
Price of present investment	Market access
Multipliers	Market access
Net assets	Cost approach
Discounted cash flow or revenues of given company	Revenue approach
Discounted cash flow of evaluated investments	Income approach
Evaluating industrial benchmark	Market access

(Smith, 1995)

Figure 2. Risk profiles of the countries in comparing with Europe
(Smith, 2006)

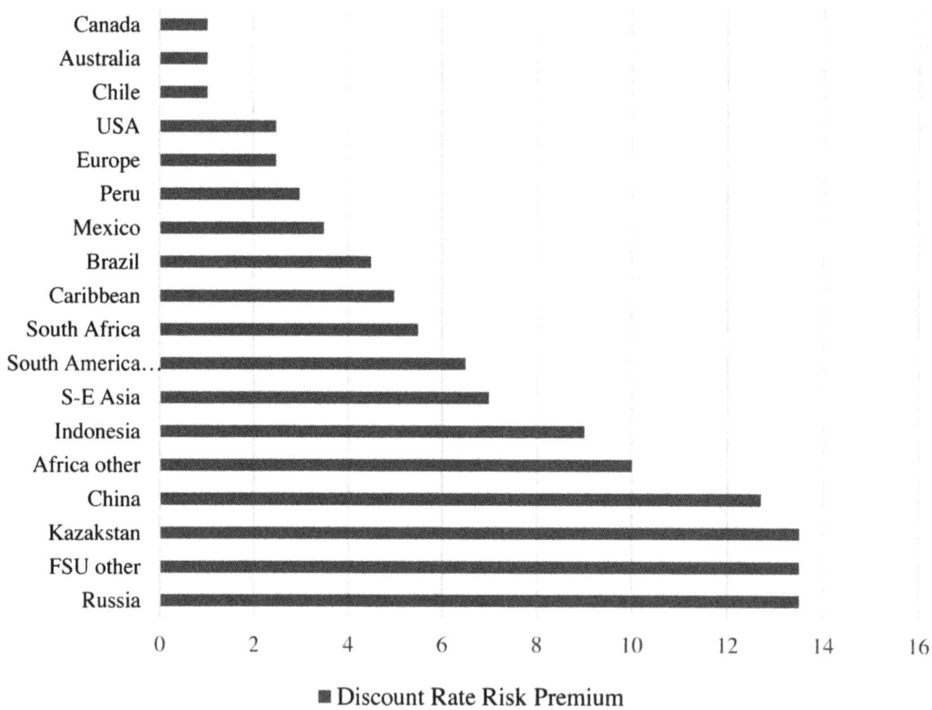

In the framework of companies' evaluation made by investors' individual risk profiles of the countries are also considered, graded normally according to the percentage scale from 0-14% (see Figure 2). This percentage is consequently incorporated into the evaluation of the country overall, its particular region and of the single act of investment. From the standpoint of a particular country, one company which is target of a private equity investment is not able to influence the risk measure. But it is important to remember that this company would later be able to compensate the country's risk through other indices of investment.

PRESENT SITUATION AT THE PRIVATE EQUITY MARKET

Today's private equity market can be divided into two groups of private equity companies. The first group presents global companies, which operate mostly at the international level and which are mainly concentrating their interest on the financially demanding transactions, for example, on a company which operates on all the continents. Such companies include, for example, The Carlyle Group, KKR, The Blackstone Group etc. These companies are often closely connected with individual financiers having vast business knowledge and also strong financial position, the people who are really able to transform initially small companies into large global entities. Majority of such companies went through a range of radical transformations, from small private firms to large publicly traded organizations with varying ownership rates. Such global entities tend to expand their activities from net investing to advisory services and consulting (Kortum & Lerner, 2000).

The second group of participants at the market of private equity include small and medium enterprises (SMEs) that are mostly characterized by well-organized operations and standard investment business models. The majority of mid-sized private equity companies are very much sector-specific. Differentiation of activities is much broader than in the case of small enterprises. During the latest financial crisis, the consequences of which are still visible at the world and many national markets, private equity companies strengthened their positions and business models at all levels. They managed to operate more effectively and thus achieved the expected revenues from their portfolios later on. All operational activities of such businesses, for example, acquiring, working with capital, logistics etc., are managed more cautiously, otherwise, their dependence on financial engineering and financial leverages could lead to difficulties or even bankruptcies. Today situation at these markets is changing and these changes, which started after 2007, will result in change of the private equity business model overall, mainly in the ways of financing, structure of transactions, volume of single transactions. Companies operating in this sector must find gradually their own new ways how to find a target company and also they must consider other types of debt financing, as well as PIPE investment (private investment in public entities). Moreover, all these companies must get prepared for possible reductions in managerial fees; they should lower their expectations as to revenues etc. (Hellmann, Lindsey, & Puri, 2004).

PERFORMANCE OF ECONOMIES AND PRIVATE EQUITY MARKET

Economic situation and private equity influence in the region will be illustrated by the results of short analysis of the situation throughout European industries, 2007 to 2016. The following graphs illustrate the economic situation from the view of production in European industries. Figure 3 provides a graphical overview of statistics on all private equity industry (investments, fundraising, and divestments) along with the data on more than 1200 European private equity firms. The 2016 statistics covers 88% of the € 600 bln in capital under management in Europe (www.investeurope.eu).

Figure 4 demonstrates the changing percentage of private equity in GDP in Europe since 2007. There is an obvious decrease of total production in European economies and then the repeated decrease in 2010, which brings in fears about the double bottom of recession (Eurostat, 2016).

Figure 3. The overview of private equity in Europe
(www.investeurope.eu)

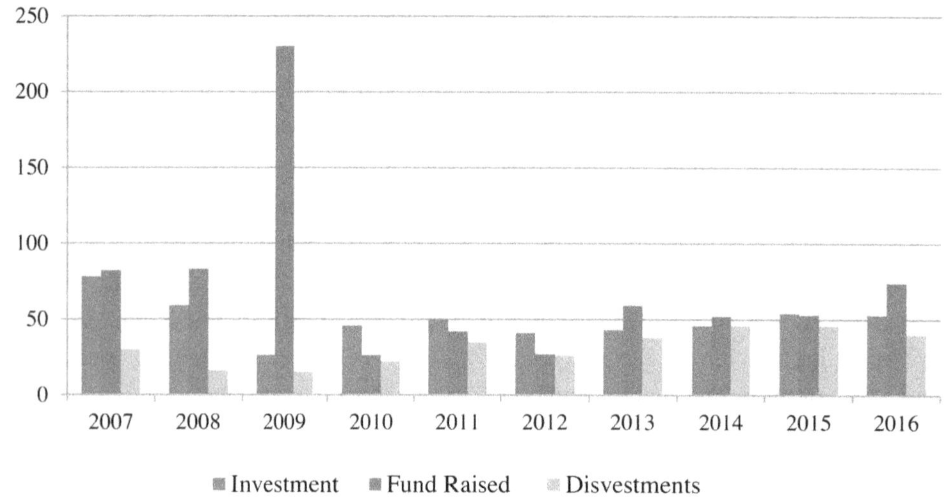

Figure 4. Private equity as % GDP in Europe
(Eurostat, 2016)

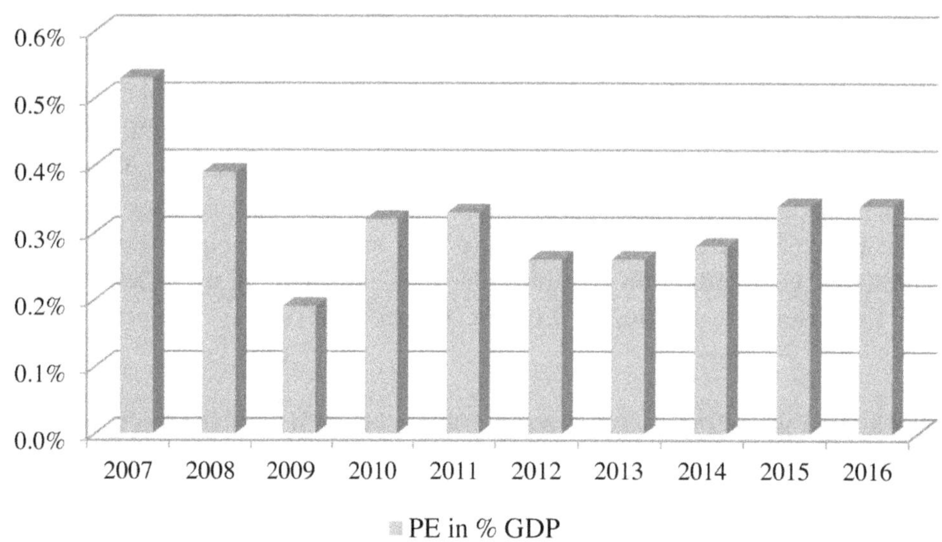

Visual illustration of private equity investors' impact on European economy is also provided in Figure 5, in which we can see the activity of private equity companies, expressed through the volume of investments in Europe. Sharp decrease, leading to negative invested means volume, was similar for all industrial sectors in Europe. As it has been already mentioned, private equity reacts more flexibly and promptly to changes at the world markets, which means also change in the volume of invested means in the framework of European industries (EVCA, 2016).

Figure 5. Activity of private equity investment in Europe
(EVCA, 2016)

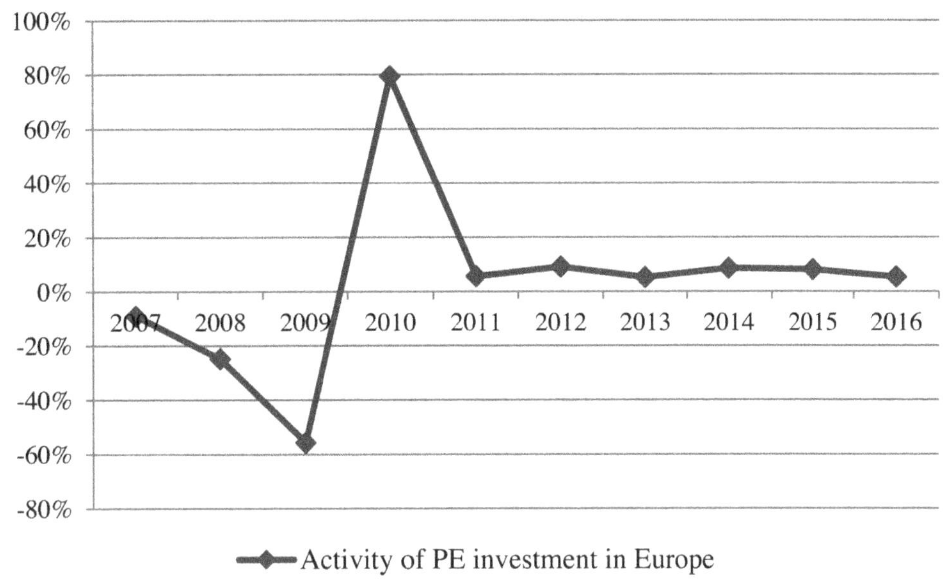

As for comparing of industrial production and activity of private equity investment we can see that the trend of volume development is mostly decreasing. Difference is visible in the range of this decrease, when industrial sectors in Europe, during 2007-2008, were still recording growth, even with a falling trend, whereas private equity investment was already demonstrating an explicit negative decreasing trend. It is important to mention here that since 2009, which became the first bottom of recession, the activity of private equity investment managed to maintain positive annual change of the invested means, same applies to annual trends of investment volumes. At the same time we can state that performance of private equity investment during the crisis years of 2007-2011 recorded the same trend with many European industries and GDP dynamics in Europe overall. As an interesting observation, we can also mention the correlation of FDI volumes' development with private equity investments as percentage of GDP in Europe. Looking at the graph below (see Figure 6) we can simply compare what was the volume of private equity investment in the previous years and what was the rate of total FDI investments. Considering that private equity investments are investments into risk projects, which are closely oriented on specifically targeted companies, the resulting rate of FDI is rather high, and for example back in 2011 the comparison rate between them was 1 to 7. Another interesting fact is that during 2000-2007 national economies achieved quite high GDP rates and in 2008-2011 the GDP level was already significantly lower, approximately similar applies to the level of investments to GDP rate.

Private equity is only one of investment types being used within European economies, however, this specific type has an important contribution into the overall volume of FDI, and this is a sign that European industrial market is very interesting for this type of investments and investors. Comparing FDI and private equity investment in Europe is illustrated in Figure 6. Eurostat exact and full data is available only for the years 2000 to 2011, not for the later years.

Figure 6. Comparing FDI volumes and private equity investment in Europe - as % of GDP (Eurostat, 2012; EVCA, 2000-2006)

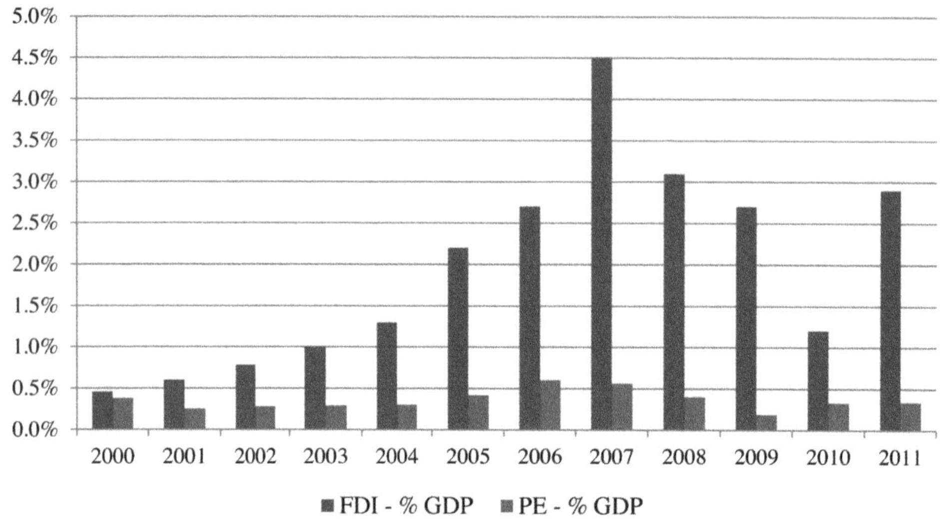

Another important side of the official statistics on private equity concerns location of the private equity firms' offices in charge of investment, as it is illustrated by Figure 7 on the data as of 2016. On the European level this directly relates to the investments made by European private equity firms regardless the location of the portfolio company (www.investeurope.eu). The presented below figure provides data on the DACH region (Austria, Germany and Switzerland), then go Southern Europe: Greece, Italy, Portugal and Spain. Further there are also Nordic countries: Denmark, Finland, Norway, Sweden, and then finally goes Central Eastern Europe.

Figure 7. Percentage rate of private equity by countries and regions of Europe (EVCA, 2016; www.investeurope.eu)

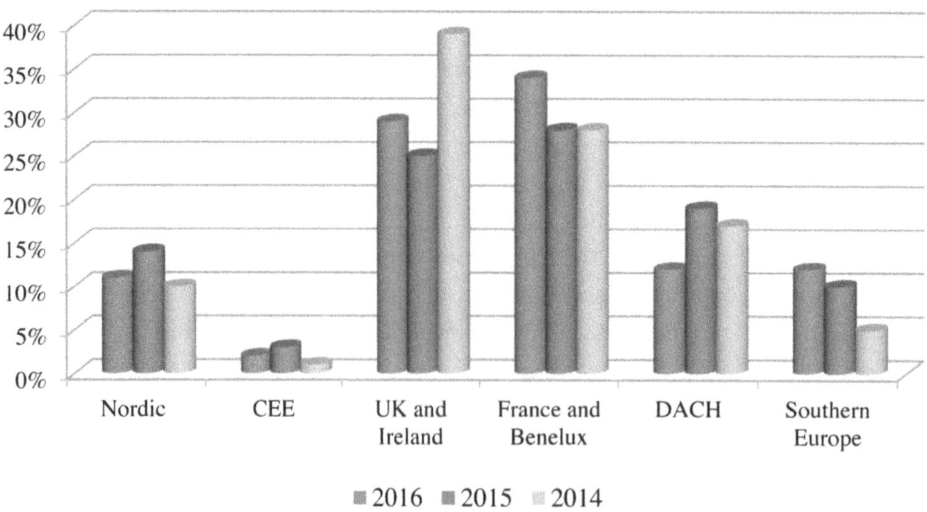

INFLUENCE OF PRIVATE EQUITY IN FRAMEWORK OF INDUSTRIES

Analysis of private equity influences and effects on the industries throughout European economies will be carried out further, using two data databases, similar to how it was realized in (Bernstein, Lerner, Sørensen, & Strömberg, 2010). One of the databases is oriented on the private equity data specifically, while the second one is oriented on more general data from various industries. For private equity data the following databases were used: Bloomberg, and also the EVCA, which represents the European Association of Risk Capital, the research department of which provides aggregate data on the private equity sector. More general data used in our analysis was obtained from the OECD database which provides detailed information for analysis of industries, namely, the STAN – Structural Analysis Database (www.oecd.org).

After data collection we carried out the analysis of the quality and adequacy of data, and our final selection of data was made from the EVCA database. Also, we contacted several other research organizations, dealing with the research of private equity activities, but as it turned out only EVCA was able to provide sufficient volumes of data which was of interest specifically for our research. In most cases associations, dealing with the issues of private equity, provide data exclusively to their members, which are mainly private equity companies, financial institutions, research institutions etc. The final selection of data includes therefore all private equity transactions, which include all level of investments at various level of their realization, as for example: seed capital, development capital, capital for a mature organization, sale of the company as a whole, PIPE transaction etc. In the course of data selection we did not distinguish between merger or acquisition transaction in all the companies under study, since we were oriented on the research of exclusively private equity sector. The obtained data divided into groups provided information on the companies, taken over with financial leverage, transformation of private companies and managerial takeovers in the time span from 1993 to 2010. The whole data set consisted of 115 086 transactions (with no filter on transaction volume), thus, our data sample was not reduced by information on transaction volumes, as it was the case in, for example, (Groh, von Liechtenstein, & Lieser, 2008), since we obtained the aggregated data with the number of transactions, volume of transactions, type of private equity investments and level of investments. Then the data was divided by industries, countries and years. Then, the data sets were used as aggregated values with regard to the level of countries, years and industries for further evaluation of private equity activity throughout the analysed period. Selection of countries had been initially oriented primarily on the OECD members (since we were operating the data from STAN database), and the final selection consisted of 22 European countries. In the evaluation we did not cover Baltic countries, Bulgaria and Romania, but we included Switzerland and Norway; such countries as Slovakia and Slovenia were analysed as combined values with neighbouring countries due to the size factor and the already traditional ways of comparing them in the European context. For the next step in analysis we used data on the transactions at their final stage, therefore, we excluded those transactions that were deferred or cancelled for some reason (Groh, von Liechtenstein, & Lieser, 2008).

Data on the industries had been fully elaborated from the OECD STAN database and selection was done for the years 1993 to 2008. We tried to obtain most actual data on this period, but not all data were available in this public database. The selected data were orientated on six main indicators that include employment, capital formation, productivity etc. Several indicators demanded due to the importance and the structure deeper analysis and such analysis was carried out using the following indicators: productivity (rough output), value added, labour costs, rough capital forming and consumption of fixed capital. Closer definition of the deeper analysed indicators is as follows:

- **Production:** Aggregated value for all produced products and services during the analysed years in real prices.
- **Value Added:** The total rate of industries on national GDP for every analysed country, known also as net output of purchased products.
- **Labour Costs:** The indicator calculated as all wages and other social payments, including pension, life insurance etc.
- **Rough Capital Formed:** Presents all acquisitions of both tangible and intangible assets minus all losses of assets. Depreciation in this case is not included, since depreciation is presented by net stock of capital.
- **Consumption of Fixed Capital:** This indicator expresses the reduction of fixed assets value that were used during the year and which value is greatly reduced due to this use (Gompers & Lerner, 1998).

Table 3. All private equity investors by sectors, as of 2014-2016

Sector/Year		2014	2015	2016
Consumer goods and services	Share of the sector, in %	13,8	14,0	28,2
	Number of companies in %	10,2	10,2	17,0
ICT	Share of the sector, in %	14,0	11,2	20,3
	Number of companies in %	17,6	19,1	32,1
Business products and services	Share of the sector, in %	13,0	15,8	19,8
	Number of companies in %	11,8	12,4	18,3
Biotech and healthcare	Share of the sector, in %	13,1	12,2	11,0
	Number of companies in %	15,8	16,2	14,4
Energy and environment	Share of the sector, in %	4,1	5,4	5,6
	Number of companies in %	6,8	5,5	4,8
Financial and insurance activities	Share of the sector, in %	5,3	10,0	5,2
	Number of companies in %	2,1	2,2	2,8
Chemicals and materials	Share of the sector, in %	2,3	1,8	3,1
	Number of companies in %	1,9	1,8	1,8
Unclassified	Share of the sector, in %	0,2	0,1	2,1
	Number of companies in %	1,3	0,9	4,0
Construction	Share of the sector, in %	2,3	1,1	2,0
	Number of companies in %	1,6	1,3	1,8
Transportation	Share of the sector, in %	2,0	2,4	1,5
	Number of companies in %	1,4	1,7	1,5
Real estate	Share of the sector, in %	0,5	0,6	0,9
	Number of companies in %	0,5	0,4	0,5
Agriculture	Share of the sector, in %	0,8	1,9	0,4
	Number of companies in %	0,9	0,7	1,0

After identification of all the needed indicators and data summarization, including private equity transactions and industrial data, we performed mapping that was necessary for comparing and further analysis. In the process of mapping we used standard industrial classification code (known as ISIC). At the following step we made review of all industries in the STAN database and established the connection of the industries with similar or correspondent industrial sectors in the EVCA database. Classification in the STAN database was much more extensive and we had to make several aggregation processes with the aim to obtain aggregate values from industrial sectors that were presented as aggregated values in EVCA database. Single mapping processes helped us differentiate between the industries that must be evaluated in the analysis with aim to avoid the situation of excessive detailing at the individual level of certain industries. The final result of mapping consisted of 33 660 data appearance with 6 570 mistakes, when all zero values were considered as insufficient according the assumption that no aggregated data recorded aggregated zero value from the view of performance of the country and industries during the analysed period (Jacobs, Smith, & Goddard, 2004).

The overall number of transactions with proper values achieved at the end the level of 27 090 data appearances, and this presents more than 80% measure of success of all the data used. As it was already mentioned previously, the total initial sample was 115 086 transactions, but availability of data reduced the preliminary sample of transactions to 27 090, all of which were then consequently evaluated. The overall number of industries that were evaluated is 15, and more specifically, we have evaluated the following industrial sectors: agriculture, industry, business products, chemicals and materials, computers and consumption electronics, building & construction industry, consumption goods and retail, customer services, transportation, communication services, financial services, real estate market, industries related to natural sciences research, industrial services, computer technologies, energy sector and living environment. Next, we have compared the mining industry, which represents part of the all mentioned above industries, but this evaluation of the mining industry specifically was carried out from the standpoint of private equity performance and attractiveness and their consequent comparison was realized individually with correspondent analysis (Groh, von Liechtenstein, & Lieser, 2008).

During the analysis we have identified certain differences between the level of private equity acting, quarters and single indicators. Table 3 illustrates these differences by individual sectors of all EU countries.

ATTRACTIVENESS OF EUROPEAN COUNTRIES FROM THE VIEW OF PRIVATE EQUITY INVESTORS

Attractiveness of European countries has been measured through calculation of private equity attractiveness and risk capital according to the process, already described in the previous parts, and the final index presents the result of the following statistic techniques: transformation of scales, standardization and geometric aggregation. The indices of attractiveness for the selected countries are presented in Table 4. The evaluated countries include: Austria, Belgium, Czech Republic, Denmark, Finland, France, Germany, Greece, Hungary, Ireland, Italy, Luxemburg, Netherland, Poland, Portugal, Slovakia, Slovenia, Spain, Sweden and Great Britain. Further, we have included also Switzerland and Norway, but we have also decided to exclude Baltic region and new EU countries, as for example Bulgaria and Romania. We have also used other techniques for better differentiation between individual countries with the aim to be able to construct the final index of attractiveness for private equity and risk capital and consequently – only for private equity by using separately the GDP average index, which determines the direction of weighted sub index, mainly due to obtaining more precise results. By using the aggregate values from 1-100 we have achieved rather significant differences in results, which reflect deeper volume of the economies in question. Our data illustrates the development in the index of private equity attractiveness and in the indexed values of the chosen European countries, where we can see increases and decreases among the analysed countries.

The best results were recorded by Luxemburg, Norway, Switzerland, Netherland and Denmark. Great Britain, France and the biggest European economy – Germany, achieved the levels quite in the middle of the scale, considering all the values for the 15 years in question. The V4 countries – that is, Poland, Slovakia, Hungary and Czech Republic – got the last places among the evaluated countries, followed by Slovenia in close proximity. The levels of private equity and risk capital in this region are considerably lower. At this, we should take into account that these countries are still at the post-communist stage of their development in many senses, which means their economies are still transforming from the planned mode to capitalistic one, and this transition has its considerable impact to their economic development. It is also true that the period of former socialistic regime finished over 20 years ago, but in terms of economic changes within a country this is still a rather short period of time.

Another interesting factor is that the indices of Portugal, Greece, Spain and Italy are better than those of the V4 countries, even though the former group of countries has significant economic problems. Construction of the single index was carried for the period between 1993-2008. Noteworthy, 2008 is only 1 year after the start of the global financial crisis, however, the reaction of private equity investors to the attractiveness of individual countries and industrial sectors came much latter than the actual economic changes in their status, as manifested in national accounts, economic performance and debt level of individual countries. This presents one of the factors proving that countries with possible problems in the future are evaluated more precisely by private equity investors and attractiveness of such countries is more vulnerable against future economic problems.

Table 4. Indices of private equity attractiveness

Country	2011	2016	Change
Slovakia	46	54,2	↑
Czech Republic	51	57,6	↑
Portugal	58	68,6	↑
Spain	73	73,7	↑
France	100	80,3	↓
Germany	103	88,6	↓
Sweden	115	84,6	↓
Austria	117	78,5	↓
Denmark	120	85,4	↓
Switzerland	120	85,6	↓
Luxemburg	150	68,9	↓

(EVCA, 2011; EVCA, 2016)

IMPACT OF PRIVATE EQUITY ON THE MINING INDUSTRY (CASE STUDY)

Evaluation of the mining companies' performance is always rather complicated as compared to commodity companies, since the former are subject to much greater cyclicality. In the mining industry there are two main cycles: pricing of commodities and economic cycle. Also, in the course of evaluation and management these companies must take into consideration various risks. Most important risks are: financial risk, risk to obtain permission for mining and its exact duration, risk connected with geological tasks, risks regarding metallurgical issues, economic risks, and risks of individual countries, political risks, geographical and social risks etc.

Among most important evaluation processes for the mining companies (prior to actual investing) are such processes that deal with the evaluation of incomes and cash-flow, costs and market situation overall. Such evaluations can be distinguished by the level of company's development and what type of company is responsible for deposits, whether this company is dealing with preparation of a single mining location and case or whether it is constantly involved in mining activities.

Short analysis of the situation in European mining industry during the period of 2007-2011 is presented in Figure 8. This graph illustrates the overall situation with production in mining. As we can see, in the second half of the time period in question there is a decrease in production volumes. However, production of European mining industry did not correlate directly with productions of other European industries. Our analysis shows that mining industry volumes in a particular year tend to have a correlation with the rate of GDP in a previous year, and this is applicable to the whole European economy.

Private equity behavior of investors in European mining industry is illustrated in Figure 9. We can see that private equity activity of the related companies is expressed by the volume of investments. Private equity activity in the mining industry in Europe has recorded several decreases, that is, negative changes in investments volumes, but during the period in question this trend was applicable to all industrial sectors in Europe, actually. As it was already mentioned above, private equity reacts more flexibly and promptly to all changes at the world markets, which also means rapid changes in the investments' volume in all European industries *(EVCA, 2012).*

Figure 8. Percentage change in production of the mining industry in Europe
(Eurostat, 2012)

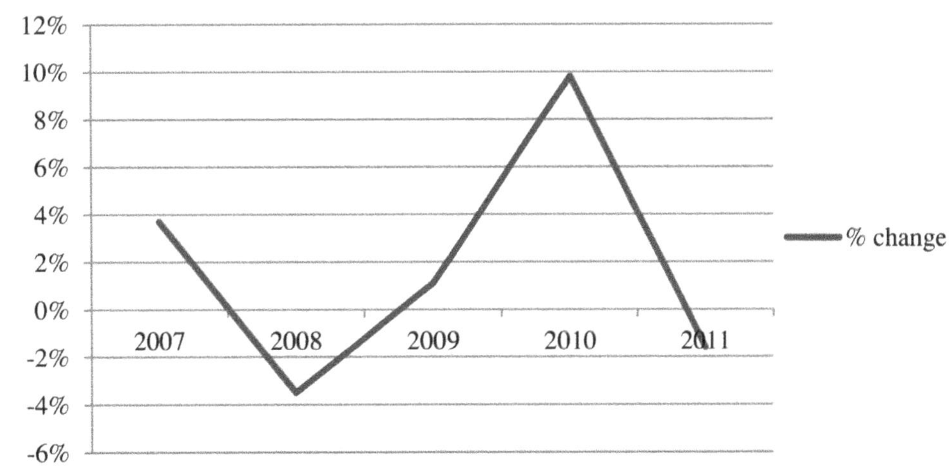

Figure 9. Activeness of private equity investments in the mining industry of Europe (EVCA, 2012)

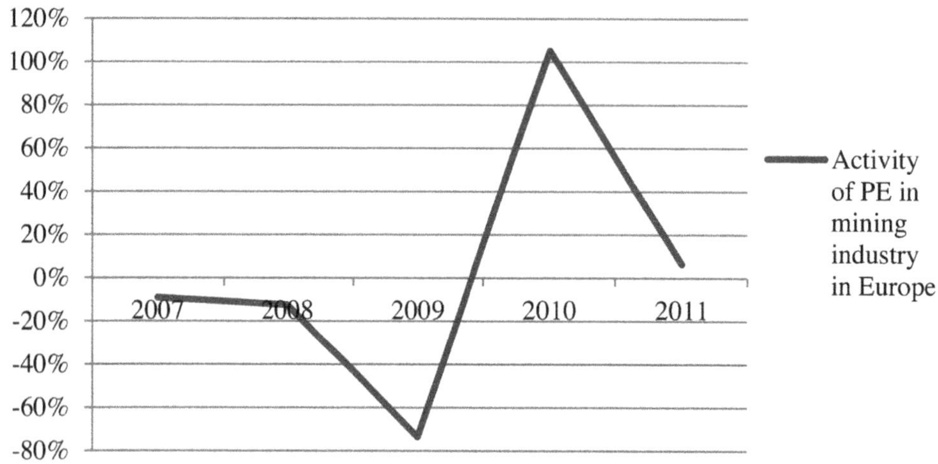

From the standpoint of buyout volume activity of private equity there is a notable disparity between the high value (12% of deals) and low volume (5%) of all energy, mining and utilities transactions as investments are mostly concentrated in a few but large buyouts (more details on this are provided in Figure 10, with some specification for individual European group of countries.

Our analysis is oriented on the evaluation of the mining industry share in the total GDP in Europe and analysis what is the rate of private equity at investments and production in the given industry. Consequently, we have analysed what is growth potential in the mining industry with private equity investors' participation as compared to the same but without private equity investors. Figure 11 demonstrates the rate of European mining industry in the total GDP of Europe.

Figure 10. Activity of private equity from the view of buyout in the energy, mining and utilities sectors (www.pwc.pl/pl/pdf/private-equity-trend-report-2017.pdf)

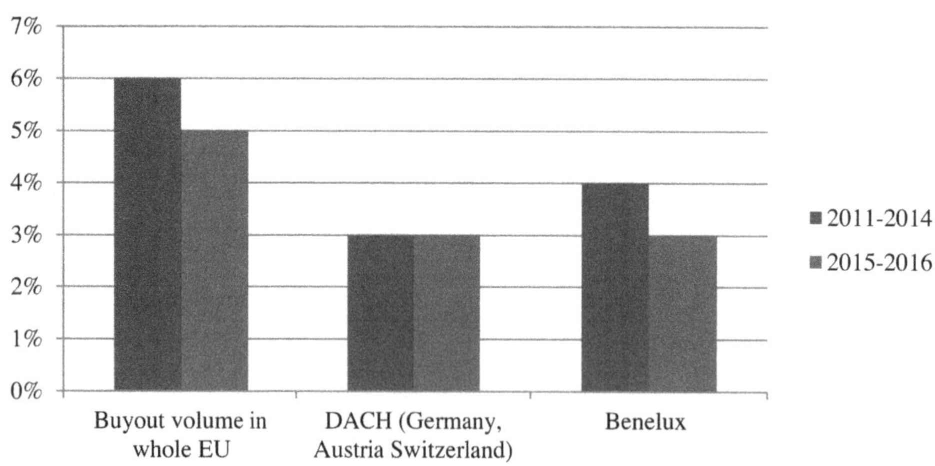

Figure 11. Rate of mining industry on GDP
(EVCA, 2012; Eurostat, 2012)

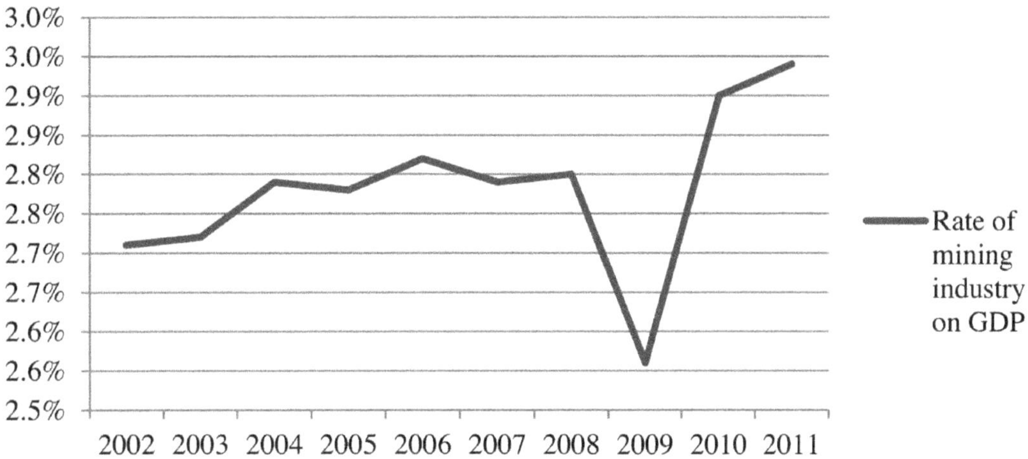

Rate of mining industry in GDP in Europe has been prevailingly stable or slightly growing during the analysed 9 years recorded, except 2009, however, later on the production of the mining industry got even higher than in the previous several years. Single decrease in 2009 was quite expected, since industrial production across whole European industrial market slowed down significantly. Figure 12 further on illustrates the rate of private equity investments, directly orientated on the mining industry and the level of the investments achieved at the time of the global crisis outbreak.

Figure 12 illustrates the level of private equity investments in the mining industry of Europe, which more or less follows the changes in the amount of private equity investments at European markets overall. This sort of development shows that mining industry is attractive from the view of private equity investors and immediately after the first year of crisis there was growth of investments into the mining industry.

Figure 12. Private equity investments in the mining industry of Europe
(EVCA, 2012; Eurostat, 2012)

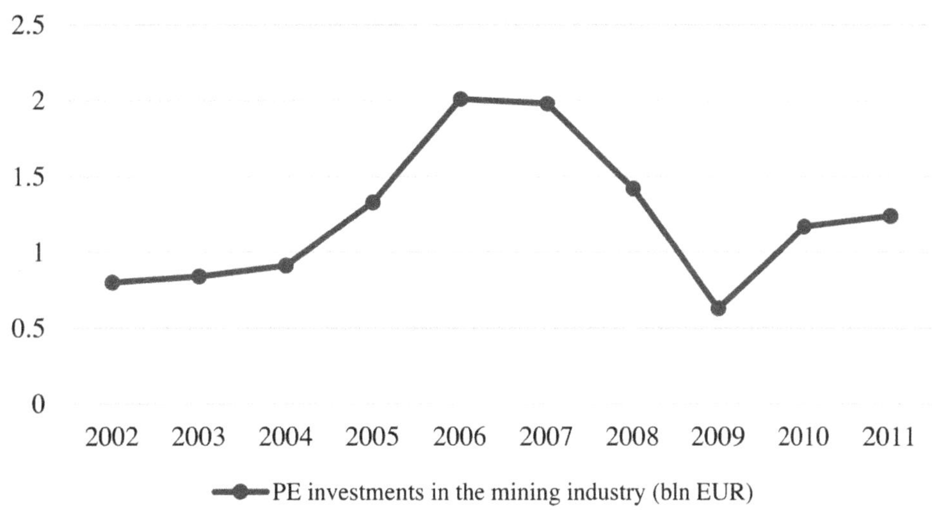

Development of investments to mining industry and mainly its share in the total GDP could be influenced also to certain level by the rates of individual industries in the total GDP. Figure 13 demonstrates the comparison of trends (data is treated as with the index score, where 2002 data is taken as 100) between the mining industry development against GDP, influenced by other industries. We can state that private equity investments have a growing trend in most years.

According to our findings, the mining industry has better performance during the analysed 10 years in comparison with the overall development of industries. Also, mining industry with the influence of private equity investors demonstrates higher performance than the mining industry alone. Trend of growth of mining industry is more expressive considering all of the evaluated factors. Lastly, assessment of the private equity investors' contribution into the mining industry development is carried out by means of comparing production and performance of the mining industry with and without private equity investors' participation. This comparison is illustrated in Table 5.

Development, production and value added of the mining industry are significantly different in the case of private equity investors acting and in the case when private equity investing is not part of companies' functioning within the industry in question (see Table 6).

Companies without private equity investors achieved very stable, but rather stagnating development throughout the 10 analysed years. In one year when companies, supported by private equity investors, achieved lower performance as compared with the base, companies without private equity achieved slightly higher performance. Company with a private equity investor would nearly always achieve higher performance and growth, which in the long term enables company's growth overall and creation of new job positions in particular. In case when company's growth is unchanging throughout more than a decade, such a company could not provide sufficient possibilities for higher employment rates or for increasing the value added.

Figure 13. Trend of mining industry share in GDP as compared to private equity trend
(EVCA, 2012; Eurostat, 2012)

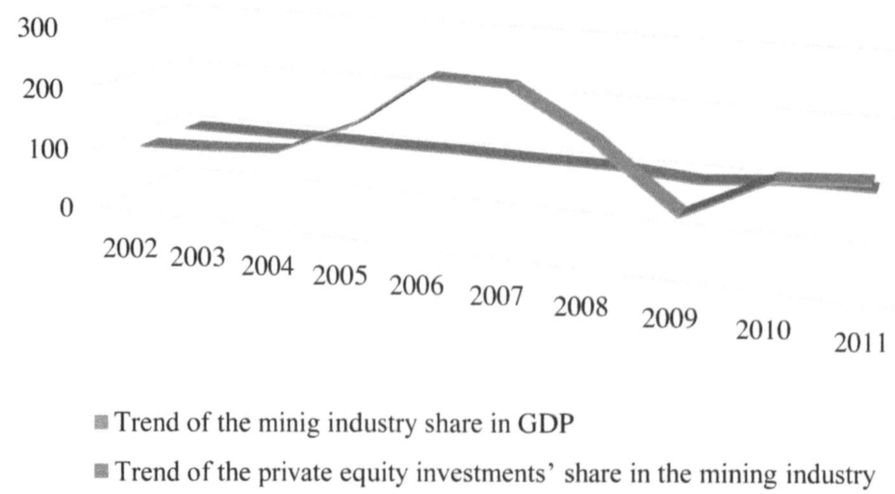

Table 5. Activity of the mining industry in Europe

Year/Analysis	Share of the Mining Industry as % of GDP	PE Investments as % of GDP	PE Investment Into the Mining Industry (bln EUR)	PE Investments Into the Mining Industry as % of GDP
2002	2,71	0,28	800 129	0,0079
2003	2,72	0,29	840 403	0,0081
2004	2,79	0,30	911 155	0,0084
2005	2,78	0,42	1 331 658	0,0118
2006	2,82	0,60	2 008 666	0,0168
2007	2,79	0,56	1 980 663	0,0157
2008	2,80	0,40	1 424 994	0,0112
2009	2,56	0,19	638 823	0,0053
2010	2,90	0,33	1 165 885	0,0093
2011	2,94	0,34	1 243 258	0,0095

(EVCA 2012, Eurostat 2012)

Table 6. Indexed movement of performance in the mining industry of Europe

Years Under Analysis (2002=100)	The Growth Rate of the Mining Industry as Compared to GDP	The Rate of PE Investments Into the Mining Industry	Development of Mining Industry With PE Investors' Participation	Development of Mining Industry Without PE Investors' Participation
2002	100,00	100,00	100,00	100,00
2003	100,38	105,03	103,57	99,99
2004	102,81	113,88	107,14	99,98
2005	102,30	166,43	150,00	99,86
2006	103,83	251,04	214,29	99,68
2007	102,81	247,54	200,00	99,72
2008	103,32	178,10	142,86	99,88
2009	94,45	79,84	67,86	100,09
2010	106,74	145,71	117,86	99,95
2011	108,29	155,38	121,43	99,94

(EVCA, 2012; Eurostat 2012)

According to all of the presented above, the mining industry has quite an investment potential from the viewpoint of private equity investors, as it is reflected in 10 years of growth of these companies, supported by private equity investors, and also as it is reflected in the overall dynamics of European mining industry's development. When comparing mining companies with and without private equity investors' participation, the latter turn out to be also quite stable, however, they do not achieve any significant growth, at least in the context of European mining sector specifically. Therefore, our analysis proves that mining industry has a significant potential for attracting private equity investors.

CONCLUSION

Financial crisis which started in 2007 had its impact to the global private equity market, thus influencing also ownership and transformation of private equity investments. During several decades in the USA and in Europe, private equity market proved private equity organizations with permanent growth in all the industries, thus having positive impact on national GDP, employment growth and other performance indicators.

The key aim of this chapter was to estimate whether private equity supports industries by its presence and what can result from this situation for the mining sector specifically as well as to find out how investors perceive private equity in various countries and whether differences in country's attractiveness has its influence on private equity activity in the selected countries and industries.

The results of our research show certain differences among individual sectors with low or any participation of private equity investors and with the sectors of high level of private investment capital. It had been verified also in case of the mining industry, where positive influence of private equity on the performance of mining companies had been confirmed. This conclusion may have its practical contribution in this as well as in other industrial sectors and for individual companies as well from the viewpoint of increasing their performance.

ACKNOWLEDGMENT

This contribution is also partial result of the projects VEGA MŠVVaŠ SR 1/0310/16 and 1/0651/18.

REFERENCES

Axelson, U., Strömberg, P., Jenkinson, T., & Weisbach, M. S. (2009). Leverage and Pricing in Buyouts: An Empirical Analysis. *Social Science Research Network.*

Bernstein, S., Lerner, J., Sørensen, M., & Strömberg, P. (2010). Private equity and industry performance. *NBER.*

Birnleitner, H. (2014). Attractiveness of Countries for Foreign Direct Investments from the Macro-Economic Perspective. In *Proceedings of FIKUSZ´14, Symposium for Young Researchers* (pp. 29-40). Hungary: Óbuda University.

Bittner, M., Soroková, T., Csikósová, A., Čulková, K., & Marasová, D. (2015). Private equity within mining industry in Europe. *Naukovyi Visnyk Natsionalnoho Hirnychoho Universytetu*, *2*(146), 138–145.

Bloom, N., Sadun, R., & Van Reenen, J. (2009). Do private equity owned firms have better management practices? *Centre for Economic Performance, London School of Economics and Political Science.*

Bloomberg. (n.d.). Europe. Retrieved from www.bloomberg.com/europe

Cetorelli, N., & Gamera, M. (2001). Banking market structure, financial dependence and growth: International evidence from industry data. *The Journal of Finance*, *56*(2), 617–648.

Chemla, G. (2005). The determinants of investment in private equity and venture capital: Evidence from American and Canadian pension funds. *Social Science Research Network.*

Csikósová, A., Mihalčová, B., & Antošová, M. (2015). *International business.* Ostrava: VŠB Ostrava.

Čulková, K., Csikósová, A., & Janošková, M. (2015). Development of Risk Payment Index in Slovakia Comparing with Chosen EU Countries. *Polish Journal of Management Studies, 12*(1), 37–47.

Dorożyński, T., & Kuna-Marszałek, A. (2016). Attracting FDI to the new EU Member States. In P. Trąpczyński, Ł. Puślecki, & M. Jarosiński (Eds.), *Competitiveness of CEE Economies and Business: Multidisciplinary Perspectives and Challenges and Opportunities* (pp. 65–87). Cham: Springer. doi:10.1007/978-3-319-39654-5_4

EIF and EVCA. (2010). *The European Private Equity Market Outlook.* European Investment Fund, European Venture Capital Association.

Eurostat. (2016). EU-28 Annual rates of change total industry MIGs NACE divisions ca 2005-2016. Retrieved October 10, 2017, from www.ec.europa.eu/eurostat/statistics-explained/index.php/File:EU-28_Annual_rates_of_change_total_industry_MIGs_NACE_divisions_ca_2005-2016.png

Eurostat. (2016). Retrieved October 10, 2017, from http://ec.europa.eu/eurostat/publications/statistical-reports

Eurostat. (n.d.). European Statistic Database. Retrieved August 11, 2012, from http://epp.eurostat.ec.europa.eu/ portal/page/portal/statistics/search_database

EVCA. (2005). Barometer May 2005. Retrieved October 1, 2017, from https://www.investeurope.eu/uploadedFiles/Home/Knowledge_Center/EVCA_Research/Barometer/May_2005.pdf

EVCA. (2007). European Private Equity: Strong 2006 Performance drives increased allocation. Retrieved October 1, 2017, from http://www.nvp.nl/data_files/performance_2006.pdf

EVCA. (2012). Central and Eastern Europe Statistics 2011. Retrieved August 11, 2017, from https://psik.org.pl/images/aktualnosci---statystyki-rynku/CEE%20Statistics%202011.pdf

EVCA. (2016). The Invest Europe Yearbook 2016. European Private Equity Activity. Retrieved October 10, 2017, from www.investeurope.eu/media/651727/invest-europe-2016-european-private-equity-activity-final.pdf

Gompers, P., & Lerner, J. (1998). What Drives Venture Fundraising? *Brooking Papers on Economic Activity.*

Groh, A. P., von Liechtenstein, H., & Lieser, K. (2008). The European Capital and Private Equity Country Attractiveness Index(es). IESE Business School – University of Navarra.

Guo, S., Hotchkiss, E., & Song, W. (2009). Do buyouts (still) create value? *Social Science Research Network.*

Hellmann, T., Lindsey, L., & Puri, M. (2004). The interaction between product market and financial strategy: The role of venture capital. *Review of Financial Studies*, 13, 4(25).

InvestEurope. (2016). European Private Equity Activity. Retrieved from https://www.investeurope.eu/media/651727/invest-europe-2016-european-private-equity-activity-final.pdf

Jackson, S., & Markowski, S. (1996). The attractiveness of countries to foreign direct investors. *Australian Journal of Management*, *21*(2), 113–138. doi:10.1177/031289629602100202

Jacobs, R., Smith, P., & Goddard, M. (2004). Measuring performance: an examination of composite performance indicators. Centre for Health Economics.

Janošková, M., Csikósová, A., & Čulková, K. (2018). Measurement of company performance as part of its strategic management. In R. D. Leon (Ed.), *Managerial strategies for business sustainability during turbulent times* (pp. 309–335). Hershey, PA: IGI Global. doi:10.4018/978-1-5225-2716-9.ch017

Jeng, L. A., & Wells, Ph. C. (2000). The determinants of Venture Capital funding: evidence across countries. *Journal of Corporate Finance*, *6*(3).

Jensen, M. (1989). Agency costs of free cash flow: Corporate finance and takeovers. *The American Economic Review*, *76*(6).

John, K., Lang, L., & Netter, J. (1992). The Voluntary Restructuring of Large Firms in Response to Performance Decline. *The Journal of Finance*, *47*(26).

Kaplan, S. (1989). The Effects of Management Buyouts on Operating Performance and Value. *Journal of Financial Economics*, *60*(32).

Kaplan, S., & Stein, J. (1993). The Evolution of Buyout Pricing and Financial Structure in the 1980s. *The Quarterly Journal of Economics*, *108*(44).

Kortum, S., & Lerner, J. (2000). Assessing the Contribution of Venture Capital to Innovation. *The Rand Journal of Economics*, *31*(18).

Muscarella, C. J., & Vetsuypens, M. R. (1990). Efficiency and Organizational Structure: A Study of Reverse LBOs. *The Journal of Finance*, *45*(24).

Priame zahraničné investície. NBS. Retrieved November 1, 2017, from www.nbs.sk/sk/statisticke-udaje/statistika-platobnej-bilancie/priame-zahranicne-investicie

Private Equity Trend Report 2017. (2017). Retrieved October 17, 2017, from www.pwc.pl/pl/pdf/private-equity-trend-report-2017.pdf

Rasmussen, P. (2008). Taming the private equity fund – Locus. *Europe Today*, 8(3).

Smith, L. D. (1995). Discount rates and risk assessment in mineral project evaluations. *Canadian Institute of Mining and Metallurgical Bulletin*, *88*(989), 34–43.

Smith, L. D. (2006). Discounted Cash Flow Analysis, Methodology and Discount Rates. *Rio Algom Limited,* Retrieved October 17, 2017, from http://web.cim.org/mes/pdf/valdaylarrysmith.pdf

OECD. (n.d.). STAN: STructural ANalysis Database. Retrieved October 17, 2017, from http://www.oecd.org/sti/ind/ stanstructuralanalysisdatabase.htm

Stowell, D. P. 2010. Private equity Impact on Corporations. In: Stowell (Ed.) An Introduction to Investment Banks, Hedge Funds, and Private Equity: the new paradigm (pp. 325-345). USA: Elsevier. doi:10.1016/B978-0-12-374503-3.00025-1

Farrell, D., Lund, S., Gerlemann, E., & Seeburger, P. (2007). The New Power Brokers: How Oil, Asia, Hedge Funds and Private Equity Are Shaping the Global Capital Markets. McKinsey Global Institute.

Zámborský, P. (2016). International business and global strategy. *Bookboon*. Retrieved August 12, 2017, from http://bookboon.com/en/international-business-and-global-strategy-ebook

KEY TERMS AND DEFINITIONS

Financing: Act of providing funds for business activities, making purchases or investing. It is part of financial relations' realization, which is aimed at creation, distribution and use of money.

Foreign Direct Investment: Investment made by a company or an individual from one country into business interests in another country in the form of establishing business operations or acquiring business assets in this other country, such as ownership or controlling interests in a foreign company.

Going Private: Transformation, after which public society (mainly traded at a stock exchange) is becoming private organization which means it is not tradable at the stock exchange and investing into its shares is no more possible.

Industrial Market: The set of all individuals and organizations that acquire goods and services that enter into the production of other products or services that are sold, rented, or supplied to others.

International Business: Cross-border transactions of goods and services between two or more countries. Transactions of economic resources include capital, skills, and people for the purposes of international production of physical goods and services, such as finance, banking, insurance and construction.

Mining Industry: Sector dealing with the extraction of valuable minerals and other geological materials from the Earth, in the course of which deposits are becoming of economic interest for a miner.

Private Equity: Type of investment, at which debt financing is used with the aim to purchase a company. It means transformation of a public company into a private one using own and debt financial sources.

Venture Capital: Risk capital provided to by investors during investments to new, beginning companies, but with the interest of the former in potential significant revenues of the latter. This type of financing is more risky than financing of the already existing companies, thus, higher revenues are usually demanded.

Chapter 6
Financial Security of Economic Activity:
Analysis, Control, Risk Management

Natalia Kazakova
Plekhanov Russian University of Economics, Russia

Anna Sivkova
Plekhanov Russian University of Economics, Russia

ABSTRACT

Under the conditions of megarisks, the general level of the world economy's instability rises, the number of unprofitable organizations with overdue debts increases, thus, creating additional threats to the financial security of states. In this regard, presented here, research results have scientific and applied importance for risk management and financial security of economic entities on the basis of the control and analytical concepts which cover: monitoring, diagnostics, prevention of crisis situations, including bankruptcy, corporate fraud and various other financial irregularities in the economy. Accounting for the specifics of economic entities in the course of analysis, diagnostics, and control over their activities is aimed at the creation of effective corporate fraud prevention and bankruptcy management systems. The conceptual principles of information and analytical support, improved methods for analyzing, and evaluating and monitoring financial security contributes to the development of a common methodology for economic analysis and control activities, ensuring their effectiveness and transparency. The comprehensive toolkit for diagnosing financial security allows identifying the areas of increased bankruptcy risks, fraudulent actions or ineffective business management; and unifies the control process, thereby reducing labor intensity and improving the quality of control measures.

DOI: 10.4018/978-1-5225-7760-7.ch006

INTRODUCTION

Public policies today are experiencing a series of problems due to increased macroeconomic, global and international risks. That's why strengthening economic security policy has to develop its own mechanisms, methods and tools.

Economic security in general is the set of conditions required for sustainable development. These conditions determine a quality status of the overall socioeconomic environment, which ensures sufficient independence of management, stability of the financial system, availability of reserves for further economic growth. Governments create and maintain their own resources, strengthen the comprehensive capacity and opportunities to reduce the negative effects from the crisis phenomena in the national, regional and global economies. The most important economic security factor is efficient functioning of businesses.

Financial security rests on strategic programs of increasing the investment attractiveness of the state economy and on financial security diagnostics system which aims to identify and increase the financial stability of reliable companies. For this, a complex of state measures would be needed to work with such companies. If companies have low level of financial transparency about their economic activities, industrial cooperation and establishing partner relationship would be difficult; investment processes overall would slow down in specific regions and maybe in the whole country. This means that financial security and protection of business entities from risks forms the foundation for future investment.

Analysis, evaluation, prediction, diagnostics and monitoring of companies' financial security forms the foundation for contemporary financial management needed for a changed economic situation. This newer economic situation can be characterized by: higher levels of financial risks, more frequent changes in the external and internal factors of the organizational environment, the growing threats to business financial interests.

BACKGROUND

Financial security is an important economic category, which is still not well-established and unambiguous in its definition. Different interpretations of the concept of company's financial security suggested by post-Soviet scientists and economists-practitioners are shown in Table 1.

Obviously, all these definitions differ from each other in depth and breadth, but, in our view, they all reflect the common key areas for assessment such as financial condition, resources' availability, development, counteraction to financial losses and threats. Some authors treat the concepts of "financial security" and "economic security" as the identical ones, but in our view, there is a big difference between them (See Figure 1).

MAIN FOCUS OF THE CHAPTER

The Concept of Financial Security of Business Entities

Financial security is one of the components of economic security, and it is so important that many authors tend to overlook the rest of the components and use financial security as a synonym for economic security. Economic security (in Greek means "governing the situation") was legitimize in the Russian

Table 1. Various interpretations of the concept of company's financial security

The Authors	The Author's Interpretation of the Concept of Company's Financial Security
Blanc I.O.	Financial security of a company represents a quantitatively and qualitatively determinant of its financial condition, provides the top-priority protection for the well-balanced financial interests from the identified actual and potential threats of internal and external nature, the parameters of which are determined on the basis of company's financial philosophy and the created preconditions for financial support of sustainable development in the current and future periods.
Goryacheva K.S.	Financial security of an enterprise is its financial state, which is characterized by the balance and quality of financial instruments, technologies and services, and resistance to threats, the ability of the enterprise's financial system to ensure the realization of its financial interests, missions and tasks, having the sufficient volumes of financial resources as well as ensuring effective and sustainable development of its financial system.
Reverchuk N.Y.	Company's financial security is protection against possible financial losses and bankruptcy, achieving the most efficient use of corporate resources.
Gaponenko V.F., Margiev Z.V.	The state of the financial-credit sphere which is characterized by balance, resistance to internal and external negative influences, the ability of this sector to ensure effective functioning of the national economic system and economic growth.
Goncharenko L.P., Akulinin F.V.	The state of the resources which prevents risks and ensures company's stable functioning.
Kazakova N.A., Zinoviev A.A., Hlevnaya E.A.	The level of maintaining the stability of company's overall condition and its financial stability, sufficiency of cash for conducting operational, financial and investment activity, the balance of cash flows, sufficient independence from counterparties and business partners.
Kazakova N.A., Ivanova A.N.	Financial environment of the company, in which it has the ability to function effectively in accordance with the goals set by business owners, to react promptly and adequately to changes in the internal and external environments, and to adapt to them without losing autonomy and reducing own efficiency.

(Source: compiled by the authors)

Federation by the Law No. 2446-1 as of March 5, 1992 "On Security" (updated by the Law No. 390-FL as of Dec. 28, 2010, later amended and supplemented by the Federal Law as of Oct. 5, 2015 No. 285-FL).

Thus, the concepts of security were determined at the legislative level for the first time back in 1992, and from the very beginning its multidimensional nature, objects and subjects, threats and methods of its provision were defined too. In accordance with the Law No. 390-FL, security activities include forecasting, identifying, analyzing and assessing security threats. This may belong to the competences of the general financial management system or be allocated to an independent risk management service, this can also be the function of the internal control or internal audit system.

The most important part in ensuring financial security of a company is constructing its optimal capital structure on the basis of the generally accepted coefficients, which makes it possible to optimize debt management along with thee methods of attracting additional financial resources at the financial market. But the main problem in implementation of the company's financial security concept is preventing risks and/or saving from them. There are no universal methods for covering various types of risks; neither is there formalization and full description of the structure of risks themselves.

Comprehensive assessment of the financial-economic condition is one of the most important criterions for assessing financial security. Many famous scientists have developed their own criteria and methodology for the financial-economic assessment of risks to economic entities. Their theories and propositions were based on the common idea that in order to conduct financial analysis with a large number of respondents and determine their reliability, it is necessary to form a group of indicators that together provide a complex description of the state and prospects of any company. On the basis of such

Figure 1. Financial security as one of the components of economic security
(Source: Compiled by the authors)

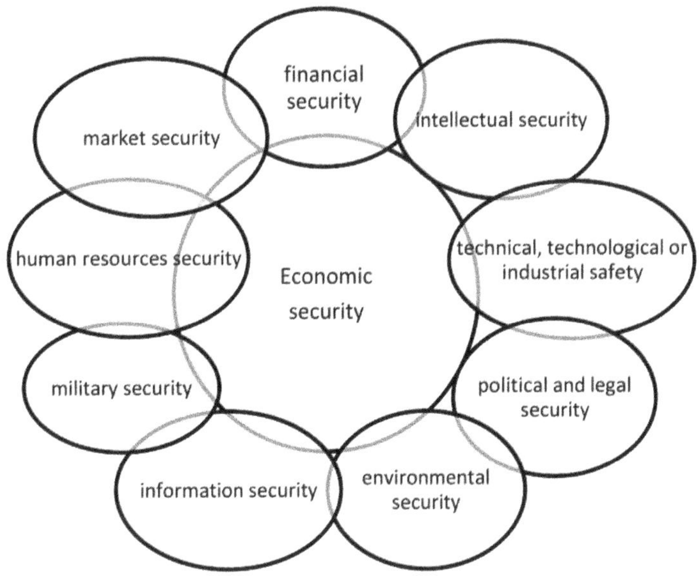

an analysis, it becomes possible to assess the potential risks to financial security of a company/business. The number of such indicators should be optimal and sufficient. The optimal number of these indicators becomes the key prerequisite for the efficiency and complexity of such an analysis. It also helps avoiding excessive inconveniences and eliminates the potential inconsistency of the analysis conclusions. It would be also important to note here that calculation of indicators should be ideally based on the publicly accessible information (Sedova, Kazakova, Gendon, & Khlevnaya, 2017).

This, in turn, requires unambiguous interpretation of the indicators and their values, and also the aggregate values of the indicators should be provided. It means there should be a special ranking system present within the methodology, according to which each indicator has its own weight value, and the amount received by the evaluated enterprise classifies it automatically to a specific group of financial-economic reliability. And this, in turn, will allow assessing in detail all the related risks to financial security. To form the list of indicators of the financial security risks for further development of the related ranking system, it would be needed to choose those aspects of enterprise's economic activity that are most important for suppliers of products, for investors, management, financial and credit organizations and other users. For the aims of our analysis we have selected the following of them: efficiency, riskiness and quality of business management, long-term and short-term prospects of company's solvency. This approach makes it possible to obtain a comprehensive description of nearly any economic entity.

According to the "ideal" recommended model, the controlling service must obey the owner and must be independent from chief managers (the general director and the like) so that to provide more reliable information. However, in fact, in the vast majority of companies, the supervisory service reports directly to the CFO.

That's why the following stages can be identified in the process of diagnostics and controlling the financial security of business entities:

1 Identification of potential dangers and threats to the company. The goal of this stage is to obtain all necessary information on the structure and the key features of the business unit in question and also on the risks that exist.
2 Assessment and ranking of risks by their hazard level, determination of their acceptable levels. At this stage, the company's industry affiliation and its specificity are taken into account, as the latter two, to a large extent, determine the degree of organization's exposure to specific threats.
3 Determining the system of indicators for quantitative assessment and parameters for qualitative assessment of the level of financial security of the company for subsequent monitoring of threats and risks. The system of indicators must necessarily correlate with the risks identified at the previous stages.
4 Development of a set of measures aimed at ensuring the financial security of the organization in the short and long term.
5 Monitoring of the implementation and analysis of the results obtained with their subsequent evaluation and adjustment.
6 Identification of hazards and threats, adjustment of indicators depending on changes in the external environment as well as changed goals and objectives of the organization.

Figure 2 shows the internal organization of interaction between the company's divisions while monitoring the security of all implemented activities.

The stages' content in the course of diagnosis and control of financial security may be different, depending on the specifics of a company's activities.

According to the classical approach used by most authors, financial security is analyzed using four typical blocks of economic analysis (Figure 3).

The conducted research results become the conclusion that it is most rational, reasonable and non-trivial to consider in terms of security of the economic entity's activities, and namely, its risks and losses.

Assessment of Financial Security Risks in the Leading and Socially Significant Sectors of Russian Economy

Contemporary economic science has already come up with the conceptual paradigm regarding financial security as the key factor in the activities of any business entity. However, when it comes to financial security of the higher

The level and the quality of state's functioning depend on the level of development of its macro- and microfinance systems. The mechanism for ensuring financial security of the Russian Federation is complicated by a combination of internal problems inherent to the transition period and external problems and contradictions of the globalization process. Identification of the financial security threats and assessing the ways how to neutralize them seems to be a general methodological imperative for Russian economic research studies in all the significant areas (Sivkova, 2016). In this regard, a number of problems arise, such as ensuring the stability of enterprises' functioning, strengthening their capacity to protect themselves against various external and internal negative impacts, realizing their economic interests at the same time; ensuring financial independence of enterprises, using competitive advantages to ensure equal participation in market relations along with continuous production modernization, effective investment and innovation policies, human resource development (Kazakova, Gendon, & Khlevnaya, 2016). From the standpoint of harmonious development of the Russian Federation, financial security

Figure 2. Internal organization of interaction between the company's divisions in the course of monitoring the security of its activities
(Source: compiled by the authors)

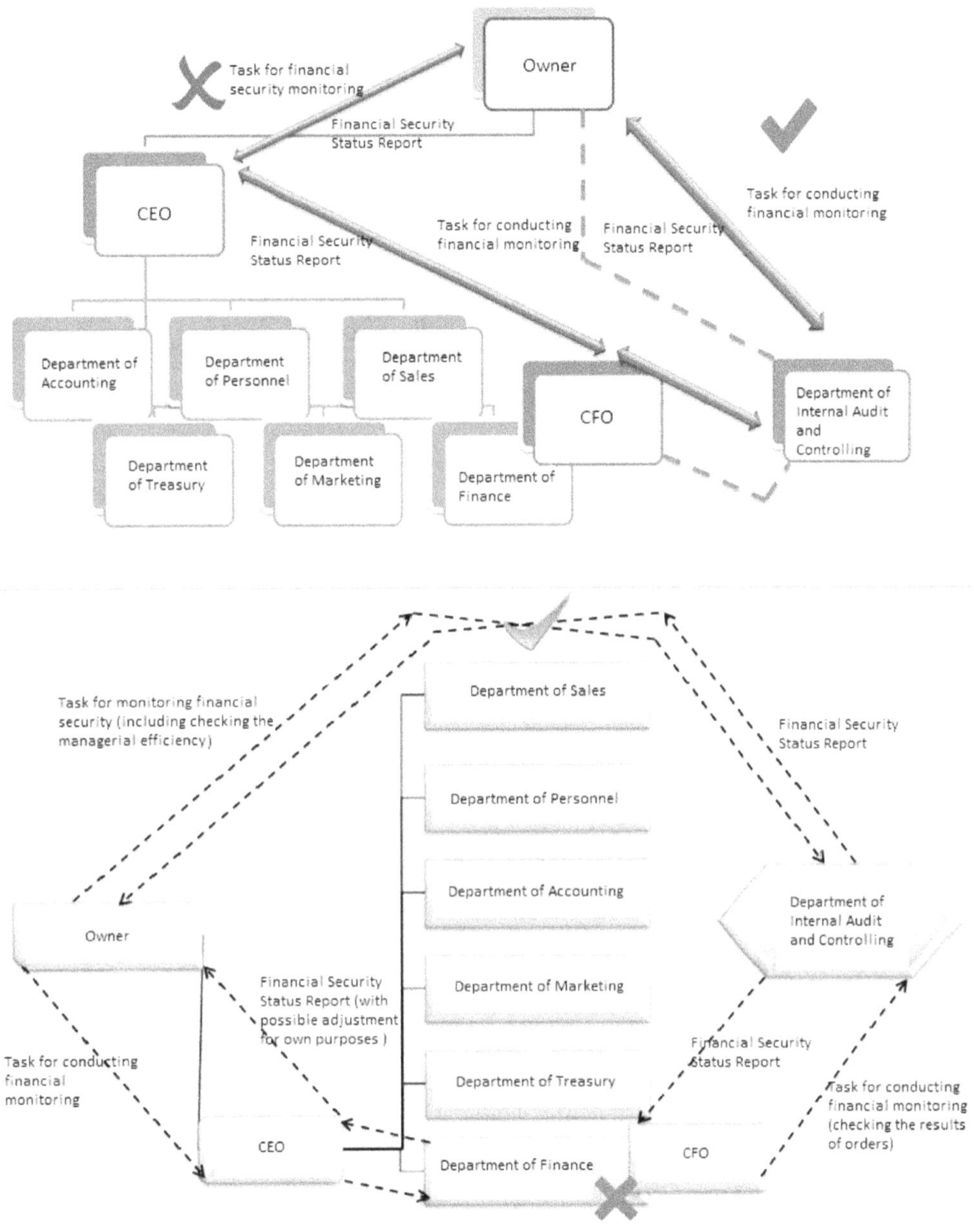

Figure 3. Typical blocks of economic analysis in the course of business security assessment
(Source: compiled by the authors)

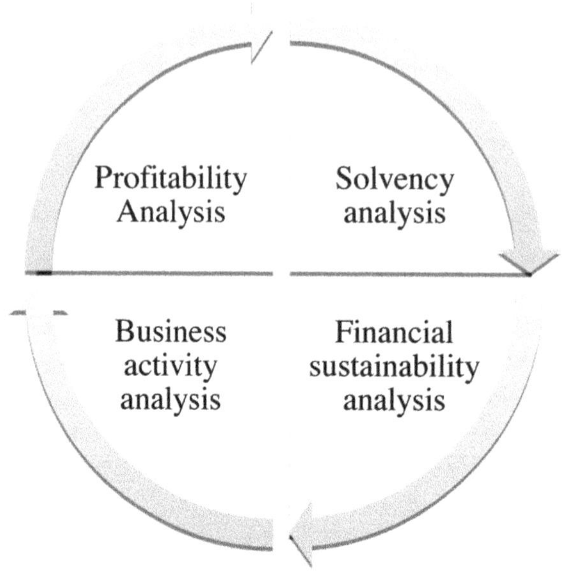

means augmenting the welfare of the state, which, first of all, provides both macro- and microlevels of economic development with specific components. Thus, the basis for any analysis of financial security should be the principle of dividing the spheres of management.

The financial security problem in the context of ongoing globalization processes has recently attracted the attention of many Russian and foreign researchers. This is evidenced by a growing number of scientific publications, monographs and articles on various related economic problems, in particular, the works by T.G. Antropova, N.S. Bezuglaya, A.V. Dadalko, M.E. Listopad and others (Kazakova, Khlevnaya, & Zinovieva, 2016). Noteworthy, all these authors have come up with rather different results, thus, several important elements in assessing and analyzing the financial security of economic entities need further improvement and development.

Development of any society and the welfare level of its citizens depends on the security of their activities and also on the conditions under which this security is being maintained. In this context it would be important to note that government and society are not the one. Government is only a small part of a society. Therefore, sometimes security of the state can be ensured by government, but that does not automatically mean financial security for the whole society. We should also note that financial security is a key component of national security, its foundation and its material basis. Also, noteworthy here is that financial security is a condition of state economy functioning when certain organizational and legal norms become the basis of public life and thus the whole society gradually comes to the state of balance. These are the norms that the state creates as the principles of coexistence, which are passed on from generation to generation (Kazakova, Sokolova, Gendon, & Dun, 2016). An important component of general security is financial security which is ensuring the relevant national interests of the state. All these elements are closely connected with financial independence, stability and security of the society, and also with financial efficiency of the state institutes' and institutions' functioning.

The concept of financial security of a business entity is focused on the balance between business processes and effectiveness of managerial decisions ensuring the sustainable development of this business. At the same time, financial security is a multi-faceted concept that may relate to any level of managerial decision-making. It includes, among other things, information and financial components, macro- and microeconomic risks, and it is also determined by the quality of company's general environment. Once an economic entity achieves a sufficient level of independence in its managerial decision-making, financial system, financial strengths due to the growth of its own production and economic resources, it will also achieve new, integrated capacities as well as extra opportunities to reduce the negative impact of crisis phenomena and counteracting intra-firm fraud (Kazakova, Bolvachev, Gendon, & Golubeva, 2017).

Financial security of domestic enterprises greatly influences the economic security of the Russian Federation overall. According to the analytical agency Kommersant, by the end of 2016 the GNP of the Russian Federation was lower by 3.5% than expected, due to the growing number of bankrupt enterprises. Basing on the analytical data of the Rosstat, we note that the intensity of their liquidation approached the peak levels of the previous crises: only 2.6% below March 2015 level, and 4.3% - below the mid 2009 level. In the third quarter the number of bankruptcies increased by 11% as compared to the second quarter of 2016, and according to the results of the third quarter 79 000 enterprises were already liquidated (Table 2).

It should be noted that the optimistic scenario for the third quarter of 2016 was not fulfilled and the real figures exceeded the forecast by manifold. This happened due to the significant influence of the external environment on Russian economy and businesses once the sanctions were imposed and the international economic situation became mostly unfavorable for Russia. As of October 1, 2016, more than 72 000 legal entities were in the process of liquidation. The largest number of registered and officially liquidated legal entities among the objects included in the register was industrial enterprises (27%) and agricultural farms (22%). These industries are still undergoing major restructuring and liquidation processes in these sectors can be actually explained by a huge number of loss-making decisions made by managers.

Russian scientists have already come up with some predictions concerning future financial security of Russian businesses and the whole Russian economy. We have decided to expand the frontiers of the conventional research in this study. Therefore, security is defined here as the state of financial stability. There is no single approach to identifying the level of security and determining the financial stability of

Table 2. The dynamics of liquidated organizations in the socially important economic sectors, in these units

#	Analyzed Period	Number of Liquidated Companies	Socially Significant Sectors of Russian Economy					
			Industry	**Agriculture**	**Socio-Cultural Sphere**	**Construction**	**Transport**	**Housing and Utilities' Infrastructure**
1.	1st quarter 2016	82254	26674	15530	12260	11443	9809	6539
2.	2nd quarter 2016	65528	18829	14228	9829	10391	7864	6151
3.	3rd quarter 2016	79289	22784	17216	11894	12573	9515	7443
4.	4th quarter 2016	96948	22546	19634	12231	13007	9821	7115

(Source: compiled by the authors from the data by the Federal State Statistics Service official website)

business entities and industries. In the majority of contemporary studies on the issues related to security, three main theoretical approaches are applied to studying this notion along with all the accompanying problems.

"Macroconceptual" financial security components are studied solely on the macroeconomic level. This level determines that the state of financial security depends on the conditions of new social and financial reality and is also closely connected with the financial system, which is called social-market economy (both in terms of its formation and implementation). Despite more than 25 years of economic and social transformations in our country, the constitutional provisions of the economic system of the Russian Federation are still based mostly on the theoretical conclusions of the economists. And these conclusions are often focused around the statement that our state, supposedly, has chosen the most effective model of the financial system. Ignorance about its actual essence is often caused by false theoretical interpretations and misunderstandings in financial policy, unreasonable assessments of economic realities etc. (Kazakova, Kisnichyan, Sivkova, & Kazakov, 2015).

This situation is yet another proof that contemporary businesses, functioning within the framework of such a financial system, are not capable of reasonable redistribution of the resources, between sectors in particular. Thus, ensuring national financial security under current national socio-financial realities should be linked, first of all, to taking the control over the number of unprofitable companies. Therefore, it is extremely necessary to formulate an appropriate financial security policy, which would include this criterion too. It is important to note here that the method used for tracking the real numbers of unprofitable companies is a serious problem today. Solution of this problem is hampered by the lack of a unified statistical nationwide database and also by the multiplicity of indicators used for tracking these numbers. As of today, the Rosstat has proposed an innovative approach to such calculations based on tracking the main demographic indicators of economic entities (Table 3).

Data provided in Table 3 is yet another proof for the non-stability situation in nearly all sectors of Russian economy. Rises and falls in the indicators are abrupt, especially in agriculture and the sector of socio-cultural services. In the transportation and utilities sectors the situation is controlled mainly through government interventions. In the 4th quarter of 2016, for all economic sectors a sharp increase in the number of unprofitable companies has been forecasted.

According to some theories, macroeconomic crisis phenomena are unpredictable as such since every economic crisis destroys the already outlived economic elements, thus freeing place for more progressive economic processes which are yet in the process of formation. Thus, the main prerequisites for ensuring

Table 3. The number of unprofitable companies in socially important sectors of the economy, these units

#	Analyzed Period	Industry	Agriculture	Socio-Cultural Sphere	Construction	Transportation	Housing and Utilities' Infrastructure
1.	1st quarter 2015	1,9	3,0	7,3	3,1	3,9	3,0
2.	4th quarter 2015	1,6	6,9	5,1	2,9	4,0	4,4
3.	1st quarter 2016	1,5	5,1	4,1	3,4	3,0	3,1
4.	2nd quarter 2016	1,0	4,1	2,9	2,8	2,2	2,6
5.	3rd quarter 2016	1,5	7,0	5,9	2,5	4,8	8,9

(Source: compiled by the authors on the data provided by the Federal State Statistics Service: official website)

Table 4. The number of enterprises and organizations that have the current liquidity ratio being less than one, this units

Current Liquidity Ratio		
Analyzed Period	**2015**	**2016**
1st of April 2016	150,15	155,22
1st of July 2016	148,24	149,30
1st of October 2016	143,00	142,10

(Source: compiled by the authors on the data of the Federal State Statistics Service: official website)

economic and financial security of any economic entity (system) are flexibility, dynamism, adaptability and the ability to overcome crisis in a relatively short time.

Financial security studies at the mesolevel tend to be limited to studying and measuring certain conditions of the financial environment only. In such a way they objectively outline the key requirements to financial security. However, the authors emphasize mainly on the efficiency and flexibility as well as on the ability to provide timely repayment of obligations or, in other words, on liquidity. This means that analyzing the state of financial security should also refer to the general characteristics of the economy of the Russian Federation (Table 4).

Table 4 shows that the lowest value of enterprises' circulating assets was reached in the third quarter of 2016. This indicates that companies experienced the greatest difficulties in financing their current activities during this period. Decreases in this indicator were also the reason for the decreasing autonomy ratio, which shows the degree of enterprise's independence from its creditors.

The third group of financial security criteria characterizes the microlevel. Developed countries direct their economic policies onto the interests of leading firms and multinational corporations. There is an additional financial security problem with internal and external factors around business obligations of economic entities in the Russian Federation. For example, at the end of the summer 2015, the number

Table 5. The number of companies with overdue accounts payable by economic sectors, these units

#	Analyzed Period	Number of Companies	Companies That Have Payments in Arrears for More Than 3 Months	Socially Significant Branches of the Economy					
				Industry	**Agriculture**	**Socio-Cultural Sector**	**Constructions**	**Transportation**	**Housing and Utilities' Infrastructure**
1.	1st quarter 2015	14346	1509	4299	7124	2116	1627	826	1022
2.	4th quarter 2015	62269	29855	3402	31969	2516	3521	221	518
3.	1st quarter 2016	18647	2149	4636	8447	2410	1718	1151	18647
4.	2nd quarter 2016	22970	4931	3501	12138	2292	1779	874	22970
5.	3rd quarter 2016	59706	27210	3367	36342	2096	4072	1437	59706

(Source: compiled by the authors on the data from the Federal State Statistics Service: official website)

of companies with overdue accounts payable was increasing very quickly. This happened mostly due to economic sanctions imposed by the European Union in the same 2015 because of the military conflict between Russia and Ukraine. One more factor of the negative influence was rapid devaluation of the ruble. Another additional factor, directly related to the imposed sanctions, was the refusal of European banks to lend to large Russian companies, mainly to industrial and agricultural ones. The most vulnerable sectors of Russian economy with high payable risks in the 3rd quarter of 2016 were transportation and utilities sectors (Table 5).

Table 5 shows the number of companies with overdue accounts payable by economic sectors. Indicators of the 3rd quarter of 2016 were more than 50% higher as compared to the 2nd quarter of 2016, and this was the highest growth in the last several years.

Analysis of Risks Related to Financial Violations in Russia and Other Countries

The most widely spread economic crimes in today's Russian practice include: fraud, appropriating, illegal or semi shadow entrepreneurship, criminal bankruptcies, tax avoidance and other crimes related to taxation and customs. The most common of them, causing direct and huge damages to businesses, are: fraud *(Article 159 of the Criminal Code),* appropriation and fraud *(Article 160 of the Criminal Code of the Russian Federation).* Many Russian researchers note in this regard the high degree the latency of the intra-firm fraud (that is, many crimes are of hidden, disguised character).

The number of fraud and other economic crimes may be in the range of about 5% of all criminal acts, according to some estimates. However, the actual volume of damages repeatedly exceeds this official data. This inflicts enormous damage done to enterprise themselves and also to the budgets of all levels, primarily due to shortfalls of taxes and duties. Damages from fraud and other economic crimes have an especially strong influence during the period of sanctions imposed on Russia. The level of financial security of the state has obviously reduced, and significantly. According to Sheila R. Ronis, financial security is an important element of national security (Ronis, 2011). And national security, in its turn, is the shield for economic viability of the people. There is no business without capital; there are no jobs without profit. And there are no taxes without work, and without taxes - there will be no military, economic or cultural potential in a country (Kazakova, Bolvachev, Gendon, & Golubeva, 2016).

Corporate fraud practices and the mechanisms used for investigation of economic crimes have been considered by many researchers, including I. Shengeliy, D.A. Markvart, D.A. Litvinov, O.B. Ivanov, V.M. Kashuba, V.S. Efimov, A.N. Brodunov, V.V. Lizyayev, V.G. Kogdenko and others. The problem of corruption-related fraud has been also widely explored in the works of foreign authors, such as K. Schipper, K. Marshan, J.T. Wells, J.M. Zack, J.L. Kovasic, etc. However, investigation of fraud schemes applied specifically in Russian conditions is still a topical problem from the standpoint of both theoretical research and practical investigations.

Famous American specialists in fraud analysis S. Albrecht, J. Wentz and T. Williams wrote about two major elements in fraud: denomination and trust. Without trust, fraud is impossible (Ronis, 2011).

The Association of Certified Fraud Examiners (ACFE) apply a proprietary approach according to which fraud and abuse in the sphere of professional activity means personal use of one's official position for the purposes of personal enrichment through deliberate misuse or abuse of the resources and assets available in the employing organization.

According to Art. 159 of the Criminal Code of the Russian Federation, "fraud" means theft of someone's property or acquisition of the right to someone's property by misconception or abuse of trust. It also states that internal or corporate fraud means fraudulent operations between an employer and a worker or between a worker and an employer.

The Ministry of Finance of the Russian Federation states that the work of the Associate of Certified Fraud Examiners (ACFE) should cover three categories of corporate fraud (also called the "fraud tree"): 1. bribery and corruption (in Russia - 40% of all detected cases, in the world - about 24%); 2. falsification of accounting records, improper collection of taxes (in Russia and in the world the rate is approximately the same - 25%); 3. unlawful appropriation of assets (this indicator is also roughly the same in the world and in Russia - up to 72%) (Federal State Statistics Service: official website).

In the world intra-firm fraud ranking Russia occupies the first place (71%), South Africa goes second (62%), Kenya - 3rd (57%), Canada - 4th (56%), Mexico - 5th (51%) (this ranking has been formed on the basis of the research carried out by PwC under the title "Economic crimes during the period of economic expansion"). Victims of such economic crimes in the last two years became over 59% of all domestic companies, this is higher than the world average indicator (43%).

Russia's first place in the ranking mentioned above can be explained by the low quality of corporations' development and corporate relations in particular: people at the highest ranks in Russian corporations, including state-owned ones, are directly involved in criminal schemes. In contrast, in the absolute majority of Western countries, such crimes belong mostly to the middle and linear levels of employees. And what is even worse, 42% of Russian respondents do not consider such practices to be a significant problem for business (Kazakova & Ivanova, 2016).

The British audit company PricewaterhouseCoopers has recently came up with the research on the world economic violations, which ended up with rather horrific results: in two years only damages caused by the internal fraud cases inside Russian companies quadrupled in volume, and the amount of losses from one such act is now five times higher than the average world indicator. According to other results of the same study, more than five thousand companies, including 120 largest Russian companies, suffer from losses due to corruption, fraud and the related violations. This number exceeds the average world indicator by more than 15%.

In today's Russian and international practice, the term "corporate fraud" is used to express unscrupulous, deliberate actions of personnel entailing various financial violations aimed at obtaining personal benefits. According to the federal standards on auditing in the Russian Federation, fraudulent actions with the aim of extracting illegal benefits are considered to be unfair, leading to significant distortions in financial statements. At the same time, financial reporting can be distorted due to low quality of documents' preparation, for example.

The fight against the intra-firm fraud is the subject of improving departmental regulations as well as the regulatory framework of large financial companies concerning mortgage lending, public healthcare financing and other areas of activity. Fraud in such cases is manifested through manipulations with financial reporting, trading operations and abuse of trust. A series of major scandals occurred over the pact decade due to the revealed corporate fraud facts. After this range of scandals the issue of identifying corporate fraud has become particularly relevant. Particularly notorious became the scandals involving such organizations such as ENRON, WorldCom, LG Group, Mercury Finance Company, British Petroleum, Hollinger International Inc. и Parmalat.

The international history of fighting unfair business practices officially began back in 1960, with the creation of the committee of experts on bankruptcy within the framework of the European Union. Its most important achievement was development of a set of measures regulating bankruptcy procedures for the companies on the territory of the European Union. But this regulation includes only mandatory bankruptcy procedures, moreover, part of its features are additionally regulated by national legislation of different countries (Hyide & Panos, 2014).

USA is one of the countries to carry out the most active work on the development of mechanisms for counteracting economic crimes. In the case of the US unlawful actions related to bankruptcy often include concealing the assets. Thus, this aspect needs to be specified as a liability: provision of falsified or incomplete data to creditors; bribery of the appointed arbitration administrator etc.

In the US detection and prevention of fraudulent activities is handled by the Financial Fraud Enforcement Task Force with the assistance of the Federal Bureau of Investigation, the Securities and Exchange Commission, the Industrial Finance Regulatory Committee, the Internal Revenue Service and the Labor Department. The most significant result from these joint efforts of the US government institutions in terms of combating corporate fraud has become the creation of the Financial Crimes Enforcement Network (FinCEN), which has an extensive database and has already become the platform for interaction between various special services (Blaskowitz & Herwartz, 2011).

In recent decades various countries and regions worldwide have been also establishing various international organizations and associations to fight and prevent this problem. The most famous international organization today in this regard is the Association of Certified Fraud Examiners (ACFE), which deals with the problems of financial fraud and namely - unscrupulous bankruptcy actions. This organization has its branch in Russia as well. The Association conducts trainings for specialists so that they become able to identify and investigate various types of economic crimes, including corporate fraud. It also develops methodological recommendations that contain examples of combating unfair economic activities. Finally, it collects statistical data and forms its own database of the identified economic crimes.

Obtaining information from monitoring of such activities should be aimed at preventing fraud within organizations, identifying its causes and eliminating fraud at the early stages of its development already.

Directions in Assessment, Diagnostics and Control Over Financial Security of Economic Entities

Security problems of company's activities are related to growing instability in the economy due to the financial crisis, fluctuations in oil prices, various political decisions and economic sanctions, which together ultimately lead to the increasing financial risks for all organizations. Financial stability is an integrated indicator of security of company's activities, as it reflects company's management effectiveness and shows how stable the organization can be under the conditions of growing micro- and macrorisks. Development of the security control methodology can be presented in several stages which include identification of security risks, determining the directions for monitoring, development of financial and economic indicators along with the security monitoring criteria, and finally - shaping the information-analytical framework for security analysis and monitoring.

Identification of Security Risks Along With the Directions in Their Control

The first stage begins directly with the procedure for identifying risks and determining future directions for controlling financial security. External threats to company are caused by geopolitical relations and more specifically - by the relations between states, for example, imposition of sanctions on certain goods or countries and other restriction of activities; instability of the domestic currency exchange rate; monetary defaults and sharp rises in the inflation level; too frequent changes in the legal framework; growth of interest rates on loans; unfair competition and fraud; high rate of financial crimes.

Internal threats to business are most frequently caused by unfair work practices of personnel, low level of qualifications and unsatisfactory quality of work; corporate fraud; insufficient supervision by management; outdated technical base, malfunctioning of equipment; low level of assets' liquidity; leakage of information and the related damages to company's reputation; lack of development plans; ineffective company policies and unjustified management decisions overall.

In order to ensure financial security of a company, it is necessary to build an internal control system with several responsibility centers. Specific features of a particular business are supposed to predetermine the directions of control, its subjects, the system of financial and economic parameters to refer to in the future, criteria for monitoring financial security, information & analytical base to be used in the course of monitoring, methods for identification of risks to financial security, principles ensuring the security of business entities. We assume here that the key objects of control over the security of economic entities' activities can be:

- Assets (property);
- Information;
- Staff;
- Information resources (databases), and;
- Reputation.

Table 6 presents the distribution of security risks of the business entity's activities between the proposed control objects.

The control centers over financial security of a business entity may include such significant management and external control subsystems as personnel department, top management, internal control or internal audit service, external controllers as the hired individuals from independent audit organizations, representatives of counterparties, tax authorities, international organizations etc. In order to reduce the security risks' levels within business entity's activity we put forward the following recommendations:

1. Ongoing professional development for all personnel directly related to accounting and financial-economic relations overall
2. Improvement of top management's skills in general
3. Continuous monitoring, analysis and assessment of the financial security level; continuous and mandatory legal support
4. Improving the effectiveness of the internal control system (double control, increased attention to atypical operations, availability of internal audit, annual voluntary audits initiated by the organization itself)
5. Strict cash, tax and payment discipline

Table 6. Security risks' distribution between the objects of control

Objects of Control (Security Centers Within a Business Entity)	Controlled Risks	Causes (Factors) of Potential Risks	Controllers
Property (assets) of the company in general	The possibility of theft of easily available assets; re-ownership of property; damage to or destruction of property; too much of financial liabilities	Dishonesty and negligence of staff; insufficient supervision by management	Heads of departments; Financial Director; Legal service; Internal auditors; Controllers; External Auditors
Information	Leakage of confidential information (recipes, production technologies, know-how, investment ideas etc.); absence or violation of regulated procedures for the transfer and use of information	Insufficient control by management; bad faith of staff; ill-conceived resolution of issues by lawyers (this especially concerns confidentiality agreements); improper distribution of the levels of secrecy of confidential information	Heads of departments; Financial Director; Legal service; IT-department
Company's staff	Damages to company in the form of selling under unprofitable terms or carrying out other unprofitable business operations; falsification of financial documents; corruption, blackmailing, threats on the part of third persons; luring important employees to other companies; abuse of office	Insufficient control by management; bad faith of staff; insufficient control by lawyers.	Heads of the departments; Financial Director; Legal service; Personnel service
Information resources (databases)	Hacking; destruction of databases; leakage of confidential information, financial losses due to additional costs spent on restoring information	Weak technical support; insecurity from viruses and unauthorized access; abuse of office	IT-department; top management; heads of the departments
Reputation	Reclamation of products or services; "creative" accounting; instability of contractual relations; false information in the media; getting into "black lists" of organizations, unreliable customers for banks, unstable taxpayers, untrustworthy suppliers, etc.	Lack of competence, integrity, qualifications of personnel; violation of normative regulations; untimely response to complaints of partners	The whole of management team; top management in particular; heads of departments
Financial indicators	Insolvency (bankruptcy); loss of financial stability; low liquidity of assets.	Lack of business planning; low quality of accounting and control.	Financial Director; Controllers; Internal auditors; External auditors

(Source: compiled by the authors)

6. Control over how marketing personnel policies are being implemented and followed
7. Improving the security of internal information systems

Financial and Economic Indicators and Criteria for Monitoring the Security of Business Entities

Security of business entities is determined by the level of maintained stability of the state and financial stability of companies, by the adequacy of funds' volume for all further operations, by the activeness of current financial and investment activities and the balance of cash flows, and also by the sufficient independence from suppliers, business partners and other counterparties.

Monitoring the security level of an economic entity includes following certain requirements:

- Measurability of financial security parameters (availability of qualitative and quantitative indicators)
- Presence of threshold values which can be used in assessment of financial security at the level of particular business

In addition, control over the security of a business entity must ensure the development of its integrated capacity, its financial stability in both long-term and short-term periods. Table 7 below systematizes financial security indicators of the company's level, distributed between control centers.

Express analysis of financial security of a business entity can be carried out on the basis of accounting data. It would be used not only to determine the position of organization, but also to assess the effectiveness of management and to ensure its financial stability.

Organization and functioning of the system of internal control over financial security of an economic entity should be based on the principles of comprehensiveness, timeliness, continuity, legality and accountability for the industrial specialization of this business.

The principle of comprehensiveness is supposed to ensure the security of both personnel and company's assets. It means that the information basis must be wide enough, however, confidentiality of information must be the priority and all data must be protected from all possible types of threats. This is achieved through the right personnel selection policy, using of technical security and information protection tools. Information analysis in this regard must be aimed at preventing potential risks to company's financial security.

The principles of timeliness and continuity assume constant monitoring, detection and prevention of the current and future risks for a company. Not only data analysis and forecasting of security threats must be constant, same applies to the development of effective protection measures.

The increasing risks of corporate fraud are often associated with the insufficiency of control measures aimed to detecting and preventing fraud cases. Another risk concerns too wide range of powers granted to one employee and/or the lack of a system for assessing staff performance. Same applies to the impunity, disregarding the rules of professional ethics, absence of or poorly developed organizational culture; easy access to internal confidential information from the outside (by former employees, for example); high risks of information distortion; the inability to control the use of internal information; general incompetence and/or insufficient qualification of personnel; various organizational problems with carrying out internal and external audit.

The most common types of fraud on the part of employees include:

- Counterfeiting (falsification) of documents;
- Conducting transactions with controlled companies;
- Collusion with customers or with suppliers; invoicing for uncompleted work or undelivered goods;
- The use of kickbacks;
- The use of shell suppliers or intermediaries;
- Artificial overstatement of prices;
- The use of employees' labor, equipment, materials or other office resources of the company for personal purposes;
- Illegal operations with property;

Table 7. Distribution of the financial security indicators between the control centers within a company

Financial Security Control Centers (Control Objects)	Indicators	Financial Description
Property (assets) of the company	Current ratio	Shows company's ability to meet current obligations from liquid assets. In the process of working on revealing the facts of fraud, the current liquidity ratio can be also the indicator of manipulations in accounting records. Embezzlement will reduce this ratio. Withholding obligations will give it a higher value.
	Short-term liquidity ratio	Shows company's ability to cover unexpected cash requirements, can act as an indicator of fraud.
	Accounts receivable turnover	Shows how many times the accounts of debtors turn around during the reporting period. In other words, it indirectly characterizes the time between the receipts and accounts receivable in accounting and receipt of cash in an actual payment. If the fact of fraud concerns fictitious sales, money for them will never be received. As a result, the turnover of receivables will decrease.
	Turnover of inventories	This ratio is the best parameter for the efficiency of purchases, production and sales. For example, if the cost of sales rose due to theft of inventory (inventory at the end of the period decreased, but it was not because some of them were sold), then this ratio will be higher than the normal value.
	Average period of inventory turnover	Increase in the number of days when inventories are left in stock (a decrease in turnover) causes additional costs, including storage costs, the risk of inventory obsolescence, decline in the market price, and interest and other costs arising from the freezing of funds in inventories. Inconsistencies and significant fluctuations of this coefficient may be the sign of possible fraud. One can use this factor when studying inventory accounts to identify possible theft.
Company staff	Staff turnover rate	Extreme instability of staff may indicate the presence of financial problems in the company and indirectly, may be the signs of possible fraud.
Reputation	The amount of costs associated with complaints for products (works or services)	Growth of other expenses due to economic sanctions, supply disruptions, increase in product returns, which may be the signs of technical, technological or HR-related troubles, financial instability, legal irregularities etc.
Financial risks	Leverage ratio	Shows the balance between the resources provided by creditors and the resources provided by owners. This is the most important for analyzing the real financial situation of a company. Maintaining a certain ratio of borrowed funds and equity is often included in the text of loan agreements. Unexpected changes in this coefficient may serve as the sign of financial irregularities.
	Profit margin ratio	The ratio of net profit to sales proceeds reflects not only changes in the gross profit margin, but also changes in trade and administrative expenses. When there is a fraud case, artificially inflated sales will not be accompanied by an increase in the cost of sales, net profit will be overstated, and profit margin will be unusually high. Fictitious expenses and fraudulent payments will lead to increased costs and reduced profitability.

(Source: compiled by the authors)

- Computer hacking and planting viruses, and;
- Use of cash for other, often shadow purposes.

Additional factors leading to higher risks to organization's financial security include:

- Overcomplicated and/or illogical organizational structure;
- Default of independent audits initiated by the company itself;

- Activities in the zones of high risks;
- Frequent changes of senior and middle managers, and;
- Large transactions with affiliated persons and interested companies.

The process of detecting corporate fraud facts is usually based on the analytical procedures identifying the signs of fraud. These can be atypical or implausible business contacts, or these can be actions or business events occurring in strange places or at unusual times; or transactions involving individuals who do not normally have to participate in these relations, and also business operations carried out through atypical procedures or methods. Another widely spread sign is too large (or too small) volume of transactions or transferred amounts; or transactions carried out too often etc.

Generally speaking, the signs of fraudulent operations may include everything that goes beyond usual/standard business operations, typical for a given sector and the specific company.

SOLUTIONS AND RECOMMENDATIONS

Stemming from the study and generalization of the experience risk diagnostics and control measures, we have developed and offer the following recommendations for the use in internal control services in order to gain better control over the financial security of economic entities in general and to identify fraud cases in particular.

1. Most frequently, fraud cases are detected in the service sector. This is mostly because provision of services is the hardest to verify among all business operations.
2. In the presence of fictitious production transactions, figures in financial statements can look reliable, but all fraudulent facts will be hidden in interim documents and intermediate reports which are not publicly available.
3. Fraudulent transactions are mostly hidden within many other actions that were actually committed (for example, there is indeed the confirmed fact of purchase, however, in a different amount).
4. If the fact of detected fraud involved the use of computer technologies or databases, then, as a rule, a specialist working in the IT department participated in it.
5. Most of the fraud cases are hidden through manipulations with primary documents.
6. Accounting signs that may be indicative of potential corporate fraud and, therefore, require detailed control, can be the following: accounts receivable grow much faster than the revenue; the wage bill increases with staff cuts; investments' volume is increasing in the absence of growth in the depreciation of fixed assets; writing off equipment before the deadline; availability of products and materials in stock not registered in accounting.
7. In order to reduce the risks of corporate fraud it is recommended to use such organizational methods: separation of duties; availability of double control over the key functions and major operations; availability of a special authorization system; systemic independent checks; strictly documented control.
8. For the detection of fraudulent operations we can recommend the following methods of internal audit: checking the accuracy of calculations (analysis of the correctness of calculations, recalculation); analytical tests (verification of causation); checking the completeness of the documentation; verification of the correctness of procedures approving documents; verification of legitimacy (le-

gality of business transactions); conducting interviews with staff related to procedures, methods and operations carried out inside the company.

FUTURE RESEARCH DIRECTIONS

On the basis of theoretical and factual study of the financial security issues, the solution must include formation of a general approach to creating sustainable development conditions for all business entities. And scientifically grounded views on this problem should contribute to the creation of the socially-oriented concept of financial security. The authors' scientific standpoint here is based on the information-analytical paradigm of ensuring financial security by developing scientifically well-grounded tools for monitoring and diagnosing financial security combining all the indicators at the three basic levels - macro, meso and micro, thus allowing for a comprehensive assessment of the actual state of economic entities from the viewpoint of their independent activity, branch specificity and, finally, the state system of financial security in the Russian Federation overall.

CONCLUSION

The key result of its study is presenting the author's conceptual approach to information & analytical provision of financial security for business entities which involves accounting for the specifics of various economic sectors, determining the directions of control along with the control subjects, the system of financial and economic parameters and criteria for monitoring security, and developing an information-analytical bases for identifying the security risks of an economic entity. In particular, we proposed such responsibility centers and objects of control over the security of business entities as: assets (property), information, personnel, information resources (databases), and finally company's reputation.

As typical diagnostics and control measures for financial security maintenance, including the detection of fraud, we recommend the following:

- Carrying out control actions: external and internal audit, control over corporate culture, double control, independent control, confirmation of authority
- Control over personnel policy (inspection of personnel activities, delineation of powers)
- Organizational arrangements aimed at delegating authority to prevent possible collusion between employees, customers or suppliers
- Carrying out information and psychological activities aimed at informing company's partners about its policy to fight violations and abuses, operation of the "hotline" to receive anonymous signals and messages, public dissemination of information on how perpetrators have been published
- Creation of an organized workflow system
- Introduction of rules for collegial decision-making and independent coordination of documents
- Transparency of contractual relations and all business processes, full legality of company's activities

REFERENCES

Blaskowitz, O., & Herwartz, H. (2011). On economic evaluation of directional forecasts. *International Journal of Forecasting*, *27*(4), 1058–1065. doi:10.1016/j.ijforecast.2010.07.002

Federal State Statistics Service. (n.d.). Retrieved from: http://www.gks.ru/

Hyide, H. K., & Panos, G. A. (2014). Risk tolerance and entrepreneurship. *Journal of Financial Economics*, *111*(1), 200–223. doi:10.1016/j.jfineco.2013.06.001

Kazakova, N., Sokolova, E., Gendon, A., & Dun, I. (2016). Methodological tools for assessing the quality of information in the system of economic security business. *European Journal of Scientific Research*, *1*(13), 677–683.

Kazakova, N. A., Bolvachev, A. I., Gendon, A. L., & Golubeva, G. F. (2016). Monitoring Economic Security in the Region Based on Indicators of Sustainable Development. *Studies on Russian Economic Development*, *27*(6), 650–660. doi:10.1134/S1075700716060058

Kazakova, N. A., Bolvachev, A. I., Gendon, A. L., & Golubeva, G. F. (2017). Value Added Analysis and Trend Forecasting in the Manufacturing Industry in Kaliningrad Oblast. *Studies on Russian Economic Development*, *28*(2), 160–168. doi:10.1134/S107570071702006X

Kazakova, N. A., Gendon, A. L., Khlevnaya, E. A. (2016) Development potential of Russian mining-and-chemical holdings. *GORNYI ZHURNAL,* (7), 89–91. doi:10.17580/gzh.2016.07.19

Kazakova, N.A., Ivanova, A.N. (2016). Diagnostika i kontrol finansovoy bezopasnosti kompanii: upravlencheskiy aspekt [Diagnostics and control of financial security of the company: management aspect]. *Management Accounting,* (5), 20-32.

Kazakova, N. A., Khlevnaya, E. A., & Zinovieva, A. A. (2016). Aktualnyye problemy kontrolya finansovoy bezopasnosti kompanii [Actual problems of financial control of the company]. *Financial Management*, (2): 3–12.

Kazakova, N.A., Kisnichyan, M.B., Sivkova, A.E., Kazakov, A.Yu. (2015). Uchet, analiz i otsenka riskov predprinimatelskoy deyatelnosti na rynke lizingovykh uslug [Accounting, analysis and assessment of risks of entrepreneurial activity in the market of leasing services]. *Leasing,* (4), 53-61.

Report to the nations on occupational fraud and abuse official website (ACFE) (2016). Retrieved from http://www.acfe.com/rttn.aspx

Ronis, S. R. (2011). Economic Security. Neglected Dimension of National Security? National Strategic Studies by National Defense University.

Sedova, N.V., Kazakova, N. A, Gendon, A. L., Khlevnaya, E. A. (2017). Prediction of development in the mining and chemical industry in Russia and in the world. *Gornyi Zhurnal,* (4), 49–52. doi:10.17580/gzh.2017.04.09

Sivkova, A. E. (2016). Metodicheskoye obespecheniye i instrumentariy diagnostiki veroyatnosti bankrotstva v kompanii [Methodical support and tools for diagnosing the probability of bankruptcy in the company]. *Financial Management*, (3): 31–38.

Statistics on the judicial practice of the RF Arbitration Courts in bankruptcy cases. (2015). Retrieved from http://sudact.ru/arbitral/stats/?law_stat_category=sRE7Jt1f1fV8&datefrom=01.01.2015&workflow_stage=DKnC6cEIq7Vv&date_to=20.11.2015

KEY TERMS AND DEFINITIONS

Current Ratio: Shows company's ability to meet current obligations from liquid assets.

Financial Security: Is level of the financial environment of a company, in which it has the ability to function effectively in accordance with the goals set by business owners, to react promptly and adequately to changes in the internal and external environment, and to adapt to them without losing autonomy and reducing efficiency.

Fraud: Means the theft of someone's property or acquisition of the right to someone's property by misconception or abuse by trust.

Leverage Ratio: Shows the balance of resources provided by creditors and the resources provided by owners, and it is also the most important indicator for analyzing the financial situation of a company.

Security of a Business Entity: Is determined by the level of maintained stability of the state and financial stability of a company, by the adequacy of funds for operations, by financial and investment activities and the balance of cash flows, and finally by the sufficient level of independence from business partners and other counterparties.

The Principle of Complexity: Is supposed to ensure the security of personnel, of company's assets, information bases and confidentiality of information from all types of threats. This is achieved through the personnel selection policy, technical security strengthening and information protection tools.

The Principles of Timeliness and Continuity: Assume the existence of a system for constant monitoring of the current and future state of the company which is ensured by constant analysis and forecasting of security threats to the company as well as development of effective protection measures.

Chapter 7
Financing at the Housing Market:
Analysis of Best Practices in the Selected Countries

Ermilova Mariia
Plekhanov Russian University of Economics, Russia

ABSTRACT

Instruments of financing at the housing market allow increasing the efficiency of branch operation, accumulating more money resources, and redistributing them among the segments of this market. The chapter is based on the analysis of the housing markets' functioning in different countries, taking into account the possibilities of their financing. Recommendations have been formulated on the use of the foreign countries' experience in Russian practice in order to improve the efficiency of financing for the housing market in Russia. It is determined that the main instrument of financing at the majority of national housing markets is mortgage lending. The author has analyzed single-level and two-level models of mortgage lending to determine the advantages and disadvantages each of them has. In the German model, such a mechanism is implemented as a system of "building saving," which involves gradual accumulation of the initial contribution.

INTRODUCTION

At present, housing market plays an important role for any state and its population. An important task for the state is not only to develop the housing market in the whole country, but also to provide citizens with affordable housing by means of using various financing instruments. The main problem is the choice of the most optimal financing instrument from the citizens' standpoint. In this regard, it is important to analyze experiences of different countries with the aim of identifying the most successful practices that can be adapted to less efficient housing markets. The above confirms that the topic of this study is relevant for many countries worldwide.

The object of the study is the process of financing at the housing market.

DOI: 10.4018/978-1-5225-7760-7.ch007

The purpose of the study is to formulate an approach to determining the financing at the housing market, as well as to identify, on the basis of foreign experience analysis, the tools that can be adapted in Russian practice.

To achieve this goal, it is necessary to solve the following tasks:

- To analyze the theoretical basis of the housing market financing with the goal of formulating one's own vision;
- To review foreign experience and identify the key trends;
- To determine the list of instruments appropriate for housing market financing.

The following hypotheses have been put forward in this regard:

- Development of housing markets depends on the possibilities of its financing;
- Foreign markets use mainly mortgage lending to finance the residential real estate market;
- An important role in the development and financing of the housing market is played by the state;
- Adapting the foreign experience of implementing various financing mechanisms will increase the availability of housing options for Russian population.

LITERATURE REVIEW

Analysis of housing markets in terms of their tools and financing mechanisms has attracted the attention of quite a wide range of both Russian and foreign researchers.

Klevtsov V.V. under the housing market understands the aggregate of national, municipal and local housing markets, related to each other via socioeconomic, political, cultural integration and unification; socioeconomic and political relations that mediate production, distribution, exchange and consumption of residential property with the appropriate financial and credit support.

In the opinion of Lazarova L.B and Murieva M.V. (2012) housing market is a complex system of interacting markets. Housing market, above all, is connected with the financial market, which includes the money market, the foreign exchange market, the capital market, the securities market and the credit market.

From the viewpoint of Sazhin Yu.V. and Inchina T.V. (2010) housing market is a complex system of interacting markets: housing land market, financial housing market, construction housing market, and also, there are primary and secondary housing markets.

Reed and Wu (2010) consider the model of real estate market development to be based on the implementation of the principle of cyclicity and risk factor accounting.

Features of financial analysis for the real estate investment were reviewed by William J. Poorvu (2003). The following assumptions were made that complicate the process of financial analysis with respect to real estate investment: an excessively long planning horizon, the impact of ever-changing environment, and also liquidity problems. In this regard, we can distinguish the following elements of the analysis:

- Cash flow,
- Tax effect, and;
- Future benefits.

Researchers (Lin, 2012) have constructed the dependence of the main participants of the housing market on the key parameters (for example, interest rate, money supply, GDP, number of applications for mortgages, rental costs etc.).

The author (Hornstein, 2009) examined the impact from innovative methods of financing on the mortgage market, the development of which both directly and indirectly affects the GDP growth. The author emphasizes that increasing incomes of population do not require expanding the range of innovative financial services, but an increase in the return on investment in real estate in the future.

Klevtsov V.V. (2012) considered mortgage as an instrument of housing finance, paying attention to some of the foreign practices in this regard, however, he did not focus on analyzing the factors that influence the development of housing markets, one of which is the interest rate on mortgage.

Korosteleva T.S. (2013) paid great attention to the tools used for financing at the housing markets, in particular, mortgage bonds, which are especially widely spread in the United States.

Analysis of the US housing market and assessment of the probability of mortgage delinquency or its non-payment depending on the use of insurance instruments is considered in the works of American researchers Park K. (2016) and Moss J. (2017).

Udland M. (2016) reveals the problems of the US housing market, such as high demand and low supply, the impact of crisis consequences in connection with a burst mortgage bubble.

McCord M., McGreal S., Berry J., Haran M. and Davis P. (2011) revealed the relationship between mortgage lending and housing affordability. These authors defined mortgage as the main source of financing at the housing market.

Mortgage models, their advantages and disadvantages are considered in the works of Poorvu, W.J. (2003), Wyman O. (2005).

Basten C. and Koch C. (2015) considered the influence of various factors on the demand and supply of mortgage lending in Europe.

Shim I., Bogdanova V., Shek J, and A. Subelyte (2013) considered mortgage rates as a factor influencing the development of the housing market. These authors proposed a combination of measures to provide mortgages and regulate the market at the same time. This kind of work has never been carried out in Russian context, although this is essential for further development of the national mortgage system.

Also, none of the mentioned authors (or other authors known to us) have formulated an approach to the definition of the concept of "housing market financing" and they also paid insufficient attention to the possibilities of adapting foreign experience to current Russian conditions, taking into account the latest trends.

METHODOLOGY OF THE STUDY

In recent years, Russian housing market has gone through different states, from a sharp rise straight before the crisis and to the drastic fall after the crisis. Today's Russian housing market needs state support, which will help solve many social problems and develop the economy as a whole. And it is important to note here that state support is needed and provided accordingly not only in the case of Russian Federation, but in a number of foreign countries too.

The key problems of the housing market are insufficiently solvent demand of the population, low per capita income, especially within those social groups that are in actual need of purchasing housing, high interest rates on loans, underdeveloped legislation, strained relations between state executive authorities and active developers, insufficient volumes of housing construction in certain regions, particularly in rural areas, shortage of borrowed and attracted financial resources and other factors. Some problems have been manifested already at the stage of the housing market formation. This especially concerns lack of clear approaches to its organization and functioning, as well as absence of exact definitions, confusion between them.

In general, housing market research has shown that one of the main indicators that influences the development of housing markets is GDP. If we draw a parallel between GDP growth and development, we can see that the countries where GDP is growing, housing markets are developing quite intensively too.

The first studies related to the analysis of the residential real estate market as an independent element of the economic system appeared during the 1960s. These initial studies were very much narrow-profile and were mainly focused on studying the housing market in general and its interaction with other subjects of national economic systems. Later, the relationship between the residential real estate market and the world economic system was considered in more detail.

One of the main categories of the housing market is housing itself, which, firstly, is understood as a benefit that meets the needs of people and preserves their life and health. Secondly, housing can be perceived as an investment tool, that is, its purchase is carried out in order to subsequently obtain material benefits from all further operations with it. Thus, housing becomes a financial and an investment asset.

Housing as an investment asset has become widespread in European countries in the middle of the XVII century, during the construction of multi-apartment rental houses, and then in the XIX century, with the construction of apartment houses, leasing spaces within which became a common practice.

During the period of the USSR, such types of housing as communal homes, cooperatives with shared participation, low-rise buildings, sectional houses, and hotel-type houses became widespread. In those times housing served as a benefit that met the population needs, and as an investment asset.

Two approaches to understanding the essence of housing are mostly frequently used in contemporary conditions, as real estate property is perceived by population and as a blessing that satisfies the needs of citizens and as an investment asset (for obtaining additional income further).

Approaches to understanding the term "housing" are also specified in national legislation.

So, in Russian legislation the concept of housing is reflected in the Housing Code of the Russian Federation, first of all. A dwelling is an isolated premise, which is real estate and is suitable for permanent residence of citizens. Thus, living quarters include a dwelling house or a part of it, an apartment or a part thereof, a room. Each of these definitions is specifically mentioned in the Code.

Based on the presented analysis of approaches to the definition of the concept "housing" it seems possible to formulate the author's own interpretation of it: housing is a benefit that is acquired as a property or is a rented property in order to meet the needs of population for a permanent or temporary place of residence and also as a financial asset that allows one receive additional income in the form of rent payments or the difference between the purchase price and the sale of the existing facility.

The concept of residential real estate market basically defines it as a segment of the real estate market. However, taking into account the specifics of development and importance for the population of the country and for the state, a much more detailed interpretation of its contents would be needed. For this this, it is necessary to analyze the points of view that already exist in this regard.

Having analyzed the existing definitions of the housing market, from the author's point of view, it is expedient to single out a number of approaches to the disclosure of its essence (Table 1).

Table 1. Author's approaches to understanding the essence of "residential real estate market"

Approach	Specification
Territorial	Residential real estate market is a set of global, national, regional and local housing markets that are closely interrelated and affecting one another.
Investment (financial)	Residential real estate market is the sphere of formation of demand and supply on the side of potential investors, which allows them receive a permanent or temporary income from the transactions with housing.
Economic	Residential real estate market is a sphere of economic relations between the participants in an economic system, related to the formation of their demand and supply, and their mutual satisfaction through the implementation of transactions with residential real estate under the current legislation.

(Developed by the author)

The results of our research show that housing market can be considered as an object of financing. At present, this concept is not described sufficiently in scientific literature, despite the importance of this term for solving certain tasks in the sphere of housing construction, which are connected, among other things, with providing citizens with affordable housing.

Housing market, from the author's point of view, can be considered as an object of financing, which is the sphere of economic relations between business entities in the process of their implementation of financing the construction, modernization or purchase of residential real estate, which allows each of its participants receive benefits, expressed either in the amount of rent payments, or in the form of difference between the cost of housing construction and the price of its sale or the difference between the price of buying and that of selling residential real estate.

The foregoing predetermines the housing market of a certain subject and object composition.

Subjects of the housing market are legal entities and individuals, directly or indirectly involved in the transactions related to residential real estate. Market entities are construction organizations, contractors, sellers, buyers, tenants, equity holders, state organizations, banks, other financial organizations, professional stock market participants, insurers, management companies etc.

Objects of the housing market include residential areas built on the own funds of developers, investors and co-investors, and also credit resources intended for temporary or permanent residence of owners or tenants.

Thus, the subject-object composition of the residential real estate market also indicates that this market can be treated as an object of financing.

Further, it is necessary to consider the concept of the form of housing financing.

Under the form (model) of housing financing we understand here the totality of organizational, functional, legal and financial-economic mechanisms operating in a single system according to a certain pattern of relationships between subjects of the housing market.

The following forms of housing finance are distinguished by economists:

- Housing finance,
- Financing of housing construction, including state (municipal) rental, and;
- State support in providing housing for families with low incomes.

The author (Bardasova, 2007), in the process of analyzing the experience of financing housing construction through lending, has structured all forms in the model, according to the refinancing mechanism within them and the sources of financing, namely:

- Shared construction and sale of housing in installments,
- Provision of employee loans for acquisition of housing by enterprises,
- Housing certificates,
- Municipal housing bonds,
- Regional schemes (programs) using resources of regional and local budgets,
- Bank crediting,
- Savings scheme and consumer unions, and;
- A classical two-level model (developed in Moscow and St. Petersburg).

Each of these variants has its advantages and disadvantages, as well as a number of accompanying problems. For example, with equity participation, the related problems are the risks of unfinished construction, inaccessibility of high effective demand, the need to attract credit resources, inaccessibility of real estate purchases for the population with low incomes, and finally low level of insurance coverage.

Regional programs using budgetary funds are implemented only in those regions where budgets have sufficient financial resources. Advantage is availability of state guarantees for low-income families, their reliability; however, these opportunities are rather limited in numbers due to funding limitations.

The housing financing mechanism has not received sufficient distribution in Russia, but it is quite widely spread in European countries.

Lending to population by organizations is an option only when the latter are profitable enough and financially sustainable, which means they have sufficient resources for this act and are ready to provide their employees with such an opportunity. However, there is no way this option can be applicable to all employees, no matter how successful a certain company/enterprise is.

Bank mortgage should become one of the most important and large-scale instruments to be used in the course of the housing market development. However, in Russia, notwithstanding some decline, interest rates are still rather high, and this fact alone does not allow the development of such type of lending. The major constraint to the development of the mortgage model is its inaccessibility to a larger share of population.

The loan and savings model is not widely spread due to lack of confidence in savings and loan funds, high inflation rate, lack of state support and state guarantees for this form of housing financing.

Mortgage loan schemes are currently the main market instruments for residential real estate in most of the countries worldwide. For example, various subjects at the Russian housing market - banks, developers, realtors, insurance organizations and others - are consistently considering housing mortgage lending as a new promising business. In particular, in Russia, this is also justified by the fact that the Strategy for the Development of Housing Mortgage Lending in the Russian Federation until 2020 indicates that the share of borrowers in the field of mortgage lending with the intention to purchase real estate should increase up to 30%. However, at present the Strategy has lost its effect, and thus the related development programs are supposed to be supported through the implementation of the priority project under the title "Mortgage and rental housing".

Thus, one of the main sources of financing at the Russian residential real estate market is mortgage lending and in the future it most probably would increase its share in the total lending in Russia. Available mortgages at the same time are one of the most difficult tasks for the Russian state. Unlike many other countries, mortgage lending is a rather expensive tool for financing for the Russian residential real estate segment. Therefore, today's state policy is aimed at solving this problem and steps are being taken to solve it (including federal and regional programs of affordable mortgages, interest rate subsidies etc.).

Due to the fact that in other countries housing markets are more developed and mortgage as a financing option is more accessible to wider population, it would be expedient to analyze the experiences of these countries along with the potential variants of its adaptation to the Russian economy context.

HOUSING MARKET MODELS

Problems and trends of the housing markets' development have been in the center of interest for various analytical agencies, exploring the development experience of these markets on the examples of major cities, such as London, UK (Report, 2016).

Housing is one of the key priorities for the UK government today. At the same time, housing is becoming less affordable for many people in the recent years.

As part of its housing policy, the UK government has two goals: to stimulate housing in the next five years and to increase the share of owned housing.

The total amount of public housing costs in England was about 28 billion pounds in 2015-2016.

The Home Building Fund is expected to be more than 3 billion pounds sterling until 2020-2021 and it provides a combination of short-term and long-term loans for development and infrastructure. From this fund, £ 1 billion will be assigned for small and mid-sized construction companies, which means that the government plans to increase the volumes of ongoing construction to 25,500 new homes by 2020. The remaining £ 2 billion is intended as long-term financing for infrastructure.

The problem of housing affordability is also relevant for Finland, despite quite high level of welfare in this country. The volume of transactions related to the housing sector in 2017 remained high. However, in the first quarter of 2017, the average transaction size was relatively low, leaving the total volume clearly lower than the same indicator back in 2016. Significant investment demand has reduced profitability, which has reached record low levels.

In the recent years, the most active groups of investors at the housing market have been companies and funds, as well as foreign investors. All these groups of stakeholders have increased their portfolios and funds. As the overall size of the housing market continues to grow, the share of institutional investors at this market continues to drop.

The analysis of prices at the housing markets of Europe revealed the following trends:

- The highest prices per square meter can be observed in the UK, France, Israel and Ireland. In Israel and Ireland in 2015 there was a significant increase in prices.
- The economies of Central and Eastern Europe are not demonstrating sufficiently high rates of growth so that to maintain the growth of their real estate markets. Russia demonstrates the lowest prices for housing among all the analyzed countries, with a price well below 1000 euro / square meter.

- Czech Republic has the highest prices among the abovementioned states, 1920 euro / square meter. As compared with the previous years, price levels in this country are slowly approaching the rates of Western Europe.
- Prices in Spain and Portugal are associated with a decline in these economies during the several recent years, same as in some countries of Central and Eastern Europe.
- Property prices rose at most markets in 2015. Out of 12 major cities in Europe, only 3 demonstrated prices' decrease as compared to the 2014 level.

Prices have been steadily increasing in Lisbon, London, Dublin and Jerusalem.

- The best market in 2015 was Lisbon, it demonstrated a truly astounding growth (+ 33%), noteworthy, a year before that, the same market had demonstrated a significant decrease (-14%).
- London took the second place (+29%), while Dublin was the third (+21%). The fourth place was occupied by Jerusalem (+13%), its strong ranking was partially caused by the strengthening of local currency against the euro.

Housing loans are correlated with housing prices. Increase in housing loans in general supports the growth of prices for residential real estate.

As a result, indebtedness of households (the share of housing debt to household income) and, consequently, their debt burden is one of the determining factors in the growth of house prices.

The lowest level of household debt can be observed in Russia, about 4.9% of housing debt to disposable household income.

The group of countries with low indebtedness also includes Slovenia, Hungary, Czech Republic, Israel, Italy, Poland and Austria, with a debt roughly equal to the borrower's income - less than 50%.

The highest level of debt is observed in the Netherlands, the United Kingdom and Ireland, in all three countries debt reaching 100% of the borrowers' income.

The highest level of debt can be observed in the Netherlands, the United Kingdom and Ireland with a debt equal to above 100%.

It should be noted that the main tool for financing at foreign housing markets is mortgage, which is used to finance, purchase, build and redevelop both residential and industrial premises.

At the same time, the level of interest rates in mortgage lending differs depending on a country, as are the ways of its establishment. For example, in the last quarter of 2015, a couple from Denmark paid interest on mortgages at a negative rate of -0.0562%. It should be taken into account that in Europe, floating rates are calculated on the basis of the Euribor (Euro Interbank Offered Rate), to which each bank adds its own margin (1.5-2.0%). The European Interbank Offered Rate is the average interest rate for interbank loans that are issued in euros. This rate is determined on the basis of data provided by credit institutions of the EU countries, the Association of Financial Markets, as well as Norway and Iceland. It is calculated for different terms (from one week to 12 months) by the European Banking Federation. Every working day, credit institutions whose indicators are taken into account send rates to their pages to the Reuters agency, which at 11:00 CET expects a new EURIBOR value and then publishes it. The calculation does not take into account 15% of the highest and lowest interest rates, the remaining values are calculated by the arithmetic mean and rounded to three decimal places. As the Euribor constantly fluctuates, buyers who take loans with floating interest rates also take certain risks.

In some European countries, such as Germany, fixed-rate loans are more common. A buyer who pays a loan for 15 years at a rate of 1.9% a year in Germany today, can be sure that in 10 years he will pay the same interest rate. In the case of cheapening of the borrowed capital cost, there is an option to refinance the debt.

In some cases, floating rates may be lower than fixed ones, thus attracting borrowers with a higher level of risk. For example, fixed interest rates in Denmark are far from negative. In fact, on average they are about 3% per year.

Thus, in European countries, mortgage rates are at a rather low level. At the same time, in countries that were formerly part of the USSR, they are high and outstrip growth not only in Europe but also in Russia.

Quite interesting from the point of view of analysis is the Canadian residential real estate market. Regulation of the housing market in Canada is initially subject to regulation by the standards and requirements reflected in the National Housing Act (1938). The financial component of this Act currently concerns the formation of the State Fund for Financing, which is supposed to provide support to the development of the residential real estate market (Table 3).

These tables show that in Canada, serious attention is paid to the development of the housing market and providing citizens with affordable housing options. However, for a number of positions a decline in indicators is observed by the end of 2015. As in many other countries, mortgage mechanisms are in demand at Canadian market (see Table 4).

Table 2. Average mortgage rates in European countries, %

1.	Belarus	21.44	22.	United Kingdom	3.27
2.	Ukraine	21.25	23.	Italy	2.92
3.	Moldova	13.26	24.	Portugal	2.90
4.	Russian Federation	12.71	25.	Latvia	2.82
5.	Montenegro	8.25	26.	Netherlands	2.63
6.	Macedonia	6.73	27.	Norway	2.55
7.	Bosnia and Herzegovina	6.57	28.	Belgium	2.47
8.	Iceland	6.55	29.	Denmark	2.37
9.	Albania	6.55	30.	Spain	2.33
10.	Hungary	6.11	31.	Estonia	2.25
11.	Kosovo	6.06	32.	France	2.21
12.	Croatia	5.36	33.	Austria	2.06
13	Cyprus	5.00	34.	Lithuania	2.03
14.	Bulgaria	4.98	35.	Slovakia	2.01
15.	Serbia	4.48	36.	Germany	2.01
16.	Greece	4.38	37.	Czech Republic	1.99
17.	Ireland	3.83	38.	Luxembourg	1.94
18.	Poland	3.76	39.	Sweden	1.87
19.	Malta	3.65	40.	Finland	1.51
20.	Slovenia	3.53	41.	Switzerland	1.43
21.	Romania	3.30			

(www.numbeo.com)

Table 3. Contents of the program of state regulation of the real estate market in Canada

Name of the Programs of Target Financing, mln USD	2011	2012	2013	2014	2015
Renovation of housing	54.3	37.6	14.9	17.1	14.1
Financing of the programs on the housing market development	3.2	4.1	3.6	3.9	3.7
Direct financing of the real estate acquisition	1.2	0.7	2.4	0.9	0.9
Assembly	499.5	-	-	-	-
Land-use infrastructure development programs at the municipal level	93.4	226.9	189.2	88.2	103.1
Total:	651.6	269.3	210.1	110.1	121.8

Data in this table clearly shows that demand for mortgages in Canada has been increasing annually, which is largely due to the lending conditions being acceptable to the larger share of the country's population.

In general, we can conclude that mortgage is in demand in many countries. Its attractiveness for borrowers and also other participants of the real estate market depends on the mortgage model and the instruments being used in the course of mortgage.

Socioeconomic development of individual countries (specificity of their legislation, mechanisms used for mortgage implementation etc.) has to a greater extent determined the features inherent in today's mortgage systems. Thus, it would be feasible to explain additionally the differences in legal regulation of mortgage in the countries of civil and common law, since these differences have predetermined the formation of a set of approaches to formalizing the relationship between the parties of a mortgage contract. These approaches are usually divided as follows:

1. Mortgage systems are similar in all the countries of continental Western Europe (except Denmark). All these countries apply the notarized certification of acts, registration in the land register, publication of information on mortgage transactions and other significant formalities. It is important to note that Russia has also introduced mandatory notarization of such transactions.

Table 4. Volumes of mortgage lending by financial and credit institutions for the period of 2010-2015, mln USD (National Housing Act)

Year	Life Insurance Companies	Certified Banks	Trust-Mortgage Companies	Credit Unions	Corporations (Securitization of Mortgage Obligations)	Companies (Securities Secured by a Pool of Mortgages)	Other Financial Companies	Pension Funds	Total Amount of Mortgage Loans Issued to the Population
2010	14360	479184	11120	121902	13808	302647	29045	14361	985305
2011	14730	580789	35047	131580	11971	232749	38051	13360	1057358
2012	14958	840337	35304	139926	9728	35572	40137	12703	1128811
2013	14680	888765	30486	149435	11114	36375	43491	13099	1187441
2014	15092	931830	24757	161020	10380	42132	48685	13210	1246890
2015	15750	978037	24903	171238	10061	51701	52888	14038	1318367

2. Mortgage systems are more flexible and less formalized in the countries practicing common law (or the so-called laws of the Anglo-Saxon type). In the mortgage system of this type, it is not necessary to notarize the act, mortgage lending is of a general nature, while the subject of pledge is not clearly defined and there is no publication on the matter.

In the Danish mortgage system, both these approaches are used in combination.

One of the important mortgage systems is American one, in view of the fact that the securities market in this country is substantially developed and many debt obligations are secured by a mortgage. Changes at the stock market strongly affect mortgage lending, and inversely, development of mortgage affects the financial market. This has been confirmed, inter alia, by the global financial crisis, when, in addition to many segments of the market, the mortgage market also collapsed. There is a popular opinion that it was mortgage lending that caused this crisis. However, in our view, it would be more appropriate to state that the global financial crisis was the result of many factors taken together, including debt problems at the US housing market, inter alia.

Specificity of economies' functioning in different countries made it possible to single out the following mortgage models, see Table 5.

Environment surrounding the financial markets has always its impact on building a balanced autonomous model. This is due to the fact that credit funds are accumulated by attracting savings from future borrowers according to the mutual assistance fund principles. This model may become an interesting option for the Russian mortgage system due to the fact that the cost of housing in new buildings in this country today is lower than the prices at the secondary market. Also important is the fact that in Russia the cost of construction is significantly lower than the established cost of housing at the market. It is necessary to take into account that there have already been attempts to create cooperatives in Russia.

However, this practice is poorly developed and requires the construction of a more complex, multilevel system, so that the effectiveness of such structures is maximized. Curiously, this type of financing is not totally new for the country, since in the pre-revolutionary Russia the system of cooperatives was fairly successfully practiced for several decades. Obviously, these historic experiences needs to be studied in detail and might be partially followed, at least as a historic reference.

Table 5. Mortgage lending models in developed countries

#	Model Name	Countries in Which This Model Is Applied	The Essence of the Model
1	Truncated open	UK, Israel, Spain	Mortgage loans are financed from various sources, including, banks' own capital, deposits, interbank loans. The rate is determined by the current economic situation.
2	Expanded open	USA	A credit organization provides a loan to a client, depending on the level of their income and credit history.
3	Balanced autonomous	Germany	Citizens form a cooperative and make contributions for a certain period of time. As soon as half of the value of future residential real estate is accumulated, the cooperative participant acquires the right to purchase housing in the order of its order. The remaining part of the cost is paid within 10 years, after which the residential property becomes their own property.

(Completed by the author)

One of the most popular classifications of mortgage lending systems is the division into single-level and two-level mortgage models.

The choice of this or that model of a mortgage system depends on the features of a particular country's development, the history of its financial system formation and the already practiced system(s) of mortgage lending, in particular. Also important is the process of implementing the procedure for loans' refinancing.

It is commonly believed that the US is implementing a two-level model of the mortgage system, and in European countries a single-level model of mortgage lending is predominantly applied. In Russia, a number of normative legal documents prescribed the development of a two-tier system. However, the existence of building cooperatives and similar structures inherent in a single-level system has predetermined the possibility of stating that a mixed model of the mortgage system is currently being used in Russia.

A two-level model of mortgage lending was formed historically in connection with the need to ensure uniformity and standardization of credit transactions at the national level. The introduction of such measures implied, as a result, an increase in the liquidity of loans and their subsequent refinancing.

A two-level mortgage model assumes that loans of the primary mortgage market are transferred with the participation of the state to open mortgage agencies.

Mortgage agencies have the right from the same mortgage loans to form pools and sell to secondary investors such pools or their shares. The received money can be immediately assigned to secondary investors.

Cash from such transactions can also be directed to the issue and placement of mortgage securities, which determines further development of the stock market and operations with mortgage-backed securities. Such operations ensure constancy of financial flows at the world financial market.

The survey on the effect of the single-tier and two-tier mortgage lending models showed their significant differences, which is mainly due to their historical development.

A retrospective analysis of the development of a two-tier mortgage lending model in the USA has shown that the mortgage lending system was formed over a long period of time as an effective model. However, a slowdown in the development processes was caused by wars and crises. Analysis of the functioning of the US mortgage lending model allows the author to determine a number of milestones in the course of its development.

At the first stage (the 1930s), rather active development of mortgage lending was first observed, then, in the course of the Great Depression, the housing market collapsed and the share of unpaid mortgage loans increased sharply. This made it necessary to take urgent measures on the part of the state, and the measures taken allowed restoring the former position of the system for quite a long term. The next important development step was the creation, back in in 1934, of the Federal Housing Administration, which partly solved the problems associated with mortgage debts.

At the next stage, 1935 to 1981, such large companies as Fannie Mae and Freddie Mac were established, which for many years were the most important financial structures of the American mortgage market, in fact, they became the formers of this market. In the late 1980s a new type of securities was introduced, they were issued by mortgage investment intermediaries, which also further expanded the mortgage market and strengthened its position. However, the crises of 1998 and then of 2008 shook its position dramatically. Especially in 2008, when the mortgage bubble burst and the US mortgage market collapsed.

It should be taken into account that the US experience showed to the whole world that the mortgage lending system, which began to develop actively during the Great Depression, after experiencing serious crises and having passed several stages in its development, moved from a mechanism with strict state regulation to a being self-regulating economic system. It is important that the state supports the mortgage system, which is due to the need to provide citizens with affordable housing. The American system of mortgage lending is one of the fastest recovering and developing models. Despite the 20% drop in house prices during the global financial crisis, American citizens have been impoverished by almost $ 5 trillion (Data: Thomson Reuters). Quite quickly problems with crediting were also felt by reliable borrowers. Thus, the mortgage crisis affected almost 40 percent of the total loans at this market.

Currently, the model of the US mortgage lending is functioning quite effectively again. In 2016, the minimum loan interest rate was observed at the level of 2.81%, as compared to the previous minimum recorded back in May 2013 (2.86% for a 15-year loan; data: usbank.com). This statistics suggests that, despite quite serious consequences of the crisis, the US mortgage market has quickly recovered, which cannot be said of the Russian market, the latter still showing quite high levels of interest rates on mortgages as compared to many other countries.

Next, we would like to analyze a single-level model of mortgage lending, which is being exercised mainly by European countries.

The essence of the European model of mortgage lending is that a bank that provides a mortgage loan independently issues securities of a bond type that are secured, on the one hand, with mortgage loans on real estate that is mortgaged by borrowers to obtain a loan being on the other. Issuance and circulation of mortgages is regulated by special legislation. Issuance of mortgage bonds is possible by the issuer, as it is specified in legislation (mainly banking organizations). Activities of mortgage banks are strictly controlled by the state and banking supervisors.

This model of mortgage lending assumes that the state comprehensively supports participants in the mortgage mechanism, determines the "rules of the game" and ensures that mortgage lending becomes an effective tool for economic development. Analyzing the development of the European model of mortgage, the author would like to outline the following stages.

The XVIII-XIX centuries - formation of the very institution of primary mortgage lending, along with the concept of pledge and guarantees for this type of loan.

At the next stage (1930s - the very end of the XX century) special organizations were emerging to carry out operations on mortgage lending, the secondary market of mortgage lending was set up, including the sector working directly with securities.

The third stage (the end of the 20th century and the beginning of the 21st century) was marked by modernization of the instruments used by the mortgage market and, in general, of all activity at the mortgage market. Further, the global financial crisis predetermined the slowdown in the course of this market development, an increase in interest rates, and also some reduction in the list of programs (for example, in the framework of programs for Russian citizens, some mortgage products in Europe were curtailed or their requirements for potential borrowers were tightened).

By now, we can talk about the post-crisis development of the European model of mortgage lending, gradual restoration of the market, more active lending overall, and in some countries (for example, in Austria) opportunities to subsidize the purchase of residential property by citizens have been increased. Interest rates today range in between 3-8% per annum, depending on the territory and other conditions of a particular mortgage.

A single-level model of mortgage lending is currently in use in Hungary, Germany, Denmark, Poland, Slovakia, France, Czech Republic, and other European countries. In Hungary, Poland, Slovakia and Czech Republic establishment of a single-level mortgage model took place much later than in other countries.

Analysis of the single-level model functioning allowed the author determine its advantages and disadvantages in comparison with the two-level one.

The merits of a single-level mortgage model include:

- Low costs of the model;
- Simplified legal regulation.

At the same time, a two-level model of mortgage lending also has its advantages, which at the same time are the disadvantages of the single-level model:

- Due to the formation of mortgage pools, credit risks that are not covered by insurance and guarantees are distributed among all loans;
- State organizations issue guarantees for certain types of mortgage lending and facilitate the receipt of a preferential mortgage loan by certain categories of citizens;
- State authorities implement a specific policy aimed at stimulation of mortgage lending, through legislative and financial support, provision of insurance and guarantees, both for citizens of the country and for also other subjects of the mortgage lending model. At the same time, the government is developing a system of regulation and control in order to stabilize the functioning of this model;
- The model assumes the possibility of entering the securities market and using more transparent pricing mechanisms, and this, in its turn, predetermines the possibility for the subjects of the mortgage market to assess all related risks more accurately along with the potential benefits from investing in certain mortgage mechanisms.

The most effective single-level mortgage lending system is probably in Germany, where mortgage banks operate having the right to issue pledge sheets only if they have already acquired valuables that can be treated as collateral.

The most common system in Germany is the so-called "building-saving". This system is implemented in several stages. At the initial stage, accumulation of funds is taking place. The investor concludes a contract with the construction savings bank and transfers a certain amount of money. Thus, the system of "building-saving" is independent from both securities market and banking market, that is, from fluctuations in interest rates and the rate of securities. Accumulation is carried out within 5-10 years. As a result, the depositor collects 40-50 percent of the amount, which is prescribed in the contract. A small percentage of the savings deposit is paid, which is significantly lower than the market rate. Further, the depositor in the order of priority is given a mortgage loan, interest rates are much lower than the market rates. Precisely because of low interest rates, the functioning of this "building-saving" system is possible even in the absence of a mass effective demand for mortgage loans.

In addition to general guarantees of the reliability of the mortgage banking and mortgage bonds, which are inherent in a single-tier model, the German system has two additional advantages:

- There is a system of banking supervision that periodically performs random checks;
- The supervisor of banking institutions is appointed as the manager in each mortgage bank.

An essential advantage of the German model is the issuance of a loan of 100% of the value of residential real estate, less often - 98%. However, the loan amount does not exceed 80% of the value of the pledged property, and the interest rate on the loan is 4-7% per annum. The loan rate is fixed during the term of the contract, but may be less than the period provided for the full repayment of the loan. In this situation, at the end of the agreed period, the lender can offer a new rate, and the borrower determines the need for its adoption. It is also necessary to take into account the pledge when obtaining a mortgage.

Attempts to use the "building-saving" model in Russian practice were carried out, but the system is not widely used as of today. This system was implemented via construction cooperatives. Despite a significant reduction in risks and more loyal credit conditions, Russian population is still not too eager to get engaged into the activities of such cooperatives.

Two-level mortgage system has become quite widespread not only in the US, but also in some other countries, including Russia. In recent years, European countries have begun to actively introduce certain elements from this system into their practice. For example, the system of refinancing loans. In Russia, the two-level model has been used to a greater extent, but as noted earlier, the elements of the single-level system are also present.

Insurance mechanism within the system of mortgage lending has also been adapted in many countries. However, its level of effectiveness varies from country to country. The system of guarantees has not received such a spread, despite the fact that it is able to reduce the risks for all the participants of the scheme.

Another trend of the foreign mortgage markets is development of mortgage lending to non-residents. This is another form of financing at the housing market. This type of lending was particularly popular in European countries. For Russian citizens, European real estate is an attractive option, especially taking into account much softer credit conditions.

Thus, a fairly wide range of instruments for housing market financing is being implemented in foreign countries, which allows not only citizens of the country, but also non-residents to purchase residential real estate. As the data in the above tables show, the lending conditions are quite loyal. In comparison with Russia, where interest rates in most cases exceed 10% per annum, mortgages are extremely attractive.

It is important to note the role of the state at the housing markets is significant both in Russia and abroad.

This role is realized through various instruments of monetary policy, participation in lending programs and introduction of legal acts to regulate both the activities of the market itself and its financing.

Active role of the state at the housing market is predetermined primarily by the vision that the development of this market is a strategic task of the state, since allows solving a number of social problems related to provision of affordable housing options and creating comfortable living conditions in the country overall.

In Russia, for example, at the state level, core documents related to financing of the housing market are being developed, including the financing by means of mortgages, development of housing market overall and its rental segment in particular.

Table 6. Mortgage lending conditions in European countries for non-residents

Country	Availability of Mortgages for Russian Citizens	Fixed Rate, %	Floating Rate, %	The Maximum Size of a Mortgage Loan in the Total Cost of Real Estate, %
Austria	Available	From 3,4	From 3,1	Until 60
United Kingdom	Available	From 3,2	From 2,8	Until 70
Germany	Available	From 3,3	From 2,9	Until 60
Greece	Available	From 4,5	From 4,2	Until 60
Spain	Available	From 4,1	From 2,9	Until 70
Italy	Hard to get	From 4,2	From 2,9	Until 70
Cyprus	Available	From 4,0	From 3,9	Until 80
Latvia	Hard to get	From 4,5	From 3,9	Until 60
Portugal	Available	From 3,5	From 2,9	Until 70
Finland	Available	From 3,7	From 3,3	Until 60
France	Available	From 2,9	From 2,3	Until 80
Czech Republic	Hard to get	From 4,5	From 3,9	Until 50
Switzerland	Hard to get	From 2,0	From 1,8	Until 65

(Gordon Rock and Lowell Finance data)

More specifically, at the governmental level, the Strategy for the Development of Housing Mortgage Lending was approved until 2030. However, later changes in the national economy conditions necessitated the introduction of amendments to this document and the strategy was re-approved for some time until 2020, with some changes. To date, this document was cancelled as such.

The federal government today carries out the process of mortgage development, which includes the two-tier model of the system, introducing the refinancing mechanism etc. Instead of the program document mentioned above, the government has approved the program "Mortgage and rental housing". This document grounds the support for not only the mortgage market, but also rental market, inter alia, by stimulating developers to build profitable houses, that is, housing that is commissioned at a cost less than the market average. In return, developers participating in the program receive various preferences from the state, such as tax incentives etc.

CONCLUSION

The conducted research has allowed us to consider in more detail the concept of housing market financing. The author has formulated her own vision on this definition.

The analysis of foreign experience has allowed investigating in detail the models of mortgage lending so that to determine the pros and cons of the one-tier and two-tier mortgage lending models.

The study has shown that the most common tool for financing at the residential property market both abroad and in Russia is mortgage lending. The author analyzed the key trends at the mortgage market and found that it is advisable to use the experience of foreign countries in improving the mortgage lending system in today's Russia. This will improve the efficiency of financing and functioning of the housing market. The author also determined that the state plays a significant role at the housing market overall and in its financing in particular. In this regard, from the author's point of view, it is important to take this into account when modernizing the mechanisms of housing financing, the key instrument of which is, again, mortgage lending.

As a result, the author proposes to consider the possibility of introducing the system of "building-savings" into the Russian practice, similar to the one which has already become quite widespread in a range of European countries. However, in the course of its introduction it would be necessary to take into account the Russian specifics too.

Let us consider how this system can be actually implemented. To begin with, we must note that in Russia the state provides support to young families in the form of maternity capital out payments. Maternity capital is paid by the state to the families after the birth of the second (third and so on) child. This capital is intended to improve the housing conditions of the family or can be later invested in child's education, for example. As of 2018, the volume of maternity capital will be 505 thousand rubles (equivalent to 8.8 ths USD).

The author suggests that these funds can be, inter alia, used under the scheme "building-savings".

Below you can see the implementation mechanism proposed by the author.

Let us consider in more detail the integration scheme proposed by the author here.

1. The depositor (a potential borrower, mother) enters into a contract with some savings, while the cash department opens a special account where money will be accumulated.
    a. At the same time or at a later date, the depositor (mother) submits an application to the Pension Fund, taking into account the fulfillment of the specified terms and conditions for the issuance of maternity capital, so that to apply for this form of financing. The data on the savings account is also transferred to the fund.
2. The lending bank on the basis of the depositor's application opens a savings account. On it, the interest is charged for the amount deposited during the entire storage period. Savings are made before reaching 50% of the total value of the residential property, which the client is planning to purchase.

Figure 1. Integration of maternity capital into the system of "building-savings"
(Author's Development).

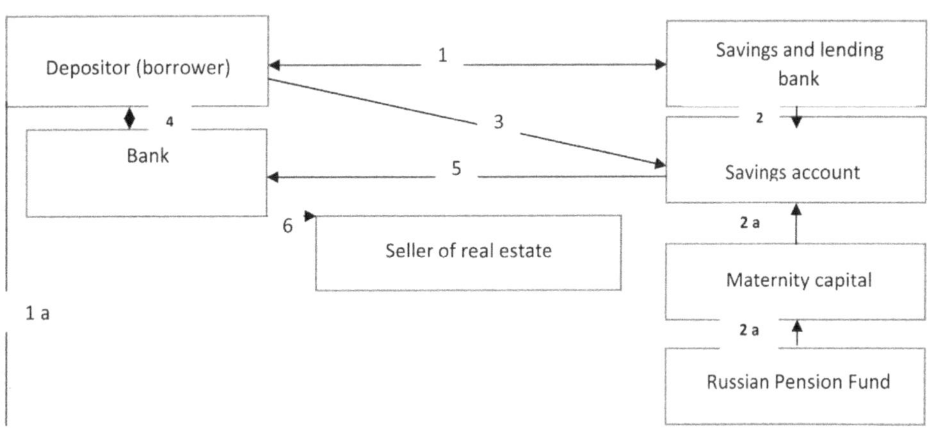

   a. The Pension Fund, after checking all necessary documents, transfers the maternity capital funds to the earlier opened account, indicating also that the beneficiary opted for the variant of housing conditions' improvement. Further, the Pension Fund is supposed to check the targeted use of the funds received (that they were indeed spent on housing, not anything else).
3. The client (borrower, mother) contributes to the special account funds before receiving at least 50% of the cost of the selected housing option. The funds of the maternity capital reduce the accumulation period, and also allow receiving additional income in the form of interest payments on the open account. This makes it possible to increase the rate of housing accessibility in a shorter period of time and, in some cases, this variant become a unique opportunity for young families to obtain own living space with the best characteristics (for example, proximity to the metro station, developed infrastructure, larger space etc.).
4. The depositor (borrower, mother) enters into a mortgage contract as soon as she accumulates at least 50% of the value of the residential real estate. Savings and loan bank and the bank issuing mortgage will act as one, since in Russia in most cases banks are very much universal organizations.
5. Funds together with the maternity capital, that is, in their full amount, are transferred from the savings account to the mortgage account.
6. The full amount of the cost of a chosen housing property, taking into account mortgage lending is transferred to the developer or other person selling residential real estate (the owner).

The presented here mechanism enables raising the efficiency of both mortgage, and Russian housing market overall. It is also potentially to attract the interest of many families who are experiencing housing problems today and thus can potentially become participants of the program. Receiving additional income from such a savings account, as described above will shorten the funds accumulation period.

Summarizing all of the above, we are ready to formulate several conclusions from the study.

Development of housing market, in any country, depends on the possibilities of financing, in the first place. In the course of this study, it was determined that in the world practice the main tool of housing financing, which provides citizens with affordable housing options is mortgage mechanism.

Analysis of foreign housing markets and mortgage variants has proved the attractiveness of mortgage lending and its affordability, in contrast to Russian practice.

Having analyzed the foreign experience in this sector, the author determined advantages and disadvantages of both single-level and two-level models of mortgage lending.

It has been also determined that Russia today is on its way to building a two-level system of residential mortgage, however, elements of the single-level model are also used in the country. Therefore, Russian model of mortgage lending can be called a mixed one.

Our research also revealed that a significant role at the housing market and in its financing in particular is played by the state, which is involved via legal acts and other forms of market regulations, first of all. The state also participates in market development programs, providing financial support to population, specifically to those citizens and families who are wishing to purchase real estate. This support is provided in the form of subsidies and also through subsidizing the interest rate on mortgages. In this regard, when adapting foreign experience to Russian market conditions, it is advisable to take into account the role of the state.

Analysis of foreign practice has also shown that it would be worthwhile to pay more attention, scientific and practical, to the mechanism behind the so-called "building-savings" system and the opportunities of its adaptation to Russian practice.

The author suggests the adaptation of this scheme taking into account the peculiarities of Russian real estate market and the possibilities of using maternity capital out payments as one of the financial sources in the presented scheme, see below.

Implementation of the presented here author's approach will allow increasing the overall efficiency of the housing and mortgage markets, and this, in turn, will increase its attractiveness for population of the Russian Federation.

REFERENCES

Basten, C., & Koch, C. (2015). The causal effect of house prices on mortgage demand and mortgage supply: Evidence from Switzerland. *Journal of Housing Economics*, *30*, 1–22. doi:10.1016/j.jhe.2015.07.001

Database NEWSru.com. (n.d.). Retrieved from http://www.newsru.com

Database Real Estate Market Indications. (n.d.). Retrieved from http://www.irn.ru

Hornstein, A. (2009). Problems for a fundamental theory on house price. *Economic Quarterly*, *95*(1), 1–24.

Information Agency Database "Interfax". (n.d.). Retrieved from www.interfax.ru

Klevtsov, V. (2012). *The mechanism of housing finance: theory, methodology, practice*. Moscow: MUESI.

Korosteleva, T. (2013). Problems and prospects of the development of the mortgage lending system. *Financial Analytics: Problems and Solutions, 11*(149), 32-38.

Lazarova, L., & Murieva, M. (2012). Russian Housing Market: Problems and Prospects for Development. *Russian Entrepreneurship*, *11*(209), 114–118.

Lin, R. F.-Y. (2012). A comparative framework for commercial and residential markets. London: University College London (UCL).

Matyukhin, G. (2008). Difficult way of mortgage lending. *Banking*, *3*, 34–39.

McCord, M., McGreal, S., Berry, J., Haras, M. & Davis, P. (2011). The implications of mortgage finance on housing market affordability. *International Journal of Housing Markets and Analysis*, *4*(4), 394-417.

Moss, J. (2017). *The similarities and differences between the US housing market in 2017*. internationalbanker.com.

Park, K. (2016). FHA loan performance and adverse selection in mortgage insurance. *Journal of Housing Economics*, *34*, 82–97. doi:10.1016/j.jhe.2016.07.004

Poorvu, W. J. (2003). *Financial analysis of real property investments*. Harvard Business School.

Reed, R., & Wu, H. (2010). Understanding property cycles in a residential market. *Property Management*, *28*(1), 33–46.

Report of UK. (2016). *Property Data Report 2016. Facts and figures about the UK commercial property industry to year-end 2015*. A publication by the Property Industry Alliance. Retrieved from http://www.bpf.org.uk/sites/default/files/resources/PIA-Property-Report-2016-final-for-web.pdf

Sazhin, Y., & Inchina, T. (2010). *Housing market management system*. Retrieved from http://www.sisupr.mrsu.ru/2010-1/pdf/sajin_2.pdf

Sergeev, D. (2008). System of mass mortgage lending in the Russian Federation: Adaptation of the world market. *Securities market*, *4*(235), 28–30.

Udland, M. (2016). *The US housing market has a major supply problem*. Business Insider. Retrieved from amp.businessinsider.com

Zhurkina, N. (2007). Modern mortgage: State, problems, solutions. *Finance*, *6*, 17.

KEY TERMS AND DEFINITIONS

Form (Model) of Housing Finance: The totality of organizational, functional, legal, and financial-economic mechanisms within the same system, functioning according to a certain pattern of relationships between the subjects of the housing market.

Housing: Benefit that is acquired as a property or as a rental property in order to meet the needs of population for a permanent or temporary place of residence and also as a financial asset that allows receiving additional income in the form of rent payments or as a difference between the price at the time of a purchase and that at the time of its resale.

Housing Market as an Object for Financing: The sphere of economic relations between business entities in the course of financing the construction, modernization or purchase of residential real estate, which allows each of the concerned participants to receive a certain benefit, expressed either in the amount of rent payments, or in the form of a difference between the cost of housing construction and the price of its sale or the difference between the price of buying and selling residential real estate (or its share) by the owner.

Single-Level Mortgage Model: Mortgage independently issues securities of a bond type that are secured, on the one hand, with mortgage loans, and, on the other, real estate is mortgaged by borrowers to obtain a loan. Issuance and circulation of mortgages is regulated by special legislation. Issuance of mortgage bonds is possible by the issuer, mentioned in the related legislation (these are mainly banking organizations). Activities of mortgage banks are strictly controlled by the state and banking supervisors.

Two-Level Mortgage Model: Loans at the primary mortgage market are transferred with the participation of the state to open mortgage agencies.

Chapter 8
Scoring Modeling in Estimating the Financial Condition of Russian Agro-Industrial Companies

Oleg Y. Patlasov
Omsk Regional Institute, Russia

Olga K. Mzhelskaya
Omsk Humanitarian Academy, Russia

ABSTRACT

The chapter presents the authors' estimations according to the scoring modeling techniques; also, internationally spread models of bankruptcy forecasting are systematized. Advantages and disadvantages of dynamic modelling methods as applied to financial condition assessment are presented here. Methodological problems of financial modelling are explained here in detail. Regression, logit-regression, and discriminant models are built on the basis of data on the Rosselkhozbank and Sberbank of Russia regulations, taking into account the agrarian specifics of organizations and regional specificity of the Omsk region. An attempt has been made to balance the simplicity of calculations and the accuracy of predictions. Graphs, to be used for express analysis, are constructed on the basis of two core financial indicators.

INTRODUCTION

Nowadays managers' tasks include not just optimal combination of production factors, based on the knowledge of production technology and own organizational capabilities, but also on taking into account the current marketing situation, financial analysis and then making the right managerial decisions. Success of entrepreneurship is thus predetermined by natural and technological factors, and also organizational and sociopolitical factors and finally, by the variety of business risks. Contemporary management requires the knowledge of bankruptcy diagnostics, business financial position assessment, its operational prospects, possible actions of creditors, internal opportunities for debt restructuring etc.

DOI: 10.4018/978-1-5225-7760-7.ch008

Depending on the economic analysis objectives, attention can be focused on the following aspect: company's liquidity and debt service indicators, important (for creditors); profitability and equity in their dynamics (for shareholders); labor costs, volume and efficiency of capital expenditures (for labor analysts); accuracy in calculations and payment of taxes (for public authorities' representatives). Arbitration managers should become convinced in the absence of premeditated and fictitious bankruptcy, and for this they should assess company's real net assets, the extent of overdue debts etc., the execution of the already announced court decisions. From the standpoint of managers, financial analysis and managerial accounting are management function; and from the standpoint of competitors' comparative analysis, economic analysis is part of benchmarking.

In the framework of economic analysis, the following forms of comparative analysis have become the most common:

1. Comparative analysis of financial ratios of the given economic subject with the average industry indicators.
2. Comparative analysis of financial indicators with the related data from competing enterprises.
3. Comparative analysis of financial indicators of separate structural units and separate divisions of a legal entity (its responsibility centers).
4. Monitoring of reporting according to the planned and/or regulatory financial indicators.

It is always easier to assess the merits and bottlenecks of any official analysis method in scientific terms, however, in practical terms, it is always not subject to correction because all corrections immediately become the prerogative of the official body that has approved and imposed this method. Complex methods of analysis are indisputably more labor-consuming, but they are necessary for organizations themselves, namely, for their more grounded managerial decision-making, whereas for external users (tax revenue offices, creditors, banks etc.) it is necessary to conduct more punctual analysis according to the already approved and well established methods.

The currently used methods of the organizations' financial condition analysis all have a serious drawback: their conclusions are often based only on the accounting reports' data, thus, they do not take into consideration the current stage of a company's life cycle and/or its potential future situation. For proper managerial decisions, it is advisable to conduct system analysis which includes, in addition to assessing the financial state of an organization, the current state of the external environment and the human factor too. The maximum effect from the conducted diagnostics is achieved when this diagnostics is of complex character, however, such procedures are, of course, much more challenging since they are time- and cost-demanding.

WESTERN BANKRUPTCY DIAGNOSTICS TOOLKIT

Different methods of predicting bankruptcy forecast various types of crises and, accordingly, estimations obtained with their help are also very different. The choice of specific methods is prescribed and adjusted in accordance with the specifics of a particular industry/branch in which the organization operates. As a result, a large number of different models for bankruptcy forecasting have been developed.

Financial analysis models differ depending on the research principles and analysis priorities. The key of them are as follows:

1. Descriptive models. They are based on scientific, theoretical literature mostly and also on the accounting toolkit (vertical and horizontal analyses of financial statements, balances' system construction, analytical coefficients' calculation).
2. Normative models are used mainly for carrying out an internal financial analysis. They are based on the required calculated indicators that are are compared with the recommended (normative) value.
3. Predictive models are used to make forecasts about future financial results and future financial condition of a firm. The models of situational analysis, of dynamic analysis, critical models can be singled out here.

Several groups of bankruptcy forecasting models can be distinguished basing on the characteristics of the used modelling techniques:

- Statistical models;
- Artificial intelligence models, and;
- Theoretical models.

The first two groups of models are characterized as positive ones, because they are focused on the symptoms of bankruptcy and are trying to explain, using inductive arguments, the reasons for some companies to become bankrupt. The last category (normative models) applies deductive argumentation to explain why a certain part of enterprises can become bankrupt.

Statistical models obtained through the use of various statistical methods to classify the problems of bankruptcy forecasting, include:

- Univariate analysis;
- Multiple discriminant analysis;
- Conditional probability analysis;
- The method of expert evaluations;
- Analogy method;
- The method of financial condition estimation, and;
- Survival analysis.

Among the artificial intelligence techniques, which have been successfully applied in bankruptcy forecasting, the following methods can be named:

- Decision tree; classification tree or recursive partitioning algorithm;
- Data mining;
- K-nearest neighbors algorithm, or k-NN;
- Genetic algorithm;
- Neural network;
- Rough sets theory, and;
- Support vector machines.

Recently a number of financial theories have been successfully applied in relation to bankruptcy forecasting problem, in particular:

- Entropy theory;
- Gambler's ruin theory, and;
- Option-priced theory.

Data obtained using various modelling techniques and their prediction accuracy indicate that the main studies in this field are mainly based on the statistical models of bankruptcy forecasting, and this can be explained by the chronology of various modelling technologies' emergence. However, these models show lower forecasting accuracy (84%) as compared to the models of artificial intelligence (88%) and theoretical ones (85%).

The adequacy degree of different types of models is determined by the errors in identifying the tested business entity. The following two types of basic errors are possible: the first type of error occurs when a financially unstable enterprise being on the verge of bankruptcy is defined as a financially secure one. And the second type of errors is connected with the erroneous classification of a financially stable company as a bankrupt organization. In foreign and domestic scientific literature the accuracy of forecasting among different types of models has been compared; high accuracy of the decision tree methods, multiple discriminate analysis, genetic algorithm etc. has been confirmed.

Currently, there are several key approaches to the theory of bankruptcy diagnostics. These methods are based on regression, discriminate factor models put forward by well-known Western economists.

The essence of this approach is to identify the factors significantly affecting financial condition of the company, to determine the type and the extent of its dependence on these factors and also formation of a probabilistic criterion for company bankruptcy.

Among the bankruptcy risk models based on logistic regression are the ones by Altman-Sabato (2007), Joo-Ha-Taehong (2000), Lin- Piesse (2004), Begley-Ming-Watts, Minussi-Soopramanien-Worthington, credit assessment (supervision of loans) model by Chesser (1974) and some others. Among other authors investigating the problems with accounting arrangement under the conditions of insolvency and bankruptcy we need to mention: Anderson H., Van Breda M.F., Caldwell D., Needles B., Reed S.F., Richard J., Hendricksen E.C..

For the prediction of bankruptcies some of the contemporary authors have also used vector machines (for example, Härdle, Lee, Schäfer, & Yeh, 2007) as well as neural networks (Tam, & Kiang, 1992; Altman, Marco, & Varetto, 1994). A number of modelling techniques raise concerns among academia since their financial ratios are calculated using the profit and loss account, and thus they often do not have a normal distribution (Ohlson, 1980; Wilson, & Sharda, 1994). Wei, Li, and Chen (2007) emphasize that LDA, inter alia, can treat the outcomes incorrectly since the covariance matrices of default and active companies are likely to be confusing in interpretation.

Linearly regression variants of LPM-models can give negative or exceeding estimated values for probabilities. Probit and logit models (respectively, with the standard normal and logistic transformation functions) are better in this sense because the transformation is monotonic, its output values are limited to zero and one, and tend to be zero and one on the distribution tails. All of the abovementioned is yet another confirmation that no event can be predicted with absolute certainty, even in the cases when probability is zero or one. Comparing logit methods with MDA, Collins and Green argue that, although the former give less error of the 1st kind, in general, their accuracy in terms of classification is not much better (Collins & Green, 1982).

C. Lennox has shown that in practice logit models allow much more effective bankruptcy risk assessments than MDA can provide theoretically (Lennox, 1999). The use of logit regression implies wide possibilities for carrying out various econometric tests allowing to evaluate the statistical significance of both the model as a whole and its individual forming variables. In contrast to MDA, logit regression allows not only making conclusions concerning the enterprise belonging to potential bankrupts, but also assessing the risk of this company's bankruptcy on a quantitative scale (Postin, Harmon, & Gramlich,1994). In addition, if we divide companies into 2 groups (bankrupt and non-bankrupt), it is necessary to establish the limits of reference to the group of financial stability when we use MDA. Logit models of bankruptcy risk do not require the development of decision-making ranges, and this simplifies results' interpretation: the resulting bankruptcy risk indicators obtained using these models are known to take values from 0 to 1 without ranges of uncertainty, and the conclusion about the degree of bankruptcy probability is made in the dependence from proximity of the calculated value of the final indicator to 0 (the minimum risk) or to 1 (the maximum risk).

Comparisons of neural network and MDA models are useful since we are able to compare a new, more stable method with known models where a priori assumptions about variables are adopted (Baestaens, Van Den Bergh, & Wood,1997). In this regard, we must note the use of neural networks when dealing with the problems of industrial corporations' bankruptcies and financial corporations' bankruptcies. In all such cases, only standard numeric variables reflecting the past state were used as input data, whereas it is preferable to use qualitative variables reflecting information about the future as well.

In contrast to discriminate forecasting models that are concentrating on linear dependence, logit models assume a non-linear dependence of bankruptcy probability from various factors (Ooghe & Balcaen, 2002).

An alternative to multiple discriminate analysis is a model with a discrete dependent variable, the basic principles of such models have been described in the works of D. McFadden, J. Tobin, and C. Gurieruks, W. Green.

The main difference between rating assessment of organizations' financial state and the integral models is that the weight coefficients in the model are obtained through expert analysis or by means of the coefficient value standardization, whereas in alternative integral models of estimation, the weight values of coefficients are obtained using mathematical tools (multiple discriminate analysis, probity regression, logistic regression etc.).

The world-known rating agencies, such as Standard and Poor's, Moody's Investors Service and Fitch Ratings, made a special contribution to the development of the investment attractiveness assessment methods, although in recent years these agencies have lost independence in risk assessments and have become politically biased, especially when it comes to credit ratings' understatement for Russia (in 2014-2015, for example).

Unfortunately, Russian university text books always present only the internationally promoted models, while other models, not that widely known in Russia, are able to show much better analytical capabilities. To these relatively new methods, practically unknown to a wider audience in Russia, belong the models by Keasey-McGuinness (Great Britain), Ooghe-Joos-Devos (Belgium), Meyers and Forgy (Myers, & Forgy, 1986); Cohen and Gilmore (Cohen, & Gilmore, 1990).

Among other related foreign studies it would be appropriate to mention: Edmister (1972); Altman, Sabato (2007); Vallini, Ciampi, and Gordini (2009), Pederzoli and Torricelli (2005).

In both scientific literature and in practical calculations, some attempts have been made to balance the simplicity of calculations and the accuracy of predictions. Insufficient accuracy of linear models has led to the necessity for transition to non-linear ones, while the insufficient predictive ability of two(three)-factor models has led to the necessity to construct 7-9-factor (or even more) models which is obviously associated with complication of calculations. Despite certain advantages demonstrated by the dynamic models, static linear models still have much wider practical application.

In order to strengthen the predictive role of static models, various proposals have been put forward regarding these models' and modeling techniques' transformation. A dynamic approach to the analysis of phenomena and processes in general as well as strategic analysis in particular is based on the concept of "instantaneous dynamics" (Voronin, 1994). According to this approach, the whole process (from its beginning to the very end) is not studied, but only certain moments (instants) of its implementation are. Therefore, the process of objects' changing is viewed as a successive change of their states. It is assumed that each state is the result of a shift from an immediately preceding state, which is primarily expressed quantitatively, since qualitative changes caused by structural shifts are mostly observed during a longer period of time. The paradigm of "instantaneous dynamics" is closely connected with the paradigm of time as a space for events. Within such a time space, there are many instantaneous events, or a sequence of instantaneous non-overlapping events, or a combination of the above mentioned. According to this interpretation, time space is considered to be one-dimensional, separate events are arranged in the order of their implementation in the form of a point or a segment on the time axis oriented "from the past through the present to the future" (the so-called "arrow of time"). For a more specific representation of events, the starting point and the scale of measurement are indicated on the time axis. In such a one-dimensional time space, it is possible to investigate only certain processes of objects' changing, which leads to a break in the links between them, or their totality as a whole, when connections and relationships are invisible. The concept of one-dimensional time is widely used in both natural and social sciences, whenever methodological aims are oriented towards analysis of complex objects and phenomena by means of separation into simple ones, and their subsequent studying separately from each other. With such an approach to the study objects (when only their structure is taken into account or only their structure is changed), all events are placed on a single time axis, so there is no need to revise the concept of one-dimensional time, which is confirmed by new scientific data in the field of natural sciences. At the same time, the one-dimensional time paradigm limits the possibilities for a holistic cognition of socio-economic systems, where the functioning importance belongs not only to individual objects, but also to their joint activities, mutual relations and interactions.

The values of time series represent the trend, cyclical, seasonal and random fluctuations. The method of simple dynamic analysis is used to construct the trend of a time series. Cyclical fluctuations are the ones referring to the trend line for the periods exceeding one year. Sometimes these fluctuations of financial indicators coincide with the business activity cycles: recession, recovery, growth and stagnation. Seasonal fluctuations are understood as periodic changes of the series values over a year, for example, when you grow plants in open ground, the main inflow of cash flows occurs in summer and in autumn. Random deviations are detected by determining the trend, cyclic and seasonal variations for the value of the analyzed indicator. When testing the forecasting model accuracy, a random deviation is taken into account. The method of simple dynamic analysis is based on the assumption that the predicted indicator varies in time proportionally.

Our research shows that official methods applied to analyze the financial state of organizations have a serious drawback - the conclusions are based on accounting data only, while the stage of organization's life cycle is not taken into account, thus, the future state is not predicted either. For crisis management, it is important to conduct system analysis taking into consideration the processes taking place in the business external environment and the human factor role too. Comprehensive methods of analysis are indisputably more labor-intensive, but they allow not only increase the reliability of the results obtained, but also to explore more deeply the hidden causes and consequences of the phenomena studied, and, thus, to improve the efficiency of crisis management for commercial organizations.

As it was noted above, the use of foreign and domestic methods for bankruptcy diagnostics have some drawbacks, in particular, the weight factors used in official methods require adjustments in relation to domestic, regional and sectoral conditions; the existing statistics does not fully reflect the actual situation of successful, average and underperforming enterprises in terms of their dynamics, structure of their equity and borrowed capital, current assets, liquidity etc. The main problem with data here is that it is rather complicated to collect all necessary financial information characterizing the actual financial situation from inside of an organization.

At present, on the one hand, the key problem with bankruptcy forecasting for individual enterprises is the absence of universally recognized effective methods to forecast bankruptcy and solvency of business entities. On the other hand, these techniques are oriented primarily to establish the fact of insolvency when the signs of bankruptcy are already too obvious.

HYPOTHESES AND PROBLEMS

There are a lot of discussions in scientific literature about the accuracy of models. When testing them, one should keep in mind the following useful questions:

1. How is the model result affected by the model's "age"? We will demonstrate that the Altman model of 1968, when compared with his latest models, shows a good result even on the example of Siberian agricultural enterprises.
2. How do the model characteristics influence its results? Let's take discriminant analysis vs logistic regression, for example. Discriminant models usually have a significant proximity due to the eroded boundaries of the integrated indicators' values as well as due to the presence of a "gray zone". Leitinen-Kankaanpaa studies (1999) were dedicated to comparing the accuracy of six alternative forcasting methods results: discriminant analysis, logistic regression, successive division method, survival analysis, decision-making analysis, and neural networks. These studies have come up with the conclusion that the results of one of the latest methods (neural networks) are also effective and accurate, as are the results of discriminant analysis, which was used more than thirty years ago (Laitinen, & Kankaanpaa, 1999).
3. What is the impact of the number of variables and their complexity on the result? In general, 2-3-factor linear models show rather low forecast accuracy; 4-5-factor nonlinear ones are relatively accurate; models with more than 6 factors are already cumbersome in calculations.
4. Is there a fundamental difference between Anglo-Saxon and European models in relation to Russia? In general, the differences between those two are not observed, however, there are some differences in Anglo-Saxon economic law and the continental one; in particular, European models are less focused on the stock quotes' performance.

5. What should be the ratio of financial and non-financial indicators in the model? In the study by Falkenstein, Boral, and Carty (2000), it is emphasized that the relationship between financial performance and the default risk is different for public and non-public companies. Pompe and Bilderbik in their work (Pompe, & Bilderbeek, 2005) note that it is more difficult to predict the bankruptcy probability for new firms than for long-established ones.

RESEARCH METHODOLOGY

Due to the fact that there are no universal methods to assess legal entities' solvency, some of the commercial banks have been developing their own regulations, thus, the conclusions from testing results for the same organization may turn out to be very much different when analyzed using different methodologies. In this regard, combination of models for assessing the legal entities' solvency allows entrepreneurs to have more possibilities to obtain a bank loan.

We have set the task to build a number of models for agroindustrial enterprises of Russia, proceeding from the commercial banks' regulations (namely, specialised banks functioning specifically in and for agriculture), primarily Sberbank of Russia and OJSC Rosselkhozbank.

Thus, in accordance with the Methodology for the Analysis and Assessment of Financial Condition for Borrowers of the OJSC Rosselkhozbank and taking into account their industry-specific features and organizational and legal forms approved by the Resolution of the Management Board of the OJSC Rosselkhozbank *(Protocol # 65 as of 25.11.2004),* the following indicators are used as the criteria for assessing the borrowers' financial condition:

- Financial soundness;
- Liquidity (solvency);
- Financial results (profit, loss),and;
- Cash flow for the term of credit.

As the estimates of the current financial condition, the following three groups of indicators are used:

- **Indicators of Financial Soundness (Independence):** Financial independence ratio; own funds ratio;
- **Liquidity Indicators:** Current liquidity ratio; absolute liquid ratio; quick liquidity ratio (or critical evaluation);
- **Indicators of Business Activity:** Turnover indicators; indicators of cost-efficiency (profitability).

In accordance with this Methodology the ratios are divided into:

- **Mandatory Ratios:** Financial independence ratio (K1), own funds ratio (K2), current liquidity ratio (K3), quick liquidity ratio (or critical evaluation) (K4), indicators of cost-efficiency (profitability) (K5), turnover of current assets (K6);
- **Voluntary Ratios (Used for Assessment if Necessary):** Absolute liquidity ratio, short-term receivables and payables; sufficiency of turnover in the bank.

Financial condition of a borrower is assessed taking into account the score points calculated using mandatory ratios. In accordance with this technique the following condition states can be singled out:

- **Good Financial Condition:** The number of scored points is equal to or more than 53.
- **Average Financial State:** The number of scored points is between 25 to 52 points.
- **Bad Financial Condition:** The number of scored points is less than 25.

Regulation on granting loans to legal entities and individual entrepreneurs by the Sberbank of the Russian Federation and its branches (approved by the Sberbank of Russia 30.06.2006, Protocol #322) concerning the assessment of borrowers' solvency in based on the following three groups of estimates:

1. **Liquidity Ratios:** Absolute liquid ratio (K1), quick liquidity ratio (K2), current liquidity ratio (K3);
2. Own funds ratio (K4);
3. **Turnover and Profitability Indicators:** Current assets turnover, receivables turnover, inventory turnover, profitability of products (profitability of sales) (K5), of enterprise profitability (K6), profitability of investments in this enterprise.

The main estimates are thus the K1, K2, K3, K4, K5 and K6 ratios (see Table 1 for more details). Evaluation of the results of these six ratios' calculation concludes with assigning a category for each of these indicators on the basis of the obtained values' comparison with the established sufficient ones.

In accordance with this methodology, we determine 3 classes of organizations' solvency:

1 Class: Lending is beyond doubt, S = 1.25 or less;
2 Class: Lending requires a balanced approach, S is in the range between 1,25 (exclusive) to 2,35 (inclusive);
3 Class: Lending is associated with an increased level of risks, S is 2.35 or above.

We have set a task to assess the solvency of 408 agroindusrial enterprises of the Omsk region on the basis of their annual accounting reports data for the period of 2003-2005 (369 organisations as of 01.01.2006, and 350 agricultural organizations in 2007). Moreover, the analysis has been carried out

Table 1. Indicators' subdivision into categories depending on their actual values

Ratios	1st Category	2nd Category	3rd Category
K_1	0,1 and higher	0,05-0,1	less than 0,05
K_2	0,8 and higher	0,5-0,8	less than 0,5
K_3	1,5 and higher	1,0-1,5	less than 1,0
K_4			
except trade and leasing companies	0,4 and higher	0,25-0,4	less than 0,25
for trade and leasing companies	0,25 and higher	0,15-0,25	less than 0,15
K_5	0.1 and higher	less than 0,10	unprofitable
K_6	0.06 and higher	less than 0,06	unprofitable

S = 0,05 * Category; K_1 + 0,10 * Category K_2 + 0,40 * Category K_3 + 0,20 * Category K_4 + 0,15 * Category K_5 + 0,10 * Category K_6.

according to the natural and economic zones of the Omsk Region: steppe zone (9 districts, 86 organizations), Southern forest-steppe zone (8 districts, 80 organizations), Northern forest-steppe zone (9 districts, 121 organizations) and Northern zone (6 districts, 82 organizations). Regression equations and graphs have been constructed basing on the analysis results.

AUTHORS' MODELS OF FINANCIAL CONDITION EVALUATION AIMED TO ANALYSE BORROWER'S SOLVENCY

At present, the most significant risk for the Russian banking sector is the credit one. Credit risk means the danger that a debtor will not be able to make interest payments or pay the principal amount of a loan in accordance with the terms specified in the loan agreement. Credit risk also means that payments can be delayed or not paid at all, which, in turn, may lead to the problems with cash flow and adversely affect bank's liquidity. Despite numerous innovations already implemented in the financial services' sector, credit risk is still the main cause of banking problems. More than 80% of the banks' balance sheets content is devoted to this risk management aspect. Taking into consideration some potentially dangerous consequences of credit risk, it is important to conduct a comprehensive analysis of the banks' capacities to assess, administer, monitor, control, implement and repay loans, advances, guarantees and other credit instruments. An overview of credit risk management includes the analysis of banks' policies and practices. This analysis should also determine the adequacy of financial information received from borrower which is by then used by a bank when making the decision to grant a loan.

Regression, logit-regression and discriminant models assessing borrowers' solvency have been built basing on the regulations of commercial banks, mainly, Rosselkhozbank and Sberbank and using the data on 369 agricultural organizations of the Omsk region as our study object. Analysis of the organizations' financial condition, determination of significant factors affecting their solvency level allows credit institutions to determine correctly the lending capacity of a particular organization, and the organization itself, after such an assessment, become more capable to manage these factors so that to increase own opportunity of obtaining a bank loan. This, indirectly, also confirms the practical importance of econometrics and multidimensional statistical research in general.

Rosselkhozbank Methodology

Having applied the data substitution method, we have experimentally determined the boundaries of the credit rating classes in points using the 100-point scale along with the Methodology for calculating financial condition indicators for agricultural producers (RF Government Decree # 52, as of January 30, 2003) as the basis: 1st class - 100 to 42,2 points (exclusive); 2nd class - from 42.2 (inclusive) to 26 points (inclusive); 3rd class - below 26 points (Patlasov, & Vasina, 2008). Indicators of the annual accounting reports data on all the Omsk region agricultural organizations for 2005-2007 have been used for the modelling here. Six basic coefficients were calculated, applying the Rosselkhozbank method.

From the obtained results it can be concluded that the solvency degree and the factors included in the model are closely related (the correlation ratio is equal to 0, 8917), and that the obtained regression equation is rather significant and cannot be the result of random sampling (the coefficient of determination is 0.82, and the calculated value of the Fisher test is higher than the tabulated value) (Table 2).

Table 2. Final results of the regression model estimation for the Omsk region as of 2007.

	Beta	Std. Err.	B	Std .Err.	t(343)	p-Level
Intercept			29,57775	1,384764	21,35942	0,000000
K1	0,685505	0,034189	37,80690	1,885584	20,05050	0,000000
K2	0,061420	0,033320	0,17393	0,094354	1,84336	0,066139
K3	0,233361	0,046195	0,23402	0,046325	5,05165	0,000001
K4	0,012488	0,045083	0,05036	0,181809	0,27700	0,781946
K5	-0,048720	0,033090	-0,23071	0,156694	-1,47237	0,141837
K6	0,036888	0,033157	0,28494	0,256119	1,11251	0,266697

Regression Summary for the Dependent Variable: Var7
R=, 89176679 R^2=, 82689464 Adjusted R^2=, 82036802
F(6,343)=96,052 p<0,0000 Std.Error of estimations: 15,706
Legend: K1 is the financial independence ratio, K2 - own funds' ratio, K3 - current liquidity ratio, K4 - quick liquidity ratio, K5 – profitability ratio, K6 - turnover of current assets ratio.

According to the analysis results, the following regression equations were obtained (Patlasov-Vasina regression model).

In 2007: Omsk region: $B = 29{,}57 + 37{,}80K_1 + 0{,}17K_2 + 0{,}23K_3 + 0{,}05K_4 - 0{,}23K_5 + 0{,}28K_6$ (Patlasov, Vasina, 2009);

Steppe zone: $B = 8{,}91 + 70{,}66K_1 + 1{,}47K_2 + 0{,}37K_3 - 0{,}53K_4 - 0{,}32K_5 + 4{,}91K_6$.

Southern forest-steppe: $B = 19{,}63 + 50{,}11K_1 + 1{,}17K_2 + 0{,}08K_3 + 0{,}61K_4 + 2{,}07K_5 - 6{,}21K_{6.}$

Northern forest-steppe: $B = 33{,}52 + 26{,}04K_1 + 0{,}11K_2 + 0{,}45K_3 - 0{,}30K_4 - 0{,}06K_5 - 1{,}03K_{6.}$

Northern zone: $B = 16{,}71 + 53{,}77K_1 + 1{,}83K_2 + 0{,}28K_3 - 0{,}36K_4 - 0{,}02K_5 + 0{,}19K_{6.}$

The research thus shows that the assessment can be carried out on the basis of two indicators that have the most significant impact on the financial condition of agricultural producers:

- Own funds ratio (K4) with the error probability (p-level) being 0.0000;
- The current liquidity ratio (K3) for which the p-level is also equal to 0.0000.

During the research, the discriminant models assesing borrowers' solvency have been also constructed on the basis of data obtained from Omsk region agricultural enterprises and farms. The Methodology for calculating the indicators of the agricultural producers' financial condition (RF Government Decree # 52, as of January 30, 2003) is also the basis for the discriminant factor model here. This made it possible to classify the research objects into three groups according to their solvency level (financial condition) (see Table 3 for more details).

Thus, the system of equations (the discriminant model) is expressed in the following way:

Omsk Region:

Table 3. Discriminant analysis results for the agroindustrial enterprises of the Omsk region in 2007 According to the Rosselkhozbank Methodology

	Wilks' Lamda	Partial Lamda	F-Remove	p-Level	Toler.	1-Toler. (R-Sqr.)
Var1	0,863778	0,437144	220,1754	0,000000	0,972505	0,027495
Var2	0,392288	0,962546	6,6539	0,001462	0,995686	0,004314
Var3	0,378736	0,996989	0,5163	0,597161	0,538042	0,461958
Var4	0,380443	0,992516	1,2894	0,276761	0,543796	0,456204
Var5	0,385852	0,978601	3,7392	0,024750	0,993623	0,006377
Var6	0,384719	0,981484	3,2260	0,040930	0,994793	0,005207

Discriminate Function Analysis Summary
# of vars in model: 6; Grouping: Var9 (3 grps)
Wilks' Lambda:, 37760 approx. F (12,684)=35,760 p<0,0000

Table 4. Initial data for the equations by groups and for the Omsk region as of 2007

	1	2	3
Intercept	-4,04859	-3,50311	-1,69006
Var1	8,90478	4,14748	-0,87928
Var2	0,00755	-0,07138	-0,01675
Var3	0,00007	-0,00812	0,00334
Var4	0,06836	0,03775	-0,00420
Var5	0,02896	0,12736	0,06012
Var6	-0,01276	-0,15009	-0,01466

Classification Functions for Var9
Sigma-restricted parameterization

$$G_1 = -4{,}05 + 8{,}90K_1 + 0{,}01K_2 + 0{,}001K_3 + 0{,}07K_4 + 0{,}03K_5 - 0{,}01K_6$$

$$G_2 = -3{,}50 + 4{,}15K_1 - 0{,}07K_2 - 0{,}01K_3 + 0{,}04K_4 + 0{,}13K_5 - 0{,}15K_6$$

$$G_3 = -1{,}69 - 0{,}88K_1 - 0{,}02K_2 + 0{,}003K_3 - 0{,}004K_4 + 0{,}06K_5 - 0{,}01K_6$$

Steppe zone:

$$G_1 = -15{,}66 + 40{,}82K_1 - 0{,}39K_2 - 0{,}19K_3 + 0{,}54K_4 - 0{,}19K_5 + 4{,}94K_6$$

$$G_2 = -7{,}98 + 24{,}02K_1 - 0{,}46K_2 - 0{,}15K_3 + 0{,}42K_4 - 0{,}03K_5 + 4{,}09K_6$$

$$G_3 = -3{,}05 + 9{,}83K_1 - 0{,}73K_2 - 0{,}04K_3 + 0{,}10K_4 - 0{,}05K_5 - 0{,}19K_6$$

Southern forest-steppe zone:

$$G_1 = -10{,}75 + 22{,}42K_1 + 0{,}59K_2 + 0{,}004K_3 - 0{,}16K_4 + 2{,}13K_5 - 2{,}99K_6$$

$$G_2 = -4{,}80 + 11{,}04K_1 + 0{,}18K_2 + 0{,}001K_3 - 0{,}12K_4 + 1{,}31K_5 - 1{,}36K_6$$

$$G_3 = -2{,}80 - 1{,}00K_1 + 0{,}19K_2 + 0{,}01K_3 - 0{,}04K_4 + 1{,}32K_5 - 0{,}19K_6$$

Northern forest-steppe zone:

$$G_1 = - 2{,}84 + 4{,}26K_1 + 0{,}03K_2 + 0{,}05K_3 + 0{,}01K_4 + 0{,}54K_5 - 0{,}64K_6$$

$$G_2 = - 3{,}36 + 1{,}56K_1 - 0{,}05K_2 + 0{,}005K_3 + 0{,}01K_4 + 0{,}49K_5 - 0{,}33K_6$$

$$G_3 = - 1{,}72 - 0{,}81K_1 + 0{,}01K_2 + 0{,}01K_3 - 0{,}02K_4 + 0{,}46K_5 - 0{,}25K_6$$

Northern zone:

$$G_1 = - 29{,}26 + 62{,}70K_1 + 1{,}64K_2 - 0{,}10K_3 + 0{,}22K_4 + 1{,}99K_5 + 0{,}06K_6$$

$$G_2 = - 11{,}51 + 21{,}98K_1 + 0{,}51K_2 - 0{,}05K_3 + 0{,}12K_4 + 0{,}69K_5 - 0{,}47K_6$$

$$G_3 = - 5{,}17 + 13{,}12K_1 - 0{,}66K_2 - 0{,}02K_3 + 0{,}07K_4 + 0{,}26K_5 + 0{,}02K_6$$

Modelling Based on the Sberbank Methodology

Applying the data substitution method, we have experimentally determined the boundaries of the solvency classes in points using the 100-point scale, using the methodology for calculating the financial condition indicators for agricultural producers (RF Government Decree #. 52, as of January 30, 2003) as the basis: 1st class - 100 to 69 points, 2nd class - from 69 (not inclusive) to 42 points, 3rd class - below 42 points (not inclusive).

The following regression equations were obtained (Patlasov-Vasina regression model) for the Omsk region as a whole according to the data as of 01.01.2006:

$$B = 32{,}601 + 6{,}36\ K1 + 0{,}77\ K2 + 0{,}38\ K3 + 23{,}\ 95\ K4 + 6{,}70\ K5 + 0{,}26\ K6\ [9],$$

where K1 - the absolute liquid ratio;

K2 - the interim coverage ratio;
K3 - the current liquidity ratio;
K4 - own funds' ratio;
K5 – profit margin;
K6 - enterprise profitability (see Table 6 for more details on calculations).

Table 5. Statistics of errors for the Omsk region as a whole in 2007

	Observed	1	2	3	Highest	Second	Third
1	1	0,961004	0,035578	0,003419	1	2	3
2	1	0,981859	0,016702	0,001440	1	2	3
3	1	0,972165	0,025803	0,002032	1	2	3
4	1	0,979272	0,018116	0,002612	1	2	3
*5	2	0,532218	0,216568	0,251214	1	3	2
*6	3	0,479990	0,238672	0,281338	1	3	2
7	1	0,962986	0,033553	0,003462	1	2	3
*8	2	0,397159	0,250741	0,352100	1	3	2
*9	2	0,861896	0,103902	0,034202	1	2	3
10	1	0,939756	0,054205	0,006038	1	2	3
	etc.						
348	1	0,706537	0,165445	0,128018	1	2	3
349	3	0,056942	0,138546	0,804511	3	2	1
350	1	0,985607	0,013601	0,000792	1	2	3

Statistics for each case of incorrect classifications are marked with *
Analysis sample N = 350

Table 6. Regression Summary for the Dependent Variable

	Beta	Std. Err.	B	Std. Err.	t(362)	p-Level
Intercept			32,60066	1,267911	25,71210	0,000000
K 1	0,032463	0,035780	6,35794	7,007490	0,90731	0,364848
K 2	0,093219	0,042679	0,76985	0,352466	2,18417	0,029591
K 3	0,217814	0,042907	0,38442	0,075728	5,07636	0,000001
K 4	0,597020	0,037425	23,94968	1,501317	15,95245	0,000000
K 5	0,115490	0,038919	6,70405	2,259234	2,96740	0,003203
K 6	0,013951	0,039893	0,25719	0,735427	0,34972	0,726752

Regression Summary for the Dependent Variable: Var7
R=, 73398633 R^2=, 53873593 Adjusted R^2=, 53109067;
F(6,362)=70,467 p<0,0000 Std. error of estimations: 16,129.

The assessment can be carried out according to two indicators that have the most significant impact on the financial condition of agricultural producers:

- Own funds' ratio (K4) with the error probability (p-level) being 0.0000. It can also take a negative value;
- Current liquidity ratio (K3) where p-level is also equal to 0.0000.

The graphs are convenient for quicker analysis of enterprises and organizations, they allow classifying them into certain groups on the basis of two factors, and then the remaining indicators need to be calculated to assign organization/enterprise to a certain credit rating class (the financial condition group) more accurately.

Table 7 presents the general results of the six-factor regression model evaluation basing on the data for the Omsk Region as a whole, as of 2007.

The following characteristics of the constructed regression equation are given: R is the value of the selective correlation coefficient; R^2- the value of the coefficient of determination (its value shows what percentage of the total variation of the dependent variable is due to the regression constructed); adjusted R^2 - the value of the coefficient of determination corrected for the number of the degrees of freedom; F is the calculated value of the Fisher test used to test the hypothesis of the regression equation signifiance; p is the magnitude of the significance level; Std. error of estimate is the standard error of estimating the regression equation.

Thus, the correlation coefficient back in 2007 was equal to 0.9273. This indicates that the solvency degree and the factors included in the model are closely related.

In 2007, the coefficient of determination was 0.8132. This means that the constructed regression equation reproduces approximately 81% of the dependence of B on the factors (K1-K6), i.e., the effective indicator depends on these factors by 81%. The remaining 19% fall on the share of random and unaccounted factors. The calculated value of the Fisher test at the degree of freedom (6.334) was 93.212, which is higher than its tabular (theoretical) value for the confidence probability P = (1-0.05) = 0.95, and this, in turn, corresponds to the significance level of p being less than 0.0000. Therefore, the regression equation obtained is significant, and it is not the result of the random selection of observations.

According to the results of analysis on the agroindustrial enterprises in the Omsk Region as a whole, the following regression equations have been obtained for several natural-economic zones using the data as of 2007:

Table 7. General results of the regression model estimation for the Omsk region as of 2007

	Beta	Std. Err.	B	Std. Err.	t(343)	p-Level
Intercept			28,88420	1,365349	21,15518	0,000000
K1	0,027762	0,052598	0,27591	0,522750	0,52781	0,597975
K2	-0,014748	0,049176	-0,05948	0,198316	-0,29991	0,764427
K3	0,225652	0,053319	0,22629	0,053469	4,23212	0,000030
K4	0,694109	0,034647	38,21893	1,907740	20,03361	0,000000
K5	-0,044456	0,033853	-2,39926	1,826987	-1,31323	0,189982
K6	0,046040	0,033586	0,35563	0,259432	1,37081	0,171331

Regression Summary for the Dependent Variable: B

R=, 92730491 R^2=, 81984902 Adjusted R^2=, 81319915

F(6,343)=93,212 p<0,0000 Std.error of estimations: 5,854

Legend: K1 is the absolute liquid ratio; K2 - the interim coverage ratio; K3 - the current liquidity ratio; K4 - own funds' ratio; K5 - profit margin; K6 - enterprise profitability.

Omsk Region: $B = 28,88 + 0,27K_1 - 0,05K_2 + 0,22K_3 + 38,21K_4 - 2,39K_5 + 0,35K_6$ [10].

Steppe zone: $B = 7,30 - 2,96K_1 + 0,22K_2 + 0,55K_3 + 70,84K_4 - 6,82K_5 + 10,64K_{6.}$

Southern forest-steppe zone:

$B = 22,70 + 1,61K_1 + 0,34K_2 + 0,02K_3 + 48,96K_4 -4,61K_5 - 0,78K_{6.}$

Northern forest-steppe zone:

$B = 33,62 + 3,36K_1 - 0,13K_2 + 0,33K_3 + 26,23K_4 + 3,83K_5 - 0,25K_{6.}$

Northern zone: $B = 14,52 + 6,93K_1 - 2,54K_2 + 0,33K_3 + 57,50K_4 + 3,85K_5 + 0,21K_{6.}$

The research results show that, despite the importance of each equation, not all the factors are significant. So, if the p-level exceeds the given level of significance (α) 0.05, then these factors are insignificant in the regression equation. Significant factors having the greatest impact on the solvency degree are those that have the highest level of significance (p-level<0.05).

After the stepwise correlation, i.e., successively excluding the factors from the model according to the principle of their least significance, we have obtained the following results (see Table 8).

Thus, we have obtained the set of equations containing the most significant factors affecting the solvency degree:

Omsk Region: $B = 28,82 + 0,23K_3 + 38,20K_4 - 2,31K_5 + 0,35K_6$

Steppe zone: $B = 6,69 - 2,61K_1 + 0,56K_3 + 70,98K_4 + 6,70K_6$

Southern forest-steppe zone: $B = 22,80 + 2,35K_3 + 49,71K_4 - 5,44K_5$

Northern forest-steppe zone: $B = 33,49 + 4,75K_1 + 0,24K_3 + 26,64K_4$

Northern zone: $B = 13,78 + 6,99K_1 - 2,52K_2 + 0,35K_3 + 57,09K_4 + 0,20K_6$

Table 8. General results of the four-factor model assessment for the Omsk region, as of 2007.

	Beta	Std. Err.	B	Std. Err.	t(345)	p-Level
Intercept			28,82849	1,356994	21,24437	0,000000
K4	0,693766	0,034468	38,20003	1,897875	20,12778	0,000000
K3	0,235861	0,034310	0,23653	0,034406	6,87448	0,000000
K6	0,045907	0,033502	0,35460	0,258781	1,37027	0,171493
K5	-0,042866	0,033621	-2,31344	1,814517	-1,27496	0,203180

Regression Summary for the Dependent Variable: B
R=, 92710060 R^2=, 81952735 Adjusted R^2=, 81511608
F(4,345)=140,44 p<0,0000 Std. error of estimations: 5,815

According to the Sberbank methodology, the fragment of the dialog box is shown as in Table 9. Thus, the system of equations (as per the discriminant model) looks as follows:

Omsk region:

$$G_1 = -5{,}05 - 0{,}16K_1 + 0{,}03K_2 + 0{,}03K_3 + 8{,}97K_4 - 0{,}68K_5 + 0{,}05K_6$$

$$G_2 = -3{,}89 - 0{,}17K_1 + 0{,}09K_2 - 0{,}001K_3 + 7{,}16K_4 - 0{,}04K_5 + 0{,}04K_6$$

$$G_3 = -1{,}20 - 0{,}03K_1 + 0{,}01K_2 - 0{,}001K_3 + 0{,}91K_4 + 0{,}01K_5 - 0{,}06K_6$$

Steppe zone:

$$G_1 = -15{,}42 - 0{,}59K_1 + 0{,}14K_2 + 0{,}04K_3 + 34{,}03K_4 + 6{,}92K_5 -2{,}51K_6$$

$$G_2 = -11{,}08 - 0{,}06K_1 + 0{,}04K_2 - 0{,}04K_3 + 28{,}23K_4 + 8{,}01K_5 - 2{,}82K_6$$

$$G_3 = -3{,}28 + 0{,}09K_1 - 0{,}05K_2 - 0{,}02K_3 + 12{,}4K_4 + 7{,}23K_5 - 3{,}79K_6$$

Table 9. Fragment of the dialog box according to the Sberbank methodology

	Wilks' Lamda	**Partial Lambda**	**F-Remove**	**p-Level**	**Toler.**	**1-Toler. (R^2)**
Var1	0,412334	0,995209	0,8232	0,439884	0,415680	0,584320
Var2	0,415740	0,987054	2,2427	0,107727	0,466326	0,533674
Var3	0,428441	0,957794	7,5352	0,000627	0,420867	0,579133
Var4	0,855155	0,479864	185,3508	0,000000	0,971287	0,028713
Var5	0,418419	0,980736	3,3588	0,035926	0,958499	0,041501
Var6	0,415083	0,988616	1,9691	0,141158	0,982213	0,017788

Discriminant Function Analysis Summary
# of vars in model: 6; Grouping: Var9 (3 grps)
Wilks' Lambda:, 41036 approx. F (12,684)=31,980 p<0,0000

Table 10. Initial data for the equations by groups for the Omsk region as a whole, as of 2007.

	G_1:1	**G_2:2**	**G_3:3**
Var1	-0,15632	-0,16826	-0,03101
Var2	0,03173	0,08752	0,01328
Var3	0,03289	-0,00081	0,00095
Var4	8,97384	7,16354	0,91444
Var5	-0,68149	-0,98190	0,01090
Var6	0,05198	0,03599	-0,05807
Constant	-5,04716	-3,89890	-1,20227

Classification Functions; grouping: Var9

Southern forest-steppe zone:

$$G_1 = -1,67 + 0,07K_1 - 0,03K_2 - 0,002K_3 + 2,93K_4 - 0,36K_5 + 0,13K_6$$

$$G_2 = -2,75 - 0,07K_1 - 0,001K_2 - 0,006K_3 + 4,10K_4 + 0,30K_5 - 0,45K_6$$

$$G_3 = -1,96 - 0,19K_1 + 0,09K_2 + 0,004K_3 + 3,09K_4 - 0,03K_5 - 0,57K_6$$

Northern forest-steppe zone:

$$G_1 = -3,29 - 0,92K_1 - 0,10K_2 + 0,11K_3 + 3,88K_4 - 0,51K_5 - 0,10K_6$$

$$G_2 = -2,68 - 0,51K_1 + 0,04K_2 + 0,03K_3 + 3,15K_4 - 0,57K_5 - 0,32K_6$$

$$G_3 = -0,97 - 0,05K_1 - 0,01K_2 + 0,008K_3 - 0,45K_4 - 0,61K_5 - 0,31K_6$$

Northern zone:

$$G_1 = -32,93 - 0,16K_1 + 0,08K_2 - 0,03K_3 + 71,09K_4 + 1,17K_5 + 0,23K_6$$

$$G_2 = -24,05 - 0,24K_1 + 0,15K_2 - 0,06K_3 + 58,26K_4 - 2,22K_5 + 0,18K_6$$

$$G_3 = -5,05 - 0,13K_1 + 0,13K_2 - 0,02K_3 + 18,62K_4 - 1,05K_5 - 0,09K_6$$

Table 11. Fragment of error statistics for the Omsk region as of 2007

#	Observed	1	2	3	Highest	Second	Third
1	1	0,593849	0,368347	0,037803	1	2	3
2	1	0,745449	0,241932	0,012620	1	2	3
3	1	0,629958	0,346817	0,023225	1	2	3
4	1	0,897464	0,094120	0,008416	1	2	3
5	3	0,154512	0,262337	0,583152	3	2	1
6	3	0,142467	0,244370	0,613163	3	2	1
7	1	0,591174	0,375289	0,033536	1	2	3
8	3	0,110079	0,206023	0,683898	3	2	1
*9	3	0,394454	0,404863	0,200684	2	1	3
*10	2	0,548031	0,390896	0,061073	1	2	3
	Etc.						
348	2	0,291505	0,383828	0,324667	2	3	1
349	3	0,018692	0,062457	0,918851	3	2	1
350	1	0,730353	0,261720	0,007927	1	2	3

(Statistics for each case of incorrect classifications are marked with *)

Analysis sample N = 350

Note: The analyst has the opportunity to see the possibility to assign all 350 (in our case) organizations to the group of financial stability; here a fragment only is given. Information about the potentially incorrect organization classification is marked with an asterisk (*) in the table above and thus should be subject for a deeper analysis.

Thus, according to the annual accounting reports' data provided by the agricultural enterprises registered in the Omsk region, the following results of discriminant analysis have been obtained: the partition was obtained for 3 groups of solvency (financial) condition, a system of equations was established to classify the organization to a certain group of financial stability. To classify an organization to a group by financial position, the above systems of equations have been used to determine the largest value - **G**, indicating the organization's belonging to a particular group of financial stability. One of the positive aspect in using this toolkit is that it demonstrates the opportunity to assign a particular enterprise to a particular financial stability group. Besides that, asterisks in the first row mean mistakes in the initial classification into groups; and if additional information on these enterprises is added to the matrix for testing, the program will automatically assign them to the appropriate financial stability groups.

In order to build the log-regression model, financial indicators calculated on the basis of the annual accounting reports data on all agricultural enterprises of the Omsk Region were used. The basis for risk factors' selection for further classification is the methodology developed and used by the Sberbank of Russia.

For borrowers' solvency assessment, the Sberbank uses three groups of valuation indicators:

- **Liquidity Ratios:** Absolute liquid ratio (K1), quick liquidity ratio (K2), current liquidity ratio (K3);
- Own funds' ratio (K4);
- **Turnover and Profitability Indicators:** Current assets turnover, receivables' turnover, inventory turnover, profitability of products (profitability of sales) (K5), enterprise's profitability (K6), profitability of investments in the enterprise.

When constructing the logit-regression model, six basic coefficients were calculated, according to the Sberbank methodology.

Applying the data substitution method, we have experimentally determined the boundaries of classes in points using the 100-point system, using the Methodology for calculating financial condition indicators for agricultural producers (RF Government Decree #52, as of January 30, 2003) as the basis. According to the research results we have determined: 1st class of solvency - from 100 to 69 points (inclusive); 2nd class of solvency - from 69 (exclusive) to 26 points (inclusive); 3rd class of solvency being below 26 points.

In order to construct the regression equation, it is necessary to form the initial matrix. Data in matrices are formed by years, natural and economic zones and for the Omsk region as a whole. Annual accounting reports data provided by the Omsk region agricultural enterprises (as of 2005-2007) were used for the study. Data processing was carried out using the SPSS software. After entering the data presented in the matrix, the following information was obtained.

The forecast results can be put in the form of the following table (see Table 13).

A significant regression equation is obtained by using all six selected coefficients simultaneously. Based on the modelling results, the following regression equation has been obtained (Patlasov-Vasina logit regression model) (Patlasov, Vasina, 2013):

$$Y = -13{,}03 + 2{,}79K1 - 0{,}64K2 + 0{,}84K3 + 16{,}49K4 + 3{,}33K5 + 0{,}58K6.$$

Table 12. Dialog box fragment of the classification table for predicting the percentage of data correctness

	Observed		Predicted		
			VAR00007		Percentage Correct
			0,00	1,00	
Step 1	VAR00007	0,00	115	4	96,6
		1,00	2	149	98,7
	Overall Percentage				97,8

Classification Table (a)
a The cut value is, 500

Table 13. Generalized results of data forecasting

	VAR00007 = 1	VAR00007 = 0	Total
Totally according to the sampling	119	151	270
Forecast	117	153	270
Correct	115	149	264
Incorrect	4	2	6
% of correct	96,6	98,7	97,8
% of incorrect	0,4	1,3	2,2

Table 14. Data for regression equation construction

		B (Regression Coefficient of B)	Standard Error	Wald	Degree of Freedom	Significance	Exp(B) Inverse Function Ln
Step 1(a)	VAR00001	2,796	3,930	,506	1	,477	16,379
	VAR00002	-,639	,529	1,461	1	,227	1,528
	VAR00003	,844	,295	8,192	1	,004	2,325
	VAR00004	16,486	4,059	16,499	1	,000	14,243
	VAR00005	3,333	1,838	3,288	1	,070	28,009
	VAR00006	,579	,541	1,143	1	,285	1,783
	Constant	-13,030	2,955	19,443	1	,000	,000

Variables in the Equation
a Variable(s) entered on step 1: VAR00001, VAR00002, VAR00003, VAR00004, VAR00005, VAR00006.
Table values and coefficients' correspondence:
VAR00001 - K_1 (absolute liquid ratio);
VAR00002 - K_2 (interim coverage ratio);
VAR00003 - K_3 (current liquidity ratio);
VAR00004 - K_4 (own funds' ratio);
VAR00005 - K_5 (profit margin);
VAR00006 - K_6 (enterprise's profitability).

In this model, rather high error has the absolute liquidity ratio, own funds' ratio and profit margin. However, this model is built under the Sberbank regulation, so it is not appropriate to exclude from the model, for example, absolute liquid ratio, profit margin as they weakly reflect the actual financial situation in the agricultural sector.

The probability of loan payment delay is calculated by the formula:

$$P = \frac{1}{1 + e^{-y}}$$

If for p we get a value less than 0.5, then we can assume that bankruptcy does not come; otherwise, financial collapse is assumed.

The advantage of modelling in comparison with regulation is the ability to take into account industry's specificity, regional characteristics, the stage of company's life cycle, company's sizr and other business conditions.

In accordance with the proposed methodology, a set of logit regression models has been created allowing to predict the financial status and the solvency of organizations under various economic conditions. These models can be used by credit analysts of banks, financial analysts and managers of organizations with the purpose of forecasting the financial state of organizations.

The proposed methods for assessing the organization's solvency are acceptable for Russian conditions, since they are already somewhat adapted to the agricultural sector. The models are created on the regional data set and are presented in the context of the natural and economic zones of the regions, thus making it possible to better take into account the regional specificity and to develop a model that allows more accurate assessment of the financial condition of agricultural organizations located in different zones.

The proposed models allow organizations assess their financial condition from the viewpoint of banks and to obtain information on compliance with the requirements set by credit institutions. If you get such information in time, it will allow making more appropriate managerial decisions that would contribute to the organizations' financial condition improvement.

The models can be as well used by rating agencies to calculate the organizations' credit ratings and also by territorial state commissions in the course of financial recovery of agricultural producers.

CONCLUSION

Financial condition of any organization is characterized by a system of indicators reflecting the process of financial resources' formation and further use. Financial resources in this case include the aggregate of own money, income, raised and borrowed funds intended for the performance of financial obligations, financing of current costs and expenses associated with activities' expansion. The task of comprehensive analysis of organization's financial condition is not limited by establishing the solvency level according to official methods. It is necessary to conduct in-depth financial diagnostics taking into account sectoral and regional specifics. To determine the direction of in-depth analysis, a preliminary express analysis is first conducted. The key advantages of the indicators' system are systemic and integrated approaches, while the major disadvantage is higher degree of decision-making complexity.

In addition to the officially approved methods, there are other methods of analyzing financial and economic activities developed by scientists and practitioners working in consulting, audit, valuation firms, commercial banks, rating agencies and other organizations.

When analyzing company's financial condition, the following groups of financial indicators are distinguished: general indicators, liquidity and solvency analysis, financial stability, business activity, profit and profitability, cash flows and financial activity, business valuation, integral rating analysis. Among the methodological problems in forecasting of potential bankruptcy of organizations the following can be mentioned:

- Financial rather than economic analysis is carried out according to a complex methodology (while aggregated factor analysis is not carried out);
- Analysis involves mainly Form 1 and Form 2 of accounting reports, other forms with analytical capabilities are disregarded;
- Internal analysis is not always corroborated by environmental factors' analysis; financial analysis of economic entities' activities should be preceded by macroeconomic analysis (situation in the national economy, sectoral trends and regional characteristics);
- The problem of adaptation of Western methods for indicators' calculation as per Russian specifics of accounting and reporting persists;
- The difference between Russian accounting system (RAS) and the International Accounting System (IAS) and IFRS is maintained;
- Within the framework of our analysis, three following areas of economic activities are not studied thoroughly: operational, investment and financial ones;
- Within the framework of such an analysis business and management are not always assessed properly;
- As a rule, when constructing a graphical model of the break-even production, only the break-even point and the security edge are examined, the points of bankruptcy, profitability, minimum and full estimated profit remain without attention; the study of the corresponding points in the break-even graphical model is not corroborated by an analysis of the corresponding types of values (the liquidation value at the point of bankruptcy, the value of net assets at the point of profitability, the market value of the enterprise's property complex at the break-even point, the market value of business under traditional approaches to valuation at the point of minimum settlement profit and the market value of business as part of a strategic approach to valuation at the point of full estimated profit);
- Analysis is conducted with the involvement of limited information sources; there is hardly any information system for integrated analysis (data on accounting, taxation, statistics, managerial accounting and reporting, marketing research, enterprise itself etc.);
- During bankruptcy diagnostics, many intangible assets are not taken into account - the assets of intellectual capital, brand value etc.;
- The audit of initial information is not always carried out with the purpose of improving the quality of the information support system for further bankruptcy forecasting;
- The problem of indicators' choice and grouping under various financial analysis techniques is preserved, many of the vitally important indicators are often disregarded;
- Indicators sometimes correspond with each other or choose the inverse coefficients in the considered techniques and financial models;

- Company's investment attractiveness analysis does not actually provide a complete picture of its innovative activities;
- In the absence of standards (recommended values) of financial ratios, the integral indicator of economic activity cannot always be determined;
- Analysis of the best and/or the most effective business types is not conducted since benchmarking tool as such is;
- Specific features at various stages of bankruptcy (observation, financial recovery, external management, bankruptcy proceedings, settlement agreement) are not taken into account;
- As a rule, sectoral methods are limited to agriculture only, thus, when being applied to trade, for example, these methods do not sufficiently capture the specificity of accounting and/or analysis purposes as such;
- Analysis of added value is rarely carried out as such.

As of today, there is still no domestic model developed and available specifically for Russian insurance companies, commercial banks and non-bank credit organizations.

In general, in order to obtain more adequate conclusions about the financial state, it is advisable to apply a set of models in the analysis.

Thus, our research shows that official methods of financial analysis organization have a serious drawback - the basis for conclusions is formed by accounting data only, while the stage of organization's life cycle is not taken into consideration at all, thus, the future state cannot be really predicted as precisely as it is expected. For the aims of financial management it would be important to conduct system analysis, covering all processes in the external environment and the role of the human factor, in addition to organization's financial state assessment. Such comprehensive methods of analysis are indisputably more labor-intensive, but they allow not only increasing the reliability of the results obtained, but also exploring the hidden causes and consequences of all related phenomena. Consequently, this more comprehensive analysis would help raising the efficiency of commercial organizations' crisis management.

ACKNOWLEDGMENT

This article was prepared with the financial support of the Russian Foundation for Fundamental Research, grant #18-414-550001.

REFERENCES

Baestaens, D-E., Van Den Bergh, W., & Wood, D. (1997). *Neural Network: Solutions for Trading in Financial Markets*. Moscow, Russia: Scientific Publishing House TVP. (in Russian)

Collins, R. A., & Green, R. D. (1982). Statistical methods for bankruptcy forecasting. *Journal of Economics and Business*, 32.

Laitinen, T., & Kankaanpaa, M. (1999). Comparative analysis of failure prediction methods: The Finnish case. *European Accounting Review*, *8*(1), 89.

Lennox, C. (1999). Identifying Failing Companies: A Re-evaluation of the Logit-, Probit- and DA Approaches. *Journal of Economics and Business*, *51*(4), 4. doi:10.1016/S0148-6195(99)00009-0

Ooghe, H., & Balcaen, S. (2002). *Are failure prediction models transferable from one country to another? An empirical study using Belgian financial statements*. Belgium: Ghent University.

Patlasov, O. Y., & Vasina, N. V. (2008). Models of financial state assessment for the purpose of solvency analysis. *Economics of Agricultural and Processing Enterprises, 12,* 87.

Patlasov, O. Y., & Vasina, N. V. (2009). Modeling the borrowers (legal entities) solvency. *Audit and Financial Analysis, 5,* 103.

Patlasov, O. Y., & Vasina, N. V. (2013). Models for the borrowers (agricultural organizations) solvency assessment. *Finance and Credit*, *39*, 18–24.

Patlasov, O. Y., & Vasina, N. V. (2014). The technique of borrower's solvency analysis and scoring modeling. *Actual Problems of Economics*, *10*(160), 490–503.

Postin, K. M., Harmon, K. W., & Gramlich, J. D. (1994). A Test of Financial Ratios as Predictors of Turnaround Versus Failure Among Financially Distressed Firms. *Journal of Applied Business Research*, *10*, 298–325.

Voronin, V. T. (1994). Time as the space for events (sociophilosophical aspect). [in Russian]. *Humanities in Siberia*, *1*, 20–25.

KEY TERMS AND DEFINITIONS

Discriminant Analysis: A classification problem, where two or more groups or clusters or populations are known *a priori* and one or more new observations are classified into one of the known populations based on the measured characteristics.

Discriminant Function: A function of several variables used to assign items into one of two or more groups. The function for a particular set of items is obtained from measurements of the variables belonging to a known group.

Discriminant Score: The score of each respondent on the discriminate function in discriminant analysis.

Discriminant Variables: Characteristics used to distinguish one class from another; they should be measured either on the interval scale, or on the scale of relations. Thus, it becomes possible to calculate the mathematical expectations, variances, etc.

Discriminant Weights: Standardized discriminant weight (discriminant coefficient) of a certain sign and weight is assigned to each variable in computing of discriminant functions. When the sigh is ignored, each weight represents the relative contribution of its associated variable to that function, while independent variables with relatively larger weights contribute more to the discriminant power of the function than do variables with smaller weights.

F-Statistics: Consists of F-enter and F-remove: 1) The use of F-value. A variable is entered into the model if its F-value is greater than the Entry value and is removed if the F-value is less than the Remove value. Entry must be greater than the removal one, and both values must be positive. To enter more variables into the model, its author is supposed to lower the Entry value. To remove more variables from the model, the Removal value must be increased. 2) The use of probability with F. A variable is entered into the model if the significance level of its F-value is less than the Entry value and is removed if the significance level is greater than the Removal value. Entry must be less than Removal, and both values must be positive. To enter more variables into the model, one should increase the Entry value. To remove more variables from the model, the Removal value must be lowered. At each step, the predictor with the largest F-enter, the value of which exceeds the entry criteria, is added to the model.

Mahalanobis Distance: A measure of how much the particular case values of the independent variables differ from the average of all cases. Larger Mahalanobis distance identifies the case with the extreme values on one or more of the independent variables.

Raw Coefficients: Coefficients providing information about the absolute contribution of a variable to the value of the discriminant function.

Solvency: Is the ability of a company to meet its long-term financial obligations. Solvency is essential to staying in business as it asserts company's ability to continue operations into the foreseeable future. Liquidity should not be confused with solvency, however. Solvency is directly related to the ability of an individual or business to pay their long-term debts including any associated interest. To be considered solvent, the value of assets, company's or individual, must be greater than the sum of debt obligations.

Standardized Coefficients: Standardized coefficients refer to how many standard deviations a dependent variable will change per standard deviation increase in the predictor variable.

Structure Coefficients: Structure coefficients add to the information provided by β weights. Betas inform us as to the credit given to a predictor in the regression equation, while structure coefficients inform us as to the bivariate relationship between a predictor and the effect observed without the influence of other predictors in the model. If the coefficient is closer to zero, the relationship between the individual variable and the discriminant function is insignificant.

Tolerance: A variable defined as 1 minus the squared multiple correlation of this variable with all the other independent variables. Therefore, the smaller is the tolerance of a variable, the more redundant is its contribution to the regression (i.e., it is redundant with the contribution of other independent variables). If the tolerance of any of the variables in the regression equation is equal to zero (or is very close to zero), then the regression equation cannot be evaluated (the matrix is said to be ill-conditioned, and it cannot be inverted).

Wilks' Lambda: A measure of how well each function separates cases into groups. It is equal to the proportion of the total variance in the discriminant scores not explained by differences among groups. Smaller value of Wilks' lambda indicates greater discriminatory ability of the function.

Section 2

The State at the Financial Market: Making the National Financial Policy Efficient

Chapter 9
Financial Instruments of Regional Economic Policy Implementation

Anastasia Ostovskaya
V. I. Vernadsky Crimean Federal University, Russia

Irina Pavlenko
V. I. Vernadsky Crimean Federal University, Russia

ABSTRACT

This study is dedicated to the rationalizing of theoretical and methodological principles as well as elaboration of practical recommendations for the improvement of the financial mechanisms of regional development. Scientific findings in the area of financial mechanisms of regional development have been subject to analysis; the purpose and the main objectives have been set and financial principles and instruments of regional development have been defined. The role of financial support has been rationalized in relation to the specifics of the social and economic interests of the region and its steady development. The main purpose of reforming the financial mechanisms has been set as such providing for the social and economic development of the regions in the Russian Federation. It has also been clarified that the financial potential of the region is a key factor in serving social and economic interests of the region by means of financial mechanisms.

INTRODUCTION

Regions showing steady economic growth make a priority goal within social and economic development strategy and are also an indicator of the strong economy of the country. For this reason, the acute problems requiring urgent solution include identifying the regional potential, applying efficient instruments for utilization of such potential, economic effect maximization and meeting regional socio-economic needs, which are expected to result in the steady development of the region. National economy encompasses a certain economic mechanism which defines the country's and its regions' rate of competitiveness and measures the economic system's potential to provide for the development of the society and to create economic goods.

DOI: 10.4018/978-1-5225-7760-7.ch009

Financial support of regional development is a problem which has been elaborated for a long period with varying success, but has never been solved completely. The system of giving financial support to the regions has always remained largely dependent on the decisions taken by governmental authorities, which leaves local authorities with no space for action or initiative in search for financial resources.

Lack of financial resources for regional development is explained by a number of factors including the following: the majority of the regions have insufficient tax basis, they are economically unappealing for investors and lack potential and infrastructure to attract financial resources from the international organizations into their project activity. Therefore, such regions are particularly vulnerable, experience lack of financing and, thus, require different financial mechanisms and instruments to support their development.

To a great extent, the efficiency of the financial mechanism in a region affects the efficiency of the regional policy, improves quality of living and functionality of the social programs.

Currently, regional development is marked by ineffective local management system, pretentiousness of the strategic planning, disproportions of socio-economic development varying from region to region and escalating social inequality. There is a well observed dependency of local and regional budgets in terms of resources distribution, i.e. financing largely comes from inter-budgetary transfers, which doesn't stimulate local authorities' initiative in searching for their own resources of covering the expense.

BACKGROUND

The shift of the Russian economy towards the market economy made a drastic change in building up and utilizing regional financial resources. This resulted in a more significant role of finance and financial policy which aims at the acceleration of economic growth and creating competitive environment. All the branches of the regions' financial system are responsible for the policy implementation as they are directed towards a common goal of mobilizing financial resources and their efficient utilization (Morozova, 2010).

Successful performance and development of the regional economy greatly depend on the conditions in the region and its ability to provide self-sustained budget for its activities, define its own priorities in development and financial stability maintenance and achieve well-balanced financial indices while expanding its economic resources (Verbinenko & Badylevich, 2012).

These factors contribute to the bigger financial functionality range of the region when it concerns socio-economic development and require strengthening financial support by means of efficient management of available and potential financial mechanisms.

Maintenance of the stable economic growth in the regions, as well as in the country, remains a priority task of socio-economic development. Thus, the urgent issues in focus are evaluation of the economic potential of the region, application of efficient instruments of its utilization, economic effect maximization and meeting the needs of the enterprises and constituent territories of the region.

The purpose of the research is elaboration of practical recommendations on strengthening the financial mechanism of regional development, whereas its objectives include:

1. Rationalizing of the financial mechanism of regional development as an important factor of national economy effectiveness.
2. Systematizing methodology of evaluation of the regional development mechanism.

3. Carrying out complex analysis of the current financial mechanism of regional development in the national economy system.
4. Describing international practices and tendencies in regional development and generating recommendations of their implementation in the Russian economy.
5. Elaborating the basic priorities in strengthening the financial mechanism of regional development.
6. Contributing to the improvement of the financial mechanism of regional development and methods of defining the practical dominants of its effectiveness.

According to our hypothesis the development of the financial system of the region presupposes optimal, rational and efficient utilization of the financial mechanism in order to meet the social and economic goals.

The role of the financial mechanism of regional development infers enhancement of national economy's competitiveness.

Advanced financial mechanism of regional development is based on defining a model of the regional financial system development.

Financial sustainability works as an indicator of efficient regional development as it shows capability of the region to develop socially and economically while effectively involving innovative tools of financial resources management with the purpose of balancing out the disproportions in financing different segments of regional economy.

MAIN FOCUS OF THE CHAPTER

Issues, Controversies, Problems

A region is a comparatively isolated economic subsystem of the national economy; it possesses the properties of any dynamic system and, therefore, functions according to general laws of economics. The foundation of the system is the resources engaged in the process of extended reproduction, i.e. in the process of achieving steady economic growth within the territory of a particular region.

It is in the regional system that "impulses" get generated for the purpose of steady development not only at the mesoeconomic level, but also at the micro and macroeconomic levels of national economy (Dobrolezha, 2007).

Regional development may be considered as functioning of the regional system characterized by positive dynamics of the basic socio-economic indices accompanied by steady and well-balanced reproduction of all the elements of its mechanism (Beer, Haughton & Maude, 2004).

Regional development requires efficient economic foundation that would facilitate social, economic and ecological stability. Economic self-reliance of the regions depends on the economic resources available for their independent functioning, meeting the needs of the territory and financing socio-economic development (Bartik, 1995).

According to our reckoning, modeling efficient financial system of the regions remains an issue and originates from the effective combination of federal and local budget financing, financing from the businesses, the population, financial and credit institutions as well as external investments.

Social and economic development certainly results from the mutual efforts of all the subjects capable of accumulating resources by means of building an efficient financial mechanism with the purpose of enhancing its financial sufficiency. For the time being, many researches have been focusing on the model of the country's financial mechanism and its functioning, which is, first of all, explained by the tangled situation in the country in terms of financial security.

As regards to the regional financial mechanism, researchers have been paying less attention to the issue, though undoubtedly its elaboration and effective use contribute to the economic stability and development of the regions and the country.

The term "financial mechanism" was introduced by Volkov (1976) in his scientific research *Long range planning of financial resources* (Volkov, 1976). The definition was based on K. Marx's social reproduction theory. According to the latter, social production includes means of production (the first segment with concentrated industries producing goods for industrial consumption) and commodities (the second segment with the industries producing material goods for the personal needs of the population). The basic elements of the social product cost structure include the cost of the consumed constant capital (C), which makes a replacement reserve, as well as the cost of the variable capital (V) and the cost of the surplus product (M) that K. Marx called "surplus value".

Herewith, extended reproduction is possible provided the new value of the first segment is bigger than the replacement reserve fund of the second segment:

$$I\left(V+M\right) \succ II\left(C\right) \tag{1}$$

Such exceedance in the absolute value terms works as a financial mechanism. The researcher describes the absolute financial mechanism as a part of national income which, after all reallocations, turns into industrial growth and the relative financial mechanism as a part of the national income directed at extending the production. In this case, the financial mechanism is understood as growth of financial resources based on the extended reproduction.

Financial mechanism is an aggregated total of "forms and methods of making and using financial funds with the purpose of meeting a range of needs of governmental institutions, businesses and population" (Joumard & Kongsrud, 2003).

As Menipaz states, "financial mechanism is a system of financial forms, methods, tools and instruments used in the government's and businesses' financial activities providing appropriate regulation, conformity to law and information support are observed, which also presupposes wise financial policy on the micro macro levels" (Menipaz & Menipaz, 2011).

Inter alia, the notion of the financial mechanism is inseparable from the financial policy of the government which defines the functions of the financial mechanism and its natural bond with the governmental regulation of the economy.

The complete definition of the financial mechanism of governmental regulation of the economy can be derived after analyzing and synthesizing the viewpoints stated above. Hence, it is a total of methodological, organizational, normative and legal forms, methods, instruments, tools and regulations working as a basis for elaborating certain measures (providing appropriate regulation, conformity to law and information support are observed), evaluating financial and economic situation in the country, and in practice such regulations are supposed to help complete certain tasks and achieve goals in the process of formation, distribution and use of centralized and decentralized targeted funds.

Financial support originates as one of the components of the financial mechanism.

Some researchers understand financial support as accumulatin of funds in a certain sufficient amount and their efficient use. Financial support requires accumulation and use of the financial resources so that all the forms of financial support could be optimized and balanced and provides for such volumes of financial resources of economic activity that would guarantee economic performance not only without loss, but also characterized by increasing efficiency and general strengthening of the country's economy (McCarthy, Jordan & Probst, 2011).

The leading role in creating efficient mechanism of socio-economic development in the regions belongs to the organization of budgetary relations, forming of stable income base and delimitation of authority between the center and the regions as well as between the government and local authorities, functional gradation of regional expenditures, preferences in economic regulation of local order placement and number of orders, small and medium enterprise development, organization of the market infrastructure, etc. The total of the instruments of implementing the financial and economic mechanism of regional development includes the following basic elements: tax rates with preference for the local budgets, restructuring of budget expenditures, principles of marketability in terms of regional order placement and number of orders, stimulation of small and medium enterprises and healthy market environment and volumes of governmental investments (through budgets and other channels). Financial, organizational and economic aspects of regional development shall be administered and regulated by legal acts and memoranda issued by governmental and local authorities in the regions. Stability of legislation and its binding authority for all legal subjects and entities are mandatory for establishing efficient legal boundaries for regional management (Pearce & Robinson, 2009).

SOLUTIONS AND RECOMMENDATIONS

The abovementioned definition of the regional financial mechanism allowed us suggesting a hypothesis of the financial mechanism workable for socio-economic development.

The basic elements of such mechanism as an economic category are listed below:

1. Capacity of the financial mechanism is characterized by the total of the financial resources available in the region and necessary to support its adequate economic performance.
2. Financial mechanism facilitates the capacity of the region to create or attract financial resources to satisfy the needs of its subjects and advances its social and economic development.
3. Financial mechanism reflects the result of the economic activity of the subjects of the region.
4. Financial mechanism makes up a reserve of economic security protecting the subjects of the region from the adverse effects of the internal and external factors.
5. Financial mechanism presupposes availability of institutions facilitating effective management of the financial resources in the regions.
6. Financial mechanism may be represented as a dynamic system which reflects economic links and relations and possesses spatial and temporal parameters.

Therefore, building up a financial mechanism of regional development involves varied elements and financial operations related to accumulation, distribution and utilization of financial resources for the purpose of socio-economic development, the basic component of the financial mechanism being financial support. The conceptual approach to structuring and implementation of the financial mechanism of regional development is shown in Figure 1.

The financial mechanism characterizes capability of the regions to utilize their financial resources in order to meet social and economic needs of the subjects and defines potential for their development. This provides for the possibility of carrying out its quantitative and qualitative evaluation with regards to its financial sufficiency.

Despite dependence of the capacity and sufficiency of the financial mechanism on the regional financial system, facilitating its ability to promptly and efficiently react to threats and withstand them is one of the priority goals and a factor of steady socio-economic development.

We shall make allowance for the formation and utilization of the financial mechanism on the basis of a complex of financial relations, and such systemic approach requires result-oriented processes, i.e. processes directed at achieving a certain set of goals.

The goals of formation and utilization of the financial mechanism include:

- Optimization of financial resource capacity and its management.
- Building security system in order to prevent the regional economy from the destructive effects of internal and external factors.
- Insuring social security and wellbeing of the population.
- Building up financial stability reserve of the economy.

The algorithm of structuring and utilizing the financial mechanism is based on definitive and scientifically grounded principles providing for its effective functioning and meeting the goals that have been set. Such principles include:

- Consistency displayed through the perception of all the constituent parts of the mechanism as a paradigm whereas the goals of one subject shall not contradict the goals of the other subjects, which results in the efficacy of such mechanism for the socio-economic development.
- Coordination and coherence of the financial mechanism enhancement strategy and the financial strategy of the state.
- Flexibility (adaptability) as an ability of getting promptly adjusted to dynamic changes in the internal and external environment by means of effective utilization of the favorable conditions and adequate management or by setting up an efficient security system against various potential and existing threats.
- Record keeping of the specifics of the regional financial development process.

The stated principles are to be applied as a complex due to the fact that their total provides for the efficient functioning of the financial mechanism, and the quality of their organization defines the quality of regional management. The suggested approach served the basis for singling out particular stages in the process of building up and use of the financial mechanism of regional development (Figure 2).

Organizational side in building up and utilization of the financial mechanism of regional development is one of its basic elements providing a link between objects and subjects. This process consists in exploring the object, identifying potential and existing, external and internal factors, their impact, planning and constant monitoring of the decision making efficacy.

Figure 1. Conceptual approach to structuring and implementation of the financial mechanism of regional development

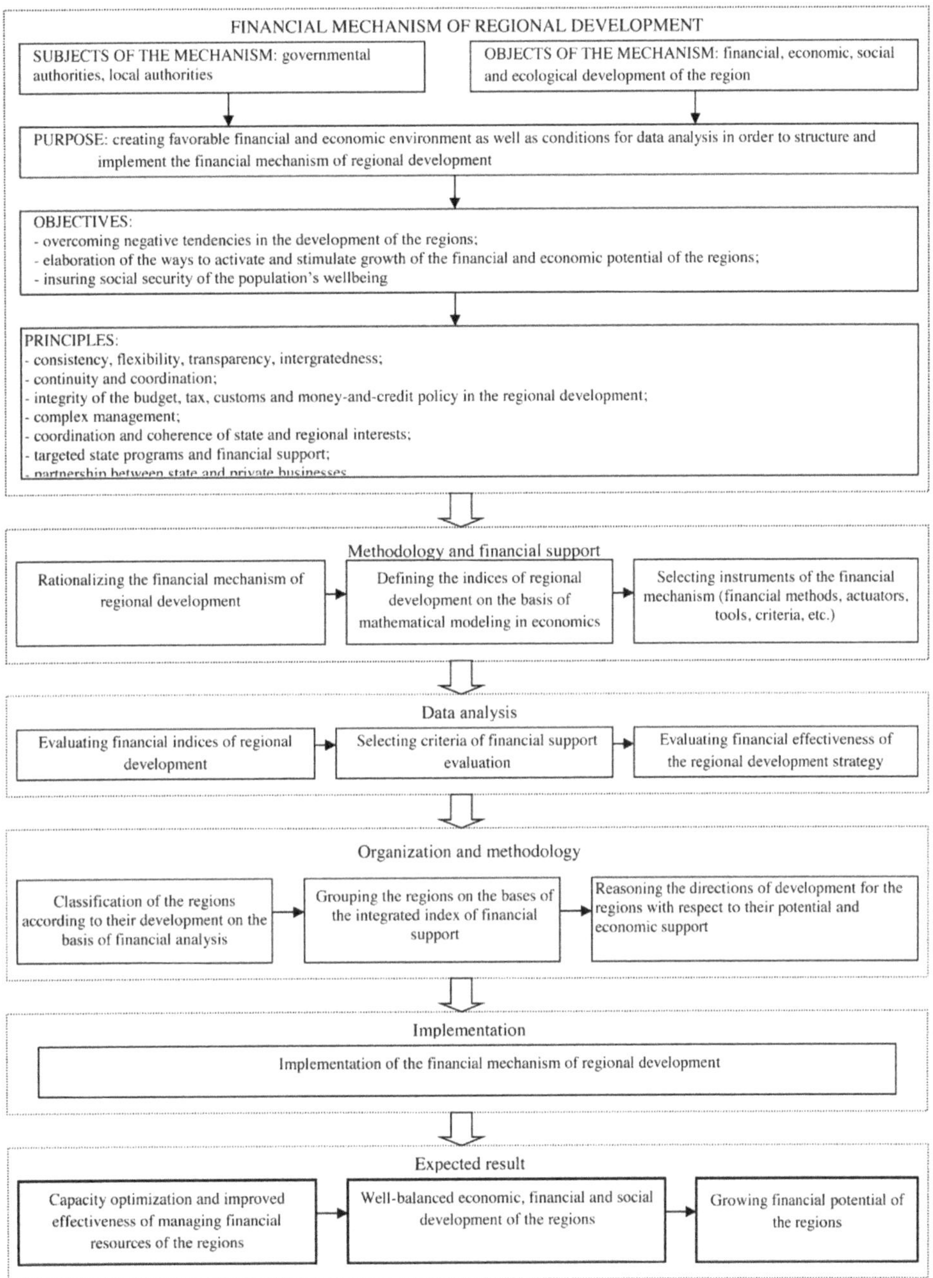

These functions shall be performed by the subjects, i.e. governmental and local authorities, businesses, households, financial and credit institutions and external investors supposedly acting to the benefit of the region's socio-economic development. Herewith, governmental and local authorities are obliged to lay the ground for the workability and efficiency of the financial mechanism functioning in the regions and to control compliance with laws.

Figure 2. Stages in the process of building up and use of the financial mechanism of regional development

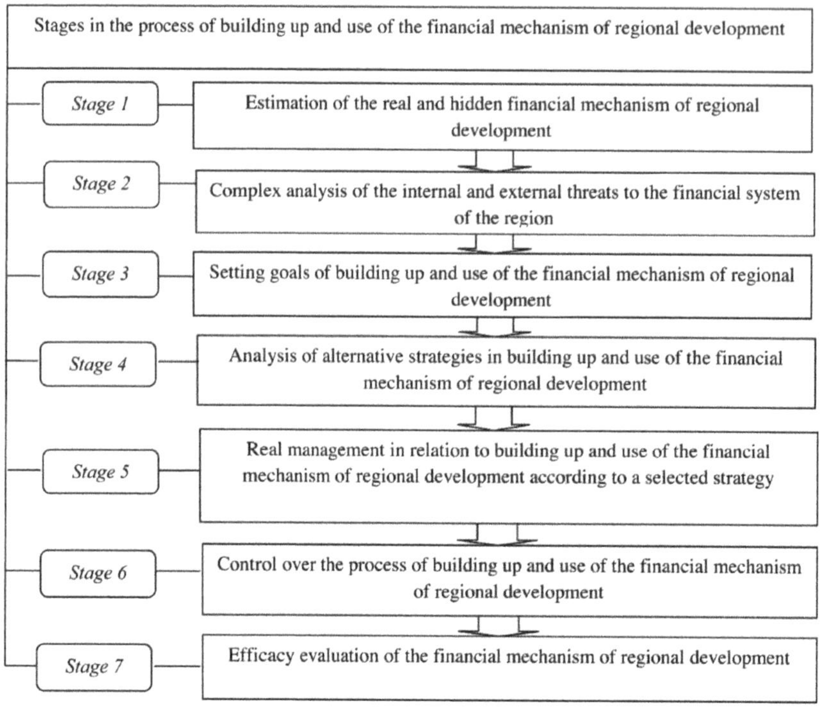

Among the objects there may be observed, firstly, a certain hierarchy in the national economy within the territory of the regions subject to the implementation of the financial mechanism; secondly, a complex of financial relations facilitating formation and utilization of the financial mechanism of regional development; thirdly, the total of all financial resources.

Correlation between subjects and objects is possible due to the definitive goals, means of their achievement and ongoing monitoring of efficacy (Figure 3).

Financial methods functioning as impact instruments in the process of formation and utilization of the financial mechanism were defined. The impact is achieved through managing the flow of financial resources owned by the subjects, efficacy evaluation, economic stimulation and responsibility for poor utilization of funds. Figure 4 illustrates the most common financial stimulation techniques effecting formation and utilization of the financial mechanism.

The efficacy of formation and utilization of the financial mechanism of regional development depends on the rational and careful application of the financial instruments by the subjects. A financial instrument is understood as a separate impact tool within a financial technique. In other words, financial

Figure 3. Correlation between subjects and objects

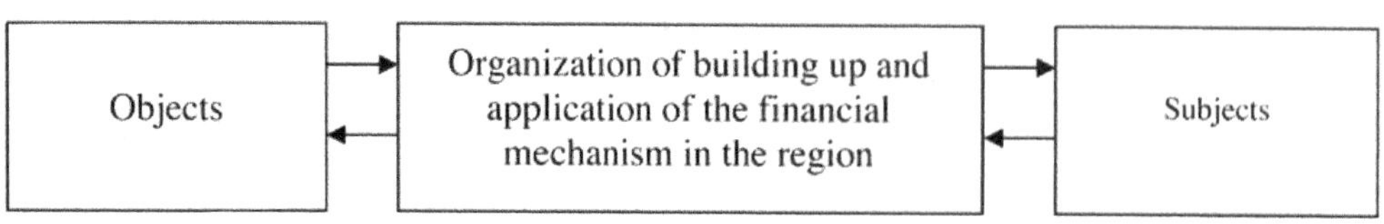

Figure 4. Financial stimulation techniques effecting formation and utilization of the financial mechanism in the regions

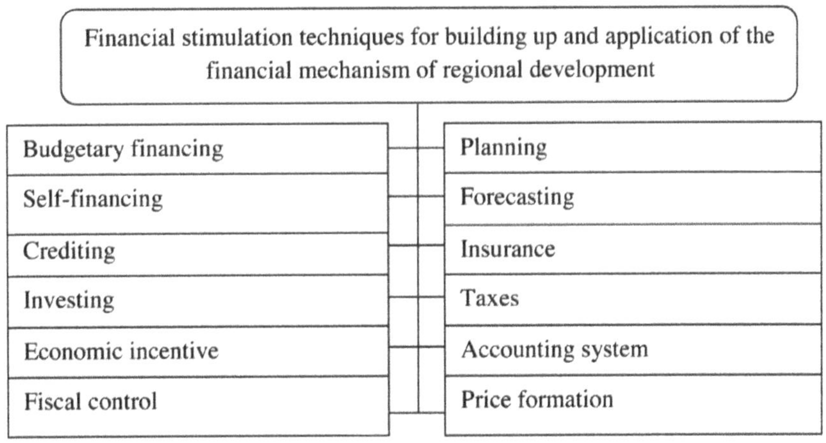

instruments are applied to influence the development of financial relations by means of creating favorable environment for the most efficient building up and utilization of the financial mechanism in the regions. Financial instruments serve to regulate financial relations, and, therefore, financial flow in the financial system of the regions. Variety of financial instruments and their diverse nature provides for building up, expansion and utilization of the financial mechanism of the regions Figure 5 (Dobrolezha, 2007).

Financial instruments include payment tools (pay orders, checks, and letters of credit); credit tools (loan agreements, bills of exchange); deposit tools (deposit agreements, certificates of deposit); investment deposits (shares, investment certificates); insurance tools (insurance contracts, certificate of insurance); other financial tools *(Dobrolezha, 2007).*

Efficient building up and utilization of the financial mechanism of regional development requires qualitative evaluation of its financial abilities, detecting threats to its financial sufficiency and factors creating financial thresholds.

Evaluation of the financial mechanism of regional development lies in exploring financial relations existing on the territory of the region and further identification of quantitative and qualitative impact factors, tracing the basic development tendencies and elaboration of the best decisions in building up, expanding and utilization of the financial mechanism in order to provide socio-economic growth of the region.

Methodology of the Study

Financial sufficiency of the regions is directly dependent on the volume of its own financial resources, budget efficacy and autonomy, which is achieved by means of effectively utilizing the financial mechanism that can fully satisfy social and economic needs of the region while leaving out external resources or minimizing their involvement.

Efficacy of the socio-economic development of the region is to a great extent conditioned by successful local budgeting which involves building up a system of financial relations directed at the accumulation, distribution and utilization of financial resources of local authorities to insure financial sufficiency of the regions and their steady development. Local budgets make one of the mechanisms of cost realloca-

Figure 5. Financial instruments with impact on financial relations in the region

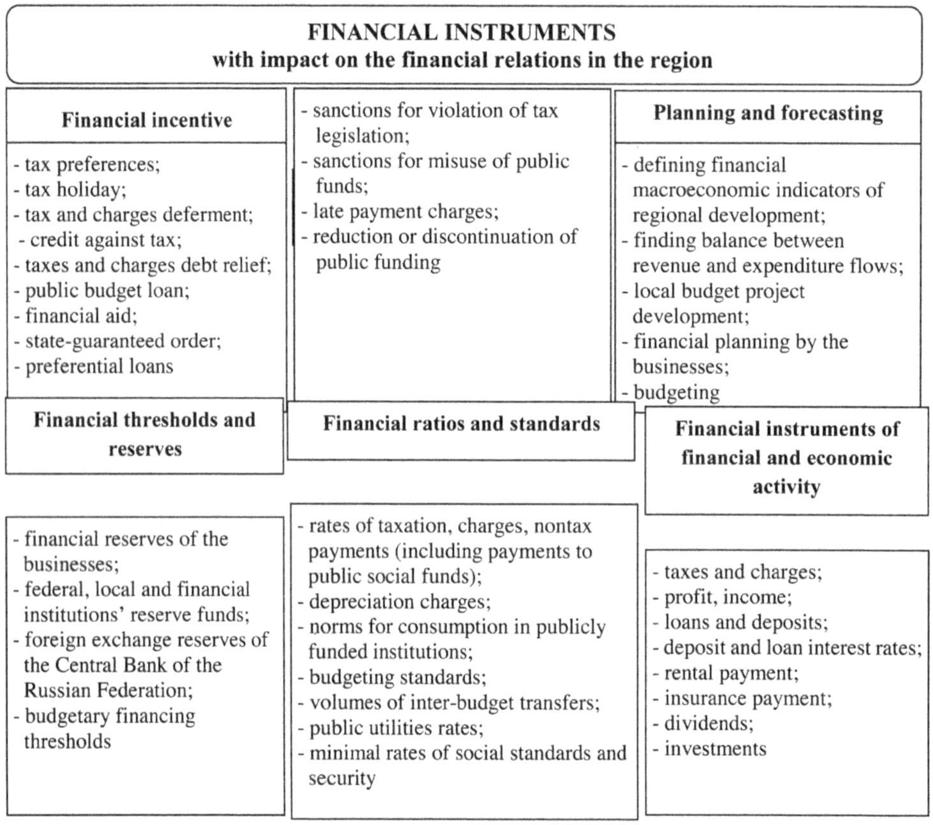

tion accepted on the territory of the regions or the whole country inasmuch by reallocating financial resources local budgets are capable of regulating the economy of the regions.

The autonomy of the local authorities is also supported by the local budget incomes, and financial sufficiency of the regions shall be primarily guaranteed by increasing these budgets while engaging innovative tools.

In this research we have elaborated an algorithm of complex financial mechanism evaluation in the regions which includes five stages (Figure 6).

When evaluating budgeting, it is reasonable to take into consideration the local incomes of the region as well as inter-budgetary transfers. Hence, the budget structure includes tax revenues (TR), nontax revenues (NTR), income from capital transactions (ICT) and inter-budgetary transfers (IBT). Therefore, the capacity of the budget mechanism of the regions (BM) is calculated according to the following formula:

$$BM = TR + NTR + ICT + IBT \qquad (2)$$

The principal indices of regional budget mechanism evaluation are presented in Table 1 (Zenchenko, 2010; Korobova, Gerasimov & Bykovskij, 2002; Cyrenov, Saktoev & Cyrenova, 2005).

Figure 6. Algorithm of complex financial mechanism evaluation in the regions

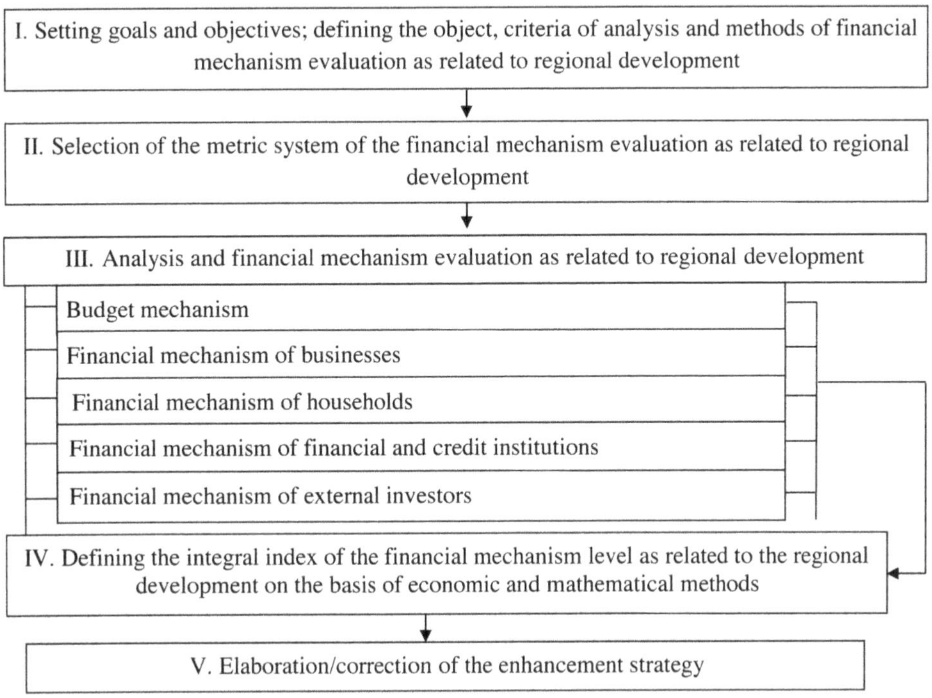

The performance evaluation from studying the indices allows for making a conclusion about the local budgets' autonomy, their capability to meet the needs of the region and stimulate its economic activity and development.

Socio-economic development of the regions predetermines growth of the financial mechanism capacity of the businesses, which is consequently expected to improve their financial sufficiency, i.e. to provide for their ability of successful financial resources management in the conditions of continuing

Table 1. Evaluation indices of regional budget mechanism

Index	Calculation Method	Recommended Value
Local budget incomes excluding inter-budget transfers, per capita	Local incomes/ Number of people	Growth is expected
Local budget expenditures excluding inter-budget transfers, per capita	Expenditures excluding inter-budget transfers / Number of people	Growth is expected
Budget sufficiency index	Local incomes/ The total income	>0,8
The total local budget benefit ratio	Aggregate income/ Aggregate expenditures	1
Tax sufficiency index	Tax revenue/ Local incomes	>0,8
Taxability index	Aggregate expenditures/ Tax revenue	≤2

disruptions from inside and outside and their ability to develop themselves in the running period and in the long term.

Capacity of the businesses' financial mechanism in the regions (BFM) is defined as a total of their own capital (OC) and borrowed capital (BC):

$$BFM = OC + BC \quad (3)$$

Evaluation of the businesses' financial mechanism has the purpose of on-the-spot correction in management and its adequate functioning and is carried out on the basis of index system combining wealth index, liquidity and financial solvency indices, financial soundness index and profitability index.

The principal indices of businesses' financial mechanism evaluation are displayed in Table 2 (Banks, 2012).

Analysis of the data allows detecting financial means for the businesses to successfully develop themselves, increase their investment potential and work in favor of their owners and the region itself.

In the financial system, financial market is in a class of its own dealing with economic and legal relations in the field with concentrated financial institutions involved in purchase and sale of financial assets and responsible for demand and supply making for the assets. They are financial institutions that are specifically engaged in accumulation and redistribution of the financial resources, which helps efficiently satisfy demand for them and contributes to the growth of economy. Accordingly, their successful operating and quality provision of financial services encourage socio-economic development of the region and the country.

Modern market economy is unimaginable without adequately and efficiently operating banks which, by means of specific tools, are capable of influencing every branch of economy. For this reason, activity of the central banks and international financial organizations is to a great extent focused on facilitating financial sufficiency of the banks globally. Thus, the International Monetary Fund has drafted a document specifying financial sufficiency indices applied to the financial institutions of the country and its

Table 2. Performance evaluation of the regional businesses' financial mechanism

Index	Calculation Method	Commentary	Recommended Value
Cover ratio	CA/CL	Shows ability of discharge current obligations	2÷2,5
Equity to total assets ratio	OC/C	Shows a share of own capital in the total capital	> 0,5
Current assets to equity ratio	OWC/OC	Shows a share of own capital in work	expected to grow
Financial leverage	BC/OC	Defines the volume of borrowed funds per 1 $ of own capital	< 1
Current and noncurrent assets ratio	CA/NA	Defines the asset structure of the business	> 1
Operating business profitability	OI/OBE*100%	Shows potential for reproduction and development	>0 expected to grow
Return on equity		Defines profitability of invested capital	>0 expected to grow

Reference designation: OWC – own working capital; TC – total capital cost; NA – noncurrent assets; OBE – operating business expenditures; OI – operating income; CA – current assets; CL – current liabilities; NP – net profit.

contractors; these indices assist in evaluation and control of strengths and vulnerability of the financial systems in order to increase their economic resilience (International Monetary Fund, 2008).

A bank being financially sufficient means its having efficient financial capital management while minimizing the risks, providing quality financial service and overcoming external and internal hazards.

In regards to financial and credit institutions, their financial mechanism capacity (FCIFM) is defined by their own capital (OC) and customer deposits (CD), i.e. the funds obtained from legal entities and individuals.

$$FCIFM = OC + CD \quad (4)$$

Evaluation of the financial and credit institutions' financial mechanism involves the indices based on capital structure and capital adequacy, structure of the obtained and borrowed funds, asset quality and dynamics of certain assets and liabilities (Prichina & Fateeva, 2010, p. 215-2017). The principal indices of evaluation of the financial and credit institutions' financial mechanism in the regions are given in Table 3.

Adequately selected instruments in the financial and credit institutions' financial mechanism evaluation allow for prompt and efficient detection of their weaknesses and potential as well as for disclosure of hidden reserves in order to enhance their functional efficiency.

Attracting foreign investments into the country's economy is one of the challenging issues today which requires focused attention. Foreign investments are not only an additional source of funding the formation of the financial mechanism in the regions, they usually come along with innovative technologies, equipment, innovative approaches to management and contacts with the institutions of the world economic system.

The main deterrents of foreign investments activity generally include lack of specific guarantees for foreign investors, high underlying inflation rates in the country, underdeveloped domestic financial market, imperfection of the legal system, bureaucratic red tape, high level of corruption, absence of preferential conditions for foreign investors (including preferential tax treatment), etc.

Table 3. Principal indices of evaluation of the financial and credit institutions' financial mechanism

Index	Calculation Method	Commentary	Recommended Value
Asset formation capital index	OC/A	Defines capital sufficiency in activation and risk covering	≥0,10
Credit activity index	CE/A	Shows a share of assets placed in credits	0,65÷0,75
Liquid assets and total assets ratio	LA/A	Shows a share of liquid assets in the total assets of the bank	0,15÷0,20
Borrowing and deposit ratio	CE/D	Defines potential of the bank for deposit attraction to finance its current operations	0,7÷0,8
Overall profitability	NP/inc*100	Shows profit per 1 RUB of received income	>0 growth
Return on total assets	NP/A*100	Shows payback of the yearly average assets by profit	>0 growth

Reference designation: A –assets; LA – liquid assets; D – deposits; CE – credit exposure; NP – net profit.

External investors' financial mechanism (EIFM) is defined by the direct foreign investments (DFI) attracted into the economy of the regions:

$$EIFM = DFI \quad (5)$$

The principal indices of external investors' financial mechanism in the regions are presented in Table 4 (Tolstova, 2012a, 2012b).

External investors' financial mechanism evaluation is crucial due to the fact that foreign investments are capable of contributing to the financial stability and economic growth in the regions in the conditions of limited internal funding.

The total financial mechanism of regional development (FMRD) is represented by the formula below:

$$FMRD = BM + BFM + FCIFM + EIFM \quad (6)$$

Defining financial mechanism capacity provides for the possibility of evaluating the economic potential of the regions and their subjects (local authorities, businesses, financial-and-credit institutions, external investors), which is expected to result in better planning of their socio-economic development.

With regard to the fact that the financial mechanism of regional development does not only reflect available financial resources, but also marks potential of their building up, growth and utilization, it is our opinion that along with quantitative indices specifying financial mechanism capacity of each constituent part, qualitative indices of its evaluation shall also be given.

The course of the study in terms of finding the factors of building up the financial mechanism in the regions as well as in Russia requires evaluation of the status and dynamics of the principal indices on the macro level; these indices are divided into five groups:

1. General economic development indices.
2. Business activity indices.
3. Wage rate indices.
4. Innovation and investment level indices.
5. Ecological indicators.

Economic foundation is the development basis of any community and it currently plays a major role by virtue of the fact that recurrent financial shocks inside of the country and on the world markets generally prevent from fully meeting the minimal needs of the subjects and hinder steady development (Table 5) ("Rating of socio-economic situation", 2016).

Table 4. Indices of external investors' financial mechanism in the regions

Index	Calculation Method	Recommended Value
Direct foreign investments per capita	DFI/Number of people	growth is expected
Gross regional product (GRP) as related to direct foreign investments into the economy of the regions	GRP/DFI	growth is expected
Share of direct foreign investments into the economy of the regions in relation to foreign investments into the economy of the country	DFI/DFI into the country's economy	growth is expected

Table 5. Income variability in the consolidated budgets of the Russian Federation's subjects in 2016

Consolidated Budget Deficit (-) / SurplusT (+) of the Subjects of the Russian Federation in 2016. Subject of the Russian Federation	Budget Income, mln. RUB.	Tax and Nontax Revenues, mln. RUB	Deficit (-) / Surplus (+), mln. RUB
Moscow	1 861,67	1783,9	115 625,6
The Republic of Bashkortostan	195,17	160,3	10 102,3
Moscow Oblast	551,73	523,3	8 004,1
Altai Krai	99,46	66,5	5 173,3
Vologda Oblast	67,22	55,4	4 683,5
Primorsky Krai	112,87	95,5	4 646,5
Rostov Oblast	190,90	155,3	4 535,9
Tyumen Oblast	142,51	134,6	4 447,0
Amur Oblast	57,80	44,6	3 510,8
Tver Oblast	63,94	52,4	3 453,6
Leningrad Oblast	136,68	127,3	2 864,1
Chukotka Autonomous Okrug	32,96	16,7	2 801,6
Murmansk Oblast	72,67	65,9	2 525,8
Krasnodar Krai	263,31	229,6	2 442,6
Ryazan Oblast	54,28	42,1	1 914,7
The Altai Republic	17,09	5,1	-55,5
Saratov Oblast	93,14	71,4	-62,5
Penza Oblast	55,32	38,9	-73,7
Novgorod Oblast	33,09	27,8	-257,6
Yamalo-Nenets Autonomous Okrug	155,16	152,1	-326,5
Tula Oblast	79,90	67,1	-358,3
The Mari El Republic	27,27	17,2	-362,2
Lipetsk Oblast	61,69	50,9	-463,3
The Republic of Kalmykia	11,64	5,4	-559,3
Tomsk Oblast	67,16	56,8	-580,7
Kamchatka Krai	72,04	28,5	-585,1
Perm Krai	133,11	117,7	-586,7
The Karachay-Cherkess Republic	21,23	8,6	-662,1
Orenburg Oblast	90,90	74,0	-686,0
Jewish Autonomous Oblast	11,35	6,5	-738,0
Novosibirsk Oblast	145,95	129,4	-744,7
Magadan Oblast	32,92	23,4	-835,9
Ulyanovsk Oblast	55,72	45,4	-1 224,5
Ivanovo Oblast	37,24	25,5	-1 246,6
Pskov Oblast	30,18	19,4	-1 515,5
Astrakhan Oblast	38,86	29,9	-1 593,7
Smolensk Oblast	43,32	35,7	-1 904,0

continued on following page

Table 5. Continued

Consolidated Budget Deficit (-) / Surplusт (+) of the Subjects of the Russian Federation in 2016. Subject of the Russian Federation	Budget Income, mln. RUB.	Tax and Nontax Revenues, mln. RUB	Deficit (-) / Surplus (+), mln. RUB
Kaluga Oblast	60,92	48,3	-2 031,0
Kursk Oblast	52,67	39,4	-2 185,6
Tambov Oblast	51,50	32,0	-2 423,2
The Republic of Buryatia	51,53	29,8	-2 528,7
The Republic of Karelia	39,32	26,4	-2 617,7
Kaliningrad Oblast	85,51	41,6	-2 817,1
Kurgan Oblast	37,90	22,5	-2 844,4
The Kabardino-Balkar Republic	31,22	16,5	-2 893,2
Kirov Oblast	54,84	39,1	-2 924,8
Belgorod Oblast	82,12	63,0	-3 059,0
Oryol Oblast	32,65	22,3	-3 228,4
Sakhalin Oblast	156,01	150,6	-3 262,7
Nenets Autonomous Okrug	14,54	12,9	-3 381,0
Sevastopol	21,82	10,3	-3 515,8

The economic situation in 2016 was heavily influenced by negative external economic factors which in the first place were fall in oil prices, progressing economic recession, decline in investments and large-scale capital outflow aggravated by the fact of settling a big share of foreign debt in the first six months of 2015.

Elaboration and refinement of the financial management mechanism in the regions requires prior analysis of their built up financial mechanism capacity, external and internal factors of its formation and utilization.

The level of economic development of the regions is defined by the volume of gross regional product (GRP) whose growth marks increase in production scale in the regions due to extensive (growing resource mechanism of the regions) and intensive (improved quality characteristics of the resource mechanism utilization in the regions) factors. Its analysis enhances further research related to socio-economic development level differentiation in the regions (Table 6) ("Rating of socio-economic situation", 2016).

The indices of economic scale and principal indices of economic efficiency are presented in Table 7.

On the basis of the generated data it is now possible to calculate the indices and rank the analyzed subjects of the Russian Federation according to their socio-economic development level as shown in Table 8.

Judging by the analyzed data, reforming domestic economy seems an imminent necessity inasmuch as the multifaceted and interrelated processes in the economy of the regions explain the need for elaboration of the statistical model defining their financial mechanism in the conditions of uneven financing. Therewith, it is a reasonable demand to create a hierarchical system of integral, roundup and specific estimates of financial mechanism capacity of each region, which would enable carrying out interterritorial analysis in dynamics (Zenchenko, 2010).

Table 6. Socio-economic indices of the regions of the registered for the ranking purpose

Federal Subjects of the Russian Federation	Goods and Services Production Value at Year-End 2016, RUB, bn.	Consolidated Budget Income at Year-End 2016, RUB, bn.	Number of Employed in the Economy, at Year-End 2016, Thousand People
Altai Krai	578.75	99.46	1059.64
Amur Oblast	263.57	57.80	389.41
Arkhangelsk Oblast	316.26	76.28	529.76
Astrakhan Oblast	316.66	38.86	482.99
Belgorod Oblast	1043.80	82.12	789.19
Bryansk Oblast	339.75	58.12	595.94
Vladimir Oblast	573.69	62.06	695.71
Volgograd Oblast	1064.00	101.49	1200.63
Vologda Oblast	691.13	67.22	570.46
Voronezh Oblast	852.80	105.61	1112.77
Moscow	8179.10	1861.67	7106.77
Saint-Petersburg	3376.07	485.87	2970.53
Sevastopl	46.01	21.82	181.27
Jewish Autonomous Oblast	29.73	11.35	77.61
Zabaykalsky Krai	219.36	55.57	477.54
Ivanovo Oblast	220.98	37.24	506.26
Irkutsk Oblast	1154.60	153.15	1137.35
The Kabardino-Balkar Republic	124.38	31.22	387.24
Kaliningrad Oblast	600.87	85.51	492.97
Kaluga Oblast	690.07	60.92	520.32
Kamchatka Krai	169.04	72.04	175.52
The Karachay-Cherkess Republic	93.36	21.23	184.20
Kemerovo Oblast	1439.20	135.62	1263.96
Kirov Oblast	355.47	54.84	643.46
Kostroma Oblast	198.95	26.97	309.51
Krasnodar Krai	2028.94	263.31	2579.39

By means of comparing the methods of distinct complex evaluation, taxonometry method was found the most adoptable for the purpose of synthesizing the overall performance index of the financial mechanism of regional development; this method is based on defining the deviation between the objects of the analysis and the reference standard.

The input information matrix is represented below in its standard form:

Table 7. Indices of economic efficiency in the regions of the in 2016

Subject of the Russian Federation	Overall Production of Goods and Services per Capita at Year-End 2016, RUB in Thousands per Capita	Investment in Fixed Capital per Capita at Year-End 2016, RUB in Thousands per Capita	Share of Profit-Making Businesses at Year-End 2016, %	Tax and Charges Debt-to-Income Ratio in the Budget of the Russian Federation, at Year-End 2016, %
Altai Krai	244.07	31.75	70.6	13.6
Amur Oblast	327.93	159.86	68.4	8.8
Arkhangelsk Oblast	280.87	80.62	72.7	8.7
Astrakhan Oblast	310.83	116.44	56.5	4.3
Belgorod Oblast	672.77	92.69	76.2	6.2
Bryansk Oblast	277.77	55.86	67.7	8.3
Vladimir Oblast	411.72	56.31	69.4	13.6
Volgograd Oblast	418.80	71.43	69.2	9.3
Vologda Oblast	582.85	101.70	74.5	8.3
Voronezh Oblast	365.31	116.09	80.1	8.2
Moscow	661.99	137.84	77.8	10.4
Saint-Petersburg	642.62	110.84	83.7	4.3
Sevastopl	108.90	28.61	69.4	1.1
Jewish Autonomous Oblast	179.97	77.85	48.5	9.9
Zabaykalsky Krai	202.92	77.72	60.8	12.2
Ivanovo Oblast	215.27	22.03	61.5	21.0
Irkutsk Oblast	478.92	107.22	75.8	6.0
The Kabardino-Balkar Republic	144.06	40.68	64.0	246.5
Kaliningrad Oblast	612.29	79.65	66.1	9.3
Kaluga Oblast	681.77	79.12	70.1	8.7
Kamchatka Krai	535.91	105.71	76.2	11.8
The Karachay-Cherkess Republic	199.86	42.60	77.2	19.3
Kemerovo Oblast	530.44	57.80	64.3	17.7
Kirov Oblast	274.58	40.98	75.1	10.0
Kostroma Oblast	306.17	40.74	69.1	20.8
Krasnodar Krai	366.08	77.40	76.9	10.8

Table 8. Ranking of the regions of the according to their socio-economic performance at year-end 2016

Position at Year-End 2016	Subject of the Russian Federation	Integral Rating at Year-End 2016	Position at Year-End 2015	Position at Year-End 2014
1	Moscow	80.891	1	1
2	Saint-Petersburg	74.541	2	2
13	Krasnodar Krai	57.217	16	15
17	Voronezh Oblast	54.946	19	24
19	Belgorod Oblast	52.353	18	18
23	Irkutsk Oblast	51.776	25	27
29	Vologda Oblast	48.467	37	41
35	Kaluga Oblast	45.139	40	30
39	Volgograd Oblast	44.222	34	36
40	Vladimir Oblast	43.846	39	35
42	Kemerovo Oblast	43.529	36	32
43	Kaliningrad Oblast	43.110	49	44
47	Altai Krai	41.947	46	45
48	Arkhangelsk Oblast	41.655	45	47
49	Amur Oblast	41.290	51	61
52	Bryansk Oblast	39.786	59	54
56	Kirov Oblast	38.333	48	52
58	Kamchatka Krai	37.908	57	60
62	Astrakhan Oblast	34.371	58	56
66	Zabaykalsky Krai	31.928	69	67
70	Ivanovo Oblast	29.476	68	65
74	Sevastpol	25.783	76	-
75	Kostroma Oblast	25.706	75	71
79	The Karachay-Cherkess Republic	22.514	78	78
81	The Kabardino-Balkar Republic	20.174	79	76

$$X = \begin{bmatrix} x_{11} & \cdots & x_{1j} & \cdots & x_{1n} \\ x_{21} & \cdots & x_{2j} & \cdots & x_{2n} \\ \cdot & \cdot & \cdot & \cdot & \cdot \\ x_{i1} & \cdots & x_{ij} & \cdots & x_{in} \\ \cdot & \cdot & \cdot & \cdot & \cdot \\ x_{m1} & \cdots & x_{mj} & \cdots & x_{mn} \end{bmatrix} \qquad (6)$$

n is the number of indices (j=1,2,...,n);

m is the number of years (i=1,2,...,m);
Xij is the value of index j which defines the index of year i.

The indices which do not make a significant difference for the final result were excluded from the preliminary list. Doing this required calculation of the coefficient of variation according to the formulae:

$$\nu_j = \frac{\sigma_j}{\overline{X}_j} \tag{7}$$

$$\sigma_j = \sqrt{\frac{\sum_{i=1}^{m}\left(X_{ij} - \overline{X_j}\right)^2}{m}} \tag{8}$$

$$\overline{X}_j = \frac{\sum_{i=1}^{m} X_{ij}^{\ 2}}{m} \tag{9}$$

X_{ij} is the value of index j for year i;
$\overline{X}_j$ is arithmetical average of index j;
$\left(X_{ij} - \overline{X}_j\right)^2$ is mean-square deviation of index j;
ν_j is coefficient of variation of j.

Such condition shall be taken into account for each j index:

$\nu_j > e$,

e is an extreme value.

Thus, in case the coefficient of variation of indices (νj) is less than 0,1, they are semipermanent and are considered equivalent. The data generated in the tables suggest that none of the indices is semi-permanent. From the standpoint that the selected indices are varied, their values can be standardized (normalized) according to the formula:

$$Z_{ij} = \frac{X_{ij} - \overline{X_j}}{\sigma_j} \tag{10}$$

The next stage required comparison of the obtained factual data to the value identified as a referenced standard. For this purpose the coordinates of the referenced standard point were defined. All the indices were to be divided into two groups: driver indices (their growth facilitates financial mechanism of regional development) and disincentive indices (such deferring growth).

In order to measure the referenced standard point (P_0), it was necessary to select the largest values among the driver indices and the lowest values among the disincentive indices:

$$P_0(z_{01},\ldots,z_{0k},\ldots,z_{0n}) \tag{11}$$

Где $z_{ok} = \max_i z_{ik}\ k \in J$;

$$z_{ok} = \min_i z_{ik}\ k \notin J$$

J is the multitude of driver indices.

The final stage of defining the integral index required a set of operations. First, the deviation between the points (Cio) that represent the analyzed elements and the referenced standard point (P_0) was calculated according to the formula:

$$C_{i0} = \sqrt{\sum_{k=1}^{n}(z_{ik} - z_{0k})^2} \tag{12}$$

i =1,2,….,m,
k =1,2,….,n;

Second, the integral index value of the financial mechanism of regional development (I_{ni}) was calculated according to the formula:

$$I_{ni} = 1 - \frac{C_{i0}}{C_0} \tag{13}$$

$$C_0 = \overline{C}_0 + 2S_0$$

$$\overline{C}_0 = \frac{1}{m}\sum_{i=1}^{m} C_{i0} \tag{14}$$

$$S_0 = \sqrt{\frac{1}{m}\sum_{i=1}^{m}(C_{i0} - \overline{C_0})^2} \quad (15)$$

Hence, the integral index allows for the complex financial mechanism level analysis in relation to the development of a specific region and suggests a set of measures in order to eliminate the problems detected in the process of enhancing the financial mechanism of each subject. The closer the integral index comes to 1, the higher is the level of the financial mechanism and, vice versa, the smaller is the index, the less sufficiency it shows.

With the reference to the integral index, we singled out five levels of financial mechanism of regional development: low, above average, average, above average and high; the strategy of enhancing the financial mechanism is selected according to the level. The extreme values of integral index are given in Table 9.

Therefore, differentiated approach with applied criterion of financial mechanism level allowed for singling out five groups of regions: regions with low financial mechanism level, regions with below average financial mechanism level, regions with average financial mechanism level, regions with above average financial mechanism level and regions with high financial mechanism level. With regards to the recurrent effect of the diverse internal and external factors of different, either positive or negative nature, on the financial system of the region, the current level of financial mechanism is largely situational and may be subject to change in the next periods. Subsequently, it is of great importance to select the correct strategy, the most efficient model of financial system development and implement it timely and appropriately.

The issues reported in the study suggest necessity of elaboration and implementation of the strategy to enhance the financial mechanism of regional development as a tool providing for the stability of the regional financial system and socio-economic development. The strategy involves a number of measures insuring a greater extent of independence for the local budgets, elaboration of the complex recuperation program for domestic businesses, implementation of the mechanisms withstanding internal and external threats to their economic activity, enhancement of the households' financial mechanism and their involvement in the investment processes, stimulation of bank activity and foreign investments in the regions through economic and administrative support and initiation of cross-border cooperation.

Table 9. Characteristic of the financial mechanism levels of regional development

Interval	Financial Mechanism Level	Strategy of Enhancing Financial Mechanism
[0;0,2)	low	Anti-recess strategy of regional development
[0,2;0,4)	below average	Financial mechanism recuperation strategy
[0,4;0,6)	average	Resources optimization strategy in building up the financial mechanism capacity
[0,6;0,8)	above average	Innovation and investment strategy of regional development
[0,8;1]	high	Financial mechanism enhancement strategy

Results and Findings

Financial mechanism forms the basis for the implementation of the national financial policy. In particular, it ensures the standard of living, stimulates entrepreneurial activity, promotes innovation, fosters environmental security, etc. It is also an integral part of the general regional mechanism as a combination of natural, production, labor, intellectual, financial, and information resources and possibilities for their use. At the same time, the institutional environment should be considered as one of the main conditions for the development of economic relations. Sustainable regional development is achieved through the effective interaction of institutions and market infrastructure.

Thus, the financial mechanism represents an aggregation of financial resources and opportunities for their formation, capacity building and effective use in accordance with internal and external conditions to meet the needs of the regions and ensure their social and economic development.

At the heart of the formation and use of the financial mechanism lies a systemic approach which involves integrated management of all its components based on the regularities of systematic development. In this process, certain elements are coordinated and implemented using an appropriate mechanism.

The main problems for ensuring the regional social and economic development in the Russian Federation today are the following:

1. Significant disproportions in regional development. As a result, the investment potential varies greatly from one region to another. For example, regions with a predominantly agricultural sector attract less investment, while the demand for their investment is annually growing (in particular, due to the aging agricultural machinery, equipment of processing plants, etc.).
2. Decrease in the level of self-sufficiency in the regions. Recently, local regional investments have been low, which, moreover, is deteriorating year by year. As a result, the share of transfers from the federal budget to the local budgets exceeded 50%.
3. Lack of financial resources in the local budgets to implement the regional socio-economic development programs. Most local budgets do not provide funding for such programs, as in some cases their funds fail to cover the existing operating costs.
4. Imperfect organizational support for regional development. Most of the legislative acts which are supposed to regulate the development of the regions are declarative in nature and do not include specific measures to accelerate this process. The existence of local governments along with state administrations makes it difficult to form and use financial resources at the local level.
5. Low activity of small business. To date, there is insufficient incentive for small businesses, which has an important role in creating GDP, promoting employment of the population, providing the regions with the necessary goods (services, works). Therefore, creating favorable conditions for small enterprises is a strategic task of socio-economic development in the regions.

Dynamic development of regions in an open economy is impossible without determining the system of priorities and ensuring the coherence of actions of all government bodies, enterprises and organizations, along with the population, and financial and credit institutions located on its territory (Menshchikova, 2010).

Solving the above-mentioned issues of socio-economic development requires the development and implementation of a regional strategy. The strategy of strengthening the financial mechanism of regional development holds a key place among its components, which is primarily due to the importance of financial support for its functioning and development.

The strategy of strengthening the financial mechanism of regional development is a model for the development of its financial system, which provides for the most rational, optimal, effective use of the mechanism for achieving regional goals. This strategy is one of the main tools for implementing a balanced financial policy of the state, while the financial goals of regional development should be formulated in the form of a certain concept (Tolstova, 2012a).

The concept is viewed as a system of key provisions (conceptual frameworks) which determine the approach to long-term socio-economic development of the regions, as well as the main mechanisms for the implementation of the specified strategic guidelines (Ul'janickaja, 2013). Based on this definition, the process of developing a strategy for strengthening the financial mechanism for regional development should include several stages to include the following: evaluation of the financial mechanism and determining its level; validation of the chosen strategy and setting specific goals to strengthen the financial mechanism taking into account the identified internal opportunities, advantages, strengths and weaknesses, threats to the financial system of the regions; drawing up a plan and determining the tools for its implementation.

Stages of formation and implementation of the strategy for strengthening the financial mechanism for the development of the regional economy are presented in Figure 7.

When implementing the strategy of strengthening the financial mechanism for the regional development, it is important to conduct a strategic analysis, a comprehensive study of external and internal factors and identify their impact in order to develop activities to achieve the goals of regional socio-economic development.

One of the most popular methods of strategic analysis is SWOT analysis, based on the approach proposed in 1963 by Professor Kenneth Andrews of the Harvard Business School. The essence of this method is to balance the internal capabilities of a system (its strengths and weaknesses) and the external situation (existing opportunities and threats) (Fedorova & Il'ina, 2013).

Considering that the strategy is formed on the basis of a conceptual approach, there are five possible options. The most appropriate option is selected according to the existing level of the financial mechanism, which is determined beforehand. Each strategy includes the main objectives that should be aligned with the goals of the regional social and economic development, the mechanisms for its implementation. The institutional environment should be taken into account as well.

Common to all strategies for strengthening the financial mechanism of regional development are the activities aimed to restore the financial stability of the regions, intensify financial flows and ensure further development.

The priority objectives include the following:

- Building up the region's own financial mechanism;
- Optimization of inter-budgetary relations;
- Stimulating business activity of enterprises and organizations, as well as self-employment;
- Assistance in attracting investment resources for regional development.

Figure 7. The sequence to evaluate the financial mechanism implementation effectiveness for regional development

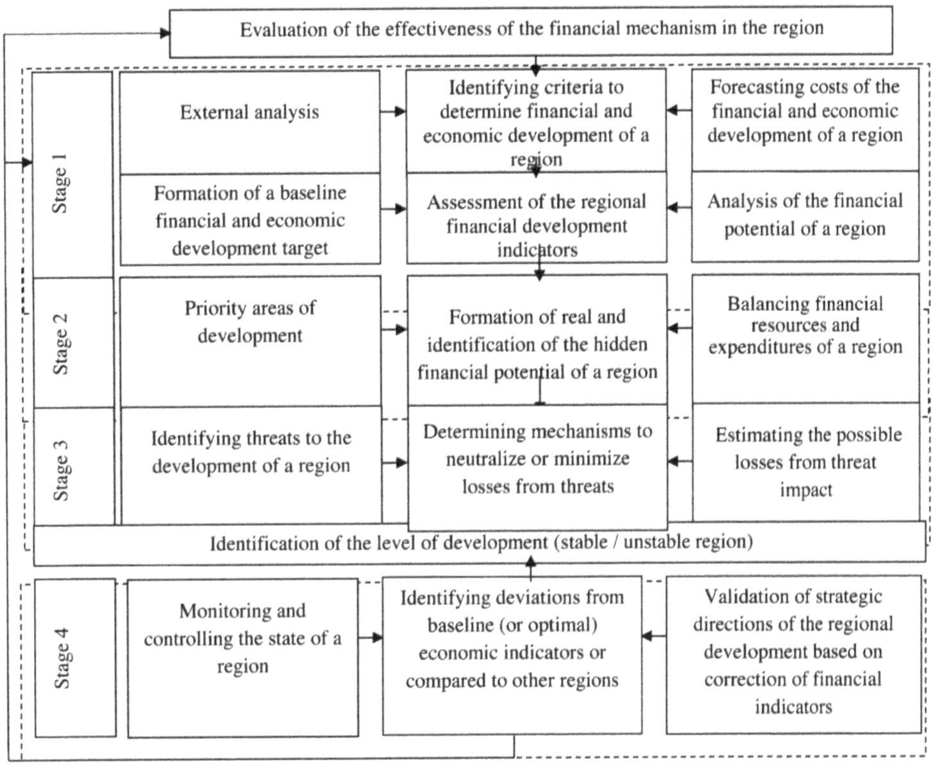

The choice directly depends on the regional financial mechanism level and represents the optimal direction for its financial system operation. The strategy foresees a sequence of actions taken by local and state authorities with the optimal combination of appropriate instruments for strengthening the financial mechanism in order to attain balanced regional development of the financial system (Table 10).

Monitoring the implementation of the strategy for strengthening the financial mechanism requires constant control and the timely identification of new factors not taken into account at the stage of strategy formation, as well as deviations which could adversely affect the financial system effectiveness.

During the implementation of a certain regional development direction, it is impossible to foresee all the factors influencing the regional financial system and identify their qualitative characteristics. Thus it is necessary to make adjustments taking into account new internal and external conditions. To evaluate the effectiveness of the strategy implementation, a system of relevant indicators is used both by individual financial mechanism components and by an integral indicator. The implementation of the strategy for strengthening the financial mechanism for the regional development is based on an integrated approach and should take into account the financial possibilities of the territory, provide for an alternative development of the financial system, depending on the level of the financial mechanism in order to meet the needs and safeguard the harmonious development of all regions.

Table 10. Strategic directions to strengthen the financial mechanism of regional development

Direction	Basis for the Application	Measures
Anti-crisis direction	The financial system of a region is in crisis (low level of all components of the financial mechanism)	• Restrictions in the provision of guarantees by local authorities to prevent possible abuse and increase in budgetary debt; • Reduction of administrative costs (expenses on local authorities, optimization of the number of civil servants); • Introduction of an exclusively targeted budget allocation; • Stimulating entrepreneurial activity in the region through the creation of an appropriate institutional environment, introduction of a tax incentive system, provision of administrative assistance to local authorities; • Liquidation of financially weak banks or their joining to more financially stable banking institutions; • Assistance in financial rehabilitation of unprofitable enterprises in the regions; • Optimization of the regional sectoral structure and diversification of its economy; • Financial support to the city-forming enterprises in order to remove economic and social tensions in the region;
Restoration of the financial mechanism for regional development	The regional economy is at the stage of recession	• Balancing the needs in financial resources and the opportunities for their formation (attraction) in the regions; • Restrictions in financing economic sectors with no or low social and economic effect; • Improvement of the investment climate in the region to attract external investors to the regional financial system; • Stimulating the investment activity in the region funded by local business entities and the population, regional financial and credit institutions; • Establishing a mesoprudential supervision system for effective risk management, aimed at minimizing (avoiding) losses from possible threats of macro, meso, and microlevel;
Fostering the sources of financial mechanism formation for regional development	The fall (a significant slowdown in growth) of the main sustainable development indicators in the regional financial system (medium level of the financial mechanism components)	• Attracting external loans to finance operating expenses and capital expenditures having the maximum economic and/or social effect; • Raising the level of capitalization of regional banks, monitoring their financial performance indicators; • Restriction of speculative operations in the financial market; • Assistance in developing the market of local borrowings, which will allow to supply the local budget with funding on innovative projects aimed at social and economic development of the regions; • Assistance in the formation of a powerful regional capital through the mechanism of partnership in financing investment projects by combining the capitals of financial and credit institutions, business entities, local authorities, the population (in various combinations);
Innovation and investment direction	Sustainable development of the regional financial system (high and medium level of the financial mechanism components)	• Stimulating innovation in the region; • Creating financial and credit institutions that will specialize in financing investment projects in the region; • Promoting the investment activity of households by issuing bonds of local borrowings to finance the development of the social sphere, housing and communal services in the regions; • Stimulating innovation and investment activity of local authorities by refusal to use the revenues from the implementation of investment projects for interbudgetary leveling, and allocating these funds for the regional development;
Building up financial mechanism capacity for the regional development	The region has a significant financial development mechanism (the highest level of all components of the financial mechanism)	• Supporting the real economy, especially the export-oriented sectors; • Promoting the interregional and cross-border cooperation; • Stimulating the development of clusters in the region

CONCLUSION

The comprehensive study of the financial mechanism of regional development conducted in this study resulted in practical findings that enable to achieve the main objectives according to the stated purpose, namely:

1. Sustainable socio-economic development of the regions requires adequate funding, which is currently limited by the insufficiency and inaccessibility of financial resources. Therefore, strengthening the regional financial mechanism remains an urgent challenge for the country's financial policy. The financial mechanism of regional development is an aggregation of financial resources and opportunities for their formation, their capacity building and effective use in accordance with the internal and external conditions to meet the needs of the regions and ensure their social and economic development.

Depending on the area of the financial mechanism formation, its components include the following: the budgetary mechanism, the financial mechanism of economic agents, the financial mechanism of households, the financial mechanism of financial and credit institutions, and the financial mechanism of external investors.

2. The financial mechanism acts as an object for assessing the financial ability of the regions being a prerequisite for socio-economic development. It is suggested to consider the financial viability of the regions as an ability for socio-economic development based on the effective use of innovative tools for managing the financial resources. This will result in resolved imbalances in financing the needs of the regions, facilitating the formation of a growing volume of the gross regional product and counteracting the permanent destructive influence of external and internal factors in short and long term perspective.
3. The basis for the formation and use of the financial mechanism is the systematic approach, which provides for the coordination of all its elements and financial relations with regard to the formation, distribution and use of financial resources in order to achieve the social and economic development goals. The main stages in the implementation and use of the financial mechanism are: assessment of the real and hidden financial mechanism; a comprehensive analysis of internal and external threats to the regional financial system; determining objectives of the financial mechanism formation and use; analysis of alternative strategies; implementation of the management decisions according to the selected strategy; control over the process of formation and use of the financial mechanism; effectiveness evaluation.
4. Evaluation of the financial mechanism of regional development is based on the principles of consistency, reliability, and objectivity, a comprehensive and systematic scientific approach, and effectiveness. This assessment should be based on the calculation of indicators, which allows tracking each component of the financial mechanism for the timely identification of threats to the regional financial interests and determining the strategic directions for strengthening their financial mechanism.

5. Based on the study of the current financial mechanism of the Russian regions, it was clarified that ineffective management of the budget mechanism is associated with an insignificant share of local budgets and a high dependence on inter-budgetary transfers. Solving these problems is possible through the effective implementation of the financial mechanism as an instrument for ensuring the stability of the regional financial system and their social and economic development, which takes into account the priorities of the regional financial development and strengthening of their financial base, the interests of the subjects, the instruments for achieving the specified objectives, the mechanisms to respond to the impact of internal and external factors.
6. The implementation of the financial mechanism for the regional development is carried out with an integrated approach and takes into account the financial possibilities of the territory, provides alternative directions for the financial system development, depending on the level of the financial mechanism to meet the needs and ensure the harmonious development of all subjects. A differentiated approach to the selection of directions made it possible to distinguish five directions: the anti-crisis direction; direction aimed at restoring the financial mechanism; direction aimed at fostering the sources of financial mechanism formation; innovation and investment direction; direction aimed at building up financial mechanism capacity. Each direction involves the use of appropriate instruments to streamline financial flows and achieve sustainable development of the regions.

ACKNOWLEDGMENT

The study was carried out with the support of the Program for the Development of the Federal State Autonomous Educational Institution of Higher Education V.I. Vernadsky Crimean Federal University for 2015-2024.

REFERENCES

Banks, E. (2012). *Finance: the basics* (2nd ed.). New York: Routledge.

Bartik, T. J. (1995). *Economic development strategies* (Vol. 95-33). Upjohn Institute Working Papers. Retrieved from http://research.upjohn.org/up_workingpapers/33

Beer, A., Haughton, G., & Maude, A. (2004). *Developing locally: An international comparison of local and regional economic development*. Bristol, UK: Policy Press.

Berk, J. B., & DeMarzo, P. M. (2014). *Corporate finance*. Pearson.

Bernstein, L. A. (1989). *Financial statement analysis: theory, application, and interpretation* (4th ed.). Irwin Publishing.

Brigham, E., & Ehrhardt, M. (2013). *Financial management: theory and practice*. South-Western Cengage Learning.

Cyrenov, A. R., Saktoev, V. E., & Cyrenova, E. D. (2005). *The mechanism of state impact on the formation of the institutional environment of the region's economy*. Ulan Ude: VSGTU Publ.

Dobrolezha, E. V. (2007). *Factors, conditions, models for the development of the region's economy: the theoretical and applied aspect*. Rostov-on-Don.

Fedorova, L. P., & Il'ina, T. S. (2013). Aspects of strategic management of a region as a socio-economic system. *Vestnik Chuvashskogo Universiteta*, *4*, 489–495.

Gitman, L. J., Juchau, R., & Flanagan, J. (2010). *Principles of managerial finance*. Pearson Higher Education AU.

Goldstein, M. (2005). The International Financial Architecture. In C. Fred Bergsten (Ed.), *The United States and the world economy: foreign economic policy for the next decade* (pp. 373–407). Washington, DC: The Institute for International Economics.

Golodova, Z. G. (2011). *Formation and management of the region's financial potential to ensure its economic growth* (Doctoral dissertation).

International Monetary Fund. (2008). *Financial Sustainability Indicators Guide*. Retrieved from http://www.imf.org/external/pubs/ft/fsi/guide/2007/pdf/eng/guide.pdf

Isaev, E. A. (2012). *Modernization of the system and development of the regional financial potential of the Russian Federation* (Doctoral dissertation).

Joumard, I., & Kongsrud, P. M. (2003). Fiscal relations across government levels. *OECD Economic Sludies*, *36*, 177–180.

Konyarova, E. K. (2006). *Reproduction management of the financial potential (on the example of the Udmurt Republic)* (Doctoral dissertation). Izhevsk.

Korobova, O. V., Gerasimov, B. I., & Bykovskij, V. V. (2002). *Regional economy: restructuring of the management system of the regional development*. Tambov: TSTU Publ.

Madura, J. (2014). *Financial markets and institutions*. Cengage learning, Inc.

McCarthy, T., Jordan, M., & Probst, D. (2011). *Six Sigma for Sustainability: How Organizations Design and Deploy Winning Environmental Programs*. New York: McGraw-Hill.

Menipaz, E., & Menipaz, A. (2011). *International Business Theory and Practice*. SAGE Publications.

Menshchikova, V. I. (2010). Strategy of social and economic development in the regional management system. *Vestnik TGU*, *6*(74), 77–87.

Moffett, M., Stonehill, A., & Eiteman, D. (2009). *Fundamentals of Multinational Finance* (3rd ed.). Pearson Prentice Hall.

Morozova, L. E., Bortnik, O. A., & Kravchuk, I. S. (2010). *Expert methods and technologies of integrated assessment of enterprise economic and innovative potential (A study guide)*. Moscow: MGUPS.

Pearce, J. A., & Robinson, R. B. (2009). *Strategic Management: Formulation, Implementation, and Control*. Boston: McGraw-Hill Irwin.

Prichina, O. S., & Fateeva, S. V. (2010). Financial and investment strategies of a region. *Terra Economicus*, *7*(3), 215-217.

Rating of socio-economic situation of the Russian Federation subjects at year-end 2016. (n.d.). Retrieved from *Rossiya Segodnya* Media Group website: http://www.riarating.ru/infografika/20170530/630063754.html

Robinson, T. R., Henry, E., Pirie, W. L., & Broihahn, M. A. (2015). *International Financial Statement Analysis* (3rd ed.). CFA Institute Investment Books.

Tolstova, M. L. (2012a). Financial strategy of the territory: Problem characteristics and organizational principles. *Vestnik Chuvashskogo Universiteta*, *2*, 467–470.

Tolstova, M. L. (2012b). System-forming principles for the formation and implementation of the regional financial strategy. *Vestnik Chuvashskogo Universiteta*, *4*, 492–495.

Ul'janickaja, N. M. (2013). Development of a regional management strategy: Conceptual approach. *Inzhenernyj Vestnik Dona*, *20*(2), 574–582.

Verbinenko, E. A., & Badylevich, R. V. (2012). Financial potential as the basis for regional development. *The North and the Market: Formation of the Economic Order*, *2*(30), 58–62.

Volkov, A. M. (1976). *Prospective planning of the financial resources*. Moscow: Finansy.

Zenchenko, S. V. (2010). *Formation and assessment of regional financial potential of sustainable development of the territory's economy: the theory and methodology* (Doctoral dissertation).

Chapter 10
Taxation System in Slovakia: National Featues and Prospects of Integration

Marcela Rabatinová
University of Economics in Bratislava, Slovakia

Juraj Válek
University of Economics in Bratislava, Slovakia

Jana Kušnírová
University of Economics in Bratislava, Slovakia

ABSTRACT

A common European area without any internal borders between the EU Member States creates greater risks in terms of tax evasion and avoidance by economic entities. Increasing tax burden during the financial and economic crisis led to an increase in tax evasion as a result of changes in the behavior of taxpayers. This chapter deals with the current problems of taxation in Slovakia in the context of effective tax collection and tax evasion prevention. The aim of the chapter is to assess the development of corporate income tax, excise tax on alcoholic beverages, and value added tax, which are considered to be the most risky ones in terms of tax evasion.

INTRODUCTION

Slovak tax system is a young one. A new tax system of the independent Slovak Republic introduced back in 1993 had many features similar with Danish tax system. The main task of the tax policy of that time was providing the sufficient volume of tax revenues in the course of transition from the centrally planned economy to the market one. The difficulty of this task was emphasized by the fact that new taxes were demanded in the period of significant changes in the structure of both revenues and expenses. The first tax reform in the early years of Slovak independence had its impact on all areas of economic policy at the macro and micro levels since the related changes in the tax policy influenced the fiscal and the social dimensions as well as general economic one. The first phase of the tax reform in Slovak Republic started in 1991. The year 1992 can be considered as the second phase of the tax reform already, because

DOI: 10.4018/978-1-5225-7760-7.ch010

the first tax act was adopted. It led to determination of the separate types of taxes, which form the new tax system of Slovak Republic, e.i., there was already a division between direct and indirect taxes.

In June 2003 Slovak government approved the document titled "The Concept of the Tax Reform in the Slovak Republic in 2004-2006". The purpose of the tax reform was to eliminate the deficiencies of the already functioning tax system. The tax reform was part of the broader reform programme, which also included the reform of public finance, social and pension reforms, labour market reform, healthcare sector reform and also reform of public administration. There was a significant drop in the rate of the corporate income tax to 19% which was applied to natural persons in the same amount as VAT. However, this decrease of the tax rate was accompanied by the significant increase of tax revenues.

The tax system often tends to become some sort of a vicious circle. Due to the presence of various tax benefits, tax rates must be maintained at a level high enough to cover the required expenses. High tax rates usually stimulate tax avoidance behavior among population as well as businesses. It reduces the tax base and creates the pressure on further increase of tax rates (Jackson & Brown, 2003). We can state that it is not possible to copy the tax system of another country while introducing own tax system, the philosophy of own tax policy of a particular state must be always unique. Introduction of own tax system also means some sort of compromise between the current trends of taxes on the international scale on the one hand and specificity of a country on the other.

Tax system is a dynamically developing organism, with its own internal and external impacts. Implementation of tax policy means practical application of tax instruments for influencing economic and social processes in the society. Effectiveness of each tax collection can be assessed from several standpoints. In the times when tax revenues are decreasing it is necessary to search for new possibilities of obtaining additional budget revenues. Changes in tax policy have a significant impact on the development of fiscal policy as well as on the formation of pension and social policies. They also influence the structure of population incomes and the character of consumption in a country.

A significant external factor which has its strong impact on the tax system of Slovak Republic is the international cooperation of tax administrations. The most important effects from the international exchange of information in this field are prevention of tax evasive behavior and additional support for voluntary compliance with tax obligations. A well functioning and effective system of the international exchange of information on taxation creates extra pressure on the individuals that tend to demonstrate tax evasive behavior. Secondly, there is an additional financial effect since international cooperation in the field of tax compliance is able to provide additional budget inflows into Slovak Republic, and since 2004 such additional inflows have actually grown manifold. Cooperation of Slovak tax authorities with their Dutch and Danish colleagues has proved to be quite effective in terms of measurable financial results for Slovak Republic. Experience of European counterparts has been used in Slovakia as the basis for the creation of own risk management model and better control under specific conditions of Slovak economy.

PURPOSE, OBJECTIVES AND HYPOTHESES OF THE STUDY

The purpose of this study is to highlight the current development problems of the taxation system in Slovak Republic, e.i., those problems that are directly related to effective collection of the selected taxes and elimination of tax evasion. The monitored period is the period from the time of Slovak Republic accession to the European Union back in 2004 until the end of 2016.

The objectives of the study are as follows:

1. To evaluate the development of corporate tax, excise tax on alcoholic beverages and VAT which are considered to be the most risky taxes in Slovak Republic in terms of tax evasion.
2. To identify the national features in the development of the monitored taxes and to evaluate the impact of Euro-integration processes on the volumes of these taxes' returns.
3. To formulate the recommendations on more effective tax collection in the future.

The main hypotheses of the study are formulated as follows:

H1: Budget revenues from corporate tax within the tax system of Slovak Republic is significantly influenced by external factors. And the latter represent thus a serious risk from the standpoint of tax return volumes.
H2: Revenues from the excise tax on alcoholic beverages are a stable source of income for the state budget of Slovak Republic, therefore, effective collection of this tax must be ensured at all times.
H3: VAT is the tax with the highest return in Slovak Republic. It is also considered to be the most risky one when it comes to tax evasion. This is because from the point of view of volumes evasion from VAT payments is potentially the largest of all taxes.

LITERATURE REVIEW

Corporate taxes in Europe today are undergoing the processes of harmonisation. This process has been ongoing since the establishment of the European Community. A common feature of all theories in this regard is that their representatives try to identify and quantify the factors with the biggest influence on the selection of this tax in each country. The absolute majority of all publications on the issues of legal entities' taxation states that comparison of tax collection effectiveness between different countries is very complicated due to various factors influencing the tax base as well as the amount of tax liability of a legal entity (Sullivan, 2011). Therefore, harmonisation of corporate income tax is a rather broad-spectrum process. Major obstacles to this harmonisation concern the differences in tax rates, application of specific conditions for taxation of the selected legal entities operating in the selected sectors of the economy, as well as providing specific economic stimuli for some of these legal entities (Hameakers, 1993; Mitchell, 2001; Wilson, 1986; Edwards & Rugy, 2002; Genser & Haufler, 2002).

The ideas of better coordination of corporate taxation were revived in the EU in the period after 2001, when many studies started offering new solutions concerning the harmonisation of the tax base of companies in the European Union. However, the European Commission is currently developing its own new conditions for the application of Common Consolidated Corporate Tax Base (CCCTB). The list of authors who have analyse the way how corporate income taxation creates the imbalance in the economic choices while reducing their efficiency, include, for example (Nicodème, 2009). This author, inter alia, has summarized the logical reasons for the corporate tax existence as such. Namely, under certain conditions, especially those directly related to capital mobility, the classical economic models clearly show that the optimal value of capital taxation in a small open economy equals to zero. Many other authors also analyze the basic "pro" and "cons" along with other issues related to the existence of corporate tax as such (Weichenrieder, 2005; de Mooij, 2005).

New challenges in the field of corporate taxation include identification of the impact factors and types of unbalances generated due to the impact of corporate tax at both domestic and international levels. Authors studying these issues do not really agree on the macroeconomic indicators which are most affected by the corporate income tax. When it comes to the issue of corporate tax rates the majority of the economists agree with the statement that reduction of corporate tax rate reduces the volume of the reported tax losses and tax evasion related to this tax and therefore, increases the fairness of taxation overall. The authors also often point out to the significant differences between the theoretical concepts of companies' taxation and the actual, real-life policies of corporate taxation (Auerbach, 2006; Mankiw, Weinzierl, & Yagan, 2009).

Alcoholic beverages belong to the category of goods with low demand elasticity according to (Ramsey, 1927), especially when compared to other products. These beverages are at the same time classified as harmful goods. Their consumption causes additional social costs. Therefore, this description corresponds with the definition of negative externalities. W.J. Corlett and D.C. Hague (1953) dealt with the situation when two consumer goods are taxed by the same rate. They tried to find out whether it is possible to increase the effectiveness through more diversity in taxation. They deduced the rule of complementarity of free time that can be used to increase the effectiveness, if the tax rate on goods with a higher degree of complementarity to free time increases (higher degree of complementarity also means lower degree of substitution). Increase in the tax on goods with higher complementarity to free time increases the work demand and thus partially compensates the original deformation. C.J. Heady and P.K. Mitra (1980) came to the conclusion that the models offered by Ramsey, Corlett and Hague lead to higher taxation of the same goods, because in case of inverse elasticity it can be proved that the goods which are more complementary to free time, have lower elasticity of demand too.

The goods of specific consumption (alcohol, tobacco and mineral oils) are generally highly taxed and according to (Heady & Mitra, 1980) it would be justifiable to prove their complementarity to free time. However, this sort of taxation is rather more related to negative externalities caused by these products. In case of alcoholic beverages, for example, the negative externalities might include the threats to life or property of third parties, higher divorce rates, damaging impact on the health of consumers etc. Therefore, the fiscal function here has same importance as the education function. This view represents Ramsey´s approach to taxation. Despite gradual but constant increase of this tax rate, consumption of alcoholic beverages and thus absolute revenues from this tax are only growing. We can relate this to the typical feature of many individuals in the societies worldwide: people refuse to give up those goods which bring them pleasure, thus getting to some extent addicted to these products. A common approach of the states is important in this regard for more efficient solution of the problem of negative externalities from the abovementioned commodities. In 1993 it was assumed that creation of the single EU market would lead to the increased tax competition among the country members, especially in what concerns regulation of the excise taxes. According to (Lockwood & Migali, 2009), this had already happened with non-sparkling and sparkling wines and beer, at least, according to the data these authors have obtained on the selected EU countries in the period of 1987-2004.

In both theory and practice selective taxation of goods means taxing production and consumption of goods that generate negative externalities, and thus, majority of governments tax the consumption of alcohol, tobacco or mineral oils by the means of selective (specific) excise taxes. On the other hand, in both theory and practice again there are arguments about whether indirect taxes should be systematically differentiated, even when negatively externalities do not really exist.

Following the classical approach of (Ramsey, 1927) and also the much later offered approach of (Corlett & Hague, 1953), many theoreticians prefer differentiated taxation of commodities, even in the case of general consumption. However, its application in real practice is problematic mostly due to impossibility of reliable estimation of cross elasticities between free time and the consumption of each product available at the market, but also due to the need of regular actualisations of these elasticities in order to take in consideration too quick changes in preferences and technologies (Sørensen, 2007; OECD, 2010).

Justification of the differentiated VAT rates' application in the context of optimal taxation of commodities is related to the application of Ramsey´s rule of inverse elasticity of demand, which requires higher taxation for goods with lower elasticity of demand, i.e., basic goods and services. The structure of VAT rates which are currently being applied in the EU does not represent the rule of inverse elasticity. On the contrary, the reduced VAT rates are applied mostly to the goods with low elasticity (food, clothes etc.). This is mostly done with the aim to reduce the tax burden on low-income households.

In practice, the uniform taxation of final consumption is preferred, while the following three reasons are usually emphasized. First, the system of VAT with the uniform tax rate is simpler and less susceptible to fraud from the viewpoint of administration, when compared to the system of VAT with differentiated tax rates. Second, the system of differentiated taxation of consumption, according to Ramsey´s principles, would require frequent changes in tax rates depending on consumers´ preferences and changes in technologies. It would implement a new element of risk and uncertainty into the tax system, which could hamper its long-term planning and investments. Third, setting differentiated taxation of consumption as a general rule could lead to the growth of lobbying by special interest groups, which would try to enforce lower tax rates for their specific economic activities.

VAT system is considered to be effective when the whole potential tax base is subordinated to the standard rate of VAT and tax administration collects the tax due in the most effective way (Ebrill, Keen, Bodin, & Summers, 2011). The question, whether consumption should be taxed by the uniform rate of VAT or the system of differentiated tax rates should be applied on various goods and services is the subject of many theoretical and practical approaches to the optimal taxation of consumption. The same question is currently being discussed at the level of the EU concerning the proposed final system of VAT which is supposed to be launched at the level of the EU in 2022 (European Commission, 2017).

METHODOLOGY

Tax system contains a number of contradictions and it is usually the system of many compromises. It is generally applicable that the less various exceptions and allowances are provided by a tax system - the simpler it is in terms of the number and the content of tax laws, and also the more transparent it is. Then it is easier to monitor and spread tax discipline, too. Slovak Republic has become the EU member in 2004, therefore, since then high level of harmonisation of VAT and excise taxes and more intensive international cooperation became natural part of its work methods. Comparison between individual approaches of the selected EU countries and the common approach of the EU countries to VAT and excise taxes can help us reveal the national features of taxation.

Within the overall structure of Slovak tax system our subjects for examination would be VAT, corporate income tax and excise tax on alcoholic beverages which are the riskiest ones in terms of tax evasive behavior. At the same time, VAT and corporate income tax belong to the taxes with the highest returns in Slovak Republic. In the course of our analysis we will be reviewing and evaluating the processes which happen to be transformative, along with their impact factors and historic causes for all related changes.

National Features and Perspective Directions of Corporate Taxation in Slovak Republic

Tax policy is usually aimed at solving the problems with employment, stabilizing prices and supporting national economic growth overall. All of the above can be supported by means of both tax and non-tax measures, when the state tries to provide the best conditions for local companies. The key features of corporate taxation in Slovak Republic are: combination of the uniform income tax rate, minimisation of tax allowances and reduction of the volume of state aid provided to companies.

Every year the government of Slovak Republic is struggling with the lack of financial means in the state budget. Therefore, the need for changes in current taxation methods and more effective collection of corporate tax are easily understandable. From 2004 to 2016 tax legislation offered several new tax and non-tax instruments and also have made the existing ones more effective with the primary aim of all changes being maximum collection of corporate tax returns.

At the time of Slovak Republic emergence as an independent state the corporate income tax rate was approximately 45%. The lowest corporate income tax rate of 19% was applied in the Slovak Republic since 2004 till 2012. Despite the fact that the majority of European countries gradually reduced the tax burden on companies due to the crisis, Slovakia increased the rate up to 23% in 2013. Last 4 years of our research period were characterized by the gradual reduction of the nominal tax rate for companies. However, reduction of corporate tax rate was realized together with the introduction of the institute of tax license (the minimal tax amount). This did not mean reduction of tax burden for many companies though. Our analysis of tax conditions in Slovak Republic has demonstrated that 38.7% of all changes in corporate income tax revenues has been influenced by changes in the tax rate imposed on companies. We can state that tax rates for companies in Slovak Republic are set quite high and further increase could rather cause reduction of tax revenues. Moreover, it could lead to the increased rate of tax evasion, more transfers of capital abroad, less economic activity by companies overall and lower motivation for the companies to invest inside own country. All of the abovementioned factors would result in the reduction of tax base and thus, also in the reduction of tax revenues under corporate tax.

The main features of the reform steps in the field of corporate taxation in 2004 was to change the then acting tax policy which was favouring certain sectors of economy or specific types of business entities. It was substituted by the flat tax policy, which created generally favourable conditions for businesses and investors. The main positives from that tax reform with the impact on corporate business primarily were related to the implementation of proportional tax rate for legal entities in the amount of 19%, elimination of a wide range of exceptions and exemptions, cancellation of the reduced income tax rates for the selected legal entities, cancellation of the tax on dividends, reduction in the number of depreciation groups of tangible and intangible assets, cancellation of the condition of reinvestments within carry-forwards and finally improvements related to companies' registration.

Together with the accession of Slovak Republic to the EU the second tax reform resulted in corporate income tax becoming the third biggest source of tax revenues in Slovak Republic after VAT and excise taxes in 2004. The inflow of foreign investments, ongoing decrease of interest rates and improving business environment also contributed to the increased corporate income tax revenues in this period. New principles for tax audit planning were put into practice in 2004 together with the tax reform. When it comes to legal entities the audits have become primarily focused on the interconnected tax entities. The year 2004 was also a breakthrough period from the viewpoint of the executed audits of corporate tax, since the number of audits of corporate income tax was lower by more than 70% in comparison with the same period of the previous year.

This reform of public finance which had such a positive start ensured that economic growth of Slovak economy during 2004-2008 was one of the highest among the EU countries and it was paradoxically accompanied by the highest growth of tax revenues. The impact of the global economic and financial crisis started to have its slightly negatively influence on the performance of Slovak economy towards the end of 2008. The industrial production was weakened and the trust of companies was shaken. May 2012 was a crucial period in terms of tax evasion, because the Action Plan against Tax Evasion was approved. The year 2009 was the most important one in the history of the independent Slovak Republic from the viewpoint of corporate income tax. The share of this tax in the total tax revenues reached the highest level of 30%. The effects from the crisis became notable for companies only at the end of 2010 and this had its impact in the form of budget revenues' drop in Slovak Republic.

The period of 2011-2012 was characterised by the recovery of the business sector and gradual growth of the companies' profits with the positive impact on the corporate tax revenues too. The period after the crisis in Slovak Republic was characterized by the fact that apart from changes in the tax policy with their impact on legal entities, the measures of non-tax character were put into practice in order to increase the effectiveness of corporate tax collection. Thus, all businesses of legal entities were influenced by the implementation of newer elements, such as registration fees for cars, additional taxation of banks and some other types of companies and also criminal liability in the field of taxation. The retrospective conditions for carry-forwards, the implementation of tax licence and the growth of the nominal corporate income tax rate in 2012 became those several selected factors with the direct negative impact on companies' profitability.

Since 2010 profitability of companies and corporate tax revenues in Slovak Republic have been continuously growing. The only exception was the year 2014 when the implementation of tax licences caused a slight drop in corporate tax revenues. Stemming from our complex analysis of Slovak corporate income tax we can state that its position within the tax system of Slovak Republic is indisputable. Considering the monitored period the corporate income tax was the second most important source of budget revenues in the country. Nowadays it is at the level of 26% share of the total tax revenues in Slovak Republic. The overview of corporate tax revenues is presented in Figure 1.

Figure 1. Dynamics of corporate tax in Slovak Republic
(Source: Statistics of Financial Administration of Slovak Republic and own calculations)

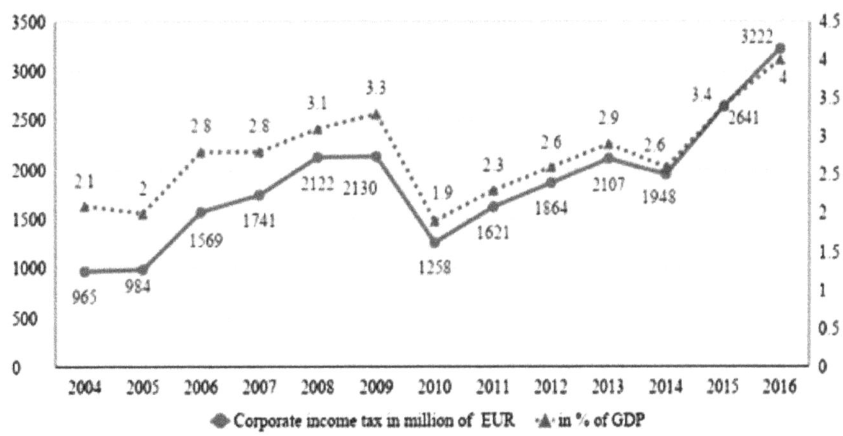

It is necessary to mention that effectiveness of the corporate tax collection in Slovak Republic is closely related to the issue of tax assignation. Slovakia is the only EU country to grant companies the right to decide about the transfer of a part of paid corporation tax to public benefit entities.

We also need to mention here that the number of registered legal entities increased nearly three times during the monitored period. Despite the abovementioned growth in the number of companies doing business in Slovakia, the number of income tax audits fell dramatically - from 37.8% to 8.2% from the total number of the executed tax audits. Such a rapid decline of tax audits on income tax may cause higher occurrence of tax evasion cases in the future, actually, since it is one of the non-financial effects of any tax audit. The volume of additional corporate tax levy grows. It proves the growth in the effectiveness of control mechanisms applied by the tax administrator. The open question here is whether this continuous reduction in the number of tax audits concerning corporate tax is appropriate, taking into account the abovementioned growth in the number of legal entities in Slovak Republic overall. Nowadays, the main objective of any tax audit - as part of financial administration - is to reach the compliance with tax obligations of companies with no delays and in the full amount. Other, additional objectives include: providing higher level of professionalism among the employees of financial administration, identifying companies under risk, increasing the number of claims on tax arrears and also improving the technological proficiency of tax administration staff.

Looking at the effective collection of corporate tax in Slovak Republic it is also necessary to take into account the effect of the related and interacting areas with the emphasis on the business of legal entities. The number of legal entities doing business and their profitability are influenced by the changes in Business Code, by the introduction of criminal liability of legal entities and by some other changes in the area of corporate income taxation in Slovak Republic.

It logically follows from the above that profit of legal entities belongs to the items which are very difficult to estimate. Corporate tax revenue is influenced by the several factors which are characterized by great variability within the economic cycle. These factors include, e.g., the option of the deduction of tax loss and withholding tax on taxable profit, changes in the deduction policy as well as changes in providing tax allowances for companies.

National Features of Excise Tax on Alcoholic Beverages and Perspectives of Integration

Distillery, brewing and wine-making industry are significantly influencing Slovak economy since these are quit economically strong sectors. Together they represent 15% of Slovak GDP and also a 17% share in the total employment of Slovak Republic. Slovakia is the country with the highest share of rural population in the EU. Tax laws in this field have undergone many changes since Slovak Republic got its independence.

The subject of excise tax on alcoholic beverages is an alcohol beverage produced in Slovak Republic, i.e., on the tax territory, delivered to this tax territory from another EU state or imported to this tax territory from a third state, outside the EU. Alcoholic beverages in Slovak Republic include: distilled spirits, wines (non-sparkling wines, non-sparkling fermented beverages, sparkling wines and sparkling fermented beverages), intermediate products and finally beer. The related tax is administered by the customs office.

The rates applicable in Slovak Republic on ethyl-alcohol (spirits) are at the medium level as compared to the rates applied in other EU countries. The rates on wine, intermediate products and beer applied in Slovak Republic are approximately in the second half of the chart when comparing to other EU countries.

The beginning of the excise taxes' harmonization dates back to the 1970s, when the EEC Council issued a decree dealing with the excise tax on tobacco products as of 21st April 1970.

Firstly, it was necessary to determine the product area to which the selective tax will apply since there was a different structure of selective excise taxes in each European country. Council Directive no. 72/43/EEC on excise tax as of 1972 defined the products which would be subject to the excise tax, namely - mineral oils, tobacco, distilled spirits, beer and wine.

The common system of excise taxes was introduced in the EU on 1st January 1993 by the Council Directive no. 92/12/EEC on the general arrangements for products subject to excise tax and on holding, movement and monitoring of such products. The system directive set general concepts, such as production, holding, transport of products subject to taxation as well as the basic principles and mechanisms of excise taxes' operation, the so-called tax regimes. The system directive no. 92/12/EEC was later substituted by a new system directive no. 2008/118/EC on the general arrangements of excise taxes. These structural directives contain a precise definition of the tax subject and tax base, special methods of taxation, tax benefits and so on. According to the Directive no. 92/83/EEC alcohol and alcoholic beverages are divided into the following groups: wine, beer, fermented beverages, intermediate products and alcohol.

The harmonisation process for taxation of alcoholic beverages was very complicated from the very beginning. These complications were caused by the historical development of this tax since some of the states had been known for their traditional production of alcoholic beverages since from the Middle Ages, or even earlier. Countries like France, Spain and Italy, are the traditional producers of wine, Belgium and Germany are more known for their production of beer, while Ireland and Scotland are world-known producers of whisky. Therefore, it was quite difficult to harmonize the excise taxes for all these diverse countries since taxation of alcohol based on traditional procedures and consumer preferences was applied in the abovementioned countries for a very long time.

Therefore, the adopted Directive no. 92/83/EEC on harmonization of excise taxes on alcohol and alcoholic beverages is based on European historical preferences and it divides all related products into beer, wine (non-sparkling, sparkling wines and fermented beverages), intermediate products and spirits. The minimal rates are set for the whole group of products by the Council rate directive no. 92/84/EEC on the approximation of the excise tax rates for alcohol and alcoholic beverages. Setting of these minimal rates respects national, production and consumer preferences of the separate member states. It also enables separate member states to tax these products by higher rates than the minimal ones, especially if they have to obtain the fiscal aims of taxation.

Demand for alcohol is not elastic due to its character of addiction and so only small changes of demand might be the result from the increasing price. The minimal price for alcohol does not have to have an important impact and in the long term it can lead to the formation of black market. Minimal price is also regressive in nature because it focuses specifically on poor alcoholics, homeless people, who buy the cheapest alcoholic beverages possible. The European Commission opts for higher excise taxes since there is a common belief that the minimal tax rate is better than setting the official lowest alcohol price. On the other hand, higher prices for alcohol products can also lead to the development of black market.

Excise tax on alcoholic beverages is important not only for the tax system of Slovak Republic, but also for many other tax systems worldwide. Dynamic development of GDP in Slovak Republic corresponds with the dynamic development of revenues from excise tax on alcoholic beverages (see Figure 2). Despite the ongoing harmonisation of excise taxes in the EU, the excise tax rates on spirits, wines and beer still vary among the individual states.

Figure 2. Revenues from the excise tax on alcoholic beverages in Slovak Republic
(Source: Statistics of Financial Administration of Slovak Republic and own calculations)

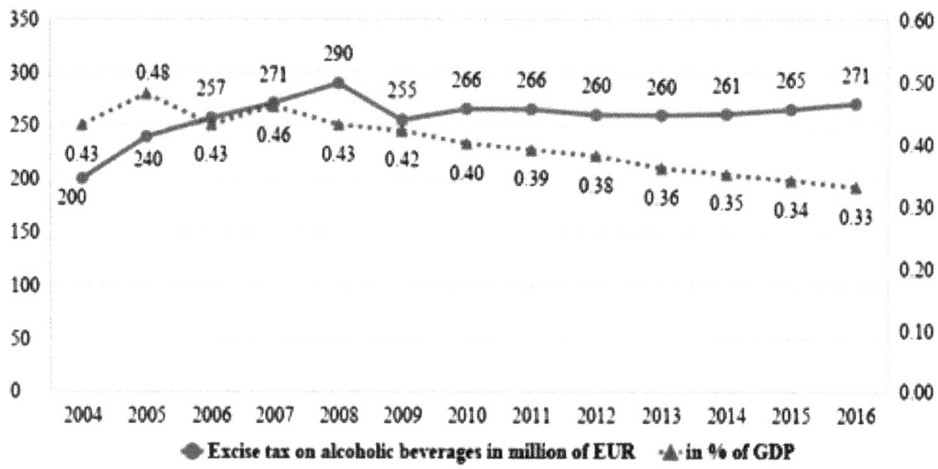

In relation to revenues from the excise tax on alcoholic beverages, tax evasion can be also monitored, especially when it comes to the excise tax on spirits. Tax evasion in this case can be caused by quite high tax burden and also by not very complicated technological process of production, with beer especially. Spirits can be made from freely available raw materials. Storing does not require special conditions and moreover, some of the required ingredients can be easily changed by substitutes, what makes illegal practices even easier. High tax burden on spirits leads both consumers and companies to the idea of illegal distillation of alcohol which, in its turn, introduces additional risks - economic ones and also those related to health (Válek & Zubaľová, 2014).

Tax evasion and the related illegal alcohol production include production of alcohol by the subjects which are not properly registered or not certified for distillation of alcohol at home, and also those subjects that are engaged in the sale of illegally produced and imported spirits, sale of spirits without trademarks, unauthorized claims for tax refunds related to spirits' sales and finally, illegal import and export of alcohol. Ownership of a device that can be used for alcohol production is considered illegal, too. Fruit kvass from an agriculturist can be fermented in a properly registered distillery plant for fruit fermentation. The plant operator collects the tax from the agriculturist when delivering alcohol, while he can also use the reduced tax rate, but on the maximum of 43 l of pure alcohol from the produced spirit on one agriculturist and their household for one production period.

According to the data of the Customs Criminal Office for the period of 2004-2010 on the amount of estimated illegally produced alcohol on the territory of Slovak Republic, the most frequent fraud cases related to illegal distillation included: operating an illegal distillery plant, production plant or filling device; ownership of an unregistered distillery device, technological device, filling device, device for alcohol production as well as an unauthorized intervention into the technological device of a legal distillery plant.

The total number of executed audits on excise taxes has a decreasing trend. The Financial Administration of Slovak Republic states that this trend is caused by the reduction in the number of initiatives by the law enforcement agencies, changes in the locality jurisdiction as well as termination of some tax subjects, increased activity of some customs offices when executing local survey and audits for several taxing periods within one tax audit. The most important deficiencies found by tax audits concerned the following positions: differences in the excise tax from the excise tax stated in the tax return due to exceeding the quantitative limit per one agriculturist; exceeding the drawing of standardized losses of spirit and their incorrect calculations, sale in the packaging of unconfirmed origin, participating in tax-free circulation without the necessary permission or acquiring goods that are subject to excise tax without proper payments.

Majority of tax audits related to the excise tax on alcoholic beverages were executed in the distillery industry, second by the number of these audits goes the wine industry. The least of tax audits were carried out in the brewing industry. The reason for this order is that it reflects the susceptibility to tax evasion by separate sectors, and indirectly, also the number of producers in each of the subsectors.

The number of fines collected in relation to the excise tax on alcoholic beverages is influenced mostly by the number of executed tax audits (see Table 1). It is clear that the majority of tax audits was executed in relation to the excise tax on spirits due to the fact that it is the excise tax on alcoholic beverages with the highest risk of tax evasion as well as due to the larger number of tax entities producing this commodity.

National Features and Perspectives of VAT Use in Slovak Republic

The year 1967 was important from the viewpoint of unification of the EU approaches to indirect taxation because in that year the first directive on VAT was adopted. It directly dealt with the implementation of VAT to the tax system of the member states. Its initial objective was the cancellation of turnover tax, which distorted the economic competition and impeded the free movement of goods and the elimination of tax audits and formalities on internal borders.

VAT is often defined as the universal consumption tax. However, its complicated system and numerous transactions related to it caused high susceptibility to VAT tax frauds and evasions which deform all the sectors of economic and social life and distort competition within the business sector. Despite the fact that all the EU countries have the obligation to apply VAT, we cannot state that harmonisation of VAT has been fully implemented. In this context we have to emphasize the fact that the preamble of the Council Directive no. 2006/112/EC as of 28th November 2006 on the common system of VAT admits that tax rates and exemptions are not completely harmonized. The process of tax rates' unification is deformed by the fact that several states have temporary exceptions to the application of common rules. However, these exceptions and allowances are not always justifiable and legitimate and their application does not automatically mean that a consumer will pay lower price.

It is estimated that approximately two thirds of the total final consumption in the EU is subject to taxation by the standard VAT rate (Borselli, Chiri, & Romagnano, 2012). Reduction of differences in the

Table 1. The amount of fines collected on the excise taxes in Slovak Republic, in EUR

	2012	2013	2014	2015	2016
Fines on all excise taxes	993,029	1,761,562	21,003,139	1,124,000	1,584,476
Beer	3,135	2,726	14,599	8,884	4,681
Wine	6,116	4,161	10,630	9,460	9,126
Alcohol	230,010	257,728	20,527,168	172,943	339,398
Other excise taxes	753,767	1,496,947	450,742	932,713	1,231,272

Source: Statistics of Financial Administration of Slovak Republic

VAT rates by 50% among the EU member states can lead to the growth of trade within the Community by 9.8%, and also to the growth of real GDP by 1.1% as well as consumption growth by 0.7% (IFS, 2011).

Harmonisation of indirect taxes in the European Union contributes to better connection of tax systems of the member states, especially in terms of VAT. Despite many positive features the European Union brings in, the common VAT system applied in the EU is still considered to be only "transitional", not fully responding to challenges of the changing global environment. It is exposed to fraudulent actions which cause serious losses of tax revenues for the budgets of the EU member states. In 2015 the estimated losses on VAT in the EU were at the level of 151 bln EUR. This is about 12.8% of the potential VAT, according to some calculations (CASE, 2017). It is also estimated that cross-border transfers in the sector of VAT especially contributed to these tax evasion schemes, roughly, in the amount of 50 bln EUR. The need to solve this problem puts additional pressure on the European Union as well as on its individual member states in order to introduce various measures against tax evasion and frauds.

VAT was introduced in the territory of Slovak Republic on 1st January 1993. This was one of the basic requirements before Slovak Republic accession to the EU. Its introduction also meant final cancellation of turnover and import taxes. In 1993 one basic VAT rate in the amount of 23% and one reduced VAT rate in the amount of 5% were introduced in Slovak Republic. But already same year both VAT rates were increased to 25% and 6% accordingly. Until 2004 these VAT rates changed several times.

The tax reform realized in Slovak Republic on the 1st of January 2004 included cancellation of the reduced VAT tax rate and introduction of the uniform VAT rate in the amount of 19% for all goods and services. It meant the simplification of the VAT mechanism and reduction of the administrative burden on both taxpayers and tax administrators. The uniform VAT rate on the level of 19% was being applied in Slovak Republic even after its accession to the EU in May 2004 and it was until the end of 2006.

Slovak Republic introduced the reduced tax rate in the amount of 10% on drugs, medical devices and some other specific commodities in 2007. In 2008 the range of goods subject to this reduced tax rate expanded. Another reduced tax rate in the amount of 6% on the so-called "yard sale" was applied during 2010. In 2011 the standard tax rate increased from 19% to 20% due to the implementation of measures focused on the reduction of public finance deficit. The increased VAT rate should have been only temporary, while the public finance deficit drops below the level of 3% of GDP.

The public finance deficit in Slovak Republic grew from 2.1% in 2008 to 8.0% in 2009-2010. The adopted consolidation measures in the volume of 1.2 bln EUR were directed to reduce the public finance deficit under 3% of GDP in 2013. The estimated amount of VAT loss was higher than the volume of the means necessary for consolidation of public finances in Slovak Republic (Reckon, 2009).

The VAT revenue has been fluctuating from 0.9 bln (1993) to 2.8 bln EUR (2003) before the accession of Slovak Republic to the EU and this fluctuation mostly had a growing tendency. After the accession of Slovak Republic to the EU the VAT revenues grew in absolute terms, with the exception of 2009 and 2012. A drop of VAT revenues in 2009 by 17% in comparison to the previous year was caused by the overall revenue losses due to the global financial and economic crisis. Despite the fact that the total VAT revenue increased in 2010, it did not reach the pre-crisis level. The VAT revenue loss also occurred in 2012. It was mostly caused by the unfavourable financial situation for the majority of business entities, growing tax evasion related to VAT and the issues related to the transition to a new information system introduced by the financial administration. The VAT revenue has been demonstrating a growing trend since 2013. That year it exceeded the level before the crisis for the first time. This fact was related to the improving economic situation and also to the implementation of measures under the Action Plan against Tax Evasion - 2012. There was a slight decrease of VAT revenues in 2016 - by 2.6%, to the level of 5.4 bln EUR (Figure 3).

In March 2012 Institute for Financial Policy of the Ministry of Finance of Slovak Republic published the study (IFP, 2012) which summarized the estimations on the total VAT revenue losses during 2005-2010 in the country. The volume of VAT losses nearly tripled in the monitored period: to compare, if back in 2005 these losses represented 18.2% of the theoretical VAT (or 1.7% of GDP), in 2010 they already reached 35.9% of the theoretical VAT volume (or 3.5% GDP).

The total VAT losses in Slovak Republic have more than doubled since 2004. They reached the highest level in 2012, more specifically - 2.6 bln EUR (or 37.8% of the theoretical VAT). Since 2013 the total VAT loss has been gradually reducing. In 2013 it fell to 33.4% of the theoretical VAT (or 2.4 bln EUR), in 2014 it was already 30.5% (or 2.2 bln EUR) and in 2015 it was 29.4% (2.3 bln EUR). Despite the fact that Slovak Republic is gradually reducing its VAT gap, it still has the second largest gap in VAT collection among the EU member states (CASE, 2017).

In May 2012 Slovak government approved "Action Plan against Tax Evasion for 2012-2016". The adopted measures on VAT were aimed at the improvement of VAT collection, prevention of VAT system misuse and creation of better conditions for legal business activities. In particular, these measures included full disclosure according to the "List of potentially risky VAT payers" formed by the Financial Directorate of Slovak Republic. Other meaningful measures were introduction of the electronic control statement of VAT in 2014 and formation of "Tax Cobra".

From the results of the control activity of Financial Administration in Slovak Republic it follows that the share of VAT-related findings in the total tax audits findings during 2004-2016 was more than 70% on average (e.g., it was 582 mln EUR in 2016, which then was 83% of the total tax findings). Tax auditors focus on inter-related companies which realized many transactions between themselves and they usually request the redemption of excessive deductions. Such a chain of companies is often used for fraudulent activities.

Despite the decreasing number of tax audits the volume of additional VAT levy nearly tripled in the monitored period and it showed the growing trend with the exception of the year 2012. The volume of

Figure 3. Dynamics of VAT revenues in Slovak Republic
(Source: Statistics of Financial Administration of Slovak Republic and own calculations)

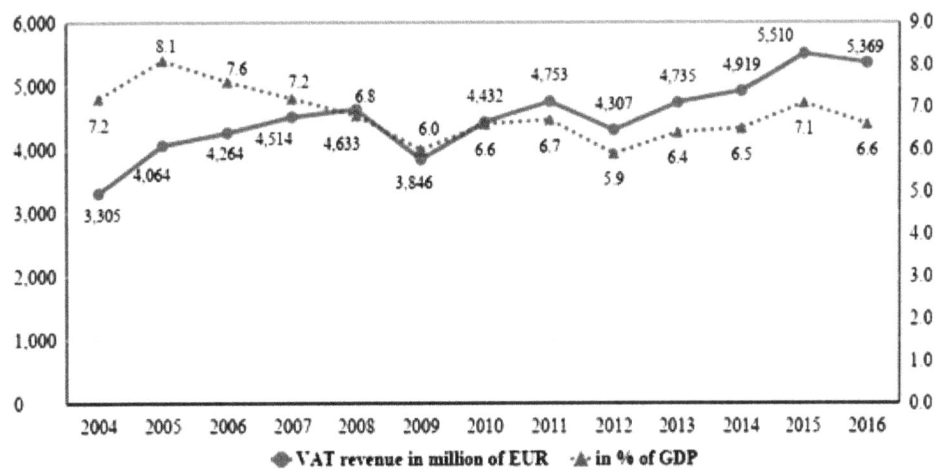

additional VAT levy can be interpreted in the context of estimated tax evasion. Based on the amount of the estimated VAT losses in Slovak Republic and the results of the control activity of the Financial Administration it can be stated that there is nearly 80% probability of non-detection of tax evasion by the Financial Administration. Ineffectiveness of additional tax levy is another serious issue for public finance, since it is very low.

RESULTS, FINDINGS AND CONCLUSION

Development of corporate taxation in Slovak Republic demonstrates that the reform steps on corporate taxation have to be realized in close connection to taxation of natural persons, taxation of dividends and the policy of support for non-profit organisations. Considering companies' taxation in Slovak Republic in its historic development perspective, there is no clear answer to the question whether to assert the proven facts or new visions within the implementation of corporate taxation reform. Our analysis of corporate taxation dynamics confirms the hypothesis H1. The most important factors impacting the corporate tax revenues in Slovak Republic are related to the macroeconomic environment. A potential future risk is the insufficient number of executed tax audits on corporate income tax.

Corporate taxation in Slovak Republic is currently significantly influenced by the EU tax policy. Current dynamics in the development of European tax policy on corporate tax confirms the fact that many European countries prefer to support small and medium-size companies by lower corporate income tax or by another form of tax stimuli. Slovakia is still facing such challenges in relation to corporate taxation as neutrality of taxation and preferential treatment of small and mid-sized companies. New challenges at the EU level in this regard concern mainly globalisation, growing international cooperation, formation and activities of transnational companies and the impact of information technologies on large businesses' development as an important factor of new methods in administration of transnational companies.

Key challenges for the future of corporate taxation concern mainly adding to the existing theoretical models a new factor accounting for more sensory behaviour of economic subjects in various tax situations, analysis of the behaviour of tax institutions and greater focus on collecting taxes from individual taxpayers, mostly because emergence and existence of tax evasion is often caused by the inability of a taxpayer and a tax administrator to reach compromises. Results of the analysis of public opinion concerning tax mechanism and tax system overall should lead to greater understanding of the real situation with taxation.

The European Union as a whole is the region with the highest consumption of alcohol per inhabitant in the world, therefore, the related negative aspects of this consumption are quite evident. Thus, it is not surprising at all that the policy of alcohol taxation in the EU is focused on regulation of consumption and simultaneous limitation of all related negative socioeconomic consequences. At the same time, management of negative externalities coming from the consumption of alcoholic beverages is a highly questionable issue, since an alcoholic beverage is often perceived as a positive thing in the eyes of many consumers. The problem is also impacted by the fact that this type of taxes is always a stable source of income for the state budget; therefore, educating against alcohol consumption might be not always a priority for all of the interested parties. Thus, our hypothesis H2 is confirmed.

On the one hand, excise tax on alcoholic beverages still has its preventive effect which, to some extent, can be understood as a penalizing effect too. Another option would be increasing taxes on the products related to alcohol consumption. Increase in the tax is connected to the alcohol volume in beverages, measured in percent. The more alcohol a particular product contains - the higher should be the tax rate. It would mean that companies would not be able to produce these products so quickly keeping the same costs. This would also indirectly lead to the reduction of offers and thus - to the increasing prices. This, in its turn, would result in the reduced demand and therefore - to smaller scale impact of all related negative externalities.

The most effective means against illegal distillation is having reasonable tax, financial and national economic policies since all three are important factors of influence on tax evasive behavior. We should take into account the fact that a person using the services of legal distillery plant should pay the tax to the state, but a person using the services of illegal distillation does not pay anything. Therefore, the state should effectively support legal distillation and should not liquidate it.

Effectiveness (profitability) of VAT system in the conditions of Slovak Republic is influenced by several factors. On the one hand, it is significantly influenced by general economic conditions in the country, especially by changes in domestic demand and also in the volumes of import and export. Negative impacts of the 2008 economic crisis found their reflection in the slowdown of economic growth of Slovak economy, and in 2009 also in the significant decrease of its efficiency. This caused the reduction of VAT returns which, in its turn, led to negative changes in domestic demand and also to decline in import and export growth rates. On the one hand, Slovak Republic as the member of the EU is obliged to respect the community laws of the EU and integrate them into its national legislation. Same applies to the directives relevant to VAT which regulate the harmonisation of VAT system at the EU level. It is mostly based on the uniform definition of taxable transactions. Regarding the harmonisation of VAT which significantly influences the effectiveness of the VAT system in Slovak Republic, effectiveness of VAT can be improved using the areas which are not yet fully harmonised with the EU legislation.

Mismatch between the growth of VAT revenues and the growth of its macroeconomic base is attributed mainly to the increase of VAT evasion and partially to the prescribed VAT which is unenforceable due to the insolvency of many taxpayers. The key issues here are: low payment discipline of taxpayers and the inability of tax administration to enforce tax arrears from tax debtors.

Stemming from this analysis we can confirm the hypothesis H3. According to this hypothesis, VAT is the most profitable tax in Slovak Republic but it is also the tax that generates the biggest tax evasion. It is estimated that one third of potential VAT revenues are undercollected in Slovak Republic. Despite the adopted measures focused on the elimination of tax evasion and frauds related to VAT, Slovak Republic still shows quite big VAT losses, approximately at the level of 2.2 bln EUR per annum. Another serious issue is the inability of Financial Administration to enforce additional VAT levy basing on the conclusions of tax audits. The expected changes in VAT system at the EU level could partially strengthen the resistance of the VAT system against tax evasion and eliminate VAT losses in the case of Slovak Republic too.

ACKNOWLEDGMENT

The chapter was prepared within the framework of the research project VEGA No. 1/0443/15 titled "The tax policy and its impact on the tax collection efficiency and the elimination of tax evasion."

REFERENCES

Auerbach, A. J. (2006). Who bears the Corporate Tax? A Review of What We Know. *Tax Policy and the Economy*, *20*, 1–40. doi:10.1086/tpe.20.20061903

Borselli, F., Chiri, S., & Romagnano, E. (2012). Patterns of Reduced VAT Rates in the European Union. *International VAT Monitor*, *23*(1), 13–21.

Bradford, D. F., & Rosen, H. S. (1976). The Optimal Taxation of Commodities and Income. *The American Economic Review*, *66*(2), 94–101.

CASE. (2013). *Study to Quantify and Analyse the VAT Gap in the EU-27 Member States. Final Report* [Report for the European Commission]. Warsaw: Center for Social and Economic Research.

CASE. (2017). *Study and Reports on the VAT Gap in the EU-28 Member States: 2017 Final Report* [Report for the European Commission]. Warsaw: Center for Social and Economic Research.

Corlett, W. J., & Hague, D. C. (1954). Complementarity and the Excess Burden of Taxation. *The Review of Economic Studies*, *21*(1), 21–30. doi:10.2307/2296257

de Mooij, R. A. (2005). Will Corporate Income Taxation Survive? *De Economist*, *153*(3), 277–301. doi:10.100710645-005-1989-5

Ebrill, L., Keen, M., Bodin, J. P., & Summers, V. (2001). *The Modern VAT*. Washington, DC: IMF. doi:10.5089/9781589060265.071

Edwards, C.H., & Rugy, V. (2002). *International Tax Competition: A 21st-Century Restraint on Government*. Cato Policy Analysis, No. 431.

European Commission. (2017). *Proposal for a Council Directive amending Directive 2006/112/EC as regards harmonising and simplifying certain rules in the value added tax system and introducing the definitive system for the taxation of trade between Member States*. COM(2017) 569 final.

Genser, B., & Haufler, A. (1996). Tax Competition, Tax Coordination and Tax Harmonization: The Effect of EMU. *Empirica*, *23*(1), 59–89. doi:10.1007/BF00925008

Hameakers, H. (1993). Fiscal Sovereignty and Tax Harmonization in the EC. *European Taxation*, *33*(1), 25–27.

Heady, C. H. J., & Mitra, P. K. (1980). The Computation of Optimum Linear Taxation. *The Review of Economic Studies*, *47*(3), 567–585. doi:10.2307/2297308

IFP. (2012). *The Estimate of the Value Added Tax Revenue Loss*. Institute for Financial Policy of the Ministry of Finance of the Slovak Republic.

IFS. (2011). *A Retrospective Evaluation of Elements of the EU VAT System – Final Report*. London: Institute for Fiscal Studies.

Lockwood, B., & Migali, G. (2009). Did the single market cause competition in excise taxes?: Evidence from EU countries. *Economic Journal (London)*, *119*(536), 406–429. doi:10.1111/j.1468-0297.2008.02235.x

Mankiw, N. G., Weinzierl, M. C. H., & Yagan, D. F. (2009). Optimal taxation in theory and practice. *The Journal of Economic Perspectives, 23*(4), 147–174. doi:10.1257/jep.23.4.147

Mitchell, J. (2001). *A Tax Competition Primer: Why Tax Harmonization and Information Exchange Undermine America's Competitive Advantage in the Global Economy. Backgrounder, No. 1460*. Washington, DC: Heritage Foundation.

Nicodème, G. (2009). *Corporate Income Tax and Economic Distortions. Taxation Papers 15*. Directorate General Taxation and Customs Union, European Commission.

OECD. (2010). *Choosing a Broad Base – Low Rate Approach to Taxation*. OECD Tax Policy Studies, No. 19.

Ramsey, F. P. (1927). A Contribution to the Theory of Taxation. *Economic Journal (London), 37*(145), 47–61. doi:10.2307/2222721

RECKON LLP. (2009). *Study to Quantify and Analyse the VAT gap in the EU-25 Member States. Report for DG Taxation and Customs Union*. London: Reckon LLP.

Sørensen, P. B. (2007). The Theory of Optimal Taxation: What is the Policy Relevance? *International Tax and Public Finance, 14*(4), 383–406. doi:10.100710797-007-9024-1

Statistics and Annual reports on the activity of the financial administration for the period 2004-2016. (n.d.). Retrieved from https://www.financnasprava.sk/sk/financna-sprava/vyrocne-spravy

Sullivan, M. A. (2001). *Corporate Tax Reform: Taxing Profits in the 21st Century*. Apress.

Weichenrieder, A. J. (2005). *(Why) Do We Need Corporate Taxation?* CESifo Working Paper, No.1495.

Wilson, J. D. (1986). A Theory of Interregional Tax Competition. *Journal of Urban Economics, 19*(3), 296–315. doi:10.1016/0094-1190(86)90045-8

KEY TERMS AND DEFINITIONS

Alcoholic Beverage: Any fermented liquor, such as wine, beer, or distilled spirit that contains ethyl alcohol or ethanol as an intoxicating agent.

Directive 92/83/EEC: An instrumental that enables the collection of excise duty on alcohol and alcoholic beverages at internal markets. At the general level, this Directive allows intra-community trade to take place free of significant tax-related trade barriers or major competitive disruptions between economic operators operating in the same sector.

Effectiveness of Tax Collection: The ability of financial (tax) administration to enforce the tax liability declared by taxpayers as well as the tax liability arising from the tax administration's control activities (including reassessment of liability after tax audits).

Tax Assignment: A situation when a taxpayer redirects a share of paid income tax to a selected organization that is not business-based. Therefore, tax assignment represents a method which can be used by both legal entities and individuals to participate in the decision-making on public benefits. Such an assignable mechanism distributes public funds from the central level to the individual one.

Tax License: The minimum tax after deducting tax allowances and considering the tax that a legal entity must pay abroad. Value of tax license depends on the annual turnover and on whether or not the entity is a VAT payer.

Theoretical VAT Revenue: VAT revenues that would be earned if all taxpayers fulfilled their duties in full compliance with the law.

VAT Gap: A difference between the VAT actually paid and the VAT that should have been paid if all individuals and companies had declared their activities and transactions correctly, in compliance with all applicable laws. It provides an estimate of revenue loss due to tax fraud, tax evasion and tax avoidance, and also due to bankruptcies, financial insolvencies, or miscalculations.

Chapter 11
Taxation Regime and Macroeconomic Systems' Dynamics

Tran Huu Ai
Van Hien University, Vietnam

Denis Ushakov
Suan Sunandha Rajabhat University, Thailand

ABSTRACT

In this chapter, the authors, operating the criteria of rigid and comfortable national taxation regimes, attempt to evaluate the stimulating impact of country's taxation systems on the dynamics of their macroeconomic growth and country's participation in the world trade. Therefore, the chapter presents the authors' conclusions concerning the efficiency of fiscal instruments for economic growth stimulation and external trade attractiveness increase as applied to the majority of contemporary states. Based on correlation of indices of tax reformations and trends of the modern countries macroeconomic development, the co-authors present their conclusions on the priority importance of the so-called "taxation comfort" in the context of country's positioning in the global rankings. Research proved a taxation effect in countries' macro-economic growth and external attractiveness stimulating, as well as this effect dependence on the level of countries material wellbeing and infrastructural conditions.

INTRODUCTION

Taxation regime of a country is among the most efficient and well known instruments of state regulation and state economic stimulation. It can also become the factor of attractiveness for foreign investors, for potential business partners from abroad and also for highly qualified (today often known as "the creative class") labor force. Cross-country comparison of the current tax rates and of the so-called "taxation comfort" (which metaphorically expresses the (in) convenience of all tax payments and other related formalities) today is actively used by a wide range of international and regional organizations and unions as a feature in overall cross-country comparisons and their consequent ranking. It is also part of various

DOI: 10.4018/978-1-5225-7760-7.ch011

aggregates indicators and indices – global competitiveness, investment attractiveness. Additionally to that, tax rates and taxation comfort assessments are also a significant factor for a variety of forecasts, foresights and strategic plans of various levels, from micro to macro.

There exist a popular idea that today, due to intensive globalization of the world economy and wide universalization of various public-level and business practices (including, inter alia, economic and fiscal regulation), the potential of a taxation regime as a factor of economic development is overestimated since its influence on country's participation in global trade and country's capacity of compete globally is rapidly decreasing. All of the above makes the following question topical as many times before: In the 21st century is national taxation system still able to stimulate the economic growth of a country and promote its trade attractiveness abroad?

- **Research Aim:** On the basis of authors' analysis of today's most widely used indicators of taxation regimes worldwide as well as indices of the same countries' macroeconomic development we will attempt here to evaluate the impact of tax reforms on the dynamics of economic growth on the sample of the selected countries.

Taking this aim into account, we set here *the following tasks:*

- On the basis of the mentioned above correlation, the determine the potential to stimulate the macroeconomic growth in the selected countries and also to estimate their external trade attractiveness from the standpoint of national tax systems according to the international ranking "Doing Business";
- To describe the tax regime rank in "Doing Business" as a factor stimulating national exports and imports;
- To determine whether the so-called "taxation comfort" (measured through the number of tax payment per year and also time spent on all taxation-related procedures and documents) is indeed able to stimulate country's macroeconomic growth as compared to the same stimulating impact a tax rate (in the same country) may have;
- To analyze the role of tax rate as a tool in stimulation of national external trade (that is, import and export);
- To text empirically the presence (or absence) of reverse dependence between the level of country's economic development, its participation in the world trade and the level of its "taxation comfort".

LITERATURE OVERVIEW

The influence of taxation regime on the economic growth dynamics and other macroeconomic indicators of the states today is an extremely topical issue because nowadays national governments tend to reconsider both instruments and strategies related to national competitiveness increase and global repositioning in the structure of global labour distribution.

Historic features of tax policies implementation and of the related national strategies aimed at stimulation of external competitiveness of countries were well outlined by H. Pemberton (2004) while examining the most important elements of the growth policy package, focusing on the array of new taxes introduced after 1960 which sought to raise growth by increasing the government's control over the economy, encouraging the more productive use of labour, or stimulating investment via changes to the structure of taxation.

Economists have long been interested in the relationship between income distribution and economic growth. Two major approaches dominate in literature on this topic. The first one is first of all associated with globally famous Simon Kuznets and comes from the assertion that the degree of inequality varies systematically with the level of income per capita, initially increasing as incomes rise and then, at some point, decreasing with further increase in income.

The second approach is associated with the name of Arthur Okun (1970) and his idea that there is a great trade-off between equality and efficiency and hence policy interventions should be aimed specifically at reducing inequality.

Taken together, these two visions have been further used by Amy Ickowitz (2001) to argue against public policies intended to create a less unequal society, since the Kuznets proposition indicates that in the long run policy interventions are unnecessary, while the Okun's proposition is that in the short run they are harmful.

Other experts on fiscal policies, Lawrence W. Kenny and Stanley L. Winer (2006) have carried out a research on 100 countries with both democratic and non-democratic regimes so that to study the role and the efficiency of taxation systems and regimes used in these countries. They assessed these regimes from the standpoint of scale effect, taxation base effects and overall efficiency of the related administrative costs. And thus, they managed to present a range of advantages of democracy for countries' fiscal strategies' implementation under the conditions of globalization. In the same vein, Philipp Harms and Stefan Zink (2003) came to the conclusion that most democracies are characterized by moderate taxation of wealth.

Following the same topic of taxes' efficiency for the public strategy of poverty eradication, Akihiko Kaneko and Daisuke Matsuzaki (2009) tested empirically the stimulating (for overall economic growth) effect from indirect taxes (namely, sales tax) and came to the conclusion about the necessity of combining fiscal and monetary instruments in economic growth stimulation. And two years prior to that, Günther Rehme (2007) proved that public finance and public financial policy has a significant role in welfare redistribution, thus contributing to potential growth and better welfare for all under the conditions of a capitalistic society.

Separately, we need to mention here the existence of socio-psychological direction in the research concerning welfare distribution and state tax policy/strategy. For example, Philipp Doerrenberg and Andreas Peichl (2013) came to the conclusion that individual morale related to taxes is higher, while the more progressive the tax schedule is. And also, that positive impact of tax progressivity on tax morale declines with income. This became the key result of their quite curious research, and at the same time this conclusion can be also treated as the fundamental principle of the progressive scale introduction in taxation and further modernization of the existing systems of fiscal administration.

Another potential methodology and vision for taxation regime modernization was suggested in the conclusions of Georg Tillmann (2010) concerning tax evading decisions of agents with different incomes. He also mentioned that governments may use different instruments to maximize the total tax receipts and to prevent the flight of capital from the country. In the same vein, Verena Kley (2011) was studying the role of tax instruments' use optimization for more fair benefits' redistribution between the citizens within one state.

S. Acharya (2015) presented taxation as a key component of national economic policy in the context of global trend of overall economic liberalization. And F. Widmalm (2001) using pooled cross-sectional data of 23 OECD countries (1965 to 1990) came to the conclusion that tax structure affects economic growth, more specifically, the proportion of tax revenue raised by taxing personal income has a negative correlation with economic growth. Moreover, she concluded that tax progressivity, measured in terms of long-run income elasticity of tax revenue, is associated with low economic growth.

The theoretical grounds for correlation between the economic growth dynamics and tax reforms on a sample of economies in transit were studied in great deal of detail by famous Russian economist E. V. Balatskii (2006). This author explained the adverse effect of tax reforms on economic growth and also offered the original classification of fiscal reforms, which includes the notions of fiscal quasi- and pseudo-traps.

Toshiki Tamai (2005) examined the relationship between wealth distribution and economic growth in an endogenous growth model with heterogeneous households and redistributive taxation. He incorporated endogenous determination of redistributive policy focusing on the relation between pre- and post-tax inequality and proved that endogenous redistributive policy affects wealth distribution and economic growth, while there exists a negative correlation between pre-tax inequality and economic growth and inverted-U relationship between post-tax inequality and economic growth in a voting equilibrium.

Valuable contribution concerning the ideal size of tax load (ideal – meaning capable of providing sustainable economic growth) on the sample of 8 leading economies was offered by Bjørn Volkerink, Jan-Egbert Sturm and Jakob de Haan (2002). These authors also grounded, inter alia, that capital taxes can reduce economic growth и high labor taxes have increased unemployment in Europe.

The problems of taxation policy modernization and the related public strategies concerning budget investments and/or indirect taxation (on the case study of European countries) have been studied by Gustavo A. Marrero (2010). This author came to the conclusion that optimal tax system becomes more intensive in income taxation relative to consumption taxation, and that public disbursements become less intensive in public investment.

Quite significant theoretical value also have more applied studies on the problems of material benefits distribution by means of various taxation levies on the case studies of the selected countries worldwide.

For example, the research on the EU economies groupped them into three clusters (North, Central and South), depending on the practiced methods and strategic guidelines of tax regulation in the countries in question (Vogel, 2014). This division has made it possible to detect a range of regularities in the influence of a national taxation regime on welfare's dynamic development.

Back in 2007 Keuschnigg, C. and Dietz, M. (2007) proved that even in such a stable and well-to-do country as Switzerland tax regulation has an extremely high potential to stimulate further the economic growth, and thus, may guarantee this growth would be up to 4-5% a year, in the long term.

Obviously, the problem of economic growth stimulation and the role of efficient taxation system in it is first of all topical and meaningful for still developing countries, in which poverty and fair distribution of economic benefits are quite painful issues, requiring significant attention of the state. In this regard, several African authors think that modernization of national taxation system should be first of all aimed to increasing the external attractiveness of a country (study on Zambia and Zimbabwe by Raghbendra Jha (2008) or on levelling the life quality levels in different regions of the same country (or in urban and rural areas, like in Botswana research by Imogen Patience and Bonolo Mogotsi (2009).

In this context Latin American studies have their peculiarity. Authors of this region (e.g., Jean-Yves Duclos, Paul Makdissi, Abdelkrim Araar (2014) in Mexico, or Enlinson Mattos and Ricardo Politi (2014) in Brazil tend to emphasize the importance of indirect taxes (sales tax, VAT) as the primary instrument in regulation of fair distribution and in fighting social inequality, thus providing additional resource for long-term economic growth.

Also, we need to mention here a comparatively new direction in tax research – studying the problems of international fiscal administration and redistribution of welfare/benefits between the states. The interest to this problem can be explained by the failures of free economy globally. For example, Petr Janský (2015) in his rather original research suggests to introduce for further use the so-called Commitment to Development Index, which ranks rich countries according to their policies which affect poor countries. This index can be used in the process of international infrastructure formation for taxes administration and international financial flows regulation. The necessity to standardize and universalize the fiscal practices on a global scale has been considered by Nuno Trindade Magessi and Luis Antunes (2014). This necessity was explained by the authors from the standpoint of the urgent need for global and joint fight against shadow economies. Potential economic consequences of the transition from international competition in the field of taxation to cross-country cooperation was quite objectively assessed already back in 2009 by Stanislaw Soltysilski (2009). This author also outlined the potential new horizons and prospects of global tax administration system development and functioning.

There are, of course, much more applied research concerning the role of taxation in economic growth stimulation carried out for various countries, but first of all, on the data of the USA and the EU and aimed mostly on theoretical explanation of tax transformations and adaptation of taxation regimes to economic real conditions in various time periods. Among these many, for example, R. Hill (2008) determined the models of taxation as adapted to the requirements of economic growth stabilization and identified that "growth maximizing tax rate even if no relationship exists between growth and the size of the state". Also noteworthy are the studies by G. W. Scully (2003) on the optimal tax rate for separate categories of taxes for economic stimulation, or for example, Cruz A. Echevarría (2015) who separately studied personal income tax rates.

Another quite successful attempt to reveal the correlation between the taxation load and the economic growth dynamics for European countries was carried out by L. Sinevičienė (2016) who determined that tax burden on capital and consumption is higher in highly developed countries; but implicit tax rate on capital is higher in the case of countries with lower GDP growth, high government sector and high government debt.

Finally, probably the most well known studies ranging the countries by the attractiveness level of their taxation systems for doing business, for international capital or investors and for participation in the world trade are traditionally carried out by the experts affiliated to the "Doing Business" project, and their annual reports have become the statistical basis for our further research.

With the due reference to all these conclusions, both purely theoretical and also empirical, concerning the stimulating role of taxation regimes for different countries worldwide, we decided to carry out our own research and started with classifying the countries into the groups, depending on the level of their welfare.

In the research which will be presented below we attempt to evaluate the efficiency of taxation regimes in the countries worldwide. And we also attempt to determine the causes of these regimes' rather different results and their certain asynchrony which is clearly observed.

RESEARCH METHODOLOGY

Here we attempt to study the correlation between the indicators of tax reforms' dynamics and the macroeconomic development trends on a sample of countries. For this matter we have used the statistics data on economic development of the selected countries, the World Bank data:

- Dynamics of GDP growth, dynamics of GDP growth per capita.
- Dynamics of export growth (in relative and absolute numbers) and the same for imports (also relative and absolute) for the selected countries.

In our analysis of tax reforms dynamics by countries we have also used the following indicators from the "Doing Business" reports:

- International ranking of the tax system in particular country;
- Time needed for all tax formalities in a country;
- The number of tax reporting periods by countries, and;
- The average size of tax rate (the synthetic indicator of tax rate for private individuals and legal bodies in a country).

Using these indicators, we have analyzes all 131 countries (see Table 1) operating this split into 5 groups of their welfare level. The time frame chosen for this study is 2009 to 2016.

RESULTS

Our correlation analysis results have demonstrated that the rank of taxation system of a country in the international ranking "Doing Business" indeed has impact on GDP level per capita, and this impact is rather long-term, not changing significantly with years (see Table 2). Improvement in this rank of a country also predetermines the growth of per capita GDP (in its dynamics), however, this impact seems to be rather short-term, it tends to fade away in 2-3 years after the country's improvement on this position.

Table 1. Countries' division by groups for further analysis

Group #	Group Title	GDP Per Capita	Number of Countries in the Group
1	Rich	Over 40,000 $	18
2	Well-to-do	25,000-39,999 $	10
3	Average	15,000 – 24,999$	20
4	Underperforming	5,000 – 14,999 $	22
5	Poor	4,999 $	61
	Total:		131

(authors' proposition)

Considering the dynamics of the international trade indicators, we can state that country's rank of the taxation system has much more impact on its exports, rather than on its imports. This proves the widely spread assumption that tax reforms, in any country, are of top priority for strong national companies (those doing business, that is selling abroad in this case), rather than for general population and its paying capacity (which tends to spend the money, "freed" as a result of tax reforms, on consumption, that is, often on purchases of imported goods).

Thus, we can conclude that even though the primary goal of any tax reform is to improve the national welfare and make population incomes higher, it also promotes the growth of national production and its competitiveness at the world markets.

Further in our analysis we would like to consider the influence of separate components of national taxation regimes (the size of average tax rate, the number of tax payments per year and the time spent on all tax formalities) on the macroeconomic indicators of countries.

In particular, we have determined that correlation between the tax rate and the dynamics of economic development and also the level of country's engagement in global economic processes is nearly absent, in both long and short terms.

At the same time, despite the stably low correlation between the time needed for tax formalities and the number of tax payments per year on one hand, and the macroeconomic dynamics on the other, it is still higher than with the tax rate (see Table 4, 5, 6).

All of the above proves the hypothesis that in today's conditions of the world economy's development organizational components of taxation system (in our case, these would be the number of tax payments per year and the time spent on all taxation formalities) are significantly more stimulating for economic growth overall and trade relations in particular, rather than the tax rate. This means that the comfort of taxation regime is more important than its rigidness, which is quite logical taking into account the limited nature of tax rate instrument for improvement of conditions for tax agents. In any case there exists a certain threshold for the tax rate decrease, and this threshold value should be taken into account in formation of countries' budget programs. For international competition between the tax rate the winners are quite evident – these are the microstates with a limited number of social programs and tiny budgets, they also usually do not have their own army (and thus, military spending either) and are actively using the

Table 2. Correlation between the taxation system rank according to "Doing Business" and countries' GDP per capita (2009-2016)

Rank	GDP Per Capita						
	2010	**2011**	**2012**	**2013**	**2014**	**2015**	**2016**
2009	0,55	0,55	0,56	0,56	0,55	0,56	0,56
2010		0,55	0,55	0,55	0,55	0,55	0,55
2011			0,54	0,54	0,54	0,54	0,55
2012				0,54	0,54	0,54	0,54
2013					0,55	0,55	0,55
2014						0,55	0,55
2015							0,53

(Calculated by the authors using the data from "Doing Business" and also World Bank data)

Table 3. Correlations between the taxation system rankings and national exports/imports (2009-2016)

Rank	Export						Rank	Import						
	2010	2011	2012	2013	2014	2015		2010	2011	2012	2013	2014	2015	2016
2009	0,57	0,57	0,58	0,58	0,58	0,58	2009	-0,16	-0,09	0,04	0,04	0,002	-0,03	0,16
2010		0,56	0,57	0,57	0,57	0,57	2010		-0,06	0,06	0,06	0,004	-0,03	0,17
2011			0,56	0,56	0,57	0,56	2011			0,05	0,06	-0,003	-0,05	0,17
2012				0,56	0,56	0,55	2012				0,06	-0,03	-0,05	0,13
2013					0,56	0,56	2013					-0,09	-0,1	0,07
2014						0,54	2014						-0,1	0,04
2015							2015							-0,06
2016							2016							-0,09

(Calculated by the authors using the data from "Doing Business" and also World Bank data)

Table 4. Correlation between the average tax rate, GDP per capita and the growth of national exports (2010-2016)

Tax Rate	GDP Per Capita						Tax rate	Export Growth						
	2010	2011	2012	2013	2014	2015		2010	2011	2012	2013	2014	2015	2016
2009	-0,16	-0,16	-0,17	-0,17	-0,17	-0,17	2009	0,11	0,2	0,08	0,05	-0,05	-0,06	-0,02
2010		-0,16	-0,17	-0,17	-0,17	-0,17	2010		0,17	0,07	0,05	-0,04	-0,01	-0,03
2011			-0,17	-0,17	-0,17	-0,18	2011			0,08	0,04	-0,02	-0,04	-0,02
2012				-0,17	-0,17	-0,17	2012				0,03	-0,01	-0,07	-0,09
2013					-0,16	-0,16	2013					-0,003	-0,05	-0,04
2014						-0,15	2014						-0,06	0,01

(calculated by the authors on the data from "Doing Business" and the World Bank)

Table 5. Correlation between tax payments per year, GDP per capita and the growth of national exports (2010-2016)

Payment	GDP Per Capita						Payment	Export Growth						
	2010	2011	2012	2013	2014	2015		2010	2011	2012	2013	2014	2015	2016
2009	-0,49	-0,49	-0,49	-0,49	-0,48	-0,48	2009	-0,32	-0,31	-0,32	-0,32	-0,32	-0,31	-0,3
2010		-0,49	-0,49	-0,48	-0,48	-0,48	2010		-0,31	-0,31	-0,31	-0,31	-0,31	-0,3
2011			-0,5	-0,49	-0,49	-0,49	2011			-0,32	-0,32	-0,32	-0,31	-0,3
2012				-0,47	-0,47	-0,47	2012				-0,3	-0,3	-0,3	-0,29
2013					-0,54	-0,54	2013					-0,36	-0,35	-0,33
2014						-0,53	2014						-0,34	-0,33

(calculated by the authors on the data from "Doing Business" and the World Bank)

Table 6. Correlation between the time spent on tax formalities, GDP per capita and the growth of national exports (2010-2016)

Time	GDP Per Capita						Time	Export Growth						
	2010	2011	2012	2013	2014	2015		2010	2011	2012	2013	2014	2015	2016
2009	-0,37	-0,37	-0,38	-0,38	-0,38	-0,38	2009	-0,17	-0,16	-0,17	-0,17	-0,17	-0,17	-0,16
2010		-0,38	-0,39	-0,39	-0,39	-0,39	2010		-0,16	-0,17	-0,17	-0,17	-0,17	-0,16
2011			-0,4	-0,4	-0,4	-0,4	2011			-0,17	-0,17	-0,18	-0,17	-0,16
2012				-0,41	-0,41	-0,42	2012				-0,17	-0,18	-0,17	-0,16
2013					-0,44	-0,44	2013					-0,19	-0,18	-0,17
2014						-0,44	2014						-0,18	-0,17

(calculated by the authors on the data from "Doing Business" and the World Bank)

migrant labour force (e.g., Singapore, Hong Kong, UAE, some microstates of the Caribbean etc.). While geographically large and thus densely populated countries cannot have the luxury of free establishing the 0% tax rate, therefore, they have to compete with each other in the field of comparative tax comfort by means of easing the tax formalities, increasing the transparence and "customer" support within tax administrations, strengthening the quality and the efficiency of taxes' distribution etc. Of course, there are no specific limits/threshold in this so-called "tax comfort", thus, governments of developing nations have to concentrate more and more efforts on this direction of work.

Following further the topic of stimulating role of taxation comfort, we should also mention one more regularity (see Table 7): there exists a mutual correlation between, for example, the number of tax payments per year and population welfare (manifested through GDP per capita). This means that not only the lower number of tax payments has stimulated the growth of GDP per capita in the countries of the world, but there is an opposite direction here too – in richer countries we can observe quite logical and predictable process of tax comfort increase. At the same time we need to note that welfare growth in a country nearly never leads to lower tax rates. And also, we observe no correlation between the dynamics of export attractiveness of a country and its level of tax comfort.

Table 7. Correlation between the number of tax payments, the time spent on tax formalities, GDP per capita and national exports' growth (2010-2016)

Payment	GDP Per Capita						Time	GDP Per Capita					
	2010	2011	2012	2013	2014	2015		2011	2012	2013	2014	2015	2010
2011	-0,5						2011	-0,4					
2012	-0,48	-0,48					2012	-0,41	-0,41				
2013	-0,54	-0,55	-0,54				2013	-0,43	-0,44	-0,44			
2014	-0,54	-0,54	-0,53	-0,53			2014	-0,43	-0,44	-0,44	-0,44		
2015	-0,52	-0,52	-0,51	-0,51	-0,51		2015	-0,42	-0,42	-0,42	-0,42	-0,42	
2016	0,07	0,09	0,09	0,08	0,08	0,09	2016	-0,09	-0,09	-0,09	-0,09	-0,09	-0,08

(calculated by the authors)

As shown in Table 8, in poor countries the average tax rate is usually much more influential than, for example, taxation comfort indicators, but still, the tax rate impact is less than the impact of the international ranking of a certain country's taxation system overall. While in case of average income countries the nearly equal stimulating effects on the local economy's development have such indicators as taxation comfort, the tax rate size and the country's rank in the taxation systems' global ranking.

We also need to mention here that in case of rich countries the ranking of a national taxation system and the tax rate size have the maximum impact on macroeconomic indicators of a country.

More detailed description of how specifically separate components of a taxation regime impact the macroeconomic indicators and external trade attractiveness is presented in Table 9.

Table 8. Taxation regime impact on macroeconomic indicators of development and external trade dynamics by country groups, 2009-2016[1]

Country Groups	Taxation Regime Indicators[2]			
	Taxation Ranking of the Group	Taxation Comfort		Average Tax Rate
		Duration of Overall Tax Formalities	Number of Tax Payments	
Rich	82	61	60	80
Well-to-do	75	41	67	65
Average	97	80	100	99
Underperforming	61	49	84	77
Poor	100	77	89	96

(calculated by the authors)

Table 9. Interdependence between taxation regime components and indicators of economic systems' development and trade dynamics by country groups, 2009-2015

Country Groups	Taxation Regime Indicators			
	Taxation Ranking	Taxation Comfort		Average Tax Rate
		Duration of All Tax Formalities	Number of Tax Payments	
Rich				5
Well-to-do	1,2,3,5	5		3
Average	3,5,7	1,3,7	7	5,7
Underperforming				
Poor	1,3	7		1,3,7

(calculated by the authors)
1- GDP in relative terms
2- GDP growth, %
3- GDP per capita
4- GDP per capita growth, %
5- Export in absolute terms
6- Export growth, %
7- Import in absolute terms
8- Import growth, %

As we can see in Table 9, the most powerful stimulating effect on economic growth overall and trade attractiveness in particular have the taxation regimes in poor, average income and well-to-do countries. On the other hand, it is also obvious that taxation regime has nearly minimal influence on the most important dynamics indicators, such as growth of export-import operations, GDP per capita growth. And in case of underperforming countries taxation has no stimulating effect as such.

CONCLUSION

The presented here statistical study determining the economic development impact factors, namely, related to taxation regimes, enables us make several conclusions so that to explain the initial hypotheses posed.

First of all, the rank of country's taxation system in the international rating "Doing Business" indeed has its long-term effect on the GDP per capita level. And this impact is much more stronger for national exports, rather than for national imports.

Secondly, correlation between the tax rate size and the dynamics of countries' economic development as well as the level of their involvement into the world economic processes is nearly absent in both long and short terms. At the same time, criteria responsible for the so-called "comfort of the national taxation regime" (traditionally measured through the time spent on various tax formalities and the number of tax payments per year) are much more meaningful factors when it comes to macroeconomic growth as compared to the tax rate as such.

Thirdly, not only the reduced number of tax payment is able to stimulate the GDP per capita growth, but also vice verse – wealthier countries clearly have higher levels of taxation comfort.

Comparing the results at two stages of our research on the worldwide statistical data, namely, concerning the stimulating effects from taxation comfort indicators, from the size of tax rate and from the global rank of a national taxation regime, we can clearly observe the most significant effect of the latter indicator.

This leads us to the conclusion that the actual current situation with taxation regimes in the countries (taxation comfort + the tax rate) has significantly less influence in terms of economic development stimulation and country's engagement in the world economy and global trade, while country's favorable ranking as determined by the expert community has much more influence. Consequently, the study carried out above proves, yet another time, that the role and the value of such rankings is growing, even though they tend to display to the actual state of affairs in a particular country, but rather its image, its attractiveness for experts, potential investors etc. Therefore, expert opinions on the efficiency of national taxation systems today may indeed determine the dynamics of countries' economic development and country's further engagement in world economic relations. These widely popular rankings shape the attitudes of potential investors and country's overall attrazctiveness for capital, incoming labor force, for transnational business – and thus, they also determine the macroeconomic dynamics of national economies' development, and this external influence of theirs in many cases is much more significant than all national/internal instruments of public economic regulation, such as tax rates or taxation regime/ conditions.

On the one hand, this conclusion describes rather well the current stage of the global economy's development which has already become "the economy of images", the some sort of "economic simulacrum", one of the manifestations of which is actually the popularity of all these rankings. Today's global economy is based on simplified mathematical methodologies which are not only distanced from actual economic situations but are also essentially pseudo-scientific! And as a result, too much of a role and ungrounded preferences are given to such subjective qualitative criteria as "innovation potential of society" or "creativity", level of economic freedom, level of human capital development etc. Therefore, rather unmeasurable notions become not only measurable, but recalculated and correlated with each other, thus forming the basis for further modernization of international redistribution of capital or labour force. And this means that intangible notions have very many tangible, economic consequences for real business, the state and the society.

On the other hand, conclusions we have made in relation to taxation regimes can be potentially also confirmed for other popular indicators (for example, the level of external trade freedom, the innovation potential of nations, ease of new business registration, protection of private property in a country etc.). And this definitely requires further and more detailed research in the same direction and overall context.

Also, the carried out research has managed to prove here that taxation indeed has certain stimulating effect on macroeconomic growth and countries' attractiveness for external trade. At the same time we can observe this effect tends to vary significantly, depending on a country's welfare level, its overall economic conditions and trade infrastructure in particular. The authors prove here that the stimulating effects from taxation ranking, components of taxation comfort and tax rates can be rather differentiated, thus, there is a necessity for a multivector approach to tax levers' application on the state level of economic stimulation. And the key requirements to this stimulating policy should be the following:

1. In rich countries worldwide significant stimulating effects for national economies have global rankings of their taxation systems as well as the average tax rate in the country. This can be explained by the fact that traditionally rich states have by default rather high level of taxation comfort. In our previous research (Ushakov, 2016) we have already proved that once a country achieves a certain level of welfare – its taxation comfort nearly automatically gets also higher, for example, bureaucracy related to taxation procedures reduces and overall, public bodies perform their regulating functions in a more efficient way – thus, further increase of tax rates becomes simply inexpedient. At the same time, we need also to note that higher tax rates in the most developed countries in the world manifest their efficiency in stimulation of national economies and export-import operations in particular.
2. For poor countries higher economic value have tax rates and also taxation system ranking (which is often predetermined by the size of taxes in the country), while taxation comfort factors usually get secondary importance. At the same time, curiously, taxation comfort has significant stimulation powers in underperforming countries and also in the countries with average income (in case of the latter – mostly because their economic growth is to a larger extent predetermined by rather liberalized taxation processes).
3. In rich and average income countries the tax rate is able to onset the development of national exports, consequently, their discriminatory tax policy (which is in most cases preferential to actively exporting enterprises) would activate and widen the country's role and engagement in the world trade.
4. Import is very much dependent upon the specifics of a particular national taxation system in poor countries and average income countries. This can be explained by the underdevelopment of internal proposition, actually. Therefore, in these countries regulation of tax rates and promoting taxation comfort would revive the growth of national consumption, however, this can actually turn to the

disadvantage of national production (though longer-term favourable effect would be still possible due to internal competition development).

5. In the three groups of countries we consider here (that is, the larger share of the world as such) taxation rank and taxation comfort indicators impact population welfare (measured through GDP per capita), however, at the same time not impacting the GDP dynamics (measured through GDP growth and GDP per capita growth).

Conclusions we have reached here for these five groups of countries can be further taken into account in the processes of national policies' modernization in part of tax instruments' implementation for economic growth intensification purposes.

REFERENCES

Acharya, S. (2015). Trade Liberalization. In Palgrave Dictionary of Emerging Markets and Transition Economics. New York: Palgrave Macmillan. doi:10.1007/978-1-137-37138-6_21

Balatskii, E. (2006). Tax reform and economic growth. *Studies on Russian Economic Development, 17*(2), 204–208.

Doerrenberg, P. & Peichl, A. (2013). Progressive taxation and tax morale. *Public Choice, 155*(3), 293–316.

Duclos, J.Y., Makdissi, P., & Araar, A. (2014). Pro-poor indirect tax reforms, with an application to Mexico. *International Tax and Public Finance, 21*(1), 87–118.

Echevarría, C. (2015). Income tax progressivity, growth, income inequality and welfare. *SERIEs, 6*(1), 43–72.

Harms, P., & Zink, S. (2003). Eating the Rich vs. Feeding the Poor: Borrowing Constraints and the Reluctance to Redistribute. *Public Choice, 116*(3), 351–366.

Hill, R. (2008). Optimal taxation and economic growth: a comment. *Public Choice, 134*(3), 419–427.

Ickowitz, A. (2001). *The Distribution of Wealth and the Pace of Development.* Studies in Development Strategy and Systemic Transformation.

Janský, P. (2015). Updating the Rich Countries' Commitment to Development Index: How They Help Poorer Ones Through Curbing Illicit Financial Flows. *Social Indicators Research, 124*(1), 43–65.

Jha. (2008). *Pro-Poor Fiscal Policy in the Globalized Economy. Pro-Poor Macroeconomics.* Social Policy in a Development Context.

Kaneko, A., & Matsuzaki, D. J. (2009). Consumption tax and economic growth in an overlapping generations model with money holdings. *Journal of Economics, 98*(2), 155–175. doi:10.100700712-009-0088-5

Kenny, L. W., & Winer, S. L. (2006). Tax Systems in the World: An Empirical Investigation into the Importance of Tax Bases, Administration Costs, Scale and Political Regime. *International Tax and Public Finance*, 3.

Keuschnigg, C. & Dietz, M.D. (2007). A growth oriented dual income tax. *International Tax and Public Finance, 14*(2), 191–221.

Kley, V. (2011). *Optimal wealth transfer taxation: a review of existing literature*. The Taxation of Capitalistic Bequests.

Kuznets, S. (1937). *Some Problems In Measuring Per Capita Labor Income*. Retrieved from http://www.nber.org/chapters/c8142.pdf

Magessi, N., & Antunes, L. (2014). Shadow Economy and Wealth Distribution. *Advances in Artificial Economics*, *676*, 169–179.

Marrero, G. (2010). Tax-mix, public spending composition and growth. *Journal of Economics*, *99*(1), 29–51.

Mattos, E. & Politi, R. (2014). Pro-poor tax policy and yardstick competition: a spatial investigation for VAT relief on food in Brazil. *The Annals of Regional Science, 52*(1), 279–307.

Okun, A. (1970). *The Political Economy of Prosperity*. Yale University Press.

Patience, I., & Mogotsi, B. (2009). *Wealth and Income Inequalities. Poverty Reduction and Changing Policy Regimes in Botswana*. Developmental Pathways to Poverty Reduction Series.

Pemberton, H. (2004). *Policy learning and British governance in the 1960s*. New York: Palgrave Macmillan. doi:10.1057/9780230504752

Rehme, G. J. E. (2007). Economic Growth and (Re-) Distributive Policies in a Non-cooperative World. *Journal of Economics*, *91*(1), 1–40.

Scully, G. W. (2003). Optimal Taxation, Economic Growth and Income Inequality. *Public Choice*, *115*(3), 299–312.

Sinevičienė, L. (2016). Tax Burden and Economic Development: The Case of the European Union Countries. *Entrepreneurship. Business Economics (Cleveland, Ohio)*, *2*, 283–298.

Soltysilski, S. (2009). Global Tax Competition and Tax Cooperation. *The Role of Law and Ethics in the Globalized Economy*, *10*, 1–7.

Tamai, T. (2015). Redistributive taxation, wealth distribution, and economic growth. *Journal of Economics, 115*(2), 133–152.

Tillmann, G. (2010). Evasion of Tax on Interest Income in a Two-Country Model. *Economics Essays.*, *4*, 345–363.

Ushakov, D. (2016). Dynamics of international economical relationships in the global context of innovative modernization. *International Journal of Environmental and Science Education*, 18.

Vogel, J. (2014). Welfare Production, Poverty and Wealth. A Comparative and Longitudinal Perspective. *Rich and Poor.*, *15*, 235–270. doi:10.1007/978-94-010-0257-8_16

Volkerink, B., Sturm, J. & De Haan, J. Tax Ratios in Macroeconomics: Do Taxes Really Matter? *Empirica, 29*(3), 209–224.

Widmalm, F. (2001). Tax Structure and Growth: Are Some Taxes Better Than Others? *Public Choice, 107*(3), 199–219.

KEY TERMS AND DEFINITIONS

Capital Flight: In economics, occurs when assets or money rapidly flow out of a country, due to an event of economic consequence. Such events could be an increase in taxes on capital or capital holders or the government of the country defaulting on its debt that disturbs investors and causes them to lower their valuation of the assets in that country, or otherwise to lose confidence in its economic strength. This leads to a disappearance of wealth, and is usually accompanied by a sharp drop in the exchange rate of the affected country—depreciation in a variable exchange rate regime, or a forced devaluation in a fixed exchange rate regime.

Economic Growth: Is the increase in the inflation-adjusted market value of the goods and services produced by an economy over time. It is conventionally measured as the percent rate of increase in real gross domestic product, or real GDP. Growth is usually calculated in real terms (i.e., inflation-adjusted terms) to eliminate the distorting effect of inflation on the price of goods produced.

National Competitiveness: The concept "national competitiveness" examines the ability of a national economy to grow. It is measured by a set of factors, policies, and institutions that determine a country's level of productivity.

Social Inequality: Occurs when resources in a given society are distributed unevenly, typically through norms of allocation, that engender specific patterns along lines of socially defined categories of persons. It is the differentiation preference of access of social goods in the society brought about by power, religion, kinship, prestige, race, ethnicity, gender, age, sexual orientation, and class. The social rights include labor market, the source of income, healthcare, and freedom of speech, education, political representation, and participation.

Tax Amnesty: Is a limited-time opportunity for a specified group of taxpayers to pay a defined amount, in exchange for forgiveness of a tax liability (including interest and penalties) relating to a previous tax period or periods and without fear of criminal prosecution. It typically expires when some authority begins a tax investigation of the past-due tax. In some cases, legislation extending amnesty also imposes harsher penalties on those who are eligible for amnesty but do not take it. Tax amnesty is one of voluntary compliance strategies to increase tax base and tax revenue. Tax amnesty is different from other voluntary compliance strategies in part where tax amnesty usually waives the taxpayers' tax liability.

Tax Avoidance: Is the legal usage of the tax regime in a single territory to one's own advantage to reduce the amount of tax that is payable by means that are within the law. Tax sheltering is very similar, although unlike tax avoidance tax sheltering is not necessarily legal.

Tax Reform: Is the process of changing the way taxes are collected or managed by the government and is usually undertaken to improve tax administration or to provide economic or social benefits. Tax reform can include reducing the level of taxation of all people by the government, making the tax system more progressive or less progressive, or simplifying the tax system and making the system more understandable or more accountable.

Tax Evasion: Is the illegal evasion of taxes by individuals, corporations, and trusts. Tax evasion often entails taxpayers deliberately misrepresenting the true state of their affairs to the tax authorities to reduce their tax liability and includes dishonest tax reporting, such as declaring less income, profits or gains than the amounts actually earned, or overstating deductions.

Tax Mitigation: "Tax aggressive," "aggressive tax avoidance," or "tax neutral" schemes generally refer to multi-territory schemes that fall into the grey area between commonplace and well-accepted tax avoidance (such as purchasing municipal bonds in the United States) and evasion, but are widely viewed as unethical, especially if they are involved in profit-shifting from high-tax to low-tax territories and territories recognized as tax havens.

Tax Reform: Is the process of changing the way taxes are collected or managed by the government and is usually undertaken to improve tax administration or to provide economic or social benefits. Tax reform can include reducing the level of taxation of all people by the government, making the tax system more progressive or less progressive, or simplifying the tax system and making the system more understandable or more accountable.

Wealth: Has been defined as a collection of things limited in supply, transferable, and useful in satisfying human desires. Scarcity is a fundamental factor for wealth. When a desirable or valuable commodity (transferable good or skill) is abundantly available to everyone, the owner of the commodity will possess no potential for wealth. When a valuable or desirable commodity is in scarce supply, the owner of the commodity will possess great potential for wealth.

ENDNOTES

1 Correlation has been calculated by the authors.

2 100 is the maximum.

Chapter 12
Model of Socioeconomic Development Based on Market Economy and Public-Private Partnership (PPP) Mechanism:
Key Approaches and Terms for Implementation

Alexey Zeldner
Institute of Economics of the Russian Academy of Sciences, Russia

Vladimir Osipov
MGIMO University, Russia & Market Economy Institute of the Russian Academy of Sciences, Russia

Tatiana Skryl
Plekhanov Russian University of Economics, Russia

ABSTRACT

This chapter systematizes the main components of the socio-market model of the economy. Its basis is formed by market economy and public-private partnership as the mechanism stimulating the attraction of private investments. Using the opportunities of the market economy and PPP mechanism creates a real opportunity for the formation of a new model of socio-market economy. This model does not imply the weakening the role of the state and infringement of democracy as such, but rather strengthening of institutions and PPP mechanisms with the aim to attract private investments and improve social relations at the same time. This chapter is thus aimed at revealing the main elements of this socioeconomic model along with the theoretical, methodological, and practical aspects of its main components: the market economy and the PPP mechanisms.

DOI: 10.4018/978-1-5225-7760-7.ch012

INTRODUCTION

Managing the public-private partnerships in the context of mixed economy is one of the key elements in the national model of social-market economy which is essentially based on partnerships between the state, businesses and civil society institutions.

The PPP management mechanism assumes a system of economic levers that provide incentives for attracting private investments and their further effective use in the course of infrastructure projects. These levers include legal, budgetary and off-budget sources, prices, taxes, loans, customs payments and other incentives for attracting investments. According to A. Kulman, economic mechanism operates within the framework of laws and rules adopted by the state, "forming an economic regime that includes elements of state legislation, corporate law, legal forms of combining labor and capital within enterprises, defining the scope of preferential taxation etc." (Kulman, 1993).

The nature of economic mechanism, formed for each of the development stages, does not eliminate the possibility of the impact of force majeure circumstances or other external factors; moreover, it allows adapting to new conditions. This approach assumes the use of the state system in management over the process of formation and functioning of PPP.

Under the current conditions of Russian economy, the PPP mechanism should be seen as a strategic development management tool which allows not only minimizing costs for all types of transaction costs, but also providing a system solution for attracting financial resources for the implementation of large infrastructural projects which later would ensure the reproduction process.

From the institutional perspective, public administration of PPP is considered as an optimal strategic approach to stimulating socioeconomic development that combines efficiency, flexibility, and competence of the private sector with the control possibilities, long-term prospects and social interests of the public sector (Spielman, & Grebmer, 2012). Management of public-private partnerships should be viewed as a process that forms a tolerant relationship between the subjects of market relations and civil society institutions in the process of public production, exchange and distribution, and with the aim of ensuring sustainable growth and development of economy and social relations.

Ultimately, competently organized management ensures the achievement of the planned results with the most efficient use of resources and preservation of the environment. At the same time, in the process of implementing large projects PPP management ensures the rule of law, transparency in the use of funds, responsibility, interest of all participants in achievement of final results, ensuring their rights and compensation for possible losses.

Managing large PPP projects often assume the possibility of project management application. The project structure, in its turn, assumes implementation of the infrastructural target tasks, one-man management and stronger responsibility for all related decision and actions. At the same time, according to the recommendations of the World Bank, own capital must cover at least 20-30% of the PPP project costs (Nikonov, 2017).

Such management of PPP projects requires a targeted approach and its phased implementation, which includes the definition of ultimate goals, working out the ways of its achievement, including through the provision of investments, and systematic monitoring over the project implementation.

LITERATURE REVIEW

Russian experiences with various forms of PPP as well as foreign experience in the same field allows us conclude that for the current development stage of Russia, a unified structure of PPP management would be more appropriate. The need for this unified management structure of PPP in Russia is also linked to the already well established bureaucratic nature of PPP projects' coordination by several departments at the same time. The importance of a unified management system is also evidenced by the world experience. According to the World Bank, PPP management is an organization established to implement and improve public-private partnerships in various sectors of the economy. According to the definition adopted by the OECD, PPP management body is an organization whose task is to assist the government in creation, support and evaluation of PPP agreements *(Dedicated Public Private Partnership Units: A Survey of Institutional and Governance Structures, 2010).*

No matter how well tuned is the management system or which development model has been selected, without well-trained personnel it would be difficult to achieve any success from PPP.

According to Lee Kuan Yew, a talented politician and economist, "if there was any formula for our success, it was that we were constantly learning how to make the system work or to make it work even better" (Lee Kuan Yew, 2010). The use of well-trained personnel in the process of national modernization is very typical for China. The human factor in China "is considered to be the foundation of the whole matter of accelerated development" (Lee Kuan Yew, 2010). The emphasis on the priority development of innovative economy is also provided by an increase in the share of expenditures on R&D in GDP. China ranks first in the world by the number of scientific and technical employees, working in the field of R&D - over 51 mln people (Nasibov, 2012).

The most important factor that has determined China's success is the human factor. This includes, inter alia, constant work with staff, their life-long learning and career growth depending on the achieved results. As it is the rule in many authoritarian systems, leaders are appointed from above, and there is no accountability of leaders to their voters or the possibility of their replacement.

However, the actual commercial and research results in China seems to be the exception to the rules common in China. How does China manage to reach such impressive level of socioeconomic and scientific development under the authoritarian regime?

According to Professor Xu Chenggang (Cheung Kong Graduate School of Business), the reason is the model of "regional decentralized authoritarianism" (Xu Chenggang, 2015). According to his hypothesis, "the Chinese focus is that the regional leaders in China are appointed from above, but they have a very significant autonomy in issues of economic policy. While in the Soviet Union enterprises were controlled by sectoral ministries from the center, in China most state-owned enterprises belong to provincial, city and village authorities. Already in the early 2000s, the share of local and regional budgets in the total expenditures of the state in unitary China was approximately 70%" (Xu Chenggang, 2015), which is significantly higher than in many countries of the world. Therefore, the central authorities in China evaluate only the very final, regional-level results of management activities.

Another significant factor concerns the selection of business leaders in this country. The principle of recruitment has deep historical traditions in China. For two thousand years, government officials in China have been selected according to the results of open competitive examinations. This system has been preserved in China to this day; moreover, it is also widely used to identify the most talented youth.

China's successes in terms of trade turnover and GDP for are directly connected to thorough and competent selection of human resources for managers' positions. It can be treated with varying degrees of irony that the Communist Party directly participates in the selection of personnel in China; however, the key result from this intrusion is that the country's interests always go first, as opposed to the goals of personal enrichment. In China each stage in personal career is tracked, and not only is the attitude to learning taken into account, but also the feedback provided by other managers and colleagues. With each promotion, all candidates are certified before appointment. In the higher echelons of the power pyramid, there is the core of fifty thousand people who were carefully selected and "sorter out" by the Chinese Communist Party, but not by the government.

To make sure that these estimates are correct, a special inspection commission from the center visits all provinces and larger cities, assessing the persons passing this certification, and having interviews with them before the actual promotion. In case of any disagreement between inspectors or any doubt, the issue is considered in Beijing. Selection is conducted carefully and comprehensively. According to Lee Kuan Yew, the author of "Singapore miracle", the overall level of Chinese leaders' competences is quite impressive (Lee Kuan Yew, 2010).

"I expected this from the leaders in Beijing, but I was surprised to find that in provincial officials: secretaries of party committees, governors, mayors and senior officials are also high-class leaders. A thick layer of talented people scattered throughout the whole continent is impressive. Those who got to the top do not necessarily have a head taller than those they went around. In such a densely populated country like China, luck plays a significant role in moving to the heights of power, even with careful selection, which emphasizes abilities and character, and not ideological purity and revolutionary zeal, as in the years of the "cultural revolution"" (Lee Kuan Yew, 2010).

In Lee Kuan Yew's opinion, the future belongs to those who possess knowledge. "We must learn and become part of a world based on knowledge". At the same time, it is necessary to adhere to the principles that helped this country succeed.

This is a public consensus, achieved through a fair distribution of the fruits of progress. This is an equal opportunity for all. This is a system of promotion by merit, in which the most worthy person takes the best place. The latter is especially important when we are talking about people who head government. (Lee Kuan Yew, 2010)

Lee Kuan Yew's approach to the formation of government was to place the most capable, not the most devoted people at the head of the most important ministries, using the target method in management: the task was posed to the minister and an opportunity was provided to solve it. The state model used in a particular country is usually very specific; therefore, it would be difficult to reproduce it in another country. However, each state model with its unique management experience makes it possible to learn useful lessons for other countries, moreover, it helps avoiding common mistakes in the process of own management model formation.

METHODOLOGY

Economic Levers and Incentives for Attracting Investments into PPP Projects

Russian economy's recovery from today's depression (taking into account, inter alia, the imposed and prolonged sanctions) is possible through reindustrialization (in fact, this would be more like new industrialization). It should be aimed at recovery of the very basis of the economy - industry - through continuous technological innovation, ensuring high competitiveness of the final product due to a larger share of innovativeness in it and reduction of material consumption in combination with costs' minimization.

Technological and innovative breakthrough is always based on the availability of investment sources. The most serious financial problems of Russian economy today include: significant budget deficit, high interest rates on long-term loans (from 15 to 25%), and consequently - their rather limited use for investment purposes (10.5% as of 2016), also, sanctions have blocked access to cheaper foreign loans and new technologies, now not really available and/or affordable for Russian market.

As a result, a slowdown in investment growth in comparable prices has been observed for several years already. Besides that, in current prices there is a small increase in investment observed, while in comparable prices there is only a decrease. For example, from 2013 to 2014, investments in fixed capital at comparable prices decreased by 2.7%, in 2015 as compared to 2014 - by 8.4% and in 2016 as compared to 2015 – by another 4%. As for the rate of accumulation (as the ratio of investments in fixed assets to GDP), over the past five years it has never exceeded 21%. To compare, in China the investment rate is twice as high *(Federal State Statistics Service Report, 2015).*

According to the economic development forecasts of Russia for the years 2017-2020 prepared by the Vnesheconombank, state capital investments, which decreased by 201% in 2016, and as compared to 2015 - by 15.3%, will go even further, by -10% at least. What concerns private investments, in 2016 they demonstrated an increase of 1.4%, and in 2017-2019 their growth is expected to be around 4,6-6,5% *(Federal State Statistics Service Report, 2015).*

Under the current economic conditions in Russia, one of the most important sources of attracting investments to launch a reproductive process is private capital. And when it come to infrastructural projects specifically, such mechanisms as concessions, leasing, special economic zones, advanced development territories etc. proved to be most effective.

The world practice has already accumulated quite solid experience of attracting private investments into the implementation of large infrastructural projects. There are examples of such practice in Russia too. Since the adoption of the Law "On special economic zones in the Russian Federation" No. 116-FZ as of July 22, 2005, several large-scale projects have been implemented in Russia to attract private investments into high-tech & innovative field, industrial production, tourism and port management. The main purpose of special economic zones that have been created for the term of 49 years is the development of innovative, high-tech industries, manufacturing industries, production of new types of products, development of tourism along with a range of related recreational activities, improvement of transport and port infrastructure, development of other technologies along with their commercialization.

The most important incentive for the investors attracted to these special economic zones concerns the guarantees against adverse changes in legislation on taxes and fees.

Since 2005 and till 2016, that is, during 11 years 36 special economic zones (SEZ) have been created on the territories of 31 Russian regions. Since 2010, activity in 10 of these SEZs has been terminated as inefficient. Now, there are 26 operating SEZs, which include 10 industrial production ones, 6 specializing in technical promotional, 9 tourist-recreational ones and one port SEZ. In 2016, the Ministry for Economic Development of Russia signed agreements with the executive authorities of 17 regions on the transfer of powers to manage 20 SEZ. Under the conditions of constant budget deficit, this is fraught with a reduction in financing of infrastructure.

Analysis of the accumulated world experience in the field of SEZ creation and functioning has shown that only tax concessions in combination with customs fail to become a persuasive enough incentive for attracting private investments into a SEZ. The most important factor for attracting domestic and foreign investors into such PPPs is the development of zones' infrastructure mainly at the expense of federal and regional budgets. The already created infrastructural objects save significant financial resources for residents. The land should be provided to residents with some sort of already prepared infrastructure. At the same time, residents are exempted from paying the land tax for 5 years from the time of getting this land, and when it is bought out, the residents receive a discount of up to 50% of its cadastral value.

The first years of SEZ establishment were relatively favorable from the viewpoint of budget fulfillment of their obligations. According to the Accounts Chamber of the Russian Federation, during the period of 2006 to 2011 the total amount of budget funds aimed at the creation and development of SEZs amounted to 87.8 bln rubles, while 46.3 bln rubles were spent on infrastructure development (52.7%). During the next three years (2011-2013) a steady reduction was observed in budget financing of SEZ infrastructure development. If in 2011 15.7 bln rubles were allocated from the federal budget for all the SEZs, in 2012 and 2013 the investments already amounted to 6 bln rubles only. After 2013, SEZ were not even mentioned in the federal budget spending items. According to the Accounts Chamber of the Russian Federation, during 2017-2019 budget investments in the amount of 13.1 bln rubles are envisaged for SEZ financing, that is, on average, about 4.4 bln rubles a year. Reduction in the volume of budgetary financing with simultaneous, in fact, synchronous non-fulfillment of obligations by the residents of SEZs concerning the extra-budgetary financing of special technical and innovative economic zones together have led not only to increased construction costs, but also to the loss of private business confidence in state obligations. A significant reduction in budget financing of infrastructure and the related construction works has led to a real stagnation in the development of many SEZs. Only those SEZs where certain financial support has been provided by regional budgets, for example, SEZ "Alabuga" and "Lipetsk", managed to maintain good performance indicators.

According to the Accounting Chamber, as of January 1, 2017, the total cost of building SEZ infrastructural objects was estimated to be 383.2 bln rubles, including the expenses of the federal budget in the amount of 127.7 bln rubles (33.3%), regional budgets contributed 104.1 bln rubles, managing companies - 24.5 bln rubles, other extra-budgetary sources provided 51.9 bln rubles. In the period from 2005 to 2016 127.7 bln rubles have been granted from the federal budget to finance the creation and development of SEZ, as well as for the maintenance of the already available infrastructure. It should be noted that many regions did not fulfill their obligations to co-finance SEZ infrastructure. Thus, as of January 1, 2016, obligations of the regional budgets were fulfilled by 38.9% only. This is the consequence of budgetary underfunding, which affects the amount of funding available for the residents of SEZ. The total volume of investments made by the residents amounted to 217.7 bln rubles, which is only 33.5% of the declared volume. At the same time, the residents of three SEZs only together attracted the larger share of all investments (77.4% of the total volume).

Another highly important stimulating factor for attracting private investors into SEZ that can actually reduce the costs for residents is allocation of tax preferences.

First of All, The Profit Tax

Since the organization of the first SEZ, the share of profit tax provided to the federal budget was 2%, while 18% were allocated to regional budgets. Moreover, for the residents of special economic zones, this rate could have been significantly decreased, but it could not be less than 13.5%. Exceptions have been made for separate types of SEZs, and this was specifically mentioned in the Tax Code. Thus, for the residents of technical innovation zones, the tax rates were reset to zero for the period from 2012 to 2018 *(item 1.2 of Art. 284 of the Tax Code of the Russian Federation).*

Since 2017, the government has changed the order of distribution of the profit tax between the federal and the regional budgets. Since 2017, the profit tax became 20%, from which 3% were allocated to the federal budget, while regional budgets got 17%.

Article 284 of the Tax Code notes that "the tax rate that is subject to enrollment in the budgets of the constituent entities of the Russian Federation may be reduced for certain categories of taxpayers by the laws of the subjects of the Russian Federation. At the same time, this rate cannot be lower than 13.5% (12.5% in 2017-2020), unless otherwise provided by this article.

Article 284 of the Tax Code of the Russian Federation also retained income tax benefits received from activities in technology-innovative special economic zones and tourist-recreational zones, united in a cluster. For these zones, payments to the federal budget were reset to zero, while allocations to regional budgets should not exceed 12.5% (items 1 and 1.2 of Art. 284 of the Tax Code of the Russian Federation). A 0% rate applies if an organization has separate accounting records of income and expenses for the activities carried out on the SEZ territory and beyond. If an organization does not keep a separate record of income and expenses associated with the activities in the special economic zone and beyond, the profits from such activities are taxed at the tax rate of 3%. The income tax rate for organizations residing in free economic zones is formed according to a similar scheme.

It should be noted that, according to item 4.1 of Art. 284 of the Tax Code, subjects of the Russian Federation can reduce the tax rate assigned to regional budget for other forms of taxpayers to the level of 12.5%, as it is used by certain regions where SEZs are located. For organizations in the advancing areas of socioeconomic development and the free port of Vladivostok a zero rate of income tax to the federal budget has been introduced. As for allocations to regional budgets, the rate of profit tax is supposed to be no more than 5% within the five years from the moment of profit receipt, and no less than 10% during the next five years *(item 1.8 of Art. 284.4 of the Tax Code).*

As a rule, practically all tax privileges used to attract investments have encumbrances that seriously affect the number of residents who actually benefit from these and other preferences mentioned in the Tax Code.

The encumbrances in the Tax Code on income tax *(Art. 284 of the Tax Code of the Russian Federation)* are related to the organizations that do not maintain separate accounting, directly related to activities in the SEZ and beyond. In this case the profit is taxed at the rate of 3%.

In our view, this position should be canceled, because it imposes a restriction on the formation of clusters. Moreover, it does not trigger a chain reaction of demand, while we are talking here about technological innovation products, the introduction of which requires extensive approbation.

Further, profits received in the special economic zone that later goes for investment purposes should be fully exempted from taxation. This would contribute to creation of more comfortable conditions for production development. In addition, for the zones developing and producing scientific and technical products, it is necessary to introduce the lending rate of 5% per annum, as it is now in the agricultural sector.

Property tax. According to the letter of the Ministry for Finance of the Russian Federation as of 21.01.2008. No. 03-05-04-01/2 in accordance with Art.381 of the second part of the Tax Code of the Russian Federation "organizations are exempted from taxation in respect of property recorded on the balance sheet of a resident organization of a special economic zone created or acquired for the purpose of conducting activities on the territory of SEZ ... within 5 years from the date of registration of the said property". Noteworthy, regional specificity should be taken into account here.

The privilege is granted to the residents of SEZ only provided there are separate accounting records for the incomes received during the implementation of technical and innovative activities and also the incomes received from other activities. In case if a resident does not keep a separate record of income, taxation of their property is carried out at the rate of 2.2%.

If certain property objects created in the course of technical and innovative activities on the SEZ territory are later used for other activities, such property is also subject to taxation according to the general procedure that naturally limits the effective use of fixed assets accumulated in such zones.

Transport tax. In accordance with regional laws, SEZ residents are exempt from "payment of transport tax, except cars, water and air vehicles". The tax code *(Ch. 28)* does not provide SEZ residents with special privileges. According to Article 357 of the Tax Code, taxpayers of transport tax are recognized as persons owning registered vehicles as the objects of taxation registered in accordance with Article 358 of the Tax Code, unless otherwise provided by this article. Moreover, there are certain restrictions for the subjects of the Russian Federation concerning the use of this tax. Tax rates can be increased (reduced) by the laws of the subjects of the Russian Federation, but no more than five times. Therefore, the issue about transport tax remains unclear and largely depends on the initiatives of a local tax inspection when it is checking the local residents.

Land relations in SEZ are regulated by Chapter 7 of the Federal Law No. 240-FZ as of 30.10.2007 "The procedure for the provision of land plots located within the boundaries of a special economic zone, and the procedure for the use of these land plots". In accordance with the mentioned law, land plots within the boundaries of an economic zone can be granted for temporary possession and use solely based on a lease agreement. In accordance with the legislation of the Russian Federation, tenants have the right to purchase the land plots under the real estate objects.

The maximum amount of rent for land plots granted to a resident of a special economic zone on the basis of an agreement on the conduct of industrial-production, technical-promotional, tourist-recreational activities is determined by the executive body authorized by the Government of the Russian Federation. Before the purchase of a land plot, the resident pays for the lease of land at a reduced rate, which is 2% of the cadastral value of this land. Lease payments and other payments for land plots located within the boundaries of a special economic zone are transferred to the budget of the appropriate level of the budget system of the Russian Federation in accordance with the legislation of the Russian Federation, although it would be more expedient to use it for the development of the related zone itself.

In accordance with the Law "On Special Economic Zones in the Russian Federation" *(No. 116-FZ amended by the Federal Law No. 340-FZ as of December 25, 2009)*, the residents are exempted from paying land tax for 5 years from the date of the land plot ownership start (*Federal Law No. 75-FZ of 03.06.2006, item 9)*.

All SEZ (except port) are created only on the land plots in state or municipal ownership. If the resident buys a plot of land with a property on it that is privately owned, they may be subject to payment of land tax because, according to the provision of Chapter 1, Article 1 of Federal Law No. 116-FZ, such land is no longer a SEZ territory. Consequently, benefits for the residents in such case are lost. It is necessary to adopt appropriate by-laws to protect the status of residents, and to improve, at the same time, the use of land within SEZ. According to the SEZ managing companies, as of January 1, 2017, 43.7 thousand hectares, or 65.5% of the total land areas under SEZ were not used.

Tariffs on insurance payments in SEZ are differentiated by their types. For the residents of SEZs that have concluded an agreement on the implementation of technical and innovative activities and make payments to individuals, there are privileges in the form of 14% insurance rate (with the total contribution of 30% in accordance with the Tax Code).

Same preferential insurance tariffs have been established for the residents of SEZ of the tourist cluster and, as an exception, only for those residents that carry out technical and innovative activities in the industrial production zones.

Special privileges for the aforementioned SEZs have been established by the Federal Law No. 272-FZ as of 16.10.2010 "On insurance contributions to the Pension Fund of the Russian Federation, the Social Insurance Fund ... the federal Mandatory Health Insurance Fund and the territorial funds of compulsory medical insurance". In other SEZs rates are applied as in the case of standard taxpayers.

As shown in Table 1, reduction of insurance premiums is temporary. For organizations and individual entrepreneurs who have the status of a resident of the technical-innovative or tourist-recreational special economic zone and make payments to individuals operating on their territory too, differentiation of tariffs on insurance premiums by years is applied. The existing tariffs for insurance premiums for these zones were preserved until 2017 inclusively, and then a smooth growth in all insurance funds will began. Already in 2018, for the residents of technical-innovation zones, it was in the amount of 21%, which naturally reduces the incentives to increase the number of employees and the wage fund.

SEZ territories are considered to be the zones of customs control, which means that the goods are placed and used within special economic zones without paying customs duties and VAT. The regime of a free customs zone is especially relevant for the enterprises using expensive high-tech equipment.

At the same time, according to the letter of the Ministry for Finance, goods sold by the residents of special economic zones are subject to taxation with the value added tax at the rates of 10 or 18%. Such a system of using VAT as applied to the goods sold by SEZ residents to other regions of Russia deprives them of the possibility of creating clusters, since this fact does not stimulate the subcontractors to purchase products with lower costs within SEZ, and this, in turn, significantly limits the demand for such products.

Table 1. Benefits on insurance premiums, operating on the territories of technical-innovation and tourist-recreational SEZ

Title of Funds	Tariffs of Insurance Premiums by Years (%)			
	2011	2012-2017	2018	2019
Pension Fund of the Russian Federation	8,0	8,0	13,0	20,0
Social Insurance Fund of the Russian Federation	2,0	2,0	2,9	2,9
Federal Compulsory Medical Insurance Fund	2,0	4,0	5,1	5,1
Territorial funds of compulsory medical insurance	2,0	0,0	0,0	0,0
Total	14	14	21	28

RESULTS, FINDINGS AND CONCLUSIONS

Peculiarities of Attracting Investments to the Territories of Priority Development

Development of the Russian Far East through the creation of a network with territories of priority development is an important stage in restructuring and modernization of Russian industries, which require, inter alia, substantial reallocation of almost all production factors, including labor resources. This means spatial displacement of production factors in the areas and territories that have new opportunities and social significance. For Russia, this is an extremely difficult problem. The issues of relocation are related to the availability of infrastructure, investment, jobs with decent wages, housing option, social security etc.

As the experience of Singapore's development and 30-year experience in the development of China's territorial zones (which provided the whole country with high rates of post-industrial development) shows, all related socioeconomic successes became possible due to following factors: 1) formation of industrial and social infrastructure through budget and private capital on the basis of public-private partnerships, and; 2) the incentive system, including economic levers, tax and customs privileges, guarantees to foreign investors to recover costs and free export of profits.

One of the key problems of the Far East as a Russian region is its poorly developed infrastructure (social, transport, energy and more). In order to Russian Far East attractive for the investors from Japan, China, South Korea, Singapore and other countries in the same region, the state should intensify its activities on outstripping financing of infrastructural projects, and not only in the field of industrial production, but also in the social sphere. It would be also reasonable to activate the PPP mechanism for these purposes.

The most important issue for the implementation of the national program covering the Far East with the network of territories of priority development (TPD) is their financing. The law on TPDs states that financial provision of infrastructural facilities is carried out by the expense of federal, regional and local budgets, and also through extra-budgetary sources of financing. It is also possible to grant subsidies for reimbursement of the interest rate on loans attracted by the investor for the construction of an infrastructure object, at 100% of the refinancing rate. Subjects of the federation contribute money as the authorized capital of the subsidiary company to the managing company, as well as by means of transferring the ownership of movable and immovable regional or municipal property.

The Fund for the Development of the Far East and the Baikal Region is also involved in financing of projects inside TPD. Initially, there were certain restrictions in this regard: investments were allowed only for the already prepared projects with market returns, but since the middle of 2015 these restrictions have been lifted. The mechanism of the investments' payback is aimed at the received taxes. However, in fact, the payback for most projects happens within 5-10 years, therefore, state companies are inevitably involved in their implementation as well as PPP.

In relation to TPDs financing, the need to provide attractive conditions for population should be also taken into account. The Far East is characterized by a steady outflow of population due to low standards of living there (high prices and relatively low salaries and pensions, permanent growth of tariffs, high prices for flights to other parts of Russia etc.). Therefore, attracting truly professional and experienced human resources to this region will require not only the growth of salaries, provision of better housing, medical care, schools, kindergartens, but also the introduction of a special Far Eastern coefficient to the salary.

The most important incentives for attracting investors are economic levers and stimulus, including tax preferences. Here we would like to mention at least some of those:

1. Zero rates of the profit tax for the first five years (the next 5 years - up to 5%, later on - 10% or above); same zero rates are also applied on land and property, as well as on import and export customs duties;
2. Free land acquisition, preferential rental rates (0.4% of the base rate) and for the use of the existing infrastructure;
3. For the first 10 years, insurance premiums are set at the level of 7.6% instead of 30%, and then the coefficient of one is applied;
4. An accelerated procedure of VAT reimbursement for all exporters, and 0% of VAT on the import of processing products;
5. Easier and quicker procedures of getting a construction permit, passage of customs, "one window" procedure for the investor, verification only with the consent of the Ministry for Economic Development.
6. An investment project is required to obtain the status of a TPD resident, the minimum investment volume is set at the level of 0.5 mln rubles. The company should be registered in the Far East and not have branches outside the TPD. The criteria for becoming the resident of the Free Port of Vladivostok are: having a brand new project and stating company's obligation to invest 5 mln rubles within three years.

As of 01.2017 the rate of income tax for all subjects of the Russian Federation is set at the level of 17%. For the residents of SEZ, it can be significantly reduced, but it still should be no less than 12.5%. At the same time, for the profit which is taxed in favor of the federal budget (3%), an exception was made for the residents of SEZ - a 0% tax rate for the period from 01/01/2012 to 01/01/2018 (Art. 284 of the Tax Code of the Russian Federation, item 1.2.). The profit tax privilege granted to TPDs has an encumbrance according to the same scheme as for SEZ.

Significant differences between TPDs and SEZs are in the established tariffs for insurance payments. TPD residents pay reduced premiums at the rate of 7.6%, of which 6% go to the Pension Fund of the Russian Federation, 1.5% are allocated to the Social Insurance Fund and 0.1% - to the Federal Compulsory Medical Insurance Fund. Benefits are valid for 10 years from the month following the month when the resident status was obtained. Only those insurers that are registered within TPD can take advantage of these reduced tariffs.

The system of tax privileges adopted for TPDs has its own specificity. On the one hand, such a regime makes it possible to increase the competitiveness of new enterprises by reducing their costs. On the other hand, opportunities for clustering are reduced, since products sold outside TPDs are subject to full taxation. From the production standpoint, this is an obvious disadvantage; moreover, this is not beneficial for employees either.

Billions of rubles are invested in TPDs in Russia. After a certain period, industrial and agricultural enterprises will start to work, ensuring a decent level of wages for their workers. However, these TPD provide reduced insurance payments, in particular, to the pension fund, to the health insurance fund and so on. With a new point system introduced, calculation of pensions and their future size depends on the insurance deposit and the amounts transferred for the employee. In accordance with the law, the state budget will compensate the funds for arrears. Nevertheless, the criteria for such arrears are not really well written, consequently, with such lowered contributions even well-earning (at least for today) workers can eventually receive reduced pensions. Such a situation can lead to the problem with attracting domestic skilled labor, especially since, according to the law on TPDs, attracted foreign labor is not quoted as such.

Population's attitude and intentions may be affected by the simplified procedure for taking-off lands and their redistribution in the course of TPD establishment: the appraisal company has been commissioned by the authorized federal bodies, which is a violation of the civil procedural legislation. Today this appraisal company determines the cost of property, however, in our opinion, such evaluation should be conducted as part of a court proceeding upon the request of either party.

An important condition for effective functioning of TPDs is stable demand for the products produced on these territories. Without solving this problem, the effectiveness of the entire project can be significantly reduced. For this matter, it is extremely important to reorganize interregional relations, to reconsider the whole system of clusters, state orders, state reserves, taking into account the available experience in organization of offset contracts.

When solving the problem of demand, one should pay close attention to the experience of India, where the policy of offset contracts was wisely applied for the development of the aerospace industry.

Foreign aircraft manufacturers, such as Boeing and Airbus, could sell India's products only if they place counter orders on Indian enterprises for an amount equal to at least 30% of each defense contract. Thus, a market worth over $ 30 billion was provided for national producers over a period of ten years. (Osipov, & Skryl, 2016)

Calculations conducted by the Russian Plekhanov University of Economics (PRUE) showed that under the existing financing conditions, construction costs of housing and transport, "the payback period of investments in TPDs will be about 38 years" with a term of economic activity of 70 years. Such a payback period of 38 years requires the revision and activation of the budget policy of the federal center in order to create territories that really demonstrate outrunning socioeconomic development in Russia and not turn an extremely important project for Russia into another unfulfilled strategy (and this trend has been preserved for a quarter of a century already, actually).

Creation of TPDs targeting the Asia-Pacific Region (APR) markets should be integrated into the overall scheme of development and deployment of the country's productive forces, taking into account all possible integration and cluster capabilities. We are talking here about their orientation on not only external opportunities, but also about the feasibility of paying more attention to domestic market overall and the creation of interregional clusters in particular.

Foreign experience in this field shows that for a well-organized arrangement of 1 square km of the industrial-production zone, the desirable amount of investments is about 40-45 mln USD, of which - 10-15 mln USD are supposed to go on customs and trade (Furschik, & Doronin, 2009).

It should be noted that the state costs for the creation of SEZs abroad are higher than in Russia. According to the survey conducted by the Institute of Oriental Studies of the Russian Academy of Sciences in 26 countries, the state costs for attracting foreign investments in SEZ averaged to 4 USD per one dollar of foreign investments. In the PRC, for example, foreign investments in 43 economic zones by the end of the 1980s amounted to $ 4 bln, while the initial own investments exceeded $ 22 bln, which is 5.5 times more. This means, essentially, that the entire infrastructure of SEZ in China was created mostly through public funds.

In order to increase investment attractiveness it is necessary to create conditions for more active role of the banking system in the investment process. The share of bank loans in the structure of investments in fixed assets in 2016 amounted to only 10.5%, this was due to high interest rates on long-term loans and the risks of non-repayment of the loan. Sanctions that have blocked access to cheap foreign loans have also contributed negatively to this situation. It is necessary to change the credit policy with respect to infrastructural projects in general and in particular for all types of zones. For the infrastructural projects in these zones, it is necessary to switch to the preferential rate for loans at 5% per annum, as it is already practiced in the agricultural sector.

In turn, effective implementation of infrastructural projects based on the use of various forms of PPP is not conducive to the existing rule regulating the ratio of loans and assets. In accordance with the Tax Code, the amount of loans from affiliated persons may exceed the amount of the net assets of the borrower by no more than three times. Otherwise, it is impossible to reduce tax profit by the amount of interest paid on such loans, and tax authorities thus can easily add this amount to profit tax. A feature of most PPP projects is that the ratio of net assets and debt financing in them exceeds the parameters set by the Tax Code. For PPP projects, given their role in attracting private capital, an exception should be made, otherwise, it will lead to a significant slowdown in the implementation of infrastructural projects.

Legal Security of the PPP Mechanism Functioning

One of the most serious problems hampering widespread introduction of the PPP forms and mechanisms is the incompleteness of legal security of this process. Until 2016, Russia had a limited number of federal laws covering various forms of PPPs. The main problems of the previously adopted federal laws are related to the provision of a mechanism for implementing PPP projects, manifested in the absence of detailed subordinate legislation that exists for concessions, as they are also necessary for the Law "On Special Economic Zones of the Russian Federation" *(Law No. 116-FZ as of July 13, 2005)* and for the law "On Production Sharing Agreements" as of 30.12.1998.

Since early 2016, the Federal Law "On Public-Private Partnership, Municipal-Private Partnership in the Russian Federation and Amendments to Certain Legislative Acts of the Russian Federation" as of July 13, 2015, No. 224-FZ, has also been implemented, however, this Federal Law, as we will show below, does not have a detailed system of by-laws.

In Russia concession projects occupy a predominant position today. As of the end of 2016, more than 1,300 PPP projects have been already implemented in the country, of which over 60% are not based on concession agreements (in the housing sector, in healthcare, education etc.). This is due to the fact that prior to the appearance of Law No. 224-FZ, the only form of PPP that was fixed in the Federal Law were concessions. In July 2014 a new law was passed - No. 265-FZ "On Amendments to the Federal Law "On Concession Agreements in the Russian Federation and Certain Legislative Acts of the Russian Federation", "where a provision was made on concluding a concession agreement on the initiative of a private individual (private initiative)".

Prior to this, the initiator of concluding concession agreements was the state (the concessioner), and now a private person can do it as well. Amendments to the concession legislation (items 4.1-4.12 of Art. 37 of the Federal Law "On Concession Agreements") came into force on May 1, 2015.

The mechanism for concluding a concession agreement on the initiative of a potential concessionaire provides the option of concluding an agreement without conducting tender procedures, up to a certain amount, if the initiator is the only applicant for concluding an agreement on such terms. However, it should be noted that these amendments do not take into account the risks of financial losses (project preparation) in case of refusal or the victory of another customer - there is no clarity in compensation of costs (there are other risks: corruption, risk of commercial secrets disclosure etc.).

Development of PPP projects under a private initiative scheme and the conclusion of life-cycle contracts, in fact, lead to much fuller and more active implementation of concession agreements. Life-cycle contracts are similar in terms of responsibilities to concessions, but there are significant differences at the same time. In concession terms, the state transfers part of its functions to the concessionaire who is then providing end services to population. This allows the state generate revenues through collecting service fees. Unlike the concessionaire, which invests its funds in a concession object or pays for operations of the concession object, under the conditions of life-cycle contracts, the state, in fact, hires a business partner to create the project and implement all related services. When life-cycle contracts are being implemented, revenues are generated from payments from the budget for the availability of services. Despite great popularity of concession projects in the world and their overall effectiveness, this form of business organization has not become widespread in Russia, even in the field of road infrastructure, where there is an acute shortage of good-quality roads. In general, legal aspects of the concession mechanism need to be further developed and expanded.

1. For the Federal Law "On Concession Agreements" it would be appropriate to adopt the corresponding by-laws that would take into account the specific features of various regional and municipal property. Thus, transferring something to a concession would be taking into account all specific risks, incentives and responsibilities, both that of a concessor and a concessionaire. In order to attract foreign investors to concession agreements and reduce all related risks, it would be also reasonable, in some cases, to turn to the international commercial arbitration in certain, highly disputable situations.
2. It is necessary to establish equal responsibility for both the concessionaire and the concessor. Currently, the state is protected better than the concessionaire, and the latter, when the construction begins, provides the state with bank guarantees. Under such guarantees, if the concessionaire fails to fulfill their obligations, the state receives compensation. Risks borne by a concessionaire, associated with high costs of the concession activity itself, are also burdened additionally by the need to pay a high concession fee to the state. At the same time, the law does not stipulate any penalty for the breach of obligations on the part of the state. It is necessary to provide additional legal backup for the situation when the state fails to fulfill its obligations. In such cases the concessionaire should be able to return money, taking into account the repayment of the loan taken for production purposes and the lost profit as well.
3. All adopted amendments to the Federal Law "On concession agreements", like the law itself, do not correlate with the current taxation system. In fact, there are no tax incentives for the implementation of concession activities as such. Even the property transferred under the concession agreement is not exempt from taxes. In accordance with the provisions of the Tax Code, transfer of immovable property from the conceding to the concessionaire is assessed as an implementation process and thus is subject to VAT. In reality, these are the operations of truly investment character, and they should not be recognized as subject to taxation. In our opinion, in order to attract private investment resources to participate in concession projects, it is also advisable to introduce changes into the Tax Code of the Russian Federation. These changes cover, inter alia, the exclusion of concessionaires from the list of entities paying property taxes in relation to property transferred to the

concessionaire, as well as in respect to the property created within the framework of a concession agreement. It is also efficient to extend to concessionaires (both domestic and foreign) those tax incentives that are introduced for the residents of technical and innovation zones.

4. There is no connection between concession agreements and the budget. In our opinion, in order to make the concessionary mechanism attractive for private investments, it is necessary to ensure some sort of state guarantees for the allocation of budgetary funds to concession projects without taking into account the limitations in the terms of budget financing. It is essential to introduce changes into the Budget Code of the Russian Federation so that to ensure continuous financing of the contracts for the entire period of construction of the concession facility along with the corresponding sanctions for the breach of contractual obligations.
5. It is advisable to introduce preferential crediting for concessionaires on the experience of agriculture under the two-thirds of the Central Bank's rates for the period of the implementation of the concession project.
6. Removing the contradiction between the Regulation on the Investment Fund and the Federal Law "On Concession Agreements" in the event that a private investor wants to resort to financing of a concession project. In the Investment Fund, there are actually two competitions for one project - one tender for the provision of financing, the other - for the project itself. Appealing to the Investment Fund is difficult before the concrete concessionaire is determined. At the same time, winning a concession tender without the Investment Fund's decision to support the project can also be problematic. In general, it should be noted that insufficiently clear legal provisions lead to a misunderstanding between the agencies responsible for concession projects.

Despite the fact that the adoption of Law 224-FZ is a significant step forward for the development of PPP practices in Russia, a number of the related problems should be noted. Their solution would contribute to the growing effectiveness of the law enforcement practices:

1. The risks of return on investments to private partner are extremely serious and require strict regulation. In accordance with the Law 224-FZ, agreement on a PPP assumes object transfer to private property, if the costs of the private partner exceed the costs of the public one. In addition to that, in such cases there will be a return of funds to a private partner at the expense of debt obligations with an indefinite period or at the expense of consumers' payments, also during an indefinite period. However, delay of funds' return means direct losses to the private partner (delay in loans, funds are subject to inflation etc.). Additionally to that, as it was already mentioned above, legislation should be updated so that to take into account the situation when default of a public partner should lead to appropriate compensation for its private partners.
2. As it was already mentioned, prior to the adoption of FZ-224, the main (in fact, the only) legally recognized form of PPP in Russia was concession agreements (according to FZ-115 as of 21.07.2005 "On concession agreements"). All other PPP projects might have been subject to regional PPP regulations; however, they were still quasi-PPP in their nature. Nevertheless, all the shortcomings of the concession law, in particular, serious risks with return on investments were significantly higher than under the adopted FZ-224. The adopted FZ-224 not only protects private investors more explicitly, but also explains the transfer of objects under partnership agreement into private ownership. In order not to create confusion in the compared laws, the law FZ-224 made a clear statement that the provisions of this law do not apply to concession agreements *(art. 2, item 2,*

FZ-224). Concession agreements are thus not regulated by 224-FZ, but only by 115-FZ. A clear distinction has also been made between concession and PPP projects.

3. Exclusion of foreign partners from the list of persons participating in PPP projects has become the consequence of the general campaign for import substitution, even though this decision is not subject to logic or common sense. Moreover, this contradicts the world practice and also deprives many well-developed project of investments (in the situation when there is acute shortage of foreign investments in the country). On the top of that, such legal changes limit access to the newest technologies available in the world, thus hindering Russia's development as such.

Another significant drawback of the new law is the fact that public facilities (water supply, heating etc.) are not currently included in the list of objects for potential PPP agreements.

4. Excluding a number of private partners from partnerships under the control of the Russian Federation (Clause 4, Part 2, Article 5) contradicts the provisions of Art. 49, 50 of the Civil Code, as it limits the scope of their activities and their legal capacity in general. Participation of the Russian Federation in the overwhelming majority of business entities (of which, again, the overwhelming majority are huge enterprises of regional importance) excludes such companies from participation in public-private partnership projects. Taking into account the fact that almost all early privatization programs provided for the state maintenance of a controlling share, it becomes clear that the PPP law itself is blocking the development of PPP projects. In addition to that, as Russian law enforcement practice has already demonstrated, even if the share of the state is the minority one, nevertheless, the state still has a significant impact on company's activities. All these norms exclude all largest Russian businesses from participation in PPP projects as private partners. These restrictions concern, among other things, the subsidiaries of economic entities (Clause 5, Part 2, Article 5). According to the Federal State Statistics Service, the total number of business entities with state participation (more than 50%) is 2,939 organizations, and to this groups belong all systemically important banks, large corporations etc. Thus, all these companies and organizations are by default excluded from the formation of public-private partnerships.
5. Banning of non-commercial organizations, established by both the Russian Federation and commercial organizations with the participation of the Russian Federation, from participation in the PPP funds and projects as private partners is groundless. Continuing the logic of all these prohibitions, it turns out that non-profit organizations created by business entities under the control of the Russian Federation are also, most likely, not able to be private partners in PPP projects.

The same applies to state institutions, state unitary enterprises, as well as property involved in their operational management. Even if we recognize such enterprises and institutions as PPP projects rather than actors, they nevertheless fall out of the PPP formation process project, since a ban on PPP agreements is established due to property encumbrance by the fact of such operational management.

Nevertheless, adoption of the Law FZ-224 is a significant achievement for Russia in terms of expanding the implementation of mechanisms used in state- and municipal-private partnership in the course of Russia's economic development. Given the growing deficit of the federal and regional budgets, as well as rather gloomy situation with municipal budgets, implementation of this law, taking into account its further amendments, can ensure a significant inflow of private capital into Russian economy and thus - improved socioeconomic indicators of the country's development overall.

REFERENCES

Abalkin, L. (2004). *The Fate of Russia: The Link Of Times*. Moscow: Institute of Economy RAS.

Crouch, K. (2016). *How to make capitalism acceptable to society*. Moscow: HSE.

Dedicated Public Private Partnership Units: A Survey of Institutional and Governance Structures. (2010). Paris: OECD.

Economy state regulation: world experience and reforms in Russia: theory and practice. (1996). Moscow: Institute of Economy, RAS.

Evsukov, S. G., Sigarev, A. V., Ustyuzhanina, E. V., & Zaytseva, E. V. (2016). Comparative analysis of pricing policies at the market for network goods. *Journal of Internet Banking and Commerce*, *21*, 6.

Furshyk, M., & Doronin, P. (2009). How to develop the concept of creation and development of regional techno-innovation Park? *Innovations*, 3.

Havin, S. A. (1993). Diversity of types of mixed economy abroad. *Questions of Economy, 1.*

Holland, C. (1993). Planning and mixed economy. *Economic Issues, 1.*

Jobs, S. (2012). *About the business: 250 statements of the person who changed the world*. Moscow: Publisher.

Keynes, J. M. (1993). General theory of employment, interest and money. *Anthology of Economic Classics, 2.*

Kolodko, G. V. (2011). *Globalization, transformation, crisis – What next?* Moscow: Master.

Kudrin, A., & Gurvich, E. (2014). New growth model for the Russian economy. *Journal of Economic Issues*, 12.

Kulkov, V. M. (1996). Mixed economy (theoretical and methodological aspects). *Bulletin of MGU*, *6*, 5.

Kulman, A. (1993). *Economic mechanisms*. Moscow: Progress.

Lee Kuan Yew. (2010). *Singapore story: 1965-2000: Trom the "third world" to the "first"*. Moscow: MGIMO-University.

Leontyev, V. (1990). To the market under state control. *Economics and Life, 16.*

Mao, T. (2003). *China and Russia. The development of economic reforms*. Moscow: Science.

Mises, L. (2000). *Human action: a treatise on economic theory*. Moscow: Economics.

Muller-Armack, A. (1965). *Soziale Markwirtshcarft*. Stuttgart, Germany: Handorterbuch der Sozialwissenshcaften.

Nasibov, I. (2012). Scientific and technical potential of China: results and prospects. *MEMO, 10.*

Nee, V. (1989). Theory of Market Transition. *American Journal of Sociology*, 100.

Nesterenko, A. (1998). Social market economy: conceptual foundations, historical experience, lessons for Russia. *Economic Issues, 8.*

Nikonov, I. (2014). *Project analysis and project financing*. Moscow: Alpina Publisher.

Oi, J. C. (1992). Fiscal Reform and the Economic Foundation of Local State Corporatism China. *World Politics*, 45.

Osipov, V., & Skryl, T. (2016). The strategic directions of the modern Russian economic development. *International Business Management,10.*

Osipov, V. S. (2011). *Managing the value chain*. Moscow: The Institute for Training State Employees.

Porokhovskiy, P. (2008). Political economy of the current crisis. *Theoretical Economics*, 10.

Russian Statistical Yearbook. (2015). Moscow: Federal State Statistics Service.

Samuelson, P., & Nordhaus, V. (1997). Economics. Moscow: Academic Press.

Silvestrov, S. N. (2009). State partnership: the Russian options welts. *Proceedings of the Free Economic Society of Russia*, 117.

Skryl, T. V. (2017). A paradigm shift in Russia's industrial policy: From a raw model to innovative technological growth points. *International Journal of Ecological Economics and Statistics*, *38*, 2.

Sokolov, I. (2012). *Public-private partnership as a tool to support innovation*. Moscow: Ranepa.

Stark, D. (1966). Recombinant property and the birth of the Eastern European capital. *Economic Issues, 6.*

Ustyuzhanina, E. (2016). The Eurasian Union and global value chains. *European Politics and Society, 17.*

Varnavskiy, V. (2013). *Mechanism of public-private partnerships*. Moscow: MGIMO University.

Walder, A. (1994). Corporate Organisation and Local Government Property Rights in China. In A. Milor (Ed.), *Changing Political Economies: Privatisation in Post-Communist and Reforming Communist States*. Boulder, CO: Lynne Rienner.

Xu, C. (2015). Political and Economic Institutions of China and Their Influences. *The Cato Journal*, *35*, 3.

Zeldner A. G. (2010). Combined socio-economic system: ownership issues. *Economic Science, 1.*

Zeldner, A. G. (2010). *Partnership of the state, business and society in a mixed economy*. Moscow: Economics.

Zeldner, A. G. (2013). *Destructive trends and constructive possibilities of overcoming them in the economic system of Russia*. Moscow: Economics.

Zeldner, A. G., & Khalturin, R. A. (2014). The role of development institutions in attracting private investment. Moscow: Institute of Economy, RAS.

KEY TERMS AND DEFINITIONS

APR: Asia Pacific region.

GDP: Gross domestic product.

OECD: The Organization for Economic Cooperation and Development.

PPP: Public-private partnership.

PRC: Public Republic of China.

SEZ: Special economic zones.

TPD: Territory of priority development.

VAT: Value added tax.

Chapter 13
Financial Systems Reforms in Western Balkans Countries

Sofija Adžić
University of Novi Sad, Serbia

ABSTRACT

Tax system and tax policy today are becoming the most important instruments of national economic policy. Globalization process is objective in nature and is also inherent in market economy, whereas the neoliberal model of globalization is constantly getting more popular in both developed and developing countries. While developing countries in this regard are concentrating mostly on a multitude of potential reforms and resolving their numerous economic and social problems which are getting only more complicated, the interest of developed countries concerns mostly newest innovative technological trends and their application in a specific economic context. That is, in order to provide better conditions for full convergence of socioeconomic systems with higher rates of economic growth reforms, tax systems and tax policies are needed to reduce the barriers to free and global movement of goods, services, capital, and manpower.

INTRODUCTION

In the today's world change is the precondition for successful development. Global economic recovery has been accelerating since the last year, mostly due to the growth of investments, acceleration of world trade volumes' growth, improved business conditions and rising consumer confidence. Disparity remains to be one of the main features of the global growth though, both among the regions within countries and also between different strata of population.

The first step taken in the Balkans towards "healing" the regional economy has been being implemented through equity and sectoral restructuring. Ownership restructuring was meant the change the vision on the concept of property as such and later lead to sectoral restructuring which assumes better capacity of economic units to maintain their competitive position and their ability to materialize the results of the innovative technical processes.

DOI: 10.4018/978-1-5225-7760-7.ch013

The goals of economic policies of each country in the Balkans can be formulated as follows: GDP growth, full employment, low inflation and positive balance of payment. Our analysis suggests that the process of privatization has become a common response to the financial problems of many firms and the countries in question overall. These actions taken by almost all Eastern European countries are often treated as a fairly drastic remedy, at least for their development cycle, where the already accumulated economic problems are supposed to be solved via rising the economic competitive superiority so that to satisfy future needs and also comply to technological and social changes. However, some of these local problems are more complex in nature and thus require a more sophisticated driver, oriented toward the future market development and even having no real criteria for assessment.

Countries' commitment to the consistent program of economic restructuring under increased efficiency and stronger business competitiveness requires the availability of an adequate financial and fiscal system and also well functioning market institutions under economically acceptable terms with an opportunity to relocate the factors production according to changing needs of certain sectors and activities. In the course of this objective realisation the role of States play manifests itself through the allocating function, redistributing function and also stabilizing function, all three resting on the foundations of neoliberalism.

Fiscal consolidation in the countries of the Western Balkans requires rising more stable balance of payments, which would exceed the inflow of direct investments. Internal demand should be also increased, which includes the recovery of private consumption due to growing employment rate and thus more earnings in the private sector. Growing foreign direct investments are in most cases directly related to the developments in the Euro zone. FDI growth has resulted in additional growth in competitiveness, thus, it is extremely important to continue with the implementation of structural reforms in the Balkans. Of particular interests for the local national economies would be promoting competitiveness in agriculture and services, and this can be the result of better innovative scientific and technological education that also contributes to the reform process.

Implementation of structural reforms in the Western Balkan countries is lagging behind the projected rate of their economic growth. However, newer inflows of foreign investments have all complementary capacities so that to contribute to domestic economies in any case. For the purposes of more balanced regional development it is necessary to reconsider the local interests in each of the countries in question.

DEVELOPMENT PERFORMANCE OF THE WESTERN BALKANS' ECONOMIES

In the course of economic reforms and establishing newer development policies in the Balkans, these countries must bear in mind their many developmental comparative advantages in terms of attracting foreign capital, while not allowing their economy to be placed in a strongly dependent, subordinate position in relation to close developed economies. The most recent economic crisis has emphasized the need to outline/reformulate newer competitive economic advantages, some of them posing quite a serious challenge for the institutions within the European Union. Belief in the long-term benefits of free movement of goods and services, people and money is countered by the short-term challenges of protectionism without any obvious positive effect. The sense of solidarity within Europe, between the East and the West, the rich and the poor, the old and the new Europe must be constantly re-examined and adequately aligned with the growing socioeconomic needs and challenges.

Economic reality of the majority of developed countries includes the challenges related to population aging, low productivity growth and limited potential growth, and therefore economic policies of these countries must be oriented towards structural reforms that are able to strengthen their internal resistance to shocks, and increase the aggregate demand at the same time. In the United States, where growth is approaching the growth of potential GDP, implementation of newer economic policy is needed so that to promptly raise the public debt limit in order to avoid internal political turmoil over budgetary policy. At the same time, in the Eurozone, countries with low public debt in GDP and small deficits should utilize the created fiscal space in their support of structural reforms and boosting investment in order to accelerate potential growth. Also, a more proactive approach to solving the problems in the banking sector of the Eurozone is needed. Banking regulations should be directed at solving the issues with problem loans, as well as at more efficient regulation over bank operations.

In our opinion, future reforms should cover the following three major areas.

The first one is economy, of course. Over the past years we have witnessed the wave of financial innovations. However, economic policy makers have failed to keep up their own pace in parallel to these innovations, thus, they also failed to prevent or fight most of the strengthening systemic risks. This failure, in its turn, endangers development processes overall, however, today, when already moving towards the real sector of economy, it threatens jobs and even people's survival. That is why it is necessary for regulatory measures to change and respond to the crisis, in Europe, the Western Balkans and the whole world. It is necessary to restructure European economy and alleviate national differences, which implies adequate management of regional development, inter alia. We need more world-class universities and more investment in the research and development sector if we want to be competitive in quality and innovation, and not in prices. Companies should accept the risk of hiring new workers under today's flexible labor market.

The second priority is campaigning for economic development with more pronounced reforms in the national fiscal systems. In the recent couple years rises of commodity prices caused central banks to react and curb inflation, while the credit crunch began to demand lower interest rates. In order to overcome recession and prepare national economies for a sustainable recovery, reforms are needed, and those covering not only key economic trends but also investment processes, first of all.

Thirdly, more work must be done to achieve productive cooperation between the processing plants of both developed and developing countries. This can be done through various forms of business and trade cooperation.

The most recent of global crises has clearly shown that any global crisis requires a global response and a more or less common approach to social and economic reforms should have real economic effects at both national and local levels. Therefore, also required is a direct connection between national and local actions which would help bridging the gap between globally interdependent economies on one side and strong national political identities on the other, with their constant attempts of reforms along with their attempts to adjust to European flexibility, elasticity and global outeach. Measures of moderate fiscal relaxation would work on two tracks in this regard. By easing the economy, through increase of the non-taxable part of wages, economic growth overall and job creation are encouraged, while the growth of pensions and salaries in the public sector increases the purchasing power of households and stimulates the internal demand.

A stable inflow of foreign direct investments, in its turn, motivates innovation activities and thus becomes another supporting source for sustainable growth, while reforms within the education system, support provided to social entrepreneurship, gender equality policy and raising the minimum labor pay are just some of the measures that the Western Balkans countries need to pay more attention at the moment. Inclusive and fairly distributed growth with the ultimate effect on poverty rate reduction must be well

Table 1. International environment: Macroeconomic indicators

	2016	2017	2018	2019
Real Growth of Gross Domestic Product %				
World total	3.2	3.6	3.7	3.7
Developed economies	1.7	2.2	2.0	1.8
Eurozone	1.8	2.1	1.9	1.7
USA	1.5	2.2	2.3	1.9
Russia	-0.2	1.8	1.6	1.5
Emerging economies	4.3	4.6	4.9	5.0
World trade growth, %	2.4	4.2	4.0	3.9
Unemployment Rate, %				
Eurozone	10.0	9.2	8.7	8.3
USA	4.9	4.4	4.1	4.2
Consumer Prices, Period Average, %				
Eurozone	0.2	1.5	1.4	1.7
Developed economies	0.8	1.7	1.7	2.1
Emerging economies	4.3	4.2	4.4	4.1
Exchange rate, EUR/USD, end of period	1.1	1.1	1.2	/
Prices of cereals, in USD, annual change	-11.8	2.7	8.6	5.6
Metal prices, in USD, annual change	-5.4	20.6	1.4	-1.0
Price of iron ore, in USD	58.6	71.7	62.0	57.1
Oil prices, in USD, annual change, %	-15.7	17.4	-0.2	0.7

(Eurostat, 2016, 2017)

coordinated with the potential paths for effective reforms. Newer macroeconomic policies must focus on building a new institutional framework and removing barriers to growth. Successfully implemented activities in the previous period are reflected in already higher efficiency of state administrations, improved legislation, increased flexibility demonstrated by the local labor markets, improved countries' external positioning, increasing foreign direct investment inflows, and finally, providing more concrete support to the growth of the SME sector in all the countries in question.

The key assumptions for achieving the envisaged medium-term scenario remain the preservation of fiscal stability, continuation of the economies' restructuring (and that of the public sector specifically), further improvement of business environment, expansion and modernization of production capacities, primarily in the sector of tradable goods, as well as maintaining continuity in approaching the European Union in all aspects and spheres.

According to the estimates of the European Commission, recovery of economic activities in the Eurozone continues at the rates much higher than planned. The expected growth in 2017 was 2.2%, while in 2018 and 2019 it is expected to be 2.1% and 1.9%, respectively. Although the growth of economic activity has strengthened and expanded to all the member states, there is still inequality in the economic cycles of individual countries, and this factor jeopardizes the synchronization of monetary and fiscal policies of the ECB. Growth of employment and significant acceleration of investment activity were triggered by strong growth in domestic demand, which was the main driver of economic activity in 2016 as well. In the forthcoming period, growth of production volumes in the manufacturing sector, new orders and positive expectations of businessmen overall serve as a strong impetus to the growth of many economies, as it is evident from Figure 1.

The three-year development scenario was created in accordance with the strategic orientation towards establishing a sustainable enough economic growth trajectory, assisted by structural adjustments and system improvements, based on export and investment activities. The goals are quite ambitiousbut also realistic, since they take into account internal specificities as well as dynamic changes in the international environment and provide a sound basis for the fastest convergence towards developed countries by improving the key GDP components. The share of gross investments in basic funds in GDP will be around 2 pp at the end of 2020, this is much higher than the same indicator back in 2014. The share of government spending in the same period will fall to around 16%, which is significantly below the European average (which is around 20%). The share of exports of goods and services in GDP in 2017 is forecasted to reach 52.5% and it is expected that at the end of the three-year period this share will exceed 57%. Removing the barriers will provide a wide dispersion of foreign direct investments, which will stimulate other boosting measures in the sector of tradable goods, as well as service activities in which high level of GVA per employee is created. External debt sustainability, external liquidity and solvency will be provided by simultaneously reducing the share of deficits in goods and services and the current account deficit in GDP to 6% and 3.9%, respectively, by the end of 2020.

Recovery of economic activity in the coming period is supposed tounfold underthe conditions of low inflation, although the production gap will be still visible. After the Eurozone reached the growth rate of 2.2% in 2017, which is the highest rate in the last decade, economic growth will continue in 2018

Figure 1. Cyclical movement of economic activity
(The Ministry of Finance, Republic of Serbia)

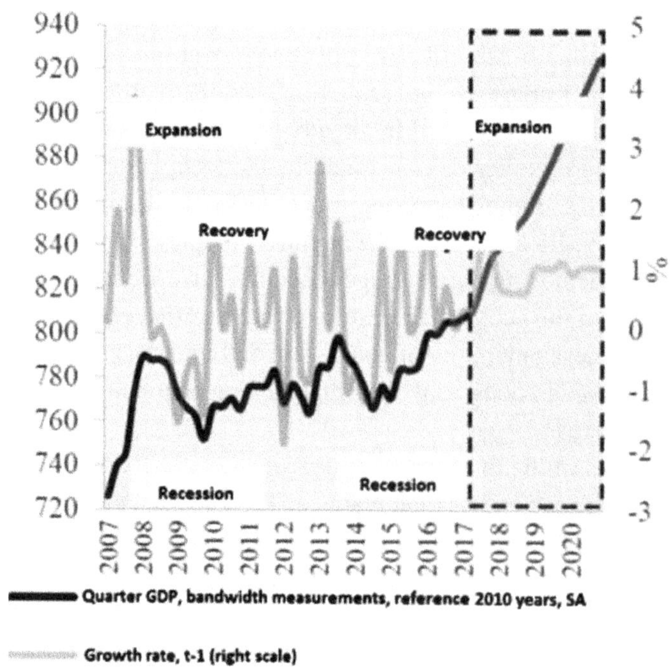

Figure 2. Contribution of production factors to potential growth rate
(The Ministry of Finance, Republic of Serbia)

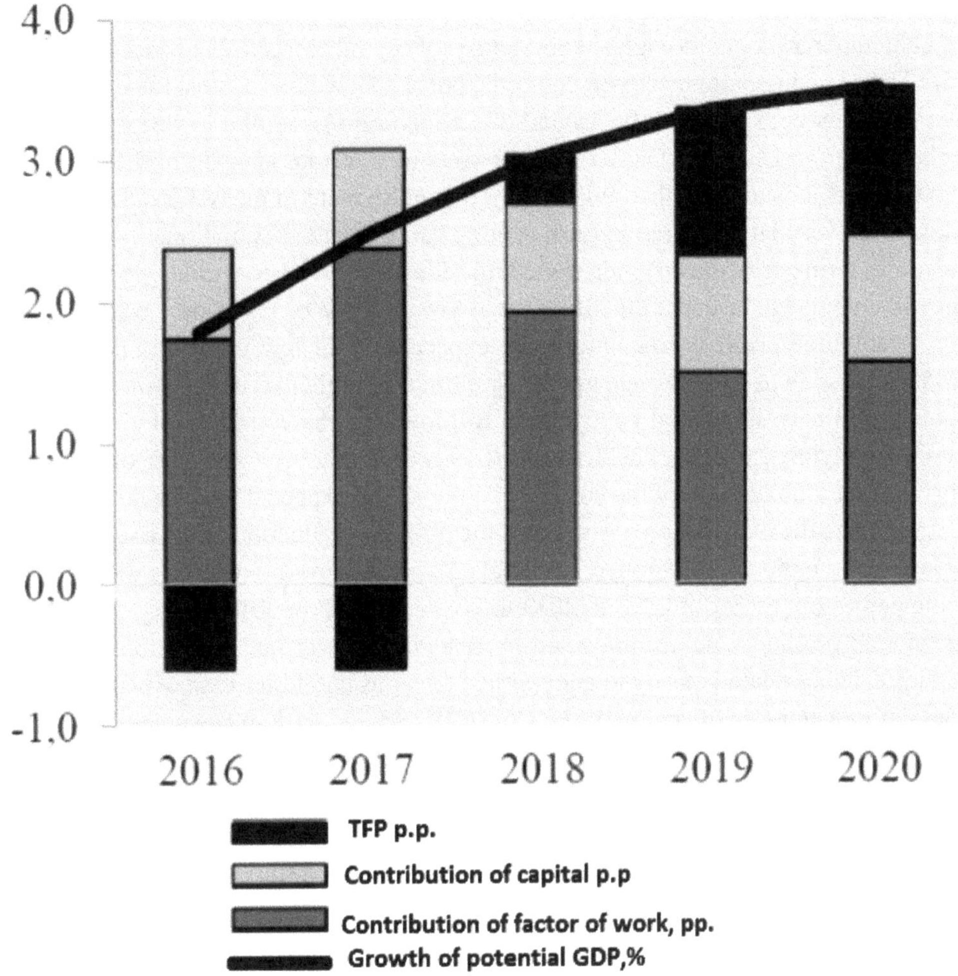

and 2019, albeit at somewhat slower pace. The projected growth is based on a slowdown in private consumption and investments, moderate acceleration of government spending and a slightly positive contribution to net exports. Thanks to adequate fiscal and monetary policies, labor market reforms and low inflation, private consumption has been the main driver of growth in the past period. In the upcoming mid-term period, normalization of the monetary and fiscal policy of the ECB is expected to be through an increase in the reference interest rate, which will stimulate savings and with the slowdown in wage growth and disposable income in 2018 and 2019 will also contribute to the slowdown in private consumption growth from 1.8% in 2017 to 1.5% in 2019. By reducing the share of public debt in GDP and interest at the international capital market, conditions have been created for a stronger impact of fiscal policy on economic growth. The growth of profit margins, increased demand and reduction in the pressure of thinning, along with the accelerated investment activity of the EC (European Investment Plan) are the main factors that will influence the growth of investment spending in the coming period (that is, in the period since 2017 to 2019). The average investment growth of 3.7% is expected, driven by the acceleration of investment in equipment due to the newer phase of the business cycle. Export growth will be supported by the growth of global demand and gradual recovery of the global economy overall.

As a result of this economic recovery, strong employment growth is expected in the coming periodon the basis of contemporary methodological experiences of liberal flows in the process of globalization. The downward trend in unemployment will continue, but at a slower pace, so at the end of the projected period, unemployment is expected to be around 8%, which represents the lowest rate since 2008, but still higher than the pre-crisis level. These tendencies require a serious analysis of the causes that lead to such movements. It is most certain that reduction of unemployment in many Western Balkan countries is a reflection of the very large migration of the young and educated population.

In the next mid-term perio, the inflation trend will follow the prices for primary products and energy sources, but will continue to be under the influence of low inflation of 1.4% and 1.6% in 2018 and 2019, respectively. Despite the positive production gap, expectations of low inflation and lower prices for primary products, as well as slower wage growth, are limiting higher inflation growth.

Fiscal policy will have its neutral contribution to growth in the coming period, although in some members it will be slightly expansive. In 2018 and 2019, a deficit of 0.9% and 0.8% of GDP is projected, respectively, with the stabilization of the structural deficit. The expected recovery of the economy and lower interest rates are the main factors influencing the projected reduction of the fiscal deficit in almost all member states of the Eurozone. Stronger nominal growth and low interest rates will keep public debt on a declining path, from 89.3% of GDP in 2017 to 85.2% of GDP in 2019.

Macroeconomic prospects are accompanied by risks that can endanger economic growth and are external in nature, being related mostly to geopolitical tensions and faster than expected increase in the restrictiveness of monetary and fiscal policies. Consequently, increase in financial risks and risk aversion on the side of investors may endanger growth in the countries which still represent the external environment in relation to the EU. In the medium term, there are also risks related to rebalancing Chinese economy, that is, the growth of corporate loans in China, which indicates a possible increase in financial risks in this country overall. And this, in its turn, will preserve the protectionist trade policy in the US which – in its turn – will have its negative impact on global recovery.

Stabilization of public finances, accompanied with legal reforms and structural reforms, substantially mitigates internal and external imbalances, making Western Balkan economy overall more resistant to endogenous and exogenous shocks. Incidentally, short-term slowing down of GDP growth cannot jeopardize its growing path in the next three-year period. Governments can lead their responsible and predictable fiscal policies in order to preserve fiscal achievements. Measures of moderate fiscal relaxation will work on two tracks. By easing the economy, through the increase of the non-taxable part of wages, growth and job creation are encouraged, while the growth of pensions and salaries in the public sector will increase the purchasing power of households and will indirectly stimulate future demand. A stable inflow of FDIs supporting innovative and other scientific &technological activities is another valuable contribution to sustainable growth, while reformd within the education system, support to social entrepreneurship, gender equality budgeting and raising the minimum labor pay are just some of the measures that should ensure inclusive and fairly distributed growth with the ultimate effect to reduce poverty.

In the current year, 2018, the real growth of economic activity has been projected to be at the level of 3.5%. Taking into account the prudence of agricultural production and construction activities, that is, moderate investment and export expectations, this projection can be considered as rather conservative.

Growth carriers of the year will be sectors of industry and services, and it is expected that these two sectors will create two thirds of the overall growth. A steady increase in manufacturing volumes, accompanied by the recovery of the electro-energy sector, will provide the overall industry growth of around 5.5%. The growth of the service sector is projected to be at the level of 2.2%. Returning agricultural production to an average perennial level will provide an agricultural growth rate of around 9%, while projects for civil engineering will accelerate their activities by 4.9%. Viewed from the expenditure side of GDP, the most important source of growth will be private consumption, which is expected to be the dominant component of the expenditure side of GDP and which will be stimulated by the measures of both monetary and fiscal relaxation. Projected growth of private consumption is about 2.7%, which will contribute to its total growth of 2 pp., it is lower than the real GDP growth and thus it will not generate any increase in internal and external imbalances. In the longer term, the role of investment as the dominant source of growth is more important. In 2018, acceleration of investment activity and their real growth of 5.1% is expected, thus contributing to the overall growth of economy. Economic growth, on the one hand, and good fiscal outcome with a sustained reduction in the deficit, on the other hand, with more favorable borrowing conditions at the international financial market, will guarantee the countries of the Western Balkans experience thecontinuation of reduction in the shares of both external and public debts in GDP in the forthcoming period.

FRAMEWORK FOR MID-TERM FISCAL POLICY OBJECTIVES

The goals of fiscal policy reforms in the Western Balkan countries in the next mid-term period include achievement of relatively low fiscal deficits of about 0.5% of GDP, further accelerating of the downward path in public debt. The main objective of fiscal consolidation, stopping further debt growth and its gradual reduction, is achieved within the framework of the precautionary arrangement implementation with a view to ensure high fiscal stability and significant debt reduction to around 50% of GDP in 2020.

Effectiveness of the implementation of fiscal consolidation measures has been confirmed by the international rating agency, which has improved the credit rating, and also by reducing costs of borrowing for the countries at the international financial market. Lowering interest rates and leveraging confidence in the lender will provide cheaper sources of financing, thus further improving the fiscal position of the country. In addition to the direct effect reflected in easier access to finance with lower costs, the indirect impact arises from the multiplicative effect of investing in infrastructure, not only for the state but also for the private sector, and their contribution to sustainable economic growth.

In the next mid-term period, fiscal policy objectives are focused on maintaining fiscal stability, which leads to further reduction of public debt. Projections of fiscal aggregates in the period from 2018 to 2020 are based on the projections of macroeconomic indicators for the stated period, the planned tax policy, which implies further harmonization with the EU laws and directives and fiscal and structural measures, including reforms of large public enterprises.

Thanks to the fiscal consolidation measures, extra fiscal space for new policies has been created, which in 2018 will be used to increase capital investment, pensions and salaries in one part of the public sector, and reduce the tax burden on wages. These measures and their fiscal implications have been designed in such a way that they do not jeopardize the stability of public finances and the pace of public debt reduction, and on the other hand, they raise the standards of living for population, stimulate private consumption and accelerate economic development in the countries of the Western Balkans.

Figure 3. Fiscal sub-index and the sub-index of macro financial competitiveness of the EU countries for 2016 and Serbia – for 2014, 2015 and 2016.

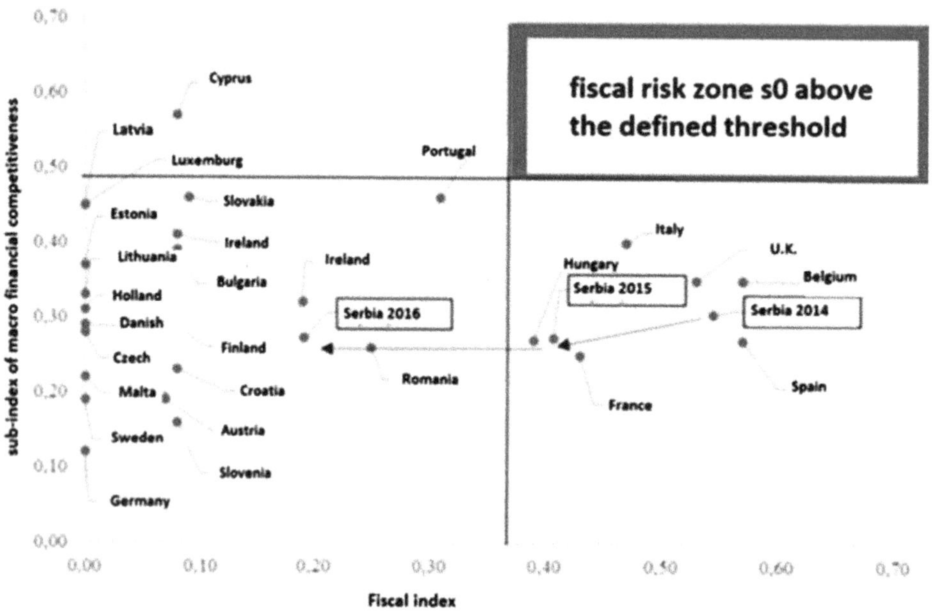

Table 2. Fiscal powers during the period of 2016-2020, % Of GDP

Description	Actual Indicator	Actual Indicator	Projection		
	2016	2017	2018	2019	2020
Publicrevenues	43.2	43.9	42.4	41.8	41.2
Publictotal expenditures	44.5	43.2	43.1	42.3	41.7
Consolidatedfiscalresult	-1.3	0.7	-0.7	-0.5	-0.5
Primaryconsolidatedresult	1.8	3.4	1.9	1.8	1.6
General debt	73.0	63.7	62.8	59.8	56.3
Realisticrate of GDP growth	2.8%	2.0%	3.5%	3.5%	4.0%

(The Ministry of finance Of the Republic of Serbia, 2017)

It should be noted that the Republic of Serbia is one of the most powerful countries in the Western Balkans in terms of economic reforms' implementation. And its significant successes in the reform process are quite evident. It is interesting to analyze the data related to:

- Projections of the movement of the most important macroeconomic indicators: GDP and its components, inflation, foreign exchange rate, foreign trade, employment and wages;
- Valid and planned changes in tax policy;
- Estimated effects from fiscal and structural measures in the coming period.

Stable revenues from profit tax are projected for the period from 2018 to 2020 (2% of GDP). Budget inflows from the corporate income tax in the forthcoming three-year period will depend on the path of economic growth, the relative stability of the exchange rate and overall profitability of the national economy. Estimating income on this basis may be uncertain due to a range economic factors, and also because of the possibilities of using tax credits and/or refunds. In 2017, a record income tax collection (2.5% of GDP) was achieved, this was mainly as a result of high profitability during 2016. One part of this year's income, however, is the result from application of new accounting regulations. Mid-term projections do not anticipate any major changes in the related legislation further on.

Movement in value added tax is characterized by a slight drop in its share in GDP, as slower growth in private consumption is projected against the nominal GDP growth. The main determinant of VAT movement is the domestic demand driven by the available income among population. Available income as the biggest determinant of spending depends on the dynamics of public sector wages, pensions, social assistance, changes in the private sector wages and other forms of income, including remittances, as well as the volumes of banks' lending to households. In the coming period, revenues from the consumption by foreign tourists will have a greater significance. Also, relaxation of fiscal policy in relation to the public sector salaries and pensions will contribute to the growth of the disposable income amog population. Nevertheless, due to the rebalancing of the economy, the share of VAT revenues in the total GDP is projected to fall from 10.7% of GDP in 2017 to 10.4% in 2020. At the same time, the projected export growth will also affect the growth of VAT refunds, therefore, the level of VAT collected. Risks in relation to VAT volumes in the coming period are similar to those of income tax and are directly connected to the movement of wages in the private sector, the growth of economic activity overall, and the share of gray sector within the national economy(or the efficiency of its reduction).

Table 3. Total revenues and contributions during the period of 2016-2020, % of GDP

Description	Actual Indicator	Actual Indicator	Projection		
	2016	2017	2018	2019	2020
PUBLIC REVENUES	43.2	43.9	42.4	41.8	41.2
Current revenues	43.0	43.7	42.1	41.5	40.9
VAT registration revenues	37.2	38.4	37.3	37.1	36.6
Taxes on citizens' income	3.6	3.7	3.6	3.6	3.5
Taxesonprofit of legal entities	1.9	2.5	2.0	2.0	2.0
VAT tax	10.6	10.7	10.6	10.5	10.4
Excise tax	6.2	6.3	6.0	5.8	5.6
Customs	0.9	0.9	0.9	0.9	0.9
Other than VAT registration revenues	1.6	1.6	1.6	1.5	1.4
Contributions	12.4	12.7	12.7	12.7	12.7
Non-tax revenues	5.8	5.3	4.7	4.5	4.3
Donations	0.2	0.2	0.3	0.3	0.3

(The Ministry of finance Of the Republic of Serbia, 2017)

The results of more efficient taxes collection and control over taxpayers are evident and it is expected that this trend will continue in the coming period, with the effects on the decreasing volumes of the gray economy not explicitly included in the mid-term projection of public revenues. Increasing level of VAT collection in the context of the anti-evasion measures' implementation already gave some results in the past period. In this segment there is still space for further improvements, of course, including the measures aimed at strengthening and modernization of tax administration.

According to the estimates, improvement in billing efficiency by about 5 pp. in the next four-year period would lead to a cumulative increase in VAT revenues up to 1.9% of GDP.

Projection of the excise revenues is based on the applicable excise policy and projected consumption of excise products. Within the excise policy concerning tobacco products further gradual harmonization with the EU directives is expected in accordance with the mid-term plan on the gradual increase in excise duties. With cigarettes, this means a gradual increase in excise duties, in order to reach the EU minimum of 1.8 EUR per pax in a reasonable time. In the forthcoming period, in parallel to the excise revenues' projection, a natural decline in the tobacco products market is predicted, on average, by about 3% per year. If there is an improvement in the conditions at the tobacco product market and reduction of the gray economy's volumes at the same time, there is a certain "positive risk" in terms of collecting this type of revenues.

Unlike with tobacco products, situation at the market of petroleum products is considerably less volatile. Better control over petroleum production have reduced the opportunities and cost-effectiveness of illegal (shadow) activities in this sector. In the coming years, due to cautiousness, no further increase in consumption of petroleum products is forecasted, although it can be expected that acceleration of economic activity will contribute to the growth of these products' consumption. In this case there is a certain "positive risk" in terms of the related revenues' collection if the trend of growth at the market for petroleum products continues.

Income from the excise taxes on alcoholic beverages, coffee and electricity are forecasted in accordance with the existing consumption patterns. The current nominal amounts of excise taxes on alcoholic beverages and coffee are adjusted to the expected rates of inflation in the mid term. In 2015, an advalore excise tax of 7.5% was imposed on electricity consumption in the period from 2018 to 2020. The annual revenue from this excise tax is expected to reach around 17 bln dinars, taking into account the current annual consumption and the current prices.

Customs revenues currently account for 0.9% of GDP and can be expected to remain at this level in the future. With the projected volumes of imports, exchange rate and consumption dynamics and also taking into account the process of customs tarifss' harmonization in the course of implementing the Stabilization and Association Agreement with the EU, a gradual nominal increase of the related revenues is planned, but no change in their share in GDP is expected.

In the case of other tax revenues, their reaction to economic activity are not significantly appreciated, their level is relatively stable and a slight decline in the share of these revenues in GDP is expected during the period in question. The most important tax revenue source in this category is the property tax, its share being about 70%. Increase in this revenue category can be expected due to the expansion of its base. Under the project of the Property Tax Reform, a list of immovable property in 40 local self-government units is being prepared, and this measure can increase the volumes of property tax collectio in some municipalities by several times. An increase in the collection volumes due to wider coverage (that is, due to the expansion of this tax base) is not included in projections for the mim term and thus

Table 4. Total expenditures in the period 2016-2020, % of GDP

Description	Realization	Estimate	Projection		
	2016	2017	2018	2019	2020
Public Expenditures	44.5	43.2	43.1	42.3	41.6
Current expenditures	40.3	39.2	38.9	38.2	37.7
Expenditures for employees	9.8	9.8	9.8	9.7	9.6
Purchase of goods and services	6.7	6.8	7.0	7.0	7.0
Interest payment	3.1	2.7	2.5	2.3	2.1
Subsidies	2.6	2.4	2.4	2.3	2.2
Social assistance and transfers	16.8	16.2	15.7	15.5	15.3
to pensions	11.6	11.2	11.1	11.0	11.0
Other current expenditures	1.3	1.3	1.4	1.4	1.4
Capital expenditures	3.3	3.0	3.6	3.7	3.7
Net lending	0.1	0.3	0.1	0.1	0.1
Activated guarantees	0.9	0.6	0.4	0.3	0.1

(The Ministry of Finance of the Republic of Serbia)

represents a positive risk. In addition to property tax, other tax revenues also include taxes on the use, holding and carrying of goods, and other minor taxes which belong to the local level.

These are projected in line with the inflation trend, as the inflation component is embedded as a significant part of these tax forms. The process of approaching the EU membership increases the potential availability of the IPA funds that are the predominant part of the income from donations. Funding based on the sectoral budget support from the EU is also included in the projected donations. Donation revenues are neutral in relation to the result, given that they are equal to expenditures on this basis.

A restrictive fiscal policy in combination with good macroeconomic performance has led to the creation of a fiscal space that will, among other things, be used for new policies on the expenditure side, primarily those related to increasing capital investments as an essential component of the overall development of the economy. Rather unfavorable structure of expenditures in the previous period was characterized by high expenditures on various subsidies and repayments based on the guarantees and resulting from inefficient operations of the public sector. Additionally, high interest rates made capital investments rather insufficient. In the forthcoming period special attention will be given to rising the efficiency from the capital investments' implementation. Also, social component of the budget will be improved through better targeting of social assistance programs and greater allocations for the healthcare and education sectors. By 2020, salaries and pensions will be stabilized in terms of GDP participation, which will be another factor that potentiall would enable a more equitable reallocation of income, reducing the pressure on public finances at the same time.

Thanks to the fiscal space created by fiscal consolidation, within the framework of the arrangement with the IMF, the central government will increase the volume of total spending up to 290 million EUR. This will have many positive effects on the fiscal sphere.

Reducing interest spending is one of the best indicators of success when it comes to fiscal consolidation. Extremely high level of public debt and high fiscal deficits have led to interest rates becoming one of the largest categories in the public expenditures overall. Good results in the previous period reduced the need for borrowing, which led to a change in the trend of interest rates. In 2017, the nominal interest rate was reduced for the first time after reaching the peak in 2016. In 2020, the level of interest expenses will fall to almost 2% of GDP. Improving the position of the Republic of Serbia at the international financial market will lead to further reduction of interest rates.

Social assistance and transfers to households represent the largest expenditure category of the central government budget. Reducing the amount of pensions and reforming the pension system have made its significant contribution to reducing the share of expenditures on pensions in GDP. Over the last three years, spending on certain types of social assistance has increased, given the implementation of fiscal consolidation measures, such as funds for severance payments. The share of social welfare expenditures is going downd from 17.8% of GDP back in 2014 to 15.3% of GDP in 2020, according to the forecasts.

Reducing subsidies that serve as an aid to inefficient segments of the public sector would make it possible to increase that share of subsidies that represent real incentives for the economy, primarily its agricultural sector, and which would lead to acceleration of economic activity overall. In the next three-year period reduction of subsidies is expected as a consequence from restructuring and rationalization of the number of employees. The aim is to divert the subsidized funds onto development programs in general and in agriculture in particular.

Other current expenditure categories comprise different expenditures, such as grants to non-governmental organizations, political parties, religious and sports organizations, fines, damages, etc. In the past, the share of this category was between 1% and 1.3% of GDP, and by 2020 these expenditures are expected to reach the level of 1.4% of GDP.

In the forthcoming mid-term period, all efforts will be directed towards achieving a desirable level of investment in the public infrastructure. The level of capital investment participation in GDP, which in the previous period was around 3%, is considered insufficient and it is desirable to increase it to at least 4%. By reducing the current consumption of the state sectora fiscal space has been created which should be used partly to boost the investment process. When it comes to capital expenditures, we are observing both inefficient and insufficient use of funds coming from the international loans.

The decline in capital investments is partly the result of a methodological change, or a change in the number and structure of institutional units within the central government. The Directorate for Building Land and Construction of Belgrade changed its status and became a public company, leaving the institutional scope of the central authorities. With the launch of a new phase of the infrastructuralprojects in 2018, acceleration of capital expenditures is expected, up to the level of 3.6% of GDP.

The level of budget borrowings and repayment of debts under guarantees is a good indicator of success when it comes to assessing the fiscal consolidation measures. The joint share of these two categories in GDP back in 2014 was 2.2%, and in 2018 it is expected to reduce to 0.5% of GDP. By the end of 2020, these expenditures will be minimal, no more than 0.2% of GDP.

Reducing budget support to public and state enterprises means: a) limiting direct and indirect subsidies; b) strictly limiting the issuance of guarantees for new loans, and; c) strengthening accountability and transparency in the operations of these enterprises which therefore are supposed to undergo significant changes.

A cyclically adjusted fiscal balance is a fiscal balance from which the isolated impact of the business cycle is excluded. In a mathematical form this relation can be ppresented as follows:

$$FB = CB + CAB.$$

Table 5 below provides the statistical data on the nature of this relationship.

The positive effect of the business cycle is visible, where there is a positive production gap. This would lead to better a fiscal result than it would have been when the economy has overall lower potential for further growth.

Certain internal and external factors have mitigated the effects from fiscal consolidation. The most important factors among them include: 1) significant improvement in tax collection efficiency; 2) collection of one-off non-tax revenues that largely neutralized the allocations on the basis of one-time expenditures; 3) relaxation of the NBS monetary policy; 4) favorable international environment (situation with oil prices, economic growth of key foreign trade partners, ECB policy), and; 5) relatively low value of fiscal multipliers.

In the period of 2018-2020 the fiscal impulse is expected to be positive as consolidation in the previous period has already created a significant fiscal space. A certain minimum degree of restrictiveness comes from further improvement in the efficiency of billing at central and local levels. The approximation of the achieved growth rates to the potential level in conjunction with the achieved fiscal results significantly reduces the need for a restrictive fiscal policy in the future. Despite relatively low values of the fiscal multiplier, a certain effect of a positive fiscal impulse on economic developments will surely exist in the next mid-term period. With the careful design of the revenue and expenditure policy in the coming period it is possible to increase this effect. The created fiscal space can also be used for simplification and harmonization of the tax system, which additionally improves the business environment and creates space for accelerating the potential growth.

Table 5. Fiscal balance and components for calculating the cyclically adjusted balance in the period of 2005-2020, % of GDP

	Manufacturing Gap	Fiscal Balance	Primary Fiscal Balance	Cyclical Component of the Fiscal Balance Sheet	Cycle Count of the Custom Fiscal Balance	Cycle Count of the Custom Primary Fiscal Balance	Structural Primary Fiscal Balance**	Criterion of the Fiscal Policy– Fiscal Impulse
2007	1.5	-1.9	-1.3	0.6	-2.5	-1.9	-1.5	1.8
2008	3.9	-2.9	-2.1	1.5	-4.1	-3.5	-3.6	1.6
2009	-0.9	-4.4	-3.8	-0.3	-4.1	-3.4	-3.5	-0.1
2010	-1.0	-4.6	-3.6	-0.4	-4.2	-3.2	-3.3	-0.2
2011	1.3	-4.8	-3.6	0.0	-4.8	-3.6	-3.8	0.4
2012	-1.1	-6.8	-5.0	-0.4	-6.5	-4.6	-4.6	1.0
2013	-1.4	-5.5	-3.1	0.5	-6.0	-3.6	-3.4	-1.0
2014	-0.4	-6.6	-3.7	-0.4	-6.2	-3.3	-2.3	-0.4
2015	-0.8	-3.7	-0.5	-0.5	-3.2	0.0	0.7	-3.3
2016	-0.4	-1.3	1.8	-0.1	-1.1	1.9	2.0	-1.9
2017	-0.8	0.7	3.4	-0.3	1.0	3.8	3.7	-1.8
2018	-0.4	-0.7	1.9	-0.2	-0.5	2.0	2.0	1.7
2019	-0.3	-0.5	1.8	-0.1	-0.4	1.9	1.9	0.1
2020	0.2	-0.5	1.6	0.1	-0.6	1.5	1.5	0.4

(The Ministry of Finance, Republic of Serbia)

Figure 4. Production gap and the cyclically adjusted structural fiscal balance in the period of 2005-2020, % of GDP
(The Ministry of Finance, Republic of Serbia)

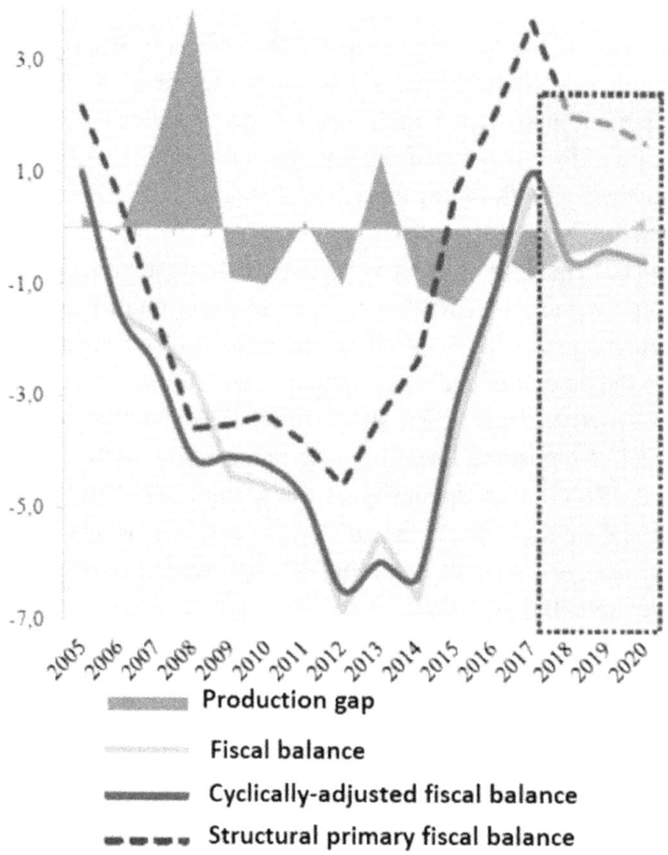

The public debt management strategy is based on the principles that define the need for a transparent and predictable borrowing process, with the permanent development of the government securities market and an acceptable level of exposure to financial risks.

Bearing in mind the projected primary surplus of budget in the Republic of Serbia for the period 2017-2020, including the volume of loan financing for project financing, the effects of change in the dinar exchange rate against EUR and USD under the basic macroeconomic scenario, the state debt of the central government should be at the level of 55.2% of GDP by the end of 2020.

It is projected that the non-guaranteed local government debt will be at the level of around 0.9% of GDP in 2017 to 1.1% of GDP in 2020 in the next period.

The public debt of the general government, according to the Maastricht criteria, should be at the level of 53.4% of GDP at the end of 2020.

Financial and fiscal risks can lead to the growth of public debt more than is predicted according to the current scenario. Risks that are present and which can lead to the growth of indebtedness and costs of public debt servicing are: risk of refinancing, foreign exchange risk, market risk (interest rate risk,

Figure 5. The nature and the effects of fiscal policy in the period of 2006-2020, % of GDP*
(The Ministry of Finance, Republic of Serbia)

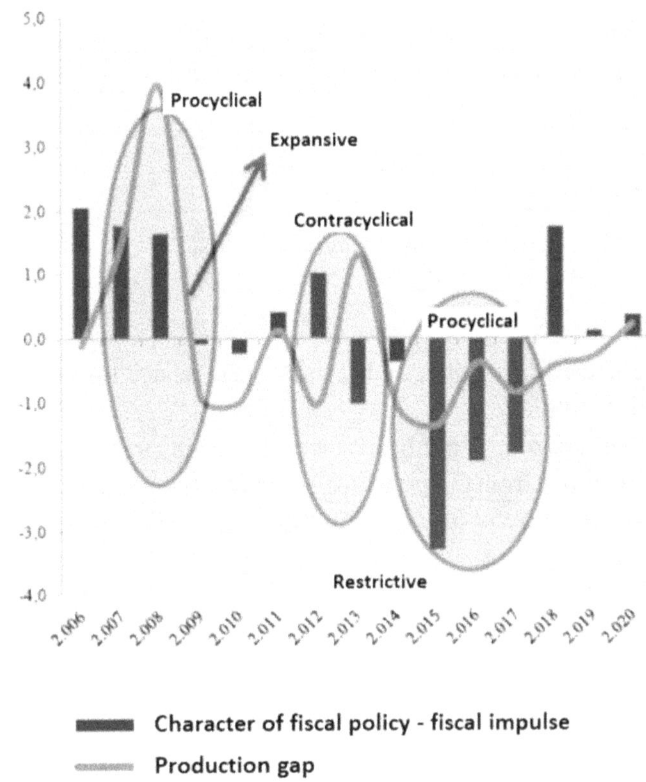

Figure 6. The nature and the effects from fiscal policy in the period from 2006 to 2017
(The Ministry of Finance, Republic of Serbia)

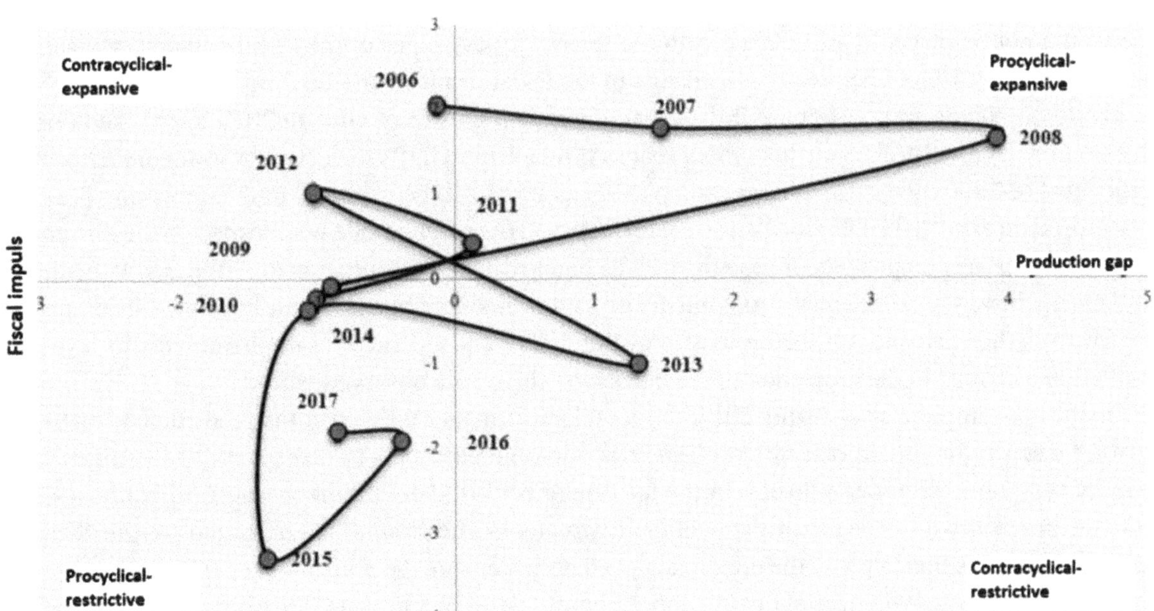

Table 6. Basic projection of general government public debt balance by 2020

	2017p	2018p	2019p	2020p
Primary surplus (central government level), in RSD billion	142.1	84.2	88.5	89.6
Interests (central government level), in RSD billion	119.0	117.8	111.9	111.3
Public debt (central government level), in RSD billion	2,807.5	2,938.7	2,979.7	2,995.1
Central government debt, as % of GDP	62.8	61.8	58.8	55.2
Non-guaranteed local government debt, as % of GDP	0.9	1.0	1.0	1.1
General government debt, as % of GDP	63.7	62.8	59.8	56.3

(The Ministry of finance RS)

inflation risk), liquidity risk, credit risk, operational risks, costs related to distribution of servicing (debt structure, concentration of liabilities).

Fiscal risks represent the exposure of public finances to certain circumstances that may cause short-term and medium-term deviations from the projected fiscal framework. This sort of deviation can occur in revenues, expenditures, fiscal results, as well as in the assets and liabilities of the state, in relation to what is planned and expected.

Identifying the highest fiscal risks that can affect government finances in the medium term is the starting point for better fiscal risk management. There are detailed data on certain fiscal risks and it can easily be determined whether and how much probability will affect fiscal aggregates in the mid-term. For others, there are not enough detailed data, but only their identification raises the awareness of the possibility that in the coming period they will lead to deviations from the planned fiscal framework.

Deviation of macroeconomic assumptions from the baseline scenario can lead to the deviation of fiscal aggregates from the projected level.

A negative scenario for the coming period implies a decline in economic activity or lower growth would lead to a significant reduction in capital inflows and reduction in foreign trade. In this case, there would be lower incomes, and consequently a larger deficit, if additional adjustments on the expenditure side would not be made. In accordance with the sensitivity estimates of the fiscal balance, any change in real growth by 1% of GDP leads to a change in the fiscal result of around 0.36% of GDP.

The Economic Reform Program (2017-2019) envisaged growth of GDP in 2017 by 3%, and further acceleration of growth to 3.5% in the coming years. Although real GDP growth will be lower than expected, at the level of 2% roughly, growth rates of up to 4% in 2020 will be expected in the upcoming period.

Lower than expected GDP growth was not reflected on the revenue side with respect to the movement of future generous components of growth, such as employment, consumption and imports. In addition, the fight against gray economy has continued, and improvement of business results of public companies has led to higher revenues on the basis of profit and dividends. Structural improvements in revenues resulted in a change in the projection of revenues over the whole observed period.

On the consumption side, during 2017, the actual performance was lower than the planned one, thus creating a space for certain one-off costs, such as one-time payments to pensioners and bonuses for a share of the public sector employees. In the upcoming period, there might be, most probably, a slight increase in costs with changes in the economic structure. The results demonstrated by the Western Balkan economies indicate that the effects achieved do not ensure the realization of the planned growth rates of 3.5%. The growth rates should be more impressive so that to meet the growing demands of the consumer societies in the framework of their new socioeconomic requirements.

CONCLUSION

Transformation of the national economies in the Western Balkans means a wide range of significant changes and requires the inevitable redefinition of the fiscal system and fiscal policy as a result of changes in the socioeconomic system overall. For the less developed countries of the Western Balkans, the conditions are restrictive in terms of defining criteria and conditions for interventions within each national state. When it comes to the fiscal system, the tax capacity of the economy is of crucial importance. It is clear that domestic income per capita is the starting point for calculating fiscal capacity. In a market-based country, the foreign-exchange relationship visible from the balance of payments is a prerequisite for assessing the performance of the economy and therefore – its fiscal capacity. Thus, it is important to plan the balance of payments for the upcoming period. It is most certain that a more stable balance of payments will reduce the foreign trade deficit, and this will, in its turn, increase the competitiveness of the economy. Balance of payments also serves as the basis for natural comparative advantages, and when it comes to the latter, the major goal is to balance the exports growth through increased competitiveness. Of course, competitiveness in a market-based country has its most decisive influence on successful economic development. The desired level of national competitiveness will determine, in addition to technological restructuring measures, the volume of the tax load in a country. The expected changes will have their positive effects within the framework of economic reform programs, which include significant reforms of the fiscal system in the context of the public finance management process.

The most important effect, in any case, concerns higher tax revenues and better tax discipline within the fiscal system. The main goal will be to bring the macrofiscal and macromonetary situations in line with each other, so that to stop the deficit and debt growth and thus reach certain stabilization of the financial sector, stop/ prevent the decliningdevelopment of banks' internal financial situation, offernew sources of financing for future growth and development under the state-level reforms. Today, Serbia is one of the few countries in the world that has managed to reverse the negative trend of falling GDP, being at the same time under the conditions of fiscal expansive consolidation. The obvious lack of social consensus is confirmed by poor investment rating and also by a very much evident need for engagement of the IMF in the near future.

It can be concluded that the fiscal system will be constantly changing in line with the fiscal policy requirements through economic policy measures. Changing dimensions and instruments must always take into account the continuously developing relationships between the systems and their subsystems. The best way of transforming the fiscal system is through a deliberate rather than an "ad hoc" policy, establishing a step-by-step, well-designed intervention of adequate measures and instruments.

REFERENCES

Adžić, S. (2008). *Economic System and Economic Policy*. Subotica.

Adžić, S. (2011). *Regional Economics of the EU*. Subotica.

Arsić, M., & Ranđelović, S. (2017). *Economics of Taxation - Theory and Politics*. Faculty of Economics in Belgrade.

Begović, B., & Mijatović, B. (2017). *Financial intermediation and economic growth*. Belgrade: CLDS.

EUROSTAT. (2017). Retrieved September, 2017 from: http://ec.europa.eu/eurostat

IMF. (2006), Fiscal Adjustment for Stability and Growth. James Daniel. Pamphlet Series, #55.

OECD. (2014). *OECD Revenue Statistics 2014*. Paris: OECD Publishing.

OECD. (2016). *Fiscal Federalism 2016: Making Decentralization Work*. Paris: OECD Publishing.

Popvić, D. (2014). *Tax Law*. Belgrade: University of Belgrade.

Raičević, B. (2008). *Public Finance*. Belgrade: University of Belgrade.

Ranđelović, S. (2013). The assessment of tax-benefit automatic stabilizers in Serbia: A combined micro-macro approach. *Economic Annals*, *58*(198), 61–88. doi:10.2298/EKA1398061R

Santini, G. (2017). *Winners and losers*. Rifin.

SGS. (2016). *Belgrade*. Retrieved, November, 2017, from http://webrzs.stat.gov.rs/WebSite/Public/PageView.aspx?pKey=82

Stiglitz, J. (2004). *The Globalization and Its Discontents*. Zagreb: Algorithm.

Stiglitz, J. (2009). *The Success of Globalization, New Steps to a Just World*. Zagreb: Algorithm.

Stojanov, D. (2013). *Economic crisis and crisis of economic science*. Faculty of Economics in Rjeka.

Supek, I. (2006). *Globalization or the Associated Covenant*. Zagreb: HAZU.

Urošević, B. (2009). *Quantitative methods in corporate finance*. Faculty of Economics, University of Belgrade.

Zweifel, P., & Eisen, R. (2012). *Insurance Economics*. Berlin: Spinger Verlag. doi:10.1007/978-3-642-20548-4

KEY TERMS AND DEFINITIONS

Developmental Performance: Within the political system, decisions made are often crucial for further development of the economy, practically all economic and systemic solutions with the control over their implementation. Numerous analyses have shown that of all non-economic factors affecting the developmental performance of any economic system, the most important ones are those originally coming from the political system.

Economic Development: Is a complex economic flow by which one country gradually liberates it from own economic underdevelopment and poverty, thus reaching higher developmental levels. This development consists of economic growth and changes in the composition of the economy.

Fiscal System: Is all forms of public revenues imposed by the state (i.e., by its public-law collectives). Fiscal policy, being part of general economic policy, is a set of fiscal instruments, public expenditure instruments and revenues used to achieve the goals of economic policy.

Innovation: Is a new idea, or a more effective device or process. Innovation can be viewed as the application of better solutions that meet new requirements, unarticulated needs, or in some cases, the already existing market needs. This is accomplished through more effective products, processes, services, technologies, or business models that are readily available to markets, governments and the society overall.

Tax System: Is a set of tax regulations, institutes and norms, bound in a unique mechanism for the purposes of achieving a certain tax policy. The tax system includes a large number of tax forms that differ in each system. This system is a set of institutes and instruments available to tax authorities for achieving certain fiscal, economic, social and political goals within the economic system.

Chapter 14
The Impact of Budget and Fiscal Policy on Entrepreneurial Activity and Country's Competitiveness:
The Case of Ukraine

Yuriy Holynskyy
Ivan Franko National University of Lviv, Ukraine

Irina Onyusheva
Stamford International University, Thailand

ABSTRACT

Ukraine's economy, as compared to other European countries, is lagging behind. An unstable political situation, significant tax pressure, various administrative barriers, complexity of tax administration and with obtaining permits, technical regulation, certification and standardization, frequent sudden inspections by state control bodies, limited opportunities for the use of financial and credit resources, weakness of material, technical, financial, managerial, and personnel components of business entities – all these factors do not promote the entrepreneurial initiative in this country. The key precondition for raising the prosperity level and effective social and economic development is strengthening the competitiveness of the national economy through the coordinated work of the state and its budget and fiscal institutions. This study reveals the theory and the methodology of the formation and implementation of fiscal policy in Ukraine. Peculiarities in the development of the entrepreneurial environment in Ukraine are analyzed, and fiscal mechanisms are defined with the purpose of activating further entrepreneurship development.

INTRODUCTION

The key precondition for rising the levels of prosperity and overall socioeconomic development is strengthening of the competitiveness of the national economy through the coordinated work of the state and its fiscal institutions. Taxes are one of the most important elements of fiscal policy, without which

DOI: 10.4018/978-1-5225-7760-7.ch014

the state cannot effectively perform its functions. Taxes also affect the development of entrepreneurial activity, the redistribution of gross domestic product, changes in the structure of demand and consumption, quality of life for general population in the country. Moreover, they determine the conditions for the national economy's interaction with the outside world.

Dynamic spread of economic globalization during the last decade, namely liberalization of international trade and capital movements, the growing role of information in the development of society and the spread of deregulation, all have led to the development of international trade, increase of the production factors' mobility and to frees flows of capital between the states.

Contemporary processes of globalization are both the driving force and the result of the processes of cultural, political and, above all, economic integration. Economic integration is characterized by some essential features that in aggregate distinguish it from other forms of economic interaction between countries: interpenetration and interweaving of national production processes; wide development of international specialization and cooperation in production, science and technology on the basis of the most progressive forms of cooperation; deeper structural changes in the economies of the participating countries; the need for purposeful regulation of the integration process, development of well coordinated economic strategy and policy; regional character of spatial integration due to the fact all necessary prerequisites for this type of integration predominantly exist between the countries that already have close economic ties due to the factor of geographical proximity.

The result of these processes is the emergence of competition not only at the market of goods and services, but also within the tax environment. Inflexible and uncooperative behaviour of the states while establishing taxes, determining their composition, structure and mechanism of collection on their territory leads to the emergence of differences between the countries in terms of tax burden. Liberalizing tax laws, governments are trying to attract foreign investments, but at the same time, they prevent the outflow of the taxpayers abroad. The key result from these constant changes in countries' taxation policies is the emergence of international tax competition.

The main purpose of this study is to describe the theoretical basis and the methodology of the formation and implementation of budget and fiscal policies in Ukraine, so that to formulate the possible ways of improving the efficiency of the related regulation which, in turn, will lead to the increase of entrepreneurial activity and thus, higher country's competitiveness of Ukraine. To achieve this purpose, the following objectives should be complete: to analyse the results of budget and fiscal policies of Ukraine and its position in the selected international ratings; to reveal the instruments of budget and fiscal policies in Ukraine; to uncover the current and potential threats to local budgets' execution and fiscal decentralisation in Ukraine; to offer the ways of improving budgetary and fiscal policies in Ukraine and provide other related recommendations on the basis of the obtained data.

LITERATURE REVIEW

There is no consensus among researchers concerning the definition of "tax competition". R. Teaser (2005), T. Field (2003), C. Pinto (2003) and D. Rohas (2006) all considered international tax competition in the broad sense and treated it as inconsistent tax-setting by an independent state, the use of low effective tax rates, and the reduction of tax burden in order to increase the competitiveness of national business, boost business activity in the country and attract foreign investments.

In a narrower sense, tax competition is considered as the impact of the tax system of one state on the tax system of the other, based on the ability of taxpayers to choose between jurisdictions with different levels of taxation and transfer part of the gross national product to another territory, with a certain impact of tax policy on the distribution of income from taxation between state budgets. This opinion has been supported by T. Goodspider (2015), P. Genschel (2001), J. Wilson (2015), D. Wildasin (2004) and some Ukrainian researchers (Krysovatyi, 2000; Bazylevych, 2004; Sidelnikova, 2010).

For example, they consider tax competition as an interstate and/or interregional struggle for economic benefits and growth of the tax base by creating more attractive tax terms and conditions for individuals and legal entities of foreign origin and/or remittances of taxpayers from other areas of their state, in particular, enterprises and multinational corporations.

The supporters of the second group are, for example, K. Edwards (1996), C. Stewart and M. Webb (2006), P. Bruchez and C. Schaltegger (2005). They define international tax competition as tax competition between sovereign states only. International tax competition covers significant territories, including countries whose borders do not significantly impede the international movement of mobile factors of production.

The essence of the concept "international tax competition" is in the rivalry of countries with the use of taxation tools for highly mobile but limited in terms of availability economic resources. Its emergence has been caused by the existence of objective differences between the mechanisms of tax regulation within national economic systems that are in line with the structural features of their reproductive systems, and also the strengthening interdependence of national tax systems under the conditions of economic globalization.

However, both groups of the researchers as mentioned above argue that tax competition stimulates the government's fiscal effort to improve national competitive advantage.

Due to escalating interdependence of the countries in the economic, political and cultural fields, development of the world information system, spread of the Internet coverage and all related technologies, tax competition today would be more appropriate to consider in the narrower sense. Systematization of the already available study results leads us to the possibility of defining international tax competition as a competition between the states on the criterion of tax policy effectiveness and favourable business climate in order to attract foreign investments, mobile capital and labour under the conditions of integration and economic globalization.

Tax competition has a mixed impact on the socioeconomic development of the state. On the one hand, it stimulates the reform of national tax systems, growth of production, and creation of favourable conditions for attracting foreign investments and labour resources. On the other hand, rigid tax competition absorbs underdeveloped economies, as it encourages jurisdictions to over-reduce the tax burden, provide privileges and make exceptions in order to attract the attention of enterprises and investors. And all of this provokes lack of funds in state budgets necessary for performing their core functions.

Also there are other researches on fiscal and budget policies' influence on country's competitiveness. Thus, (Dar & Amirkhalkhali, 2017) have been trying to observe the economic growth in most developed countries since the recent financial crisis. They summarised that changes in the composition of expenditures in infrastructure investment projects will contribute to long-term growth and this can increase the overall productivity. The main purpose of this article is to highlight the impact of fiscal policies on productivity change and its effects on economic growth. Economic growth is impacted adversely by the size of total government outlays relative to GDP while the growth of government consumption has an unambiguously positive impact on the total factor productivity and economic growth.

Rangan Gupta et al. (2017) have revealed there is a link between fiscal policy and asset prices in a conflict situation (what is very actual for Ukraine too). Also, this article analyses the impact of the conflict situation and various actions of the American government on the fiscal policy of the state. This article describes the correlation between returning assets, government surpluses as a percentage of GDP, and the degree of partisan conflict based on the developed Azimont index (2015). The authors emphasized there is no link between fiscal surpluses and profits, namely in party's conflicts. The conflict situation only affects the ability of the government to implement policies that lead to financial crisis. Various changes in income lead to changes in fiscal surpluses, and as a result, this affects the changes in interest rates in the budget, which are related to prices.

J. Soukup (2017) describes the relationship between the innovative capabilities of European countries and the levels of their competitiveness. The analysis of statistics has shown there is a strong relationship between these two concepts, which depends on economic development of the countries. One can conclude that it is country's competitiveness that influences the introduction of innovations in various areas of entrepreneurial activity. It creates conditions for economic development, based on know-how and technological changes. Another part of the article points to the link between innovations and economic growth, which is measured by the growth rate of GDP. This connectivity is very weak as innovation indicators are not the tools to measure the overall performance on economic growth.

Competitiveness has been a popular study object for the research at all levels and researchers have already noted its direct correlation with the GNP level as the key factor affecting the level of the country's competitiveness, its welfare, and competitiveness of national human capital (Onyusheva, 2017).

Another important paper for Ukrainian case describes the impact of economic security on national competitiveness (Simanavičienė & Stankevičius, 2017). Each country must independently defend its national interests and create a favourable environment for innovations, investments and intellectual development. These authors conclude that an economy that is constantly evolving is capable of resisting independently both internal and external threats. Analysis of the current economic situation can reveal trends in economic interests and identify the measures necessary for enhancing competitiveness. The authors defined the most important indicators for increasing competitiveness (the structure of GDP, the growth of investments, natural resources' availability, inflation etc.).

S. González (2017) in her article describes the struggle of avoiding the payment of taxes and tax competition within the country. This author evaluates the use of state aid in the fight against tax competition. It is recommended to use state aid in cases of tax distortion and double taxation. One of the requirements of state aid of the European Union is provision of the selective tax privileges. The mentioned above author believes that state aid is useful, but in a limited way, because it focuses on national tax systems and selective preferences. Tax privileges due to tax disparities between different tax jurisdictions should be excluded from the scope of application of state aid assessment. Also, there are examples of double taxation from the point of view of state aid. This is possible only when each country applies its tax legislation that is consistent with international standards.

METHODOLOGY OF THE STUDY

In this study the following research methods were applied: document analysis method – applied to obtain information, quantitative and qualitative analysis of strategic documents, ratings, programs, current Ukrainian legislation, publications of other researchers, and publications of international organisations.

Statistical data analysis method – applied to demonstrate the importance of budget and fiscal policies in shaping the country's competitiveness and to analyse data from international ratings and official data on budgets' execution in Ukraine. The logical analytical method is used further to analyse the information collected on the basis of the formation of the intermediate and final conclusions.

RESULTS AND FINDINGS

Results of Budget and Fiscal Policies of Ukraine as Reflected in International Ratings

Various international organizations together with research institutions use the indicators of fiscal policies while constructing the international ratings to determine the competitive advantages of countries. Using these international ratings economic entities can assess the socioeconomic environment interesting for them, the effectiveness of various tax systems, the possible consequences from the tax policies' implementation, and the conditions for doing business in a particular country.

The main indicators for the assessment of the tax system competitiveness in the structure of the considered indices are: the total number of taxes and fees in a country, tax rates on income (profit) of individuals and legal entities, the overall level of tax burden, efficiency of tax authorities' work, and the stability of tax legislation.

One of the most popular rating is Doing Business calculated within the framework of the Doing Business project by the World Bank and the International Finance Corporation (IFC). The index of doing business allows businesses assess how favourable is certain business climate, prospects for business development in a particular country, effectiveness of the fiscal function of the state and the ease of administrative procedures. This index consists of 10 indices. The latter, in turn, are based on the analysis of specific examples of labour and timing costs from the enterprises' perspective. These indicators serve to estimate the number of procedures, time and money expenditures associated with the implementation of transactions in accordance with all applicable regulations.

In this rating, Ukraine is ranked 76th among 190 countries. During 2014-2017, Ukraine has gone up in the ranking by 20 positions. The most significant improvements have taken place in the field of taxation (+65 positions in 4 years) and also in the field of electricity networks (+57 positions) (World Bank, 2018).

Implementation of the Ukraine-2020 Sustainable Development Strategy has been supposed to provide that Ukraine will belong to the top-30 positions of the World Bank's Doing Business rating. However, at the moment, Ukraine has not the best indicators in terms of business climate, though in the recent years there have been some serious improvements concerning the role of the state in Ukraine's economic development.

The highest subrankings Ukraine got on the following positions: credit indicators (29th place), construction permits (35th place) and taxation (43rd place). The most problematic groups of indicators for Ukraine that restrain the development of entrepreneurial activity in the country are: resolving insolvency (149th place), connection to the electricity supply system (128th place), international trade (119th place), investors' protection (81st place) and registration of enterprises (52nd place).

The rather modest ranking on the "Taxation" index has been caused by the complexity of taxation administration and high tax rates overall. Comparison of Ukraine's achievements with the indices of the selected European and Central Asian countries and also the states that are the OECD members shows that Ukraine has good results in terms of "amount of tax payments" and is almost on the same level with the majority of them when it comes to the index of "procedures after reporting" (time spent on calculation of VAT refund, time required to obtain this refund, time required to correct errors, adjust the reporting, conduct and complete the tax audit procedures).

These seemingly positive figures should be approached critically, however. Thus, a decrease in the number of tax payments is largely "artificial", taking into account changes that were made recently in the composition of property and resource taxes. For example, fee for vehicle registration, land tax, and the tax on real estate different from land are now all transformed into property tax, which consists of:

- A tax on immovable property, different from land,
- Transport tax, and;
- Land tax.

Thus, reform of the Ukrainian tax system often does not involve reduction in the number of taxes, but is merely combining them in terms of naming only.

One of the most interesting report in this regard is "Paying Taxes 2017: The Global Picture", which is part of the Doing Business Report by the World Bank in collaboration with PricewaterhouseCoopers. Its aim is to assess the quality of tax systems for businesses. Their annual report examines the tax regimes in 190 countries. In the ranking as of 2014, Ukraine was ranked 164th, in 2016 ranking it was already 107th, in 2017 ranking - 84th, in 2018 – even the 43rd place in terms of simplicity of the tax system.

Due to significant and purposeful improvements in the tax system, adoption and massive amendments of the Tax Code, modernization of business conditions overall, the tax environment has improved significantly indeed. Ukraine has moved up by dozens of positions in four years only, however, the current level should not be treated as the final achievement.

This year's rating includes one more indicator - assessment of processes after tax payments, including tax audits, receiving budgetary claims, administrative appeals. Taking these elements into account too allows more accurate and correct assessment of the tax system's functioning. The tax burden on profits in Ukraine is 8.7%, practically the same rate as in Russia (8.8%) and the French Riviera (8.8%). The tax rate on labour is 43.1%, almost same as in Italy (43.4%). The burden of other tax payments is 0.1%, just as in Uganda, Slovenia, Palau, Hong Kong and Fiji.

It should be noted that there is a trend towards technological optimization of tax administration due to the increasing numbers of taxpayers reporting electronically. The indicators of tax burden are also used in calculation of the Economic Freedom Index, which assesses the level of liberalization of the interaction between the state and business, taking into account four main components of the freedom of economic activity (Tyrrell & Riley, 2017). The logic behind this Index is based on the idea of Adam Smith that the welfare of a country depends on the degree of freedom of its market and the freedom of economic activity on it. The Index of Economic Freedom provides an objective assessment of the government's activity and the legislative framework of the state, shows the limitations in economic development and the problem areas of socioeconomic growth. The research is conducted by The Wall Street Journal in collaboration with The Heritage Foundation. According to the latest data on the index of economic freedom, Ukraine is ranked 74th (Tyrrell & Riley, 2017).

The level of the economies' freedom is calculated using the arithmetic mean of 12 indicators (previously there were 10 indicators). After analysing the dynamics of the economic freedom indices for

2015-2016, one can conclude that at the critical level in the case of Ukraine have the following indices: judicial efficiency (22.6 points), freedom of investment (25 points), conscientiousness of power (29.2 points) and freedom of the financial sector (30 points). Ukraine scored high results in terms of freedom of trade (85.9 points) and tax burden (78.6 points). This can be explained by the relatively low rate of personal income tax (18%) and corporate income tax (18%), inflation rate declines, and a relatively low average weighted customs duty (2.1%).

A strong commitment to structural reforms to reduce corruption and open the economy further to Western investment and financial institutions will be crucial in helping to stabilize the economy. The government has launched a comprehensive set of reforms to restore growth, but progress is not yet evident...

– this was the conclusion of the experts from the research centre of the Index of Economic Freedom (Ukraine: Economic Freedom Score, 2017).

Consequently, international competitiveness ratings are peculiar indicators of the country's investment climate, informing foreign investors about the most promising areas for business placement and investments. Ukraine has moved up in recent years in most international rankings. In order to improve the reputation in the eyes of the worldwide business community there is a need for further improvements in fiscal policy, more improvements of the social and political situation, and, most importantly, economic stability.

Our analysis shows that Ukraine has improved its position in international ratings on the parameter of tax burden. However, still quite low general positions in most ratings indicate that harmonization and coordination between the key components of fiscal policy are still inadequate. Thus, the whole fiscal system can be characterized as volatile and ineffective. It should be noted that the adoption of the Tax Code has had its positive effect and somewhat improved the economic situation of the state, but further reforms the tax system are clearly needed. On the way to European integration, it is necessary to work on other problem areas and realize the stimulating potential of fiscal policy. Analysis of the world rankings and Ukraine's position in it may help formulate a mechanism needed for the transformation of fiscal policy, and the latter, in its turn, will stimulate future economic growth and improve the business environment.

However, while "borrowing" the mechanisms and schemes that are already being used in developed countries, it is important to be guided not only by the idea of improving the rank of Ukraine in the world ranking, but also to assess the potential effectiveness and compatibility of these borrowed innovations in the existing socioeconomic environment of Ukraine.

Instruments of Budget and Fiscal Policies of Ukraine

State regulation of the economy is carried out with certain fiscal leverage instruments in the process of fiscal policy implementation. Effectiveness of the state regulatory policy which is aimed at economic development, depends on the correct choice of leverage or the combination of levers in complex. In contemporary economic literature, fiscal policy is associated with government regulation of state spending and taxation. For example, well-known American economists K. McConnell and S. Brue argue that fiscal policy is a change in government spending and taxation, aimed at achieving full employment and non-inflationary internal production (Rios, McConnell, & Brue, 2013). R. Dornbusch and S. Fischer suggest the following definition: fiscal policy is a government policy that deals with the volumes of government procurement, transfer payments and taxes (Dornbusch & Fischer, 1986). Some other researchers under fiscal policy understand the process of changes in the taxation system, government expenditures in order to: first, reduce the fluctuation of business cycles; and secondly, contribute to rapid growth of high-employment economy and without high and uncontrolled inflation.

Some Ukrainian researchers (Krysovatyi, 2000) consider fiscal policy as the regulation of state expenditures and tax revenues to ensure full employment, price stability and economic growth, as well as state influence on the economic situation by changing the taxation system of government expenditures. They argue that fiscal policy is the government's influence on the economy through taxation, formation of the volume and the structure of public expenditures in order to ensure adequate level of employment, prevent and limit inflation and the adverse effects of cyclical fluctuations. Other Ukrainian researchers (Bazylevych, 2004; Sidelnikova, 2010) believe that the budget and tax (fiscal) policy cover government measures aimed at ensuring full employment and production of non-inflationary GDP through changes in government expenditures, tax systems and approaches to formation of the state budget as a whole.

Fiscal policy can be also defined as a set of measures by which the state influences the economy through the structure of tax revenues to the state budget, directions of public expenditure and the methods of attracting borrowed funds.

In general, economic theory deals with two main forms of the fiscal policy functioning: automatic and discretionary, and the tools of these forms are: cost policy, income policy, tax system, transfer policy. Among the instruments of fiscal policy, researchers have identified primarily tax revenues, state expenditures and transfer payments.

The choice of fiscal adjustment instruments is primarily determined by the chosen model of market development. Thus, one of the key features of taxation in the United States, for example, is its relatively moderate level, but the level of spending by the state on the social sphere is also moderate. The European model is characterized by larger guarantees from the state, accompanied however by higher level of taxation. The highest level of GDP centralization is typical for Scandinavian countries, which are characterized by the largest public sector and the highest social guarantees.

It should be noted that the choice of vector in fiscal regulation, the use of its instruments is determined by the peculiarities of the institutional environment, as well as fiscal traditions that have been evolving for decades. Consequently, implementation of the fiscal control mechanism involves the use of two main groups of levers – budgetary and tax, which are implemented through the use of appropriate instruments. In scientific literature, different approaches to interpretation and classification of fiscal instruments are considered. In particular, fiscal instruments can be categorized as: restraining (budget deficit, excessive tax burden, minimal level of local taxation etc.), equalizing (various subsidies and subventions), stimulating (tax privileges, reduction of tax rates etc.). Also, there are budget levers, which include budget expenditures (budget loans, budget investments, subsidies, subventions, subsidies, expenditure structure) and budget deficit (size of deficit, method financing of the deficit), as well as tax levers: tax rates (tax burden, investment tax credit, investment tax discount, reduction of tax rates, decrease in the value of the taxation object), tax privileges (tax holidays, tax exemptions for certain transactions, exemption from taxation of individual taxpayers), alternative tax regimes (simplified tax system, special free economic zones), changes in tax payment deadlines (deferred payment, instalment payment), tax sanctions (fines, penalties, cancellation of preferential tax treatment).

Fiscal instruments are divided into: systemic (level of taxation, structure of the tax system, application of alternative taxation systems), complex (special tax regimes for certain groups of taxpayers, special tax regimes for certain sectors of the economy), local (tax objects, taxpayers, tax rates, tax calculations, tax credits).

Instruments of fiscal policy include fiscal norms and periods for fulfilling obligations to the state. Such standards are rates, tariffs, taxis, inflation rates etc. The mentioned periods include the terms of submission of declarations, terms of payment, payment of debts etc. Incentives include benefits, instalment payments, and tax credits. Levers of influence on payers are fines and penalties. The instruments of fiscal policy include the degree or the nature of its levers, in particular, the rigidity of the use of such instruments, high rates of taxation, high levels of fines or the liberalization of this policy, in particular, reduction of the level of fines imposed on business entities.

It can be noted that over the past years the role of indirect taxation in Ukraine has intensified. Thus, during the investigated period, tax revenues to the Consolidated Budget of Ukraine increased by 2.6 times, while the volume of indirect taxes alone - by 2.9 times. Thus, the share of indirect taxes in the overall structure of tax revenues increased from 49.6% in 2010 to 55.0% in 2016.

Among the indirect taxes, the largest share belongs to the value added tax - 65.9%. This tax forms one third of the overall budget revenues and tax payments. The share of excise tax in indirect taxes is 28.4%, in budget revenues - 13.0%, in tax revenues - 15.6%.

The transfer of a larger share of taxation on consumption is a popular pan-European trend, it is used to increase the share of profits at the disposal of taxpayers.

Among the direct taxes, the tax on personal income is dominant; its share in Ukraine is 47.3%. During the investigated period, the receipts of this tax into the Consolidated Budget of Ukraine increased by 2.7 times. The corporate income tax covers 20.5% of all direct taxes, 7.7% in budget revenues, and 9.2% in tax revenues. In recent years, the fiscal role of corporate profit tax has decreased though.

Domestic personal income tax and corporate income tax rates are among the lowest in Europe – 18%. For example, less than in Ukraine the corporate income tax is in Ireland (12.5%), however, the offset there is represented by higher PIT rates (up to 48%) and VAT (23%). Similarly, lower corporate income tax in Slovenia (17%) is accompanied by the offset of higher PIT rates (up to 50%) and VAT (22%). In Romania, the rate of corporate tax and personal income tax is 16%, while the VAT rate is 24%.

The lowest tax rates in the EU (10%) - in Bulgaria - over the past few years did not provide significant economic growth but only sharply increased the budget deficit and, as a result, led to increasing public debt. Among the 28 EU Member States, 17 countries have the VAT rates above the Ukrainian level, equal level (20%) have 7 countries, and only 4 countries in Europe have VAT rates lower than in Ukraine (Luxembourg, Malta, Germany and Cyprus). Thus, with the exception of small island countries and the Baltic countries, Ukraine has the most attractive tax rates, which should become an important prerequisite for attracting foreign investments and creating new jobs.

The state, using the tools of fiscal policy and the methods of its implementation, should regulate the reproductive process on the production, technical and technological basis of enterprises, promoting at the same time the creation of the market most favourable and adaptive conditions for all market participants to get involved in innovation and investment activities. Provision of state privileges must be oriented on the priority of financially advantageous for the state spheres and sectors.

In addition, fiscal policy in Ukraine is aimed at the maximal withdrawal of funds from taxpayers, which actually deprives business entities of profit - the main motive of their activities. As a result, this narrows the possibility for accumulation of funds that could be later invested in the development of the production base, therefore, it also may lead either to bankruptcy of enterprises, or to their decision to move to the shadow sector of the economy.

Excessive tax burden leads to more and more shadowing of business activities. While reducing tax burden contributes to economic growth of the state through increased real incomes, additional household savings, effective demand etc.

Shadow economy has its negative impact on all socioeconomic processes taking place in society, causing serious mistakes while determining the main macroeconomic indicators, leading to inadequate assessment of the most important processes and trends, tactical and strategic failures in ensuring the competitiveness of the economy. According to many experts, the level of shadow economy in Ukraine is very high. This negatively affects the volume of revenues to the budgets of all levels, the ability of the state to implement large-scale investment and social projects, social protection of employees and disadvantaged social groups, as well as the effective use of natural and financial resources of the country.

In order to reduce the level of shadowing in Ukraine, it is necessary to redirect the tax policy on the implementation of the following priorities: ensuring equal taxation conditions for all economic entities, reducing tax burden, ensuring effective tax administration and stability of public finances overall.

The objective of the fiscal policy is to establish such an optimal level and taxation conditions that ensure efficient business activity of economic entities and the reasonable balance between the interests of the state and the taxpayers.

According to the Annual Business Climate Assessment (ABCA) conducted in 2015-2016, the index of business climate in Ukraine is at the level slightly above 0 on the scale from -1 to +1 (Freik, Bespalko, Fedets, & Kuziakiv, 2017). The survey of entrepreneurs allowed create the list of the main obstacles to business development. The first place in the rating is occupied by the group of factors, which includes the consequences of the military aggression of the Russian Federation and the general instability of the political situation in the country (59% of all respondents mentioned them). The second place is occupied by the problems related to tax legislation, in particular: complexity of tax administration, frequent changes in legislation, frequent changes in tax and other forms of reporting (54% of the respondents' answers).

Instability and frequent changes in tax legislation create tensions in fiscal authorities' relations with taxpayers, reduce economic activity of business entities, thus slowing down economic growth in the country in general.

Typical tax administration problems can be identified as follows: insufficient transparency of the system of electronic administration for VAT and delays with returning budget compensations prior to its implementation, unilateral cancellation (by the fiscal service) agreements on the recognition of electronic documents; violation of the moratorium on tax audits of taxpayers with an income volume of up to UAH 20 million for the previous calendar year; appointment of tax audits in the absence of sufficient grounds, procedural violations during audits or making unreasonable decisions on their results; ineffectiveness of the administrative appeal procedure - limited time to appeal for taxpayers, formal approaches on the side of tax authorities, limited personal liability of tax officials.

Tax and customs services are currently on the top of the anti-rating of public authorities in terms of corruption, although in other parts of Europe they usually have much high degrees of trust, professional image and authority. Under all these conditions, shadow economy and corruption are more economically advantageous for Ukrainian entrepreneurs, since both of them help avoid punishment for tax evasion.

Thus, under the negative influence of systemic deformations on the economy, for most enterprises and entrepreneurs, the only way to ensure business continuity becomes concealing part of income from taxation, thus violating the principles of business social responsibility and legal obligations to the state and the society.

One of the most acute problems with Ukrainian fiscal policy is financing of budgets and cost optimization, especially during the economic crisis. Improving fiscal policy should increase the competitiveness of Ukraine's economy, activate the innovation and investment component of its development, and positively influence the structural processes in the real sector economy, thus providing more dynamic economic growth overall as well as increasing level in life quality.

Formation of an innovative model of the economy is impossible without the use of complex state incentives, primarily fiscal ones. This is because investment in innovation is associated with additional risks, thus the expected profit is supposed to compensate for that. Advantages of tax instruments today are an integral part of any tax system in any country of the world. Noteworthy, 26 of 34 OECD countries offer tax incentives for the businesses that are implementing R&D activities.

Among the countries outside OECD, this practice is also actively used by Brazil, China, India, Russia, Singapore, South Africa and some other countries. Tax incentives, such as investment tax credit, research tax credit, investment tax discount are most effective and most common tools for supporting and stimulating innovations. Prevalence of these instruments of tax support for investment and innovation activities can be explained by their attractiveness for both the state and the enterprises.

Tax preferences for capital investments are often realized in the form of an investment tax credit to those enterprises, which are performing direct investments in new technologies, techniques, equipment etc. An investment tax credit is available only after the fact of implementing new equipment into operations, and the size of this credit is determined as a percentage of the cost of the equipment being introduced: for electronic equipment and equipment in Japan it is 5.3%; for new technology, technologies, materials of the first year in operation in the UK - 50%. In the United States, tax deduction for such investments is limited to energy-saving equipment exclusively.

Improving the quality of effectiveness assessment in using tax incentives involves improving the process of disclosure of statistical information and tax analytics by sectors of the economy, defined in the state programs. This will ensure transparency and openness in the formation of budget investments. Tax benefits should be based on the assessment of innovation and investment activities in top-priority sectors of the economy. It is expedient to determine the nature of tax incentives and the object of their influence, to create a single register of investment and innovation projects with a view to applying direct and indirect measures of state support for stimulating the economy. The improvement of the effectiveness of tax privileges will be facilitated by the improvement of financial instruments, including methods for analysing, evaluating and financing innovative and investment activities of organizations (based on foreign experience).

The purpose of fiscal policy is to ensure appropriate level of socioeconomic development for the society, taking into account the balance of public finances, implemented through the institutions of budgetary regulation and state financial control.

State regulation in today's conditions is a macroeconomic regulator of reproductive processes, aimed at implementation of strategic priorities of socioeconomic development of the state. Long-term forecasting of budget expenditures is an important instrument in state regulation of economic and social processes, since it substantiates the directions of using budget funds in the future, taking into account the determined goals and priorities of the country's socioeconomic development in the medium and long term.

Regulation in the field of budget expenditures through the use of a combination of budgetary tools of influence on the process of formation and execution of the budget allows copying with the challenges faced by the country at the present stage of social development, achieving at the same time the necessary macroeconomic proportions and indicators of economic growth. Increasing certain levels in the competitiveness of country's economy, in quality of public services, and in living standards requires the implementation of a strategy optimizing the amount of budget expenditures, while increasing their effectiveness.

Taking into account the level of budget filling in today's conditions, the urgent task would be to reduce budget deficit and increase the efficiency of using budget funds. This implies an increased share of public expenditures in the innovation sector of the economy; improving the public procurement system; program-target method use for optimizing the number of budget programs, determining their optimal structure and content; prevention of duplication in the functions assigned to various spending units; improvement of the budget program management process; raising the level of responsibility of the main spending units for violating the requirements of budget legislation.

The current stage in the development of budget relations in Ukraine is characterized by an increasing role of budgetary expenditures in the process of regulating the socioeconomic development of the state and regions.

Budget expenditures are involved in formation of consumption and accumulation funds in the state, therefore, they are an important area of influence on economic and social processes. In general, fiscal policy in the field of public expenditures is a rather powerful instrument for influencing socioeconomic development, especially in the context of economic reforms and limited financial resources of the state.

To determine the role of budget expenditures as a fiscal policy tool, efficiency of the budget resources' distribution, impacts of certain their components on economic situation of the state, peculiarities of the budget expenditures' formation in recent years in Ukraine were analysed.

The analysis of the dynamics of the share of expenditures on economic activity in the total expenditures of the consolidated budget shows that for the last nine years the largest their share - 17.9% was observed in 2007, and the lowest - 7.9% - in 2016. Also observable is the decrease in the share of budget financing of the economy to GDP - from 5.6% in 2007 to 2.8% in 2016.

At the same time, in 2016, capital expenditures were only 8.8%, thus demonstrating a gradual fluctuation between 3.9% in 2014 and 10.1% in 2007. This reflects the practice of redistributing budget resources, mostly on the side of current expenditures.

The extremely low share of capital expenditures in the budget indicates the prevelance of a short-term development strategy, while most of institutional changes in a developing economy can be achieved through directing budget funds on capital expenditures, in particular, on innovations. Since there is a need to reorient the economy of Ukraine onto a more innovative way of development, attention should be paid to the efficiency of financial resources' redistribution in the state, in particular, on stimulating innovative projects, partly through budget expenditures on innovation and preferential taxation of certain areas of activity and industries. Budget expenditures on infrastructural changes, as well as the costs of innovation, also have their positive impact on long-term economic development. Spending on innovations can help maintain the scientific and industrial potential of the country on a required level.

We have also analysed the dynamics of the key macroeconomic indicators for the years 2007 to 2016, which affect the budgetary system of Ukraine, as well as its interaction with fiscal policy. Inter alia, we have studied GDP and its components, namely, consumption, accumulation, export and import of goods and services.

The structure of Ukrainian economy shows that the volume of investment in the country is insignificant as compared to the level of consumption. This is yet another proof for the need to perform structural reforms and thus guide national economy on the more innovative path of development, thus ensuring more active economic growth.

The generally known constraints to the country's economic development and its low investment attractiveness are inconsistency and unpredictability of the legislative and regulatory environment in Ukraine.

To the major problems at the current stage of the fiscal policy implementation in Ukraine belong: prevalence of fiscal tasks over the regulatory potential of tax instruments, inefficient use of state financial resources mobilized through both tax and debt sources, imbalances in the inter budgetary fiscal and social transfers, which adversely affect macroeconomic stability.

Potentially increasing competitiveness of the national economy depends, first of all, on active investment and fiscal policies and, therefore, further improvement of fiscal instruments becomes a particularly important aspect of socioeconomic transformations in Ukraine. The main precondition for the state's competitiveness is a well regulated, effective, stable fiscal policy that meets European aspirations and contributes to attracting potential investors to Ukrainian economy.

Threats of Local Budgets' Execution and Fiscal Decentralisation in Ukraine

Taxes are mandatory payments to be made by legal entities and individuals to budgets of various levels. Historically, they are the oldest form of financial relations between the state and the members of society. Foreign economic activity, including the inflow of foreign investments, can be regulated using taxes. With the help of taxes, the state receives the resources needed to carry out its public functions. Taxation system determines the final distribution of incomes inside a society.

The main objective of tax revenues is to provide the state budget with financial resources to finance public expenditures. Formation of tax revenues is carried out by budget mobilizing taxes, duties, and other compulsory payments. The size of such tax revenues depends on the state of the country's economy, as well as on a country's needs for redistribution of GDP and financial support in the course of state programs' implementation.

However, the state lacks state budget revenues to fully finance expenditures, especially in Ukraine in recent years, since the deficit of the State Budget of Ukraine has grown rapidly. Threats to financial and economic security of the state have its disabling effect on the taxation of economic activity of business entities, as well as unplanned budget losses due to the lack of tax revenues.

The effects from the unbalanced tax policy can generate the following threats to financial and economic security of the state:

- The growing share of the shadow economy;
- Constantly increasing level of the tax debt;
- Illegal use of tax privileges;
- Illegal manufacturing and further same illegal sale of the supposedly excisable goods;
- Tax evasion, and;
- Carrying out fictitious foreign economic operations.

Also, there are additional factors lowering the levels of both financial and economic security. They include:

- Ill-conceived tax policy;
- High level of taxation imposed on business entities, which restrains the growth of entrepreneurial activity (especially in the field of innovation production);

- Corruption in tax administration.

Another threat to financial and economic security of Ukrainian economy is the uneven distribution of tax burden in the country, which is caused, above all, by the imperfection of the mechanism used for granting tax privileges. The major problem with the domestic taxation system is the extremely large number of taxes and the permanent variability of their list.

The instruments of fiscal regulation are not an effective means of rising the level of economic security in Ukraine, in opposite - it generates a number of additional threats to the domestic economy.

An important role in the system of budgets execution is allocated to local budgets. The problems with forming the revenue base for local budgets, the lack of financial resources for local authorities and the instability of their sources of income are acute in Ukraine.

Ukraine lacks an effective system of fiscal regulation over the economic security of its regions. The main threats in this regard are as follows:

- Excessive centralization of the financial system, redistribution of a significant amount of financial resources through the state budget;
- Insufficient financial support of local authorities and their high dependence from the state budget when it comes to formation of revenues (70-80%);
- Lack of real decentralization, as it is evidenced by the growing role of transfers in the formation of local budget revenues and the declining share of local revenues in the consolidated budget of the country.

Local budgets in Ukraine depend on the financial assistance in the form of intergovernmental transfers. The lower levels of government authorities in the country are entrusted with the functions of providing public services of vital importance; however, their execution is not supported with the sufficient volume of financial resources. In addition, local budgets' capacity to form their own revenue base is limited by an ineffective institutional environment (Holynskyy, 2013).

One of the main reasons for unsatisfactory financial situation of local authorities in Ukraine is the inefficient functioning of the local taxes and fees institute, which is influenced by such exogenous and endogenous negative factors as: limited list of local taxes and fees; general ineffectiveness of the tax imposed on the real property other than land; restriction in the rights of local authorities in part of having own fiscal policy and, in particular, in establishment of local taxes and fees; lack of incentives for local self-governments to increase the revenue base in the areas under their administration.

The Tax Code of Ukraine has modernized the system of local taxes and fees. But these relatively recent changes in it did not contribute to strengthening the financial base of local budgets. Such a situation requires immediate development and implementation of a state program which would increase the level of economic security. Inter alia, this program is supposed to include the use of fiscal instruments. Priority in this regard belongs to the development of appropriate regional targeted programs, fiscal decentralization, clear division of powers between national and local authorities, improvement of the system of intergovernmental fiscal transfers etc.

Thus, an important way of improving the efficiency of fiscal regulation over the economic security of Ukraine's regions is fiscal decentralization. Fiscal decentralization in Ukraine stems from the numerous changes taking place due to the newer versions of the Tax and Budget Codes and other legislative acts.

The first steps in this tax reform concerned the reduction in the number of taxes overall. In particular, the number of local level taxes reduced due to combining 17 taxes into 7.

Ways of Improving Budgetary and Fiscal Policies in Ukraine

Increasing budget revenues without creating additional barriers to economic growth would be possible within the following policy areas:

- **Increasing the Tax Burden on Consumption, Rather than on Capital:** In terms of the threat of critical imbalance in the system of public finances, it is necessary to be prepared to increase some taxes. At the same time, it should be clearly understood that the increase of direct tax rates reduces the financial result and limits the innovation and investment opportunities of entities. Because of this, most of the developed countries, while trying to solve the problem of budget deficit, increase indirect taxes, primarily taxes on consumption. Fiscal efficiency of taxes on consumption is higher, since they are charged only in case of actual consumption. This means that this type of taxes cover not only official sources of income but also those received within shadow economy. Therefore, in the case of Ukraine it would be necessary to shift emphasis from taxation on capital to consumption taxation, since here there is a great potential for tax revenues' growth.
- **Refusal to Further Reduce the Tax Rate on Profit:** In Ukraine, the profit tax rate is already one of the lowest in comparison with the EU countries, therefore, its further reduction is no longer appropriate. This can be also substantiated by the fact that the reduction of fiscal pressure on profit will not automatically lead either to an increase in investments, or to expansion of current activities' volume. The accumulated experience of European countries suggests that the reduction of income tax rate and introduction of a single income tax rate were effective while the inflow of foreign direct investments grew intensively. And when revenues halt, it turned out that the countries with the lowest tax rates were affected by the global financial and economic crisis more severely than the others. This is due to the fact that reduction of the income tax rate did not contribute to a corresponding increase in the volume of attracted investments into the country, and a larger share of additional profits was used for other needs, in particular, on dividends.
- **Refusal to Further Reduce the Basic VAT Rate:** Experience of many other countries testifies that in order to increase tax revenues to the EU budget they raised the VAT rate first of all. In particular, Italy, Spain, Ireland, Czech Republic and Hungary have made such a decision during 2012-2013. Even if by reducing the tax rate it will be possible to save budget reimbursements over a certain period of time, the VAT rate in Ukraine will be the smallest in comparison with other post-socialist countries of Central and Eastern Europe, and this fact in the future will reduce the share of indirect taxes that is unusual for market economy as such. It is necessary to raise the VAT rate temporarily to 23% with the simultaneous introduction of a 10% rate for essential goods. The majority of the EU countries that, in the times of crisis, faced the need to finance additional budget expenditures, ended up with introducing the increased rate (23%) of VAT on luxury goods permanently. It would be expedient to add the following items to the list of objects under higher VAT rate: purchasing cars with larger engines, yachts, jewellery, valuable watches etc.

Optimization of the Tax Privileges System

Tax benefits should be directed towards the development of those segments of the economy, which in the future will lead to increased incomes or reduced costs due to production modernization, issuing new products or improving significantly their quality, thus raising the competitiveness level overall. In addition, it is also important to ensure:

- The list of industries subject to tax incentives is regularly reviewed. These and other tax benefits should be provided to enterprises that own, use or develop high technologies, since the latter is the best guarantee for the long-term high rates of economic activity. And this, in its turn, would be replenishing the state budget via tax revenues;
- There are exact and specific criteria for granting tax privileges. One of the consequences from the current ineffectiveness of providing tax benefits is the significant loss of budget revenues. Therefore, it would be necessary to take the following into account while changing the system of tax privileges in Ukraine:
- When tax benefits are provided, type of enterprise activity should be considered, potential impact from these benefits should be assessed along with the relevance of their use. Also, potential budget losses from these benefits' imposing must be calculated along with the impact on the country's socioeconomic development;
- Strategic objectives of imposing particular tax privileges must be clearly defined. Future compensation for the tax revenues not received by the budget should be accurately calculated, accounting for production modernization, introduction of new products or improvements in quality and competitiveness of the already existing ones;
- One of the main preconditions for granting tax privileges should be mandatory finishing of an investment project;
- Stronger control over the use of tax incentives. Tax evasion schemes exist in Ukraine in their wide variety, so it is necessary to find effective methods for monitoring the use of tax breaks. Due to the abuse of tax privileges and purposeful use of tax-deductible funds to increase production, re-equip material and technical base, introduce the latest technologies, it is necessary to consider the following:
- To ensure adequate state control over all related processes and to increase the responsibility for the misuse of the funds released from taxation;
- To introduce systematic reporting of the Cabinet of Ministers to the Parliament (Verkhovna Rada) on the amounts of tax incentives, as well as on economic and social efficiency of the granted tax benefits during a certain period.

Improving the Effectiveness of Combating Income Concealment

Tax revenue office has quite wide powers to control the authenticity of the declared by citizens incomes and property, but work in this direction remains to be quite ineffective. At the same time, shadow incomes of citizens are nearly the only large source of potential budget revenues today. Shadow income of the society has a significant fiscal potential and what is more important, its integration into the tax system would not create barriers for further economic development.

- Deepening progression of the personal income tax, the key sources of which are wages and other forms of remuneration. Social privilege should be introduced into this system in the form of a reduced tax rate for low-income groups of population;
- Introduction of a Capital Tax on the Level of 1% of the Market Value of Shares Owned by Residents of Ukraine;
- Extension of the List of Minerals, Mining and Sale of Which Are Charged with Additional Rent

In addition to oil, gas and gas condensate, Ukraine produces a significant amount of other valuable minerals, which are the property of the Ukrainian nation, actually, but at the same time they somehow do not generate income from the industrial development. It seems expedient to add iron ore, manganese ore, uranium ore, some varieties of coking coal, ores of non-ferrous metals etc to the list of minerals, mining and sale of which are subject to a special rent. This will significantly increase the volume of budget revenues.

Extension of the Group of Excisable Goods

In particular, objects of taxation in the category of excise goods should include the purchases of food products that are:

- Of premium category;
- Harmful to health.

This would allow not only increasing budget revenues, but would also provide additional positive stimulus, in particular, those related to restriction on harmful food products.

CONCLUSION

Fiscal regulation in Ukraine can be successfully applied to strengthen financial security and increase country's competitiveness through the following measures: reducing the level of income redistribution through budget and extrabudgetary funds, reducing the fiscal burden on business, increasing the efficiency of state budget expenditures, improving the government's debt policy (acceleration of external debt repayments and optimization of foreign borrowings, gradual transfer of external debt to the domestic market, attraction of financial resources at the lowest possible cost and insurance of financial risks in order to ensure stability and integrity of the financial system overall), improvement of the system of state debt planning, which should include planning future debts for at least several years, improving the system of tax control, improving the system of charging and refunding VAT from the state budget (changing the basis of VAT, minimizing benefits for taxpayers etc.).

REFERENCES

Altshuler, R., & Goodspeed, T. J. (2015). Follow the leader? Evidence on European and US tax competition. *Public Finance Review*, *43*(4), 485–504. doi:10.1177/1091142114527781

Bazylevych, V. (2004). *Macroeconomics*. Znannya.

Bruchez, P. A., & Schaltegger, C. A. (2005). *International tax competition and trends in tax policy: Some implications for Switzerland*. Eidgenössische Finanzverwaltung.

Dar, A., & Amirkhalkhali, S. (2017). Fiscal Policy, Total Factor Productivity and Economic Growth in Advanced Economies. *Applied Econometrics and International Development*, *17*(2), 5–18.

Dornbusch, R., & Fischer, S. (1986). The open economy: implications for monetary and fiscal policy. In *The American business cycle: Continuity and change* (pp. 459–516). University of Chicago Press.

Edwards, J., & Keen, M. (1996). Tax competition and Leviathan. *European Economic Review*, *40*(1), 113–134. doi:10.1016/0014-2921(95)00057-7

Field, T. F. (2003). Tax Competition in Europe and America. Tax Notes, 98(14).

Freik, N., Bespalko, V., Fedets, I., & Kuziakiv, O. (2017). *Annual Business Climate Assessment 2016: National and Regional Dimensions*. Retrieved from The Institute for Economic Research and Policy Consulting: http://www.ier.com.ua/en/sme_development/ABCA?pid=5789

Genschel, P. (2001). *Globalization, tax competition, and the fiscal viability of the welfare state*. MPIfG Working paper.

González, S. M. (2017). *State Aid, Tax Competition and BEPS: Comments on the European Commission's Decisions on Transfer Pricing Rulings*. University of Leicester, School of Law Research Paper No. 17-00.

Gupta, R., Lau, C. K. M., Miller, S. M., & Wohar, M. E. (2017). *US Fiscal Policy and Asset Prices: The Role of Partisan Conflict*. Academic Press.

Holynskyy, Y. (2013). Improvement of Cash-flow Planning by the Treasury of Ukraine. Economic Annals-XXI, 51-54.

Krysovatyi, A. I. (2000). *Taxation and Market: the Conditions and Possibilities of the Combination*. Vydavnytstvo Karpiuka.

Mongrain, S., & Wilson, J. (2015). *Tax competition with heterogeneous capital mobility*. CESifo Working Paper Series No. 5688.

Onyusheva, I. (2017), Analytical and managerial issues of human capital in conditions of global competitiveness: the case of Kazakhstan. Polish Journal of Management Studies, 16(2), 198-209.

Pinto, C., & Pinto, C. A. (2003). *Tax competition and EU law*. Kluwer Law International.

Rios, M. C., McConnell, C. R., & Brue, S. L. (2013). *Economics: Principles, problems, and policies*. McGraw-Hill.

Rohác, D. (2006). Evidence and Myths about Tax Competition. *New Perspectives on Political Economy*, *2*(2), 86–115.

Sidelnikova, L. P. (2010). Tax and Credit Finance: Fiscal Philosophy of Choice. Hrin' DS, 13.

Simanavičienė, Ž., & Stankevičius, A. (2017). *Economic security and national competitiveness*. Retrieved December 10, 2017 from https://repository.mruni.eu/bitstream/handle/007/15011/Simanavi%C4%8Dien%C4%97.pdf?sequence=1&isAllowed=y

Soukup, J. (2017). The Impact of Innovation on Competitiveness and Economic Growth in EU Countries. *ICFE*, *2017*, 295.

Stewart, K., & Webb, M. (2006). International competition in corporate taxation: Evidence from the OECD time series. *Economic Policy*, *21*(45), 154–201. doi:10.1111/j.1468-0327.2006.00156.x

Teather, R. (2005). *The benefits of tax competition. Hobart Paper 153*. London: The Institute of Economic Affairs.

Tyrrell, B., & Riley, P. (2017). *2018 Index of Economic Freedom: Freedom to Trade Is a Key to Prosperity*. Retrieved from The Heritage Foundation: https://www.heritage.org/sites/default/files/2017-11/BG3266.pdf

Ukraine: Economic Freedom Score. (2017). Retrieved December 10, 2017 from The Heritage Foundation: https://www.heritage.org/index/pdf/2017/countries/ukraine.pdf

Wilson, J. D., & Wildasin, D. E. (2004). Capital tax competition: Bane or boon. *Journal of Public Economics*, *88*(6), 1065–1091. doi:10.1016/S0047-2727(03)00057-4

World Bank. (2018). *Doing Business 2018: Reforming to Create Jobs*. Washington, DC: World Bank; doi:10.1596/978-1-4648-1146-3

KEY TERMS AND DEFINITIONS

Fiscal Policy: A set of measures by which the state influences the economy through the structure of tax revenues to the state budget, directions in public expenditure and methods of attracting the borrowed funds.

Tax Burden: The amount of income, property, or sales tax levied on an individual or a business.

Tax Competition: A form of regulatory competition which exists when governments are encouraged to lower fiscal burdens to either encourage the inflow of productive resources, or discourage the outflow of those resources. The essence of the concept "international tax competition" is in the rivalry of countries for mobile but limited economic resources using the tools and specific features of national taxation systems.

Tax Harmonization: The process of adjusting tax systems of different jurisdictions in the pursuit of a common policy objective.

Tax Incentive: An aspect of a country's tax code designed to encourage a particular economic activity.

Chapter 15
Environmental Accounting Implementation and Stimulation of National Business Global Competitiveness:
The Case of Thailand

Prateep Wajeetongratana
Suan Sunandha Rajabhat University, Thailand

ABSTRACT

Today's system of accounting does not contain sufficient volumes of information about environmental incomes and losses of organizations; therefore, it is nearly impossible to evaluate precisely the efficiency of environmental actions taken and environmental protection systems being implemented in order to maintain and/or increase the environmental balance. One of the key elements in the mechanism increasing the quality of economic performance is the system of environmental accounting. This chapter explains both theory and methodology of environmental accounting and also determines its role and place within the system of existing types of accounting and reporting in accordance with the IFRS requirements and also the Kyoto Protocol. The presented organizational economic mechanism of environmental accounting allows implementing the latter at concrete enterprises to promote and support more efficient managerial decision making.

INTRODUCTION

Human activity has rather significant impact on the processes of global warming all over the planet. Researchers today are not questioning climate change anymore – they are discussing already what can be and must be done so that to stop these processes or at least hinder them. The most acute problem at the contemporary stage of the environmental policies' development worldwide is the determination of

DOI: 10.4018/978-1-5225-7760-7.ch015

key principles and mechanisms in overcoming the greenhouse effects so that to guarantee safety for both today's and future generations on this planet, in full accordance with the Kyoto Protocol implementation.

Thailand today is ranked 21st in the world by the volume of atmosphere pollution (Environmental Performance Index, 2016), the country is also 91st in the world ranking of environmental efficiency (also 2016 data). One of the causes for such a situation is Thailand's loss of economic potential in the course of environmental reforms' implementation in the country as well as changes in the strategic vision of the kingdom – from the priority of dynamic industrial growth to the formation of a sustainable economic system which would not only guarantee Thailand a favourable rank in the overall global structure of labor distribution but would also provide more comfortable life condtions for local population (inter alia, including environmental conditions and nature protection).

Despite the global nature of nearly all environmental problems and the volume of the negative impacts on the whole humankind, up to truly catastrophic consequences, as of today neither Thailand separately, nor the ASEAN region overall, do not have available the well thought-out strategies for further development of economies and societies which would have taken into account the factors of so needed environmental balance and minimization of pollution.

This is why today pressing become the issues related to taking action on environmentalization of carbon dioxide emissions and certification for lower emissions etc. The key instrument to solve this task at the level of a separate enterprise is actually environmental accounting, in its development and further implementation.

As of today environmental aspects in accounting and reporting regulation are present, however, they are displayed sporadically, moreover, there is no precise explanation concerning the all related accounting terminology, neither there is any methodology for further environmentalization of accounting, nor specific requirements on how to present environmental information in accounting documents. Thus, there arises the necessity to consider the environmental elements of the financial/accounting system as a component of accounting process overall, on the level of enterprises and organizations.

In today's conditions of Thai economy national enterprises simply must develop own environmental policies and also their own comprehensive programs and plans for these policies' further actual implementation. And if they would also have a forecast component in their policies and programs, this would only increase the overall level of environmental safety in the country. Moreover, ideally enterprise-level environmental policy and program must have not only forecast and actual implementation parts – but also certain space must be dedicated to the analysis of the results, their control and audit.

The purpose of the research is to develop, after analyzing the results of the survey of both professionals and researchers in the accounting field, a methodology covering all vital theoretical, organizational and methodological issues so that to create and implement a system of environmental accounting which would help promote and maintain the environmental balance.

Under this wider objective we would like also to outline the following objectives:

- To develop comprehensive methodological grounds for introducing environmental accounting into a larger accounting analytical system.
- To explain in detail the theoretical fundamental of environmental balance as a notion and under conditions of world economy globalization specifically.
- To develop and provide methodological grounds for "green investment flows" modelling as applied to environmental accounting.
- To develop methodological grounds for organization of environmentally oriented accounting.

In the course of our research we plan to verify the following hypotheses:

The system of environmental accounting at any business enterprise today must be, first of all, oriented on external users (the society, local community, public authorities, investors etc.) and least of all – on the interests of own management.

Most of today's Thai enterprises do not see environmental accounting as a factor of own competitiveness strengthening and stimulation (neither at the internal market, nor at the external ones). This means that the state must take extra actions on shifting the emphasis on the direct correlation between environmental activities and enterprise competitiveness.

Environmental accounting, just as traditional accounting, must be based on the balance (but in this case – environmental balance). And in Thai business balance is understood as a stable chain of production processes which is consuming and restoring natural resources.

Taking into account all specific features of environmental accounting, we see as more probable not an autonomous version of such a system but more like some sort of environmentalization strategy aimed managerial accounting at the national, all-Thai level.

Efficient and sustainable development of the Thai system of environmental accounting assumes that information (primarily environmental one) is presented not as much in its cost, financial form but rather in its quantitative form.

As a potential basis for development and implementation of the national system of environmental accounting can serve the already available standard - (IAS) 27 Separate Financial Statements. However, this idea most probably would not gain much popularity among the expert community, for a range of reasons.

The key factors in environmental monetization in today's Thai business are paybility and marketing priority (that is, the opportunity to use own environmental progress and all related innovations in more intensive commercialization of proposition and its promotion).

Greenhouse emission quotas should take into account the specific role in production and thus, it would be logical to assign them to the accounts "intangible assets" and perform the depreciation of their costs accordingly.

BACKGROUND

One of the most internationally recognized authors in the field of sustainable relations between economic activities and the environment, accounting for natural resources and ecosystems, valuation of the environment and accounting of environmental costs is Ichiro Kaneda (2001) from Niigata Sangyo University, Japan. He was the first to suggest expanding the system of national accounts (SNA) so that it would become the System of Integrated Environmental and Economic Accounting (SEEA), and this, in turn, would make it possible for the accounting system to take fully into account all the issues related to natural resources and ecosystems.

Nearly in parallel to Ichiro Kaneda's work, the neighbouring China (in the early 2000s this country has faced numerous serious problems related to unstable development) offered its own concept of the economic progress' environmentalization. This Chinese concept was based on the famous Input-Output Analysis, and also the System of National Accounts and Social Accounting Matrix. It was develop to present a Social and Ecological Accounting Matrix (SEAM) for sustainability planning, and using all the above the research team from Xiaoming PAN Institute of Systems Science, affiliated to the Chinese Academy of Sciences has carried out a truly collosal theoretical and applied research which demonstrated that SEAM can establish a concrete base for sustainability planning and an operable framework for sustainable development indicators (*Social and Ecological Accounting Matrix: An Empirical Study for China,* 2000). Further, the necessity of having large volumes of information for substantiation of managerial decisions to be included in financial reporting, aggregation of information in order to assess costs and risks from natural disasters and also the problems with financial accounting of the natural resources' consumption have been well described by Carmen-Veronica Zefinescu (2015). This author also suggested her own conceptual framework as well as methods for assessing and accounting the consequences from such activities of companies in relation to changes in the natural environment.

Doina Maria Tilea (2016), in the same vein, has noted that environmental accounting is a relatively novel interdisciplinary approach which aims to integrate environmental and accounting issues. This author has also grounded the need for the formation of an effective model necessary for integration of the environmental aspects into the decision-making processes and financial processes of business entities in order to present the most accurate picture of the entity's impact on the environment in accounting.

Throughout the last decade the issues related to accounting of environmental assets and all related business spending (aimed at maintaining the environmental balance) were always in the center of attention in quite many general economic and financial studies in nearly all countries of the world. We think especially noteworthy is, for example, the study by I.C. Stanciu et al. (2011) dedicated specifically to accounting of environmental costs. These authors have grounded theoretically the concepts of environmental costs and also described in detail how environmental management accounting may be useful in determining environmental costs. M. Tamborra and M. Pavan (2005) discussed the methodology used for estimation of damages caused by air pollution and the cost of defensive expenditures, presenting the results of their detailed analysis and drawing important policy conclusions for environmental accounting practices throughout the EU.

In another research on the same topic, C. Sendroiu and A. G. Roman, (2007) noted that companies and managers usually believe that environmental costs are not that very much significant for their business operations. And too often it does not occur to them that some of the production costs have an environmental component within them. These authors have come to the conclusion that by identifying and controlling environmental costs, environmental accounting systems can help environmental managers justify cleaner production projects, and also identify some new ways of saving money and improving their environmental performance at the same time.

The problems of environmental accounting in the context of sustainable development provision have been also studied by F. Boghean (2007) who interpreted environmental accounting as a tool which, used prudently, can make an important contribution to social decision-making. Inter alia, this author suggested incorporation of natural resource and intangible environmental costs and benefits into green accounting at the firm level as well as at the level of national economy.

In our opinion, a separate direction in all studies related to environmental accounting concerns evaluation of opportunities for introduction of the environmental accounting system on the case studies of separate countries. For example, A. Deaconu and A. Buiga (2011) have carried out a thorough and rather detailed analysis of the retrospective forms of accounting development in Romania. This analysis was based on the distinction between accounting systems of Continental-European type and those of Anglo-Saxon type, and separately the authors described the development and implementation of national standards related to environmental accounting as a relatively new and still urgent direction in overall modernization of the whole national system of accounting.

Problems related to actual introduction of environmental accounting systems have been also studied separately for various industrial sectors and also branches in agriculture, also in quite many countries worldwide. For example, the research study of A. Tanc and K. Gokoglan (2015) investigated the sensitivity of manufacturing companies operating in the organized industrial zone of Diyarbakýr (Turkey) to environmental accounting approaches within the scope of so popular today social responsibility. Or, for example, J. Kouřilová (2003) took quite an interesting approach in treating the environment overall as external assets in relation to farm accounting and showed how specifically this is influencing the results of farm activities. This study was carried out on the data from several EU countries. Our study further will be most surely based on the results and conclusions many honorable and respected rerseachers worldwide have already reached. However, at the same time we plan to take into account the specificity of Thai accounting system in its compliance with the international standards of financial reporting. We also hope to suggest a new algorithm, applying which it would become possible to implement the system of environmental accounting in the Kingdom, special emphasis would be put on distribution of greenhouse emission quotas and their further use.

THEORETICAL FRAMEWORKS OF THE STUDY

Operating the theoretical fundamentals borrowed from the literature overview above, here we would like to present the analytical comparison between financial, tax, managerial and environmental accounting.

Environmental accounting here we have determined as a separate direction in accounting of any economic subject, and this direction is supposed to provide the accounting system overall with all the needed environment-related information. Important note in this regard is that as of today such information is still not systemic. This means that an additional subsystem is needed to display and monitor the spending on environmental protection and more specifically – so that to have the cost indicators of environmental factors in their interrelation between the environment and economy. This system is supposed to operate the real, actual data on the environmental conditions (provided as a result of thorough monitoring and comparison with the developed in advance accounting norms of environment quality). This sort of information, regularly updated, is supposed to serve as the information basis for further development of the environmental accounting system at an enterprise.

The Figure 1 above clearly shows how exactly we have established and envision the interrelation and interdependence between classical business accounting and environmental accounting.

Figure 1. Interrelation and interdependence between business accounting and environmental accounting (Made by co-authors)

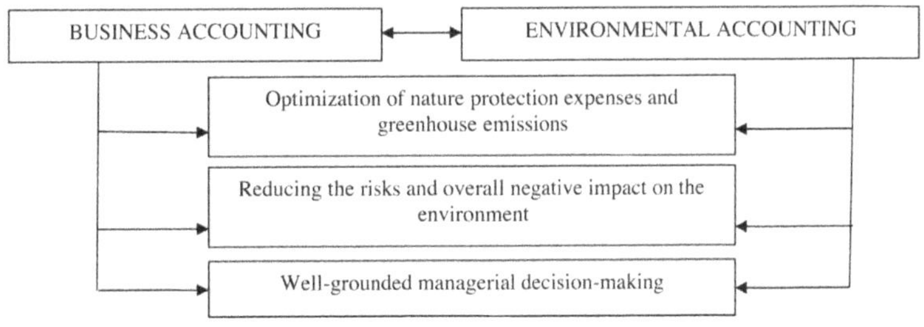

Practical introduction of environmental accounting at enterprises is hindered today due to lack of the needed methodologies which would take into account all potential states and overall dynamics of changes in the environment. The very concept of environmental accounting is determined through its principles, functions, aims and tasks. After a comprehensive analysis of the key determining features of tax accounting, financial, managerial and environmental accounting we are able to determine the key goals of environmental accounting as a notion and as a phenomenon in accounting (both in science as well as in actual business practice). So, its key goals are: coordinating the balance between the economic and the environmental components of business, determining all possible environmental risks and the related problems and also determining the ways to overcome these risks and solve these problems (see Table 1).

Environmental accounting serves to estimate fully the environmental factors and on the basis of this estimation it is supposed to result in environmental reporting of a certain predetermined form and contents, oriented and serving both external and internal users. This sort of information can be useful for owners themselves, their creditors, investors, tax and/or public authorities, current and future clients, overseas partners etc. Table 1 presents the comparison between the types of accounting which has been carried out so that to determine exactly the interrelation between financial, managerial and environmental accounting (also presented graphically in Figure 2).

As it can be seen in Figure 2, business accounting includes financial accounting, managerial accounting and finally environmental accounting. The key objects in environmental accounting are all operations and activities of an enterprise/organization related to the environment and its condition (current and future/potential). While financial and environmental accounting are supposed to be performed in full compliance with normative guidelines which bear the regulatory function in accounting. For violations in methodology of financial and/or environmental accounting there exists a certain responsibility described in laws.

Environmental accounting covers only the environment-related activities of an enterprise, while financial accounting is performed for an enterprise overall and thus treats it as one single economic unit. Managerial accounting is usually performed by: sectors of a particular market, by places of expenditures' formation, by centers of responsibility, by causes and/or responsibility centers for specific fluctuations in profit/losses, and only in case of obvious necessity managerial accounting will be performed for an enterprise overall.

All these considered above types of accounting differ not only by contents, but also by frequency of reporting and types of documents to be presented.

Figure 2. Interrelation between financial, managerial and environmental accounting
(Made by co-authors)

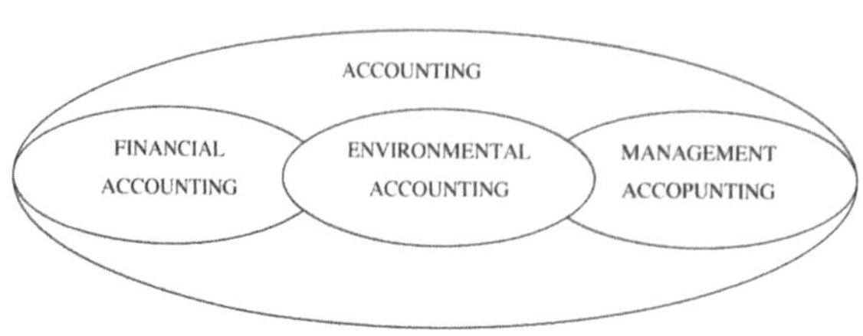

Table 1. Comparative description of financial, managerial and environmental accounting

1. Financial Accounting	
Notion	Accounting of availability and movement of money assets and financial resources
Goal	Gathering trustworthy information for further financial reporting, later – control over it so that to reveal the financial reserves
Key task	Collecting information for further analysis of enterprise performance and its financial condition
Key users of information	External users: tax administration, credit institutions, including banks, supplies, clients – current and potential, investors – also current and potential, etc.
Ways to disclose information	Double entry
Degree of freedom in selecting the accounting method	Is limited due to general rules and principles of accounting
Key objects in accounting	Organization as a whole
Key reporting documents	Balance; report on profits and losses; report on capital movement; report; cash flow report
Frequency of reporting	Month, quarter, year
Degree of trustworthiness	Trustworthy, confirmed by other documents and reports
Mandatory or not	Mandatory
Key internal document to set the order of accounting	Accounting policy for the aims of financial accounting
2. Managerial Accounting	
Notion	The system for collection, registration, generalization and further presentation of information on the economic activities of an organization to be used in further planning, control and management over all reported activities
Goal	Information support for all activities of an organization so that to have more appropriately grounded managerial decision-making
Key task	Gathering information for both operational and strategic planning and management of the whole enterprise
Information users	Top managers of an organization
Ways to disclose information	In any systemic way. The use of accounting elements is not mandatory at all. Mostly quantitative methods are used
Degree of freedom in selecting the accounting method	No particular limitations but preference is given to costs' comparison with profits in the context of more/less efficient decision-making
Key objects in accounting	Structural units; centers of responsibility; other important business units
Key reporting documents	Various reports, including internal cost sheets and internal budgets; mostly internally developed forms are used
Frequency of reporting	Shift, day, week, month
Degree of trustworthiness	Raw estimates and approximate evaluations are allowed to be used
Mandatory or not	Non-mandatory.Can be used or stopped being used by a decision of top managers/administration
Key internal document to set the order of accounting	Accounting policy for the aims of managerial accounting
3. Environmental Accounting	
Notion	The system for collection, registration and generalization of information with the aims to detect, evaluate, plan/forecast, analyze and control all environmental costs and environmental liabilities of an enterprise
Goal	Coordination of economic and environmental components of business so that to determine all related risks and potential problems along with the ways to overcome/avoid them
Key task	Collection and registration of information for further estimation of environmental costs and liabilities
Information users	Both internal and external users
Ways to disclose information	Continuously documented accounting using both natural and cost indicators
Degree of freedom in selecting the accounting method	No limitations
Key objects in accounting	All environment-related activities of an enterprise/organization, and also liabilities for such activities and their cost
Key reporting documents	Environmental declarations
Frequency of reporting	Month, quarter, year
Degree of trustworthiness	Trustworthy, confirmed by other documents and reports
Mandatory or not	Mandatory
Key internal document to set the order of accounting	Accounting policy for the aims of environmental accounting

(Made by author)

Table 2. Description of the sample in our survey, divided into three groups

Group #1: Scientists and Researchers		
Number of people in the group		**43**
Distribution of affiliations (in %)	Thailand-based universities	63
	Research centers and associations	19
	Foreign universities	14
	Other	4
Time of the survey		November 2016 – February 2017
Methods used for data collection (%)	Questionnaires sent via email	52
	Questionnaires sent via postal mail	27
	Interviews	13
	Questionnaires were delivered personally[1]	8
Experience and feedback demonstrated	Have faced problems related to environmental accounting	27
	Have experience of working with the enterprises that have negative impact on the environment	14
Group #2: Professionals with Applied Knowledge in the Fields of Business and Managerial Accounting		
Number of people in the group		**69**
Time period of the survey		December 2016 – March 2017
Affiliations of the respondents	Private companies	69
	State-owned companies	31
	Thai companies	82
	Foreign companies, joint ventures	18
	SMEs	76
	Large	24
	Companies from the financial sector	14
	Transport & cargo enterprises	32
	Construction & development	9
	Services sector	8
	Agricultural enterprises	3
	Trade & retail	21
	Other various businesses	13
	Enterprises having damading impact on the environment	37
	Enterprises already using certain elements of environmental accounting (accounting of resources used, environmental taxes and duties, taxes on emissions, trade and further accounting of emission quotas' trade)	14
Methods used for data collection	Questionnaires sent via email	63
	Interviews	12
	Questionnaires sent via regular mail	11
	Questionnaires delivered personally	14

continued on following page

Table 2. Continued

Group #3: Representatives of Public Authorities		
Number of people in the group		**29**
Time period of the survey		January – April 2017
Affiliations of the respondents	Ministry of Finance	12
	Ministry of Trade and Commerce	31
	National Committee for Accounting and Audit	14
	NGOs and professional associations	19
	Other	10
Having experience in the fields or regulation/control over the environmental accounting (on the level of the whole country or on the level of a specific business unit)		59
Methods used for data collection	Questionnaires sent via email	36
	Interviews	32
	Questionnaires sent via regular mail	24
	Questionnaired delivered personally	8

(Made by author)

RESEARCH METHODS AND PROCEDURES

The practical part of our research is dedicated to determining the fundamental principles, instruments and rules of environmentally oriented accounting. For this matter we have gathered data from three categories of the respondents:

Group # 1: Scientists and researchers working on modernization and further improvement of business and/or managerial accounting;
Group #2: Professionals with profound practical knowledge in the fields of business accounting and managerial accounting;
Group #3: Representatives of public authorities, responsible for regulation of accounting processes at the enterprises of all property forms and types.

More details on our sample divided into three groups are presented in Table 2.

Thus, the research has been carried out during 6 months in total, since November 2016 till April 2017. At some parts, students of the Faculty of Management, Suan Sunandha Rajabat University (Dusit, Bangkok) were involved for assistance with data collection. Also, personal contacts of the author of this study have been widely used, namely, among corporate representatives, other researchers, public authorities' officers etc.

The questionnaire had the following structure:

- 24 closed questions or questions with multiple choice answers (selection between 2-5 options);
- 5 open questions which assumed the respondent is free to explain his/her point of view on a particular problem;

- 3 test tasks in the course of which the respondent was supposed to solve a specific task related to environmental accounting organization.

Questionnaires were available in two languages – Thai and English.

Data collected from these questionnaires has been further used in data analysis which involved the following research methods:

- **Cost-Benefit Analysis (CBA):** So that to determine the economic efficiency of the suggested instruments of environmental accounting and of the related actions of environmental accounting implementation in real practice of contemporary Thai companies; CBA was also used to determine the level of influence of environmental accounting on the competitiveness of Thai businesses and Thai products at world markets as well as to assess the attractiveness of Thailand as a jurisdiction for business development;
- **Modelling:** This method was used while describing the potential correlations between the elements of environmental, managerial and financial accounting between each other and also with the instruments of state control and regulation over each of them;
- **Expert Evaluation Methods (Delphi etc.):** Those were applied in the process of presenting the author's vision on the components of environmental accounting and on the options of its integration with the already well established Thai system of financial reporting as well as with the system of international financial reporting. In the result of this method application, recommendations from the experts which had previous experience in the field of environmental accounting implementation have been assessed thrice higher than the recommendations provided by the respondents which had no such previous experience;
- **System Analysis:** Was used as the instrument for development of one common approach to environmental accounting organization and its implementation in actual business practice. In the course of this method use, despite the fact that there was a group of priviled experts (one of the three groups, see above) in the overall sample, the shares of each group answers were identical in formulation of the final decision by the researcher;
- **Sociological Methods (Survey, Interview, Observation):** Were applied as the basic instruments for data collection (general information on the groups of respondents is outlined in the tables above).

All obtained data were processed using classical statistical methods with application of Excel and SPSS.

RESEARCH RESULTS

The starting point in determination of the structure, principles and contents of environmental accounting is the question: Who are/will be the users of this information? Peculiarities of users, level of their competences and other (both subjective and objective) factors predetermine the whole system, structure and level of formalization in the environmental business accounting.

Regarding the potential users in our survey we have obtained the following variants of answers (the questionnaire initially suggested choosing five out of ten options and range them in the order of decreasing interest in the information related to environmental accounting at an enterprise).

As Table 3 demonstrates, representatives of business sector are more prone to treat environmental accounting as an additional element of financial responsibility and financial reporting. This also means that for businessmen social value of environmental accounting is not that important. Internal users of this type of accounting are, noteworthy, hardly mentioned as such, only a few representatives from Group #1 (researchers) placed them into this priority list. Representatives of the public sector view environmental accounting mostly as an additional competence of the state power; this is why they include sectoral regulators into this list (we tend to think, however, that involvement of this groups of potential stakeholders might lead to increased bureaucratic load mostly). Overall, these results are not surprising at all. All three groups of our respondents have provided quite obvious and expected answers, thus revealing their true interests, essence and dominating values (the latter would be: fairness and justice – for the first group, efficiency – for the second, and formalism – for the last group).

Despite the fact that internal users got to the top-5 only in the Group #1 results, taking into account the specificity of our expert evaluation procedure (in which the share of experts' votes is three times larger than of the rest), the internal users still make it to the top-5 overall. But of course, the priority of external users is still obvious (this confirms our first hypothesis). This external priority makes the whole system of environmental accounting more formal and better regulated, more "obedient" to regulations, external requirements and regular audits.

On the basis of top-5 interest groups we then suggested to formulate the fundamental principles of environmental accounting implementation. For this, we got the following answers and recommendations, again divided by groups (Table 4).

As demonstrated in Table 4, Thai business considers least of all the responsibilities related to environmental accounting, while most of all sees it as yet another formality which potentially may limit

Table 3. Survey results: interest in environmental accounting by groups of potential stakeholders, %

Group 1 (Researchers)		Group 2 (Business Representatives)		Group 3 (Public Sector Representatives)	
Tax authorities	39	Tax authorities	49	Society	42
Society	21	Investors	19	Environmental protection authorities	24
Environmental protection authorities	20	Environmental protection authorities	18	Tax authorities	18
Investors	14	Society	9	International organizations	10
Internal users, including stockholders	6	Creditors	5	Regulators of specific sectors (ministries, inspections etc.)	6

(Authors calculation and presentation)

Table 4. Survey results: fundamental principles and values of environmental accounting, in %

Group 1 (Researchers)		Group 2 (Business Representatives)		Group 3 (Public Sector Representatives)	
Double entry	34	Separate entity assumption	74	Formalization	64
Separate entity assumption	18	Financial indicators	9	Responsibility	16
Trustworthiness	16	Regularity	7	Double entry	8
Responsibility	11	Double entry	6	Standardization	7
Continuity	9	Trustworthiness	4	Financial indicators	5

(Calculated by author)

business operations. It is also obvious that representatives of business still do not see much of significant differences between traditional business accounting and environmental accounting (this is one of the reasons why double entry principles got such a low score in Group #2 votes).

Analyzing the today's state of environmental accounting in Thailand, we also need to mention that today a large share of companies and enterprises in the country are at the stage of capital accumulation. This means they would prioritize getting new competitive advantages, entry to new markets, going global etc., thus, all of them are orienting on rather short-term incomes and least of all are ready to pay attention to the environmental requirements and procedures (and this confirms our second hypothesis).

However, even under such unfavorable business conditions the state could be still able to use some factors which potentially may motivate local businesses environmentalize their productions. These may include legal limitations on the most environmentally damaging productions and also, indirectly, consumer load and consumer changing preferences (since it is already globally acknowledged that consumers would nearly always prefer "clean product).

Therefore, business success of any enterprise depends on its compliance with the environmental rules and regulations, and this, in turn, emphasizes the necessity for using the adequate managerial instruments, to which, inter alia, belongs managerial environmental accounting.

One of the central principles in accounting is the balance of the whole system, starting from the higher level of national accounts and to the level of a particular enterprise accounts. Therefore, before defining the key principles of environmental accounting we need to determine what environmental balance is essentially, for the economy and society, and how it would be possible to track its changes/ maintenance/achievements.

In order to form the model of optimal/balanced development for an economic-environmental system we first need to study the structure of this system and its major tangible and intangible flows which are emerging once this system starts its functioning and which are at the same time the result of two sybsystems' interaction – economic and environmental ones. At this, the key indicator must be always the quality of the environment. This indicator shows the level of anthropological load on the environment and at the same time it can serve as some sort of feedback channel since it is always used within the system of environmental planning. From the standpoint of accounting, quality of the environment as the indicator of economic-environmental system shows how new type of costs are being formed – additional costs caused by emissions and other pollution factors.

Therefore, thorouth and detailed enough analysis of socioeconomic and natural processes' interaction can serve as the basis for further research on what are the optimal preconditions for the formation of well balanced economic-environmental system. This also assumes there must be such an economic model which allows minimizing the overall costs of separate economic subjects and of the society as a whole spent on production and environmental activities.

At this, every nature-exploiting production unit must participate not only in the production of tangible values but at the same time – in reproduction of natural values (restoring disturbed lands, deforested areas, polluted water basins etc.).

On the basis of the suggested here concept we see it as being possible to introduce the ecobalance notion into the system of national accounts.

Throughout the course of our research we preferred to keep open the question regarding what is environmental balance. This allowed us obtain the following results (only the most popular answers are presented in the table below):

Table 5. Survey results: Definitions of "environmental balance", in %

	Definitions	Group #1	Group #2	Group #3
1	The state of equilibrium between the used natural resources and those being restored	48	39	41
2	Such a state of the system at which it does not need attracting additional resources so that to compensate for the lack of some/any of them	12	28	21
3	The harmony between the spacial and biological structure	10	13	11
4	Ecologically sustainable chain of production processes which is supposed to function in a well-orchestrated manner and be zero damage to the environment at the same time	9	9	6
	Various other replies	21	11	21

(Calculated by author)

Taking into account both our survey results and also the latest theoretical achievements, we can introduce into further scientific use and circulation our own definition of environmental balance. We see it as the category which describes the ability to display the system of environmental activities of an enterprise in environmental accounting (thus, our third hypothesis is rejected). Environmental balance, in this case, is the balanced conditions of an environmental system which serve better utilization and restoration of natural resources as recorded in business accounts. At the same time, we need to keep in mind that disrupting the environmental balance could lead to irreversible climatic changes and not only on the local level, but for the whole planet.

One of the key tasks during the transition to better balance economic & social development is to evaluate the correlation between economic activities and the natural environment. At this, we need to keep in mind that the latter is always one of the key factors in economic growth and at the same time it also tends to hinder this economic growth. Therefore, achieving and maintaining the dynamic balance between natural and social environments is of vital importance. In general, formation of the very concept of balanced development should be based on environmental limitations which are related to the limitedness of natural resources, slowing down reproduction of renewable resources, rather limited capacities of the environment assimilation. In this regard, we had a special, rather real-life question in our survey which concerned the major obstacles and problems on the way of environmental accounting implementation in Thailand (this was a closed question, however, with an additional option to provide a comment). We got the following answers (Table 6).

From Table 6 it is rather obvious that the most serious obstacle in the course of environmental accounting development and actual implementation is, first of all, lack of exact monetary/financial equivalent for natural assets. Thus, assets which do not have any money equivalent cannot become an accounting object. For the same reasons, raw materials and other similar items being supplied to an enterprise are recorded in accounting documents, while all other components of the surrounding environment (for example, air, waste heat etc.) are not present in accounting records, first of all, because as of today they can be measured in natural units only. And to the best of our knowledge, as of today there is no feasible enough methodology or method to "translate" these indicators from natural units into some sort of universal money/financial terms.

Another reason why these indicators are still not included into accounting documents concerns, in our opinion, the commonly popular statement that a resource can be called an asset if it is under enterprise control (normally, this would mean the enterprise has some sort of property rights for this resource).

Table 6. Survey results: Problems and obstacles to environmental accounting implementation in Thailand, in %

Group #1 (Researchers)	Group #2 (Business Representatives)	Group #3 (Public Sector Representatives)
Measuring environmental issues in monetary terms	Any natural resource is not a full-scale asset in relation to a particular enterprise (e.g., the latter has no property rights for it)	Gaps in legislation and regulation
Any natural resource is not a full-scale asset in relation to a particular enterprise (e.g., the latter has no property rights for it)	Gaps in legislation and regulation	Lack of methodologies for calculations
Lack of practical skills on double entry in environmental accounting	Lack of practical skills on double entry in environmental accounting	Any natural resource is not a full-scale asset in relation to a particular enterprise (e.g., the latter has no property rights for it)
Lack of methodologies for calculations	Lack of methodologies for calculations	Lack of practical skills on double entry in environmental accounting
Gaps in legislation and regulation	Lack of international experience which, speaking theoretically, could have been borrowed and/or copied	Lack of international experience which, speaking theoretically, could have been borrowed and/or copied

(Calculated by author)

This, however, does not automatically mean that all enterprises need to reject the very idea of trying to calculate and measure the environmental aspects of their performance. Lack of such accounting and control at contemporary enterprises leads to uncontrolled pollution of the environment (including soil, air, nearby waters and also presence of wastes which are impossible or hard to utilize). Personal awareness could have been helpful in this regard, but unfortunately, the level of environmental awareness among both producers and consumers is still at very low level, thus, neither manufacturing, nor consumption patterns in Thailand today can be called truly environmentally friendly. Moreover, even provided the local community has enough awareness to raise questions concerning the impact of local producers on the environment – there is technically no capacity to provide/obtain such information on local enterprises and their practices.

In this research we have managed to determine and present the most pressing issues related to the environmental accounting implementation, however, our results only re-emphasize the importance and topicality of the more general problem. Obviously, today it is too early to suggest introduction of a separate type of accounting (which, speaking theoretically, could have been based on the natural assessment of assets, or on the presumption of natural asset owner), but it is already quite possible to appeal for at least partial "environmentalization" of traditional business accounting (thus, one more of our initial hypotheses is confirmed).

Expanding the borders of traditional environmental accounting provides the enterprises with more opportunities for more detailed and more objective accounting of various spheres and activities, in particular, taking into account the degree of enterprise's impact on the environment. This, in turn, would allow timely detection of all risks related to excessive anthropogenic load on the environment and thus would also allow timely prevention measures, thus shaping the environmental nature of all further development of this enterprise.

Environmental accounting must also cover those activities, methods, systems and financial operations which are initially predetermined by the environment as well as all environmental impacts of all structural business units inside the enterprise.

Traditional business accounting, but environmentally predetermined, is presented graphically as a system in Table 7.

Environmentally differentiated financial accounting is supposed to operate such categories as costs and incomes, on the same profit & loss accounts. It also uses the reports on financial results along with standard tax statements and the balance sheet of assets and liabilities.

To the environmentally predetermined costs belong, for example, the following: fines for illegal pollution/emission or costs spent on the improvement of the environment condition.

This system makes it possible to implement environmental accounting even within the already formed and functioning accounting system, without any radical changes in Thai legislation.

The next set of questions all three categories of our respondents answered looked more like a test, additionally there were also several open questions (with some space for further comments and expert opinions). These test tasks and questions concerned a rather specific topic of environmental accounting, namely, accounting in the process of quotas trade (under the Kyoto Protocol).

In the table further we present some of the most important questions using which we have tried to collect the expert opinions, along with the variants of answers and their popularity in three expert groups.

On the basis of these answers' popularity we have tested further the hypotheses and therefore, were able to formulate our own conclusions and original recommendations concerning the system of environmental accounting which could be designed specifically for Thai enterprises.

It is quite obvious from the table above that there is no unanimity among the expert groups and inside them concerning the potential use of international financial reporting standards in environmental ac-

Table 7. The system of environmentally differentiated traditional business accounting

Environmentally Differentiated Traditional Business Accounting	
Financial actions predetermined by the environment and/or environmental impacts of the enterprise	
Environmentally differentiated financial accounting	Environmentally differentiated managerial accounting

(Made by co-authors)

Table 8. Survey results: National (Thai) accounting standards as per Kyoto Protocol quotas' trade, answers in %

<table>
<tr><th colspan="2" rowspan="2">As of today IFRS does not consider at all such a complex issue as CER – accounting of certified emission reductions. In your opinion, which of the already available international standards can form a logical and feasible basis for a national (Thai) accounting system for emission quotas trade?</th><th colspan="2">Researchers</th><th colspan="2">Business</th><th colspan="2">State</th><th colspan="2">Total</th></tr>
<tr><th>NQ[2]</th><th>Q[3]</th><th>NQ</th><th>Q</th><th>NQ</th><th>Q</th><th>NQ</th><th>Q</th></tr>
<tr><td>1</td><td>(IAS) 20 Accounting for Goverments Grants and Disclosure of Goverment Assistance</td><td>0,36</td><td>0,41</td><td>0,24</td><td>0,49</td><td>0,24</td><td>0,29</td><td>0,28</td><td>0,39</td></tr>
<tr><td>2</td><td>(IAS) 23 Borrowing Costs</td><td>0,22</td><td>0,19</td><td>0,21</td><td>0,21</td><td>0,39</td><td>0,44</td><td>0,27</td><td>0,28</td></tr>
<tr><td>3</td><td>(IAS) 27 Separate Financial Statements</td><td>0,19</td><td>0,16</td><td>0,29</td><td>0,19</td><td>0,19</td><td>0,23</td><td>0,22</td><td>0,19</td></tr>
<tr><td>4</td><td>(IFRIC) 1 Changes in Existing Decommissioning, Restoration and Similar Liabilities</td><td>0,14</td><td>0,13</td><td>0,14</td><td>0,09</td><td>0,08</td><td>0,04</td><td>0,12</td><td>0,08</td></tr>
<tr><td>5</td><td>(IFRIC) 10 Interim Financial Reporting and Impairment</td><td>0,09</td><td>0,11</td><td>0,12</td><td>0,02</td><td>0,1</td><td>0</td><td>0,1</td><td>0,04</td></tr>
</table>

(Calculated by the authors)

Table 9. Survey results: quantitative and cost measurements of eco-related information in enterprise accounting, answers in %

	Information concerning the environment-related activities of an economic subject must be present in accounting documents and other reports in both volume/quantitative and financial measurements	Researchers		Business		Public Sector		Total	
		NQ	Q	NQ	Q	NQ	Q	NQ	Q
1	Yes, this is mandatory	0,69	0,98	0,21	0,37	0,49	0,74	0,46	0,69
2	No, financial measurement only is sufficient enough	0,31	0,02	0,79	0,63	0,51	0,26	0,53	0,3

(Calculated by author)

counting. However, we need to note here that actual, real decision-making in this regard must take into account the opinions of, first of all, those who already has previous experience in this field.

Also obvious is that the majority of experts express their preference of (IAS) 20 Accounting for Goverments Grants and Disclosure of Goverment Assistance. This implies that this standard indeed can be used further as the fundamental one while developing the national (Thai) environmental accounting standard. At the same time the author's preliminary hypothesis concerning the perspective use of IAS 27 Separate Financial Statements have not found enough support among the expert community.

From the table above it is obvious that both groups – experts and non-qualified majority – have supported our initial hypothesis concerning the necessity to present environment-related information in all accounting documents and reports not only in its financial/cost-related form, but also as measured quantitatively, that is, in volumes etc. This is quite a logical and predictable choice considering all the problems accompanying the implementation of the environmental accounting system and the specificity of environmental assets as such.

As for the key factors in monetization of the environmental factors in economic activities of enterprises, our respondents mentioned them in the following order: payable character of the natural resource use; payments for pollution/emissions; the necessity to pay off debts and other environmental payments. However, this order of classification has become possible only due to expert assessments predominantly. Obviously, business representatives are more prone to payable green technologies (since, in their opinion, such technologies are some sort of investments in assets). But at the same time the representatives of the public sector were mostly choosing environmental expertize and audits as the key instruments of nature use monetization and as an integral part of environmental accounting implementation in Thailand. Therefore, our initial hypothesis concerning the top priority of green technologies in the process of nature use monetization must be rejected.

Taking into account separately the opinions of the most qualified majority proves our initial hypothesis that greenhouse emission quotas must be, most probably, treated as "intangible assets" of enterprises. Also noteworthy here is that representatives of the public sector emphasized attention mostly on payments to the budget, while business representatives were "voting" mostly for circulating assets. But at the same time, here we would have to agree with the qualified experts' opinion that accounting as intangible assets would be most appropriate here, since greenhouse emission quotas assigned to this particular account would mostly appropriately demonstrate the importance of this production factor. This variant would also provide opportunities for depreciation and also for taking into account this factor in the process of prime cost formation. And in case greenhouse emission quotas are assigned to any other account, this would be nearly impossible to do.

Table 10. Survey results: Payments for natural resource use, answers in %

	Payments for natural resource use should be separated from other types of payments within the accounting system for the following key reason:	Researchers		Business		Public Sector		Total	
		NQ	Q	NQ	Q	NQ	Q	NQ	Q
1	The use of natural resources should be prepaid as such	0,32	0,49	0,24	0,54	0,43	0,49	0,33	0,5
2	Enterpises should pay for the pollution of the natural environment	0,21	0,21	0,19	0,29	0,17	0,17	0,19	0,22
3	Enterprises need to determine in advance their costs assigned for environmental payments	0,17	0,18	0,14	0,09	0,13	0,19	0,14	0,15
4	All "green technologies" have their cost	0,09	0,09	0,16	0,04	0,17	0,09	0,14	0,07
5	Access for Thai enterprises to the market of emission quotas has a certain price	0,12	0,02	0,13	0,03	0,07	0,05	0,16	0,02
6	All environmental expert assessments, audits etc. are always available at a certain fee	0,09	0,02	0,14	0,01	0,03	0,01	0,08	0,01

(Calculated by author)

Table 11. Survey results: Accounting options for emission quotas, answers in %

	Accounting of greenhouse emission quotas which are actually state subsidies must be carried out as:	Researchers		Business		Public Sector		Total	
		NQ	Q	NQ	Q	NQ	Q	NQ	Q
1	"intangible assets"	0,69	0,79	0,29	0,39	0,1	0,59	0,36	0,59
2	"fixed assets"	0,14	0,09	0,13	0,14	0,02	0,12	0,09	0,11
3	"other liabilities"	0,09	0,04	0,05	0,1	0	0,15	0,04	0,09
4	"payments to the budget"	0,05	0,04	0,05	0,13	0,88	0,12	0,32	0,09
5	"circulating assets"	0,03	0,04	0,48	0,24	0	0,02	0,17	0,1

(Calculated by author)

In a rather similar way, the experts have supported our initial hypothesis concerning the possibilities of greenhouse emission quotas' depreciation, just as in the case with any other intangible asset in real business practice. Taking into account the opinions of qualified experts in the field has also allowed determining the prospects of using the account "Settlements on greenhouse emission quotas" with their subsequent detalization and opening subaccounts for various types of emissions. This can be a nominal account so that to demonstrate better the circulation of enterprise's assets spent on the purchase of quota and its further use. However, our hypothesis concerning the possibility of opening the account called

Table 12. Survey results: Managing the CER, answers in %

	The initial cost of CER may change due to depreciation. In case the related market is active enough, the cost of CET must be settled as:	Researchers		Business		Public Sector		Total	
		NQ	Q	NQ	Q	NQ	Q	NQ	Q
1	Through calculation of depreciation	0,74	0,89	0,59	0,75	0,36	0,64	0,56	0,76
2	Through gradual writing down of an assets	0,12	0,01	0,09	0,09	0,14	0,18	0,11	0,093
3	Through discounting	0,06	0,06	0,12	0,07	0,26	0,12	0,14	0,08
4	Through quota's market price adjustment	0,08	0,04	0,2	0,09	0,24	0,06	0,17	0,06

(Calculated by author)

Table 13. Survey results: forms of quotas trade, answers in %

	Which form of internal trade in quotas would be most appropriate for Thailand?	Researchers		Business		Public Sector		Total	
		NQ	Q	NQ	Q	NQ	Q	NQ	Q
1	Administered permissions (assumes the establishment of a special public body to distribute these quotas between the owners of industrial pollution venues; further, this body is supposed to sanction every deal in this quotas' trade between all interested private subjects)	0,72	0,79	0,81	0,84	0,87	0,91	0,8	0,84
2	Market form	0,28	0,21	0,2	0,09	0,13	0,09	0,23	0,13

(Calculated by author)

"Environmental costs/expenditures of the enterprise" have not found enough support among the experts in the sample.

Finally, full unanimity has been demonstrated by the representatives of business, public sector and science in relation to potential forms of quotas' trade: the absolute majority in all three groups thinks that the administered model would be much more feasible and efficient (rather than market-based one) when it comes to distribution and further trade in quotas for greenhouse emissions. This confirms our initial hypothesis.

On the basis of the obtained results we are now ready to provide our conclusions along with some recommendations, of both theoretical and applied nature.

CONCLUSION AND RECOMMENDATIONS

According to the most recent version of the Kyoto Protocal requirements Thailand today needs to establish (and in the shortest time possible) an efficient national system for greenhouse emissions' trade. This system would enable the country to fulfill all its obligations under the Kyoto Protocal, actively participating in internal trade in quotas and spending the minimum on it at the same time.

At the same time, the International Financial Reporting Standards still do not cover such a complex issue as CER – Certified Emission Reduction, even though today the meaning and the potential value of these certificates cannot be overestimated. More and more companies, especially those from the countries with the so-called catching-up economic development, own such certificates and engage in trading them, in full accordance with the CDM (Clean Development Mechanism) under the Kyoto Protocol.

Therefore, we can state that this Protocol as such is forming the new fundamental economic mechanisms for further international cooperation in the field. And these mechanisms are actually based on the idea that all human-related climatic effects and changes do not depend on a place of already happened emission. This, in turn, predetermines the so-called "flexibility mechanisms" of the Kyoto Protocol. Flexibility in this particular context should be understood as follows: for all further global environmental effects it is not that important what was the initial place of emission and what actions specifically have been taken to reduce the volume of these greenhouse emissions into the atmosphere.

CER represent the units of decreased greenhouse emissions, produced and certified by the UN in full accordance with the CDM descriptions under the Kyoto Protocol. Accounting of CER is actually quite possible to perform using the IAS 20 "Government grants and Disclosure of Government Assistance".

However, to use it, the management of an enterprise has to prove that their CER has been indeed provided by the state authorities.

As of today the system of environmental accounting is itself an object of state regulation, and this finds its manifestation, inter alia, in some of special measures taken both at the international scale and also on the level of separate countries, including Thailand. Thus, at the state level there is a pressing need for thorough analysis of opportunities and prospects for state regulation measures' implementation in the field of environmental accounting so that those would be in full compliance with the Kyoto Protocol requirements.

Environmental accounting is only a segment within a more general system of accounting, while the latter is supposed to serve all levels of management and control over the economic and environmental processes at economic objects.

In our opinion, all information about the environment-related activities of a managing subject must be disclosed in accounting and reporting of an enterprise, moreover, it must be disclosed in both cost as well as quantitative/volume measures.

Additionally we need to mention that timely and trustworthy accounting of environmental liabilities of an enterprise concerning its greenhouse emissions is an integral part and a vital precondition for radical changes in managerial priorities and all further managerial decision-making concerning environment-related issues.

Therefore, environmental account must cover information on both money and tangible flows, since both of them, in their tight interrelation, describe how economy and the environment are actually co-existing today.

This, in turn, means that performing the environmental accounting should be always dynamic and flexible to the maximum, so that to comply with also quite dynamic environmental component in the economic activity of enterprises.

In our view, the model of the overall accounting process in environmental accounting must be adequate to the current model of general business accounting for enterprises. But at the same time, it must have its own preferences in methods and instruments for presentation of environment-related accounting information.

Such type of model would help fulfill all necessary environmental requirements and therefore would increase the quality of the overall accounting system, thus also promoting its manageability.

As we see it now, introducing and conducting environmental accounting must be based on the same methodological principles with traditional accounting, that is, it must comply with all other regulations and legal acts applicable to accounting today in Thailand. It is also must be fully compatable with the general methodological principles of accounting as such (see above – Table 3).

Compliance with all these principles above would allow much more rational organization of information processing concerning enterprise's environmental liabilities in relation to greenhouse emissions' reduction. For this, an enterprise is supposed to have a special environmental fund for further investments in own fixed assets, more specifically – in nanotechnologies (for example) or other high efficient environment-related innovations, tools and measures.

Managing a separate account for nature resource use within the general system of accounting can and should be explained by the payable character of natural resources in general. All enterprises should be prepared in advance to pay for the use of all natural resources as well as for polluting the natural environment. Moreover, all enterprises must be ready to calculate these costs in such a way so that not to have environmental debts.

Table 14. Fundamental methodological principles of environmental accounting

Principle	Its Explanation
The regulatory balance generalization	There must be a conceptual model of automated processing of accounting data
Data integration in first-entry accounting	Data from all types of accounting must be integrated
Interconnecting all registers and stages in the accounting process	There must be one common scheme for both input and output indicators which is basically the information process in accounting as such
Automated formation of registers	All data obtained from first-entry accounting must be integrated using all possible means of technical, software and also mathematical support
Saving the double entry principle	All previous document workflow ways remain the same
Expanding the analytical & control functions	The model of the environmental accounting system must display the order of presentation and further interpretation of all synthetic and analytical environmental accounts
Wider possibilities for development	The system must have an option to expand and diversify its basic functions

(Calculated by author)

In case Thailand indeed opens a market for emission quotas' trade, their sales and purchases should be carried out through the national stock markets or this can be done directly from the enterprises which have managed to save their own quotas.

A certificate for emissions must comply with all requirements put forward to all other intangible assets. At the same time and additionally to that, the certificates for greenhouse emissions must comply with the following criteria: strict determination; control over resourses; explicit future economic benefit.

CER should be used in such situations: when there is high probability that the enterprise would be able to fulfill the requirements under CER; when there are guarantees that subsidies/state grants would be really obtained; when the cost of CER is sufficiently high so that the enterprise would get future economic benefits in any case – applying CER or selling it. At the same time, we need to keep in mind that CER are often taken into account only after the "production" of emission or even at much later stages.

The IAS 20 "Accounting for Government Grants and Disclosure of Government Assistance" assumes there are two variants of initial recognition:

By the nominal amount: production costs should be proportionally and consequently assigned to costs of "green product" manufacturing and/or, in applicable, to the cost of CER too;

Using the notion of fair value. In this case, CER should be treated by its fair value, while state grant should be accounted by a difference between nominal amount and this fair value.

If CER does not comply with the definition of "non-current assets held for sale", it should be disclosed by its cost exclusive of depreciation and/or impairment in case the related market is inactive. Increasing or decreasing balance cost of CER must be disclosed in accordance to the requirements provided in IAS 38.85 and 38.86.

In case an enterprise is getting its quota for greenhouse emissions as a state grant, its accounting should belong to the "intangible assets" account, according to IAS 38 (see Table 15 for more details).

Further on, the initial cost of CER may change, mostly due to the depreciation factor. If the related market is active enough, the cost of CER would be fully depreciated in the due term and this would be recorded accordingly on the credit side of the account"Depreciation of intangible assets", with further details recorded on the expenses account.

CER should be actually tested for impairment according the requirements described in IAS 36. If CER falls under IAS 5, then depreciation is not calculated for it. All valuations in this regard are supposed to be carried according to IAS 5.

When subsidy/grant is valuated by its nominal cost, the income cannot be account prior to the date of the factual sale of CER. And if subsidy/grant is accounted by the principle of fair value – it is disclosed as Other incomes, on the date when this subsidy/grant is accepted. Consequently, there is a certain time gap in the accounting of income, if CER is disclosed by its nominal value or by its fair value, according to IAS 20.

For the accounting of greenhouse emission quotas' circulation (their receipt, movement, trade due to savings etc.) we suggest here for all involved in this field economic subjects to introduce the account "Settlement on greenhouse emission quotas", with further itemization and opening of subaccounts for six types of emissions, all separately:

- Quota for carbon dioxide emissions;
- Quota for methane emissions;
- Quota for methane oxide emissions;
- Quota for hydrofluorocarbon emissions;
- Quota for perfluocarbon emissions;
- Quota for sulfur hexafluoride emissions.

Key accounting procedures related to getting, using and selling quotas for greenhouse emissions would allow presenting in the greatest detail the movement of funds and assets on the accounts, and this is part of the overall control over enterprise's expenses.

Initially, CER is disclosed in the records on incomes and expenses as "Other income", and on the date of disposal CER sale is also allocated to "Other income".

Within the today's systems of greenhouse emissions trade enterprises also often use the mechanisms of quotas' banking an quotas' loaning. Both of these mechanisms enable using quotas from various budget periods and this increases the overall flexibility of these trade systems.

In our opinion, the system of greenhouse emission quotas' distribution must be transparent to the very maximum, and the results of its performance must be in a timely manner published in open sources, established in advance.

Internal trade in quotas may be organized using one of the models – administered permissions or a market-based model. The former assumes there must be created a special public body, responsible for distributing quotas between the owners of pollution sources of various capacities. And later, the same public body is supposed to sanction each deal involving these quotas' exchange between private entities. The presence of such a public body would allow performing strict legal control over this trade in quotas, on both national and international levels.

In our opinion, the key distinctive feature of environmental accounting is its close correlation between the general financial reporting of an enterprise, but at the same time environmental accounting must be much easier, more readily understandable for a wide range of potential users.

Inclusion of controlled environmental indicators into the general financial reporting of enterprises would promote the creation of the enterprises' database which further can be used for detection, detailed description, fair and realistic assessment of direct and indirect effects all enterprises, included into this database, have on the environment.

Table 15. Accounting of operations related to getting a greenhouse emission quota

#	Operations in Their Rrder	Debit Side of the Account	Credit Side of the Account
	Getting greenhouse emission quota as a state grant or a subsidy		
1.	Getting the quota as a state grant	Investments in non-current assets	Special purpose financing
2.	The certificate for greenhouse emission is entered into the books by its initial value	Intangible assets, subaccount "Quota for emissions"	Investments in non-current assets
3.	Depreciation calculations using the method of writing-off the cost proportionally to the volumes of production (and accordingly, emissions too)	Recurring operaitons	Depreciation of intangible assets
4.	The total of quota is disclosed as deferred income (simultaneously with #3)	Settlements on greenhouse emission quotas	Deferred income
	Accounting of greenhouse emission sale to a third party (Enterpises have the right to choose one of the variants below):		
	Variant 1		
5.	Disclosing the income from quota sale	Settlements with creditors and debtors	Other income
6.	Writing the quota off at sale	Deferred income	Settlements on quotas for greenhouse emissions
	Variant 2		
7.	The quota is sold to a third party using the established saving scheme	Settlements with various debtors and creditors	Settlements on quotas for greenhouse emissions
8.	Financial result obtained from the saving on the quota is determined	Deferred income	Other income
	Purchasing a quota from a different enterprise or a different state		
9.	Booking the greenhouse emission quota obtained as a state grant or state subsidy	Investments in non-current assets	Special purpose financing
10.	The certificate for greenhouse emission is entered into the books by its initial value	Intangible assets; subaccount "Quota on greenhouse emissions"	Investments in noncurrent assets
11.	Depreciation accruals	Recurring operations	Depreciation of intangible assets
12.	A quota is purchased from a third party due to insufficient volume of own quota	Settlements on greenhouse emission quotas	Settlements with various debtors and creditors
13.	Writing the missing quota off to Other expenses	Other expenses	Settlements on greenhouse emission quotas

(Made by the author)

Environmental reporting is a relative new phenomenon in the field of rational nature use management & organization, it is even newer for the IT scope of enterprises' activities. However, environmental reporting today tends to become rather quickly one of the major channels through which an enterprise is able to present its business and environmental standing and vision as well as to explain its goals, mission and practices in the field of rational nature management. And what is important here, all this information should be easily accessible to all current and potential stakeholders.

Already today, the situation with information accessibility and trustworthiness is like this: if accounting and reporting does not contain detailed enough information on enterprise's environment-related liabilities and activities already undertaken – most of potential investors and/or creditors (especially foreign ones) would have partial distrust to these financial reports as such. Moreover, if investors have information (from other, external sources, for example) that a given enterprise indeed has environment-related liabilities but chooses not to disclose them or does not indicate those liabilities in its financial statements – there is a high probability that the investor/creditor would increase the interest rate due to high risks and less trust to business owners. This is yet another proof that all environment-related information on enterprise activities must be present in its reporting and statement, and it must be presented in the most transparent and obvious way.

Presence of such information in enterprise's documents also has its useful internal functions. For example, disclosing environment-related information in the annual accounting report can help top managers assess more fairly and objectively the performance of middle management. Disclosure of such information also helps establish better contact with the local community and promotes better image formation, among potential business contacts and in the society in general.

In addition to everything above, reporting with the emphasis on the environment also has the following useful features:

- Environmental spending should be singled out from the total expenses of an enterprise. And if disclosure of this type of expenses is standardized – this would allow a wide circle of its potential users compare the information on environmental-economic state of various enterprises (within the same area, for example, or within the same sector, within several linked together branches etc.);
- Environmental accounting is able to provide the evaluation of the overall volume of environmental damage caused by a particular enterprise (this damage is comprised of payments for emissions plus the total volume of environmental credit indebtedness);
- Environmental accounting is an integral part of operational control over all environment-related activities of enterprises, since it already contains all necessary information on the financial side of environment-related activities, and;

Table 16. Aggregated environmental balance of company A

Assets	Total	Liabilities	Total
Intangible assets in their original cost (quota on greenhouse emissions)	1000	Resource capital	1000
Depreciation of intangible assets	200	Losses from the impairment of intangible assets	200
Sale of saved units in emissions' total volume	125	Expenses of emissions' reduction (as losses)	50
		Financial profit	75
Assets, total	1325	Liabilities, total	1325

(Made by the author)

Table 17. Report on incomes and losses of Company A

Article	Amount
Income from the sale of saved emission volumes	125
Expenses on the reduction of greenhouse emissions	50
Financial profit (income)	75

(Made by the author)

- Environmental accounting promotes better decision-making since it operates the data adjusted to all environmental factors.

As of today there is no truly efficient standard in Thailand that would regulate the accounting of environmental spending and rational nature use and/or their disclosure in accounting. One of the major reasons for such a gap in Thai accounting regulations is the lack of actual demand for such a standard, there is very little understanding and awareness of such issues in the country. Besides, there is hardly any suitable best practice globally which could have been used as a benchmark in this regard. On the top of that, another reason is that reforms in Thai system of accounting are going much slower than it was supposed to be and thus, there is a certain lagging behind all other important economic changes in the country.

In order to boost foreign investments and solve all problems related to the investment processes inside the country, thorough research of the accounting balance structure, of debit and credit debts would be always of primary importance. In parallel to that, special attention is also dedicated to the environmental indicators of enterprises. Therefore, if an enterprise is able to disclose its environmental liabilities etc. in its accounting balance – the potential investor would get the most detailed economic & environmental information concerning enterprise performance. And this, in turn, may contribute to trust and thus promote positive investment decision-making.

Today reporting of all Thai enterprises and organizations covers very limited amount of information concerning the environments – only some stastistical reports. In the light of all recent international decisions related to the Kyoto Protocol, it is quite obvious that it is necessary to develop new forms of reporting which would help collect, compile and record all necessary details related to greenhouse emissions in the country.

One of the ways to disclose the inflow of state subsidy/grant related to greenhouse emission quota in the financial reporting of an enterprise as well as its further income from the reduction of these emissions is presented Table 16 in the form of an aggregated environmental balance, and further Table 17 shows how to disclose the related profits and expenses, on the example of an abstract company A.

Actual practical use of the methods and algorithms suggested here in the environmental reporting of enterprises would enable carrying out further environmental analysis or even environmental audit so to evaluate and compare the real performance indicators of enterprises and thus manage them better in the future.

The formulated here theoretical conclusions and applied propositions are able to promote better, more efficient and more feasible decision-making in the field of accounting and audit, with a special emphasis on achieving the environmental balance at the level of separate enterprises and at the overall national level as well.

REFERENCES

Allowance Trading. (n.d.). U.S Environment Protection Agency.

Boghean, F. (2007). Environment Accounting For Sustainable Development. *Theoretical and Applied Economics*, *6*(511), 257-264.

Cap and Trade: Key Terms Glossary. (2011). Climate Change 101. Center for Climate and Energy Solutions.

Deaconu, A., & Buiga, A. (2011). Accounting and the Environmental Factors - an Empirical Investigation in Post-Communist Romania. *Journal of Accounting and Management Information Systems*, *10*(2), 135–168.

Environmental Performance Index Reveals Dire State of Fisheries, Worsening Air Pollution. (n.d.). Retrieved from http://environment.yale.edu/news/article/2016-yale-environmental-performance-index-released/

Environmental Protection Agency. (1995). *An introduction to environmental accounting as a business management tool: Key concepts and terms*. US Environmental Protection Agency.

Global Assessment of Environment Statistics and Environmental-Economic Accounting. (2007). United Nations.

Handbook of National Accounting: Integrated Environmental and Economic Accounting. (2003). United Nations, European Commission, International Monetary Fund, Organization for Economic Co-operation and Development and World Bank.

Idowu, S. O., & Filho, L. W. (Eds.). (2009). *Professionals' Perspectives of Corporate Social Responsibiliry*. Springer-Verlag Berlin Heidelberg; doi:10.1007/978-3-642-02630-0_2

Illge, L., & Schwarze, R. (2009). *A Matter of Opinion: How Ecological and Neoclassical Environmental Economists Think about Sustainability and Economics. DIW Discussion Papers, #619*. DIW Berlin.

Jasch, C. (2006). How to perform an environmental management cost assessment in one day. *Journal of Cleaner Production*, *14*(14), 1194–1213. doi:10.1016/j.jclepro.2005.08.005

Johnson, D. L., Ambrose, S. H., Bassett, T. J., Bowen, M. L., Crummey, D. E., Isaacson, J. S., ... Winter-Nelson, A. E. (1997). Meanings of Environmental Terms. *Journal of Environmental Quality*, *26*(3), 581–589. doi:10.2134/jeq1997.00472425002600030002x

Kaneda, I. (2001). Conceptual Issues Including Environmental, Natural Resources, And Ecological Accounting. Encyclopedia of Life Support Systems.

Kouřilová, J. (2003). Agro environment and accounting. *Acta Universitatis Bohemiae Meridionales*, *6*(1), 37–40.

Maria Tilea, D. (2016). Environmental Accounting - Essential Tool for Decision Making. *Knowledge Horizons - Economics, 8*(1), 154-156.

Netherlands Environmental Assessment Agency. (n.d.). *The Emissions Database for Global Atmospheric Research (EDGAR): CO2 emissions (kt)*. Author.

Schaltegger, S., & Burritt, R. (2000). *Contemporary Environmental Accounting: Issues, Concepts and Practice*. Sheffield, UK: Greenleaf Publishing.

Sendroiu, C., & Roman, A. (2007). The Environmental Accounting: an Instrument for Promoting the Environmental Management. Theoretical and Applied Economics. *Asociatia Generala a Economistilor din Romania,* 8(513), 45-48.

Social and Ecological Accounting Matrix: an Empirical Study for China. (2000). Xiaoming PAN Institute of Systems Science Chinese Academy of Sciences.

Stanciu, I. C. (2011). Accounting Policies Regarding Environmental Costs. *Ovidius University Annals. Economic Sciences Series. XI, 1*(May), 1986–1991.

Status of ratification. (n.d.). UNFCC.

Stavins, R. N. (2001). *Experience with Market-Based Environmental Policy Instruments*. Discussion Paper 01-58. Washington, DC: Resources for the Future.

Tamborra, M., & Pavan, M. (2005). Environmental Expenditures. In *Green Accounting in Europe*. Edward Elgar Publishing. doi:10.4337/9781845428136.00021

Tanc, A. & Gokoglan, K. (2015). The Impact of Environmental Accounting on Strategic Management Accounting: A Research on Manufacturing Companies. *International Journal of Economics and Financial Issues, 5*(2), 566-573.

Tax Treaty Issues Related to Emissions Permits/Credits. (n.d.). OECD.

Teeter, P., & Sandberg, J. (2016). Constraining or Enabling Green Capability Development? How Policy Uncertainty Affects Organizational Responses to Flexible Environmental Regulations. *British Journal of Management*. doi:10.1111/1467-8551.12188

Thompson, D. (2010). *The Power of Prices and the Failure of Markets. The Edmonton Sustainability Papers*. City of Edmonton.

Tilt, C. A. (2007). Corporate Responsibility, Accounting and Accountants. In Professionals' Perspective of CSR: An Introduction (pp. 11-32). Springer Berlin Heidelberg.

van den Bergh, J. C. J. M. (2001). Ecological Economics: Themes, Approaches, and Differences with Environmental Economics. *Regional Environmental Change, 2*(1), 13–23. doi:10.1007101130000020

Zefinescu, C. (2015, July). Green Costs in the Context Of Sustainable Development Trends. Constatin Brancusi University of Targu Jiu Annals - Economy Series, 118-122.

ENDNOTES

1. Delivered by the students of the Faculty of Management, Suan Sunandha Rajabat University, Bangkok.
2. Non-qualified weight of answers in % (disregarding the professional expertize and experience).
3. Qualified weight of answers in % (taking into account the experts' opinion).

Compilation of References

Abalkin, L. (2004). *The Fate of Russia: The Link Of Times*. Moscow: Institute of Economy RAS.

Acharya, S. (2015). Trade Liberalization. In Palgrave Dictionary of Emerging Markets and Transition Economics. New York: Palgrave Macmillan. doi:10.1007/978-1-137-37138-6_21

Adžić, S. (2008). *Economic System and Economic Policy*. Subotica.

Adžić, S. (2011). *Regional Economics of the EU*. Subotica.

Aguiar, S., Aguiar-Conraria, L., Gulamhussen, M. A., & Magalhaes, P. C. (2012). Foreign Direct İnvestment And Home-Country Political Risk: The Case of Brazil. *Latin American Research Review*, *47*(2), 144–165. doi:10.1353/lar.2012.0013

Alfaro, L., Chanda, A., Kalemli-Ozcan, S., & Sayek, S. (2004). FDI and Economic Growth: The Role Of Local Financial Markets. *Journal of International Economics*, *64*(1), 89–112. doi:10.1016/S0022-1996(03)00081-3

Algin, A. P. (1991). *The borders of economic risk*. Moscow: Knowledge.

Aliev, A.A. (2016). Methodological approach to assessing financial potential of innovation development using the example of the Socar oil and gas company. *Economic Analysis: Theory and Practice* (7), 153-161.

Al-Khouri, R., & Abdul Khalik, U. (2013). Does Political Risk Affect the Flow of Foreign Direct Investment into the Middle East North African Region. *Journal of Global Business and Technology*, *9*(2), 47–63.

Allowance Trading. (n.d.). U.S Environment Protection Agency.

Altshuler, R., & Goodspeed, T. J. (2015). Follow the leader? Evidence on European and US tax competition. *Public Finance Review*, *43*(4), 485–504. doi:10.1177/1091142114527781

Al-Yousif, Y. K. (2000). Do government expenditures inhibit or promote economic growth: Some empirical evidence from Saudi Arabia. *The Indian Economic Journal*, *48*(2), 92.

Amano, R. A., & Wirjanto, T. S. (1998). Government expenditures and the permanent-income model. *Review of Economic Dynamics*, *1*(3), 719–730.

Arsić, M., & Ranđelović, S. (2017). *Economics of Taxation - Theory and Politics*. Faculty of Economics in Belgrade.

Asiedu, E. (2006). Foreign Direct Investment in Africa: The Role of Natural Resources, Market Size, Government Policy, Institutions and Political Instability. *World Economy*, *29*(1), 63–77. doi:10.1111/j.1467-9701.2006.00758.x

Auerbach, A. J. (2006). Who bears the Corporate Tax? A Review of What We Know. *Tax Policy and the Economy*, *20*, 1–40. doi:10.1086/tpe.20.20061903

Avtonomov, V. C. (1993). Man at mirror of economic theory (Essay on the history of Western economic thought). *Science*.

Axelson, U., Strömberg, P., Jenkinson, T., & Weisbach, M. S. (2009). Leverage and Pricing in Buyouts: An Empirical Analysis. *Social Science Research Network.*

Baek, K., & Qian, X. (2011). An Analysis on Political Risks and the Flow of Foreign Direct Invesment in Developing and Industrialized Economies. *Economics. Management and Financial Markets*, *6*(4), 60–91.

Baestaens, D-E., Van Den Bergh, W., & Wood, D. (1997). *Neural Network: Solutions for Trading in Financial Markets*. Moscow, Russia: Scientific Publishing House TVP. (in Russian)

Balabanov, I. T. (1996). *Risk management*. Moscow: Finance and Prospects.

Balassa, B. (1978). Exports and economic growth: Further evidence. *Journal of Development Economics*, *5*(2), 181–189. doi:10.1016/0304-3878(78)90006-8

Balatskii, E. (2006). Tax reform and economic growth. *Studies on Russian Economic Development*, *17*(2), 204–208.

Banks, E. (2012). *Finance: the basics* (2nd ed.). New York: Routledge.

Barinov, A. E. (2001). Design and credit risks: The problem of their insurance. *Risk Management*, *4*, 19–22.

Barro, R. (1998). *Determinants of Economic Growth: A Cross-Country Empirical Study.* The MIT Press.

Barro, R. J. (1990). Government spending in a simple model of endogeneous growth. *Journal of Political Economy*, *98*(5, Part 2), S103–S125.

Bartik, T. J. (1995). *Economic development strategies* (Vol. 95-33). Upjohn Institute Working Papers. Retrieved from http://research.upjohn.org/up_workingpapers/33

Basten, C., & Koch, C. (2015). The causal effect of house prices on mortgage demand and mortgage supply: Evidence from Switzerland. *Journal of Housing Economics*, *30*, 1–22. doi:10.1016/j.jhe.2015.07.001

Bayraktutan, Y., & Tarı, Ö. M. (2016). Politik Riskler, İki Taraflı Yatırım Anlaşmaları ve Uyuşmazlıklar Bağlamında Doğrudan Yabancı Yatırımlar [Foreign Direct Investments at the Context of Political Risks, Bilateral Investment Agreements and Disputes]. *Uluslararası Ekonomik Araştırmalar Dergisi [International Journal of Economic Studies]*, *2*(4), 87–104.

Bazylevych, V. (2004). *Macroeconomics*. Znannya.

Beer, A., Haughton, G., & Maude, A. (2004). *Developing locally: An international comparison of local and regional economic development*. Bristol, UK: Policy Press.

Begović, B., & Mijatović, B. (2017). *Financial intermediation and economic growth*. Belgrade: CLDS.

Benáček, V., Lenihan, H., Andreosso-O'Callaghan, B., Michalíkov, E., & Kan, D. (2014). Political Risk, Institutions and Foreign Direct Investment: How Do They Relate in Various European Countries? *World Economy*, *37*(5), 625–653. doi:10.1111/twec.12112

Bernstein, S., Lerner, J., Sørensen, M., & Strömberg, P. (2010). Private equity and industry performance. *NBER.*

Bernstein, L. A. (1989). *Financial statement analysis: theory, application, and interpretation* (4th ed.). Irwin Publishing.

Bertonesh, M., & Nait, R. (2004). *Cash flow management*. St. Petersburg: Piter Publ.

Bhalla, B. 1983. How Corporations Should Weigh Up Country Risk. *Euromoney*, June, 66–72.

Birnleitner, H. (2014). Attractiveness of Countries for Foreign Direct Investments from the Macro-Economic Perspective. In *Proceedings of FIKUSZ´14, Symposium for Young Researchers* (pp. 29-40). Hungary: Óbuda University.

Bittner, M., Soroková, T., Csikósová, A., Čulková, K., & Marasová, D. (2015). Private equity within mining industry in Europe. *Naukovyi Visnyk Natsionalnoho Hirnychoho Universytetu*, *2*(146), 138–145.

Blaskowitz, O., & Herwartz, H. (2011). On economic evaluation of directional forecasts. *International Journal of Forecasting*, *27*(4), 1058–1065. doi:10.1016/j.ijforecast.2010.07.002

Bloom, N., Sadun, R., & Van Reenen, J. (2009). Do private equity owned firms have better management practices? *Centre for Economic Performance, London School of Economics and Political Science*.

Bloomberg. (n.d.). Europe. Retrieved from www.bloomberg.com/europe

Bocharov, V. V. (2008). *Corporate finance*. St. Petersburg: Piter Publ.

Bodie, Z., & Merton, R. (2007). *Finance*. Moscow: Williams Publ.

Boghean, F. (2007). Environment Accounting For Sustainable Development. *Theoretical and Applied Economics*, *6*(511), 257-264.

Borselli, F., Chiri, S., & Romagnano, E. (2012). Patterns of Reduced VAT Rates in the European Union. *International VAT Monitor*, *23*(1), 13–21.

Bradford, D. F., & Rosen, H. S. (1976). The Optimal Taxation of Commodities and Income. *The American Economic Review*, *66*(2), 94–101.

Brigham, E., & Ehrhardt, M. (2013). *Financial management: theory and practice*. South-Western Cengage Learning.

Bruchez, P. A., & Schaltegger, C. A. (2005). *International tax competition and trends in tax policy: Some implications for Switzerland*. Eidgenössische Finanzverwaltung.

Busse, M., & Hefeker, C. (2007). Political Risk, Institutions And Foreign Direct Investment. *European Journal of Political Economy*, *23*(2), 397–415. doi:10.1016/j.ejpoleco.2006.02.003

Cap and Trade: Key Terms Glossary. (2011). Climate Change 101. Center for Climate and Energy Solutions.

CASE. (2013). *Study to Quantify and Analyse the VAT Gap in the EU-27 Member States. Final Report* [Report for the European Commission]. Warsaw: Center for Social and Economic Research.

CASE. (2017). *Study and Reports on the VAT Gap in the EU-28 Member States: 2017 Final Report* [Report for the European Commission]. Warsaw: Center for Social and Economic Research.

Cetorelli, N., & Gamera, M. (2001). Banking market structure, financial dependence and growth: International evidence from industry data. *The Journal of Finance*, *56*(2), 617–648.

Chemla, G. (2005). The determinants of investment in private equity and venture capital: Evidence from American and Canadian pension funds. *Social Science Research Network*.

Clark, E., & Marois, B. (1996). Managing Risk. In *International Business: Techniques And Applications*. USA: Thomson Business Press.

Collins, R. A., & Green, R. D. (1982). Statistical methods for bankruptcy forecasting. *Journal of Economics and Business*, 32.

Cooray, A. (2009). Government Expenditure, Governance and Economic Growth. *Comparative Economic Studies*, *51*(3), 401–418. doi:10.1057/ces.2009.7

Corlett, W. J., & Hague, D. C. (1954). Complementarity and the Excess Burden of Taxation. *The Review of Economic Studies, 21*(1), 21–30. doi:10.2307/2296257

Crouch, K. (2016). *How to make capitalism acceptable to society*. Moscow: HSE.

Csikósová, A., Mihalčová, B., & Antošová, M. (2015). *International business*. Ostrava: VŠB Ostrava.

Čulková, K., Csikósová, A., & Janošková, M. (2015). Development of Risk Payment Index in Slovakia Comparing with Chosen EU Countries. *Polish Journal of Management Studies, 12*(1), 37–47.

Currie, D. M. (2011). *Country Analysis: Understanding Economic and Political Performance*. NY, USA: Routledge Taylor and Francis.

Cyrenov, A. R., Saktoev, V. E., & Cyrenova, E. D. (2005). *The mechanism of state impact on the formation of the institutional environment of the region's economy*. Ulan Ude: VSGTU Publ.

Danilova, E. P. (2010). *Investment behavior of business entities in terms of socio-economic changes (in Tyumen region)*. Tyumen: TSU Publishing House.

Dar, A., & Amirkhalkhali, S. (2017). Fiscal Policy, Total Factor Productivity and Economic Growth in Advanced Economies. *Applied Econometrics and International Development, 17*(2), 5–18.

Database NEWSru.com. (n.d.). Retrieved from http://www.newsru.com

Database Real Estate Market Indications. (n.d.). Retrieved from http://www.irn.ru

Daude, C., & Stein, E. (2007). The quality of institutions and foreign direct investment. *Economics and Politics, 19*(3), 317–345. doi:10.1111/j.1468-0343.2007.00318.x

Davoodi, H., & Zou, H. (1998). Fiscal decentralization and economic growth: a cross-country study. *Journal of Urban Economics, 43*(2), 244–257. doi:10.1006/juec.1997.2042

de Mooij, R. A. (2005). Will Corporate Income Taxation Survive? *De Economist, 153*(3), 277–301. doi:10.100710645-005-1989-5

Deaconu, A., & Buiga, A. (2011). Accounting and the Environmental Factors - an Empirical Investigation in Post-Communist Romania. *Journal of Accounting and Management Information Systems, 10*(2), 135–168.

Dedicated Public Private Partnership Units: A Survey of Institutional and Governance Structures. (2010). Paris: OECD.

Demirhan, E., & Masca, M. (2008). Determinants of foreign direct investment flows to developing countries: a cross-sectional analysis. *Prague Economic Papers, 4*(4), 356–369. doi:10.18267/j.pep.337

Devarajan, S., Swaroop, V., & Zou, H. F. (1996). The composition of public expenditure and economic growth. *Journal of Monetary Economics, 37*(2), 313–344.

Dobrolezha, E. V. (2007). *Factors, conditions, models for the development of the region's economy: the theoretical and applied aspect*. Rostov-on-Don.

Doerrenberg, P. & Peichl, A. (2013). Progressive taxation and tax morale. *Public Choice, 155*(3), 293–316.

Doing Business. (2017). Doing business 2017. Retrieved from http://www.doingbusiness.org/reports/global-reports/doing-business-2017

Dornbusch, R., & Fischer, S. (1986). The open economy: implications for monetary and fiscal policy. In *The American business cycle: Continuity and change* (pp. 459–516). University of Chicago Press.

Dorożyński, T., & Kuna-Marszałek, A. (2016). Attracting FDI to the new EU Member States. In P. Trąpczyński, Ł. Puślecki, & M. Jarosiński (Eds.), *Competitiveness of CEE Economies and Business: Multidisciplinary Perspectives and Challenges and Opportunities* (pp. 65–87). Cham: Springer. doi:10.1007/978-3-319-39654-5_4

Dreher, A. (2006). The influence of globalization on taxes and social policy: An empirical analysis for OECD countries. *European Journal of Political Economy*, *22*(1), 179–201.

Dreher, A., Sturm, J. E., & Ursprung, H. W. (2008). The impact of globalization on the composition of government expenditures: Evidence from panel data. *Public Choice*, *134*(3-4), 263–292.

Drury, K. (2005). *Management and production accounting. Introductory course* (Tutorial). Unity.

Duclos, J.Y., Makdissi, P., & Araar, A. (2014). Pro-poor indirect tax reforms, with an application to Mexico. *International Tax and Public Finance*, *21*(1), 87–118.

Dutta, N., & Roy, S. (2008). Foreign direct investment, financial development and political risks. *Munich Personal RePEc Archive*. Retrieved from http://mpra.ub.uni-muenchen.de/10186/

Dzidrov, M., & Dzidrov, M. (2010). Political and economic risk analysis case study of Macedonia. In *The Conference on Web-Based Business Management*. Retrieved from http://file.scirp.org/pdf/18-1.8.14.pdf

Ebrill, L., Keen, M., Bodin, J. P., & Summers, V. (2001). *The Modern VAT*. Washington, DC: IMF. doi:10.5089/9781589060265.071

Echevarría, C. (2015). Income tax progressivity, growth, income inequality and welfare. *SERIEs*, *6*(1), 43–72.

Economy state regulation: world experience and reforms in Russia: theory and practice . (1996). Moscow: Institute of Economy, RAS.

Edwards, C.H., & Rugy, V. (2002). *International Tax Competition: A 21st-Century Restraint on Government*. Cato Policy Analysis, No. 431.

Edwards, J., & Keen, M. (1996). Tax competition and Leviathan. *European Economic Review*, *40*(1), 113–134. doi:10.1016/0014-2921(95)00057-7

EIF and EVCA. (2010). *The European Private Equity Market Outlook*. European Investment Fund, European Venture Capital Association.

Elleuch, N., Ilhem, M., Jaouadi, Z., & And Jaouadi, S. (2015). Examination of the impact of political and country risk on foreign direct investment inflows in Tunisia. *European Academic Research*, *2*(11), 14434–14445.

Environmental Performance Index Reveals Dire State of Fisheries, Worsening Air Pollution. (n.d.). Retrieved from http://environment.yale.edu/news/article/2016-yale-environmental-performance-index-released/

Environmental Protection Agency. (1995). *An introduction to environmental accounting as a business management tool: Key concepts and terms*. US Environmental Protection Agency.

Erkekoglu, H., & Kilicarslan, Z. (2016). Do political risks affect the foreign direct investment inflows to host countries? *Journal of Business, Economics and Finance*, *5*(2), 218–232.

Erramilli, M., & Krishna, C. P. (1993). Service firms' international entry-mode choice: a modified transaction-cost analysis approach. *Journal of Marketing*, *57*(3), 19–38. doi:10.2307/1251852

Esfahani, H. (1991). Exports, imports, and economic growth in semi-industrialized countries. *Journal of Development Economics*, *35*(1), 93–116. doi:10.1016/0304-3878(91)90068-7

European Commission. (2017). *Proposal for a Council Directive amending Directive 2006/112/EC as regards harmonising and simplifying certain rules in the value added tax system and introducing the definitive system for the taxation of trade between Member States*. COM(2017) 569 final.

Eurostat. (2016). EU-28 Annual rates of change total industry MIGs NACE divisions ca 2005-2016. Retrieved October 10, 2017, from www.ec.europa.eu/eurostat/statistics-explained/index.php/File:EU-28_Annual_rates_of_change_total_industry_MIGs_NACE_divisions_ca_2005-2016.png

Eurostat. (2016). Retrieved October 10, 2017, from http://ec.europa.eu/eurostat/publications/statistical-reports

EUROSTAT. (2017). Retrieved September, 2017 from: http://ec.europa.eu/eurostat

Eurostat. (n.d.). European Statistic Database. Retrieved August 11, 2012, from http://epp.eurostat.ec.europa.eu/ portal/page/portal/statistics/search_database

EVCA. (2005). Barometer May 2005. Retrieved October 1, 2017, from https://www.investeurope.eu/ uploadedFiles/Home/Knowledge_Center/EVCA_Research/Barometer/May_2005.pdf

EVCA. (2007). European Private Equity: Strong 2006 Performance drives increased allocation. Retrieved October 1, 2017, from http://www.nvp.nl/data_files/performance_2006.pdf

EVCA. (2012). Central and Eastern Europe Statistics 2011. Retrieved August 11, 2017, from https://psik.org.pl/images/aktualnosci---statystyki-rynku/CEE%20Statistics%202011.pdf

EVCA. (2016). The Invest Europe Yearbook 2016. European Private Equity Activity. Retrieved October 10, 2017, from www.investeurope.eu/media/651727/invest-europe-2016-european-private-equity-activity-final.pdf

Evsukov, S. G., Sigarev, A. V., Ustyuzhanina, E. V., & Zaytseva, E. V. (2016). Comparative analysis of pricing policies at the market for network goods. *Journal of Internet Banking and Commerce*, *21*, 6.

Farrell, D., Lund, S., Gerlemann, E., & Seeburger, P. (2007). The New Power Brokers: How Oil, Asia, Hedge Funds and Private Equity Are Shaping the Global Capital Markets. McKinsey Global Institute.

Federal State Statistics Service. (n.d.). Retrieved from: http://www.gks.ru/

Feder, G. (1983). On exports and economic growth. *Journal of Development Economics*, *12*(1-2), 59–73.

Fedorova, L. P., & Il'ina, T. S. (2013). Aspects of strategic management of a region as a socio-economic system. *Vestnik Chuvashskogo Universiteta*, *4*, 489–495.

Field, T. F. (2003). Tax Competition in Europe and America. Tax Notes, 98(14).

Freik, N., Bespalko, V., Fedets, I., & Kuziakiv, O. (2017). *Annual Business Climate Assessment 2016: National and Regional Dimensions*. Retrieved from The Institute for Economic Research and Policy Consulting: http://www.ier.com.ua/en/sme_development/ABCA?pid=5789

Furshyk, M., & Doronin, P. (2009). How to develop the concept of creation and development of regional techno-innovation Park? *Innovations*, 3.

Gastanaga, V. M., Nugent, J. B., & Pashamova, B. (1998). Host country reforms and FDI inflows: how much difference do they make? *World Development*, *26*(7), 1299–1314. doi:10.1016/S0305-750X(98)00049-7

Gengher, E. (2011). *Best Practice in Accounts Receivable Reconciliation*. Analytical report of Citi Group. Retrieved from http://www.citigroup.com/transactionservices/home/about_us/articles/docs/accounts_receivable.pdf

Genschel, P. (2001). *Globalization, tax competition, and the fiscal viability of the welfare state*. MPIfG Working paper.

Genser, B., & Haufler, A. (1996). Tax Competition, Tax Coordination and Tax Harmonization: The Effect of EMU. *Empirica*, *23*(1), 59–89. doi:10.1007/BF00925008

Gitman, L. J., Juchau, R., & Flanagan, J. (2010). *Principles of managerial finance*. Pearson Higher Education AU.

Global Assessment of Environment Statistics and Environmental-Economic Accounting. (2007). United Nations.

Global Venture Capital and Private Equity Country Attractiveness Index. (2016). Retrieved from https://www.iese.edu/research/pdfs/ESTUDIO-143-E.pdf

Goldstein, M. (2005). The International Financial Architecture. In C. Fred Bergsten (Ed.), *The United States and the world economy: foreign economic policy for the next decade* (pp. 373–407). Washington, DC: The Institute for International Economics.

Golodova, Z. G. (2011). *Formation and management of the region's financial potential to ensure its economic growth* (Doctoral dissertation).

Gompers, P., & Lerner, J. (1998). What Drives Venture Fundraising? *Brooking Papers on Economic Activity*.

González, S. M. (2017). *State Aid, Tax Competition and BEPS: Comments on the European Commission's Decisions on Transfer Pricing Rulings*. University of Leicester, School of Law Research Paper No. 17-00.

Grier, K., & Tullock, G. (1989). An empirical analysis of cross-national economic growth, 1951–1980. *Journal of Monetary Economics*, *24*(2), 259–276. doi:10.1016/0304-3932(89)90006-8

Groh, A. P., von Liechtenstein, H., & Lieser, K. (2008). The European Capital and Private Equity Country Attractiveness Index(es). IESE Business School – University of Navarra.

Grosse, R., & Trevino, L. J. (1996). Foreign direct investment in the United States: an analysis by country of origin. *Journal of International Business Studies*, *27*(1), 139–155. doi:10.1057/palgrave.jibs.8490129

Grosse, R., & Trevino, L. J. (2005). New Institutional Economics and FDI Location in Central and Eastern Europe. *Management International Review*, *45*(2), 123–145.

Guo, S., Hotchkiss, E., & Song, W. (2009). Do buyouts (still) create value? *Social Science Research Network*.

Gupta, R., Lau, C. K. M., Miller, S. M., & Wohar, M. E. (2017). *US Fiscal Policy and Asset Prices: The Role of Partisan Conflict*. Academic Press.

Hamada, J., Haugerudbraaten, H., Hickman, A., & Khaykin, I. (2004). Pricing Political Risk within an Economic Capital Framework. In S. Wilkin (Ed.), *Country and Political Risk: Practical Insights for Global Finance*. Risk Books, England.

Hameakers, H. (1993). Fiscal Sovereignty and Tax Harmonization in the EC. *European Taxation*, *33*(1), 25–27.

Handbook of National Accounting: Integrated Environmental and Economic Accounting. (2003). United Nations, European Commission, International Monetary Fund, Organization for Economic Co-operation and Development and World Bank.

Harms, P., & Zink, S. (2003). Eating the Rich vs. Feeding the Poor: Borrowing Constraints and the Reluctance to Redistribute. *Public Choice*, *116*(3), 351–366.

Harrison, A. (1996). Openness and growth: A time-series, cross-country analysis for developing countries. *Journal of Development Economics*, *48*(2), 419–447. doi:10.1016/0304-3878(95)00042-9

Havin, S. A. (1993). Diversity of types of mixed economy abroad. *Questions of Economy*, *1*.

Hayakawa, K., Kimura, F., & Lee, H. (2011). How does country risk matter for FDI. Institute of Development Economies.

Heady, C. H. J., & Mitra, P. K. (1980). The Computation of Optimum Linear Taxation. *The Review of Economic Studies*, *47*(3), 567–585. doi:10.2307/2297308

Hellmann, T., Lindsey, L., & Puri, M. (2004). The interaction between product market and financial strategy: The role of venture capital. *Review of Financial Studies*, 13, 4(25).

Hill, R. (2008). Optimal taxation and economic growth: a comment. *Public Choice, 134*(3), 419–427.

Hines, J. R. Jr. (2006). Will social welfare expenditures survive tax competition? *Oxford Review of Economic Policy*, *22*(3), 330–348.

Hinterhuber, H. (1996). *Strategische Unternehmensführung*. Berlin, Germany: Walter de Gruyter.

Holland, C. (1993). Planning and mixed economy. *Economic Issues, 1*.

Holynskyy, Y. (2013). Improvement of Cash-flow Planning by the Treasury of Ukraine. Economic Annals-XXI, 51-54.

Hornstein, A. (2009). Problems for a fundamental theory on house price. *Economic Quarterly*, *95*(1), 1–24.

Hyide, H. K., & Panos, G. A. (2014). Risk tolerance and entrepreneurship. *Journal of Financial Economics*, *111*(1), 200–223. doi:10.1016/j.jfineco.2013.06.001

Ickowitz, A. (2001). *The Distribution of Wealth and the Pace of Development*. Studies in Development Strategy and Systemic Transformation.

Idowu, S. O., & Filho, L. W. (Eds.). (2009). *Professionals' Perspectives of Corporate Social Responsibiliry*. Springer-Verlag Berlin Heidelberg; doi:10.1007/978-3-642-02630-0_2

IFP. (2012). *The Estimate of the Value Added Tax Revenue Loss*. Institute for Financial Policy of the Ministry of Finance of the Slovak Republic.

IFS. (2011). *A Retrospective Evaluation of Elements of the EU VAT System – Final Report*. London: Institute for Fiscal Studies.

Illge, L., & Schwarze, R. (2009). *A Matter of Opinion: How Ecological and Neoclassical Environmental Economists Think about Sustainability and Economics. DIW Discussion Papers, #619*. DIW Berlin.

IMF. (2006), Fiscal Adjustment for Stability and Growth. James Daniel. Pamphlet Series, #55.

Information Agency Database "Interfax". (n.d.). Retrieved from www.interfax.ru

International Monetary Fund. (2008). *Financial Sustainability Indicators Guide*. Retrieved from http://www.imf.org/external/pubs/ft/fsi/guide/2007/pdf/eng/guide.pdf

InvestEurope. (2016). European Private Equity Activity. Retrieved from https://www.investeurope.eu/media/651727/invest-europe-2016-european-private-equity-activity-final.pdf

Isaev, E. A. (2012). *Modernization of the system and development of the regional financial potential of the Russian Federation* (Doctoral dissertation).

Jackson, S., & Markowski, S. (1996). The attractiveness of countries to foreign direct investors. *Australian Journal of Management*, *21*(2), 113–138. doi:10.1177/031289629602100202

Jacobs, R., Smith, P., & Goddard, M. (2004). Measuring performance: an examination of composite performance indicators. Centre for Health Economics.

Janošková, M., Csikósová, A., & Čulková, K. (2018). Measurement of company performance as part of its strategic management. In R. D. Leon (Ed.), *Managerial strategies for business sustainability during turbulent times* (pp. 309–335). Hershey, PA: IGI Global. doi:10.4018/978-1-5225-2716-9.ch017

Janský, P. (2015). Updating the Rich Countries' Commitment to Development Index: How They Help Poorer Ones Through Curbing Illicit Financial Flows. *Social Indicators Research, 124*(1), 43–65.

Jasch, C. (2006). How to perform an environmental management cost assessment in one day. *Journal of Cleaner Production, 14*(14), 1194–1213. doi:10.1016/j.jclepro.2005.08.005

Jeng, L. A., & Wells, Ph. C. (2000). The determinants of Venture Capital funding: evidence across countries. *Journal of Corporate Finance, 6*(3).

Jensen, M. (1989). Agency costs of free cash flow: Corporate finance and takeovers. *The American Economic Review, 76*(6).

Jensen, N., Biglaiser, G., Malesky, E., Pinto, P., Pinto, S., & Staats, J. (2012). *Politics and Foreign Direct Investment.* USA: University of Michigan Press. doi:10.3998/mpub.3425019

Jha. (2008). *Pro-Poor Fiscal Policy in the Globalized Economy. Pro-Poor Macroeconomics.* Social Policy in a Development Context.

Jobs, S. (2012). *About the business: 250 statements of the person who changed the world.* Moscow: Publisher.

John, K., Lang, L., & Netter, J. (1992). The Voluntary Restructuring of Large Firms in Response to Performance Decline. *The Journal of Finance, 47*(26).

Johnson, D. L., Ambrose, S. H., Bassett, T. J., Bowen, M. L., Crummey, D. E., Isaacson, J. S., ... Winter-Nelson, A. E. (1997). Meanings of Environmental Terms. *Journal of Environmental Quality, 26*(3), 581–589. doi:10.2134/jeq1997.00472425002600030002x

Joumard, I., & Kongsrud, P. M. (2003). Fiscal relations across government levels. *OECD Economic Sludies, 36*, 177–180.

Ju, J., Wu, Y., & Zeng, L. (2010). The impact of trade liberalization on the trade balance in developing countries. *IMF Staff Papers, 57*(2), 427–449. doi:10.1057/imfsp.2009.19

Kakwani, N., & Krongkaew, M. (2000). Economic growth, poverty and income inequality in the Asia-Pacific region. *Journal of the Asia Pacific Economy, 5*(1-2), 9–13.

Kaneda, I. (2001). Conceptual Issues Including Environmental, Natural Resources, And Ecological Accounting. Encyclopedia of Life Support Systems.

Kaneko, A., & Matsuzaki, D. J. (2009). Consumption tax and economic growth in an overlapping generations model with money holdings. *Journal of Economics, 98*(2), 155–175. doi:10.100700712-009-0088-5

Kansal, V. (2015). Political Risk: Conceptualization, Definition, Categorization and Methodologies. *The Journal of Politik Risk, 3*(4).

Kaplan, S. (1989). The Effects of Management Buyouts on Operating Performance and Value. *Journal of Financial Economics, 60*(32).

Kaplan, S., & Stein, J. (1993). The Evolution of Buyout Pricing and Financial Structure in the 1980s. *The Quarterly Journal of Economics, 108*(44).

Kavoussi, R. (1984). Export expansion and economic growth: Further empirical evidence. *Journal of Development Economics, 14*(1), 241–250. doi:10.1016/0304-3878(84)90052-X

Kazakova, N. A., Gendon, A. L., Khlevnaya, E. A. (2016) Development potential of Russian mining-and-chemical holdings. *GORNYI ZHURNAL,* (7), 89–91. doi:10.17580/gzh.2016.07.19

Kazakova, N.A., Ivanova, A.N. (2016). Diagnostika i kontrol finansovoy bezopasnosti kompanii: upravlencheskiy aspekt [Diagnostics and control of financial security of the company: management aspect]. *Management Accounting,* (5), 20-32.

Kazakova, N.A., Kisnichyan, M.B., Sivkova, A.E., Kazakov, A.Yu. (2015). Uchet, analiz i otsenka riskov predprinimatelskoy deyatelnosti na rynke lizingovykh uslug [Accounting, analysis and assessment of risks of entrepreneurial activity in the market of leasing services]. *Leasing,* (4), 53-61.

Kazakova, N. A., Bolvachev, A. I., Gendon, A. L., & Golubeva, G. F. (2016). Monitoring Economic Security in the Region Based on Indicators of Sustainable Development. *Studies on Russian Economic Development, 27*(6), 650–660. doi:10.1134/S1075700716060058

Kazakova, N. A., Bolvachev, A. I., Gendon, A. L., & Golubeva, G. F. (2017). Value Added Analysis and Trend Forecasting in the Manufacturing Industry in Kaliningrad Oblast. *Studies on Russian Economic Development, 28*(2), 160–168. doi:10.1134/S107570071702006X

Kazakova, N. A., Khlevnaya, E. A., & Zinovieva, A. A. (2016). Aktualnyye problemy kontrolya finansovoy bezopasnosti kompanii [Actual problems of financial control of the company]. *Financial Management,* (2): 3–12.

Kazakova, N., Sokolova, E., Gendon, A., & Dun, I. (2016). Methodological tools for assessing the quality of information in the system of economic security business. *European Journal of Scientific Research, 1*(13), 677–683.

Kelly, T. (1997). Public expenditures and growth. *The Journal of Development Studies, 34*(1), 60–84.

Kenny, L. W., & Winer, S. L. (2006). Tax Systems in the World: An Empirical Investigation into the Importance of Tax Bases, Administration Costs, Scale and Political Regime. *International Tax and Public Finance,* 3.

Keuschnigg, C. & Dietz, M.D. (2007). A growth oriented dual income tax. *International Tax and Public Finance, 14*(2), 191–221.

Keynes, J. M. (1993). General theory of employment, interest and money. *Anthology of Economic Classics, 2.*

Kirikkaleli, D. (2016). Interlinkage Between Economic, Financial, and Political Risks in the Balkan Countries: Evidence from a Panel Cointegration. *Eastern European Economics, 54*(3), 208–227. doi:10.1080/00128775.2016.1168704

Klevtsov, V. (2012). *The mechanism of housing finance: theory, methodology, practice.* Moscow: MUESI.

Kley, V. (2011). *Optimal wealth transfer taxation: a review of existing literature.* The Taxation of Capitalistic Bequests.

Knight, F. (1994). Concept of risk and uncertainty. *THESIS, 5,* 12-28.

Kogdenko, V.G. (2013). Corporate financial policy: features of development and implementation. *Financial analytics: problems and solutions,* (25), 2-13.

Kolodko, G. V. (2011). *Globalization, transformation, crisis – What next?* Moscow: Master.

Kolstad, I., & Tondel, L. (2002). *Social Development and Foreign Direct Investment in Services. CMI Report 2002:11.* Bergen: Chr Michelsen Institute.

Konyarova, E. K. (2006). *Reproduction management of the financial potential (on the example of the Udmurt Republic)* (Doctoral dissertation). Izhevsk.

Korobova, O. V., Gerasimov, B. I., & Bykovskij, V. V. (2002). *Regional economy: restructuring of the management system of the regional development.* Tambov: TSTU Publ.

Korosteleva, T. (2013). Problems and prospects of the development of the mortgage lending system. *Financial Analytics: Problems and Solutions, 11*(149), 32-38.

Kortum, S., & Lerner, J. (2000). Assessing the Contribution of Venture Capital to Innovation. *The Rand Journal of Economics*, *31*(18).

Kouřilová, J. (2003). Agro environment and accounting. *Acta Universitatis Bohemiae Meridionales*, *6*(1), 37–40.

Krifa-Schneider, H., Matei, I., & Matei, I. (2010). Business Climate, Political Risk and FDI in Developing Countries: Evidence from Panel Data. *International Journal of Economics and Finance*, *2*(5), 54–65. doi:10.5539/ijef.v2n5p54

Krivov, V. (2000). The problem of risk management decisions. *Risk Management*, *4*, 15–17.

Kruja, A., & Dragusha, B. (2014). The Impact of Political Risk on Foreign Direct Investment. *Iliria International Review*, (2), 73–92. doi:10.21113/iir.v4i2.33

Krysovatyi, A. I. (2000). *Taxation and Market: the Conditions and Possibilities of the Combination*. Vydavnytstvo Karpiuka.

Kudrin, A., & Gurvich, E. (2014). New growth model for the Russian economy. *Journal of Economic Issues*, 12.

Kudryavtseva, T. J., Ivanova, E. A., Kozlova, E. A., & Skhvediani, A. E. (2017). Pricing and assessment of competitiveness of innovative medical devices in the context of commercialization strategy. *Academy of Strategic Management Journal*, *16*(1), 110–122.

Kulkov, V. M. (1996). Mixed economy (theoretical and methodological aspects). *Bulletin of MGU*, *6*, 5.

Kulman, A. (1993). *Economic mechanisms*. Moscow: Progress.

Kuznets, S. (1937). *Some Problems In Measuring Per Capita Labor Income*. Retrieved from http://www.nber.org/chapters/c8142.pdf

Laitinen, T., & Kankaanpaa, M. (1999). Comparative analysis of failure prediction methods: The Finnish case. *European Accounting Review*, *8*(l), 89.

Lazarova, L., & Murieva, M. (2012). Russian Housing Market: Problems and Prospects for Development. *Russian Entrepreneurship*, *11*(209), 114–118.

Lee Kuan Yew. (2010). *Singapore story: 1965-2000: Trom the "third world" to the "first"*. Moscow: MGIMO-University.

Lennox, C. (1999). Identifying Failing Companies: A Re-evaluation of the Logit-, Probit- and DA Approaches. *Journal of Economics and Business*, *51*(4), 4. doi:10.1016/S0148-6195(99)00009-0

Leontyev, V. (1990). To the market under state control. *Economics and Life, 16.*

Lin, R. F.-Y. (2012). A comparative framework for commercial and residential markets. London: University College London (UCL).

Lindert, P. (1996). What Limits Social Spending? *Explorations in Economic History*, *33*(1), 1–34. doi:10.1006/exeh.1996.0001

Lockwood, B., & Migali, G. (2009). Did the single market cause competition in excise taxes?: Evidence from EU countries. *Economic Journal (London)*, *119*(536), 406–429. doi:10.1111/j.1468-0297.2008.02235.x

Madura, J. (2014). *Financial markets and institutions*. Cengage learning, Inc.

Magessi, N., & Antunes, L. (2014). Shadow Economy and Wealth Distribution. *Advances in Artificial Economics*, *676*, 169–179.

Makarov, A.S. (2008). The financial policy of the organization, its types, instruments of formation and implementation. *Finance and credit,* (10), 54-60.

Malizia, E. E., & Ke, S. (1993). The influence of economic diversity on unemployment and stability. *Journal of Regional Science*, *33*(2), 221–235.

Mankiw, N. G., Weinzierl, M. C. H., & Yagan, D. F. (2009). Optimal taxation in theory and practice. *The Journal of Economic Perspectives*, *23*(4), 147–174. doi:10.1257/jep.23.4.147

Mao, T. (2003). *China and Russia. The development of economic reforms*. Moscow: Science.

Maria Tilea, D. (2016). Environmental Accounting - Essential Tool for Decision Making. *Knowledge Horizons - Economics, 8*(1), 154-156.

Marrero, G. (2010). Tax-mix, public spending composition and growth. *Journal of Economics*, *99*(1), 29–51.

Mattos, E. & Politi, R. (2014). Pro-poor tax policy and yardstick competition: a spatial investigation for VAT relief on food in Brazil. *The Annals of Regional Science, 52*(1), 279–307.

Matyukhin, G. (2008). Difficult way of mortgage lending. *Banking*, *3*, 34–39.

McCarthy, T., Jordan, M., & Probst, D. (2011). *Six Sigma for Sustainability: How Organizations Design and Deploy Winning Environmental Programs*. New York: McGraw-Hill.

McCord, M., McGreal, S., Berry, J., Haras, M. & Davis, P. (2011). The implications of mortgage finance on housing market affordability. *International Journal of Housing Markets and Analysis*, *4*(4), 394-417.

McGowan Jr, C. B., & And Moeller, S. E. (2009). A model for making foreign direct investment decisions using real variables for political and economic risk analysis. *Managing Global Transitions International Research Journal*, *7*(1), 27–44.

McKellar, R. (2010). *A Short Guide to Political Risk*. England: Gower Publishing Limited.

Memba, S. F., & Njeru, A. (2016). Effect of accounts receivable on financial performance of firms funded by government venture capital in Kenya. *Journal of Economics and Finance*, *7*(1), 62–69.

Menipaz, E., & Menipaz, A. (2011). *International Business Theory and Practice*. SAGE Publications.

Menshchikova, V. I. (2010). Strategy of social and economic development in the regional management system. *Vestnik TGU*, *6*(74), 77–87.

Mises, L. (2000). *Human action: a treatise on economic theory*. Moscow: Economics.

Mitchell, J. (2001). *A Tax Competition Primer: Why Tax Harmonization and Information Exchange Undermine America's Competitive Advantage in the Global Economy. Backgrounder, No. 1460*. Washington, DC: Heritage Foundation.

Moffett, M., Stonehill, A., & Eiteman, D. (2009). *Fundamentals of Multinational Finance* (3rd ed.). Pearson Prentice Hall.

Mongrain, S., & Wilson, J. (2015). *Tax competition with heterogeneous capital mobility*. CESifo Working Paper Series No. 5688.

Morozova, L. E., Bortnik, O. A., & Kravchuk, I. S. (2010). *Expert methods and technologies of integrated assessment of enterprise economic and innovative potential (A study guide)*. Moscow: MGUPS.

Moss, J. (2017). *The similarities and differences between the US housing market in 2017.* internationalbanker.com.

Muller-Armack, A. (1965). *Soziale Markwirtshcarft.* Stuttgart, Germany: Handorterbuch der Sozialwissenshcaften.

Muscarella, C. J., & Vetsuypens, M. R. (1990). Efficiency and Organizational Structure: A Study of Reverse LBOs. *The Journal of Finance*, *45*(24).

Mustaque, K. M., & Akbar, M. I. (2013). The Impact of Political Risk on Foreign Direct Investment. *MPRA.* Retrieved from http://mpra.ub.uni-muenchen.de/47283/

Narayan Rath, B., & Akram, V. (2017). Export diversification and total factor productivity growth in case of South Asian region. *Journal of Social and Economic Development*, *19*(1), 196–210.

Nasibov, I. (2012). Scientific and technical potential of China: results and prospects. *MEMO, 10.*

Nee, V. (1989). Theory of Market Transition. *American Journal of Sociology*, 100.

Nesterenko, A. (1998). Social market economy: conceptual foundations, historical experience, lessons for Russia. *Economic Issues, 8.*

Netherlands Environmental Assessment Agency. (n.d.). *The Emissions Database for Global Atmospheric Research (EDGAR): CO2 emissions (kt).* Author.

Nicodème, G. (2009). *Corporate Income Tax and Economic Distortions. Taxation Papers 15.* Directorate General Taxation and Customs Union, European Commission.

Nigh, D. (1986). Political Events and the Foreign Direct Investment Decision: An Empirical Examination. *Managerial and Decision Economics*, *7*(2), 99–106. doi:10.1002/mde.4090070205

Nikonov, I. (2014). *Project analysis and project financing.* Moscow: Alpina Publisher.

Noorbakhsh, F., Paloni, A., & Youssef, A. (2001). Human Capital and FDI Inflows to Developing Countries: New Empirical Evidence. *World Development*, *29*(9), 1593–1610. doi:10.1016/S0305-750X(01)00054-7

OECD. (2010). *Choosing a Broad Base – Low Rate Approach to Taxation.* OECD Tax Policy Studies, No. 19.

OECD. (2014). *OECD Revenue Statistics 2014.* Paris: OECD Publishing.

OECD. (2016). *Fiscal Federalism 2016: Making Decentralization Work.* Paris: OECD Publishing.

OECD. (n.d.). STAN: STructural ANalysis Database. Retrieved October 17, 2017, from http://www.oecd.org/sti/ind/stanstructuralanalysisdatabase.htm

Oi, J. C. (1992). Fiscal Reform and the Economic Foundation of Local State Corporatism China. *World Politics*, 45.

Okun, A. (1970). *The Political Economy of Prosperity.* Yale University Press.

Onyusheva, I. (2017), Analytical and managerial issues of human capital in conditions of global competitiveness: the case of Kazakhstan. Polish Journal of Management Studies, 16(2), 198-209.

Ooghe, H., & Balcaen, S. (2002). *Are failure prediction models transferable from one country to another? An empirical study using Belgian financial statements.* Belgium: Ghent University.

Osipov, V., & Skryl, T. (2016). The strategic directions of the modern Russian economic development. *International Business Management,10.*

Osipov, V. S. (2011). *Managing the value chain.* Moscow: The Institute for Training State Employees.

Park, K. (2016). FHA loan performance and adverse selection in mortgage insurance. *Journal of Housing Economics*, *34*, 82–97. doi:10.1016/j.jhe.2016.07.004

Patience, I., & Mogotsi, B. (2009). *Wealth and Income Inequalities. Poverty Reduction and Changing Policy Regimes in Botswana*. Developmental Pathways to Poverty Reduction Series.

Patlasov, O. Y., & Vasina, N. V. (2008). Models of financial state assessment for the purpose of solvency analysis. *Economics of Agricultural and Processing Enterprises, 12,* 87.

Patlasov, O. Y., & Vasina, N. V. (2009). Modeling the borrowers (legal entities) solvency. *Audit and Financial Analysis, 5,* 103.

Patlasov, O. Y., & Vasina, N. V. (2013). Models for the borrowers (agricultural organizations) solvency assessment. *Finance and Credit*, *39*, 18–24.

Patlasov, O. Y., & Vasina, N. V. (2014). The technique of borrower's solvency analysis and scoring modeling. *Actual Problems of Economics*, *10*(160), 490–503.

Pearce, J. A., & Robinson, R. B. (2009). *Strategic Management: Formulation, Implementation, and Control*. Boston: McGraw-Hill Irwin.

Pemberton, H. (2004). *Policy learning and British governance in the 1960s*. New York: Palgrave Macmillan. doi:10.1057/9780230504752

Pinto, C., & Pinto, C. A. (2003). *Tax competition and EU law*. Kluwer Law International.

Poorvu, W. J. (2003). *Financial analysis of real property investments*. Harvard Business School.

Popvić, D. (2014). *Tax Law*. Belgrade: University of Belgrade.

Porokhovskiy, P. (2008). Political economy of the current crisis. *Theoretical Economics*, 10.

Postin, K. M., Harmon, K. W., & Gramlich, J. D. (1994). A Test of Financial Ratios as Predictors of Turnaround Versus Failure Among Financially Distressed Firms. *Journal of Applied Business Research*, *10*, 298–325.

Priame zahraničné investície. NBS. Retrieved November 1, 2017, from www.nbs.sk/sk/statisticke-udaje/statistika-platobnej-bilancie/priame-zahranicne-investicie

Prichina, O. S., & Fateeva, S. V. (2010). Financial and investment strategies of a region. *Terra Economicus*, *7*(3), 215-217.

Private Equity Trend Report 2017. (2017). Retrieved October 17, 2017, from www.pwc.pl/pl/pdf/private-equity-trend-report-2017.pdf

Raičević, B. (2008). *Public Finance*. Belgrade: University of Belgrade.

Ramsey, F. P. (1927). A Contribution to the Theory of Taxation. *Economic Journal (London)*, *37*(145), 47–61. doi:10.2307/2222721

Ranđelović, S. (2013). The assessment of tax-benefit automatic stabilizers in Serbia: A combined micro-macro approach. *Economic Annals*, *58*(198), 61–88. doi:10.2298/EKA1398061R

Rasmussen, P. (2008). Taming the private equity fund – Locus. *Europe Today*, 8(3).

Rating of socio-economic situation of the Russian Federation subjects at year-end 2016. (n.d.). Retrieved from *Rossiya Segodnya* Media Group website: http://www.riarating.ru/infografika/20170530/630063754.html

RECKON LLP. (2009). *Study to Quantify and Analyse the VAT gap in the EU-25 Member States. Report for DG Taxation and Customs Union*. London: Reckon LLP.

Reed, R., & Wu, H. (2010). Understanding property cycles in a residential market. *Property Management*, *28*(1), 33–46.

Rehme, G. J. E. (2007). Economic Growth and (Re-) Distributive Policies in a Non-cooperative World. *Journal of Economics*, *91*(1), 1–40.

Report of UK. (2016). *Property Data Report 2016. Facts and figures about the UK commercial property industry to year-end 2015*. A publication by the Property Industry Alliance. Retrieved from http://www.bpf.org.uk/sites/default/files/resources/PIA-Property-Report-2016-final-for-web.pdf

Report to the nations on occupational fraud and abuse official website (ACFE) (2016). Retrieved from http://www.acfe.com/rttn.aspx

Rios, M. C., McConnell, C. R., & Brue, S. L. (2013). *Economics: Principles, problems, and policies*. McGraw-Hill.

Robinson, T. R., Henry, E., Pirie, W. L., & Broihahn, M. A. (2015). *International Financial Statement Analysis* (3rd ed.). CFA Institute Investment Books.

Rodionov, D. G., & Rudskaya, I. A. (2017a). Econometric modeling as a tool for evaluating the performance of regional innovation systems (with regions of the Russian Federation as the example). Academy of Strategic Management Journal, 16(2), 12-21.

Rodionov, D. G., & Rudskaya, I. A. (2017). Regional Innovative Environment in National Economic Development (The Case of Russia). *International Journal of Economic Development*, *32*(4), 20–28.

Rohác, D. (2006). Evidence and Myths about Tax Competition. *New Perspectives on Political Economy*, *2*(2), 86–115.

Roll, R., & Talbott, J. (2001). Why Many Developing Countries Just Aren't. The Anderson School at UCLA. Retrieved from https://ssrn.com/abstract=292140

Ronis, S. R. (2011). Economic Security. Neglected Dimension of National Security? National Strategic Studies by National Defense University.

Russian Statistical Yearbook. (2015). Moscow: Federal State Statistics Service.

Sakaki, S. (2004). Income distribution management to sustain long-term economic growth: Does the equalization of income distribution contribute to long-term economic growth? *The Annals of Regional Science*, *38*(2), 199–218.

Samuelson, P., & Nordhaus, V. (1997). Economics. Moscow: Academic Press.

Santini, G. (2017). *Winners and losers*. Rifin.

Sazhin, Y., & Inchina, T. (2010). *Housing market management system*. Retrieved from http://www.sisupr.mrsu.ru/2010-1/pdf/sajin_2.pdf

Schaltegger, S., & Burritt, R. (2000). *Contemporary Environmental Accounting: Issues, Concepts and Practice*. Sheffield, UK: Greenleaf Publishing.

Schneider, F., & Frey, B. S. (1985). Economic and Political Determinants of Foreign Direct Investment. *World Development*, *13*(2), 161–175. doi:10.1016/0305-750X(85)90002-6

Scully, G. W. (2003). Optimal Taxation, Economic Growth and Income Inequality. *Public Choice*, *115*(3), 299–312.

Scully, G. (2001). Government Expenditure and Quality of Life. *Public Choice, 108*(1), 123–145. doi:10.1023/A:1017518926640

Sedik, W. M., & Seoudy, H. (2012). The Impact of Country Risk and New Institutional Economics on Foreign Direct Investment A Panel Data Analysis for Middle East and North Africa Region (1999-2010). In *The 16th Meeting of the International Society for New Institutional Economics*, University of Southern California.

Sedova, N.V., Kazakova, N. A, Gendon, A. L., Khlevnaya, E. A. (2017). Prediction of development in the mining and chemical industry in Russia and in the world. *Gornyi Zhurnal,* (4), 49–52. doi:10.17580/gzh.2017.04.09

Sendroiu, C., & Roman, A. (2007). The Environmental Accounting: an Instrument for Promoting the Environmental Management. Theoretical and Applied Economics. *Asociatia Generala a Economistilor din Romania,* 8(513), 45-48.

Sergeev, D. (2008). System of mass mortgage lending in the Russian Federation: Adaptation of the world market. *Securities market*, *4*(235), 28–30.

SGS. (2016). *Belgrade*. Retrieved, November, 2017, from http://webrzs.stat.gov.rs/WebSite/Public/PageView.aspx?pKey=82

Shabunina, T. V., Shchelkina, S. P., & Rodionov, D. G. (2017). An innovative approach to the transformation of eco-economic space of a region based on the green economy principles. Academy of Strategic Management Journal, 16(1), 176-185.

Shari, I. (2000). Economic growth and income inequality in Malaysia, 1971–95. *Journal of the Asia Pacific Economy*, *5*(1-2), 112–124.

Shestovskikh, T. S. (1998). Risk in the structure of economic behavior. *Sociological Research*, *5*, 116–119.

Sidelnikova, L. P. (2010). Tax and Credit Finance: Fiscal Philosophy of Choice. Hrin' DS, 13.

Silvestrov, S. N. (2009). State partnership: the Russian options welts. *Proceedings of the Free Economic Society of Russia*, 117.

Simanavičienė, Ž., & Stankevičius, A. (2017). *Economic security and national competitiveness.* Retrieved December 10, 2017 from https://repository.mruni.eu/bitstream/handle/007/15011/Simanavi%C4%8Dien%C4%97.pdf?sequence=1&isAllowed=y

Simonenko, N. N., & Simonenko, V. N. (2017). *Short-term and long-term financial policy of the firm: Textbook. M.: Master*. SIC INFRA-M.

Sinevičienė, L. (2016). Tax Burden and Economic Development: The Case of the European Union Countries. *Entrepreneurship. Business Economics (Cleveland, Ohio)*, *2*, 283–298.

Singh, H., & Jun, K. W. (1995). Some New Evidence on Determinants of Foreign Direct Investment in Developing Countries. *World Bank*. Retrieved from http://ssrn.com/abstract=623885

Sıssanı, M., & Belkacem, Z. (2014). The Effect of Political Risk on Foreign Direct Investment: The Case of Algeria, *Hyperion. Economic Journal (London)*, *3*(2), 29–35.

Sivkova, A. E. (2016). Metodicheskoye obespecheniye i instrumentariy diagnostiki veroyatnosti bankrotstva v kompanii [Methodical support and tools for diagnosing the probability of bankruptcy in the company]. *Financial Management*, (3): 31–38.

Skryl, T. V. (2017). A paradigm shift in Russia's industrial policy: From a raw model to innovative technological growth points. *International Journal of Ecological Economics and Statistics*, *38*, 2.

Smirnova, E. (2001). Manufacturing risk: The nature and management. *Risk Management, 1*, 3–5.

Smith, L. D. (2006). Discounted Cash Flow Analysis, Methodology and Discount Rates. *Rio Algom Limited,* Retrieved October 17, 2017, from http://web.cim.org/mes/pdf/valdaylarrysmith.pdf

Smith, L. D. (1995). Discount rates and risk assessment in mineral project evaluations. *Canadian Institute of Mining and Metallurgical Bulletin, 88*(989), 34–43.

Social and Ecological Accounting Matrix: an Empirical Study for China. (2000). Xiaoming PAN Institute of Systems Science Chinese Academy of Sciences.

Sokolov, I. (2012). *Public-private partnership as a tool to support innovation.* Moscow: Ranepa.

Soltysilski, S. (2009). Global Tax Competition and Tax Cooperation. *The Role of Law and Ethics in the Globalized Economy, 10*, 1–7.

Sørensen, P. B. (2007). The Theory of Optimal Taxation: What is the Policy Relevance? *International Tax and Public Finance, 14*(4), 383–406. doi:10.100710797-007-9024-1

Soukup, J. (2017). The Impact of Innovation on Competitiveness and Economic Growth in EU Countries. *ICFE, 2017*, 295.

Stanciu, I. C. (2011). Accounting Policies Regarding Environmental Costs. *Ovidius University Annals. Economic Sciences Series. XI, 1*(May), 1986–1991.

Stark, D. (1966). Recombinant property and the birth of the Eastern European capital. *Economic Issues, 6.*

Statistics and Annual reports on the activity of the financial administration for the period 2004-2016. (n.d.). Retrieved from https://www.financnasprava.sk/sk/financna-sprava/vyrocne-spravy

Statistics on the judicial practice of the RF Arbitration Courts in bankruptcy cases. (2015). Retrieved from http://sudact.ru/arbitral/stats/?law_stat_category=sRE7Jt1f1fV8&datefrom=01.01.2015&workflow_stage=DKnC6cEIq7Vv&date_to=20.11.2015

Status of ratification. (n.d.). UNFCC.

Stavins, R. N. (2001). *Experience with Market-Based Environmental Policy Instruments.* Discussion Paper 01-58. Washington, DC: Resources for the Future.

Stewart, K., & Webb, M. (2006). International competition in corporate taxation: Evidence from the OECD time series. *Economic Policy, 21*(45), 154–201. doi:10.1111/j.1468-0327.2006.00156.x

Stiglitz, J. (2004). *The Globalization and Its Discontents.* Zagreb: Algorithm.

Stiglitz, J. (2009). *The Success of Globalization, New Steps to a Just World.* Zagreb: Algorithm.

Stoever, W. (2002). Attempting to resolve the attraction-aversion dilemma: A study of FDI Policy in the Republic of Korea. *Transnational Corporations, 11*(1), 49–76.

Stojanov, D. (2013). *Economic crisis and crisis of economic science.* Faculty of Economics in Rjeka.

Stowell, D. P. 2010. Private equity Impact on Corporations. In: Stowell (Ed.) An Introduction to Investment Banks, Hedge Funds, and Private Equity: the new paradigm (pp. 325-345). USA: Elsevier. doi:10.1016/B978-0-12-374503-3.00025-1

Streltsov, A. V. (2000). Risk assessment when updating production facilities. *Risk Management, 2*, 13–15.

Sullivan, M. A. (2001). *Corporate Tax Reform: Taxing Profits in the 21st Century.* Apress.

Supek, I. (2006). *Globalization or the Associated Covenant*. Zagreb: HAZU.

Talbott, J., & Roll, R. W. (2001). Why many developing countries just aren't. *The Anderson School at UCLA*.

Tallman, S. B. (1988). Home Country Political Risk and Foreign Direct Investment in The United States. *Journal of International Business Studies*, *19*(2), 219–233. doi:10.1057/palgrave.jibs.8490856

Tamai, T. (2015). Redistributive taxation, wealth distribution, and economic growth. *Journal of Economics, 115*(2), 133–152.

Tamborra, M., & Pavan, M. (2005). Environmental Expenditures. In *Green Accounting in Europe*. Edward Elgar Publishing. doi:10.4337/9781845428136.00021

Tanc, A. & Gokoglan, K. (2015). The Impact of Environmental Accounting on Strategic Management Accounting: A Research on Manufacturing Companies. *International Journal of Economics and Financial Issues, 5*(2), 566-573.

Tanninen, H. (2010). Income inequality, government expenditures and growth. *Applied Economics*, *31*(9), 1109–1117.

Tax Treaty Issues Related to Emissions Permits/Credits. (n.d.). OECD.

Teather, R. (2005). *The benefits of tax competition. Hobart Paper 153*. London: The Institute of Economic Affairs.

Teeter, P., & Sandberg, J. (2016). Constraining or Enabling Green Capability Development? How Policy Uncertainty Affects Organizational Responses to Flexible Environmental Regulations. *British Journal of Management*. doi:10.1111/1467-8551.12188

Thompson, D. (2010). *The Power of Prices and the Failure of Markets. The Edmonton Sustainability Papers*. City of Edmonton.

Tillmann, G. (2010). Evasion of Tax on Interest Income in a Two-Country Model. *Economics Essays.*, *4*, 345–363.

Tilt, C. A. (2007). Corporate Responsibility, Accounting and Accountants. In Professionals' Perspective of CSR: An Introduction (pp. 11-32). Springer Berlin Heidelberg.

Tolstova, M. L. (2012a). Financial strategy of the territory: Problem characteristics and organizational principles. *Vestnik Chuvashskogo Universiteta*, *2*, 467–470.

Tolstova, M. L. (2012b). System-forming principles for the formation and implementation of the regional financial strategy. *Vestnik Chuvashskogo Universiteta*, *4*, 492–495.

Trevino, L. J., & And Mixon, F. G. (2004). Strategic factors affecting foreign direct investment decisions by multinational enterprises in Latin America. *Journal of World Business*, *39*(3), 233–243. doi:10.1016/j.jwb.2004.04.003

Tyrrell, B., & Riley, P. (2017). *2018 Index of Economic Freedom: Freedom to Trade Is a Key to Prosperity*. Retrieved from The Heritage Foundation: https://www.heritage.org/sites/default/files/2017-11/BG3266.pdf

Udland, M. (2016). *The US housing market has a major supply problem*. Business Insider. Retrieved from amp.businessinsider.com

Ukraine: Economic Freedom Score. (2017). Retrieved December 10, 2017 from The Heritage Foundation: https://www.heritage.org/index/pdf/2017/countries/ukraine.pdf

Ul'janickaja, N. M. (2013). Development of a regional management strategy: Conceptual approach. *Inzhenernyj Vestnik Dona*, *20*(2), 574–582.

Ulrich, H. (1990). *Unternehmungspolitik*. Bern, Stuttgart: Haupt.

UNCTAD. (2017). *World Investment Report 2017: Investment and The Digital Economy*. Geneva: UN Publication.

Urošević, B. (2009). *Quantitative methods in corporate finance*. Faculty of Economics, University of Belgrade.

Ushakov, D. (2016). Dynamics of international economical relationships in the global context of Innovative Modernization. *International Journal of Environmental and Science Education, 18*, 10160–10165.

Ushakov, D. (2016). Dynamics of international economical relationships in the global context of innovative modernization. *International Journal of Environmental and Science Education*, 18.

Ushakov, D. (2017a). Information Technologies Within Market Economy: How Communication Tools Became A Field Of Activity. *The EUrASEANs*, *1*, 7–18.

Ushakov, D., Elokhova, I., & Kozonogova, E. (2017). Post industrialization prospects in the dynamics of socioeconomic transformations: Cluster approach. *International Journal of Ecological Economics and Statistics*, *38*(2), 46–57.

Ustyuzhanina, E. (2016). The Eurasian Union and global value chains. *European Politics and Society, 17.*

van den Bergh, J. C. J. M. (2001). Ecological Economics: Themes, Approaches, and Differences with Environmental Economics. *Regional Environmental Change*, *2*(1), 13–23. doi:10.1007101130000020

Varnavskiy, V. (2013). *Mechanism of public-private partnerships*. Moscow: MGIMO University.

Verbinenko, E. A., & Badylevich, R. V. (2012). Financial potential as the basis for regional development. *The North and the Market: Formation of the Economic Order*, *2*(30), 58–62.

Verkhovin, V. I. (1994). Economic behavior as a subject of sociological analysis. *Sociolinguistic Studies*, *10*, 120–125.

Verkhovin, V. I. (2009). Investment behavior. *Economia e Sociologia (Evora, Portugal)*, *2*, 148–160.

Vogel, J. (2014). Welfare Production, Poverty and Wealth. A Comparative and Longitudinal Perspective. *Rich and Poor.*, *15*, 235–270. doi:10.1007/978-94-010-0257-8_16

Volkerink, B., Sturm, J. & De Haan, J. Tax Ratios in Macroeconomics: Do Taxes Really Matter? *Empirica, 29*(3), 209–224.

Volkov, A. M. (1976). *Prospective planning of the financial resources*. Moscow: Finansy.

Voronin, V. T. (1994). Time as the space for events (sociophilosophical aspect). [in Russian]. *Humanities in Siberia*, *1*, 20–25.

Voronkova E.K. (2011). The balance of the economy and the investment policy of the Russian Federation. *Business in law,* (6), 300-306.

Walder, A. (1994). Corporate Organisation and Local Government Property Rights in China. In A. Milor (Ed.), *Changing Political Economies: Privatisation in Post-Communist and Reforming Communist States*. Boulder, CO: Lynne Rienner.

Weichenrieder, A. J. (2005). *(Why) Do We Need Corporate Taxation?* CESifo Working Paper, No.1495.

Wei, S. J. (2000). How taxing is corruption on international investors? *The Review of Economics and Statistics*, *82*(1), 1–12. doi:10.1162/003465300558533

Wheeler, D., & Moody, A. (1992). International investment location decisions: The Case of US Firms. *Journal of International Economics*, *33*(1-2), 57–76. doi:10.1016/0022-1996(92)90050-T

Widmalm, F. (2001). Tax Structure and Growth: Are Some Taxes Better Than Others? *Public Choice, 107*(3), 199–219.

Wilson, J. D. (1986). A Theory of Interregional Tax Competition. *Journal of Urban Economics*, *19*(3), 296–315. doi:10.1016/0094-1190(86)90045-8

Wilson, J. D., & Wildasin, D. E. (2004). Capital tax competition: Bane or boon. *Journal of Public Economics*, *88*(6), 1065–1091. doi:10.1016/S0047-2727(03)00057-4

World Bank. (2014). *World Investment and Political Risk (WIPR)-2013: World Investment Trends and Corporate Perspectives, The Political Risk Insurance Industry, Breach of Contract*. Washington, D.C.: MIGA, World Bank Group.

World Bank. (2018). *Doing Business 2018: Reforming to Create Jobs*. Washington, DC: World Bank; doi:10.1596/978-1-4648-1146-3

Xu, C. (2015). Political and Economic Institutions of China and Their Influences. *The Cato Journal*, *35*, 3.

Yao, S. (2007). Economic growth, income inequality and poverty in china under economic reforms. *The Journal of Development Studies*, *35*(6), 104–130.

Zámborský, P. (2016). International business and global strategy. *Bookboon*. Retrieved August 12, 2017, from http://bookboon.com/en/international-business-and-global-strategy-ebook

Zefinescu, C. (2015, July). Green Costs in the Context Of Sustainable Development Trends. Constatin Brancusi University of Targu Jiu Annals - Economy Series, 118-122.

Zeldner A. G. (2010). Combined socio-economic system: ownership issues. *Economic Science, 1*.

Zeldner, A. G., & Khalturin, R. A. (2014). The role of development institutions in attracting private investment. Moscow: Institute of Economy, RAS.

Zeldner, A. G. (2010). *Partnership of the state, business and society in a mixed economy*. Moscow: Economics.

Zeldner, A. G. (2013). *Destructive trends and constructive possibilities of overcoming them in the economic system of Russia*. Moscow: Economics.

Zenchenko, S. V. (2010). *Formation and assessment of regional financial potential of sustainable development of the territory's economy: the theory and methodology* (Doctoral dissertation).

Zhurkina, N. (2007). Modern mortgage: State, problems, solutions. *Finance*, *6*, 17.

Zubkov, V. I. (2001). Risk in the structure of economic behavior. *West. Ros. Univ. of Peoples'. Friendship*, *2*, 76–93.

Zweifel, P., & Eisen, R. (2012). *Insurance Economics*. Berlin: Spinger Verlag. doi:10.1007/978-3-642-20548-4

About the Contributors

Denis Ushakov holds degree of Doctor of economy (macroeconomic) from Russia' Academy of entrepreneurship, Moscow, Russia (since 2009), academic title of Professor (Russia) and Assistant Professor (Thailand). He works now as a lecturer in International College Suan Sunandha Rajabhat University, Bangkok, Thailand, is a Member of Russian Academy of Natural Science, International Association of organizational innovations. His scientific interests include economy of tourism: theory of tourism market's function, modern trends of development, corporative management; multinational corporation in service's production: organization, strategic management, global competitive resources; government regulation of the service's market; innovative modernization in economical Government's regulation, production's organization. He published 72 research papers in federal Russian scientific magazines; 52 research papers in International journals; participated in 42 scientific conferences; prepared 10 training manuals for students of the service professions.

* * *

Sofija Adžić is a full professor at University of Novi Sad, Faculty of Economics in Subotica, Serbia. Her research interests and subjects include economic system and economic policy, regional economy of the EU, and industrial policy of the EU. She has actively participated on 118 international conferences in Serbia, Bosnia and Herzegovina, Brazil, Bulgaria, Montenegro, Greece, the Nederland's, China, Croatia, India, Italy, Japan, South Africa, Hungary, Macedonia, Malaysia, the Russian Federation, Slovakia, Slovenia, Spain, USA, Thailand and the UK. All of these papers were published in conference preceding, monographs, scientific and professional journals. She has published 9 textbooks, 9 scientific monographs and participated in 55 collective monographs. In addition, she has published 162 scientific papers in national and international journals. She has participated in the development of 26 macroeconomic and 18 microeconomic projects.

Fatih Ayhan, PhD., Assistant Professor, Head of department of the Business and Management section at Bandirma Onyedi Eylul University, Gonen Vocational High School, Balikesir, Turkey. He works now as a lecturer in Bandirma Onyedi Eylul University since 2017 (Balikesir, Turkey). He holds degree of Doctor of economy (macroeconomic) from Selcuk University, Konya, Turkey (Since 2016). His scientific interests include labor economics, unemployment and employment policy, migration, international trade policy, Exchange rate volatility, tourism economics, political risk, economic growth and development. He published 6 research papers in different international scientific journals; participated in 17 international scientific conferences; participated in 7 different lessons for students of the vocational higher school.

Adriana Csikósová, PhD, deals with the issues of economics, international business, marketing and market research. She developed concept and introduced the subject of marketing, international business, and she guarantee them and lecture at Technical university of Košice. She was investigator of several projects in area of environmental and social aspect of social marketing, strategic management of the region, taking into account aspects of sustainable development in the region. The good orientation in this issue tells its publications and scientific research activity at home and abroad.

Katarína Čulková, PhD., works on Department of Earth Sources, Faculty BERG, Technical University Košice, Slovakia. Her pedagogical, scientific and publication activity is orientated to the area of Financial analysis, Financial management and Financial investment in production companies and individual sectors of national economy. In her scientific and research activity she participated at solving problems of sustainable development in the region and presently she is part of project, orientated to the evaluation of economic efficiency of raw material policy of the state.

Elena Danilova is a candidate of sociological sciences, an associate professor of the Tyumen State University, Russia. Her research interests and topics include economic behavior, investment activity, and regional economy. She took an active part in international conferences in Russia, the Czech Republic and Thailand. All documents were published in collections of conferences, monographs, scientific and professional journals. She published 27 scientific and 5 educational works. Participated in the development of major regional and interregional projects.

Mariia Ermilova, PhD of Economics, Associate Professor, Department of Financial Management, Plekhanov Russian University of Economics (since 2012), Head of Central office of the Association of Education and Science Managers (since 2017). Her science interests are focused around financing of housing market. She published more than 100 articles in Russian federal and international journals, 3 textbook and 3 training manuals for students; 2 monographs; participated more than 50 conferences.

Elena Gromova, Ph.D., is an Associate Professor in Economics at the Department of Finance and Pricing, Faculty of Finance, Plekhanov Russian University of Economics, Russia. Her scientific interest is finance policy company, investment attractiveness of companies in connection with future growth opportunities and competitive advantages. She has actively participated on international conferences, published 7 textbooks and participated in 3 collective monographs. She actively participated in 10 microeconomic projects.

Yuriy Holynskyy, PhD, is an Associate Professor at the Department of State and Local Finance, Faculty of Financial Management and Business, Ivan Franko National University of Lviv, Ukraine. His scientific interests are public finance, problems of budgets maintenance, state treasury services and functioning, fiscal policies at emerging markets. He is also the author of scientific monographs and book chapters on public finance published by the Ivan Franko National University of Lviv, Ukraine.

Mária Janošková is PhD candidate of economical sciences, assoc. prof. at Technical university of Košice, Slovakia. Research and Professional Experience: She works at Institute of Business and Management of Technical university of Košice, Slovakia. Her pedagogical and science activity is concentrated to Management of company, Strategic management, Human resources management, Business and

Corporate Social Responsibility. In her scientific and research activity she deals with Strategy management, Human resources management with emphasize to Knowledge management and human capital, problems of Corporate Social Responsibility in practice, as well as transfer of managerial knowledge to the business practice. She published some scientific monographs, chapters of monographs, articles in international journals, participated in International scientific conferences.

Natalia Kazakova, Doctor of Economic Sciences (since 2008), is a professor of the Financial Management Department (since 2009), Director of the Center for Financial Studies, Plekhanov Russian University of Economics, Russia. Scientific interests are related to the development of information and analytical support for financial security and are aimed at developing tools for financial analysis, diagnosis and controlling of business processes, assessing and managing the risks of financial and economic activity, analyzing the effectiveness of using budget funds, assessing the results of intellectual activity. Her scientific papers have been published in national and foreign journals (more than 200 publications), including 4 SCOPUS-indexed international journals. She has also written 37 textbooks on finance, accounting and the world economy and 10 monographs.

Igor Keri, Ph.D. is an Associate Professor in Economics at the Department of Financial Management, Faculty of Finance, Plekhanov Russian University of Economics, Russia. His scientific interest is finance policy company, modern capital budgeting techniques, evaluation of strategic investment projects of private and state companies. He actively participated on international conferences, published 3 textbooks, participated in 5 microeconomic projects.

Krongthong Khairiree, assistant professor, Ph.D. (Mathematics Education, Deakin University, Australia), Dean of International College, Suan Sunandha Rajabhat University, Bangkok, Thailand and Executive Board Member of National Institute of Educational Service (Thailand). Her scientific interests are concentrated on business research methods, business statistic, statistical analyze of industries and national economies. She published 48 research papers in Thailand and international scientific journals, participated in 50 scientific conferences; prepared training manuals for students on business mathematic and statistic.

Jana Kušnírová holds PhD in Finance from the University of Economics in Bratislava, Slovakia (2011). She works as a lecturer at the Department of Finance, Faculty of National Economy, University of Economics in Bratislava. Her scientific interests include corporate income taxes, tax debts, tax optimization and tax evasion. She has published more than 15 papers in research journals, chapters in monographs and participated in 37 international scientific conferences.

Olga Mzhelskaya is the head of the Humanities and Foreign Language department at Omsk Humanitarian Academy, Russia. She is PhD in Philological Sciencies. Research interests: linguistics and humanitarian research of communication processes, sociology and management in education, business consulting. She has published 60 scientific papers, 2 monographs and 12 text books and manuals. Twice she has been a laureate of All Russia Best scientific book contest organized by Russian Fond of Education Development.

Krasovskaya Nadezhda, Ph.D., is an associate professor of the Department of Management, Marketing and Logistics of the Financial and Economic Institute of the Tyumen State University, Russia. Her research interests and subjects include organic food, rural tourism and financial behavior. She has actively participated on international conferences in the Russian Federation, Poland, Czech Republic and Bulgaria. Her scientific papers were published in journals of a list of international databases and citation systems, list of journals of the highest attestation commission of Russia and national editions. She has published 8 textbooks. She is one of the authors scientific monograph «Characteristics of the socio-cultural development of the Tyumen region». She has participated in the development of micro-economic project.

Irina Onyusheva has earned PhD in Economics from the University of International Business (Almaty, Kazakhstan) in conjunction with George Washington University (Washington, DC, USA) and City University London (London, United Kingdom). She is an Associate Professor, Professor of the Regional Academy of Management (Republic of Kazakhstan), Professor of the Multidisciplinary Russian Academy of Natural History (Moscow, Russia), Corresponding Member of the Academy of Pedagogical Sciences of Kazakhstan (APSK), Academician of the International Informatization Academy (IIA). She works as a MBA lecturer in Stamford International University, Graduate School, Faculty of Business and Technology, in Bangkok, Thailand. Irina has a rich worldwide teaching and research experience as well as managerial one in the field of higher education. She is also internationally certified as a project manager by the IPMA (Level C). She is an active participant of international academic mobility programs, national and international scientific conferences, workshops and trainings. Her research field and scientific interests include: formation, ensuring and increasing economic competitiveness at both micro- and macrolevels; human capital development, HR management; knowledge economy; project management. She is the author of more than 80 research publications and conference proceedings abstracts, including those indexed in the international databases. She is the author of an individual scientific monograph titled "Human capital in the context of national economic competitiveness: formation factors and development prospects" (2015) which was awarded as "Best educational edition in economics" in the framework of the XXVI international book fair of education publications (Sochi, Russia, October 8-11, 2015), and also got Gold medal "European Quality" (ESIC, Germany-Russia, April 4, 2016).

Anastasiya Ostovskaya holds PhD in public administration from the Classic Private University of Zaporizhzhya, Ukraine (2010). She works as Associate Professor at the Department of Public and Municipal Administration, Institute of Economics and Management, V.I. Vernadsky Crimean Federal University. Her scientific interests include public regulation of territorial socio-economic development and financial instruments of territorial socio-economic development control. She has published more than 60 papers including 2 monographs, 21 papers in research journals, 1 paper in an international journal and participated in 35 international and All-Russian scientific conferences.

Oleg Patlasov is a Vice-Rector for International Affairs in Omsk Humanitarian Academy, Vice-Rector for Licensing and Accreditation in Omsk Regional Institution. He is an Honorary Worker of Higher Professional Education, Professor, PhD in Economics, Federal Expert in Scientific and technical sphere of the Russian Federation. Professor Patlasov O. is a member of editorial boards in National and

Foreign peer-reviewed scientific journals. His main scientific interests are: crisis Management in commercial organization, marketing, audit and personnel controlling, risk management, financial modeling, entrepreneurship. He has more than 300 scientific published papers.

Irina Pavlenko holds PhD in economics from the Poltava University of Consumer Cooperation in Ukraine, Poltava, Ukraine (2009). She works as Associate Professor at the Department of Business Management, Institute of Economics and Management, V.I. Vernadsky Crimean Federal University. Her scientific interests include conditions for innovative development, efficient functioning and development management of hotel facilities in Crimea; global cyberspace formation and perspectives of digital economy development in Russia and internationally. She has published more than 200 papers including 10 monographs (1 single-author monograph), 83 papers in the research journals, 4 papers in the international journals and participated in 101 international and All-Russian scientific conferences.

Marcela Rabatinová holds PhD in Finance from the University of Economics in Bratislava, Slovakia (2006). She works as a lecturer at the Department of Finance, Faculty of National Economy, University of Economics in Bratislava. Her scientific interests include personal income tax, value added tax, tax policy and tax evasion. She has published more than 12 papers in research journals, chapters in monographs and participated in 26 international scientific conferences.

Nadezhda Sinelschikova, PhD, is an Associate Professor in Economics at the Department of Financial Management, Faculty of Finance, Plekhanov Russian University of Economics, Russia. Her scientific interest is finance policy company, investment projects of private and state companies.

Anna Sivkova is a third-year post-graduate student of the Financial Management Department and an assistant at the Department of Financial Control, Analysis and Audit, Plekhanov Russian University of Economics, Russia. Her scientific interest is financial analysis, bankruptcy analysis, bankruptcy risk diagnostics, business process diagnostics, financial and management reporting. She often takes part in international scientific conferences where she made reports on her subject. Her scientific papers have been published in more than 30 national journals.

Ai Huu Tran, PhD, lecturer of Faculty of Economics, Van Hien University, Ho Chi Minh City, Vietnam. Member of editorial board of International journals. Research interests – markets of agricultural products, SMEs functioning and government support, organic food markets, ecological economics, environmental issues of economic development and corporate social responsibility. He published 32 research papers in Vietnam scientific magazines; 39 research papers in International journals; participated in 21 scientific conferences. Participating in many provincial and ministerial scientific research projects in Vietnam. Participate in the innovation and accreditation of high quality programs of university.

Juraj Válek holds PhD in Finance from the University of Economics in Bratislava, Slovakia (2011). He works as a lecturer at the Department of Finance, Faculty of National Economy, University of Economics in Bratislava. His scientific interests include environmental taxes, excise taxes, tax policy and tax evasion. He has published more than 15 papers in research journals, chapters in monographs and participated in 35 international scientific conferences.

Prateep Wajeetongratana, PhD., Assistant Professor, dean of Faculty of management science at Suan Sunandha Rajabhat University, Bangkok, Thailand, member of organizational board of "Actual economicsts" society, reviewer of 5 International journals. His scientific interests are modern marketing and alternative management theories, sufficient economy and sustainable corporative management. He published more than 40 papers in Thai and International journals, organized more than 15 conferences, prepared 5 training manuals for students.

Larisa Zamuraeva, Ph.D., is an associate professor of the Department of Management, Marketing and Logistics of the Financial and Economic Institute of the Tyumen State University, Russia. Her research interests and subjects include competitiveness of regions and organizations, regional economy and financial behavior. She has actively participated on international conferences in the Russian Federation and Poland. Her scientific papers were published in journals of a list of international databases and citation systems, list of journals of the highest attestation commission of Russia and national editions. She has published 10 textbooks. She is one of the authors of scientific monograph "Actual problems of managing the strategic development of the region: domestic and foreign experience." She has participated in the development of microeconomic project.

Index

N

O

P

R

S

T

U

V

W

www.ingramcontent.com/pod-product-compliance
Lightning Source LLC
LaVergne TN
LVHW062122300926
849161LV00010B/2518